BEING
BERNARD BERENSON

ALSO BY MERYLE SECREST

Between Me and Life: A Biography of Romaine Brooks

BEING
BERNARD BERENSON

A BIOGRAPHY

MERYLE SECREST

HOLT, RINEHART AND WINSTON
New York

Published by Holt, Rinehart and Winston, 383 Madison Avenue, New York, New York 10017.

Published simultaneously in Canada by Holt, Rinehart and Winston of Canada, Limited.

Library of Congress Cataloging in Publication Data

Secrest, Meryle.
Being Bernard Berenson.

Includes index.
1. Berenson, Bernard, 1865–1959. 2. Art historians—United States—Biography. I. Title.
N7483.B47S42 709'.2'4 [B] 78-31433

ISBN 0-03-018411-8

FIRST EDITION

Designer: Christine Aulicino
Printed in the United States of America
10 9 8 7 6 5 4 3 2 1

Grateful acknowledgment is made to the following: to Jonathan Gathorne-Hardy, for permission to quote from the unpublished writings of Robert Gathorne-Hardy; to John Russell, for permission to quote from the published and unpublished writings and letters of Logan Pearsall Smith; to Barbara Halpern for permission to quote from the letters of Mary Berenson and from a letter of Hannah Whitall Smith; to Bernard Perry and Ralph Barton Perry, Jr., for permission to quote from the Berenson family letters in their possession; to Philippa Offner for permission to quote from the unpublished writings of Richard Offner; to Agnes Cora Ruth Stillman for permission to quote from her thesis on Senda Berenson; to Philippa Calnan for permission to quote from the letters of Charles Loeser, also by permission of the Houghton Library, Harvard; to the Collection of American Literature, Beinecke Rare Book and Manuscript Library, Yale University, for permission to quote from Mary Berenson's letters to Mr. and Mrs. Hutchins Hapgood; to the Walter Lippmann Papers, Yale University Library, for permission to quote from Mary Berenson's letters to Mr. and Mrs. Lippmann; to the Houghton Library, for permission to quote from Mary Berenson's letters to Sir William Rothenstein; to Michael Colefax, for permission to quote from a letter of Lady Sibyl Colefax; to Clotilde Marghieri, for permission to quote from her unpublished letters to Bernard Berenson; to Daphne Hoffman Mebane, for permission to quote from her letter to the author; to Julian Trevelyan, for permission to quote from his letter to the author; to Creighton Gilbert, Jacob Gould Schurman Professor of the History of Art at Cornell University, for permission to quote from his letter to the author; to W.H. Haslam, for permission to quote from his letter to David Buchanan; to Philip F. Siff, for permission to quote from his letter to the author; to Henry and Frances Francis, for permission to quote from their letters and journals; to David L. Hurwood, for permission to quote from the memoir of Bella Wolfson by Henry Hurwitz; to Barbara Ivins, for permission to quote from the letters of her father, W. M. Ivins, Jr.; to Mme. G. Powell-Pouzzner, for permission to quote from a family memoir; to Norris Darrell, Gerald Gunther, and Mrs. James H. Chadbourn, for permission to quote from a letter of Learned Hand; to Harvard University Archives, for permission to quote from the diaries of Mrs. Arthur Kingsley Porter; to Avery Library, Columbia University Libraries, for the letters of Cecil Pinsent.

Grateful acknowledgment is also made to Norman MacKenzie, for permission to quote from *The Letters of Sidney and Beatrice Webb*, Cambridge University Press, ©1978; to Baron Cecil Anrep, for permission to quote from *Sunset and Twilight*, Harcourt, Brace & World Inc., New York, ©1963; from *Rumor and Reflection*, Simon & Schuster, New York, copyright 1952; and from *Sketch for a Self-Portrait*, Pantheon Books, New York, copyright 1949; to Simon & Schuster, for permission to quote from *The Bernard Berenson Treasury*, edited by Hannah Kiel, ©1962 Simon & Schuster, New York; to Houghton Mifflin Company for permission to quote from *The Selected Letters of Bernard Berenson* edited by Arthur K. McComb, ©1963 by Houghton Mifflin Company, Boston; to Wayne State University Press for permission to quote from *The Letters of Dr. Richard Maurice Bucke to Walt Whitman*, edited by Artem Lozynsky, ©1977, Wayne State University Press, Detroit, Michigan; to Alfred A. Knopf Inc., for permission to quote from *The Flowers of Friendship: Letters Written to Gertrude Stein*, edited by Donald C. Gallup, New York, copyright 1953; and to Mrs. Pamela Diamand, for permission to quote from *Letters of Roger Fry*, edited by Denys Sutton, Random House, New York, ©1972 by Mrs. Pamela Diamand.

letter to the author; to W.H. Haslam, for permission to quote from his letter to David Buchanan; to Philip F. Siff, for permission to quote from his letter to the author; to Henry and Frances Francis, for permission to quote from their letters and journals; to David L. Hurwood, for permission to quote from the memoir of Bella Wolfson by Henry Hurwitz; to Barbara Ivins, for permission to quote from the letters of her father, W. M. Ivins, Jr.; to Mme. G. Powell-Pouzzner, for permission to quote from a family memoir; to Norris Darrell, Gerald Gunther, and Mrs. James H. Chadbourn, for permission to quote from a letter of Learned Hand; to Harvard University Archives, for permission to quote from the diaries of Mrs. Arthur Kingsley Porter; to Avery Library, Columbia University Libraries, for the letters of Cecil Pinsent.

Grateful acknowledgment is also made to Norman MacKenzie, for permission to quote from *The Letters of Sidney and Beatrice Webb*, Cambridge University Press, ©1978; to Baron Cecil Anrep, for permission to quote from *Sunset and Twilight*, Harcourt, Brace & World Inc., New York, ©1963; from *Rumor and Reflection*, Simon & Schuster, New York, copyright 1952; and from *Sketch for a Self-Portrait*, Pantheon Books, New York, copyright 1949; to Simon & Schuster, for permission to quote from *The Bernard Berenson Treasury*, edited by Hannah Kiel, ©1962 Simon & Schuster, New York; to Houghton Mifflin Company for permission to quote from *The Selected Letters of Bernard Berenson* edited by Arthur K. McComb, ©1963 by Houghton Mifflin Company, Boston; to Wayne State University Press for permission to quote from *The Letters of Dr. Richard Maurice Bucke to Walt Whitman*, edited by Artem Lozynsky, ©1977, Wayne State University Press, Detroit, Michigan; to Alfred A. Knopf Inc., for permission to quote from *The Flowers of Friendship: Letters Written to Gertrude Stein*, edited by Donald C. Gallup, New York, copyright 1953; and to Mrs. Pamela Diamand, for permission to quote from *Letters of Roger Fry*, edited by Denys Sutton, Random House, New York, ©1972 by Mrs. Pamela Diamand.

For K, with love

This self, what is it? For about seventy years I have been asking that question.

—*Sketch for a Self-Portrait*

Before his death, Rabbi Zusya said, "In the coming world, they will not ask me: 'Why were you not Moses?' They will ask me: 'Why were you not Zusya?'"

—Hasidic tale

CONTENTS

CONTENTS

ACKNOWLEDGMENTS

THE IDEA OF A BOOK on Bernard Berenson took shape in London one evening at dinner, in the agile mind of Francis King, the British author and critic. It developed in extensive conversations with Kenneth Clark, the distinguished British art historian, who suggested that I might see the book in terms of the rise, and fall, and rise, of a man. That portrait was given further dimension by Berenson's other lifelong friends, Count Umberto Morra and John Walker, both of whom met Berenson before World War II.

From an article in *Yiddish* magazine, "Bernard Berenson of Butremanz" by Michael Fixler, I found the first outlines of a theory about the effect of assimilation into a Gentile culture which I have tried to advance in this book. From Alfred Werner's equally penetrating article, "Bernard Berenson's Guilt Feelings," in *The Reconstructionist*, I gained some insights into the blend of nostalgia, shame, and guilt which such an assimilation exacted. I am indebted to both of these writers.

These and other clues gave me the sense of direction I needed. I went to the neo-Jacobean cottage of Jonathan Gathorne-Hardy in Wiltshire to rummage about in ancient trunks for memorabilia of the Pearsall Smith family, and to the Marchesa Serlupi's beautiful villa outside Florence to view the shell-pocked façade and the rooms in which Berenson hid for thirteen months during World War II.

I traveled to the California coast to talk with Mr. and Mrs. Ralph Barton Perry, Jr., and examine their family souvenirs, and to Williamstown, Massachusetts, to spend an afternoon with Michael Reinlander, one of the last of Berenson's scholar-apprentices. When I had almost finished the manuscript I learned the whereabouts of Berenson's principal advisor in matters of restoration, Giannino Marchig, and visited him in his beautiful villa on the shore of Lac Léman outside Geneva.

I found so many unexpected associations and coincidences that I was hardly surprised to learn that a near neighbor had found, in a trunk, letters from his parents describing their visit to "i Tatti" in the thirties.

ACKNOWLEDGMENTS

Invaluable information was provided by those friends of Berenson in the United States, Italy, Great Britain, and France who were kind enough to talk to me. My deepest thanks go to them: Sir Harold Acton, Sir Geoffrey Agnew, Mrs. Kinta Beevor, Mr. and Mrs. James Berenson, Mrs. Adelyn Breeskin, J. Carter Brown, John James Byam Shaw, Countess Elena Carandini, David Carritt, Mrs. Patricia Botond Chapman, Countess Anna Maria Cicogna, Count Vittorio Cini, Lord Clark and the late Lady Jane Clark, Sir Ashley Clarke, Prince and Princess Clary von Aldringen, Mr. and Mrs. Giovanni Colaccichi, Mr. and Mrs. Michael Colefax, the late Henry Coster and Mrs. Coster, Allyn Cox, Mr. and Mrs. Norris Darrell, Richard Davis, Miss Alice De Lamar, Everett Fahy, John Fleming, James Thomas Flexner, Mrs. Edward Fowles, Mr. and Mrs. Henry Sayles Francis, Judith Friedberg, Mr. and Mrs. William N. Gates, Miss Martha Gellhorn, Jean Gimpel and Mrs. Florence Gimpel, Mr. and Mrs. Bertram Goldsmith, Marco Grassi, Mrs. Renato Guttuso, Mrs. Sherman Post Haight, Mrs. Barbara Halpern, Mr. and Mrs. Hamish Hamilton, Prof. Fred Hartt, Prof. Francis Haskell, Mrs. Mary Hemingway, Philip Hofer, Mr. and Mrs. James Hogg, Hugh Honour, David Hurwood, Heyward Isham, Hanna Kiel, Dr. Edward S. King, Mrs. Livia Pappini di Kusmich, Lady Peta Lambe, Sir John Leslie, Rosamond Lehmann, Princess Dina Lieven, Mrs. Hannah R. London, the late Countess Marina Luling-Borchetti, Henry McIlhenny, Prof. G. Marchig, Clotilde Marghieri, Igor Markevitch, Mrs. Yehudi Menuhin, Prof. and Mrs. Ulrich Middeldorf, the late Dr. William Milliken, Prof. Bruno Molajoli, Miss Agnes Mongan, Mrs. Alan Moorehead, Count Umberto Morra di Lavriano, Raymond Mortimer, William Mostyn-Owen, Mrs. Norbert Muhlen, Mrs. Kenneth Murdock, the late Benedict Nicolson, Luisa Vertova Nicolson, Mrs. Richard Offner, Mr. and Mrs. Bernard Berenson Perry, Mr. and Mrs. Ralph Barton Perry, Jr., Sir John Pope-Hennessy, Mario Praz, Mascia Predit, Dr. Nathan Pusey, Michael Reinlander, John Russell, Prof. Meyer Schapiro, Marchesa Serlupi-Crescenzi, Mrs. Caroline Sizer, William Jay Smith, Freya Stark, Mr. and Mrs. Julian Trevelyan, Hugh Trevor-Roper, William Royall Tyler, John Walker, Gordon Waterfield, Sir Ellis Waterhouse, and Irene Worth.

For those of his friends who were generous enough to let me borrow letters, I am particularly indebted. As I have mentioned, Bernard and Barton Perry were willing to let me peruse not only the letters of Berenson and his wife Mary but the travel diaries of his sisters, Senda and Bessie, and the family correspondence in their possession, as well as in the collection of Ralph Barton Perry in the Harvard University Archives.

My deepest thanks also go to Mrs. Norris Darrell, for the complete exchange between Berenson and Learned Hand; to James Thomas Flexner for the papers of Simon Flexner; to Henry and Frances Francis for excerpts from their diaries and journals, and letters from Berenson and also from Bessie Berenson and Alda von Anrep; to Hamish Hamilton, for the complete exchange between Berenson and himself; to Mrs. Yehudi Menuhin, for the same; to Lord and Lady Clark, for the letters to them from Berenson, Mary Berenson, and Nicky Mariano; to Mary Hemingway, for the complete exchange between Berenson and Ernest Hemingway; to Rosamond Lehmann, for permission to read her letters from Berenson at King's College; to Clotilde Marghieri, for an exchange of letters; to John Walker, for selections from Berenson's letters to him; to Benedict Nicolson, for his collection of letters; to Hugh Trevor-Roper, Michael Colefax, Prof. Fred Hartt, Barbara Howes, and Lady Peta Lambe for similar loans; and to Princess Olga of Yugoslavia for letters of Berenson to Prince Paul. I am also indebted to Jonathan Gathorne-Hardy for the loan of letters of Hannah Whitall Smith, Alys Russell, Logan Pearsall Smith, and other family memorabilia; to William Royall Tyler for Berenson's letters to Edith Wharton; to Mrs. Pamela Diamand for the letters of Mr. and Mrs. Bernard Berenson to Roger Fry; to Mrs. Michael Eland for the letters to Maurice Brockwell; to Mrs. Paula Schindler for the letters of Berenson to Frau Mally Dienemann; to Charles Hapgood for extracts from the diary of Neith Boyce Hapgood; to C. Russell Scott for letters, photographs, and memorabilia about Geoffrey Scott; to David Hurwood for permission to quote from his father's memoir; to Patricia Chapman for permission to quote from her unpublished memoir; to John Russell for permission to quote from the unpublished writings of Logan Pearsall Smith; to Mrs. Barbara Halpern for permission to quote from the letters of Mary Berenson; to Barbara Ivins for permission to quote from her own writings and those of her father, and to read Berenson's letters to him; to Philip Siff, for a memoir of Alter Berenson; to Mme. G. Powell-Pouzzner for permission to quote from a private memoir; to Prof. Roberto Pane, for a charming memoir; to Paul Draper, for permission to read the letters of Geoffrey Scott to his mother, Muriel

Draper; to Mark Velsey, for permission to read the letters of his parents, Seth and Elinor Velsey; to Norman Mackenzie for extracts from the letters of Sidney and Beatrice Webb; to Gordon Waterfield, for letters from the Berensons to his mother, Lina Waterfield; to Philippa Offner, for permission to quote from the unpublished writings of the late Richard Offner, and to Dr. Cecil Anrep, for permission to study Berenson's letters to Isabella Stewart Gardner at the Archives of American Art. My special thanks also go to Derek Hill for his generous loan of two photographs of Berenson.

For permission to read the letters of Mrs. Gardner to Berenson, also at the Archives of American Art, the Smithsonian Institution, Washington, D.C., I wish to thank the present director of Fenway Court, Rollin Van N. Hadley. The following universities, museums, libraries, and other collections have made material available for this study:

Fogg Art Museum, Mrs. Phoebe Peebles, archivist: Letters to Edward W. Forbes, director, owned by Mrs. Rosamond F. Pickhardt; to Paul J. Sachs, associate director, owned by Mrs. Richard Stillwell; and to Grenville L. Winthrop.

Washington University Libraries, St. Louis, Missouri: Letters to William Jay Smith.

Stanford University Libraries, Stanford, California: Letters of Berenson to Albert Guérard.

Truman Library, Independence, Missouri: Letters of Berenson to President Truman.

Smith College Archives, Northampton, Massachusetts, Mary B. Trott, assistant archivist: 1971 thesis of Agnes Cora Ruth Stillman on Senda Berenson. Faculty files on Senda, her husband Herbert A. Abbott, her brother-in-law Ralph Barton Perry, and her sister Elizabeth Berenson. Rachel Berenson, class file of 1902. Mary Whitall Smith, class file of 1885.

Kent State University, Kent State, Ohio, Dean H. Keller, curator of special collections: Letters, diaries, and notebooks of Logan Pearsall Smith.

Boston Public Library, James Lawton, Department of Rare Books and Manuscripts: Letters of Berenson to Hugo Münsterberg and Sir Sydney Cockerell.

Goteborgs Universitetsbibliotek, Goteborg, Sweden, Miss Ola Christensson: Letters of Berenson to Axel Boethius.

Princeton University Library, Richard M. Ludwig, librarian, and Mrs. Ann Farr: Letters from Berenson to Frank Jewett

Mather. William Seymour Theatre Collection, Mary Ann Jensen, curator: Letters to Otto Kahn.

American Philosophical Society Library, James E. McClellan, assistant manuscript librarian: Mr. and Mrs. Berenson to Simon Flexner.

King's College, Cambridge, England, Penelope Bulloch, archivist: Letters from Mr. and Mrs. Berenson to Roger Fry. My warm thanks for the special help of Kate Miller.

University of Glasgow Library, Glasgow, Scotland, J. Baldwin, Keeper of Special Collections: Letters to D. S. MacColl.

Columbia University Libraries, Kenneth A. Lohf, librarian: Letters of Mr. and Mrs. Berenson and Nicky Mariano to Mr. and Mrs. Henry Scherman, Max Lincoln Schuster, Prince Paul of Yugoslavia, Jacques Barzun, Louis A. Freedman, and Marguerite Carrière. Letters of Logan Pearsall Smith.

Columbia University, Avery Architectural Library, Carol Falcione, reference librarian: Letters to Kenyon Cox and letters in the Henry Hope Reed collection.

Colby College, Waterville, Maine, J. Fraser Cocks III, special collections: Letters to T. S. Perry and Lilla Perry; Mr. and Mrs. Berenson to Violet Paget; an essay on "Plagiarism" by Violet Paget.

Boston Museum of Fine Arts, Joyce Tyler, acting archivist: For the files on Berenson, Langton Douglas, Frederick Mason Perkins, and others.

"I Tatti," Florence, Italy, Craig Hugh Smyth, director, and Fiorella Superbi, photographic librarian: Permission to examine letters which have entered the Archive since the death of Nicky Mariano, including those to Frank Jewett Mather, Prof. Sidney Freedberg, Mrs. Margaret Scolari Barr, and Prof. Alexander d'Entrèves. Permission to reproduce photographs in the "i Tatti" Archives.

Yale University, Sterling Memorial Library: Letter of Mary Berenson to Prof. Weir; letters of Mary, Nicky Mariano, and Berenson to Walter Lippmann, with the special assistance of Robert O. Anthony, advisor to the Walter Lippmann papers.

Harvard University Archives, Harley P. Holden, curator, and Bonnie B. Salt, curatorial associate: Berenson letters in the papers of President A. Lawrence Lowell; articles and short stories of Berenson in the *The Harvard Monthly*; Berenson letters to the Ralph Barton Perry family; letters from the Berensons to Prof. and Mrs. Arthur Kingsley Porter; the diaries of Mrs. Porter.

ACKNOWLEDGMENTS

Harvard University, Houghton Library, Rodney G. Dennis, curator, and Patrick Miehe, curatorial assistant: Letters to Witter Bynner, by permission of James Kraft; letters to Francis Henry Taylor, M. T. Chanler, J. J. Chapman, R. W. Curtis, W. P. Garrison, M. A. de W. Howe, Agnes Mongan, C. E. Norton, Miss Norton, T. S. Perry, Corinne Roosevelt Robinson, and Barrett Wendell; letters of Sir William Rothenstein to Berenson, Mary Berenson to Sir William Rothenstein and Geoffrey Scott, ditto.

Yale University, Beinecke Rare Book and Manuscript Library, Donald Gallup, curator, and Peter Dzwonkoski, assistant curator: The Berensons to Theodore Sizer, "Minnie" Jones, Gertrude Stein, Leo Stein, Hutchins and Neith Hapgood; the 1903 diary of Neith Hapgood; letters to Edith Wharton and to Royal Cortissoz. Geoffrey Scott: Letters from Scott to W. H. Haslam, letter from Miss Anna Dorothea Scott to Haslam, Haslam's recollections of Scott, and a letter from Haslam to David Buchanan. Letters of Scott to Muriel Draper.

Philadelphia Museum of Art, Johnson Collection, Joseph Rishel, curator, and Irene Konefal: Letters of Berenson to John J. Johnson.

Walters Art Gallery, Baltimore, Edward S. King, research associate: Letters of Berenson to Henry Walters.

Manuscript Division, Library of Congress, John C. Broderick, chief: Letters of Mary Whitall Smith Costelloe to Walt Whitman; the Berensons to Hendrik C. Andersen; letters of Logan Pearsall Smith.

Archives of American Art, Garnett McCoy, director, and Arthur Breton, manuscript curator: Letters of Mrs. Isabella Stewart Gardner, W. M. Ivins, Jr., René Gimpel, by permission of Jean Gimpel, D. V. Thomson, Ralph Curtis to Mrs. Gardner, and the August Jaccaci papers. I would like to add my particular thanks here to Messrs. McCoy and Breton for their help and add that the Archives is an invaluable source of information for art history of the period.

My further thanks are due to the following men and women who gave help, advice, information, and their valuable time: Miss Dina Abramowicz, librarian, Yivo Institute for Jewish Research, New York; Philip Rhys Adams, R. Ainsztein, Dr. Jacob Marcus, American Jewish Archives; James E. McClellan, American Philosophical Society; Pamela Askew, Mrs. Ralph Backlund, Carlos Baker, Sir Cecil Beaton, Marisa Berenson, Charles Beveridge, Yvon Bizardel, David Blelloch, Daniel Boorstin, Carol Bradley,

Acknowledgments

David Brown, curator, and J. Carter Brown, director, National Gallery of Art; David Buchanan, Donald A. Bullard, Sophie Burnham, Mrs. Bryson Burroughs, Philippa Calnan, Tony Carroll, Tom Carter, National Gallery; Central Archives, History of the Jewish People; Countess Laetitia Cerio, Jean Chalon, Gerald Clarke, Michèle Cliff, Prof. James Clifford, Elle Milani-Comparetti, Mrs. Charles D. Compton, Douglas Cooper, Edward A. Craig, Alda and Elena Croce, Fitzroy Davis, Lavinia Davies, Colnaghi's; Rupert Hart-Davis, Mrs. Jean Demos, Jacqueline Derby, Derner Institute, Munich; Mrs. Caroline Despard, Barbara Lee Diamonstein, Moussa M. Domit, director, North Carolina Museum of Art; Dr. Jerome Edelstein, librarian, National Gallery of Art; Prof. Colin Eisler, Countess Barbara Emo, Alan Fern, Mrs. Betty Foy, National Gallery of Art; B. H. Friedman, Herbert Friedmann, Henry Gardiner, director, Fine Arts Gallery of San Diego; Prof. Creighton Gilbert, Michael Gill, Prof. Myron Gilmore, Morton David Goldberg, Gaby Goldscheider, S. A. Goudsmit, Dr. Elio E. Grandi, Prof. Mina Gregori, Prof. Gerald Gunther, Richard Hall, Ron Hall, Lily Harmon, Marguerite Harris, W. H. Haslam, Joan Haslip, Anthony R. A. Hobson, Michael Holroyd, Michèle Isbell, Jonathan Trumbull Isham, Masao Ishizawa, Museum Yamato Bunkakan, Nara, Japan; John Jamieson, Lawrence Jeppson, Ben B. Johnson, Los Angeles County Museum; Mrs. R. Keith Kane, Justin Kaplan, Francis King, Robert Kimball, Elizabeth Shelton Knight, Mary Lago, Mary Lethbridge, Michael Levey, director, National Gallery; Peter Luling, Dr. Irma Lustig, Mrs. Nesta Macdonald, Michael Maclagan, Dr. Lawrence Marwick, Jonathan Marwik, Stephen C. Massey, Christie's; A. Hyatt Mayor, Ursula McCracken, Mr. and Mrs. J. Harvey McKenney, Mrs. Daphne Hoffman Mebane, Mrs. Millard Meiss, Lillian Miller, Pamela T. Morton, Rowland Burton-Muller, Jack Murphy, Edward Croft-Murray, Vicomte Charles de Noailles, Nigel Nicolson, Lucy Oakley, Department of European Paintings, Metropolitan Museum of Art; Iris Origo, Maître George Pannier, Andrew Patrick, Elizabeth Pennington, the *Manchester Guardian*; Mrs. Herbert Pratt, Prof. Ugo Procacci, Fondazione Horne, Florence; Elbertus Prol, Peter Quennell, Dr. Edgar P. Richardson, Gerald Reitlinger, Prof. Giles Robertson, Frank A. Ruhemann, Mrs. John Barry Ryan, Linda St. Thomas, Smithsonian Institution; Margaretta Salinger, Russell M. Scott, Roy Slade, Mrs. William A. Slade, Mrs. Everett W. Smith, Francis Steegmuller, Prof. Leo Steinberg, Yuri Suhl, Mrs. F. Carroll

ACKNOWLEDGMENTS

Taylor, John M. Taylor, Dr. Joshua Taylor, Lisa Suter Taylor, Michael Thomas, Anne Turner, BBC-TV; Richard Turner, Hugo R. Vickers, Alfred Werner, William White, the late Walter Muir Whitehill, Mrs. Michael Wood, Russell Woollen, Herman Wouk, Frank Wright, and Mahonri Sharp Young.

In conclusion I want particularly to thank Sir Ellis Waterhouse, whose knowledge of Old Master paintings is perhaps unparalleled, and who bore my endless questions and demands upon his time with the utmost patience and good humor. Similar thanks are due to the immensely knowledgeable art historian and businessman David Carritt.

I also want to thank two men whose support has been life-enhancing, to use a Berensonian phrase. First, Lord Clark, whose interest and vital help made this book possible; who is the most stimulating of mentors and the kindest and most generous of friends.

I would also like to thank my husband, Thomas Beveridge, who helped me, encouraged me, listened to me, took care of me, and never let me give up hope.

PREFACE

ONE TRADITIONALLY BEGINS a biography by thanking all those heirs of the subject who have opened their caskets and hearts to make such a work as complete as is humanly possible

This was not the case for me. Shortly after I began work on this study I learned that I could not have access to any of the thousands of letters, diaries, and other memorabilia in the Berenson Archive at "i Tatti." The reason is a curious one.

Under the terms of Berenson's will, his secretary, Nicky Mariano, was given complete freedom to dispose of his Archive as she saw fit. If she died first, the Archive would be given to Harvard University at Berenson's death and sealed for twenty-five years (until 1984). Nicky Mariano, who outlived Berenson by nine years, chose to publish diaries and notebooks from his Archive and to appoint an official biographer. She died in 1968 without leaving a will.

As a result, the Archive did not pass to Harvard but was inherited by Nicky's sister, Alda von Anrep, and then Alda's son, Dr. Cecil von Anrep. He takes the position that he is not free to grant me access to the Archive. Similarly, the issue of publication rights to letters of Berenson outside the Archive seems legally obscure. I have avoided quoting from them directly.

Harvard University has indicated that it will take control of the Berenson Archive sometime in 1984. In the interim, I present some evidence and beg the reader's indulgence about inevitable gaps and omissions. Only a few clues to Berenson's childhood are in print. As to his business dealings with Joseph Duveen, the art dealer for whom he worked for thirty years, that correspondence is locked away at the Metropolitan Museum of Art in New York and cannot be made public until the year 2002. However, forty years have elapsed since Lord Duveen died. In the last decade museums have begun to publish *catalogues raisonnés* which offer a great many clues to the buying history of these paintings for those who have learned how to interpret them.

I hope my preliminary studies in this area will inspire some-one to undertake a comprehensive study of Berenson's attributions, one that is long overdue. When that takes place the compiler will need to distinguish between those attributions for which Berenson received payment, usually substantial, and those for which he did not.

One might assume that everything to be learned about a man lies locked in his personal effects, forgetting that what is likely to be found are letters from others. His own are scattered everywhere and, in the case of Berenson, one does not need to look far, since he detested the telephone. A clue to their numbers may be gained from scanning the Acknowledgments.

Similarly, Berenson's network of friendships was equally extensive. A great many people remember him, some with memories stretching back for sixty years. More than one hundred were willing to be interviewed.

Finally, Berenson's only direct heirs, his nephews Barton Perry and Bernard Perry, have generously allowed me to read their collections of family letters. These have provided an unparalleled insight into Berenson's private world.

In retrospect, I believe I was fortunate to have been presented with these obstacles. Because of them, I have perhaps searched further and more persistently than I might otherwise have done. Too, perhaps we overemphasize the biographical importance of assembling every available scrap of information about another human being. Everything we do reveals some aspect of ourselves. We are consistent, and each act is a clue to the whole. Or, we are inconsistent; our words and actions do not accord with our secret selves. This, too, reveals us.

MERYLE SECREST
Chevy Chase, Maryland

HIGH WALLS

The mansion's self was vast and venerable
With more of the monastic than has been
Elsewhere preserved: the cloisters still were stable,
The cells, too, and refectory, I ween:
An exquisite small chapel had been able
Still unimpair'd, to decorate the scene;
The rest had been reform'd, replaced, or sunk
And spoke more of the baron than the monk.

—BYRON, *Don Juan*, "Canto the 13th, LXVI"

ONE MIGHT BEGIN, perhaps, with a landscape by Giorgione. This tapestry of cypresses and palms is steeped in a sheen of golden light, suffusing the limbs of statuesque Muses with warmth, powdering the opalescent shadows and dappling the wings of swallows wheeling in the luminous air.

As one lingers over the painting's details, there appear vistas of steps vanishing up a hill, ascending levels of lawns framed with hedges and clipped boxwood as regimented as pawns on a chessboard, leading the eye to a sixteenth-century villa on the horizon.

One can walk in these Renaissance gardens almost undisturbed nowadays, except for an occasional half-wild cat, who purrs and bites. One's feet crunch against gravel and one's footsteps bounce echoes from the high concealing walls. White doves whirr upward at the sound, with a scattering of wings.

These are gardens to avoid, rather than explore. There is something too precise about that parade of sunlit terraces; something bleak and formidable about that unbroken severity of design. So one skirts each edge, where *allées* of cypresses and ilex have been planted and sloping paths are almost black with shadow; the slithery, streaked bark is soft with moss, where it is always damp and silent; or one finds a stream garlanded with willows, or banks of flowers massed in the cutting garden. There is a jungle of thistles and the faint smell of onions coming from the kitchen beyond.

To visit "i Tatti" is to experience more than the pleasure of stepping into the frame of a Renaissance painting. It is to be transported into a dreamland of the aesthetic imagination: Altamura. To Bernard Berenson and those friends who imagined it at the turn of the century, Altamura was to be a monastery, but one devoted to the Spirit of Delight, to the arts of living. It had its own pursuits, its own code of conduct, its own religion, its own maxim: "Nil dulcius est, bene quam munita tenere/ Edita doctrina sapientum templa serena" ("There is no greater pleasure than to have a quiet sanctuary well-stocked with learned instruction"). This villa, transformed from a modest farmhouse on the hills of Settignano not far from Florence, was the setting in which its inhabitants might "dwell in the contemplation of eternal essences . . . behold Beauty with the eye of the mind and . . . feed on the shadows of perfection."

Like a palace or a church, "i Tatti" has been swept clear of extraneous detail, so that each remaining object carries symbolic weight. The white entrance is uncluttered, directing the eye to a Greek statue of a boy, lacking an arm. The statue faces the small, late-seventeenth-century chapel in which its former owner and his wife are buried. Entering the villa, one finds shining corridors, whose severe, unadorned walls act as a perfect foil for the exquisite paintings, sculpture, and objets d'art displayed: Siamese, Egyptian, Chinese, and Persian, but most of all, Renaissance Italian.

Berenson's old magnifying glass still sits on the mat of rose brocade in his study; the black paint on the handle is worn, revealing the wood beneath. Above it is the famous, incomparable painting of the Madonna and Child by Domenico Veneziano. There is a luminous quality to the marble flesh, in fastidious contrast to the surrounding tones of soft rose and gold and delicate, dull blues; and the painting hangs against a panel of the palest green brocade. The colors in the room are equally muted: golds, greens, and rose. The chairs are dowdily comfortable, like those of an English country house, and the decor is half lost in shadow, despite a bright morning light. From the shuttered windows, one catches a glimpse of a high, pale sky, Greek gods in marble, and a persimmon tree.

A visitor, a bride on her honeymoon, was right in complaining that the house was cheerless. Berenson did not mind. He liked its classical restraint, its overtones of the monastic, contemplative, cloistered life, barricaded against the world. Like a frozen reflection, the villa preserves its master's relentless search for perfection, the alabaster austerity of his mind. While he lived, not one object might be moved two inches to the right or left before he, with trembling fingers, would return it to its rightful place. Now, like silhouettes in an old photograph, these objects stand petrified by time, turning to stone. *"Those are pearles that were his eies . . ."*

Hundreds came to see him, while he lived: kings, presidents, and princes; those who collected art and those who collected each other; movie stars and politicians, students and scholars. Like Shaw, he was referred to by his initials, and was considered a consummate connoisseur and aesthete, author of The Four Gospels, four slim but crucial studies of the Venetian, Florentine, Central and North Italian painters of the Renaissance. These had been written at the turn of the century. There was a gap of decades, and then B.B. had sprung into prominence with a flood of new books on aesthetics, history, World War II, and his own life—the distillations of old age.

B.B. became the universal man, the last man in the West "still trying to live life as a hard, gemlike flame." He was a mass-media sage, to be compared with Titian and Michelangelo, whose continuing service to art put him on a rarefied plane far above mere professors or professionals. The city of Florence, in which he had, in defiance of probability, lived out the war years, made B.B. its honorary citizen. The Sorbonne gave him an honorary degree and so did the University of Florence. Cecil Beaton took his photograph. Pietro Annigoni sketched him, and Derek Hill painted him. Jacqueline Kennedy sat at his feet, Hemingway wrote him letters, and President Truman came for tea.

What caught the popular imagination, and made B.B. a myth in his own time, was the image of the aesthete and scholar, disinterestedly pursuing excellence in a world of chaos, dedicating a lifetime to Beauty and Art. His generous decision to leave "i Tatti" to Harvard University after his death added further luster to the flawless image. B.B. not only provided his alma mater with an exquisite house and art collection, but an extraordinary library of 55,000 volumes, the collection of a lifetime. One can discern the Altamuran ideal in his expressed desire that "i Tatti" become an institution dedicated to the leisurely contemplation of Beauty; specifically, the artistic achievements of the Italian Renaissance.

By the mid-1950s, the prince of Altamura had long since forgone the delights of dining out, except on his still frequent pilgrimages to the Italian towns and villages whose art he had first encountered half a century before. But he was by no means cloistered behind his high walls. He loved to entertain, the more the better, and maintained a daily social round which would have exhausted others less disciplined, less eager for information and for the stimulus of fresh viewpoints.

So, despite his despairing comments that the avalanche of attention "will kill me yet," he invited guests for lunch, tea, dinner, and sometimes the weekend as well. Enough of them were writers to provide a clear picture of the kind of experience that a visitor, arriving for a stay at "i Tatti" in the mid-1950s, might reasonably anticipate.

"I had come in through the great iron gates of 'i Tatti' and had confronted the butler, and had seen my dusty luggage borne away through corridors of paintings, and, tense as a cat among the dishes and the Venetian fingerbowls, had kept afloat through dinner, and had then woken in the morning to observe the valet who, thermometer in hand, had come to run my bath, and who had brought my breakfast tray with its little posy of flowers and copies of *Il Corriere della Sera*, the *Zuricher Zeitung* and the *London Times*, only two days old."

Guests would meet, almost immediately, Berenson's nominal secretary and the real mainstay of the household, Nicky Mariano, an enchanting half-Baltic, half-Italian gentlewoman of indeterminate age who had arrived at "i Tatti" after World War I to act as librarian and had never left it. As B.B.'s wife Mary slipped into chronic invalidism, Nicky Mariano gradually took over the management of Altamura and, after Mrs. Berenson died in 1945, became the only mind behind the man. She was in effect the second Mrs. Berenson, whom B.B. called "the necessity, the solace, the happiness of my life." She helped to write his books, she ran the staff of servants, oversaw the accounts, wrote the business letters, and acted as hostess to the platoons of guests.

Newcomers who might feel in awe of their host were unanimous in their praise of Nicky Mariano's incomparable ability to set them at their ease; her sympathy, gaiety, and tact; her ability to juggle seating charts, dates, and menus; to see that they arrived like clockwork and departed in a glow of warm feelings.·

However, Nicky Mariano's embracing warmth of newcomers was never allowed to deflect her from her larger role as B.B.'s *ange gardien*. It was she who arranged for a guest's departure with such tact that he did not realize that its exquisite timing had been orchestrated by her, until he had walked out of the door and through the gates. It was she who guarded B.B.'s privacy, read to him in a dozen languages, and ministered to his needs; and she was the one who slept outside his door at night if he were ill.

Visitors to Altamura found themselves at once in the ambiance of an Edwardian country house. Suitcases would be unpacked, clothes folded into drawers or neatly hung, and toilet articles laid out. After the morning breakfast tray had been delivered and removed, guests might lounge in bed all morning if they wished, although the subject of frequent attention: servants arriving to tend to the bedroom fire, pick up and deliver clothes, or minister to special needs.

After lunch, the blinds were drawn, the immaculately made beds turned down, and a robe laid out for the guest. The assumption at Altamura was that, since its owner took an afternoon nap, everyone else also did. Very few guests took advantage of the opportunity, and so the beds were remade, to be turned down once again at night. Before bed, a servant would indeed appear with a thermometer to run the guest's bath. A maid at Altamura was on duty from 6:30 in the morning until 10:30 or 11:00 at night.

Guests would assemble for lunch or dinner about fifteen minutes before the meal and might find themselves seated in a room, staring uncomfortably at another guest, to whom they had not yet been introduced. Elizabeth Gates, a distant relative, recalls visiting "i Tatti" in the 1950s with her husband Bill and sitting in polite silence with the British novelist Rosamond Lehmann, an old friend of the host. Bill Gates reached for a bottle of vermouth, to offer the novelist a glass, and—out poured a spider.

The incident, which was the start of a warm friendship, provides an incidental commentary on the cavalier attitude, in the court of Altamura, toward the cocktail hour. Vermouth or some other Italian aperitif was the rule, spirits never, not even for guests. Habitués soon learned to bring their own bottles of Scotch and drank secretly in their rooms, from toothbrush glasses.

The host, a man of precise habits, contrived to arrive last, a split second before the meal was served. This exercise of prerogative had given rise to the expression that one went to have an audience with B.B. It was also said that he was the only man ever to have kept Queen Helen of Rumania waiting. He certainly kept the King of Sweden, another habitué of his court, waiting on numerous occasions. The royal archaeologist didn't seem to mind.

"The first time Sir Lewis and Lady Namier visited 'i Tatti,' Lady Namier didn't know what B.B. looked like," recalled their mutual friends, Hugh Honour and John Fleming. "Seeing a tall and imposing man coming towards her, she naturally assumed that it was her host. He announced gravely, 'I am the King of Sweden.' Lady Namier was just about to retort, 'And I am the Queen of Sheba,' when Berenson himself arrived."

He was a small slim figure, always impeccably dressed and groomed, with a fresh flower in his buttonhole, or, if it was evening, wearing black tie. (He would magnanimously tell younger male guests that a dinner jacket was just a habit with him, and he didn't care what they wore; but it is also true that Nicky Mariano made a point of suggesting that they bring one.) One sensed a tough, resilient personality—"the masculinity of the little jockey"—inside a body that was as fragile as glass; he looked, said the Australian writer Alan Moorehead, as if a puff of wind would blow him away.

The fastidiously timed arrival was, no doubt, calculated for its imperial effect, but there was a further reason. The actress Irene Worth remarked on the sureness of Berenson's entrance into a room, of the involuntary hush that fell on the conversation, in short, of his mastery of dramatic timing. "He did it," she said, "through Presence."

Berenson would extend a small dry hand to each as he made his way around the room, graciously remembering to compliment one on his book, or another on his new appointment. Then, at a magical signal, he would lead the way into the dining room.

In the mid-1950s, "il Bibi," as the Italians called him, was, at the age of almost ninety, physically and mentally agile. His temples might be deeply hollowed, the skin around his alert blue eyes fretted with fine wrinkles, and his hands, so exquisitely slender, might betray the marks of age; but his mind had lost none of its prodigious powers, and his memory was almost as faultless as it had been fifty years before.

His neatly clipped beard had nautical overtones reminding some of King George V, and the precisely enunciated English which B.B. spoke furthered the Edwardian parallel. Some believed that he had a cultured Boston accent, others, a cultured British one. It is agreed, however, that B.B. used some Edwardian mannerisms of speech that could only have originated in England.

"What he actually says is ' 'uge,' just as he says 'grea' deal,' in the way that other gentlemen of the old school drop their final 'g's or say, 'Don't you know?' or recall Edward VII, who had 'such a vulgar back,' " Cyril Ray, a British journalist, reported. His voice was quiet and gentle, and did not resonate, probably accounting for his lifelong reluctance to make public speeches. He never talked on the telephone.

Guests differed in their assessment of the Altamuran cuisine. Some thought it unpretentious, but good, country cooking. Others found it indifferent and blamed that on the fact that B.B. never ate the same menu. He always had special food for his "nervous stomach," and hardly any of that: a thimbleful of rice, two drops of wine, and a sliver of steamed fish. One seldom actually caught him eating. It was as if the act itself were so repugnant to the sensibilities of a truly cultured man that it could only be done furtively, behind locked doors.

For B.B., meals were the principal setting for the game of conversation, which for him was the goal of life. Some likened it to a performance of chamber music in which B.B. took the part of first violin. He talked of anything and everything. "Which route did I think Milton took to Vallombrosa in 1638, and how much did I earn, and how much did my wife, and how much went in taxes? A word about smoked buffalo's milk cheese, and another about the two great disasters that had befallen Europe in our time—the collapse of the Austro-Hungarian and that of the Turkish Empires," Cyril Ray wrote.

The tragedy nowadays, B.B. told a British friend, Barbara Skelton, and her husband, was that journalists controlled world affairs and, since they had absolutely no historic sense, they failed to understand the present. " 'Even politics were governed by journalists; diplomats did not count any more. . . . Too many people wrote; and they wrote solely for the present; no one gave a thought for the future. . . . ' " If he had unlimited money, B.B. continued, he would leave a trust fund for writers *not* to write. . . .

B.B. would keep talking through the hors d'oeuvre, the entrée, the salad and cheese courses, the fruit and coffee, day after day, year after year. What he needed, he said, was "someone to crank me up," and there were plenty of people ready to put a dime in the talking machine, for the pleasure of hearing what would come out of it. It was always a solo performance.

"I learned how with adroit questions to keep the dialogue going, how to protect B.B. when talk became ponderous . . . how to interject a light remark when the going was hard, how to applaud with laughter an aphorism, how to underline with gravity the profound," wrote John Walker, former director of the National Gallery of Art in Washington and a former Berenson protégé. Walker gives Nicky Mariano credit for having taught him the art of this delicately perilous game.

"When I had become a part of 'i Tatti,' I realized that Nicky and I were like stage managers of a production which required that one never permit a moment of silence. Always, the conversational ball must be kept in the air so B.B. could show his most brilliant strokes. It was fun, but it was tiring."

A rather different picture is presented by another former protégé of Berenson and former director of the National Gallery in London, Kenneth Clark, in his autobiography:

"The luncheons were very seldom harmonious, but this did not matter much, as most of the time was spent in listening to Mr. Berenson. Sometimes two celebrated monologists, Ugo Ojetti and Carlo Placci, were allowed to come on and do short turns; and occasionally a rich old American lady . . . could contain herself no longer and would give us her impressions of Florence. . . . But in general Mr. Berenson talked without interruption, except for shouts of laughter and applause. . . . "

B.B.'s omnivorous curiosity had ranged far beyond the narrow confines of the specialist and, because his naturally retentive memory had been further trained by the disciplines of attribution, his ability to call up ideas, personalities, and visual impressions was dazzling.

He had the same facile ability to improvise. Like Jean Cocteau, he had been given *le don de la réplique*, and, like that poet, sometimes could not resist a diverting idea in order to discover what he thought about it. Because he "thought in sentences just long enough to be spoken," his observations were invariably epigrammatic and his play of ideas had the darting quality of a dragonfly. He pronounced upon ideas the way he pronounced upon art, and if so few traces of his conversational brilliance survive it is because, as Cyril Connolly has noted, the spoken word is a highly perishable commodity.

There was no doubt, however, about the exhilarating effect he had on others. He seemed to have, Iris Origo noted, the gift of sharpening the faculties of everyone who came near him and one could not help being infected with some of his exuberance, whether or not one agreed with him.

Irene Worth went to "i Tatti," she said, because Berenson was a superb host and a challenging friend. "If he liked you, he was stimulated, and he stimulated you, and the whole thing sparkled." Another friend, Frances Francis, found B.B. incomparable for "the spark he ignited in one's brain."

What might seem stimulatingly fresh and provocative to some, others found offensive. "He started asking me impertinent questions about Hemingway," said the writer Martha Gellhorn, Hemingway's third wife. "He said, 'Why did Hemingway leave you?' In the first place, he didn't leave me, and in the second place, it was none of his business. I put him down rather sharply." Hemingway's widow Mary recalled the same not-so-subtle probings into her own relationship with the famous novelist; B.B. wanted to know how good a lover her husband was, and managed to "flummox" her in short order.

Other women guests might suddenly be asked, "And now my dear, what do you do that is *useful?*" or, if they had babies, as did the poet Barbara Howes, they might be asked if breast feeding was sexually pleasurable. All of these questions, in the most innocent tone of voice, could exasperate, astonish, or amuse, but they guaranteed a prompt response.

The problem implied in Kenneth Clark's reminiscence was one that others, who did not mind being prodded by the prince of talkers, found more difficult to deal with. B.B. might honestly believe, as Nicky Mariano wrote, that he enjoyed being contradicted, but in fact he always had to have the last word.

". . . I admitted the truth of his remarks. That cemented our friendship. There was nothing he loved more than a discussion which ended in agreement—agreement that he was right," John Walker commented, somewhat wryly. Even this might not have mattered so much had not B.B. been so conservative in his judgments and arbitrary into the bargain.

Proust had made a very poor impression; he had a voice like a peacock's screech. Ezra Pound was not insane, just lamentably ignorant and vulgar. T. S. Eliot was a terrible humbug. Auden was equally bad, and as for modern art, the only word to describe that was "un-art." Such judgments were delivered with the same finality with which B.B. would dispatch the notion that a certain rival critic had written anything of value, or that the mass of humanity could be educated, or that universal suffrage might be desirable: "Rubbish!"

Elizabeth Hardwick found hints in Berenson of personal animosities and a tendency to think himself undervalued. Iris Origo discussed his ability to "smell the smoke and stench of animal competitiveness," among intellectual equals like Salvemini, and to weigh the merits of Santayana, Bertrand Russell, and Benedetto Croce, other old friends, and find them all wanting. His ability, in fact, to drop old friends whom he now considered tiresome could be breathtaking in its callousness, Iris Origo observed.

Yet, he needed them. There was a core of friends who had become *unsereiner* (one of us) and B.B would say that he wanted "life-enhancing" friends, rather than "life-diminishing" ones, terms implying an ability to choose, which in fact he seldom exercised. In the sea of life, Berenson found himself enisled. Only the daily reassurance of an audience of fresh faces could temporarily assuage his inner isolation.

B.B's guests might, or might not, find him indispensable in their own lives. Some were reduced to agonies of shyness. Some, hoping to display their erudition, were sharply deflated. Others were bewildered, or resorted to bluffing, or marshaled their own wit and gave as good as they got. Still others attempted to deflect the barbed comment with a soothing, placating humor. A few were able to hold their own, observing the phenomenon with interest and detachment. These were always the people who intrigued B.B. most.

The particular conversational game being played to perfection at Altamura was one which Wilde would have recognized and, indeed, is still practiced in some London and Paris circles. It required one to be cleverly amusing and, if possible, original as well—superb in attack and faultless in defense. Invisible points were silently and continually being awarded and a player could find himself checkmated and off the board with devastating swiftness.

No wonder Alan Moorehead spoke in terms of trying to "stay afloat" and even the imperturbable John Walker found it tiring. An occasional innocent, like the young Ralph Barton Perry, Jr., son of B.B.'s sister Rachel, would wander into the group and sit silently through the barrage of comment in five different languages, because no one bothered to translate. They were not, as he said, very nice about that.

A few were always spared the rigors of battle. The young, if they were personable and not too self-important, might be treated with flattering partiality. A Vassar history student of beauty and intelligence might be singled out from her group, told that she had remarkable qualities, and urged to return. Women generally, if they had the slightest pretension to charm, were B.B.'s favorite audience. Society women, he wrote, were so much more receptive, appreciative, and likely to please than his intellectual equals; they didn't try to compete, and if they only vaguely understood, what did that matter, so long as they had "enough brains to feel fascinated."

B.B. was always at his best with women. His conversation was at its most vivid, erudite, and stimulating. There was something rather endearing about the way he would ask this woman, and then that one, to sit beside him at tea, and hold her hand gently, and stroke her hair, and fix on her one of his beautifully caressing glances.

For the fact is that B.B. was a flirt, an elderly one to be sure, and one who thought of himself as an indulgent father and grandfather only, but in whom women might correctly discern the unmistakable outlines of a seducer. Although he wrote in his diaries that he and Nicky became closer every day; that he was "every day more dependent, more grateful, more devoted," Berenson still felt the need for numerous flirtations conducted, in many cases, on paper, and which were, in any case, in his head, as one lady put it.

"I was one of B.B.'s last flirtations," said Diana Menuhin, wife of Yehudi. "I was his cheerer-upper. I would write him scandalous letters and we would go for walks and he would be rocking with laughter and holding on to the boulders for support.

"I tried to discourage him from flirting. The story in Florence was that B.B. would make a pass, and one would push him away, and then one would have to rush and catch him. It was all very amusing, but Nicky didn't think so. She was devastated. One would think he were her lover of twenty-six, not an old man of almost ninety."

B.B. also appeared persuaded that he might still woo and win a maid. He liked to challenge his young women guests with, "If I were ten years younger, would you have had an affair with me?" blissfully ignoring the fact that, at his age, a mere decade would hardly have made much difference. He liked to set up trysts in foreign cities during which Nicky, who accompanied him everywhere, would discreetly vanish.

"He used to stay in a hotel in Rome to which I'd be invited for dinner; there were practically pink-shaded lamps," Martha Gellhorn remembers. "I am an exceedingly unswoony lady, and at a given moment, he'd sit next to me on the sofa and I'd say, 'Nothing doing. Keep your little hands to yourself.'"

When the volcano, as B.B. termed it, is at last extinct, some men look back on the act of sex with tender nostalgia. B.B. seemed unable to realize that his younger women friends, and there were many, loved him for his mind and not for the frail, aged shell he inhabited. Or perhaps he realized it too well, and it is this which gives his diaries the avidity, the bite, and the immediacy of one for whom the hunger is unappeasable, because so freighted with regret.

B.B. wrote in the summer of 1956, three years before he died, "How unaware I was till extreme old age of the animal, the female in women I considered of my own world. . . . Now I scarcely approach a woman of 'my world' without feeling the moment she gives her hand how cold or how warm she is. And the majority are women glowingly hot even. Were I still potent, I could bed with many, and think the better of them. . . ."

What people found alluring about his character, seductive in the widest sense, was his vitality, his appetite for life. That was indomitable. He had learned to live life for its own sake and renewed himself by a daily contact with nature that was no less vital for having become ritualized.

Every morning, at the end of a complicated toilette that took an hour, a car would be backed in front of the door. B.B. would descend to a butler, waiting beside a row of gloves, scarves, and hats and seven or eight camel's hair coats, each more beautiful than the next. B.B. would choose one of each, pull on his gloves, tuck his scarf neatly inside the lapels of his coat, and tilt his hat to a properly jaunty angle. He would select a boutonniere from the vase of assorted flowers brought to him each morning and set off with Parry, his Welsh chauffeur, in a peculiar contraption: a jeep, rebuilt with a station-wagon top. Parry would roar to the top of a hill and B.B. and his small party would descend and walk down a precipitous path through the woods, meeting Parry at a predetermined spot lower down. Those who accompanied him found a changed being, no longer combative and aggressive, but completely enraptured by the beauty of the natural world.

"Every hundred yards he would stop in ecstasy," Kenneth Clark wrote, "sometimes at a distant view, more often at a group of farmhouses, or the roots of an old olive tree, or at a cluster of autumnal leaves and seed pods. He would be completely absorbed in what he saw, speechless with delight."

Iris Origo remembered scrambling up a steep hill of pine trees and cypresses and reaching a spot from which one could see the valley of the Sieve below. "Suddenly, B.B. stopped and, looking as fixedly as a pointer who had sighted his bird, said, 'Look,' pointing to a farmhouse below us, with cypresses and behind it a little dove-cot, 'Look, a Poussin.' It was the first time it had occurred to me to look at landscape in terms of art."

The philosopher Santayana has charged B.B. with preferring the reflected light of Paolo Veronese to the truth in the Venetian sky outside, but the accusation is not valid. B.B. made no such choice. To him, the beauty of nature was on a par with that encountered in a famous art gallery, and he gave it the same aesthetic response. Irene Worth noticed that his private sitting room would be decorated with a tiny little jar containing some exquisite weeds, or the husk of an acorn, or a pebble—humble objects displayed side by side with his most precious ivories.

Berenson once told a friend that he would die happy if he could believe that he had managed to make others feel his delight in the natural world. Doubting this, he sometimes felt as if he were the only guest at a banquet. In fact, this heartfelt love of nature is what B.B. probably communicated best, and his friends instinctively understood it and liked him the better for it.

Taking Irene Worth on one of his last walks, B.B. scrambled up a hill to one of his favorite views. They stood, looking silently down on the scene half hidden in the valley below. Then B.B. said, "Just as you are beginning to learn how beautiful it is, you have to learn to say goodbye to it."

BERNARD BERENSON DIED in 1959 at the age of ninety-four. Two years later his alma mater took control of the "Villa i Tatti" and renamed it the Harvard University Center for Italian Renaissance Studies. In the years that followed, the legend of Bernard Berenson began to suffer an inevitable decline. His once unchallengeable authority became suspect and his conclusions were attacked by other, younger scholars. His methods, depending as they did upon the trained eye, were largely abandoned in favor of the scientific analysis more in tune with a technological age. Even his aesthetics, once a revelation, seemed hopelessly outdated. The myth he had established also underwent a curious sea change.

As long as he lived, B.B. had been able to convince his adoring public that he was a gentleman, an aesthete, and a scholar, whose luxurious style of living might perhaps be the result of inherited wealth, but in any case was not a topic one discussed at Altamura. Even *Time* magazine, in 1955, believed the façade, writing that the steady sale of The Four Gospels had made their author prosperous enough to acquire "i Tatti" in 1900. The truth is that his books earned barely £100 a year, B.B.'s wife told his sister Senda, in the summer of 1902. Mary added a word about her husband's conviction that art history required more training, and paid less, than any other profession.

In fact, Bernard Berenson made his fortune from the art market, to which he sold his expertise. He worked for a living, to the day he died, in a world which has always been notorious for its unscrupulousness, and in which the art he loved was a commodity, to be sold to the highest bidder. The stakes were indeed high for those few, like B.B., whose word could give the work of art its price tag in the marketplace; and that is what B.B. did for sixty years.

Through luck, the penniless graduate of Harvard University, wandering through Europe, had become chief advisor to Isabella Stewart Gardner. Through astute business dealings, combined with brilliant scholarship, he assembled a priceless collection of art for her museum in Boston, Fenway Court. Through his reputation as an enfant terrible, Berenson had established his preeminence as an Authority and, by the turn of the century, would not only draw up a manifesto for Altamura, but begin to make it a reality. His word that the painting was a genuine Titian was as good as any signature—better, since that signature might be a forgery, while B.B.'s eye (it was claimed) was infallible.

In 1909, B.B. became the handsomely paid expert of Lord Duveen, the master art dealer, some said master scoundrel, of his day; and for thirty years, B.B. authenticated the paintings of the Italian Renaissance which Duveen sold for vast prices. It was money that provided the concealed plumbing in his House of

Life, although visitors never saw B.B. at work, and Duveen's name was never mentioned. This income, an estimated $100,000 a year after World War II, paid for the forty-room villa, squadrons of servants, and nonstop entertaining.

That there was a gap between the Altamuran appearance and the grubby reality was known while B.B. lived. It was also known that, as a young man, B.B.'s aspirations had been in another, nobler direction. He was a Faustian figure, it was said in London. He had been, Cyril Connolly wrote, "taken up to a high place and shown all the kingdoms of the earth, at which he replied, 'I accept—for the sake of the library,' and there was rejoicing in heaven."

"Ah, Berenson," an old Bostonian exclaimed to the playwright S. N. Behrman, who wrote a biography of Duveen, "he is so gifted that he might have become anything he liked. He could have been God—he chose to be Mephistopheles."

Here, then, was a complex figure: outwardly successful, brilliant, respected, and feared; inwardly prey to emotional complexities which he only dimly sensed, to an uncomfortable awareness of the conflicts set up by his masterful façade and the secrets hidden behind it. He had realized, he wrote, that at some point in his life, he had taken a terribly wrong turning. He told everyone that his life had been a failure. He spilled out his story like the mariner condemned to carry the dead weight of an albatross, as if seeking absolution.

One of those closest to him, Rosamond Lehmann, said, "If he told me once, wiping his eyes, he told me six times that his life had been a failure."

Berenson was not taken seriously. Surely a man this brilliant, this legendary, must be joking? So the chorus of praise continued and few seemed aware that his postwar autobiography, *Sketch for a Self-Portrait*, is a public confession that he had weighed his soul and found it wanting.

He was a failure, he wrote, because he had allowed himself to be sidetracked into making attributions. He had once dreamed of life lived as a sacrament. He had, as a youth, great promise. He had planned to become a writer, perhaps a novelist or a poet—a second Goethe—and he had sacrificed all of this to pedantic name-giving. And so he had frittered away his talents, instead of living up to the best that was in him.

There were other, darker reasons for the feelings of failure, oblique hints that time wasted on pedantic scholarship was not the real cause for inner misgivings. Had Berenson, as some said, given way to unrelenting pressure from Duveen and willfully given false attributions? Had money corrupted his judgment?

How he wished he had never been in the art world, he wrote despairingly to Frances Francis. He hated the jungle. The moment one took a single step, one was swallowed up into its maw.

How often he recalled the New England of his youth, morally, spiritually, and artistically pure, and how he longed to return to its nobly simple ways. He was afraid that such a life could not be lived again because he was not worthy of it. He, too, had touched pitch and had been defiled.

This theme of inner anguish runs in close counterpoint to a second theme of B.B.'s final years. In his diaries, B.B. described a dream in which he was struggling in a deep wood of trees shaped like question marks which were pushing out all other growths, all other symbols, until at last only the question marks remained, "questioning what and questioning whom?"

The question, it seems fairly evident, was being addressed to himself. At the end of his life, Berenson no longer recognized the mythical figure he himself had created. In a panic, he suddenly began to ask himself whether there was still time to find out who he really was, or whether there was anyone at all behind the mask.

"Yet who is the real *I*, where does he hide from ME? I know who he is not, but how and what . . . HE is, I have never discovered, although for more than 70 years I have been looking for him."

BEYOND THE PALE

The green trees when I saw them first through
one of the gates transported and ravished me their
sweetness and unusual beauty made my heart to
leap and almost mad with ecstasy.... Eternity was
manifest in the light of the day and something
infinite behind everything appeared....

—THOMAS TRAHERNE, "The Third Century"

IN HIS SLENDER MEMOIR, almost Byzantine in its convoluted train of thought, its contradictory self-descriptions, and its ambivalent conclusions, Bernard Berenson makes only the most fleeting references to his childhood. No letters and diaries have been published and one is left with those oblique souvenirs of a past, which appears, on the surface at least, to have detached itself from its owner and slid noiselessly down the stream of memory into near oblivion.

The smoke screen of anonymity thrown up between the reader and this reluctant observer of a long life (Berenson was seventy-six when he wrote his autobiography) has succeeded in obscuring all but the barest facts about him: that he was born, went to school, and, at a certain unrecorded moment, emigrated to the United States. So the child in him has been silenced and, apart from two or three important clues which deserve a later examination, would be lost to us, were it not for a peculiar historical accident.

The expression "beyond the pale" describes those who have dared to step outside accepted social boundaries and have become outcasts. In Russia, the Pale had a literal, territorial meaning. It delineated that area in which its Jewish minority might be allowed to live according to its own laws and customs, if subject to restrictions that fluctuated in severity, depending upon the czar and the temper of the times.

The Pale of Settlement was a strip of land covering 386,000 square miles which cut a vertical swath through the western territories of Russia from the Baltic to the Black Sea and, at various periods, called itself Poland, Lithuania, Hungary, Bulgaria, and Rumania, depending on the temporary rulers.

The Jews were always there. By the turn of the century, about five million of them inhabited the Pale, still only 12 percent of the total population. They had been there ever since the Crusades and the very antiquity of their settlement had wrung a kind of grudging acquiescence from their peasant neighbors, as long as they remained within its limits.

For centuries they had lived the life of the shtetl, whose outlines were as narrowly defined as its physical boundaries. The same rituals attended their birth, followed their first steps, decreed their clothes, their meals, their introduction to school, and their position within the family and community. The same 613 inflexible laws determined when they awoke and their final prayers before sleep. These laws marked the days into clear divisions; they gave shape to the weeks and months and the inexorable turn of the seasons. A Jew ignored them at his peril, since it was decreed that their neglect would bring about his death.

What might appear to be an intolerable regimentation was the secret inner strength of shtetl life. It provided a sense of unity, fellowship, and common purpose for this "ragged kingdom of the spirit," and the inner strength which sustained and upheld it.

There was a price to be paid, however. It is one faced by any society which dare not risk the stimulus of alien thought: an increasing rigidity and narrowness of outlook. In "this prison house of the Jews," as Chaim Weizmann called it, the pattern of life had remained unchanged for so many generations that an emigré to the United States, leaving even later than Berenson, might well declare, "I began life in the Middle Ages."

Because of these unvarying patterns, one can make some assumptions about Bernard Berenson's early life and reconstruct its probable outlines, much as an anthropologist can, with some accuracy, speculate about an epoch, life-span, and culture from a few fragments of bone.

Bernhard Berenson entered this ragged kingdom of the spirit on June 26, 1865. He was born in Lithuania, the northernmost area of the Pale, in a tiny village called by a bewildering assortment of names, depending upon who laid claim to it: Butrimants and Baltrimancz (Yiddish), Butyrmantsy (Russian), Butrymance (Polish), and Butrimonicai (Lithuanian). This settlement, somewhere between a village and a town (by 1897, there were 2,394 inhabitants, 1,900 of them Jews), faded from the Soviet Atlas following the devastations of World War II. It probably differed in no important respects from a thousand other shtetls inside Lithuania.

Berenson's family name was actually Valvrojenski and his father, Alter, and mother, Eudice Michliszanski, aged nineteen and eighteen respectively, had barely been married for a year when he was born. His mother's family history has been documented, thanks to *Their Exits and Their Entrances*, a private study of the Abravanel, Michliszanski (called Mickelshanski), Freeman, and Lourie families, written by a distant relative in 1972. The genealogical study contains inevitable gaps and omissions but appears to be the first determined attempt to chronicle the origins of those who, arriving in the New World, appeared bent upon severing all ties with the Old, and as fast as possible. A resurgence of interest by succeeding generations in histories that first-generation Americans have effaced from memory, seems to be the rule, but by then, it is often too late.

Eudice, only daughter of Salmon and Guedela Michliszanski (meaning, "from the family of Michael"), was the youngest of six children in a family chiefly engaged in the cattle trade, with relatives in Dowig and Puyn as well as Butrimants. Still others lived in Warsaw, Cracow, Berlin, and Amsterdam. In the eighteenth century, a fur-trading member of the Michliszanski family had married Lina Abravanel and added much luster to the Michliszanski name.

The Abravanels claimed descent from the house of David, and an unusually large proportion became jurists, bankers, physicians, and scholars. Numbers of them, of Sephardic origin, were descended from Don Isaac Abravanel, a Jewish theologian, biblical commentator, and financier who was born in Lisbon in 1437. Don Isaac became financial advisor to the Portuguese and Spanish courts, and wrote commentaries, renowned for their historical and social insights, on the books of the Bible, drawing heavily on relevant Christian studies. Don Isaac's son, Leon Ebreo, followed his father's scholarly example into philosophy and wrote a much admired treatise on Plato, "Gli Dialoghi d'Amore." Members of the family moved to Venice and are buried in the cemetery of the Giudecca on the Grand Canal. This city was to have great significance for their distant descendant Bernhard.

In addition to the kinship connection with Don Isaac Abravanel, Eudice was also related to another distinguished scholar through her mother Guedela, who had been born a Hurwitz. He was Isaiah Hurwitz, a sixteenth-century German cabalist, rabbi, leader in Polish-Jewish affairs, and author of an important work on mysticism, *Shene Luhot ha-Berit*. Guedela's brother was also a rabbi (Reb Aryeh H. Hurwitz) and perhaps this helps to explain the persistent belief that Bernhard was descended from rabbis.

His family was certainly distinguished on his mother's side, but almost nothing is known about the Valvrojenskis, whose name indicates that they might have originated in the town of Valvro. They came from the neighboring town of Dowig and were apparently prosperous enough to establish Alter as an iron-monger and grain and lumber merchant, but it is generally held that the Valvrojenskis were of minor social importance compared with the Michliszanskis.

Bernhard would have been told, at an early age, about his mother's family, since this was where the emphasis was placed in the shtetl culture. A boy might know everything about them and nothing about his father's ancestors, a reversal of the usual Western European pattern. There was, however, the same emphasis on the pivotal position of the oldest boy, his father's legal heir, and the importance of inherited position. Berenson is emphatic on the subject: "I knew from infancy that I was to be the first in my village and it bred in me a sense of being anybody's social equal that I have never lost. . . ."

That this was a community in which snobbism was endemic can be seen in the memoir written by Henry Hurwitz, whose father, Marks, was a cousin of Eudice. Hurwitz was also born in Butrimants, also emigrated to Boston, a decade or so after the Valvrojenskis, and, like Bernhard, graduated from Harvard. In an unpublished memoir of his mother, born Bella Wolfson, Hurwitz recalled that his father and grandfather, Reb Aryeh Leib Halevi

Ish-Hurwitz Neched-Shelah, a merchant and one of the lay heads of the village, shared the prejudices of the Lithuanian-Jewish bourgeoisie (or, *baalebatishe*). This upper stratum of cultured families disdained manual labor and no Jew could engage in it without losing caste. So the cobblers, tailors, masons, and tin-smiths on which the village depended were consigned to the lower benches near the door of the synagogue, while the elite clustered around the *bimah*, the platform on which the prayer-leader conducted the Reading of the Law, or lined the east wall. Everyone in Butrimants, whether *baalebatishe* or skilled worker, felt superior to the rough, illiterate Gentile peasantry of the surrounding countryside.

The use of actual surnames was considered irrelevant by members of the shtetl, who had been versed in the elaborate interconnections of their friends and neighbors for generations. Family names only appeared on formal documents like passports. In daily life, capsule descriptions were attached to first names (Yankel-the-Wig-Maker) or outstanding characteristics (Moshe-the-Six-Fingered), much as boys in British public schools quickly substitute graphic nicknames for the colorless originals.

The same medieval tradition probably obtained in Butrimants. This would explain the casual way in which the name of Valvrojenski was dropped from the Berenson family tree and why the only name that has stuck is the one whose usage was necessitated by the New World. No one knows how, or why, "Berenson" came into being. Although it is rumored that Bern-hard himself chose the family's new name, his first biographer, Sylvia Sprigge, was able to coax no information from her then-living subject and even his youngest sister Bessie could only offer the lame explanation that Berenson had seemed simpler.

A clue to the possibility that "Berenson" may owe its origins to a place name is suggested by a reference, in *Their Exits and Their Entrances*, to the fact that families emigrating to the New World often assumed the name of the city in which they had been born. A town to the southeast of Butrimants, not far from the scene of a Napoleonic defeat, bore the name Beresin. (It no longer exists.) Perhaps the similarity is accidental. Whatever the reason, "Berenson" has a vaguely German sound; it does not automatically identify its members as Jews, and it is easy for foreigners to spell.

The teen-age marriage of Alter and Eudice seems somewhat

premature nowadays, but it was perfectly acceptable in the shtetl. Such alliances were made for sensible social reasons, to channel the first stirrings of sexuality safely into those directions laid down by the *Schulchan Aruch* (Jewish Code of Law), i.e., toward the bearing of children. Much younger marriages had been common a few decades before. During the days of the Terror in the reign of Nicholas I, thousands of young Jewish boys were rounded up and shipped off to military schools and punishingly long terms of duty as soldiers, with the tacit purpose of converting them to Catholicism or bringing about their deaths, whichever came first. Accounts of the conscriptions are heartrending. However, even Czar Nicholas I would not conscript a married man, and so boys of barely twelve were given nominal wives, to protect them from such a fate. The family provided for its boys just as it found a purpose in life for its girls, and if the emphasis was practical, rather than romantic, that, too, would be taken care of. "First marry; then love," went the shtetl saying.

A boy who had the good fortune to be the first child in a shtetl family was showered with attention. His birth was joyfully announced in the synagogue by his father, in contrast to the dispirited reception with which his sister would be received. He was groomed to be head of the family and was the chief mourner at the deaths of his parents. He was indoctrinated from birth by a society which apportioned automatic rights and privileges to the male, reserving scholastic, intellectual, and spiritual pursuits to him alone.

In this male-oriented society, young men were taught to give daily thanks to God for not having been made female. They might well be grateful. A woman's status was not even that of a human being. She was a man's property, to be disposed of at will. She was expected to care for the children and perform the menial chores, but her husband would make all the important decisions. Custom allowed her an outlet for her feelings—women were encouraged to be "emotional"—and a certain role as the movers and deciders in daily affairs. The highest praise a woman might receive in Jewish writings was that she had been an exemplary helpmate for her husband. This, after all, was why she had been created.

The ideal shtetl mother was a paragon of loving self-sacrifice. The highest praise a mother could receive was that she would be willing to commit suicide for her children. No one questioned the wisdom of such passionate self-abnegation. A Jewish son had almost a moral obligation to find his mother the personification of everything that was adorable and noble. It was enough if he admired his father for his mind.

Such close emotional ties were strengthened by actual physical ones. The sacred law decreed that a husband might not remain in his wife's bed all night, and displays of affection between married couples were considered extremely vulgar. No such prohibition separated mother from son. It was normal for her to lavish caresses upon him, normal for the boy to sleep with his mother until puberty. A recent study of the Eastern European family found that "Mother is the embodiment of warmth, intimacy, food, unconditional love, security, practical reality." No wonder that observers likened the mother-son relationship to that of lovers, in all but physical terms, and no wonder that she became the "looming figure who would inspire, haunt and devastate generations of sons," as Irving Howe wrote in *World of Our Fathers*.

Those who remember Alter and Eudice have only the fragmentary souvenirs of their endearing old age when, receiving friends in their Boston living room, they still exhaled the quaint but unmistakable air of difference. Eudice, who lived to a great age, survived the decades remarkably unchanged. One can see from photographs of her in middle life what an alert, sprightly woman she was, what suppressed gaiety there was in her eyes, what a sense of perfection, and what self-regard in the ramrod correctness of her small body.

"Bernard Berenson always said, 'My mother was born tidy and so was I,'" said Elizabeth B. Gates, who visited Eudice and Alter as a child. "She was the tidiest little person imaginable, in black bombazine, as neat as a pin. She had a natural chic, although very old-fashioned, rather in the way that B.B. did. She had enormous dignity. Very charming, but with a whim of iron."

Ralph Barton Perry, Jr., Berenson's nephew, added, "My grandmother was an absolute angel, a saint. She radiated life." His wife, Harriet, added: "She was the sweetest one in the family and she had the most trouble with the language; she spoke broken English all her life." Ruth Berenson Muhlen remembers that "there was always a cookie jar," and Elizabeth Gates recalls tea in glasses from a Russian copper samovar that stood on the table. "There was a kind of formality about it, although very simple."

She was, her daughters sighed in mock despair, the family charmer, her fine features and broad cheekbones unravaged by age. Hospitable, gregarious, perfectionistic, impulsive, she was the prototype of the adorable mother described in the sociological studies, and immensely resourceful. She was also deeply religious, to the end of her days.

Alter presents a more enigmatic and intriguing profile. Equally tiny (about five feet three inches tall) and equally handsome, he was a rebel against the culture that had molded him. The fact that Alter was widely read, although not highly educated, indicates that he placed the same emphasis as did his society on intellectual pursuits, believing that philosophical contemplation was the highest goal to which a man could aspire. But Alter no longer believed that scholarship should be devoted exclusively to studies of the Scriptures. He had become an unbeliever, or as his family termed it, "a free thinker," a member of Haskalah. His curiosity had escaped from its traditional confines and leapt into the world of Western thought, and it was to be his undoing.

Haskalah, a Hebrew word meaning the Enlightenment, the brainchild of Moses Mendelssohn, was the revolutionary outcome of the rationalist spirit which swept across Europe in the eighteenth century. It proposed that a child's education, which had been limited to the study of the Torah, should be broadened to include secular studies, and thus examine those currents of Western thought that divided when they reached the shtetl and flowed harmlessly past it.

As obvious as the idea might appear to a Westerner, it was violently opposed by the rabbinate on the grounds that such studies would deflect young people from a strict adherence to Jewish laws and customs, perhaps even from a sense of their uniqueness. This fear was justified, since its adherents did indeed begin to adopt the language, dress, customs, and even the loyalties of their host countries.

Butrimants, although in no immediate danger of such intellectual infection, was within easy distance of the historically important town of Vilna, a center for art and ideas since the fourteenth century, where the Haskalah spirit began to take hold in 1820. Adherents of the movement dressed in a German style and spoke pure German among themselves, instead of Yiddish. It is perhaps significant that, asked to record his native tongue on a college questionnaire, Berenson wrote "German."

So Alter, an otherwise impeccable product of the Lithuanian-Jewish tradition, spoke learnedly of Darwin, Emerson, Browning, Karl Marx, and Voltaire in his Boston living room. Philip F. Siff, an old friend of Berenson's youngest sister Bessie, was living a

few doors away on Winchester Street in Brookline when he was a freshman at Harvard in 1918, and came to know Alter well.

"He formed the habit of dropping in to see me of an afternoon after I had returned from Cambridge, smoked a few cigarettes and listened attentively to the wisdom I had acquired in the course of the day and was prepared to dispense. He was then a man in his seventies, I believe and . . . of course, retired. . . . To me he seemed as old as Methusaleh. I recall that our conversations indicated on his part the possession of an acute and widely read mind, if perhaps with little formal education."

Elizabeth Gates recalled that "Uncle Albert stood and read books from a lectern standing in the living room. He seemed like someone out of a Russian novel."

Alter was, above all, a Litvak (a Jew from Lithuania), a personality which is portrayed with such consistency that the stereotype is worth examining. It was said that the Litvak valued the intellect over the emotions so highly that he became erudite to the point of pedantry. His finely honed mind, trained as it was on the Talmud and Tanach, resulted in an immensely skillful casuist, even a martinet of logic and conduct. Because of this reputation for learning, along with an equal tendency to contest everything, the Litvak came to be called a *tsaylem kop*, literally, "a 'crosshead' (from the Christian cross)—which is to say, by a peculiar derivation, a critic or skeptic, the bold enquirer, perhaps overweening in his intellectual prowess," Henry Hurwitz wrote. *Tsaylem kop*, used derogatorily, also meant, according to Leo Rosten in *The Joys of Yiddish*, "a sharp trader, a corner-cutting type—and one whose piety is shallow."

Everyone knew that Alter no longer went to the synagogue. But when his grandson, Bernard Berenson Perry, dared to publish, in his hand-printed newspaper, *The Cambridge Almanac*, the news that "Albert Berenson says There is No God," there was a family uproar. Eudice had never reconciled herself to her husband's defection, just as Alter could not resist challenging her continued allegiance to Judaism. The family battle that flared up at the slightest provocation may have been the main cause of the estrangement of their later years. However, to imply that Alter was an atheist is untrue. He was an authority on the life of Jesus and a follower of the Swedish philosopher, scientist, and mystic, Emanuel Swedenborg.

If something is known about the later years of Alter and Eudice, almost nothing is known about their life in Butrimants.

One can infer, however, that life there was not markedly different from that in Svislovitz, a similar Lithuanian shtetl in the Pale, during the same period, described in *Forward from Exile*, the autobiography of Shmarya Levin.

Levin's memoirs record that life for most Jewish families was wretchedly hard. If the father had regular work, he toiled for twelve to sixteen hours a day. If not, he lived from hand to mouth, picking up jobs as a petty merchant, broker, or commission-man. Men in this society seldom made enough money to support their families and so their wives took in washing, gathered berries in the fields, or plucked down from slaughtered fowls to make cushions. If the family ran a small business, as Alter and Eudice did, the wife was tied to it from dawn until late at night. Henry Hurwitz recalled that while his father was seeking his fortune in the new land of Boston his mother kept a *krom*, a hardware store, to provide for their three children. He remembers seeing her hacking away at a big iron wheel with a hammer for the peasants who were her major customers. On market days, the family yard would be full of them and their heavy horses and wagons, and the house choked with thick smoke from their *lulkes*, clay pipes filled with makeshift tobacco from home-cured leaves or grist. His mother not only mended wheels and found new parts for their carts, but often provided hot tea as well, "sometimes I dare say, in the terrible cold of those Lithuanian winters, a little schnapps too."

In Russia, restrictions on the occupations Jews might legally undertake, the cities in which they might live, and discriminatory taxation, ensured that most Jews would never gain wealth or social position; as a rule, they were poorer than the average Russian peasant. In one province it was common for several families to occupy a single room and, in another, an entire family might have to survive the day on a pound of bread, a herring, and a few onions.

Levin wrote, "So poverty stood with lifted whip over Jewish parents, driving them in a blind circle all day and separating them from their children."

The necessity of earning a living must have separated Bernhard from his mother, because he records that his maternal grandmother, Guedela Michliszanski, cared for him as an infant. She was his first mother, perhaps because "my own mother, only 18 when I was born, was herself too much the young girl—lovely and perhaps giddy—to play the mother." Berenson remembered affectionately how his "giant" of a grandfather used to carry him around on his right shoulder like Saint Christopher and traced, to those early experiences of grandparental devotion, a particular fondness for old people.

"I . . . remember the pity and tenderness" felt for "the old, helpless, friendless, neglected peasants that I must have seen." He was haunted by that through life, and "more unhappy to think of the suffering of the aged than of younger people."

Bernhard used to say that he remembered sitting on the knee of his great-grandfather, who had witnessed Napoleon entering Russia. Perhaps this was the origin of his later absorption with "the scheme of universal history [which] I imbibed . . . before I was ten years old," and his eagerness to be an eyewitness to great events. The mysterious maneuvers of soldiers had a similar effect. He recalled that, at the age of five or six, lime blossoms were scenting the air as "the Russian mounted cavalry band" led "the troops past the garden." At that age, "I should have abandoned everything to join the troops I used to see drilling and parading."

There are some slight indications that Bernhard did not talk until the age of four, and then spoke in complete sentences; and there was a family belief that he read at a precociously early age. He was so brilliant that, it was concluded, he was destined to be a rabbi, "and all the women tiptoed around him."

The young Bernhard was convinced that he was the center of the universe. When he learned to the contrary at the age of seven, the unpleasant discovery left a permanent scar. He took his sense of uniqueness for granted, and was only annoyed to discover that his young playmates couldn't talk to themselves as he could. He immediately concluded that they must be stupid creatures and that he preferred his own company to their lumpish ways. Bernhard would soon have a much more delightful companion, a small sister, Senta (later, Senda), born on March 19, 1867, and named for the heroine of Wagner's *The Flying Dutchman*.

In winter, Alter took to the forests to fell timber, the main support of the villages around Vilna. Great forests were being destroyed by the Polish nobility in distant Warsaw and, for countless poor communities, lumberjacking was the main source of employment. The fiercer the winter the better, since logs could be dragged over the firmly packed snow to river banks and transported downstream on rafts far to the west, along the Neiman, the Dvina, the Bug, and their tributaries.

A young Jewish subcontractor, supervising peasant workers,

left home in late fall with supplies of food and warm clothing, not to return until he floated back on the crest of rushing waters in the great spring thaws. A young boy might follow his father a certain distance into the forest, gathering wild pears, nuts of all kinds, guelder roses, berries, mushrooms, and wild apples. He might also observe the wildlife that a Jew was forbidden to shoot: hares, martens, mink, and even bears. Such excursions led to a lifelong love of forests; "I used to think," Berenson wrote, "that if I loved humans as I loved trees, I should be a saint. . . . " But once the first snow fell, the merest sprinkling, that left few traces on the earth and tinged the sky a yellowish gray, the boy would have to turn toward home.

Those who have known harsh winters, have experienced at first hand the inexorable grip of arctic winds, subzero temperatures, and a wilderness of snow, retain all their lives a special gratitude for the miracle of spring. Years after he had moved to the relatively benign climate of northern Italy, Berenson still prefaced his letters with a minute catalogue of spring's arrivals, watching for it with an eager impatience that revealed the indelible impressions of childhood.

He described, years later, what the end of winter felt like in Boston: "Washington's Birthday, a school holiday, and I recall as a boy Washington Street in Boston, free from snow but with an icy wind blowing dirt in one's face, and shreds of dirty paper in the air. Yet it spelled the end of winter. So even in windy, icy Boston and its coasts, the taste of snow in the air gave place to something like the odour of violets. . . . " He would castigate himself, half in despair, half in rapture, with the words, "Where were my eyes yesterday?"

Berenson remarked that he relived his childhood in *Years of Childhood*, the autobiography of the nineteenth-century Russian writer Serge Aksakoff. One of the most telling passages in the book describes the transformation which the advent of spring brings about to the Russian landscape, and conveys the excitement with which Aksakoff viewed the event for the first time. Even before he was allowed outside, Aksakoff could observe the changes from window to window: the patches of bare earth growing broader and longer, the pool in the wood widening, and the marmots' burrows every day rising higher and higher above the snow.

When finally allowed outside, Aksakoff was in ecstasy. This was the moment when "the fragrant bird-cherries were breaking into blossom . . . when the larks hung all day right over the courtyard, pouring out a stream of unvarying song . . . when all the slopes were covered with tulips, purple and blue and white and yellow . . . when there was movement in the water, noise on the earth and the very air trembled. . . ."

One can go only so far in drawing on other memoirs to sketch in the missing outlines. "Yes, but what was it really like?" is an insistent question, perhaps an unanswerable one. Berenson, so reluctant to observe the autobiographical niceties, fortunately did describe the most important experience of his childhood, and one that reveals the origins of his own delight in nature. It paralleled, and perhaps even surpassed, that of the young Aksakoff a century before.

"Was I five or six? Certainly not seven. It was a morning in early summer. A silver haze shimmered and trembled over the lime trees. The air was laden with their fragrance. The temperature was like a caress. I remember . . . that I climbed up a tree stump and felt suddenly immersed in It-ness. I did not call it by that name. I had no need of words. It and I were one."

It-ness was to become the leitmotif of a long life spent in the contemplation of beauty. Later, Berenson was to elaborate on what he meant by that term in the broadest possible manner, but this first reference is unmistakably concerned with the insight into the mystery of existence that the seventeenth-century English poet, Thomas Traherne, refers to: "Eternity was manifest in the light of the day and something infinite behind everything appeared. . . ." Berenson stops short of calling it a transcendental experience, but this is what it was.

Few of us can remain unmoved in the presence of a beautiful landscape or a painting of ravishing harmony and grace. Berenson's response was no different in kind, but so much more intense as to indicate an extraordinary visual precocity. A child who can summon up such an instant of perfect harmony, who is born to see, and instinctively understand and identify with what he sees, is rich indeed.

> Oh how divine
> Am I! To all this sacred wealth,
> This life and health
> Who raised? Who mine
> Did make the same? What hand divine?
> —Thomas Traherne, "The Rapture"

Small sounds, in those far-off days, were easily distinguishable. Every family had its samovar, sometimes made of copper, which sat on the hearth, its tube fed with glowing coals until the water for tea came to a boil. Throughout the drinking of the tea, the sizzling, whistling sound of the samovar could be heard in the background, and a part of one's mind was focused on it, because when it slowed and stopped, this was the signal that more coal was needed. The hiss of the samovar wove its strands through the earliest memories of childhood. At the age of six or seven, Berenson began a poem, "Ringing silence is swimming all around."

He was reading voraciously. He loved narrative best: the heroes of the Old Testament, the Franconia stories of Jacob Abbot, Robin Hood, the Greek myths retold by Hawthorne, Oliver Optic, Elijah Kellogg, Mayne Reid, and Robinson Crusoe. He soon showed a particular fondness for studies about historical, anthropological, and ethnological origins, and traced that back to his early introduction to the Hexateuch.

All young Jewish boys from the ages of four to thirteen went to *cheder* (elementary school), where the main emphasis was placed on the Talmud and the rabbinics. (Girls, it was thought, did not need to study, and it was enough if they could recite their prayers and read Yiddish translations of the Bible.) Berenson's characteristic "pen-shyness" keeps him silent about the moment when he was first introduced to school, but others have described that traumatic event in considerable detail. The boy, barely four years old, indulged and petted and fondled and adored beyond the wildest dreams of childhood, at that moment becomes "a man."

Shmarya Levin described the Sunday morning in early spring, just after Passover, when he had been introduced to his *melamed* (teacher), given the place of honor at a fine feast, handed a prayer book smeared with honey, told to lick off the honey, and then discovered that he was being showered with a rain of copper and silver coins. They were being thrown down by the angels, his grandfather said, since they knew that the little boy would be a diligent pupil.

"When the ceremony was over, my father wrapped me from head to foot in a silken tallith and carried me in his arms all the way to the cheder. My mother could not come along—this was a man's business. . . . The child was carried in the arms of his father all the way to the cheder. It was as if some dark idea stirred in their minds that this child was a sacrifice, delivered to the cheder: a sacrifice must be carried all the way."

The boy soon discovers that a sacrifice is exactly what he has become. The *melamed* pictured in the memoirs is a man of little intelligence, kindliness, or humor, whose only qualification is the ability to teach by rote, and whose only instrument for instilling knowledge is the whip. The boy goes home in misery, telling pathetic stories about interminably long hours, scanty food, cold rooms, and daily beatings. No one takes his side. No one seems to see the illogic of expecting a child barely past babyhood to assume the responsibilities of adolescence. He must act like a man even if he does not feel like one. The more he can smother his pain, fear, and feelings of helplessness, the better. Everyone will approve if, like Bernhard, he can announce to his mother at the age of seven that he has grown up.

Tradition also taught that a boy's education was ultimately the responsibility of his father. The community merely saw to it that the boy received the necessary minimum of information. A few years after Bernhard had enrolled in the *cheder*, the idea of emigration must have seeded itself in Alter Valvrojenski's mind. An adherent of Haskalah, one who has glimpsed a whole world of ideas outside the teachings of the Talmud, would be bound to find shtetl life cramped and confining.

Education in America was free for everyone and the idea of America was in the air. It was the golden land, one to which 7,500 Jews in the Pale had been drawn in the previous fifty years (1820–1870). Everyone knew someone who had left—the young, bright, capable men, the most adventurous in the group. In America there was almost unimaginable freedom. One could own property, become a citizen, and vote; one could worship according to one's conscience. The law protected rather than persecuted.

A few Hebrew periodicals might caution that a young man without skills lived a hand-to-mouth existence, that his wages were meager, his toil incessant, and his bed a hovel. These warnings were drowned out by the extravagant boasts that came in the letters of emigrés, who could not help exaggerating their successes and minimizing their defeats. Everyone knew that there were steamship agents traveling through the Pale, offering *billeten* to London, Boston, Philadelphia, and New York at cut rates. At the end of Passover, what some now said instead of "May we be next year in Jerusalem," were the words "Next year—in America!"

Life in the shtetl had always been precarious and its inhabitants banded together not just to support the world within, but in
fear of the world without. Although the reign of Alexander II was
relatively benevolent, bigotry remained an unpleasant reality.
Mary Antin described the continual tension between the Pale's
Jewish and non-Jewish inhabitants. When a Gentile child threw
mud at her, her mother explained, as she wiped her dress, that
there was nothing to be done, because Gentiles did as they liked
with Jews. The little girl quickly assumed the same numb fatalism,
accepting such abuse "as one accepts the weather." Bernhard
alludes to this all-pervasive aspect of life in the Pale only indirectly, with the comment that he retained into adulthood the
ability to become indignant with very little provocation. Such an
emotion was likely to be followed by impotent resentment and "a
despairing sense of helplessness," feelings familiar to anyone who
has felt unfairly treated.

The best left first perhaps, but the rest followed. Alexander
II was assassinated in 1881 and with him went the last hope of a
barely tolerable existence for the Pale's inhabitants. The accession
of Alexander III ushered in an era of brutal religious and nation-
alist persecution. Large-scale, anti-Jewish propaganda was followed by wide-scale pogroms in cities and villages and further
restrictions of those slender rights to Russian secondary education
that the Jews had painstakingly acquired. That year marked the
turning point and, by 1910, over a million Jews had left the Pale.
But by then the Berensons were safely in Boston.

Perhaps the great famine of 1868, which devastated the
Russian countryside, or the cholera epidemic a year later, which
his family fortunately survived unharmed, helped reinforce Alter's determination to leave. There was another reason: their
house had burned down. Writing her husband's biography, Mary
Berenson described the fire as accidental. Perhaps it was. Or
perhaps the family belief that the fire was the result of a pogrom
by "drunken Cossacks on a Saturday night" was closer to the
truth. Senda was trapped in the burning house and was barely
rescued by her mother.

A personal disaster can sometimes rouse one from an uneasy
compromise and provide the determination and energy needed to
bring about a real improvement. Nevertheless, the wrench from
the only life they knew was bound to be agonizing. Any family's
departure from the shtetl was treated exactly like a funeral. The
whole community assembled for the leave-taking, marched

mournfully to the station, and wept the bitter tears of those who know that they will probably never see the emigrés again.

A decade later, Bernhard would begin to realize exactly what this departure from the only life he had ever known was to mean in terms of inner anguish. As a young man, he would take many journeys, endless homeless wanderings, set in motion by this first immense venture into the unknown. All of them attempted, in some dim, little understood, and circular fashion, to bring him back to himself, "a long pilgrimage." But at the moment when it happened, he felt only that it was the most exciting event of his life.

"I recall how as a little boy of six or at utmost seven I longed, yearned, to go and see what was beyond the horizon. Moving, going to another . . . village even, used to make me feverish with excitement," he wrote. He added, "I could follow up any road, any bypath, with the same zest that I would read a story, for the fun of going on and on. . . ." His one fear, when Bernhard left the Pale never to return, was that his journey might come to an end.

THE AVENGING
ANGEL

Upon him who is ashamed of his family there will
be no blessing.

—JEWISH PROVERB

ALTER VALVROJENSKI, the new Albert Berenson, left
Butrimants for the New World some time in 1873, the year
his second son Abram (Abie) was born, and his wife and children
followed at the very end of 1875. Albert set off with a young
companion, Louis, the orphaned son of his sister who had died in
childbirth, and whom he and his wife had unofficially adopted
some years before. Louis, whose name may have been
Koussevitsky originally, then in his early teens, also took the
name of Berenson and went on to sire thirteen children (nine
survived); his descendants cluster in the Boston area. He was, one
of his grandchildren, James Berenson, recalled, "a vigorous,
handsome man of six-one or six-two, with flashing black eyes."

Their destination was Boston, an apparently accidental
choice. There is no record of the trip, but others have recorded in
minute detail the emotions of leaving, the interminable train
rides, the hazardous border crossings, the delays, indignities,
disappointments, crises, and the final ordeal of steerage, only
slightly more endurable than passage in a slave ship. There is also
no information about the route taken. However, Irving Howe, in
World of Our Fathers, has traced the route of Jews emigrating from
western or north western Russia across the German and Austrian
borders to one of the major ports of embarkation. To judge from

the *Boston Evening Transcript* of 1875, ocean steamers crossed the Atlantic from Hamburg, Rotterdam, Liverpool, Antwerp, Havre, and Glasgow in swarms, jockeying for space on the New York docks (seven arrivals in a two-day period).

Boston was not quite as popular for transatlantic arrivals, but the papers were full of advertisements for departures to dozens of foreign ports, along with "regular packets" to San Francisco, New Orleans, and Philadelphia, and a mail line to Halifax. The Cunard Line, whose terminus was in Boston, sailed to Liverpool, with cabins available at $80, $100, and $130 (gold) and, "steerage passage at low rates." The North-German Lloyd Steamship Co. rates were even less: $100, first cabin, $60, second cabin, and $24, steerage. Even the poorest could afford the trip.

It is unlikely that Albert and Louis had passports, which would, in any event, have been refused to would-be emigrés; Russian Jews of draft age were particularly anxious to avoid drawing attention to themselves. Years later, Berenson canceled a trip to Russia that he had been planning with Sir Robert Witt, when he learned that he might be treated as an evader of the czarist draft laws. The best route was the riskiest one: to cross the Austrian or German border illegally. The fact that Albert and Louis traveled without the encumbrances of a woman with small children points to this possibility.

Until the 1870s few Jews had arrived in Boston. The influx was from Ireland, from which waves of desperate, starving families had fled in the 1840s. The Irish stayed, because they were too poor to leave. By 1875, there were 60,000 of them. A few German Jews arriving in the 1840s had organized the congregation of Ohabei Shalom and built a modest synagogue, but they were so invisible that Jews are not even mentioned in a history of Boston written by Justin Winsor in 1880. By 1930, however, there were 130,000 Jews in greater Boston and some fifty Jewish congregations.

Until the 1850s, Boston had been a thriving seaport and industrial city of some 200,000 people, packed tightly into a narrow peninsula that was bordered on three sides by water and, on the fourth, by a narrow strip of land connecting it to the mainland. The city had grown rich on the China trade and its wealth had been further increased by judicious investments in industry and railroads. Wheat, corn, and meat were imported for the mainland and every imaginable kind of article exported, from boats to shoes and clothes.

The great waves of unskilled Irish, Italian, and German immigrants rolling across the Atlantic in the mid-nineteenth century provided cheap labor for factories and brought further wealth to the city. The foreigners also brought problems—pollution, disease, crime, and alcoholism—and changed the city past recognition. In fifty years (by 1900) Boston had become a metropolis of over a million people, covering a ten-mile radius; and 35 percent of its inhabitants were foreign-born.

These changes were in full swing in the 1870s, as the city's government began to fill in the enormous marshes to the south, to finance sewers and reservoirs, and to build roads, bridges, and railways. The housing boom was at its height, new suburbs were springing up and old neighborhoods were in a state of flux. A city in such upheaval presents bewildering difficulties for the naïve and inexperienced, and endless opportunities, economic and social, for those who are quick-witted enough to profit from them.

Those who could afford it had already moved to the suburbs and paid five cents to ride into town on one of the new horsecars, which were Boston's first attempt at mass transportation. These were metal carriages, running on tracks and pulled by horses; the line already extended to the city's limits four miles south of City Hall.

As Bostonians left the old walking city, center of the city's business life, the immigrants moved in. They needed to work close to their jobs, since they could not afford the bridge tolls or horsecar fares. They were looking for old brick townhouses on the European model, or detached residences that were now down-at-heel, but potentially valuable for the space they occupied. By the 1850s, real-estate speculation and the demand for such close-in housing had turned the North End and Fort Hill, once rather grand neighborhoods, into monstrous slums.

A report of a committee of the Bureau of Labor Statistics in 1870 recorded that the immigrants' houses were not occupied by one family alone, or even by two or three families. Each room of the house, from attic to basement, would be filled with a family and sometimes two or more.

In the Fort Hill area, people lived anywhere and everywhere. They crammed themselves into attics, often only three feet high, or crowded into basements. Windowless hovels perhaps five feet high were in great demand, since they were usually warmest in winter and coolest in summer. Such hordes of people might have access to a single toilet, out of repair and gushing its filth over the surrounding streets. Life was hardly any more nasty and brutish in Henry Mayhew's London.

One assumes that Albert and Louis immediately jammed themselves into the North End or one of its equivalents and began to look for work. This was easily found if you were a seaman or boat builder or had industrial skills, or could read and write in English. Albert's only skill, beyond that of timber cutting, was in trade, the age-old barter of the East European shtetl.

The first step to a store of one's own was to begin as a peddler, an honorable American tradition since the earliest days, and the course that the German Jews had followed some twenty years before. For a modest investment, a peddler was ready to do business, with his stock on his back. It was physically demanding work, requiring strong arm and back and leg muscles, since one might tramp for weeks into Massachusetts, New Hampshire, and Maine; but, by collecting small installments every week and persuading his regular clients to buy still more merchandise, a shrewd trader could save enough money to send for his family. With unremitting effort, he might even build up enough capital to open a small warehouse and start employing peddlers of his own.

It was a hard life, but Russian Jews were versed in the arts of business and possessed an elastic conscience: "They had little scruple about fleecing their Gentile neighbors at a bargain." They knew when to urge and when to desist; how to give lip service to the authorities and keep their opinions to themselves; how to slip through the net of punitive government excise taxes and fines that would otherwise have ruined them; how to size up a market; when to cheat and when to give honest measure, if they wished to survive. Sleeping in the open air presented no novelties for Albert, who had survived the harsh winters of the Lithuanian forests, and, with the most modest improvement in his living quarters, an immigrant might consider himself almost unimaginably rich.

"What would the sophisticated sight-seer say about Union Place, off Wall Street, where my new home waited for me?" wrote Mary Antin, who arrived in Boston a few decades later than Bernhard Berenson and moved into the same neighborhood.

He would say that it is no place at all, but a short box of an alley. Two rows of three-story tenements are its sides, a stingy strip of sky is its lid, a littered pavement is the floor and a narrow mouth its exit.

But I saw a very different picture. . . . I saw two imposing rows of brick buildings, loftier than any dwelling I had ever lived in. Brick was even on the ground for me to tread on, instead of common earth or boards. . . . The three small rooms into which my father now ushered us . . . contained only the necessary beds, with lean mattresses; a few wooden chairs, a table or two, a mysterious iron structure, which later turned out to be a stove; a couple of unornamental kerosene lamps; and a scanty array of cooking utensils. . . . And yet, we were all impressed with our new home . . . it was chiefly because these wooden chairs and tin pans were American chairs and pans that they shone glorious in our eyes. . . .

Something of the sort must have greeted Eudice, arriving in Boston in late 1875 with Bernhard, age ten, Senta, age eight, and the two-year-old Abie, to a drab tenement at 32 Nashua Street, and later an equally modest home at 11 Minot Street. Although most immigrants were crowding into the North End of Boston, the streets where the Berensons first settled were in the far reaches of the West End. This area, one of the last to be settled, was still open country until the close of the eighteenth century. A number of imposing row houses around Bolton Square were built at that time and new streets laid out. It was a pleasant and desirable neighborhood until, under the pressure of the new arrivals, it too became a slum.

Nashua Street was a block-long road with houses and tenements on the south side and a railroad station, the Boston and Lowell, on the north side. Minot Street was nearby, a few doors from the corner of Mary Antin's Wall Street and close to a public horsecar line running across Cragie's Bridge and the Charles River toward Cambridge.

The houses no longer exist. They were demolished in an urban renewal effort of the 1950s which also swept away a charming polyglot neighborhood of Greek bakeries and Italian groceries and of Greek revival houses restored by young doctors and their wives. The ironically named renewal also took with it all of Nashua Street, now almost entirely parking lots, and half of Minot Street. Number 11 is now a parking garage.

All that was to come. The Berensons, settling in the West End in the 1870s, were not discouraged by the cramped quarters and drab surroundings. Everyone knew that this was just a start and that things would improve. Hope, the ray of comfort that had shed its meager warmth over generations of shivering men and women, assumed a new and luminous meaning, when a man could see his friends growing visibly better fed, housed, and clothed. Every day there was proof that what people said was true. If you were willing to work forty-eight- to fifty-five-hour weeks, and save remorselessly, and if you educated yourself and your children, things would improve.

Perhaps because Boston presented such opportunities to the quick-witted and ambitious, the European concept that collective action must be taken to attack social ills had gained no support in the 1870s. The poor struggled as best they might and the successful reaped their just rewards: affluence, leisure, and social status. Nineteenth-century capitalism taught that the rich were more worthy, because they had worked harder, and therefore could feel humbly proud of their superiority. Survival of the fittest! It was all very Victorian. The message was not lost on Bernhard.

There had been a fire in Boston which flattened sixty-five acres and a disastrous recession two years before, but there was still plenty of money to spend and no lack of opportunity. The social elite bought houses in the Highlands with stables capable of accommodating four horses, and a carriage house. They advertised for governesses in French ("On demande une bonne d'enfant...") and built houses of unimaginable splendor in the Back Bay that reflected the regal grandeur of Baron Haussmann's Parisian boulevards, using the mansard roofs so very much in style in Paris. They were absurdly rich. Even when accustomed to their excesses, Bernhard Berenson called them "squillionaires." They staggered under the weight of jewels and commanded armadas of servants and dined with gold flatware and bought sculpture and painting and held musicales and balls and traveled to London, Paris, and Rome. The poor could scarcely envision the immensity of their opulent style of living concealed, but hinted at, behind those imposing fronts on Beacon Street, with their French Academic uses of brownstone, their pavilion-type bay windows, their carefully framed and decorated doors, and their flights of stone steps, of an imperial and intimidating grandeur. One sensed, without knowing it, how exclusive that life was; and what an impregnable wall of privilege separated the socially secure from the bemused throngs of immigrants groping for a foothold in the Boston slums.

The standards of Eudice Berenson were just as impeccable, but of a different order. No self-respecting Puritan ever had a more enduring hatred of dirt, and no librarian a more fixed and innate sense of order. One sees her squaring her shoulders and scattering dust and disorder with a brusque brush, plumping up the featherbeds, mending and polishing, placing the precious copper samovar in the exact center of the starched lace tablecloth, and arranging the solid silver teaspoons, smuggled out of Russia, in meticulous rows. In an autobiographical short story, Bernhard provides a portrait that was no doubt faithful, in ambiance if not in physical detail, to the atmosphere Eudice had created:

"The floor was clean and sanded. The large oaken table glowed with scrubbing. The spaces between the double windows were ornamented with suspended apples and oranges.... The light was streaming in through the windows, and reflected from the tiles of the Dutch stove that stood across the room.... His mother—may she rest in peace—was seated, knitting, in front of this stove...."

Eudice would have explored the great Faneuil Hall markets, where beef liver could be had for ten cents a pound, salt codfish for less, and every kind of fish, at varying prices: scallops, salmon, smelts, perch, hake, bluefish, oysters, flounder, and lobsters (10 cents a pound). One learned to cook squirrels (30 cents a pair) and tame pigeons (25 cents each) and perhaps looked longingly at the imported Dutch cheeses bought by the rich at the insane price of $1.50.

One imagines Eudice cooking for the Sabbath, perhaps a cholent of beef brisket, rubbed with salt, pepper, and cinnamon and baked for hours with prunes and sweet potatoes until it fell apart; the kitchen would be fragrant with the smell of black bread and mushroom soup and homemade *kichelach*, egg-and-sugar cookies tinted with saffron. Eudice was confined to the house. There were now two *Amerikannerke*: Elizabeth (Bessie), born in 1878, and Rachel, in 1880.

An immigrant peddler could barely support seven people, even if his nephew Louis was contributing to the household (Louis lived with the Berensons until he had saved enough money to start a small business on Salem Street). There was, however, a respectable way in which Eudice could earn income, a natural result of the accelerating arrivals of Russian Jewish immigrants, following the purges of the early 1880s, and that was to take in lodgers. Relatives newly arrived from the Pale, or friends of friends, would be grateful to squeeze three or four at a time into the spare room; and Eudice was so gregarious, and such a clean, tidy, busy little person, and she cooked so beautifully, that she was always in demand. Or perhaps, like Bella Hurwitz, Eudice

cooked midday dinners for peddlers at 35 cents (for a full meal). On the nights when Albert came home, Eudice would wash his swollen feet.

> An old man remembering his East Side [New York] childhood would say that on coming home from school he had a recurrent fear that his cot in the dining room would again be occupied by a relative just off the boat from Europe and given shelter by his parents. How many other Americans could share, even grasp, this order of experience? Space was the stuff of desire; a room to oneself, a luxury beyond reach. . . .
>
> Only in the kitchen could the family come together in an approximation of community. . . . Sitting around the wooden kitchen table that was covered with a white or checkered oilcloth, fathers read newspapers, mothers prepared food . . . boarders gobbled meals. The father's eyes often fell on the youth . . . who is studying Virgil. . . .

The story goes that Bernhard sat on the top floor of 11 Minot Street in a small, unheated room, sweltering in the summer and shivering in the winter, his nose glued to books in a dozen different languages. He was the family genius, for whom a brilliant future was predicted, who would rather dispute learnedly with his professors, like Christ among the Elders, than mingle with boys of his own age, who was cloistered from the street urchins muscling their way to a half dollar as carefully as he was excluded from any role in the family's bitter economic struggle to survive. Bernhard was allowed only to grow vegetables, a task he performed with great enthusiasm. There was a small plot of ground behind the house and Bernhard would forage for manure in the street, in the wake of the horse-drawn traffic.

Louis, now in his early twenties, who had been toughened by the freezing winter tramps of the peddler, who was street-wise and dollar-smart, was in another category. It was enough if he helped his relatives and took care of his wife. Bernhard had been marked for a different fate from childhood. If not a rabbi, then perhaps he would become a *talmid chachem*, an expert on the Talmud, the wisest of the wise.

Bernhard accepted the verdict and, in the fashion of intellectuals in the making, lived his real life in a library, the Boston Public. On Saturday afternoons he visited the Old Corner Book Store. Books were an endless source of discussion, analysis, review, and comment. Life and the emotions were not to be spoken about. How could he, in any event, make any kind of complaint, when his mother worked selflessly, when his father toiled pathetically long hours at menial labor, and he, the oldest child, saw four young ones to be fed and clothed? "I have seen the toil to which my father has subjected himself to earn even the necessaries of life for himself and his five children, of whom I am the eldest," Berenson was to write in an application for a traveling fellowship, "and I have never been anything but miserable at the thought of the burden I have been to him from the expenses of my apparently unremunerative education." Only one cry escaped from him, only one clue was ever given to the effect of those years at 11 Minot Street. It was then, he said, that he was living alone with his thoughts, his anguish, and despair.

It is axiomatic that no man is ever shorter than his mother. Bernhard was hardly any taller, a manikin, rather than a man, but with a disproportionately large head that made him seem more physically imposing than he was. He had his mother's militarily correct bearing: shoulders back, chest out, hands neatly folded into place. He had something else: an apparently innate ability to project his personality. In a photograph with a group of friends at Harvard, Bernhard is noticeable for his poise and his air of vivid high spirits. There is a kind of passionate radiance about his wide-cheeked, Slavic good looks. He wears an impeccable suit, its collar braided in silk. The careless tangle of his curls, worn fashionably long at the neck, and the dreamy languor of his half-smile, full of expectancy, complete the image, that of a Byronesque hero, or a young poet.

The Little Mother, as she was called, or Aunt Julia, or Aunt Eudice, the pivot around which the family revolved, had adapted with relative ease to life in the New World. Her husband, however, had a more uneasy response to the radical shift of cultures and the stresses of surviving in the no-holds-barred arena of nineteenth-century capitalism.

On the one hand, he was now free to profess his skepticism openly, like other members of Haskalah whose break with Judaism became more or less complete, once beyond the Pale. His nephew, Louis, had adapted so well that he was soon employing his own fleets of peddlers, newcomers with unpronounceable surnames whom he cannily renamed Berenson, so as to avoid paying for new license permits. Albert attempted to emulate that example and opened a dry goods store in his house on Minot Street, but failed miserably.

Albert's character lacked, perhaps, the necessary ruthlessness to survive in a brutal business world; he lacked the resilience, and he lacked the heart for it. He was too much a product of the culture that taught that the head of a prominent family was someone to be looked up to and respected, that scholarship was the noblest goal to which a man could aspire. But in America what mattered was how much money you made.

Louis learned that lesson quickly. Louis soon owned a warehouse and then bought real estate and made a fortune in the rapidly expanding Boston market. Louis had a white mansion on Highland Place in Roxbury, and there his wife Sarah would sit, presiding over a long, elliptical table, dispensing tea from a brass samovar and coffee from a Russian silver pot, while the Little Mother remained in a mean little house in the West End.

Here, Albert was a nobody, a nothing, despised as a peddler and despised as a Jew. That he, a learned man, should be forced to grub for food from the streets, the very earth, maimed Albert's spirit and beat it into the ground. In his photographs the older Albert has the slumped shoulders of a man who feels himself defeated by life.

There are so many references to his carping tongue ("Father as usual and expected was as cranky as 'ell—It is really very funny. Everything we had was great, but he had a knock for everything") that one cannot escape the conclusion that Albert's bitter disappointments soured his marriage and his relationship with his children.

Eudice bore the brunt of his sarcasm and so, apparently, did his sons. It was years before Abie could manage not to fly into a rage at his father's taunts. Bernhard avoided the very mention of his father's name. That, too, was consistent with the family's shtetl origins. A father did not expect his sons to like him. A father was expected to set the standards of scholarship and spiritual achievement to which his sons should aspire. If they were high standards, even perfectionistic ones, so much the better.

There were other reasons for the tensions between Albert and his sons. It has been suggested that a Jewish mother's relationship with her sons, the oldest in particular, can be obsessive. After the failure of her marriage, Eudice turned more and more to her children for consolation, with such anxious exclusiveness that the merest hint of a shift in their affections would be enough to precipitate a major scene. "All she asks for, she says, in reward for a lifetime of angelic goodness and sacrifice, is her children's love—but they have given all that to their father. There's no use arguing. . . ."

It would be surprising if Albert did not resist the favoritism, feel obscurely that his sons were to blame for his wife's coldness, and resent his exclusion from the warm family circle. A friend remarked that Albert Berenson seemed unappreciated at home, and paid so little heed by the others that "often he would just go on talking to himself in a kind of *sotto voce.*"

Despite it all, Albert was proud of his son. How could he help but be? The child who spoke learnedly with savants was growing into a young man of striking charm and intelligence, with a mind that did not merely shine but glittered, diamond-faceted and knifelike. Bernhard was, as he said, wild with intellectual curiosity. He was just as eager to impart what he had learned, with embellishments of his own, since his mind turned instinctively toward evaluation and interpretation, the natural *tsaylem kop.*

Bernhard was cleverly amusing and innately convivial. He was ambitious. He could be generous. He had the rarest gift, the ability to discover beauty. The ugliness of city streets, the grime and filth, left him mute; but the ability of a rainstorm to transform the daily world filled him with eloquent wonder. He would describe the look it gave to stems, to grass, to the surface of a stone, and the way it turned clouds into corroded silver. He would, he wrote, abandon himself to the rain. This poetic ability to heighten, even transform, reality was coupled with an avidity for aesthetical experience that was almost painful.

Bernhard was developing certain rigidities of character: a punctiliousness in dress, a fastidiousness about cleanliness amounting to obsession, an insistence on promptness as inflexible toward others as to himself, and, finally, a kind of melancholic inability ever to be satisfied by food. It was always too hot, or too cold, too much, or too little; and digestive upsets seem to have been frequent. This, not surprisingly, was a family complaint, "The Berenson Stomach," the Little Mother being the chief sufferer. Rachel, writing to Senda, said that their mother was having a bad attack of indigestion. She ate little, but was being teased by her children, who told her that she ate too much, and between meals. "Sympathetic and consoling words on all sides," Rachel concluded sarcastically.

For Eudice, such attacks of indigestion appeared to coincide with emotional upsets. Bernhard absorbed the pattern, along with a general tendency to fret anxiously over every minor ailment and believe the worst. That belief, that the men in the family were frail reeds whom the least wind would buffet, and who must be protected by their wives, was also part of the Berenson creed.

"When I married Bart," remarked the delicately tiny Harriet Perry of her sturdy husband, "my mother-in-law, B.B.'s sister, said she hoped I was not so healthy that I couldn't sympathize with someone who wasn't." Away from his mother's anxious hovering, Bart discovered that he was perfectly capable of doing hard physical labor. His uncle Bernhard, however, never accepted the idea that exertion could be conceivable for someone as fragile as himself, and periods in which his robust health would inspire intense activity were always followed by remorseful illnesses during which he was convinced that he would die.

At the basis of this obsession was the Jewish fear of tempting fate. Bernhard had learned that to be optimistic about one's health was tantamount to inviting a jealous evil spirit to make instant retribution; one must be guardedly noncommittal on principle. Berenson said of his wife Mary, "Mary frightens me when she says she is well; she says it and feels it with such exaltation that one senses that she may be on the verge of some misfortune. It is the hubris of the Greeks. . . ."

The combination of his mother's smothering love and his father's faultfinding was leading to curious developments in Bernhard's personality. On the one hand, he had the charm of the spoiled child, as well as that same child's predilection to fly into a temper tantrum if love and admiration were not continually forthcoming and the taste of its honeyed sweetness no longer in his mouth.

On the other hand, his father's perfectionistic demands had the effect of turning Bernhard into his own severest critic. Nothing he ever did was quite good enough, no act ever unspotted by petty motives. If he was generous, it was not because he was truly altruistic, but because it gave him a warm glow. If a meeting was not a success, "I feel that it is all my fault, and I never can manage to blame anyone else." The warning to beware of those in whom the urge to punish is strong seems particularly apt in Bernhard's case. He judged the behavior of others as hypercritically as he did his own, parceling out guilt with a free hand, finding the canker of self-centeredness in every act, and unearthing each fatal flaw of character. He might, however, be too politic to reveal the unrelenting inner judgment, at least outwardly.

Behind everything was the conviction that he must be perfect. Every aspect of his life and thought must be flawless, a work of art, even if he might be dimly aware that he could never learn enough, master enough, or accomplish enough to appease the inner tyrant.

His constant self-belittlement was fueled by the daily exhortations to upright and moral behavior that permeated the shtetl, or what the psychoanalyst Karen Horney has termed "the tyranny of the Should." Henry Hurwitz observed that his mother's comments were peppered with such observations as "It is not becoming," "One doesn't do that" (a curious echo of the British, "It isn't done"), and "That isn't nice." One followed the straight and narrow path because to break the law of God was tantamount to desecrating His image. The more learned and prominent a member of the shtetl was, "the greater . . . his responsibility to serve as an example of honor. The concept of *noblesse oblige* is strong in Jewish life, but the aristocracy of Jews is one of knowledge plus morality in practice."

Perhaps because he was hemmed in by a sense of obligation, Bernhard could be ruthlessly unmindful of other people's feelings. He tended to observe their behavior calculatingly, in order to manipulate them for his own ends. The trait gave him detachment, but also a tendency toward hypocrisy. The same insensitivity accounted for his ability to criticize others at length and be astonished at their resentment. He also bristled the moment they attempted to return the favor. With his nimble wit and the enviable articulateness that anger lent his tongue, Bernhard was double- and triple-armed against attack, although often remorseful about the lashings he was capable of inflicting.

The power of the intellect and rational thinking seemed to him in every way superior to the treacherous swamplands of feeling. Aesthetic response was the only emotional experience that seemed to be safe. But then he began to worry about his increasing detachment from his own feelings and an apparent inability to be close to anyone. This need to block out painful emotions may have had some roots in a traumatic event of childhood. His maternal grandmother, Guedela Michliszanski, who had cared for him in Butrimants while his mother worked, died before he was five. Bernhard was devastated.

"She had meant more to me than all other people put together, including my mother. I not only missed her day and night, but could not understand what had happened. . . ."

During the agonizing months that followed, Bernhard had a strange dream. In it he saw his dead grandmother, encased like a mummy and stretched out on a slab of black marble, in a dark interior paneled with polished black stone. Standing against the wall in this tomblike setting were "a number of Osirises, like those we still see at Karnak in the temple of Ramses."

The dream was so vivid that he was never able to forget it. "And yet—at that time I could scarcely have heard of Egypt or if I had, it was a word that could have meant nothing to me. I could not have known anything about mummies or Osirises, and least of all could I have seen pictures of hypogees. The only explanation would be that I must have had this accurately visualized dream when I was already conversant with Egyptian funeral rites and . . . transferred it to my earliest years. It is an explanation hard to accept."

The dream has startling similarities with that experienced by C. G. Jung, and described in his autobiography, *Memories, Dreams and Reflections*. As he lay on the point of death Jung had a vision of an enormous block of dark granite in which an entrance had been carved. It led to an ancient temple, this time Asklepios, the birthplace of Hippocrates. Entering the temple Jung realized that he had reached the transitional point between life and death and that he was about to join a company of equals. He was, however, commanded to return to life by his doctor who, in the dream, appeared in the symbolic guise of a Greek king.

For Jung in maturity the vision provided the raw material for some fruitful speculations. But, for the five-year-old Bernhard, the experience was premature. Its implications were too profound. He was asking questions, but getting frightening answers; "after one died, one went before awesome judges who assigned one to terrible punishments. . . ." Just at that age, his closest friend, a little girl, also died. The double shock of fate had the effect of making the subject of death a taboo. "It was unwise to think and talk about death," he wrote. Step on a crack, break your mother's back. One had better superstitiously avoid any chance of being overwhelmed by the terrors of the unknown and not read authors like Dickens, whose ability to paint evil characters made one shrink, "as from the sulphur and brimstone of hell."

But perhaps the most disturbing development of his childhood was the sign that conflicting parental pressures had weakened Bernhard's ability to face life with a sense of inner worth. The little boy in him might be smothered with love and every temper tantrum forgiven, but the inquiring young mind, the explorer going on intellectual odysseys, would be subjected to exacting mental disciplines with the constant threat of being weighed and found wanting. Although Bernhard belonged, he was not acceptable—a contradiction of such transparent illogic that he would have challenged it immediately, had it ever reached consciousness.

His self-confidence was spurious, rather than real, undermined with inner criticisms and doubts, vulnerable to the least challenge from without. Others' opinions mattered far more than they must do for anyone who wants peace of mind, and this emotional vulnerability was further eroded by the all-pervasive anti-Semitism of society itself. Buffeted by the hatred of others, the already self-doubting boy came to accept the verdict as valid, to loathe and despise himself. He wrote to the widow of a Jewish rabbi, Frau Mally Dienemann, that Jews tended to think of themselves as prejudice painted them. In old age, he was still using the present tense.

"How I used to loathe myself for being one of those whom I knew, as Dante describes, Heaven rejects and Hell disdains," he wrote to Mary Costelloe, his future wife. There was an easy solution. He no longer need remain an outsider, paying, for his loyalty, the price of being despised and rejected, denied a whole world of literature, poetry, music, and art. The early paradise he was constructing in his imagination to supplant the "squalor and sordidness, meanness and brutality" of his daily life was within his grasp, and so were the limitless intellectual vistas toward which his whole nature yearned, if he was willing to forgo membership in a world that seemed in the vicelike grip of rabbinical orthodoxy, a reactionary and even anachronistic world.

"I had ears, but could not hear because of my ear locks; I had eyes and could not see because they were closed in prayer. . . . I am Rabbi Nehemiah no longer, they call me Nehemiah the atheist now." It was, everyone said, the era of the great awakening. Names were being changed as easily as shirts. Greenbaum became Greene, Levy became Lamar, and Warschawsky was changed to Ward. Just as rapidly, the immemorial customs of the shtetl were crumbling before the impact of life in the New World. In such a setting, skullcaps, prayer shawls, and untrimmed hair seemed pathetically dated. The word among the new generation was: assimilation.

Bernhard could find a further precedent in the example set by his father, who at first refused to let his wife go to the synagogue, and who encouraged his children to ignore Jewish customs. That solution was to become a Christian. At the age of fifteen Bernhard was baptized into the Episcopal Church by Phillips Brooks, the famous minister of Trinity Church, Boston. It was, as Heine termed the act of baptism, his "passport to European civilization."

Bernhard did not delude himself that he was experiencing a genuine spiritual conversion. As he was to write later, "He had known what . . . the search for God is, in the childhood of his youth; but he had never known God, who had finally grown to have no more importance in his mind than any other scientific hypotheses."

The new *geshmat* (convert) was not, however, converting to Christianity simply from the cynical knowledge that to be an Episcopalian in Boston was the surest available route to social acceptance. He had always had a genuine admiration for Christianity's benevolent influence, as well as its inspiring effect on the arts. Christianity, he wrote in a short story, was a work of art in itself, "more beautiful than Greek art, more sublime than the Himalayas. . . . He could not assist in the service of the church without having an image, at least in his mind, of the wonderful spirit that must have inspired them who first formed and read it. . . . But . . . he would not be bound by it, or for it. . . ."

So Bernhard tried to steer a middle course between admiring what Christianity had accomplished, and standing apart from an ultimate identification with it. He would marry for the second time, but he would not wear the ring.

However, he had not taken into account the havoc that unruly emotions can have in the best organized of lives, and with the most logical of solutions, particularly when the act of changing one's religion is fraught with as many symbolic overtones as it was in his case. That Bernhard did examine these feelings is evident from an obviously autobiographical short story, "The Death and Burial of Israel Koppel," written for *The Harvard Monthly* and published in the summer of 1888, the year after he graduated. The fable is worth examining in detail, because it demonstrates that, on some level, Berenson had begun to realize the price he was paying for his solution.

Israel Koppel, Berenson wrote, was a young man of twenty-two (apparently his own age when he wrote the story) who had just returned from Vilna, where he had spent four years studying Gentile subjects and Russian. Back in his native village of Lida, Koppel found himself the object of scandalized public scrutiny because he had "cut his earlocks, discarded skull-cap and long coat, and actually was wearing trousers, and a jacket reaching to the hips only."

A few days later Koppel was lounging in the living room reading a Gentile book when, to the horror of his doting mother, he suddenly fell back in his chair with a thud. He was dead. His poor mother was so frightened at the sight that, when her shawl fell from her clean-shaven head (it was customary for married women to shave their hair), she did not bother to cover herself but rushed to the synagogue to find her husband and tell him the terrible news.

Some people thought it was God's judgment on Israel for trying to become a Gentile. The immediate concern of Israel's devout parents, however, was to have their son buried quickly, so that he would be spared "the torments that devils inflict upon a body before its burial." Since a doctor would insist on waiting for three days, he wrote, a barber was called in. The barber held a feather to Israel's nose and found that it did not stir. The boy was truly dead. Preparations for his burial began at once.

A procession accompanied the corpse through the town to its eternal resting place. It had to pass a disgusting sight, a Polish church, and the mourners stopped singing and mumbling long enough to mutter a curse: " 'Despising shalt thou be despised, and loathing shalt thou be loathed; for 'tis taboo, a dog are you!' " and to spit on the doorway.

Despite the high price Koppel had been obliged to pay to have his renegade son buried, the final resting place was not to be in the place of honor, in the center under the tallest pines, but beside a young oak, whose "sere and bleached leaves . . . were shivering on their twigs." The coffin was lowered, Israel's father rent the right flap of his coat, threw four shovelfuls of earth on the boards, recited the Aramaic hymn of the exaltation of the Lord, and went home.

The bereaved parents began the seven days of mourning and went to bed. Koppel fell asleep, but was soon awakened by a nightmare which, he thought, came about because he had forgotten to repeat the night's prayer. "He recited it now: the psalms; the description of Solomon's throne and its guardians; the invocation to the guardian of Israel who neither slumbereth nor sleepeth; and the invocation to Gabriel, Raphael, Michael and the divine Presence, to watch by his bed."

Koppel fell asleep again and the same dream returned. He felt an infinite weight. He seemed to be in darkness. Something was ringing in his ears with a sharp hissing sound, the same sound he heard one winter, walking home through the snow, when the sky was freezing blue and the earth a dazzling white. It seemed to be the voice of silence itself. It was the silence of the grave.

Koppel again woke up and dressed himself. He poured water over his nails to wash off the devils that hung from them during the night. He tried to concentrate on the psalms for the dead. Instead he fell asleep for the third time, to dream once more that he was lying in a grave. As he was sleeping he wondered whether the dream had not been caused by "a picture of Mephistopheles lowering over Faust's open grave, in a copy of Goethe's *Faust* that he had just been reading."

The writer, skillfully fusing the identity of the father and son, introduced his central concept. Israel Koppel had died, been buried, and been brought back to life by Dumah, the angel of vengeance.

"He long ago had given up belief in what he considered superstitions about the future life. Since he had begun the study of Gentile lore, these Jewish superstitions had seemed something to laugh at. Were they true after all? Had the Lord slain him in the bloom of his youth for his disbelief? . . . He could recall no inquisition from the Angel of Death, and no punishment for forgetting his name, ancestry, and station. . . . He surely was not perfect, judged by any law; and, according to Jewish beliefs, he had been guilty of unspeakable sins. . . ."

The dreamer slowly became persuaded of his own guilt and convinced that he would have to endure horrible tortures. "He already felt the iron chains crushing the joints of his body. Now they are tearing him limb from limb. . . . Oh, the horror and pain! When would it end? . . . He prayed to God to forgive him. Out of the depths of his innermost soul, he prayed for forgiveness. Ah, the dreadful agony; it even would not let him pray. . . ."

Koppel the father again awoke, convinced at last that he was receiving desperate messages from his son. He forced the rabbi to open up the new grave and found his worst fears realized. His son's contorted face told him that he had been buried alive.

Someone in the crowd muttered, "God forgive us, what a

judgment!" and someone else shouted, "Served him right!"

The short story's symbolic message is unmistakable. The young man who has dared to rebel against his culture's "narrow labyrinth of ritual-theological casuistry" will be crushed to death by the weight of its retribution.

A parallel message is being stated with even greater emphasis, and that is the guilt which someone caught in Israel Koppel's dilemma will be bound to feel. The very inflexibility of Judaic law was its greatest strength in times of peril when not just spiritual, but actual bodily survival depended upon the group's ability to sustain its own cohesiveness in spite of severe pressures from the outside world. However, that same rigidity of outlook guaranteed an agonized conscience for anyone who dared to question its dictates, as Berenson could not help doing.

Even the most innocent appreciation of natural beauty, which for Berenson was as automatic as breathing, was a deadly sin: ". . . Not in vain is it written in the Talmud: 'He who turns aside from the study of the Law to say: How beautiful that tree is! How well-marked that furrow is! That one deserves to die.'"

Translated into the terms of Berenson's short story, it is therefore significant that Israel Koppel does not even try to fight his way to freedom. He concludes that the burial is his punishment for having committed "unspeakable sins," for having forgotten his name, his ancestry, and his station. He secretly concedes the justice of the sentence. It served him right. Even though he prays for forgiveness, the words die in his throat. He is doomed.

Here, in stark outline, is the dilemma that confronted the young Berenson. In attempting to free himself from the burden of his Jewish identity and the fate of the social outcast, Berenson ran the even graver risk of being crushed beneath an overwhelming sense of guilt. This reiterated guilt gives his short story its power, and perhaps the act of writing was an attempt at expiation.

"Upon him who is ashamed of his family, there will be no blessing," goes the Jewish proverb, and the young Berenson was ashamed of his poverty, ashamed of being Jewish. This is why he never wanted to recall his early years, or talk about his origins. This is why his first biographer felt the need to apologize for lifting the veil on 11 Minot Street, "which Berenson himself never lifted privately or in print." She did so, Mrs. Sprigge said in a placating aside obviously meant for her subject's eyes, to throw into sharper focus the radiance of his achievements.

Theodor Reik, the noted Jewish psychiatrist, concluded that it was impossible to be ashamed of one's family, one's culture, and one's race, without being also ashamed of one's self, since one was intimately, almost inextricably, bound up with the other. This, then, is the underlying message of the proverb. There can be no real happiness in life for a man who lacks the sense of self-worth which makes life worthwhile. "Strange that the folklore of an oriental people coincides here with the viewpoint of Goethe: any life can be lived . . . if one remains oneself."

The mind is its own place, John Milton wrote, equally capable of making a heaven out of hell, or a hell from heaven. When Bernhard became ashamed of what he was, he betrayed himself. When he buried his Jewish past, his sense of guilt guaranteed that he would never be able to lay it to rest. When he refused to remain the person he had been, the "despair of not wanting to be oneself" set the stage for years of torment, as he groped to replace his loss, and to answer the inner meaning of the Hasidic tale, "Why were you not Zusya?"

A TRUE
GENTLEMAN

BERNHARD BERENSON LIVED in Boston for barely twelve
years and never again returned to live there, yet the formative influence of that decade was decisive. If culture can be said to
have an incalculable effect on character, that effect was all the
more crucial in the case of one who had spurned his heritage and
was in the process of building a new persona, and as fast as
possible.

In a few years, nothing of the shtetl Jew from the Pale
remained (Berenson was careful to introduce himself as a Lithuanian national, speaking pure German and not that German Jewish
jargon containing so many Hebrew and Slavic idioms). In its place
was the very model of a proper Bostonian, circa 1885: polished,
impeccably mannered, exquisitely educated, and fastidiously aesthetical. He absorbed, he wrote years later, "all that could be
picked of the educated New Englander's *Weltanschauung*, to the
obliteration of nearly all that had gone before. . . ." No one knew

about his past and his Harvard classmates were never invited to 11 Minot Street.

Exactly how this radical transformation was achieved is not known. However, one can safely guess that Albert and Eudice actively encouraged it, to the extent of their own self-abasement. There is a story that when Albert at the back door learned that his son was one of the guests in the fancy drawing room of—some said Isabella Stewart Gardner, others, Louisa May Alcott—the peddler Berenson packed up his wares and fled. The story may be apocryphal, but it contains a kernel of truth. Albert would willingly have effaced himself from the earth to ensure that his children would not be the victims of his shame.

They all thought likewise. They were all climbing out of the trap that poverty and the shtetl had set for their parents and they were all renouncing their religion. Their Little Mother was the only dissenting voice. "Mama says that [the Little Mother] advised against sending me to college, for then I'll never marry, or I'll marry a Christian, like her daughters, and bring sorrow to the family." Senda became a physical education instructor and married a professor at Smith; Rachel took a master's degree in archaeology and married a professor from Harvard. Bessie studied sculpture and dance in Paris. Only Abie seemed paralyzed by the past, or perhaps did not care enough to evade it, preferring the comfort of belonging to the jagged, stony path of assimilation.

He, less brilliant than the others, who made scarcely any effort to hide his origins, was the one everyone felt embarrassed about. Rachel had to tactfully suggest to him that his English simply would not do and that he must try to improve, because B.B. disapproved so much. "I never would have ventured such a suggestion on my own hook," she wrote to Senda by way of explanation.

Abie, sensing their disapproval, was on the defensive. "I've read considerable [*sic*] the past few weeks," he wrote to Senda in the summer of 1900, "of course, the late novels, but as long as they interest me, it is far better than not reading at all."

They were all snobs, all jockeying for position in a society in which worth was precisely assessed and distributed. It is probably true that anti-Semitism did not reach its full flower until the pogroms of the 1880s in Russia brought refugees to New York and Boston in their hundreds of thousands. Long before that, Jews in Boston and New York felt the lash of customs designed to exclude them from any real acceptance by their adopted society.

They soon discovered the vast gulf separating the American promise from its reality.

"This latent anti-Semitism, if it did not eventuate in street fights as it did in the East Side of New York City, did create a tension nonetheless harmful, if more subtle. No matter how ardently these young Jews strove to become Americans . . . they found themselves excluded from schools, universities, social and country clubs, hotels, and residence in certain districts of the city by so-called 'gentlemen's agreements,'" wrote the author of *Their Exits and Their Entrances*. There was also "the more humiliating snobbery of the Jews who came from Germany in 1840–50 toward their fellow-Jews (Ostjuden) who came from Russia. . . ." This form of snobbishness "was acutely painful to my sisters and myself, for we were not invited to the college dances given by the matrons of German-Jewish descent at the Reform Temple Israel in Boston. . . ."

A Jew, if he surfaced in fashionable literature at all, was painted in shades no less black than those reserved for the grasping merchant of Venice. He was the most loathsome kind of social opportunist, feared for the narrow wedge his race had managed to drive into the once impregnable drawing rooms of the social elite. Since such newcomers always had money, there would always be some member of society depraved enough to pay off his obligations with an invitation to dine. The portrait of Simon Rosedale, the wealthy and unscrupulous outsider in Edith Wharton's *The House of Mirth*, is a fair description of the reception such ambitions might receive.

"In her little set, Mr. Rosedale had been pronounced 'impossible,' and Jack Stepney roundly snubbed for his attempt to pay his debts in dinner invitations. Even Mrs. Trenor, whose taste for variety had led her into some hazardous experiments, resisted Jack's attempts to disguise Mr. Rosedale as a novelty, and declared that he was the same little Jew who had been served up and rejected at the social board a dozen times within her memory. . . ."

Served up, and rejected. That such an attitude, poisoning the atmosphere of polite society, should have been acceptable to such a penetrating social critic as Edith Wharton is a telling comment on the tenor of the times. The potential victim can always scent the ferocity lurking beneath the veneer and must, like Mr. Rosedale, cultivate a bland insensitivity ("the instincts of his race fitted him to suffer rebuffs and put up with delays"), while making calculated use of the corruptibility of human nature; or he must be at pains to dissociate himself from the outcasts and align himself with those who ruled in the world of "us" and "them." A public disavowal may be necessary. Berenson, writing ostensibly about contemporary Jewish fiction (for the *Andover Review* in 1888), made such a statement.

"It is only by a study of Jewish institutions and literature that we shall begin to understand the puzzling character of the Jews. Begin to understand, I say, for comprehend them we never shall. Their character and interests are too vitally opposed to our own to permit the existence of that intelligent sympathy between us and them which is necessary for comprehension. . . ."

This must be one of the most pathetic self-denouncements ever written.

To become accepted by the ruling class, an outsider must cultivate the right schools as assiduously as the right friends and the proper address. Berenson lacked the latter, but he had all the academic qualifications necessary to enter the Boston Latin School, traditionally the best possible entrée into Harvard, and hence into Boston society. In 1881, Berenson managed to become admitted at the age of sixteen, when the curriculum included Latin, Greek prosody, Milton, Pope and Dryden, the history of the Middle Ages and of modern times, geography, Racine and Corneille, Krauss's grammar, geometry, physics, mechanics, and astronomy. He also studied drawing, but there is no evidence that he had any talent whatsoever.

Berenson unaccountably left at the end of a year (the lame explanation given was to study for university entrance exams) but an important preliminary step had been taken in the battle to shake off the stigma of origin. Samuel Eliot Morison wrote in *Three Centuries of Harvard* (1936) that, for a freshman entering Harvard, "family and race did not matter: an Irish-American, Jew, Italian or Cuban was not regarded as such if he went to the right school and adopted the mores of his fellows; conversely, a lad of Mayflower . . . ancestry who entered from a high school was as much 'out of it' as a ghetto Jew."

Berenson has not left behind a memoir of that brief, formative period, but one of his contemporaries has: George Santayana. The philosopher and writer was a year older than Berenson and may have met him at the Boston Latin School; he does not record it. Their friendship dated from their Harvard days and, after a moment of enthusiasm, cooled to a wary cordiality. Superficially, they had much in common. Both were the products of cultured and impoverished foreign families, they traveled in the same international intellectual circles, and both ended their days in Italy, although in vastly different surroundings.

In contrast to Berenson, however, Santayana was fascinated by his childhood and has left an evocative portrait of the Bedford Street building in which the school was then housed.

It seemed a vast, rattling old shell of a building, bare, shabby and forlorn to the point of squalor; not exactly dirty, but worn, shaky and stained deeply in every part by time, weather and merciless usage.... When up three or four worn granite steps you entered the door, the interior seemed musty and ill-lighted, but spacious, even mysterious.... No blackboard was black; all were indelibly clouded with ingrained layers of old chalk; the more you rubbed it out, the more you rubbed it in. Every desk was stained with generations of ink-spots, cut deeply with initials and scratched drawings....

And the teachers ... were surely not out of keeping with their surroundings: disappointed, shabby-genteel, picturesque old Yankees, with a little bitter humor breaking through their constitutional fatigue. I daresay that for them as for me, and for all the boys who were at all sensitive, the school was a familiar symbol of fatality. They hadn't chosen it, they hadn't wanted it, they didn't particularly like it; ... but there it stood ... and there was nothing else practicable but to go on there, doing what was expected and imposed upon them.

This first experience of the blend of discomfort, tradition, and exacting learning that was the hallmark of the best preparatory schools on both sides of the Atlantic gave Berenson his first real taste of exclusiveness and privilege. It must have been a heady experience and one which made him acutely aware of the power of education to open doors. He learned that one looked to one's school for what it could teach, and to one's professors for what entrées they might provide into that other, exclusive world, which had taken such a compelling hold on his imagination. The evidence is that Berenson, so intelligent, irresistibly handsome, with such charming wit and fastidious tastes, was quickly singled out as one of those attractive young men whom it would be a real kindness to befriend. He, for his part, played the right role assiduously.

It might have been a certain Professor Lindsay, probably one of Berenson's teachers during his year at Boston University, who first noticed and encouraged the young student. Perhaps it was Barrett Wendell, professor of literature at Harvard, who brought the young student into his house and first taught him how to use knives and forks in the proper way. Perhaps Thomas S. Perry, the American scholar then teaching literature at Harvard and socially well-placed, first befriended Berenson, or perhaps it was the famous Harvard professor, Charles Eliot Norton. One cannot tell from Berenson's letters of that period, which are curiously identical in tone. In 1885, Berenson told Professor Lindsay that he was anxious to renew the friendship of the one man whom, so far in his life, he longed to see again. In 1886, he was writing to Norton that, in the past few days, he had realized more strongly than ever how important a place Norton had come to play in his life. In 1887, he wrote to Perry that he was the one person in all the world whom he, Berenson, most admired. In the case of T. S. Perry, a friend of Henry James, who called him "perhaps the most learned man in America," Berenson may genuinely have meant his words. Forty years later, he recalled the house in Boston at 312 Marlborough Street to which the Perrys had first invited him, where he passed so many happy hours and experienced such wholehearted kindness.

Berenson's most stunning social success, however, was with a woman: Isabella Stewart Gardner, whom he met in his last year at Harvard (1886–87) through Norton, or perhaps the Perrys, since they were all socially intertwined. She was forty-six years old, with money, brains, and taste. Isabella had amused herself in the early years of her marriage to the wealthy John Gardner by collecting ballgowns, jewels, and houses. Then, falling under the influence of Norton, she turned her attention to art and music. She began to study Dante and amass paintings, rare books, and manuscripts.

Isabella Gardner also collected men, the younger and handsomer the better. She was never pretty. Her white skin, sandy red hair, and trim waistline were the only physical characteristics of which she was proud. Her famous portraitists, among them Sargent and Whistler, found the task of conveying the magnetic charm of a moon-faced, mousy little woman plainly intimidating. The best portrait of Mrs. Gardner, by Anders Zorn, resolves the dilemma by portraying her in movement, her features blurred. She is shown in the act of throwing open the doors of a Venetian palazzo, simply clad in pale yellow, but with a magnificent rope of pearls, studded with a single ruby, swinging below her waist. One senses at once the vitality and infectious enthusiasm, as well as the charm, which mitigated against such queenly dictates as, "C'est mon plaisir."

Isabella Gardner was, indeed, autocratic and high-handed. She had a genius for self-dramatization and young men flocked around her in such numbers that they were dubbed the "Isabella Club." She had begun her postmarital flirtations with the gloriously handsome future novelist F. Marion Crawford, then young and penniless. It ended when he decamped and her husband whisked her off to Cambodia.

This action on Gardner's part was uncharacteristic. He preferred his office, with lunches and dinners at the club, leaving Isabella quite free to dally with a young pianist (Clayton Johns), a young composer (Charles Loeffler), or a future museum official (Morris Carter). All of them were uneasily poised between enjoying her audacity, being flattered by her interest, and shrewdly aware of the attention they would automatically receive. Isabella, who liked to dance all night and wear twenty-five-carat diamonds in her hair, who had been known to invite a prizefighter in boxing shorts to tea so that the other women guests might admire the artistic ripple of his muscles, was someone Boston society had never quite accepted, but found impossible to ignore.

After Crawford, it is doubtful whether Isabella's attentions were even slightly amatory. In her way, she loved her distant, openhanded husband and was devastated when he died. Gardner seemed content to play the role of indulgent father to his eternal adolescent, ravenous for an adoring circle of admirers; and if young men found it expedient to join the charade, Isabella for one was not likely to scrutinize their motives any more closely than she did her own.

So the invitation to 152 Beacon Street for Berenson, one more in a succession of talented, dreamily handsome, and assiduously grateful young men, was completely predictable. As has been noted, it was also becoming habitual for Berenson to prefer women patrons and confidantes. It is a preference that can easily be traced to the loving attention he had received from the women in his family. If his father was hypercritical and his younger brother too callow to appreciate him properly, this could not be said of his sisters, who were earnestly attempting to follow him down the path of scholarship and social acceptance.

In those teen-age years of poverty in Boston, when he

dreamed every night of Lithuania "with radiant vividness," Senda was his closest companion. Together they took daily strolls through the streets, arm in arm. Recalling those days, Senda wrote, "I thought then how wonderful this big brother of mine was—how I looked up to him—how strange it seemed—he knew so much—and I feel much the same way now. What an odd little pair we must have been—by the way—that first year after we reached Boston—two queerly dressed, odd, foreign little youngsters going about the streets of Boston arm in arm."

When Berenson talked about being an outsider and spoke of the way smoke from the wood fires of Lithuania went up vertically, Senda understood the pauses between words, better than anyone. Now it seemed fabulous vistas were opening in his life, because a rich older woman had focused her jeweled glance in his direction.

One imagines the young Berenson making his first visit behind the heavy double doors of 152 Beacon Street, actually two row houses joined together, the second having been bought to provide extra rooms for recitals and dancing parties. Since the floors of the new house were on a slightly higher level, small flights of steps were built to connect it with the other. Mrs. Gardner's biographer, Morris Carter, noted that "this device, which sounds so obvious, seemed at the time immensely clever and original."

Everything about the new brownstone in the Back Bay had the novelty of difference in the relatively provincial Boston of the 1880s. There was the marvelous sweep of staircase facing the entrance, with a tiger's skin thrown nonchalantly over the banister; there were towering palms bending titanic branches over fans, photographs, and feathers; a heterogeneous mixture of Louis XIV, Italian Renaissance, and Victorian Gothic furniture; an all-yellow drawing room; embossed, brocaded walls; and a sprinkling of Old Masters and ostentatious door hangings. In the new music room, painted white, were more palms, plaster busts, and friezes of choirboys playing instruments, copied from the organ loft of the Duomo in Florence. The decor presented a profusion of detail so claustrophobic that it can only be described by Edith Wharton's term, "upholstered."

The effect on a poor boy from the West End making his first visit to a house of this imperial splendor may be imagined. All those walls soaring up to paneled and chandeliered ceilings, those galleries of paintings, acres of carpeting, and platoons of chairs printed themselves indelibly on his imagination. He was as if transfixed at that impressionable moment when the world of luxury and refinement first spread its tantalizing pleasure before him and, for the rest of his life, it provided the ideal to which he would aspire.

Such wealth and privilege was important for the social acceptance it symbolized, and because it made perfection possible. It was all attainable, if he used his wits and made proper use of what he termed his "Pandora's box of personal gifts and characteristics." Berenson was not the first to discover how much malice will be forgiven, in those Wildean drawing rooms, provided that the owner possess a rapid flow of anecdote and wit.

The world that Mrs. Gardner opened to him brought other illuminating insights. A newcomer must become consummately well-versed in the thousand trifling formalities of etiquette which told the late Victorians, more pointedly than words, which new arrivals were gentlemen and which, *arrivistes*. But such dictates of conduct, as inflexible as those of Butrimants, had the comfort of all absolutes. Berenson fitted himself into them with relief. Fundamentally conservative, what he wanted was an acceptable social image and Boston society provided the mold. Berenson described that process as the attempt to bring sensation, feeling, reactions, and desire into "a certain harmony." Elsewhere, he wrote, of a similar society (the British), " 'One knows' that there are the rules: the rules of tennis, the rules of golf, the rules of life, and it is to these that one must cling. Thus they promote . . . a comfortable, decorous system. . . ."

Berenson accepted the task of assuming a new persona confidently, as a challenge to which his ingenuity and adroit intelligence were equal. He immediately brought his remarkable powers of observation to bear on the conduct of these "barons," as he later called them, and recounted, in 1933, one of the first important lessons he learned. One evening at dinner the dreadful drawings of a wealthy amateur were being inspected in the company of John La Farge, a distinguished American painter. While Berenson and the other guests maintained a "glacial silence," La Farge pleasantly suggested, since the light in the room was bad, that he take the portfolio with him and look at it the next morning in daylight.

"I was stunned to hear such a neatly jesuitical discourse, in which any outright lie was avoided, and I said to myself—how incompetent I am; what a clod, a boor, a newborn babe who knows absolutely nothing about dealing with people, or extracting myself from messy situations."

Besides being the model of tact, a true gentleman lived a quiet, cultivated life, enjoying things in an unhurried way, with "ample time for thought and conversation, delight in each other's personalities, and aspiration. . . ." His essential nature might ultimately be indefinable, but could be recognized by small, telling signs. Take for instance the day that Berenson's friend G. appeared at the Garden Show, covered with dust. "Here is a sign that he is a gentleman; only true gentlemen . . . know how to rise above their own appearance."

A true gentleman, serene enough not to need to make an impression, was also financially secure. Indeed, a further mark of his pedigree was his unspoken reluctance ever to discuss the subject of money. Conversely, the man obliged to earn a living could never pretend to that status.

The true gentleman could also be expected, in Boston at least, to set a high moral tone. He espoused values, standards, responsibility; he personified Fair Play. The young Berenson, taking due note, found himself exposed to the "double dose" of Hebraism, first Jewish and then New England.

All of this had a profound effect on "the infant prince of a neolithic Lithuanian ghetto." He wrote, "When I was young, aristocracy and *le monde*—society—fascinated me . . . I was attracted by its seeming access to a larger, more intense, as well as freer life. Its manners, its customs, its habitations, its relations to others seemed more beautiful intrinsically than ours."

The leisured example of eighteenth-century aristocracy had found its adherents among the merchant barons of nineteenth-century Boston and it was the one to which Berenson instinctively turned. "Mary has ruined my life by inducing me to write books," he remarked. "If I had not written books, what would I have become? I would have become a true gentleman." Umberto Morra, Berenson's Eckermann, does not record the tone of wry amusement with which the remark was probably made, but the undertone of earnestness is clear enough.

Last, and most important, a true gentleman espoused Culture. An English editor, E. L. Godkin, observed in 1871 that "Boston is the one place in America where wealth and knowledge of how to use it, are apt to coincide," referring to the enthusiastic new patronage of the arts. One invited Henry James to tea to read his latest play aloud. One held musicales, donated paintings, established scholarships, commissioned John Singer Sargent to paint one's portrait and John La Farge to design stained-glass windows. It was all very elegant, generous, and public spirited, if based on the premise that the poor proposed and the rich disposed.

That the pursuit of Culture might be snobbish, exclusive, and high-handed, Berenson took as a matter of course, a historical fact since the Renaissance. Culture had been his chosen study since the age of thirteen: "the history of the development of ideas and of the means of expression—what in Germany is called the history of culture," leading him inevitably to study language, literature, and art. Culture was the only worthwhile aim of a noble life. One should bend every effort "to live resolutely in the good, the whole, the beautiful."

He was already writing, trying to become a novelist, an essayist or a poet, or a critic and historian of literature. He had haunted the Boston Public Library (he later told Kenneth Clark that his mind functioned better between the ages of twelve and sixteen than it ever did again) and read everything, "especially popular science, then Oriental history and antiquities, books of travel and all books about Russia." He could speak German, Hebrew, and Yiddish, and had been familiar with Lithuanian, Polish, and Russian from childhood. Now he was studying Greek, Arabic, Assyrian, and Sanskrit, as well as the more mundane subjects of philosophy, physics, chemistry, and English.

Berenson seemed to be preparing himself for a future whose outlines were not even dimly visible and, because he was so talented, and had such a multiplicity of choices, he was in danger of frittering away his opportunities under the enticement of a momentary enthusiasm. He was in equal danger of becoming transfixed by indecision.

There were, however, some fixed stars in the firmament of his interests and foremost among them was poetry. He had loved it since childhood and, when he first discovered the poems of Matthew Arnold at the age of sixteen, they seemed a revelation.

"It was as if I had all at once, after living speechless for sixteen years, been endowed with a voice. Every verse seemed like an utterance from my innermost heart."

When Berenson discovered him, Arnold was making his reputation in Britain as one of the major spokesmen for the crisis of faith which the Industrial Revolution had engendered. His poems contemplate the death of God and the Sea of Faith which is, in his most famous poem, "Retreating, to the breath/ Of the night-wind, down the vast edges drear/ And naked shingles of the world."

Here was Berenson's own anguish, ideally expressed, by a poet who seemed his very mouthpiece. Here, too, was his own unutterable sense of isolation: "Yes! in the sea of life enisled/ With echoing straits between us thrown/ Dotting the shoreless watery wild,/ We mortal millions live *alone*."

This discovery, however, had the paradoxical result of giving Berenson fresh heart. Friendship seemed possible, for the first time. "I was not a creature apart, alone, with no hope of finding a fellow. Here was one surely; and others there must be."

Berenson was irresistibly drawn, he wrote, to "all the great epics of despair, all the Greek tragedies; in short, everything which showed man crushed by destiny, and yet triumphing over it by his cosmic irony." The same mood of "triumphant despair" had led him, perhaps, to the great poet who expressed thoughts even more central to the silent inner questioning: Johann Wolfgang von Goethe. Berenson, the man whom heaven rejected and hell disdained, the outcast condemned by Dumah, the angel of vengeance, had discovered Goethe's masterpiece, *Faust.*

In the Christopher Marlowe play, a retelling of the medieval legend, Faust sells his soul to the Devil in exchange for all the riches of the world. Too late, he realizes the folly of his act and is condemned to hell.

In Goethe's masterpiece, Faust has become a symbol of man's emancipation from authority. Faust is a free spirit, who dares to trespass on the realm of the traditionally forbidden. He personifies the Age of Enlightenment, of choice over blind faith, of human autonomy, and his fate is no longer predictable. Mephistopheles cannot be sure of his victory and, at the very end of Goethe's verse drama, Faust cheats the Devil of his due.

If Berenson, too, was an outcast from heaven, then why not take sides with Mephistopheles, that infinitely world-weary sophisticate who "criticizes the universe like a bad book," as Madame de Staël wrote?

"I am very religious by nature," Berenson wrote to Mary Costelloe, "but my religion is of the opposition; is with Prometheus rather than with Zeus, perhaps with Satan rather than Jehovah." (The name of Satan is derived from a Hebrew word meaning "one who plots against another.") Elsewhere, Berenson wrote, "The devil is the dramatic element in the universe."

Goethe, the incomparable mind behind the poetry, was his ideal, a poet of infinite gifts who, like Berenson himself, energetically explored life in every direction—who might be in the middle of rewriting one play and become enamored of another, who managed to travel through Italy, writing a new work, while also "sightseeing, collecting coins, gems, minerals, plaster casts, taking drawing lessons, attending lectures on perspective and making botanical experiments." It was possible to transcend physical limits, be everywhere, see everyone, do everything, if one were a genius. It was possible to transcend oneself. For the medieval ideal of a pious search for God, that of his own childhood, Berenson substituted the Renaissance ideal of genius, of man's fulfillment here on earth. He was cherishing vague but luminous hopes of becoming "a poet, a novelist, a thinker, a critic, a new Goethe in short."

Fortunately for Berenson, entering Harvard as an undergraduate in 1884 (Berenson spent his freshman year at Boston University), one did not have to narrow one's field of study too soon. Since the average newcomer was extremely well prepared with a classically oriented education that included four years of Greek, six years of Latin, and ten of mathematics, he was now to be given the leisure to broaden his perceptions and follow his inclinations. This new policy followed the arrival of President Charles William Eliot five years before. The notion that certain courses should be elective was heretical to some, but for someone of Berenson's intellectual voracity, it seemed heaven-sent.

Under Eliot, the university itself was expanding rapidly. It was growing physically, as the country's spectacular new prosperity translated itself into an increasing scramble for schooling. It was also adding further luster to its enviable intellectual reputation with a faculty that included Barrett Wendell, Arthur George Sedgwick, Henry Adams, Charles Eliot Norton, Charles R. Lanman, "the best teacher of languages . . . that I ever encountered," and the psychologist and philosopher William James, from whom Berenson derived many of his subsequent theories of aesthetics. Charles Eliot Norton had just joined the faculty, in 1874, to teach the first course in fine arts that the university had ever offered.

Berenson moved into rooms at 64 Mount Auburn Street, a

block from the campus, considered *the* place to stay. It was "much more desirable, indeed, than . . . the dormitories in the [Harvard] Yard." The street was, however, very run-down and the new arrival was expected to furnish his rooms himself.

Returning home to 11 Minot Street in winter, Berenson would cross Cragie's Bridge connecting Cambridge with the West End in the thinnest of overcoats, reveling in the eighteen-degrees-below-zero weather and the buffeting, icy winds. "Nearly blew over, . . . but such a feeling of getting the better of it . . . !"

The society in which Berenson found himself, although polyglot, presented a similar challenge to one bent on mastering the hostile elements. Samuel Eliot Morison, Harvard's historian, noted that ambitious freshmen had to watch their steps carefully. "No 'Harvard individualism' for them! You must say, do, wear, the 'right thing,' avoid the company of all ineligibles and, above all, eschew originality. . . ."

Further divisions were made in Harvard's select circles according to affluence and social status. Logan Pearsall Smith, Berenson's future brother-in-law, who sat next to him in class but did not meet him for several years, recalled with chagrin how delighted he had been to be elected to the right societies at Harvard.

"It was in the essence a snobbish pleasure; why should I boggle at the word? Indeed the atmosphere of Harvard was at that time . . . richly colored by the sense of social differences. The prestige possessed by members of the most exclusive clubs, the delight of being seen in their company, and the hope of being admitted into their select circles—these were the animating motives of life at Harvard as I knew it. . . ."

In that social life, Jews played no part. George Santayana remarked of his wealthy Jewish friend, Charles Loeser, that despite Loeser's obvious breeding, the fact that he had been born a Jew, and that his father was a merchant, disqualified him from leadership in that supposedly democratic American society. Jews were in a minority and did not begin to figure in campus life until enough of them, the talented sons of Russian Jewish immigrants, arrived to form the first Menorah Society (1906).

This did not altogether matter. Even though you might be poor and might or might not be identified as being Jewish (and no Jew is listed in the 1887 graduating class), a great deal would be forgiven of an intellectual aristocrat. John Reed, a playwright who arrived some years later, observed that, although the snobs held the power, the real life of the university went on outside their ranks, the intellectual life in particular.

Berenson plunged into that intellectual life with zest. He began to contribute to the new magazine, *The Harvard Monthly*, which had been founded by George Santayana to provide an outlet for literary work of quality. By 1886, Berenson had become its editor and was contributing a number of short stories and philosophical speculations loosely grouped around book reviews.

In imitation of his idol, Goethe, Berenson was also writing poetry. It was embarrassingly bad. The man who possessed exquisite visual sensibilities seems to have completely lacked that sensitivity to the sound and rhythm of his adopted language, which is indispensable to poetic achievement. He seemed to show an almost perverse instinct for the least expressive metaphor, and his attempts at alliteration are painful. When it came to using English, Berenson was tone-deaf.

One of his poems, "Ghazel [a kind of Oriental lyric poetry]: Thought and Temperament," is, however, valuable for the insight it provides into his mood. The work begins with a variation on the sentence he wrote as a child, "Ringing silence is hissing around me," and draws a portrait of himself, bound Prometheus-like to a rock, from which he surveys a bleak world. He contrasts the cheerless scene, the "flat uncurled/ Frozen mists from wan seas that had drowned me/ With gloom," with his inner state of mind. The griefs that would "ground me/ On slimy shallows of shoreless sorrow," have no effect because, despite everything, he has refused to succumb to Despair.

"The gadfly of my early youth was my compulsion to discover the meaning, the essence of literature," he remarked later. "No critic, no philosopher, no writer gave me the explanation I was seeking and then suddenly in a flash I realized that to find it I would have to turn to the visual arts. . . ."

More precisely, it was poetry that led to his study of art, because "the problem which was with me every day was of severing off what counted in poetry and distinguished it from mere versification." The problem might be resolved in painting, Berenson thought, because "with painting, I would have my 'object' firmly before my eyes, not fluid and mobile and in a certain sense delusive. . . ."

It was in this frame of mind, already occupied with defining the essence of great Art, that Berenson joined the classes of Norton, those classes established at Harvard, it was declared, so as to transform "young barbarians at play" into urbane and civilized young men. Norton, a friend of Ruskin and Longfellow, was author of a volume of Italian studies and an authority on Dante. His ideas on fine art, derived from John Stuart Mill, centered around the value of studying art in developing feeling and imagination. His lectures pursued their stately course from the golden age of Athens to the Gothic style in Venice and Florence. Norton made only fleeting references to theories of aesthetics. He ended with the Renaissance on the apparent assumption that art after 1600 was beneath consideration.

That Berenson was on social terms with Norton outside the classroom is evident. It is also clear that Norton couldn't stand him. Perhaps he disapproved of what looked like social climbing, or shrank from the note of insincerity in his pupil's praise.

"I cannot forget that when still an undergraduate at Harvard, Charles Eliot Norton said to Barrett Wendell who repeated it: 'Berenson has more ambition than ability.' Norton never changed his mind," Berenson wrote. When Berenson sent Norton his first book, on the Venetian painters of the Renaissance, Norton wondered why it should have fallen to Berenson's lot to write on that subject. Norton took the same severe exception to his other books on Italian art and advised the Harvard library against buying copies.

To Berenson, Norton's classes had less to do with art than with the deportment proper for young men about to enter elegant society. He did, however, accord Norton the grudging tribute that his teacher had obliged him to read Dante aloud for a complete academic year, an invaluable introduction to thirteenth-century Italy.

The interests of both men differed markedly. Norton was, from the start, content with a "historical and illustrative" viewpoint. Berenson yearned for a more daring approach and one that fed his fascination for definitions. He found it in the work of Walter Pater. This exciting new writer, a fellow of Brasenose College, Oxford, a student of Greek philosophy and the theoretician for the Pre-Raphaelite movement, had already written a masterly collection of essays on Renaissance painters and then, in 1885, wrote his best-known work, *Marius the Epicurean*.

The language of *Marius* is so indigestible, the plot so negligible, and the thought so convoluted that it is difficult nowadays to understand its appeal, or how it could have survived so many reprintings for the next forty years. However, the book had an immediate attraction for Berenson, with his acute visual perceptions. For Marius, a Roman pagan, learning to see with a discerning eye counts for everything. Every day, Marius must renew his ability to view the world freshly. He must learn to discriminate with infinite fastidiousness, and further that educative process by meditating upon beautiful objects; "... to keep ever by him if it were but a single choice flower, a graceful animal or sea-shell, as a token and representative of the whole kingdom of such things. ..."

In *Marius*, a new religion was being proposed, one dedicated to a concrete and accessible Beauty, instead of an abstract and hypothetical God. One found Beauty primarily in the natural world, and one's pilgrimage was saved from hedonism by a kind of monastic idealism, "a ministry, in spirit at least, towards a sort of hieratic beauty and order in the conduct of life."

This rarefied philosophy presented the same uncompromising and austere façade that the young critic had so much admired in the poems of Matthew Arnold. These, he declared, were as beautiful as Praxitelean marbles in a moonlit Italian garden. Marble flesh chills the touch, and there is something bloodless about Arnold's poetry and Pater's idealism. It was, however, this very ethereality that Berenson admired. He reveled in the thin air, like that of a "limitless snow-field," just as he shrank from contact with life's bestial realities.

Berenson read every obscure word that Pater wrote, from *Emerald Uthwart* to *Demeter*. He discovered *The Renaissance*, Pater's collection of essays on art and poetry, and stayed up all night reading the book for weeks on end, until he knew it by heart. Even Pater's essay on Giorgione, which Berenson liked least, contained pages of beautifully phrased criticism. He found himself drawn to Venetian painting most of all, and came to decide that this most perfectly personified the Italian Renaissance. His response to that art was not cerebral at first, but that of an appreciator par excellence. Bertrand Russell, his brother-in-law, was to complain mildly some years later, "pictures still don't give me the funny feeling in the stomach they give you."

Bit by bit, the name of Walter Pater became hallowed and the reclusive Oxford aesthete attained an almost godlike status. He had taught him, Berenson wrote, how to "extract from the chaotic succession of events in the common day what was wholesome and sweet, what fed and sustained the spirit," and to turn his back on "frozen mists from wan seas" and "shoreless sorrows." He was looking ahead, hopefully, to his graduation and the moment when "I could begin to realize what was in me," even if that hope was tempered by the realization that most extravagant ambitions are unfulfillable.

Berenson even wrote to Pater at the age of twenty-one and, although the letter does not survive, it made enough of an impression to identify its writer when the two men finally met. That meeting was "against my will and . . . very disappointing," Berenson wrote later. By then, no disappointment could alter the fact that Pater's aesthetic had found its most enthusiastic adherent. Berenson had turned to art.

5

A PAINTER'S EYE

Simply to be alive and there was a delight; and as
he bathed in the fresh water set ready for his use,
the air of the room about him seemed like pure
gold ...

—WALTER PATER, *Marius the Epicurean*, Vol. I

WITH CHARACTERISTIC SHREWDNESS, Bernhard Berenson concealed his hand when he applied, in the spring of his graduating year, for a traveling fellowship to spend a year in Europe. Europe had been dinned into his head, he wrote elsewhere. He was longing to make the tour then considered an indispensable part of a gentleman's education, but he had no money. Work, however, was equated with grinding struggle in his mind.

Instead of a job, he proposed further study to fit himself for the role of a critic or literary historian. He stood a good chance of being awarded the Parker Traveling Fellowship and he knew it. He cited his 85 percent grade in Hebrew, his 80 percent grade in Prof. William James's course, his 98 percent score in medieval German literature and art, his courses in Arabic, Assyrian, and Sanskrit. He wished, he wrote, that he had concentrated still more on his English (85 percent), but that did not matter, since he was so well-motivated for study outside the classroom. "Few men sleep less and devote themselves to their true interests, more than I do," he concluded stiffly.

If he did not get the fellowship he dared not expect his

parents to support him any longer. He would have to find a job; but he intended, nevertheless, to devote every spare moment to literature.

The subject of art was broached with studied casualness. He intended to include it since "it is there that I feel myself weakest," and he made a passing reference to his belief that such study would help resolve certain problems of aesthetics. Art was to be incidental to his main study, Berenson asserted, in deference to the knowledge that the fellowship would be given for the study of literature. Yet art provided the main course for the self-imposed itinerary: Paris in mid-July, for its art galleries and churches; the fall at Berlin University to study the practical problems of art and Arabic; spring in Italy, for further study of art and Italian literature.

The field was narrowed to that of Berenson and one other candidate. Perhaps his true intentions could be discerned through the smoke screen. At any rate, he was not chosen. Just as all seemed lost, a sympathetic group of friends rescued him. Among them were the kindly Perrys and Isabella Stewart Gardner who, typically, enjoyed manipulating the lives of her protégés. (Berenson resented, for many years, the fact that his prosperous cousin Louis refused to subscribe.) The band of friends provided a purse of $750 for a year's travel in Europe. Berenson graduated with a B.A. cum laude in June of 1887 and, a few weeks later, left 11 Minot Street, never to return. He was off to Paris, to satisfy his "thirst for existence in exquisite places," and to put into immediate practice that fastidious aesthetic creed that Marius had espoused.

When Berenson left Boston, Rachel was seven years old, Bessie, nine, Abie was fourteen, and Senda, twenty. Senda was perhaps the person he most hated to leave. Intellectually, Senda could not approach her older brother, but emotionally, she could share his enthusiastic response to the arts. They had shared the same childhood and the same struggle to overcome it; it gave them a lifelong empathy. Unlike him, Senda had, as a young girl, been crippled by a physical weakness that made her back ache intolerably at the least exertion. She went to the Boston Latin School but was never able to complete a year. She studied piano at the Boston Conservatory of Music but was unable to practice, because of her back.

A friend persuaded Senda to enter the new Boston School of Gymnastics, the first American school to adopt a Swedish system and to stress the healthful benefits of exercise. At first, Senda was miserable and the simplest exercise made her ache all over. "After five minutes of standing erect, I had to lie flat on three stools." After three months, however, she was beginning to feel an improvement and, by the end of the year, "I . . . was doing all the gymnastics required." Senda concluded, "It is impossible to tell how my life had altered. I had changed an aching body to a free and strong mechanism." Helping others to make the same discovery became her vocation.

This, however, was not to come about until 1890, three years later. The leave-taking was undoubtedly painful and Senda's first letter, June 19, 1887, was written on the day after Berenson sailed.

Two days before that, Berenson had sent Isabella Stewart Gardner a hurried note to thank her for her parting good wishes. When Berenson wrote again, it was from the rue du Vaugirard on the edge of Montparnasse.

Montparnasse in those days, according to Logan Pearsall Smith, was "curious, shabby, provincial yet cosmopolitan . . . with its little shops, its vast mysterious convents, its broad boulevards close by." When Smith moved to Paris, Whistler was living around the corner and painting a portrait of the famous Comte Robert de Montesquiou, whom Marcel Proust was to immortalize and whom Berenson was to know well. All that was in the future. Berenson, alone and friendless, was acutely homesick: ". . . was it exhaustion because of the very crowded life I had been living; was it mere topsy-turviness resulting from being plunged so suddenly into the most horrible of solitudes, a great city where you do not know one friendly soul—whatever it was, for a few weeks, I barely lived. I kept to my room, slept a good deal, and sometimes I did not sleep at all but analyzed a fever and ague that were playing hide and seek within me."

Berenson was suffering from an attack of self-doubt brought about by having read Tolstoy's *A Confession.* What was there to live for, he asked Mrs. Gardner, apparently hoping to be told. Ordinary people did not mind the unoriginality of their lives but, for one of his stamp, condemned to write or die, the future looked bleak, since his every thought had already been expressed by minds far greater than his own. Such an attitude of fashionable despair is familiar to anyone who, beginning a career as a writer, suddenly encounters the possibility that he is not a genius. The particular competitiveness of that urge was, perhaps, peculiarly Berenson's.

His second letter a month later was less freighted with introspection and more hopeful. He was becoming familiar with Paris in all its moods and loved the shifting play of light patterning its walls. He had a charming view, over the treetops, of the Jardins du Luxembourg. The leaves were falling. Their soft, russet colors had a nostalgic charm, although they were not as achingly vivid as those of New England. He was already becoming nostalgic about that.

By Thanksgiving Day Berenson was so busy looking at art, going to the theater, or loafing, that he had almost no time to read books and had written nothing at all. But he had begun to meet people and was being introduced around as a Russian, while insisting that he was thoroughly Lithuanian.

Berenson had also met a fascinating young Frenchman who had been born in Boston. They had walked and talked in the Bois de Boulogne and Berenson, starved for a dialogue, had launched on a long examination of metaphysics. But he seemed to have offended his new friend. He had merely observed that the newcomer talked like a man possessed by a vision, trying to convince someone who does not see it. The remark had been innocent, but the stranger had insisted upon thinking himself made fun of. Why was it, Berenson wanted to know, that people sensed sinister undertones in his perfectly genuine overtures? Mrs. Gardner's response to that might have been revealing, but none of her early letters has survived. Berenson concluded gloomily that he might as well give up trying to be understood by others.

Berenson went to see the great Sarah Bernhardt in a performance of Sardou's new play, *La Goseau*, and suffered such agonies throughout a torture scene, that he could hardly bear to watch. He also went to see an exhibition of paintings by Pierre Puvis de Chavannes, a painter much admired for his simple areas of color and rhythmic linear patterns, and was captivated. In a city of uninspired art, said Berenson, as yet unmoved by that ravishing new movement, Impressionism, Puvis de Chavannes seemed as brilliant as a comet. Berenson sat, happy and forgetful, musing for half an hour in front of *Femmes au bord de la mer* and absorbing Puvis de Chavannes' uncanny ability to paint the sea as it really was, and as no one else had ever seen it before.

The National Gallery of London, which he visited for the

first time in the winter of 1888, was a revelation. He could not believe, Berenson wrote, that there were so many wonderful paintings in the whole world. He was charmed by Orcagna, Fra Angelico, and the Giotteschi (followers of Giotto), as well as the Pre-Raphaelites. As for the loan collection at Burlington House, well, he would have traveled far just to see an inferior Giorgione, and here was an important one, not to mention better Velásquezes and Frans Halses than he had ever seen in his life.

In London Berenson made contact with the visiting Perrys and with "Ned" (E.P.) Warren, a wealthy Bostonian who was forming what would become a famous collection of classical antiquities for the Boston Museum of Fine Arts. For the next decade, Warren and his assistants, usually reçent college graduates, scoured Italy and Greece in search of prize finds. Berenson was suggesting, half in earnest, that they take a trip to Russia together, and Warren was jokingly refusing on the grounds that he could not go all the way to Siberia to rescue Berenson from the prison he would certainly end up in.

Berenson was in Oxford for the spring term, he told Mrs. Gardner, the university that he had yearned to attend five years before. He had never quite relinquished that dream and now he found that he had been absolutely right to imagine himself happy there. The beauty of the city was incomparable. All the books he could ever want were there, and so were the most congenial people in the world. The men of Oxford, he found, possessed that rare combination of intelligence, wit, and learning that he found irresistible. One could not even begin to compare a Harvard man with these paragons of virtue; but Berenson had already made up his mind on that score. Harvard men, he declared, were incapable of being men, without also being brutes or fiendish rakes.

Berenson had discovered "a double-headed nightingale," as Logan Pearsall Smith phrased it. This was Michael Field, a pseudonym for an extraordinary pair of writers, the Misses Katherine Harris Bradley and Edith Emma Cooper. This aunt and niece respectively had become personalities on the literary scene for their plays written in Elizabethan verse. Browning had praised their first work, *Callirrhoe*, and although the pair continued to produce other plays with devastating frequency (twenty-eight in all), their subsequent verse never evoked the same admiration. Like Browning, Berenson was intrigued by *Callirrhoe*, but had reservations about the rest.

He was living life aimlessly, without ambition, Berenson

Bernhard Berenson in Cambridge, 1887 (Both photos courtesy of "i Tatti")

Left: *Berenson's father, Alter, in Boston* (Courtesy of "i Tatti")
Right: *Berenson's mother, Eudice, in Boston* (Courtesy of "i Tatti")

Left: *Berenson's sister Senda* (Courtesy of "i Tatti")
Right: *Berenson's brother Abie* (Courtesy of "i Tatti")

Left: *Berenson's sister Bessie* (Courtesy of "i Tatti")   Right: *Mary Whitall Smith (the future Mary Berenson) taken in the winter of 1884–85* (Courtesy of the Library of Congress)

The young connoisseur in the 1890s (Courtesy of "i Tatti")

Berenson at Beaulieu while staying with Ralph Curtis, circa 1910 (Courtesy of "i Tatti")

Studying the reproduction of an early drawing, winter of 1909 (Courtesy of "i Tatti")

Drawing by Rene Piot, believed to be Belle da Costa Greene (Courtesy of "i Tatti")

Mary Berenson with the children of her first marriage, Karin and Ray Costelloe (Courtesy of Princeton University Library)

Summer of 1901: the newlyweds pose with his mother, Mrs. Berenson, seated, and sister Bessie at far right

The villa "i Tatti" as it looked shortly after Berenson acquired it (Courtesy of "i Tatti")

The small chapel on the grounds of "i Tatti" where Berenson and his wife are buried (Courtesy of "i Tatti")

The famous Rene Piot mural for the library, now hidden from view (Courtesy of "i Tatti")

Berenson's study, as it looked before 1915 (Courtesy of "i Tatti")

The dining room before 1915, with a table set for six (Courtesy of "i Tatti")

The limonaia (plant house), scene of so many afternoon teas

View of the formal garden from the limonaia

Left: *View from the terrace* Right: *The front door of "i Tatti," showing the Greek statue in the entranceway*

Left: *Pellegrina Von Turco at Poggio allo Spino, 1924* (Courtesy of "i Tatti") Right: *Geoffrey Scott in the early 1920s* (Courtesy of "i Tatti")

wrote. He had arrived from Boston full of ambition to be a scholar, but had quickly realized the futility of this. Now he was content to be nothing. He expected to drift back to 11 Minot Street in due course and find a job. He had a certain modest hope that he was changing for the better, which was negated by his distinct feeling that he was falling to pieces. He really didn't mind that, and would have no regrets, were it not for his kind friends (a probable reference to the Perrys) who were anxious to know what direction his life was taking. Perhaps nihilism was at the root of his problem. If he ever became a father, he would make sure that his son did not become a nihilist. Really, there was nothing worse.

As Berenson traveled onward to Bruges, Ghent, and Brussels, his fascination with art became all-absorbing. He was looking at buildings as objects of art, at churches as art, and at museums and galleries everywhere. With such treasures all around, it was an effort to visit a city for one picture, but he was glad that he had visited Ghent, to see Van Eyck's *Adoration of the Lamb*, and Bruges, to see the St. Ursula shrine by Memling.

He arrived in Berlin to take some university courses and discovered that his fears had been justified. How far he had come, he mused; once, he had thrilled to the very name of Deutschland. Now, he found the landscape flat and ugly, like South Boston. The society was formal and flat. Even the language repelled him. However, while in Berlin, he strengthened still further his love for Italian art. He had thought of writing on the strangely neglected subject of Spanish art. He had imagined that it, or Dutch painting, might rival the Italian, but had changed his mind. The Venetians were incomparable.

While in Berlin, Berenson was appalled to discover himself trapped in a display of unforgivable weakness. Since the age of ten, when he had experienced his first Fourth of July in Boston, Berenson had feared and avoided crowds. He had allowed himself to be overruled in Paris and had joined a street celebration of Bastille Day. It was an unnerving experience. Then, in Berlin, a similar incident occurred.

Out for a walk one day, Berenson was caught in a crowd awaiting the arrival of Crown Prince William. Before he knew it, he was in the thick of the group, listening to the cheering. "I got a lump in my throat, and tears in my eyes. I was horrified, for I disapproved of William's conduct . . . and despised his popularity. Yet I could not resist mass emotion. . . ." Rather than be betrayed by such pardonable human feelings, Berenson went to some lengths to avoid being in crowds from that time on.

In the late spring of 1888, Berenson took a trip into the Spreewald (bordering the River Spree) and came back enchanted with his journey along miles of narrow canals, past thickly wooded landscapes, traveling in something resembling a gondola. It made him feel closer to Lithuania than he ever had before. If one substituted wagons for boats, even the life of the peasants had an odd resemblance. "I felt a nearness of relationship to the people that was almost sentimentality. . . ."

Then Berenson observed that he and a Norwegian friend had attended a service at the handsome Jewish synagogue, the finest building in Berlin, and had found a great deal to admire in the service and the singing of a boys' choir. Everything would have been perfect, were it not for the congregation, Berenson concluded. Many of them "seemed to be selling old clothes."

Such a remark suggests that Mrs. Gardner did not know of his Jewish origins, as indeed his emphatic, "I am a Lithuanian," would suggest. Its ridicule is so crude that it indicates not only Berenson's sense of alienation from the very past he found so lyrically reminiscent in the Spreewald, but the extent of his self-hatred.

With the exception of Paris, Oxford, and Berlin, Berenson's grand tour consisted of a butterflylike flutter across Europe. His goal was Italy, but he could not resist going there by way of Basle, sampling the Holbeins and the cathedrals, Dresden, to savor its artistic offerings, and Vienna where, in the Belvedere gallery, he was arrested by the particular way in which the artist Denner had painted a fine down of hairs on an old man's chin.

Then Berenson crossed the Alps, climbing the Grand Salève on foot to see Mont Blanc. At this point one yearns for a suitably Verdian overture with which to herald the effect of the Italian landscape on Berenson. Being denied it, one can say only that, having discovered Italy, Berenson was never to leave.

The world around him was transformed. The murmurous lapping of waves on the shore of Luino haunted his imagination. The first sight of an Italian cathedral at Como left him almost delirious with delight. The collection at the Poldi-Pezzoli Museum in Milan was incomparable. He had his first encounter with Leonardo da Vinci's *Last Supper* and was fascinated by the way that artist had painted hands. At Parma, home of the Renaissance painter Antonio Correggio, Berenson lived and breathed in that artist's exquisitely soft, tender, and voluptuous ambiance. In those dreamily beautiful first days, it seemed to him that life itself was lived more completely in Italy than elsewhere. Like Marius, Berenson had been shown a hidden window which afforded a breathtaking view of a secret valley, and suddenly saw, with the force of a vision, the way life might be lived.

Then, in the autumn of 1888, Berenson arrived in Venice. Now that access to Venice can be made by land, one is denied that sensation of "something apart, sacred almost," given to the nineteenth-century visitor who rocked across the waters and witnessed vaporous piazzas and domes looming out of an October mist.

Berenson arrived intending to stay for two weeks and could hardly bear to to leave. He was responding to the ravishing spirit of a city which seemed in complete harmony with the hallucinations of his beauty-starved adolescence. He never lost that love. Fifty years later, he could still write, "Venice was pure ecstasy. I lived, enchanted. I felt as if I had painted it all myself. Not a nook or cranny that it did not make me happy to look at, and to caress with my eyes."

As for the art of Venice, "it was enough for me to see the great Venetian masters once to be exalted and transported by them. . . . As Greek art is a summit of human creative achievement, so also is Venetian painting; it is an act of aesthetic purity. . . ."

Berenson was particularly entranced by the work of Giorgione, the poetic Venetian artist who died young and with whom he seemed to identify. Giorgione, Berenson decided, was master of the art of "picnic" pictures: tableaux of elegant young men and women enjoying background music and conversation before a ravishing landscape. These paintings, Berenson subsequently wrote, were "perfectly in touch with the ripened spirit of the Renaissance. . . ." He must also have been assessing that painter with the theories of his mentor, Walter Pater, in mind. Giorgione, Pater declared, had learned to choose, with great discrimination, those subjects which could be most perfectly expressed in color and form. As a result, he had arrived at "pictorial poetry," in which there was a "perfect interpenetration of the subject with the elements of color and design." This, Pater averred, was the essence of great art.

Berenson was already evolving his particular method of looking at paintings. He was aware how quickly the eye tired, so would walk rapidly through a collection to decide where he wanted to concentrate his energies. Arriving at perhaps a single painting, he would stare at it meditatively with his painter's eye for perhaps a half hour, saying nothing, until he had absorbed every detail of the composition into himself and had, as it were, fused himself into the work. His superbly trained memory would do the rest and, years later, he might conjure up not only the physical minutiae of the paintings themselves, but recall in which room they had been hung and in which corner of that room.

A clue to the close parallel between his response to art and his childish response to nature is contained in the following: "... the feeling which accompanied me in my visits to the galleries was absolutely one of religious awe, a religious and reverential terror. ... I had a mystical attitude toward art, and I still realize that the aesthetic experience is mystical, a mysticism which has no need to believe in objectivity, in the reality of the object, and which is thus a pure mysticism. ..."

He loved, and therefore, remembered.

He was content, in that blissful period of his life, to live for the sake of Beauty. Traveling onward to Sicily (in the probable company of Ned Warren), he responded like a latterday Marius to the glories of ancient ruined cities and crescent-shaped beaches, to orange groves translucent with golden light and to the colors embedded in the ruined stones, the stained, dull greens and blotched reds. He marveled at the crystally clear, chill light of a greenish moon. He was intoxicated by the particular droop of a stalk of papyrus. He lingered in the penumbral gloom of churches, savoring the atmosphere of a sanctuary "like the satisfaction of a vow."

Here, indeed, was the young poet, the fledgling aesthete, in love with art, with Italy and with nature. He did not want to write a book; only to "wander, absorb and dream."

> In autumn, on the skirts of Bagley Wood—
> Where most the gipsies by the turf-edged way
> Pitch their smoked tents, and every bush you see
> With scarlet patches tagg'd and shreds of grey,
> Above the forest-ground called Thessaly—
> The blackbird, picking food,
> Sees thee, nor stops his meal, nor fears at all;
> So often has he known thee past him stray,
> Rapt, twirling in thy hand a wither'd spray
> And waiting for the spark from heaven to fall.

Berenson's artless letters charmed his patron into providing the funds for a further year of delicious idleness. So, like Matthew Arnold's "Scholar-Gipsy," he wandered with "a free onward impulse," safe from the contamination of the hard-boiled, real world, dreaming of the spark which would fall from heaven and show him how to "combine his learning and his sense of poetry into one compendious philosophy." In the meantime his patron, Mrs. Gardner, took her first adventurous steps into buying Old Masters. In Seville, she acquired a *Madonna and Child* by Zurbarán.

Berenson traveled to "the remotest recesses of Arcadia," finding himself constantly greeted in Italian because, to the Greeks of that time, all foreigners were Franks, "and a Frank was no longer a Frenchman but an Italian." He was haunted by the smell of incense in Greek churches. Everything Greek had fascinated him since "I started to spell out Xenophon or look at a Greek statue." Perhaps this first visit made him yearn to become a Greek scholar, "a student of Greek letters, thought and art."

Then he returned to Italy, to spend the winter in Rome (1888–89) which was to give a crucial focus to his life. The experience would deflect him from his first, large question, "What makes a masterpiece?" to the subsidiary problem of, "Who painted what?" To understand why requires a knowledge of the state of the scholarship of Italian painting at the moment when Berenson began to study it.

Before the advent of the photograph there was no way to study the oeuvre of a single painter except with an exceptional memory, the aid of published engravings, or with the equally unreliable, but widely employed, method of making tedious sketches from the original work. Unless a painting was known to have rested undisturbed in a historically impeccable collection, it was surrounded by the cobwebbed confusion of centuries of misconception, speculation, and outright deceit.

Walter Pater's essays on the Renaissance, a liberating influence on Oscar Wilde, Proust, Yeats, and Roger Fry as well as Berenson, are riddled with errors. His famous essay on Leonardo da Vinci uses, as its examples of that painter's genius, works which, it has been unanimously agreed, Leonardo did not paint. They include a head of Medusa in the Uffizi Gallery which Pater asserted was an exquisite example of Leonardo's genius: "Leonardo alone . . . realises it as the head of a corpse, exercising its powers through all the circumstances of death."

Similarly, the critic Eugene Muntz published, in 1898, an exhaustive study of that same painter, yet, of the master's drawings used as illustrations, not one of them has since proved to be authentic. That such glaring errors were possible pointed to the need for wholesale revisions by a penetrating mind, one who could decide, once and for all, who really painted what, and who could base his conclusions on methods that were less rhapsodically subjective and more reliable. By the 1890s the tools, that is to say, detailed sepia photographs of public and private art holdings, were coming into general use, and more reliable methods of stylistic analysis were beginning to be developed in Italy itself.

The pioneers in this process were two men whom Berenson met in Rome in that winter of 1888–89. They were Giovanni Morelli, a major figure in the first attempt to catalogue, identify, and care for Italy's works of art, and Morelli's former secretary, Giovanni Cavalcaselle. With his journalist friend J. A. Crowe, Cavalcaselle had carved out a heroic niche as author of a six-volume history of Italian painting (in 1864–66) which had done much to clear away the debris of centuries of ignorance, confusion, and neglect. The intellectual underpinning for the process of attribution in which Crowe and Cavalcaselle were engaged was provided by Giovanni Morelli. Berenson became another convert, attended Morelli's lectures in Rome, and met him three or four times before Morelli died, at the age of seventy-five, in the winter of 1891.

Morelli's books, which Berenson read while at Harvard, were the influencing factors upon Berenson, rather than his personality. How much Berenson learned from them can be discerned from the first essay he ever wrote, in about 1894, which echoes, almost point for point, the underlying principles that Morelli had outlined in a pioneering work, *The Work of the Italian Masters in the Galleries of Munich, Dresden and Berlin* (1880).

In his essay on connoisseurship (defined as "the comparison of works of art with a view to determining their reciprocal relationships"), Berenson made Morelli's first main point, and one which he was to reiterate ever after: that written evidence, or what the art world calls "provenance," has very little value for Renaissance art.

Even if authentic, documentary descriptions tended to be minimal and provided no proof either way, since the descriptions might just as easily apply to an exact copy. Some of the greatest painters, notably Titian and Signorelli, customarily signed contracts promising to paint the principal characters in the work themselves and then gave the whole project to their apprentices. They even signed the finished results. Or the signature might be, and often was, forged. What had been traditionally written and believed about a work was equally unreliable. The only evidence, Berenson said, was the picture itself.

"All that remains of an event in general history is the account of it in a document or a tradition; but in the history of art, the work of art is the event."

Berenson went on to echo Morelli's second main point, that it was in the minute, unimportant details (those areas of a painting likely to be executed subconsciously and automatically) that an artist revealed his unmistakable signature. Therefore the best way to test the authenticity of a work was to see how that artist had painted ears, or hands, or folds of draperies, or the particular way in which he modeled noses. Berenson concluded that such mechanical tests were useful in inverse proportion to the greatness of the artist. A sense of quality alone would help the connoisseur here, but that was an art, and outside the scope of his essay.

In the twentieth century, new tests would be applied to determine the real from the fake as X-ray photography and the study of pigments came into their own. But, when Berenson entered the field, such tests were unknown. The only weapons at hand were a magnifying glass and a few simple chemical tests. These would only eliminate the more glaring fakes which could, in any event, be detected on the basis of style.

In the 1890s, Berenson's physiological method, which owes everything to the pioneering studies of Morelli, provided an audaciously novel way to approach works that had seldom been subjected to such close scrutiny. It was one which almost immediately placed him in a prominent and controversial position. The ideas of Morelli and Cavalcaselle, to which Berenson later added his own aesthetic, would change his course from that of becoming a second Goethe into an enfant terrible of art.

However, the decision to devote his life to connoisseurship had not yet been taken when Berenson arrived in Florence in the spring of 1889. He was still telling Mrs. Gardner that he did not quite know what to do with his newly acquired knowledge, once he returned to Boston. In the interim, he seemed to be absorbed with the pleasures of going to *festas*, reading Dante with his coffee every morning, studying paintings with minute thoroughness, and meeting people.

Together with Enrico Costa, a young Italo-Spanish disciple of Morelli, Berenson was exploring the delights of the city which, until King Victor Emmanuel moved his court to Rome in 1870, had been the capital of Italy. The great families of Florence had not yet abandoned their beautiful palazzi and had the means to hold frequent, ostentatiously lavish balls. Roads were being widened, delicious suppers were given at the new restaurants in the piazzas, and the king might, at any moment, be encountered driving along the Cascine, a wooded stretch by the river, to observe those members of Florentine society who might be frequenting this impromptu meeting place.

Even after the court had left the Pitti Palace, something of the same frivolity, mingling with the indolent charm of a Renaissance city, had proved irresistible to British and American expatriates. One might live in a picturesque villa, surveying some invariably breathtaking view of the city below, and go down into the town in an open pony carriage. In those peaceful days before trams, automobiles, taxis, or buses, the driver of a horse and cart might have to pull up short to avoid colliding with a Florentine who, in the inimitable fashion of its citizens, was walking across the street, his head buried in a newspaper.

Soon after his arrival in Florence, Berenson walked out to the hamlet of Santa Brigida to visit the shrine of San Martino and was captivated by the unspoiled, almost otherworldly, beauty of the countryside. At that period one could still encounter villagers who spoke in verse and Berenson was astonished to find a woman addressing him in this fashion. He wandered through a village fair, almost medieval in its pageantry, and was shown magical pictures, by the new stereopticon process, of a mechanical marvel called the Brooklyn Bridge.

One of the first expatriates Berenson was to meet was Vernon Lee, the nom de plume for Violet Paget, a gifted and eccentric English writer who had won critical acclaim for *Studies of the Eighteenth Century in Italy*, and almost equal hostility from the aesthetic circles she frequented in London for a novel, *Miss Brown*, a thinly disguised satire of that world. The undergraduate critic Bernhard Berenson, writing in *The Harvard Monthly* in 1885, had favorably reviewed *Miss Brown*.

Vernon Lee was also a lesbian. Depressed, and in a state of melancholic inability to work caused largely by the marriage of one of her closest friends, she had moved to the Villa il Palmerino on the hills outside Florence shortly before Berenson arrived, and was developing theories of aesthetics with another close friend, Kit Anstruther-Thomson.

> I was in Florence for the first time—very young (very hand-some, according to her, and I am convinced; also very seductive, but this I have no way of knowing) and I had a letter for her which she told me to deliver at her house at about ten o'clock some evening when I had nothing else to do.
>
> I went one evening and found a flock of women around her . . . all striking more or less Botticellian poses, all breathing an aura of acute Renaissance. What was I going to do in the midst of them? I had to interest them and stupefy them with something which they would never have thought of. I knew a little bit about Arab poetry, and I spoke about (that). . . .

This is why, Berenson said, Vernon Lee always claimed later that the only thing which had interested him when they met, was Arab poetry.

Berenson was also in contact with Charles Loeser, the wealthy young Jew who had been in his class at Harvard. As his close friend, George Santayana, later described him, Loeser was one of the few Jews who did not mind saying so, and had no ambitions to insinuate himself into the fashionable world. He was the son of a prosperous Brooklyn merchant, and one of those rare beings with no personal ambition whatever. Art and books and the pursuit of the beautiful were his only goals. By the 1890s, Loeser had moved to Europe and was being received by the Anglo-American Florentine colony, although he seemed to have few friends.

Loeser was also distinguished by an almost profligate generosity. "Only once, when we were looking at some modern pictures, I stopped before one that I liked and said that it was painted as I should have wished to paint. 'Why don't you do it,' Loeser cried impulsively. 'Why don't you stay in Paris and paint? I will help you.'" Santayana did not take advantage of that offer, but recorded many other examples of Loeser's thoughtful and generous ways. So, when Berenson wrote to Mrs. Gardner in April of 1889 that "a friend has quite surprised me with an offer of enough money to keep me abroad another year," it is entirely likely that the friend was Loeser.

Berenson concluded his letter with a nonchalant reference to his travel plans—to Spain in the autumn and then to London until the following summer—and reminded Mrs. Gardner that they had a date to look at paintings in the National Gallery a year later.

The letter is noticeable for its rather shallow cleverness, in marked contrast to the confiding, naïve, and uncritical accounts of his first months in Europe. That, however, cannot have accounted for the explosion greeting the arrival of his letter at 152 Beacon Street. Mrs. Gardner was angry. She was very angry.

Berenson later made only a guarded reference to "the opinion you must have had when you put a stop to our correspondence," but it is not hard to see, from the sequence of events, what probably happened. Mrs. Gardner must have decided that her protégé was letting his friends down. Not only had he spent two years frittering away his time in idle amusements, instead of preparing himself for a useful career, and disappointing the people who genuinely wanted to see him succeed in life, but he now proposed to continue doing nothing, and live on someone else's largesse, for yet another year.

Berenson had made a serious misjudgment of Mrs. Gardner's character and one that he was careful not to repeat. He assumed that he could go on being the brilliant young aesthete indefinitely in her eyes, that her love for him was maternally indulgent and without limit. He was wrong. She who could be so generous, could also be demanding and accusatory, if her protégés failed to live up to what she expected of them. Another of her vassals, Morris Carter, was once warned, "Sooner or later she will punish you. She is like an Indian; she never forgives and she never forgets."

Mrs. Gardner forbade Berenson from writing to her and he did not try. He must have destroyed her letters. They did not meet for five years.

6

ENTER MARY

It led to Mary Costelloe's falling in love with me.

—BERNARD BERENSON, *Sunset and Twilight*

AS AN ADOLESCENT, Berenson was living in an androgynous state. No longer a child, he was not yet able to uncover in himself those mysterious inchoate yearnings that direct the emotions toward a loved object. He was not so much homosexual, as asexual. He was an Ariel of intellect, a sprite of verve, humor, and malicious intelligence, who had somehow skittered from the clutch of that so-human dilemma, and had transcended fallibility.

Berenson himself furthers the impression. He described to Morra the "moment of perfect liberty" when, he said, a boy was liberated from the chains of maternal love, but did not yet know those of romantic love. It was a moment to be cherished, since the complete freedom and lucidity it offered would never be found again.

That such freedom for the intellect should require a detachment from feeling is a conclusion typical of him. That he should regret the passing of that moment is perhaps even more revealing. Whatever the mind had to offer was to be preferred over whatever human feeling might provide. Such apparent invulnerability makes one extremely attractive to a certain kind of woman and, by the time he was a student at Harvard and tutoring his distantly related female cousins, Berenson was gaining a reputation as the kind of boy girls fell in love with.

(9 5)

Once in college, Berenson's attitude was modified by his discovery that he could experience infatuation. It was, however, a vague, idealistic yearning for an ideal woman, rather than a real human being. Berenson was prepared to unite with such a being but, for reasons which will become clear, the kind of woman likely to satisfy these youthful aspirations remained comfortably remote.

For the most part, the subject of love was one which Berenson approached with the detached interest of a scientist prodding the nerve of a dissected frog's leg in the hope that it may still be made to jump, hovering over the corpse with charts and diagrams, analyzing and dissecting, while its essence eluded him. This, in fact, was the theme of a short story Berenson wrote while at Harvard, "The Third Category."

The hero was a young Protestant swell named Christie, a name which probably had deliberately ironic overtones, who liked to codify people and place them in logical compartments according to their effect on himself. Christie had consequently subjected the young women he knew to this scrutiny and found that they fell into three categories. In the first group were those who made delightful temporary flirtations, and in the second, women who were very dear to him, but ineligible as wives. The kind of woman one married was in the last, rarefied, third category.

Christie, this monster of calculation, was not entirely devoid of tender feelings. It was only that, for him, love had nothing to do with the matter. It was an exquisitely private affair.

"It was no woman that he loved, as he readily saw, but loving itself. The emotion of love, its intoxication . . . [was] . . . a passion of which this intoxication and these emotions were the end, to which passion, the woman he had fancied he loved, was as fuel to flames. He very soon became indifferent. . . ."

Christie was merely able to see, more clearly than most young men, the illusory nature of infatuation. He intended to choose, with a clear head, a woman whose qualities would harmonize with his own passion for neatness, punctuality, and beautiful art, and evade those with whom the potential for conflict might be great.

One sees here, in slightly modified form, the echoes of shtetl customs, or of certain European circles at the turn of the century, for whom the compelling argument was that marriages be based on enduring and practical considerations, rather than on romantic and transient ones.

The woman Christie intended to marry should be "goldenly mediocre, womanly, a little bit womanish even. He wished her to be beautiful, but not strikingly so. . . ." She might, in fact, be a chestnut-haired girl like Miss Cecily Grampian, sister of a friend of his, of a well-placed family, with a "sweet, speaking smile," a modest way of dressing, and an altogether bland nature; clever enough (as he wrote years later) to know when she was being outclassed. ". . . Cecily took pleasure in Mr. Christie's greater breadth of life and thought. In intercourse with him she seemed to get sight of thoughts and aspects of life that were, although too often, shudderingly cold, fresh and grand."

It is hard to escape the impression that Berenson is both examining his feelings and finding mocking fault with them, in this portrait of a young egotist who "found no room in the universe for another than himself" and who, while cynically courting a beautiful young girl, still imagined himself capable of love.

The same tone of derisive self-mockery is apparent in the short story's denouement. Christie took Cecily to a service in a Christian church. He admired the event for its aesthetic beauty but remained untouched by its content. Cecily, however, responded avidly to the sermon's message, which concerned the example of self-sacrifice set by Christ. Only those who were willing to lose their souls, it seemed, might save them; Cecily was ecstatically prepared.

Christie observed Cecily, a placid nonentity, suddenly becoming a woman of unsuspected dimensions, "a much more real, more living, more intense soul than his own." Christie could not deal with the transformation. He freed himself from the relationship in the most ruthless possible way and, learning that Cecily had fallen in love with him, departed in a glow of self-satisfaction.

The author of this short story seemed torn between the detached life of the mind, with its Ariel-like expanses of chilly freedom, and the life-giving warmth of the human touch. He could see that he was the poorer for his inability to make close contact with others. He longed to forget and lose himself, to transcend himself in art, religion, and all-embracing love. But he feared the ecstatic sacrifice it required and the threatened death of the Self:

So shrinks from Love the tender heart
As if from threat of being slain
For when true Love awakens, dies
The Self, that Despot, dark and vain.
Then let him die in night's black hour
And freely breathe in Dawn again!

—Delaleddin Rumi,
Persian poet (thirteenth century)

Berenson must have made a paradoxical impression on the young women he met, with his slim, agile body, his beautiful Slavic features, full-lipped, pouting mouth, eager smile, charming desire to please, and utter inviolability. Late in life, he became preoccupied with the hidden longings of those early years and his conclusions are illuminating. He realized then what he had not understood as a young man: that he was classically split between sex and love. The body of any female social equal was sacred and taboo. Sex even defiled the act of being in love, which was, for Berenson, as sacred as a great work of art. It was therefore out of the question.

Psychoanalysis teaches that "suspiciousness, obsessive scrupulosity, moral sadism and a preoccupation with dirtying and infectious thoughts and substances go together." If Berenson can be said to have had these traits of character, it is certainly true that from childhood on, he had a horror of "the animal in me." "I have never got over my disgust with everything that comes out of the body, whether from nose, mouth, bladder or bowels," he continued. "Even the supremest of all physical pleasures is somewhat spoiled for me by the ejaculation it ends with. . . ."

Berenson solved this quintessentially Victorian dilemma in the only way open to a young man of his time. He turned to prostitutes. Wherever he traveled he would make pickups of what he delicately termed the "not-lady" class. With such encounters, he recorded complete sexual satisfaction.

Then, in 1890, Bernhard Berenson met Mary.

In "The Third Category," one finds a passage describing another kind of woman Mr. Robert Christie admired. She was "a woman of magnificent form. Her very presence had that tonic effect on Mr. Christie which he used to ascribe to brazen trumpets blown in the cool of the early morning. She was a Valkyr," reminding him of "his love for Wagner and that wild, storm-saturated, old-Norse atmosphere, that spirit of triumphant struggle with the woes of existence. . . ."

Mary Whitall Smith was born on Valentine's Day a year before Bernhard Berenson (in 1864), the daughter of Robert Pearsall and Hannah Whitall Smith. Her father, Robert, suffered probable epilepsy following a fall from a horse, and "gave more than once occasion to fear for his sanity." There was a strange "Uncle H." whose periodic spells of insanity were caused, the family said, by his lifelong habit of chewing tobacco. He swallowed the weed, because he was too gentlemanly to spit it out; this, it was concluded, poisoned his system. Mary's brother Logan became a manic-depressive and Bertrand Russell and Berenson, brothers-in-law for a time, decided that "there was . . . a strain of insanity in all of them."

None of this rippled the ostensibly serene surface of the Philadelphia Quakers Hannah and Robert, who owned a farmhouse beside the Delaware where bloodstains from the War of Independence could still be observed on the ancient floorboards. They had social status and plenty of money from a family glass-manufacturing business. Mary, the oldest of three surviving children, grew up surrounded by servants, pets, and a large, adoring circle of relatives. Logan was a year younger and Alys, later Mrs. Russell, was born in 1867.

Robert and Hannah were exceedingly pious and yet, in opposition to the traditional New England pattern, they were what one would have called permissive parents. Even though grandparents are notoriously more lenient, one can discern, from the manner in which Hannah dealt with her two granddaughters, Mary's children, the fashion in which Mary herself was probably treated.

Children must, whatever happened, have "a happy childhood tucked under their belts." Hannah herself had been allowed to "race and romp and screech and scream and climb trees and roll down hills, and paddle, and dig in the mud . . ." and so must her children. Such treatment was given so that children might acquire the habit of being happy, which Hannah thought essential. She also thought it essential to defer to children: " 'It stands to reason,' she would say, 'that young people *must* know better than we do.' " They should, of course, be good, but Hannah took that for granted and the only thing that seemed to make her angry was the account of a practical joke, told with too much relish.

Hannah was the most solicitous of mothers and her excessive concern, with its undertones of anxiety, may well have its tragic origins in her maternal experiences. Her first child, Nelly, died at the age of five. A second, Frank, died aged eighteen. A third child, Rachel ("Ray"), was eleven when she died, and a fourth child died at birth.

There was, however, an aspect of the childhood of Mary, Logan, and Alys that was less than benign. Robert and Hannah believed in the "old doctrines of the corruption of man and his inevitable doom unless he finds salvation in the conviction of sin," and applied it with zeal. Since their children's futures hinged upon their being saved from damnation, it followed that the sooner they were converted, the better. One must begin at the beginning and Hannah was on her guard:

"Logan and I had our first regular battle to-day," she wrote in 1866, when Logan was not yet four months old, "and he came off conqueror, though I don't think he knew it. I whipped him until he was actually black and blue, and until I really *could not* whip him any more, and he never gave up one single inch. However, I hope it was a lesson to him. . . ."

That a parent could propose to teach a baby lessons by beating him black and blue is so irrational that it can only be attributable to religious dementia.

Mary was already saved. At the age of six, Logan's big sister undertook to save him as well. Her brother recalls, in *Unforgotten Years*, that Mary and her friend took him into the bathroom where they "prayed and wrestled with my carnal nature, until the great miracle of Conversion was accomplished in me.

" 'Oh Lord,' prayed the future Mrs. Berenson, 'please make little Logan a good boy; and don't let him tell any more lies!' "

For a true believer, the states of Justification and Sanctification followed. One so received, the doctrine stated, was immune from further sin and might rejoice, as Logan was finally able to do, "in the consciousness that [he] can commit no wrong. . . . [Since] I attained the state of Sanctification at the age of seven, I have never felt the slightest twinge of conscience, never experienced for one second the sense of sin."

One may assume, from this evidence of Mary's evangelical zeal, that she too underwent the states of Conversion, Justification, and Sanctification and that she, too, arrived early in life at the comforting conviction that, from now on, she could do no wrong.

A wave of Revivalism taking the old Quaker doctrines by storm convinced Hannah to become an evangelist. She and her husband plunged into the new movement and, for many years, saving souls was the absorbing interest of their lives. Hannah was a compelling speaker and a fertile writer. Her tract, *The Christian's Secret of a Happy Life*, written under the initials of H.W.S., became a best-seller, selling one million copies in the United States alone.

Robert Pearsall Smith was equally successful as a speaker and, when he and Hannah crossed the Atlantic to England in 1874, their fame had already preceded them. But, in 1876, something happened which was to have a profound effect on the relationship between Robert and Hannah. Robert applied Paul's admonition to Christians to salute one another with a holy kiss too enthusiastically, and was discovered with one of the spinster members of his audience seated in his lap. The resulting scandal obliged the Smiths to return to the United States. Hannah was as committed to her faith as ever, but he was broken and embittered.

"A more sensitive, tender-hearted, generous man never lived," Hannah wrote in the summer of 1876, "and this blow has sorely crushed him in every tender spot. It would have been so impossible for him to have treated anyone . . . as he has been treated. . . ."

Despite the spirited defense, the marriage of Hannah and Robert, which had never been happy, deteriorated further in the years that followed. Hannah had married, at the age of nineteen, from a sense of religious duty. Sex was something she despised and feared.

"Tell us about sex," one of her children said. "If I told you," she answered, "it would burn your spirits up." Long before the feminist movement Hannah was urging a group of visiting Quaker schoolgirls to postpone the slavery of marriage for as long as possible. "Girls," she exhorted them, "don't be too unselfish."

Childbearing transformed Hannah into a blissful mother. As a wife she remained dutiful but unenthusiastic. Robert's public display of the need for love can be seen as a transparent, if misguided, grasping for affection and a despairing admission that all was not well with his marriage. However, it must have appeared to Hannah like a public humiliation. It confirmed her view that "men are brutes and fools," and that sex martyred women. Not surprisingly, her only son became a homosexual and her husband took a mistress.

Bertrand Russell, who had a low opinion of Hannah's pretensions to sainthood, wrote:

> Her treatment of her husband, whom she despised, was humiliating in the highest degree. She never spoke to him or of him except in a tone that made her contempt obvious. It cannot be denied that he was a silly old man, but he did not deserve what she gave him. . . .
>
> He had a mistress and fondly supposed that his wife did not know of her. He used to tear up this woman's letters and throw the pieces in the waste-paper basket. His wife would fit the bits together, and read out the letters to Alys and Logan amid fits of laughter. . . .

The poet Walt Whitman, who knew the Smiths, thought Robert a warm, jovial fellow who liked good food and drink, although a pronounced hypochondriac. Whitman also saw the unmistakable signs of an unhappy marriage: "There was some trouble in the family too—some infelicity; for some years Pearsall [Robert] and Mrs. Smith had no words—no relations with each other."

Mary, whom the family always called Mariechen, a name originally coined by a German nurse, was growing up to be a young woman on the Wagnerian model that Mr. Robert Christie so much admired in "The Third Category." She was tall and imposingly built, the kind of girl whose hair might stream out fanlike away from her neck, whose clothes blow about. She was not really pretty, but her serene, open face inspired immediate and instinctive trust. She was, like her brother, "tall, delicate-featured and always smiling," Beatrice Webb noted in her diary.

Mary had the Quaker's charming, old-fashioned way of using "thee" and "thou" and spoke with a disarming lisp. She was optimistic and generous, the kind of large-hearted, womanly woman whom Walt Whitman said he especially liked.

Mary had abandoned her evangelistic pursuits along with short skirts, but retained an eagerness to shoulder new burdens. She spent time, money, and advice freely. She seemed destined, a reformer in search of a cause, as her mother had been, easily made indignant by injustice, ready to battle against poverty, ignorance, and the forces of evil. Her charm, high spirits, radiant energy, and sense of fun ensured that she would be immediately noticed. She was a natural leader.

Mary's faults were on the same generous scale. She had been brought up to believe that she must always be good but, like Logan, had also acquired the paradoxical conviction that she could never again be bad. It made for extraordinary confidence and the obtuse belief, which Logan shared, that the truth was whatever she said it was.

Hannah had taught her children to be considerate ("One must not do things that made other people uncomfortable"), while also inculcating them with the strange admonition that it was a waste of time to be "offended or hurt in one's feelings for any reason whatever."

Such concepts, jointly held, tended to have an outcome that Hannah had not anticipated. One should, of course, always think the best of others, but if their behavior seemed absurd or outrageous, then one might condemn with impunity, since the object of one's censure had no right to feel hurt.

Such an attitude perfectly fitted Hannah's children for the verbal warfare of the British drawing room in which, Henry Adams discovered, "men and women treated each others' advances much more brutally than those of strangers." However, instead of the gentle tolerance Hannah had undoubtedly hoped for, Mary and Logan's sunny friendliness could shift without warning to a hypocritical piousness, barely hiding a malicious and self-righteous glee.

Because Mary had been made to believe as a child that whatever she wanted was hers by right, she was recklessly determined to gratify any impulse, no matter how fleeting, and unscrupulously ready to manipulate others to that end.

Hannah wrote to a friend in the fall of 1882, "The other day, when I was fixing up Mary's room at College, she wanted me to buy her a leather-covered arm chair. I did not think she needed it, and was going to refuse, when she coughed. Immediately I thought, 'Now perhaps she will die of consumption, and then how I shall wish I had bought her the chair.' So forthwith I bought it."

Hannah, however, realized how adroitly her own fears had been used against her. She concluded, "And when it [the chair] came home I said, 'There, daughter, thee coughed up that chair.'"

Mary had arrived at Smith College, Northampton, Massachusetts, to take up residence in Miss Denistown's boarding house in the autumn of 1888. She and her frail, fair-haired friend Florence

Dike Reynolds would take daily rides through the countryside around Northampton and even into Hadley, racing the horses and jumping ditches and hedges.

Mary could be counted on to appreciate a joke, and she was always ready to catch the eye of a handsome young man. Hannah was well aware of it. Hannah remarked in a letter that she was in the process of finding a tutor for Mary, but that she certainly did not want a single young man, since he would be sure to end up flirting with Mary. The whole subject of Mary's flirtatiousness touched on a sore nerve, as is evident from the following incident.

"In the house of her sister, Mrs. Thomas, a friend was commenting on Mary's flirtations: she felt the adoration of men necessary, her friend said, but she was not intentionally cruel; 'She is,' concluded her critic, 'very much like Goethe in temperament.'

" 'How dare you say such a thing to me?' said H.W.S., silencing the whole table. 'You call yourself Mary's friend, and you compare her to Goethe, the most notoriously immoral man who ever lived.' "

What Hannah considered a personal affront, Logan viewed with tolerance. He seemed delighted by this new ability of his sister's and related at length how Mary met her first husband. Five members of the British Association, then touring the United States for the summer, were given hospitality in the Smith home in Philadelphia. Three of them fell in love with Mary.

Two of the suitors gave up, but the third, a fervent young Catholic of Irish descent practicing law in London, was more favorably received. He talked ". . . of T. H. Green, and Arnold Toynbee and Toynbee Hall and its new philanthropy; of English Liberalism and its great leader Gladstone; and of the great radical, Joe Chamberlain, under whose banner it was his hope and purpose to march to triumph for the great causes he had espoused . . ." In that remote American home, Logan concluded, these names "sounded like the names of heroes shouted from afar."

Mary was listening. Here was a cause worthy of her energies, and an opportunity to "bring the Kingdom of Heaven down to earth, in England." The concept, at once grand and deceptively simple, was the only one which could have roused her interest, Logan continued, aware that no simplistic exhortation to return to Faith alone would succeed with Mary. Her early religious beliefs had been destroyed forever by philosophy and the discoveries of modern science. But, to transform Faith into political idealism, to bring Salvation to the human race—this indeed was a noble prospect. It provided, her brother concluded sagaciously, "a high-flying courtship and a splendid wooing."

To prepare for this, Mary transferred to Radcliffe where she could study philosophy seriously. Mary's professor in philosophy immediately joined the ranks of her suitors, but by then, Mary was determined to follow her Irish barrister to England.

Miss Pearsall Smith married Benjamin Francis Conn Costelloe in the fall of 1885, when he was thirty and she was twenty-one. They had their wedding breakfast at Balliol College hall, Oxford. Frank was running for Parliament as Liberal candidate for East Edinburgh (he was defeated) and they chose a new house on the Embankment overlooking the Thames, barely two blocks from the Houses of Parliament.

Frank was doing well as a barrister, but his political activities, tracts, and speeches took up a great deal of his day and the Costelloes saw lean times financially, to judge from a fragment of a letter sent by their mutual friend, Dr. Richard Maurice Bucke, to Walt Whitman.

Dr. Bucke described the simple style of living at 41 Grosvenor Road. The house was "furnished comfortably, but very plainly. It would not suit you, for it is very narrow and all up and down stairs—altogether there are no less than 5 flats [floors] to it. . . ." Food was substantial but very plain. "For breakfast we had a bit of bacon and egg and toast—for lunch a chop and potato— for dinner, soup, a joint and a pudding."

The family was gathering around them. Robert and Hannah had decided to join Mary, and their benign reception—all of Robert's transgressions forgotten—encouraged them to settle in England permanently. They bought Friday's Hill in Haslemere. Logan was traveling on the Continent and only Alys, studying at Bryn Mawr, was still in America.

Frank was elected to the London County Council, along with other "strong reformers and liberals—'progressists' is the new word for them." Mary was, she wrote to Walt Whitman, "into it heart and soul with him, for I think it is really important and worth devoting one's self to." She campaigned with the Feminists, among them the lady authors writing jointly as Michael Field, demonstrated in London in support of the unemployed, and campaigned for Frank when he attempted unsuccessfully to gain a seat in Parliament in the summer of 1898.

Mary was also the mother of two little girls: Rachel (Ray),

probably named for her dead sister, born on June 4, 1887, and Karin, born on March 10, 1889. That summer there were no letters from Mary Costelloe, and Whitman, feeling a subconscious unease, sent her a note. Mary answered from Friday's Hill.

She had been, Mary wrote, "in low spirits" all summer, variously ascribed to "overwork" and "nervous prostration." Despite weeks of rest she was feeling worse and was going off with her mother for an indefinite stay in the Pyrenees, leaving her husband and two babies in England.

Referring to Whitman's "Song of the Open Road," Mary wrote, "My road has seemed so shut up—I am laid aside in the midst of all the work I care for—fit for nothing—and, oh! the horror of feeling one's mind, as well as one's physical powers, under an eclipse. . . ."

Perhaps Mary was really as contented as she seemed to be, or perhaps her nervous breakdown was the result of marital stresses which she was not ready to acknowledge, any more than her husband. A bare hint that she sometimes found Frank trying is contained in the Whitman correspondence. Discussing the unpredictable nature of British politics, Mary complained, with a touch of malice, that "Frank is an incurable Optimist and *always* sees things are 'for the best.'"

Whitman wondered how Mary, a religious radical, could have endured the narrow and tenacious views of her Roman Catholic husband, but then reflected that, politically at least, they were in accord. Costelloe was even a thoroughly enlightened "woman's-rightser," which was just as well, since Mary was "very radical indeed" about the cause of woman's suffrage, "almost along with the Anarchists."

The poet was, in fact, surprised by the extent to which Mary had thrown herself into her husband's world. But, he concluded, "it is just like Mary: just what might have been expected of her impetuosity, ardor. . . ."

Whitman was right in believing that impetuous ardor was characteristic of Mary, but even he could not have predicted the next twist in the plot. Bernhard Berenson appeared. Mary fell in love. Frank Costelloe, the house in Grosvenor Road, the two children, her life, her goals, her future, all vanished. Mary took up her new cause: Berenson and Art.

There are two versions of exactly what happened, Mary's and Bernhard's. Since her version, written as part of an *Unfinished Life* of Berenson, has already been told it can be dealt with briefly.

Since his version is not generally known, it is worth recounting.

According to Mary, Berenson was invited to spend the Easter weekend of 1890 at Friday's Hill. At dinner she wore a new pink satin dress and was mesmerized by the conversation of "this beautiful and mysterious youth," who talked about Provençal poetry, the Greek anthology, Russian novels, and Wagner's operas. Even Hannah was admiringly silent and next day they all ordered large photographs of Giorgione and Botticelli paintings.

She was, Mary concluded, "like a dry sponge that was put into water." Politics, social causes, and speeches—all these were forgotten. In their place were, suddenly, Berenson's values, "real values for me, however wicked and self-indulgent they might be." They talked all weekend and, a week later, Berenson was writing to Mary from Cambridge that he wanted to give her his whole life, "except for that part of it which belonged to his work on Italian painting, in which he hoped she would join him."

Berenson did not write an account of their meeting, except for the cryptic comment that "by mere chance I met Gertrude Hitz, who introduced me to the Costelloes in London. A flimsier chance led me, footsore I remember, past their house, where I carelessly left a visiting card. It led to Mary Costelloe's falling in love with me."

Berenson elaborated on this account in a conversation with Frances Francis, wife of the museum curator Henry Sayles Francis, after World War II. He had first seen Mary, Berenson told her, striding across the Harvard Yard in a sealskin coat and took the trouble to ascertain that she was the sister of Logan Pearsall Smith.

When he was in London in the winter of 1889–90, Berenson went to call on the Costelloes. Mary received him with her second daughter, Karin, nursing at her breast. Mary, of course, would have found nothing untoward about receiving a visitor in this fashion. She took her bodily functions as matter-of-factly as she had once splashed about in the mud. Furthermore, she believed with Hannah that motherhood was sacrosanct, as well as everything connected with it. Berenson, however, was horrified. His essentially prudish nature was shocked by what seemed like coarse and animal behavior. Berenson left no written account of this first encounter and, given his prejudices, one can see why he would not have wanted to discuss it.

Berenson was determined never to visit the Costelloes again. At the same time, something about Mary's uninhibitedness must have attracted him because, sometime later, he found an excuse to call again at 41 Grosvenor Road. His shoelace had broken and Berenson stopped to repair it. It was then, he said, that Mary invited him to spend Easter weekend at Friday's Hill.

"I must have been particularly scintillating that weekend," he told Mrs. Francis, "because when I went back to London, Mary followed me and for two years I put her off."

Mary even appeared at his lodgings with a suitcase, telling him that she had left home for good to live with him. Berenson sent her away.

This ungentlemanly account is supported by Berenson's diary entry that he had no very favorable first impression of Mary. The comment, "It led to Mary Costelloe's falling in love with me," is perhaps meant to be taken at face value. He was his usual self, being "scintillating" simply out of a compulsion to be liked. But he was not in love, only unable to resist an attractive woman. He felt about her "as the European powers do about an unclaimed strip of the African coast," i.e., ironically aware that his interest had more to do with a need to triumph, than with love.

To Mary, however, Bernhard was a magical being and when he gave her one of his mysteriously caressing glances she took him seriously. Her ardent response aroused all of his native caution and Bernhard hastily retreated, but by then the damage had been done.

When Mary came to write about the event, years later, the truth had faded. All that remained was the fact that she had been so bewitched by Berenson as to break all the codes of her world. She had even left her children. Such guilt is hard to endure, unless one can prove, to one's own satisfaction, that one has been swept off one's feet.

The role of pursuer, which would unnerve some women, suited Mary perfectly. She was never deterred by the thought that she might be rejected. Her superb self-confidence swept all inner doubts aside. She seemed, in her optimism, almost to welcome initial indifference providing, as it did, such a delicious challenge to her powers of seduction.

Four years later, en route to join Berenson, Mary shared a hotel suite in Paris with Bertrand Russell for ten days, when he was already engaged to marry her sister Alys. Mary was enthusiastic about him. She wrote to her parents from Paris that he had one of the most alert and rational minds she had ever encountered. She, Mary, did not have much intellectual originality herself, but she considered that she had a good eye for quality, whether in art or humankind, and she was predicting great things for "Bertie." Mary found it necessary to add that she was quite sure he would be absolutely monogamous.

Russell's biographer, Ronald W. Clark, has painted a very different picture of that joint stay in Paris. He concluded that the mental tête-à-tête being enjoyed by Mary and her future brother-in-law became rapidly less rarefied and more concrete. In other words, they had an "affair." This was also the conclusion of Alys, to judge from her tear-stained letters.

Was Mary unsure of Berenson and flirting with other men to arouse his possessive jealousy? Arrogantly set upon having her own way, whatever the cost to others? Did she seek out men who presented the ultimate challenge, since they were clearly inaccessible, by circumstance or temperament? One only knows that she, daughter of a mother who taught that men victimized women, played as calculating a game as Casanova, as if she had decided that, where men were concerned, attack was her best defense.

At this early stage, Berenson considered himself a friend of both Costelloes. He saw Mary simply as his first disciple and a potentially valuable assistant, and she was as eager to adopt his goals as she had been to further Costelloe's political ambitions. They all took a trip to Paris together in the summer of 1890 and again at Christmas, when they spent several days in Rome. Early in 1891, Mary visited Florence, in the company of Alys and Hannah, and saw it for the first time through Berenson's eyes. Berenson was back in London in the spring of 1891 and, that summer, the Costelloes were again on the Continent with their self-appointed guide. That autumn of 1891, Berenson and Mary took their first trip alone together through Italy.

"The news about Mrs. Costelloe is not very good," Sidney Webb wrote to his wife Beatrice from London.

> . . . She is at Verona—your Verona—he, too, there or thereabouts. But C. [Frank Costelloe] still thinks and trusts it will be all right; asserts that she has not the faintest idea or intention of leading any but an independent life; and that any move on *his* part, [an apparent reference to Berenson] towards anything else, would bring about disillusionment at once. C. is playing a very magnanimous game: he has just sent her authority to sign cheques on his account! And talks of taking the children out to her in Florence. As he says, it is not worth playing unless he plays to win completely, to have her return to him wholly and spontaneously. . . .

Webb, who also knew Mary's parents, was not willing to take as tolerant a view as did her own husband at the spectacle of Mary's running off with another man. The same month, he also wrote, "I am writing this in Costelloe's cottage—tragically 'empty' of its mistress—whilst he has taken the two children to church. I think the *wickedness* of his wife has come home to me stronger than ever. . . ."

The Pearsall Smith family's reaction to Mary's irresponsible behavior was ambivalent. Although technically in favor of "free love," with advanced views on the subject, in reality Alys was a straightlaced Puritan and so shocked that she refused to meet Berenson. Russell himself had to arrange a meeting after their marriage.

Hannah was just as horrified as were Alys and the Webbs, but for other reasons. To Hannah, a husband's only real usefulness was in the siring of children; it was therefore inexplicable that a mother should prefer a lover to her own children.

At the same time, Hannah found herself the victim of her own reiterated belief that young people must know best, however rash their decisions might seem. Too, she must have viewed Mary's departure as a providential opportunity for her to assume the role she loved most. She and her husband took a house on Grosvenor Road four doors away from Frank, Ray, and Karin, and she joyously became the mother for the children her daughter had abandoned. The girls, age four and age two, already accustomed to nurses, seemed, on the surface, to adjust with few qualms.

By the time Frank Costelloe and Mary had officially separated in 1893, Hannah had become "the background" of everything in the lives of Mary's daughters. At the same time, she was writing daily letters, comforting in their completeness, so as to include their mother in every aspect of her children's lives. Mary must, nevertheless, have been in anguish at having chosen someone else in preference to Ray and Karin. In later years, the fact that she always spoke of "going home" when returning to England, and that she could never seem to do enough for her daughters, were major sources of conflict between her and Berenson, and an indication of the extent of her remorse.

7

"CONOSCHING"

All the days carried to the evening the buoyancy of morning.

—BERNARD BERENSON,
The North Italian Painters of the Renaissance

WHENEVER HE TALKED about learning how to look at art, Berenson would couch his concept in terms of a fable, the Indian story of the God of Bow and Arrow who taught his little boy how to hit a mark.

"He took him into a wood and asked him what he saw. The boy said, 'I see a tree.' 'Look again'—'I see a bird'—'Look again'—'I see its head'—'Again'—'I see its eye'—'Then shoot!' " It was the same, Berenson said, with art. " 'One moment is enough, if the concentration is absolute.' "

In the autumn of 1890, Berenson was traveling through the great galleries of Vienna, Dresden, Berlin, and Buda-Pesth, and everywhere he went, he was exercising that trained eye which, the young Marius had learned, was indispensable to an epicurean.

"We must look and look and look," Berenson later wrote, "till we live in the painting and for a fleeting moment become identified with it. If we do not succeed in loving what through the ages has been loved, it is useless to lie ourselves into believing that we do. A good rough test is whether we feel that it is reconciling us with life."

That art should be expected to heal the breach for one at odds with life may be making far too ambitious a demand upon it for most of us. It seems clear, however, that painting actually had this effect upon the young Berenson. In the presence of great art, his self-doubts, guilts, nihilistic philosophy, and jaundiced view of the world were swept away in a torrent of passionate response. He was, he told Mary, almost dizzy with happiness.

"What a wonderful thing it is," he wrote from Dresden, "to be on a ladder, face to face with Giorgione's Venus!" Recalling his first glimpse of the Piazza San Marco in Venice, he wrote, "When I passed through the arch and had my first look at the Campanile and at San Marco, I thought they would fall on me. . . ."

By day, he took "pictures as if they were flowers," and by night, he dreamed of paintings: "two unknown Giorgiones. I can see them at this minute, in color and tone." Faced with the demanding process of gathering information, he demonstrated a perfectionistic patience. Far from being overwhelmed with minutiae, his enthusiasm even appeared to increase as his knowledge grew.

Berenson had come to appreciate the value of the Greek proverb,"*Khalepà tà kalà*" ("The beautiful things are difficult"), he told Umberto Morra. To appreciate the panoramic vistas at the summit fully, one must be willing to scale the heights of knowledge, step by tedious step.

It is perhaps perfectly apt that Berenson's field of knowledge should become the Renaissance. Born to a culture which pursued, with stately single-mindedness, the obsessive path to God, he chose to concentrate his energies on the trecento and quattrocento, i.e., that historical moment when the narrow preoccupations of the Middle Ages were being superseded by an era of Enlightenment.

The Renaissance, symbolizing as it did the release from ecclesiastical authority and a new emphasis on human values, and, in art, on the expression of deep emotion and a heightened awareness of nature, was his choice of subject matter for the next thirty years. Nowadays the concept of the Middle Ages as a long night of medieval ignorance, dispelled by a Renaissance dawn of freedom, beauty, and knowledge, is in disfavor. But to Berenson, who had inherited the views of the eighteenth-century German classicist Johann Winckelmann, as expounded by Walter Pater and championed by Ruskin and the Pre-Raphaelites, the Renaissance had become a symbol of all that his spirit yearned toward. It stood for youth's freedom to grasp the whole of life with all the ardor of its intellectual energy and curiosity, those years, he wrote, "when we seemed so full of promise ... to ourselves and ... everybody else."

He was later to call that longing "*Dahin*-ness," from Goethe's poem, "Mignon's Song."

> Kennst du das Land, wo die Zitronen blühn ...
> Kennst du es wohl? — Dahin! Dahin
> Möcht' ich mit dir, o mein Geliebter, ziehn.
>
> Know'st thou the land where the fair citron blows ...
> Know'st thou it well? 'Tis there, 'tis there,
> That I with thee, beloved one, would repair!
>
> (Translation by Edgar A. Bowring)

In all of Europe, Italy was the country which best personified, for Berenson, that dawn of intellectual and emotional freedom, that *"Dahin"* lure of a magical land.

"I wonder whether I really love Italy so much as I think, or whether I like it *faute-de-mieux*," he wrote to Mary from Berlin in October of 1890. "No, I am sure it is real love. I could kiss the stones in an Italian street."

When Berenson first discovered Italy it was still possible to trace the course of the Renaissance there, for someone with the necessary energy of will.

"I knew a Rome," he wrote in old age, "where country not only embraced town but invaded it almost to Piazza di Spagna. From the terrace before San Giovanni in Laterano the fields stretched uncontaminated, with only an ancient wine-shop here and there...." When he went to Sicily in 1889 the only hotel in Taormina was a small pink building beside the Roman theater, and when he went walking, one moonlit night, to the temples at Girgenti, he was greeted by two carabinieri who had ridden down from the city on horseback to warn him to return to the safety of the city walls.

The same mood of rapturous discovery colors his descriptions of painting itself and betrays him, despite his brave attempt to conceal his feelings: "It must seem funny to anybody else with a spirit at all so Mephistophelian as my own to see me breaking my equivalent for a heart on pining to see clearly how certain pictures came about."

For one so passionately involved, it was almost painful to

think that such objects of beauty were mere commodities for the rich, to be bought and sold like carpets.

"At times I think it would be better for people if they were not allowed to own pictures. . . . Owning them, or to fancy that one owns them, seems to make such fools of people generally. . . ."

The moralist in him concluded that wealth itself was corrupting; ". . . echoing the language of the prophet, [it] chokes up their hearts and finally kills all that is fine in them. . . ."

Berenson had arrived at a heady decision, one implied in his remark that he was "pining" to penetrate to the origins of the paintings themselves. He had decided on his life's work. In May of 1890, sitting at a rickety café table in Bergamo with Enrico Costa, drinking thin coffee and chewing on sour bread, Berenson declared,

> You see, Enrico, nobody before us has dedicated his entire activity, his entire life, to connoisseurship. Others have taken to it as a relief from politics . . . others still because they were museum officials, still others because they were teaching art history.
>
> We are the first to have no idea before us, no ambition, no expectation, no thought of reward. We shall give ourselves up to learning, to distinguish between the authentic works of an Italian painter of the fifteenth or sixteenth century, and those commonly ascribed to him. Here at Bergamo, and in all the fragrant and romantic valleys that branch out northward, we must not stop till we are sure that every Lotto is a Lotto, every Cariani a Cariani. . . .

One does not know just why Berenson decided to devote his life to connoisseurship. Berenson follows his description of this declaration with the ironic comment, "To this in the swift course of two or three years had vaulting ambitions or, at least, dazzling hopes shrunk." The brilliant young student, with a whole world to choose from, was showing himself to be an opportunist, leaping at the first practical solution which offered itself.

Yet everything he had learned since arriving in Europe was leading to this, the inevitable result of a realization that no one had fully applied the Morellian doctrines. Connoisseurship offered a host of new opportunities and, practically speaking, it was one of the few avenues then open to him.

He had hoped for a professorship. "I must ask myself . . . seriously whether the 'ultimate professorship' in a remote University would not be the sort of thing into which I should fit naturally. . . ." As a Jew, however, even though a converted Christian, he might well have found himself barred from such academic appointments.

What he really wanted was to live the life of a gentleman scholar, free to indulge in his "selfish passion for training oneself to have enjoyment of one exquisite and beautiful thing, leading on to the enjoyment of one even more beautiful. . . ." However, to be a latter-day Marius took a sinecure or money. He had neither.

He wanted to write, to "come out of his cave," as Mary was urging him to do, but shrank from the effort, convinced that he was doomed to fail because of the impossibility of saying exactly what he meant. And, "I am so deadly sick of lying and lies." And, who cared about his opinions? ". . . my impressions scarcely have any interest. . . ." Still, he determined to take the plunge and, "Perhaps before I am left to my own resources I may have attained sufficient skill in writing to earn my living."

To become an authority, a connoisseur, was the best of all compromises. Here was a calling which would require all his taste, discernment, and knowledge, which would make use of his exquisite ability to see freshly, as if for the first time. All of these considerations were, nevertheless, subservient to his love of art. He had discovered in himself an emotion "so wonderful, so delicate, so subtle, that I can scarcely define it. . . ."

There was a further factor. Berenson had often traveled in the company of Ned Warren and must have known that collector's dedication to the cause of the Boston Museum. It would have been the most natural thing in the world for Warren to suggest casually that his friend be employed in scouting for art on his behalf. This is exactly what happened, to judge from a letter E. P. Warren sent to the director of the Museum of Fine Arts in Boston, July 13, 1890, two months after Berenson made his fateful decision.

Warren wrote that Berenson had discovered what he considered to be a great find in Venice and had bought it as his agent. It was a Madonna and Child, apparently by Bronzino. Berenson said that a bad copy of the same painting was hanging at Hampton Court.

Berenson makes no reference to it but it seems likely that, in 1890, he began other tentative forays into the marketplace, a move that was to have far-reaching consequences.

Finally, there was Julian Klaczko. This Polish political commentator and art critic, born forty years before Berenson, had a life which uncannily parallels his own. Klaczko was born of Jewish parents in Vilna, that center of Haskalah and political and artistic ferment, a few miles from Butrimants. Klaczko, too, escaped the confining influence of shtetl life and embraced Western thought. He was deeply involved in politics (he ended his career as an official in the Austrian government) and just as involved in art, specifically Italian art, of which he had a specialist's knowledge. In the 1880s and 1890s, Klaczko was publishing articles in Parisian magazines of art and culture and his books on Italian art were appearing in France. Since Berenson read almost every word on the arts that was published in Europe, it is highly likely that he had at least a superficial knowledge of Klaczko's life. The curious parallels between the two men have a further aspect: both converted to Catholicism.

Three years in Europe had their effect on Berenson's appearance. He had grown thinner, friends from Boston discovered, and perhaps a little taller, and had cut his hair. As a result he looked more mature, but somehow shorn and bereft to those who remembered the cascade of beautiful curls framing his face.

Emotionally, the effect of his prolonged absence from 11 Minot Street had been to intensify the feeling that he did not belong anywhere. His first wrench, from the experiences and loves of childhood, had turned him, at twenty-two, into "a complete Bostonian patriot." But, arriving in Europe, "I was far too Bostonian and American to be taken for out-and-out English, and on the Continent languages betrayed me everywhere as a foreigner."

No one wanted him anywhere, a not wholly unmixed blessing, since he found himself unable to identify with their "patridiocy." He was not a Jew and no longer an American, but neither was he a European. He could luxuriate in complete anonymity.

This, in effect, is what Berenson did, taking an almost perverse pride in his freedom from the manners and mores of his surroundings. Detachment, however, has its reverse face, and he was beginning to feel more and more alienated and homeless, "far from the land, the men, the women, the customs, the ideas . . . the commonplaces, the catchwords, the gossip, the old and new memories where he grew to youth and matured to manhood. . . ." Despite himself, Berenson could not overcome a longing to make contact, touch another human being, to make a patch of earth his own, to belong, at some level, somewhere.

Berenson had been holding long conversations with Frank Costelloe, whose conviction of salvation as a Catholic was absolute. Frank, it seemed, had decided that religion was exactly what Berenson needed. "Tell Frank that I really 'mean business' at last," Berenson wrote to Mary. "I almost hated him the other evening for using that phrase. But I do mean business now, I have begun to go to school. . . ."

Berenson the outcast had sustained his Mephistophelian stance for as long as he could bear it emotionally. He was no longer willing to remain in limbo, suspended between heaven and hell. He yearned to be forgiven by Dumah, the angel of vengeance, to lose his soul in order to save it. Catholicism suddenly seemed inevitable. Although the rationalist in him might still shrink in distaste from dialectics and ridicule superstitious belief, the spiritual side of his nature, which had already given him a glimpse of the transcendental in great art, clung to that sense of wonder.

He wrote in *Rumor and Reflection*, ". . . when I come up against people with no feeling for the numinous, no awe before the universe, no ever-present sense of the precariousness of human life—I feel . . . remote from them. . . ."

In the winter of 1890–91, Berenson moved to the monastery of Monte Oliveto Maggiore in the remote hills southeast of Siena. Describing a later visit, Berenson's brother-in-law Logan Pearsall Smith wrote,

> In wind cold, bitter, we drove up wrapped in furs [through] barren, desert-white country—miniature mountains, valleys, real ravines—then through streets of crowded town and out under an arch we saw the sunset country, wooded and rich and there in a glowing shadow, the great monastery—noble buildings of old brick in that promontory of land.
>
> Ring bell, the men cluster. Smell of box, pictures. Fatigue, hardly saw sunset, trees, mountains. Following white brother [monk] down flickering hall. Sweet sleep, conscious, quiet sleep. Then dawn . . . I am called, "Come," a person mysterious in dawn. I stand drugged—cold wind blew on me, and through eyes dim with sleep, I saw the sharp outlines of the mountains . . . the sunset light, the red tower, & there in the sunset light we saw—we heard—the green bell ringing out over the deserted Italian city.

The solitude, beauty, and austerity of Monte Oliveto, set among leaden hills and barren canyons which reminded him of Doré's engravings, were as much in harmony with Berenson's mood as they had been with Logan's. There were white, cloistered rooms and aromatic fires and books on the table. There was the glittering valley below, shimmering like a mirage through the morning haze, and the silence, broken only by the ripple of falling water and the reverberating monastery bells.

Berenson was living simply, exactly as he liked. By night, he and the old abbot, Don Gaetano di Negro, would sit in front of a blazing wood fire while Don Gaetano told him stories about his early days in Rome serving under Pope Gregory. By day, Berenson would join the abbot on his trips into the surrounding countryside. While the abbot talked to the local priest, Berenson would wander through the country church, examining the old paintings and altarpieces.

On one of his frequent return visits to Monte Oliveto Maggiore with Logan, Berenson discovered Monistero, a huge building on the road to Maremma. It seemed the ideal spot to establish Altamura, which was beginning to take vague shape in his mind, a place to live "with a few choice spirits in a sort of Thélème. . . ." Nothing came of the idea.

Berenson was preparing himself to be received into the Catholic Church and, at the same time, collecting material for his first books. He was making a parallel pilgrimage, in search of Venetian painters in general and Lorenzo Lotto in particular. To that end, he was willing to travel to the most obscure and forgotten churches of Bergamo and the remotest villages of the Marches. Berenson avoided the crowded and dirty public horse buses, preferring to walk or hire a light *bághero* ("buggy"). The hotels were verminous and scarce, food nothing more than stale bread, onions, and a few anchovies; ". . . but every morning I awoke to a glamorous adventure [and] tasted the freshness of a spring or autumn morning in a Bergamesque valley. . . ."

At the end of his search for Lotto, Berenson felt that he had memorized that painter's work with some kind of ineradicable inner fixative. However, since Lotto's paintings are erratic in style and can also be identified from documents and his own signature, Lotto was the poorest possible choice for an illustration of Berenson's theories of stylistic analysis. Nevertheless, the resulting work, *Lorenzo Lotto: An Essay in Constructive Art Criticism,* caused something of a stir, and Berenson's work on the Venetian painters as a whole was to gain him further attention.

In January of 1891, Berenson was received into the Catholic Church. "The vaccination . . . did not 'take,' " Mary recorded, perhaps too pessimistically. Although Berenson no longer practiced his religion after the first year or two, being as repelled by the act of ecstatic merging with the Ineffable as he was attracted by it, he remained nominally Catholic and through the Church identified with "the land where the fair citron blows."

To become a Catholic gave him, if temporarily, an outlet for his incoherent longings to identify with the beautiful. Art and the church had become inextricably fused in his mind. Art had become redemption.

"I wanted so much to . . . thank God that he had led me to him so much just by those beautiful pictures. Without them I should have been nowhere. . . . How I used to loathe myself for being one of those whom I knew, as Dante describes, Heaven rejects and Hell disdains. . . . How glad I am to take sides, to give up the fancied freedom. . . ."

One morning Berenson left Monte Oliveto Maggiore for his next destination, Perugia. "Harnessing horses in cold air that was sweet and cold—caressing cold . . . Drive down. Monte Oliveto disappeared among the mountains & we did not see it again. Drive through the clear still resounding morning air—winter trees, lawns began to appear under the sun—people up going to market in the little walled town that shone through the mist of the valley below, driving pigs and great oxen. . . ."

By spring Berenson was back in London, visiting galleries and churches with Mary. His religious conversion, for which she was indirectly responsible, seemed to have brought them closer. Berenson was beginning to see her as a pupil-assistant-secretary-lover-friend, a role that more than one woman was destined to play, and was treating her accordingly. One of his techniques was to sit her on top of a ladder in the Uffizi Gallery in Florence and make her study a painting for hours on end. For relaxation, they invented a game, "conosching."

"Mary would say, 'Come and conosce,' while she gathered together a heap of photographs of Italian pictures and spread a sheet of paper over each, leaving only a face, hands or a landscape visible. We then had to guess the artist," wrote her friend Lina Waterfield.

As Walt Whitman and Frank Costelloe had already discovered, Mary was a delightful disciple, intelligent, curious, and irreverent, the kind of "adolescent-minded" woman who was radiantly open to new ideas. Since Mary knew nothing about art she presented no threat to Berenson's budding expertise. Her fresh responses and alert, curious mind, provided the perfect foil.

Mary was dividing her time between visits to Grosvenor Road and Friday's Hill and extended trips through Italy with Berenson, using Florence as their point of departure. She loved the early morning breakfasts in a *caffè*, lingering just long enough over the morning coffee for a final scrutiny of the day's itinerary, then the wanderings into the depths of the countryside in search of a half-abandoned church or dusty altarpiece.

"What a passion it was for us in those days," she wrote, "to whisper to each other a new name for an old thing! I can hardly understand it now, for it has become so much the *thing* we care for, and not the name. But then! We used to wonder if Adam had half as much pleasure from naming the animals as we from naming those ancient paintings."

Besides ingenuity, the guessing game required considerable energy and even more patience. "He tells me he has often spent a week and hundreds of francs and ruined his stomach and temper in order to see one second-rate picture," Senda wrote to her family ten years later. "And the times he has gone to little towns on purpose to see one picture in each—and had to go away without as much as a glimpse at them.

"Say a picture is in the library or small picture gallery or some such place—the janitor has the key of course—he locks the place of course—and he is never there, of course." At some point Berenson's patience would give out; this was invariably the moment when Mary would dissolve in devilish glee.

As a companion Mary was so delightful that Berenson found himself inventing small surprises, for the pleasure of her reaction. "In the Uffizi Bernhard insisted on leading Mary blindfold to the spot in the adjoining room from which she could best see, for the first time, the *Primavera*.

"In Rome they walked up the steep, narrow road leading to the Aventine, 'so intoxicated with new enchantments of thought and feeling' (I am quoting Mary) 'that a peasant who passed them said to his companions, *"Stanno per baciarsi."* ' " ("They're just going to to kiss.")

Whether he cared to admit it or not, Berenson was falling in love. He began to write letters to Mary early in the autumn of 1890, just after their trip to Paris with Frank. He wrote from Frankfurt, his first stop, and continued on an almost daily basis whenever they were apart. (By the autumn of 1944, there were some 3,300 letters.)

His letters continue the dialogue of ideas: "I have a lot to say about Ibsen, that even you have not heard, and all with regard to his women. . . . It is so simple that you will say, 'Oh, is that all!' when I tell you. . . ." He mused about changes of attribution: "I am beginning to think that the big St. Sebastian attributed to Pollajuolo [in the Pitti Palace, Florence] may be by Jacopo de' Barbari. . . ." and gossiped about mutual friends: "[Paul] Bourget has put his tail under his hind legs, and skulked back to his kennel. . . . Good riddance. He counts no more."

His tone was often flirtatious: "I can't get my feet warm these days. . . ." He was also commanding. On her trip back to Florence in 1892, Mary was to make productive use of her four-hour wait in Milan. First, she was to go to Biffi's in the "Galleria" for breakfast and then engage a carriage by the hour to take her to several churches to look at frescoes and cloisters; then she might end up in the Brera or the Poldi-Pezzoli Museum as she chose.

"Be sure you have some lunch before you get into the train," he instructed her firmly. How long it would seem until they met, "thou precious darling . . ."

Berenson's letters give the impression that the closer he and Mary became, the more the boundary between their personalities was blurring in his mind. From a polite and charming friend he was metamorphosing, little by little, into a dictatorial father-teacher-lover. He was as stern with her as he was with himself. Mary must not only see what he saw, eat where he decreed, and enjoy what he had enjoyed, but she must bow to his decisions and even dislike the people he disliked.

"I have feelings of unease about Miss S. [Eugénie Sellers]. I am willing to try her however, but on the indispensable condition that you do not in the least degree attempt to make of her a friend for yourself. If she can be the friend of us both, well and good. If not, she must remain a distant acquaintance. . . ." When Mary occasionally allowed herself to rebel against Berenson's commands, it was usually over an attribution. They would stamp off to eat at separate restaurants and then "meet again to make it up, before the same picture over which they had quarrelled."

Above all, Berenson decreed that Mary must adapt her life to accommodate his needs. That she might have emotional needs of her own does not seem to have occurred to him. "Remember," he wrote, when she seemed to be spending too much time with her children, "I am by nature a person who gets fonder of people when they are with him, and less fond when they are away."

Although they could not marry and although the clandestine nature of their liaison offended Berenson's sense of social decorum, both seemed to need the freedom for independent action that such an arrangement provided. When Berenson returned to the United States in the autumn of 1894, making his first visit in seven years, Mary sailed to Paris for a ten-day idyll with another man, her future brother-in-law.

Mary was, as Bertrand Russell discovered, almost pointedly in favor of "free love." Russell wrote to Alys, then his fiancée, that Mary had "been making me talk about sexual morality and my reasons for preferring chastity to vice." At the same time, Mary was writing letters to Berenson about procreation and marriage which he uncomfortably labeled "sophomoric."

". . . For the present it is enough to point to the fact that the entire course of civilization has been away from promiscuity," he wrote. "You see I am getting fearfully orthodox. But I must say that, putting aside cant and hypocrisies, the one-man, one-woman ideal is the highest practical social ideal. Even in its merely physical aspect it is superior as dining regularly is to foraging for a meal in the woods. . . ."

Whether Berenson was obliquely pledging himself to faithfulness, or simply reacting to what may have seemed like an uncomfortably flirtatious note in her letters, is not known. His ambivalent views about sex, disguised as morality, make it unlikely that he would have been a skillful lover, however brilliantly satisfying he might prove as a companion. Even to discuss life's "gross sexuality" was obviously painful and he shrank from it. Mary found the whole subject marvelously interesting.

Their outlooks differed in another respect. Mary's idealistic belief in a perfectable society was still verdant. To Berenson, however, socialism was the enemy of culture. "In the last thousand years whenever art has had its day, it has owed it to a merchant aristocracy—the very utmost opposite, therefore, of a democracy . . . to tell you the wickedest thing I am ever likely to, I am afraid that art would not flourish in the Millenium. . . ."

Certainly, Berenson continued in a letter three days later, he believed in the Catholic concept of duty. He also believed in being useful; he believed in beauty even more. In that respect he was an "engrained" pagan. Without spontaneity, beauty, and love of the sensuous, life was scarcely endurable. Even to visit England now filled him with gloom. It was connected in his mind with moral obligation, in contrast to Italy, which personified a blissful hedonism.

Berenson's protests mirrored the nineteenth-century capitalistic view that all men had equal opportunities and that, if some could not better themselves, they deserved to be poor. He did not ask for any quarter, nor would he give any. The very idea of philanthropy was suspect; it smacked of hypocrisy.

Not realizing that Berenson had already adopted the prejudices of the class he aspired to join, Mary kept trying to convert him into a social reformer. She sent Fabian pamphlets by Sidney Webb and Bernard Shaw. He resisted them all and she finally lost heart. She abandoned her work in social reform, tacitly accepting the Berensonian doctrine that she might only be interested in those causes which interested him.

If the Whitmanesque democrat in Mary met with hostility, the guardian angel aspect of her nature was more favorably received. Her marriage to Costelloe had brought her into contact with political and social London; her parents introduced her to the intellectual one. At Friday's Hill in Haslemere, a colony of artists and musicians, Robert and Hannah were soon making friends with their neighbor Mr. Tennyson and receiving Beatrice and Sidney Webb, William James, Beatrix Potter, Bernard Shaw, the artist and writer Sir William Rothenstein, and Israel Zangwill, who was to have a great success with *Children of the Ghetto* (1892).

The beautiful and statuesque Alys, who liked to sit around a camp fire singing Negro spirituals, was inseparable from the budding young philosopher Bertrand Russell while Logan, already a writer, was gathering his own circle of literati and inviting them to Friday's Hill. Berenson's ingratiating charm had its predictable effect. In 1891 he was invited to give a series of lectures on Venetian paintings in the National Gallery.

The series served to show him that lecturing was not his natural medium and, although he gave other lectures (notably, in Paris), he soon abandoned the attempt. To begin with, his soft voice did not carry. Then, being obliged to sustain a monologue without the stimulus of interruptions appeared to make him uneasy. So did any kind of communication during which he could not assess the other's response. This may have accounted for his refusal ever to use the telephone or have his voice recorded.

However, the lectures did introduce him to the Misses Katherine Bradley and Edith Cooper who wrote ornate plays in Elizabethan prose under the pseudonym of Michael Field. They heard him lecture and invitations to their London salon soon followed. They called him "The Faun," because he loved their poem, "The Faun's Song," which he had found in a book in the Old Corner Book Store in Boston. They opened select doors for him among the influential intelligentsia, the London worlds of Wilde and Ricketts and Shannon and Rothenstein. They paid him the compliment of wishing to learn from him, and were undeterred by his stiff remark that, "if you knew how little I care to make converts, you would not be developing lessons from my doctrines. . . . My religion consists of this: If you have summons to intellectual instinct, you will have lived."

The Michael Fields, friends of Logan, were as entranced by Mary and paid her the compliment of allowing her to influence their writing. In *Reperusals and Re-Collections*, Logan noted that, through Mary's influence, the Michael Fields were persuaded to relinquish the worst excesses of their Corvo-esque style, words like "crapulence," "defloration," "construpation," "libidinousness," and "priapean." For a time Berenson suffered in silence the price of friendship, which was to read the torrents of Elizabethan blank verse with which they deluged their friends, each new attempt at drama more catastrophic than the last.

The reason was not his fondness for the aunt, Katherine Bradley, whom he described as "a goat cropping in the garden of the Muses," but for her painfully sensitive niece, Edith Cooper. She "drew me out." Her compliant spirit provided the uncritical and accepting warmth which Berenson was to find vital, if his imagination was to take flight.

For all their otherworldliness, the Michael Fields had certain vulnerabilities which their friend William Rothenstein sidestepped with delicacy. "They knew few people, but from these few they expected—everything, all they had to give . . . but those to whom they gave must be worthy of their trust every moment, whether in their company or out of sight. . . ."

The Faun, less sensitively attuned to the nuances of character, committed an unforgivable act. He had, he recorded, successfully avoided giving an opinion as one terrible play followed another, until the day he was obliged to read the worst Michael Field drama of them all.

"It was about the widow of Crescentius and how she was to revenge herself on Otto the Holy Roman Emperor, her husband's slayer. The plot was of an indecency that only pure-minded, elderly, mid-Victorian virgins could have imagined; and the blank verse and the rhetoric would have filled with horror and indignation the worst understudies of Beaumont and Fletcher."

Even then, Berenson and Mary avoided comment, until goaded past endurance by the Michael Fields, who dared them to say what they really thought. That did it. Berenson "told them in as temperate a language as I could muster, but tell them I did."

Sometime later a postcard reached Fiesole from London: "All is not lost though Fiesole condemn. Vulgar journalists sail out of our lives." Berenson concluded, "We did. For years we did not meet."

Since Oscar Wilde was one of the habitués of the Michael Fields' salon, Berenson may have met the former disciple of Walter Pater there. Berenson never tired of quoting Wilde (he particularly liked Wilde's telegram of regret, "I cannot come. Lie follows.") and their friendship appears to have been close, at least for a time. Berenson told Kenneth Clark that Wilde would call on him in the evenings in the little house on Lord North Street, dating from Queen Anne, just behind Westminster Abbey, where Berenson had taken rooms. Berenson described how Wilde never took more than three or four puffs at a cigarette, then threw it away and lit another.

Wilde was, Berenson used to say, not only the wittiest of talkers but the kindest man imaginable. They would have shared many opinions, not the least being their aesthetic, jointly derived from Pater and his Epicurean, Marius. For Wilde, as for Berenson, raw emotion was indigestible; it must be transmuted and refined into another self which one hammered, as it were, out of the crude human clay. And Wilde was a consummate example of a posed self (of conventional respectability) versus a real self (of unacceptable sexual preferences). If Wilde said, "the first duty in life is to assume a pose; what the second is no one has yet found out," Berenson would be bound to laugh in agreement.

However, once Wilde was unveiled, Berenson withdrew in horror at the self he found exposed.

Berenson said, "We broke over Douglas. I told him I never wanted to see Douglas again and that Douglas would cause his ruin and even after I said that, Wilde invited me to dinner and Douglas was there." It was then, Berenson added, that Wilde gave his reason for continuing that friendship: "Bernhard, you forget that in every way I want to imitate my Maker and, like Him, I want nothing but praise."

For Berenson, that one friend should refuse to take his side against another was tantamount to a betrayal. The larger issue, however, was bound to be Berenson's squeamish dislike of what he would have considered a sexual abnormality, as well as his fear of guilt by association. (He was always terrified, Kenneth Clark added, that people would also accuse him of sodomy.)

Berenson broke off the friendship brutally and recalled that, when he and Wilde subsequently met, "We cut one another dead." He regretted it later, and Wilde's trial and subsequent imprisonment "gave me a shock I never got over."

It is unlikely that Berenson's abhorrence was attributable to anything more profound than prudishness. Homosexuality never attracted him, although his small size and Byronic good looks guaranteed that, in his youth, he was courted more often by men than by women. He said, of sexual relations with men, "I shouldn't have liked it," and was careful to make clear to at least two friends that Wilde never approached him sexually, even though they spent many nights together. He gave the reverse impression to others. "One gets a bit hazy," the collector and art historian Henry P. McIlhenny of Philadelphia said, "but B.B. always told me that Oscar Wilde had made a pass at him. He was very proud of it."

Berenson and Mary visited Hampton Court and Mary, under her pseudonym of Mary Logan, published a small catalogue of the Italian paintings in that little-known gallery. It was a modest, unpretentious work, important only for its sequel. Among the paintings on view at Hampton Court was *The Shepherd*, the head of a young boy holding a pipe, which Berenson called a Giorgione.

"One might suppose that anyone with an eye for paint could see even from a photograph that this picture was much restored," Kenneth Clark remarked. Berenson, unversed in the fiendishly clever art of the restorer, did not see it. He used the faked-up picture as the frontispiece for his first book, *The Venetian Painters of the Renaissance*, published in 1894.

"I should add," Lord Clark concluded, "that I was with Mr. and Mrs. Berenson when they revisited Hampton Court after many years. We stood in front of this picture for a long time in silence. At last Mrs. Berenson said, 'Bernard, we must have been in love.' Berenson remained silent, but nodded gravely, and we walked on."

Berenson's knowledge of art was already becoming almost "too professional for drawing-room conversation," Mary observed. He was attempting a feat which would have defeated anyone less passionately determined, i.e., to locate and identify every work by every Italian Renaissance master wherever it was to be found in Europe.

Taking a random example,

let us say Paolo Farinati—which suggests a fairly vague mental picture. You will find a list of about 100 works in village churches, in galleries, in private collections all over the world.

Every one of those works Berenson had seen, and they had formed a clear image of Farinati in his mind, so that he could apply it instantly in going round a collection. Now multiply this by 300, for that is the number of painters listed, [in the *Italian Pictures of the Renaissance*] and remember that all these images had to be clear and usable, and each judgment not only involved a feat of memory, but was often a piece of condensed criticism. It meant saying, "given the character and capacities of this particular artist, this is the kind of picture he might have painted."

The result is an extraordinary achievement of scholarship, intuition, and retentive prowess, all the more remarkable when one considers how few tools Berenson had at his command. The compiling team of Crowe and Cavalcaselle had their own dogged sketches, made on the spot, as references and engravers' prints. Berenson had only his own notes and a few photographs. He was perhaps the first writer to understand their usefulness for the connoisseur. A systematic study of an artist's work was possible for the first time, now that photographs of that work could be laid side by side and a plausible sequence established.

If, up to this moment, most connoisseurship had consisted of inspired guesswork, if not outright quackery, it could now attain the accuracy of a science. To do that, Berenson must have a library of photographs. These were hard to obtain.

"Tourists know how impossible it is for love or money to get good photographs of any pictures save the few favourites," he wrote, praising a photographer who had just reproduced every important painting in the Poldi-Pezzoli Collection in Milan.

To the end of his life Berenson dunned friends, colleagues,

collectors, dealers, and museums shamelessly for photographs, in tones varying from entreaties to demands, begging and coaxing as if vainly trying to acquire every print ever developed. His dependence upon them led to his being dubbed, by the art critic of *The Nation* of New York, as the "wielder of the photograph and the foot-rule."

Berenson was very poor. In Rome, in 1888, he slept in the studio of a friend from whom he rented a trestle bed, and often lived all day on *caffè latte* (for five soldi) and a handful of chestnuts. How he survived those years of poverty, between 1890 and 1895, is something of a mystery. He was still getting financial support from 11 Minot Street and Mary, who had a small private income, paid some of their traveling costs. (In 1891, they were traveling on five lire a day each.) In those years, Berenson was eking out a precarious living by conducting tourists to Florence around the art galleries for one lira each. He lived in fear of being discovered and beaten up by the other guides.

Berenson was also beginning to dabble in the art market. His letters from Florence to Mary in London in 1892 urge her to look at the new Botticelli at Mond's, to visit Deutsch, another dealer, and to get J. P. Richter, an art historian and dealer, to show her his collection.

Further evidence that he was scouting for other collectors besides Warren is provided by the diary of Emma B. Andrews, a relative who traveled with Mr. and Mrs. Theodore M. Davis of Newport, Rhode Island. Davis, a wealthy investor, collector, and amateur archaeologist, was to become famous when, excavating in the Valley of the Kings at Thebes in Egypt in 1905, he discovered the tombs of the parents of Queen Tiy, mother and inspirer of Ikhnaton, the famous "Heretic King." Two years later, Davis unearthed the tomb of Amenhotep III. Early in the 1890s Davis was traveling in Egypt with occasional forays into Paris, Italy, and London to buy paintings. Mrs. Andrews records their first meeting with Berenson in Rome in the spring of 1893.

Davis was considering buying from a private art collection that was being "rather mysteriously" offered for sale by its owner and was advised by a British envoy attached to the Vatican to consult Berenson, a "promising young art critic."

Mrs. Andrews wrote,

> So ... he came and we have been going about with him and seeing for the first time with discerning eyes.

For the first time I have seen the ravishing sweetness of the frescoes of Melozzo da Forli. . . . We had one charming morning at St. Peters, Mr. Berenson and I, wandering around the great church, talking of its history, of its builders, of its treasures. . . . Then we went to the Colonna Gallery, and looked at the few best pictures. . . . Another morning Nettie and I, Howard and Mr. B. had a perfect morning among the pictures at the Vatican. . . . In the afternoon we all went to the Villa Borghese to see the Borghese collection transferred to the Villa from the Palazzo—and again it was a great pleasure to see through eyes more knowing and discriminating than ours. . . .

When Mr. and Mrs. Davis and Mrs. Andrews traveled on to Florence, Berenson arrived at their hotel promptly to guide them over the pavement of tombstones, almost worn smooth, at the church of Santa Maria Novella, then to the chapel of the Strozzi, the Giotto frescoes in the Santa Croce, the Duomo, and the Pitti Palace. They went to the Belli-Arti and obediently looked at *Three Archangels with the Young Tobias* with a critical eye, since Berenson told them that it was not a Botticelli after all. When they went on to Venice, their ever-helpful guide even marked their books, to save them time at the art galleries. And, when Davis expressed an interest in buying art, Berenson knew just whom to contact.

"Theodore, Nettie and I went on a delightful little excursion this afternoon," Mrs. Andrews wrote from Venice. "Mr. Berenson had given Theodore a card of intoduction to a Count Nardi—living at Mira, some distance from Venice—who had some good pictures, one of which he thought Theodore could buy. . . ."

Little by little Berenson was aspiring to the role of an authority. It is one which might not seem easily acquirable to anyone less resourceful and naturally contentious, but for Berenson, it was a simple matter of seizing opportunities to be heard. Even though the critics Ruskin, Symonds, and Vernon Lee wrote palpable rubbish, they managed to make their readers aware of art and, "once the public get the ring of this monosyllable, they will follow anybody who shouts it at them, you and me, if we shout loud enough," he wrote cynically to Mary in 1892.

Such opportunities presented themselves, as an interesting exchange of letters demonstrates. In 1891–92 Berenson, then in Milan and Venice, took issue with the writer W. J. Stillman, then in Florence, in the pages of *The Nation*, the New York magazine devoted to politics, literature, science, and art.

Berenson opened the attack. In a recent article on Tintoretto that Stillman had written for *The Century*, another arts magazine, the writer, Berenson declared, was misinformed. The painting, *Finding of the Body of St. Mark* by Tintoretto, was wrongly attributed. In addition, it was not at the church of Santa Maria dei Angeli at Murano in Venice, as stated in the article, but in the Brera Museum in Milan. He signed himself "B.B."

In reply Stillman conceded that he had wrongly attributed the painting to Jacopo (the elder) Tintoretto, when it should have been given to Domenico (the younger). However, this was his only error. The painting which he called *The Apparition of St. Mark in the Church of St. Mark*, was still at Saint Mark's in Venice, and had never left it.

The argument disintegrated into a tedious and labyrinthine quarrel from which the only conclusion possible is that the two men were discussing different paintings. Berenson never concedes this.

"The intention of my first letter was to prove that Mr. Stillman had failed to see one of the most important masterpieces of the artist whose work he was reviewing," he wrote. That Berenson's intention was also to demonstrate his superior knowledge at the expense of a supposed authority on Italian art must have been evident to the editor of the magazine. A note at the bottom of Berenson's second epistle read, "We can print no more letters on this subject."

To really make one's mark, however, one must do more than administer sharp little jabs in the letters column of a fashionable journal. One needed a body of work, a statement of purpose. Berenson had been dreaming about writing a beautiful book on Venetian art. The result, in 1894, was scarcely that. "We opened the wrapper [of Berenson's first book] when we were lunching together at Gilli's in the Piazza della Signoria, & the cover was *so awful*—a large-hipped gondolier in a red & white background with gilt ripples on the water—that we felt like going & drowning ourselves in the Arno!" Mary recalled.

The book was slim and small, designed to be slipped in the pocket during an artistic pilgrimage, and Berenson's approach, in writing *The Venetian Painters of the Renaissance*, was similarly unpretentious. The result is a modest historical survey, unencumbered with aesthetical aspirations. None of the theories that were to be developed so successfully in later books appears here. They were still too unformulated to be risked in writing. Berenson wrote to the Michael Fields in the autumn of 1895, "I think hard, but unbeknownst, so to speak, even to myself. The problem before me is simple: Granting that the pleasure element is always sensuous, as we must, what is the specific element of sensual pleasure in each of the arts?"

Venetian art was his first choice of subject, because he responded most immediately and instinctively to it. Why he should have preferred Venetian art to the Florentine art of the Renaissance which is, by general agreement, superior, is unclear. What Berenson has to say about that art does not take us very far. ". . . they are more *painters* than the Florentines," he wrote to Mary in 1890. His preference is understandable only in the context of the effect Venice first had on him, as the tangible realization of a mystical inner vision. Venice had come to personify the quintessence of the Renaissance for him, and so did everything connected with it.

The Venetians, he wrote, painted from a natural love of beauty, a spontaneous delight in life. Their models were the men and women they saw around them, "handsome, healthy, sane people like themselves." The emphasis is as much on the life depicted, ideally represented as one devoted to beauty and worldly pleasure, as on the qualities of art itself. These, however, he found in abundance. Their artists, he wrote, were masters at portraying art that was true to life and in tune with human sympathy, in portraying the material world and not simply the spiritual. They were as versed in the arts of light, shadow, and spatial effects as they were in form and color.

Berenson does not particularly emphasize the heightened and dazzling response to light that perhaps best characterizes the work of Giovanni Bellini and other Venetian masters. He does not approach, in penetrating insight or facility of imagery, the level of prose attained by his idol, Walter Pater. He did, however, achieve what he set out to do, make a presentation of Venetian art that was accessible to the intelligent amateur. He manages to convey his own pleasure and, in an occasional felicitous phrase, i.e., that the work of Carlo Crivelli "expresses with the freedom and spirit of Japanese design a piety as wild and tender as Jacopo da Todi's," he hints at an ability to evoke lyrically the mood of a painting that he was to develop in the following decades.

At the end of his short essay was the first of the Lists that were to make him famous, paintings grouped by author and location, all works he had seen himself and judged by the new, "scientific," Morellian principles. A deceptively laconic note was appended. It warned the reader that these attributions were not based on official opinions, "and are often at variance with them." The authoritative air of the judgments: "No argument, no explanation, just a name, pronounced with almost magical finality," was to have far-reaching implications for the art world and the future course of his life.

Then Berenson made a second, more devastating attack on entrenched opinion. As luck would have it, a major exhibition of Venetian art of the Renaissance was being shown at the New Gallery in London some months after the publication of his book, at the close of 1894. The 300 paintings, for the most part in the hands of British nobility, inherited from the days of Charles I or the results of eighteenth-century Grand Tours made by their ancestors, carried the attributions of their owners. These, not surprisingly, were optimistic. They might be based on the embroideries of family tradition, or have survived unchanged since the 1850s, when Dr. Waagen, the great German expert, had established the authenticity of every masterpiece in England. Such optimism was further fueled by the desire of the titled owners to possess the genuine article—a point of pride, and as good as money in the bank. However, the organizers prudently dissociated themselves from such assessments. There was a gentlemanly note to this effect in the catalogue.

That such an exhibition could still be held in London in the 1890s made it transparently clear to Berenson, and also to Mary, that attributions among Italian paintings in British hands were as chaotic as Morelli and Crowe and Cavalcaselle had found them to be in Italy. The opportunity was there and Berenson seized it. With Mary as his assistant, Berenson prepared a lengthy commentary which Herbert Cook, a wealthy collector, paid to have printed. Berenson's essay was distributed at the exhibition itself.

In his essay, Berenson coolly demolished the optimism. Of thirty-three Titians on view, only one was actually painted by the master, he wrote, a Madonna owned by Mr. Ludwig Mond. Five were copies of well-known works, two were copies of lost works, and most of the rest were by imitators. None of eight paintings purporting to be by Bonifacio Veronese was genuine, and neither were thirteen listed under the name of Paolo Veronese. Of eighteen or nineteen paintings given to Giovanni Bellini, only three were actually painted by him. As for Giorgione, there were only thirteen in all of Europe, including the *Head of a Shepherd*

from Hampton Court on exhibition, Berenson wrote, and therefore the seventeen other supposed Giorgiones on exhibition were
false.

For example, the *Portrait of a Lady Professor of Bologna* owned
by Louisa, Lady Ashburton, and wrongly ascribed to Giorgione,
was "neither of a Lady, nor of a Professor, nor of Bologna."

As for the predella in three parts on the Death of the Virgin
owned by Mrs. B. W. Currie, and attributed to Alvise Vivarini, if
it were really by that master, it "would go far to justify the
neglect into which he has fallen."

Berenson dismissed paintings with words which stopped
short of calling them actual forgeries: "The 'Veronica' . . . is a
weak thing of Antonello-Alvisesque character, possibly by Filippo
Mazzola. The 'Portrait of Hans Memling' . . . is a poor copy of the
Antonello portrait in the National Gallery. The drawing for an
'Adoration of the Magi' is not worth notice." And so on.

Berenson boldly offered his own attributions. "Although
Montagna may have supervised the execution of these figures,"
he wrote of drawings attributed to Bartolommeo Montagna, "the
hand that I recognize in them is that of one of his pupils, interesting not only on his own account but for the race of artists whom
he begat, I mean the elder Francesco da Ponte. . . ."

The exhaustive details marshaled to support Berenson's opinions clearly demonstrate his Morelliesque thinking: "Another
Alvisesque trick that I must not forget to mention . . . is the
exposure of the last joints only of the fingers, as in the Madonna's
right hand here." One finds, however, very little reference to the
condition of the painting itself or to evidence of the restorer's
hand.

That other professionals shared Berenson's poor opinion can
be seen from two unsigned articles published in the London
Times. The *Times* critic, while more polite, and finding more to
praise, did venture that "doubtless a second examination of the
gallery shows that the number of wrong attributions is larger than
it ought to be, and it may be hoped that many of the owners,
when they get their pictures home again, will wisely take off the
labels bearing Giorgione's and Titian's name. . . ."

All of this must have been immensely interesting to the
student of Italian art, but one can guess at the intense rage of the
owners who read such impudent verdicts, so maddeningly authoritative, and such an affront to one's pocketbook as well as
one's pride.

The dealers themselves, accustomed to the sanctity of Ruskin, Pater, and Dr. Waagen, must have found the devastating exclusivity of Berenson's judgments equally offensive. Even when a painting was signed, as in the case of the Madonna lent by Lady Ashburton and clearly labeled IOANNES BELLINVS P. (Giovanni Bellini), one could not jump to conclusions, Berenson wrote, since Bellini ran a factory. Pupils who had become particularly expert would be allowed the honor of adding Bellini's signature to their own work. Such was the case with this Madonna, Berenson stated. It was actually by Niccolo Rondinelli. He reached this conclusion from an examination of the draperies, the colors and physical types, all of which agreed, "detail for detail," with authentic works by Rondinelli.

The essay can be taken as evidence of the scrupulous integrity of Berenson's judgments when untainted by any other considerations than those of scholarship. His reasoning shows that he was then what the art historian Meyer Schapiro has called a contractionist, i.e., a connoisseur who will accept a work only when it clearly demonstrates the master's hand in the smallest details and who is not satisfied by the mere evidence that it has come from his workshop. Schapiro added, ". . . how many museums and private owners of masterpieces were humbled by his keen attributions, which forced them to change their labels from Titian to Palma and from Palma to Amico di Nessuno!"

The essay, which Mary described as having been published in "a curious kind of innocence," had the predictable result. Perhaps they had not realized, Mary continued, just how tenaciously the owners would cling to their great names and how fiercely they would resent Berenson's deflating opinions. The comment is surely naïve, and reveals more about Mary's need to excuse their actions than explain their real motives.

She urged him to do it, Mary continued, because she realized how important it would be for his future to make his name known to the great collectors of Italian art. Together they were being labeled publicity hounds, out to make their names on the bones of other people's reputations. He must, the London trade decided, be "hunted down and exterminated." Just the same, people were beginning to know who Bernhard Berenson was.

Berenson's leap into the limelight in 1895 was probably just as Mary had described it, an attempt to establish himself with collectors, his potential employers. It launched him as a controversial figure and an increasing number of articles began to appear under his signature in international art magazines. The Paris *Gazette des Beaux Arts* was particularly hospitable, thanks to the zeal of its remarkable editor, Salomon Reinach. Himself a noted archaeologist and historian of art and religion, Reinach was so convinced of his young friend's importance that he stayed up nights translating his articles into French. Such new prominence satisfied Berenson's gadfly fondness for administering a well-aimed jab at complacent officialdom. To do this gave him, he told Mrs. Gardner, a devilish glee. Most of all, his new position as Someone, an Authority, fueled a deep emotional need.

What must have made Berenson truly insufferable to the art world of his time was that this cocksure, self-styled expert really did have an almost magical ability to identify the real authors of paintings, and had prepared himself impeccably for his task. He was unassailable on scholarly grounds and, since he was in the pay of no dealer, on moral grounds as well. The essay and books made his reputation, and these and other Lists that followed acquired the weight of holy writ. They became the "Railroad Timetable of Italian Art," as another distinguished art historian, Roberto Longhi, described it. The direction which the Lists opened before Berenson also limited his future development disastrously—and he soon knew it.

THE TSAYLEM KOP

'Twas whispered by Fry, it was muttered by Dell
And at Holmes for a space was permitted to dwell
And B.B. heard faintly
The sound of a sell.

——"A Christmas Attribution," circa 1910

THE YOUNG AUTHORITY, newly prosperous, posed for his photograph in the late 1890s. His delicious curls, long since shorn, revealed a pair of close-set ears. His hairline was slowly receding. In contrast to the fashion for muttonchop whiskers, with a clean-shaven chin, Berenson had grown a beard, trimmed to an immaculate point, and which included a luxuriant moustache.

He wore a lounge suit of a smooth fabric with a faint sheen to it, perhaps dove gray, in the very latest style. His jacket was cut away in a curve over the hip in the young, shorter manner, and buttoned high over the chest. His collar was fashionably high and tied with a handsome bow. The final button of his waistcoat, of the same fabric as his suit, was nonchalantly left undone.

The same meticulous attention to detail showed itself in the small boutonniere of his lapel and the slender edge of white shirt cuff allowed to extend beyond his coat sleeve. Two strings around his neck, leading to his breast pocket, strongly suggested a monocle. There was a slim band of gold on his right little finger.

The expression in the eyes was curiously changed. The young

poet's air of dreaming eagerness had disappeared, replaced by a look of remote but calm authority, that of a man sure of himself, his judgment, and his bank balance.

Berenson had moved from Bergamo and Venice to lodgings at the Villa Kraus in Fiesole. The decision to live in Florence, a city that he was never again to leave, was a logical one, since he had already made connections with the overlapping circles of influential expatriates who had settled there, attracted by its beauty and intellectually bracing climate. Perhaps it was no coincidence that Florence was also one of the main centers for the sale of Italian Renaissance art in Italy.

At the end of the nineteenth century, handsome prices were being paid for Italian art, but these were limited to those masterworks of Titian, Raphael, and Leonardo da Vinci, for instance, which afforded superb examples of the master's style and were therefore in demand by millionaires in search of rarity, or by wealthy European museums such as the Kaiser Friedrich in Berlin. In the 1880s and 1890s, the Berlin Museum paid £10,000 (for the then dollar equivalent, multiply by five: $50,000) for Fra Angelico's famous *Last Judgment* and Pierpont Morgan paid £100,000 for a famous Raphael altarpiece.

Whenever American buyers were not in the running to bid up the prices, Italian Renaissance paintings could be bought for much less. Small trecento and quattrocento works, the periods which were to become Berenson's specialty, were considered a scholar's taste and could be bought for the price of their frames, or less. A notorious illustration is provided by the sale of the collection of Henry Doetsch which, until its owner's death, had been on view at his house in New Burlington Street. Amassing some 450 paintings, many of them Italian, had reportedly cost Doetsch over £100,000. There were some fine examples. However, many of the attributions were, like those of the New Gallery, unrealistic. Christie's, the auctioneers, took the unusual step of having the works reattributed by a respected scholar, Dr. J. P. Richter, a collector and dealer, before the sale.

Despite this precaution, opinion was against the paintings. It was stated that Richter had badly compromised himself by inflated attributions. Christie's announced from the rostrum that they would not stand behind the attributions and the London public would not bid. "In many cases," the London *Times* reported, "paintings realized less than a quarter of the amounts which must have originally been paid for the frames." Even though Berenson had included some of the paintings in his new Lists, and was quoted by Richter, no one believed. A genuine Girolamo Savoldo, *Portrait of a Nobleman*, went for £126, two Guardis for £63 the pair, and a portrait by Jacopo Bassano for £23. A genuine Lorenzo Lotto altarpiece, full-sized, of the Holy Family and Saints, sold for £53.11s.

The Doetsch sale is an interesting example of the waves of public doubt that were likely to overwhelm the tight and secretive art world of the time. As in the stock market, the intangibles of price depended upon the amount of confidence that could be placed in an expert opinion. Insiders knew, however, that the chances of buying what the work purported to be were somewhat analogous to picking up a nugget of gold on the Bond Street sidewalk.

As has been noted, the Great Master usually ran a school. It was a paint factory, a business proposition. The products could, and often were, accepted as by the master because they bore his signature, even though they might, in fact, be the work of apprentices. To add to the confusion, such paint factories turned out large numbers of copies. Writing to Sir Dudley Carlton in 1618 Peter Paul Rubens said, "As this reproduction is not yet quite completed, I am going to retouch it throughout myself. So it can pass for an original if necessary." Of other copies by his apprentices, Rubens wrote, "I have retouched them to such an effect that they can hardly be distinguished from the original . . . they are perfect miracles at the price."

In addition, paintings that have existed in a miraculously preserved state for 500 years are so rare as to be almost nonexistent. Most have been retouched, some so extensively that, were the additions removed, only a ghost of the original would remain. The difference between honest amendments, in which a restorer attempts with painstaking self-effacement to replace what time has eroded, and unscrupulous fakery, in which a worthless old canvas has been extensively repainted in order to pass it off as an Old Master, is clear enough in principle. However, before the advent of infrared photography and the chemical analysis of pigments, it could be almost impossible to detect. In the final analysis, the only arbiter could be that elusive sense of quality that Berenson described: the connoisseur's eye.

A copyist who begins to make a fraud from scratch has been with us since Roman times, when there was a flourishing demand for Greek objects. A number of the resulting works have deceived the most discriminating tastes and have been belatedly discovered in museum collections. The forger may make an exact copy or, if he has imagination as well as skill, construct his own composition from fragments of a master's other works, to create the illusion that a new masterpiece has been discovered. At the turn of the century a man in Brussels was in the business of manufacturing old Flemish paintings, which brought high prices as originals. Somewhere in Modena, the painter Malatesta was said to be imitating Titians and touching up paintings to resemble Titian. The amazing forgeries of G. F. Ioni looked, to his contemporaries, like perfect examples of the quattrocento style and his fakes in due course found their way into American collections.

Prosperous forgers imply widespread corruption among dealers and it was well-known that rich Americans in particular, among them P. A. B. Widener, Theodore Davis, and John G. Johnson, had been sold worthless paintings. All kinds of fraudulent works might be encountered at the London and Paris art dealers, complete with a plausible provenance. However, if the client was to question too closely, he might be told that "if dealers were to make their private dealings publicly known, they might as well go out of business right away, because no client would ever trust them." Such a breathtaking admission can hardly have inspired confidence. An American journalist, writing to his boss in New York, concluded with exasperation, "the impression you get when you have been to see half a dozen dealers is that the whole business is crooked and rotten and the information you get from [them] is not of any great value. . . ."

The American editor was Carl Snyder and his superior was August Jaccaci, a French-born writer and art historian of considerable enterprise who undertook, in collaboration with the aging John La Farge, to publish a series of sumptuous books on the new American collections. He began with that of Isabella Gardner and dispatched Snyder to Europe, in the winter of 1903–04, to persuade the leading experts to write essays in praise of Mrs. Gardner's masterpieces. In the process Snyder, a man with no knowledge of art but considerable experience as an investigator, unearthed some art-market gossip about personalities, paintings, and pettifoggery.

All kinds of hanky-panky were being rumored, Snyder wrote. It was said that, in Brussels, a dealer who was about to sell a genuine Old Master had it certified by a number of critics, who all signed their autographs on the back of the painting. The painting was on a panel of wood, which the dealer then had delicately sawed in half lengthwise. He now had two objects to sell: the original painting and a fresh surface, obligingly covered on the reverse with a dozen gilt-edged signatures. It was a simple matter to supply a bogus masterpiece to accompany the testimonials.

It was said in London that dealers themselves were in collusion to fix prices. When a fine Romney was discovered on the Isle of Wight, a gentleman dealer with London connections was the first to claim it. To his dismay, however, a member of a London firm, representing what was known as "The Bond Street Ring," arrived on the scene and announced that there would be a "knock-out" for the Romney, forcing the original dealer to take part. The "knock-out" was conducted as follows: A ring of dealers who wanted the picture met beforehand to make private bids. Whichever dealer made the highest bid was allowed to buy the painting. Since there was no apparent interest, the owner would sell at a low price, usually for a few pounds. The winning dealer paid into the pool the difference between the sales price and his bid, to be split up by the losers. In a "knock-out" everyone won except, of course, the seller.

Another story related by Snyder was making the rounds. It concerned the critic of the London *Times*, "Humpy" Ward. Snyder wrote,

> Obach had an exhibition which Ward attended and as he left he said casually, "Oh, how much for such-and-such a picture?"—mentioning one of the finest in the exhibition. Knowing perfectly well what was meant, Obach's reply was, "Oh to you, Mr. Ward, that picture would only be, let us say, a hundred pounds" (when the sale price was—say—three hundred). And Ward says blandly, "Oh very well, send it round." And in the *Times* next morning is a long and laudatory article about the exhibition.
>
> A year or so later Obach's had another, and identically the same thing occurred, but this time Ward fell upon a picture that Obach's didn't want to let go, or at least weren't in the mood to be blackmailed. And so their reply was, "Oh, we are very sorry, Mr. Ward, but we are afraid that picture is sold."
>
> The next day they got one of the worst slatings in the *Times* they had had in their history. Their reply was to send Ward a bill for the other picture which they had sent. . . the year before. But he never paid it.

The casual lack of integrity displayed by a prominent critic and further evinced by the art market itself was fed upon by the art historians. No matter how serious a student of art, and many were extremely reputable scholars, there was hardly a man alive who did not also act as a dealer and tout his own wares.

In addition, there was hardly a man in the game not willing to provide a glowing certificate for the wares of other dealers, often for amiably small sums. Naturally enough, they all disagreed with each other.

"I remember a rubbed-down copy of an old man's portrait by some follower of Bassano, which was sold with a certificate by the great historian of Italian art, Adolfo Venturi, stating, with much eloquence, that it was a portrait of Michelangelo by Titian," wrote Kenneth Clark.

Edward Fowles, Duveen's right-hand man, recalled that, on one visit to see Dr. Wilhelm von Bode, director of the Kaiser Friedrich Museum and an internationally respected scholar, he mentioned that he had seen a Madonna by Petrus Christus at a certain dealer's. " 'So what did you think of it?' [Bode] asked. 'Well,' I replied, 'if it did not bear your certificate, I would never have thought it was by Petrus Christus.' He laughed. 'You don't understand the intricacies of the German language, Fowles. After a brief description of the subject, I say, in fact, "I have never seen a Petrus Christus like this." ' "

The cognoscenti might be cynically aware that the testimonial was useless, but this knowledge usually did not trickle down to the unsuspecting client. "The art dealer with his trail of bleating or venal critics," as Berenson called them, were all in collusion and the fact was taken for granted, one assumes, because the sums involved were minor.

However, the knowledge that such corruption was widespread, even among those who had reputations worth defending, and that any man had his price, contributed to the general contempt in which the art world was held and, within it, some uneasy consciences. These were often salved by the human, if not very commendable, device of making oneself look relatively virtuous by painting the reputation of one's rivals with a black brush.

SHORTLY AFTER his arrival in Fiesole in the early summer of 1895, Berenson wrote to tell T. S. Perry that it was unutterably lovely there. The roses, wisteria, and lilacs were all in bloom. The summer air was deliciously warm by day and balmy by night. The sunsets were exquisite and, after dark, one could hear the nightingales.

Berenson was spending very little time in Fiesole, nevertheless. He had already visited Siena, Perugia, Bologna, Modena, Bergamo, and Assisi and, two months later, was writing to the Perrys from the Hotel zum König von England in Munster after having seen multitudes of bad paintings in Munich.

He was hunting for pictures, this time for an important client. After a lapse of five years, Berenson and Mrs. Gardner were again friends, although on a new footing: that of advisor and client. Berenson appears to have taken the first conciliatory step by sending her, in April 1894, his newly published *Venetian Painters*. He received a prompt reply. Obviously, Mrs. Gardner was delighted that he had made good and ready to forget her harsh words. She even reproached him coquettishly for not having written, blithely ignoring her part in the break.

Mrs. Gardner had already bought a considerable number of works by Corot, Delacroix, Courbet, and Constant Troyon and was including the work of contemporary painters she liked: Whistler and Sargent. Her husband had been elected treasurer of the Boston Museum of Fine Arts in 1888, which had served to arouse her interest in Old Masters and, when her father died three years later, Mrs. Gardner inherited $2,750,000.

When Mrs. Gardner finally met Berenson again in London in the summer of 1894, his newly acquired knowledge and uncanny eye made him a fascinating guide through the National Gallery. It made her feel, Mrs. Gardner said, as if she were seeing through his eyes and not her own. It led her to ask "whether . . . pictures like those I took her to see could still be had. Fatal moment, destined to have such an effect on my career. . . ."

Nothing, he replied, could be easier.

Berenson already knew that a good living was to be made from advising collectors. Now the opportunity presented itself with golden clarity. Mrs. Gardner was eager to buy and he was consummately well-prepared to advise her, almost as if he had been training himself expressly for that purpose, although the idea had probably never crossed his mind. What could be more delightful than to be paid to study a painting, the one task he loved best in the world, and to which he had pledged his life?

Perhaps Berenson entered the art market in the belief that, with his perfectionistic scholarship, his superbly low opinion of others' motives, and his debating skills, he could play the game without becoming mired in it. The Litvak, the *tsaylem kop*, the clever skeptic with a sharp tongue and a nimble wit, was one of his cultural frames of reference and such business dealing was considered a perfectly natural way to survive.

"Predominantly mercantile, Jews were long confined to evaluations, money lending and the jewelry trade, all concerns in which a feeling for authenticity, rapid appraisal, and close observation was necessarily highly developed." Berenson had grown up watching Cousin Louis rise from poverty to affluence on his wits alone.

However the closer he came to the logical outcome of his attributing, the more hopelessly ambivalent he became about it. In old age, he was to identify the summer of 1895 as the moment when he made a fatal wrong turn, and "swerved from purely intellectual pursuits to the archaeological study of art." In his book Berenson cannot bring himself to name the real reason for his unease, and so attacks his decision to begin work on *The Drawings of the Florentine Painters*. This is patently unconvincing as a reason, since that book is considered his finest work of scholarship. It almost looks like a red herring flung in the path of his own search for the truth.

Nowhere in the self-analysis is there a hint of the bald reality, so simple, so obvious, and so impossible to discuss if one were to maintain the myth of the scholar-aristocrat: that he was desperate for money. If he were to become a gentleman of leisure he must have money, a great deal of it.

From this moment on, Berenson was hopelessly torn, vulnerable to the inner accusation and therefore irritably on the defensive to any shadow of suspicion coming from the outside world, bitterly aware that he had betrayed his truest self. A part of him would always blame Mary for encouraging him in that direction, just as he would always resent Isabella Stewart Gardner for seducing him into prostituting his poet's self. The fact that he owed her everything, including his gratitude, did not make it any easier.

Berenson does not mention in his autobiography (perhaps he had forgotten?) that, by the summer of 1895, the wrong turn had already been made. It had been taken, in fact, during that visit to the National Gallery the year before. It was then that he launched himself in the direction that would result in Fenway Court, the Isabella Stewart Gardner Museum in Boston. The idea of an art museum, however, was still a dream in the founder's mind when her "blind guide" (as he later termed such advisors) set himself the agreeable task of providing her with pictures worth looking at since, he told himself, there were barely a score of such in the United States. Whatever was bought would yield him a commission: 5 percent of the purchase price. He only wanted unique, beautiful, irreplaceable works. "My ambition now is to have done with all but the few great masterpieces of art, and in art as in life to meticulously keep away from the sordid, the second-rate, and pettily personal."

To acquire superb paintings was not quite as simple as he made it sound to Mrs. Gardner. The normal course would be to wait for such works to go on sale in London, Paris, Florence, and Rome. This process might, however, take years and Berenson was dealing, not with a state-supported museum willing to wait for a century, but with a capricious woman who might have changed her mind by next week. He must seize the initiative. In this respect he was at a decided advantage. As a scholar, compiling lists, he had come to know where the aces were and this, in the poker game of buying and selling art, counted for everything.

For his first target Berenson chose to approach the Earl of Ashburnham who, it was rumored, had some paintings to sell. He knew that the Earl's collection contained a panoramic study of *The Tragedy of Lucretia*, a story which Dante, Mrs. Gardner's particular love, had told, and that the painting was attributed to Botticelli (although some experts doubt whether it is by the master's hand alone). It was impressive—almost six feet wide by some three feet in depth—and although rather more illustrative of Botticelli's later fascination for architectural line than of his earlier, more engaging love of ravishing curves, it is still a handsome work, guaranteed to appeal to an owner's pride.

Berenson had an idea that the Earl might be willing to sell but he was not sure of this when he made his approach to Mrs. Gardner in August 1894. The first step was to determine whether she wanted the picture. Assured that she did, he somehow persuaded the Earl that he had a wealthy buyer prepared to pay American prices. He offered £3,000 ($15,000) and the Earl snapped it up. The painting arrived in Boston four months later. One assumes that Berenson received his first 5 percent commission: $750, or the exact sum which had kept him in Europe for a year in 1887.

Almost at once Berenson was besieging Mrs. Gardner with

other ideas. She wanted the Gainsborough *Blue Boy*—why not? There was a marvelous Bellini, worth any price. Berenson eagerly assured Mrs. Gardner that she could buy now and pay later; he could arrange everything. He almost bought her a rare Tintoretto, but her check arrived two weeks too late. Another wonderful Giotto Crucifixion slipped through his hands for the same reason.

He was soon signing himself "B.B." Occasionally he still talked about landscapes and books and clouds as beautiful as paintings and how he gazed at them in a daze of delight. These days, what he mostly talked about was money.

Berenson was assessing the market and also probing to find out how much Mrs. Gardner was willing to pay. Mrs. Gardner was cautious for another reason. If he wished to tell someone else about a painting at the same time, he need not bother to tell her at all, Mrs. Gardner said, evidently suspecting him of this and haughtily refusing to be placed in the position of competing buyer. If this had been Berenson's intention, he quickly renounced it. He did, however, guilelessly request that she let him know when some other "blind guide" had acquired a work she wanted.

They prowled around each other like sparring partners, unsure whether, as she wrote, to throw pillows at each other or ideas. She was eager, wistful, imperious, with a coquettish way of letting him know that she did not altogether trust him. Feeling this thread of doubt just beneath the surface, Berenson was hypersensitive to the slightest reproach, anxious to put his actions in the best possible light and never, for a moment, to turn his back.

They were well-matched and both knew it. Berenson knew, from past experience, how quickly a relationship with Mrs. Gardner could twist itself out of shape. His letters were judiciously phrased. Some nicely calculated compliments to himself—that he could build her an unrivaled collection of masterpieces—were interspersed with effusive praise for her daring, her taste, and her traits. He pandered to her voracious appetite for admiration, her competitiveness with the Boston Museum of Fine Arts, and her fantasy that she was a latter-day Queen of Sheba and he an adoring slave groveling at her feet. Evidence that such obsequious praise was cynically intended is contained in a letter in which Berenson explained to a friend he thought he was losing that, "I could promise, and flatter, and cajole, if I did not love you enough to take you in good earnest." Berenson could not love Mrs. Gardner—she had too much power over him—and the fact that he could manipulate her in this way made him secretly contemptuous.

In an unscrupulous attempt to ingratiate himself Berenson even invented the fiction that they had common Scottish ancestors. He knew, as did everyone else, that Isabella Stewart Gardner preened herself on being somehow related to Mary Stuart and Robert the Bruce. Berenson, on a trip to Scotland in 1896, fondly remarked how much more vivid and alive their ballads would seem to him now and, the following year, referred to their close relative, presumably Robert the Bruce as (he had been told) a rather unpleasant fellow. The fiction may have been motivated by an oblique attempt to place himself on a more equal footing with this Boston plutocrat by establishing their common aristocracy. However, since Berenson could not tell the truth, he was obliged to add one more flourish to a false self-portrait and contribute one more straw of guilt to the inner burden he was already carrying. Incredibly enough, Mrs. Gardner appeared to believe him.

Berenson was slowly winning her over. He knew it when she wrote enthusiastically, in the summer of 1896, about the fun they were both going to have with her museum. The audacious dream was becoming an eventuality in her mind (Fenway Court opened seven years later) and Berenson was collecting in earnest. He was sincerely ambitious for her museum and must have seen what a monument such a collection would be to his expertise, but more than his *amour-propre* was involved. He was becoming as excited by the challenge and delighted with the results as was his benefactor herself.

One of Berenson's first coups was perhaps his most famous buy for Mrs. Gardner: Titian's *The Rape of Europa*, for £20,000. The painting, based on a story by Ovid in which Jove, disguised as a bull, carries off an altogether willing maiden named Europa, had already been offered to the National Gallery in London for far less than the price Mrs. Gardner paid. But the subject was considered too risqué for that staid institution. It was a stroke of luck for Berenson, who made the painting even more attractive with the reminder that it had been intended as a gift for a Stuart, Charles I of England. It was only just that this masterpiece should revert to the Stewarts. The argument proved irresistible. Her own excitement upon its arrival was furthered by the gratifying effect that first sight of this masterpiece was having on others. A painter friend, she recorded ecstatically, burst into tears.

Other successes followed. A Rembrandt early self-portrait (£3,000), a famous Guardi, *The Riva degli Schiavoni*, a Velásquez portrait of Philip IV (£15,000), Van Dyck's *A Lady with a Rose*, Rembrandt's *A Lady and Gentleman in Black*, a portrait of the Earl of Arundel by Rubens, and a famous bust of Bindo Altoviti by Benvenuto Cellini were among his spectacular purchases.

To buy them took money as well as diplomacy and the evidence is that Berenson offered top prices. He angled for, and almost landed, the finest Velásquez in the world at the bait of £8,000, but at the last moment the fish skittishly refused to bite.

In later years, Berenson complained of Mrs. Gardner's miserly ways and held his head when he contemplated the wiles that had been necessary to persuade her to part with a single penny. This may have been true at the end of her collecting, with a lavish museum under construction and her fortune dwindling daily, but it cannot be said of the years before 1900. Anyone who, like her, was ready to pay at least £20,000 for Gainsborough's famous *Blue Boy* or £30,000 for Rembrandt's equally famous *The Mill* (neither offer was accepted) was prepared to spend handsomely.

Berenson took full advantage of that fact. In 1901 he offered, for instance, £11,000 for a *Portrait of a Man* by Dürer. Mrs. Gardner paid the bill. Others thought the price outrageously inflated. Dr. Bode of the Kaiser Friedrich Museum said that he had bought better Dürers for far less. But he echoed the general opinion that an American must expect to pay more for famous works, since there were so few Dürers on that side of the Atlantic, a factor which presumably placed the buyer in a poor bargaining position. Such was precisely Mrs. Gardner's position, for another reason: It was axiomatic, in the art market, that the size of the purse dictated the price to be paid.

Mrs. Gardner might have expected to pay a few hundred dollars for those minor masterpieces of the Italian Renaissance whose value was appreciated by scholars, including Berenson, but for which the Henry Doetsch and other sales had demonstrated a minimal market. An examination of the prices she paid for paintings in this category shows, however, that they began at a relatively handsome level and rose. A Cima da Conegliano Madonna was bought for Fenway Court for £500 and a portrait of *Isabella d'Este* by Polidoro Lanzani for £600. In 1900 a Giotto *Presentation of the Christ Child* which, it was said, had been bought by J. P. Richter for £80 from a man who had found it in a country house and bought it for £1, was sold to Mrs. Gardner for £1,500.

The painting which most delighted Berenson's aesthetic sensibilities, *St. George and the Dragon*, by Carlo Crivelli, was bought in 1897 for £3,500. An exquisite little Madonna by Pinturicchio, which Berenson thought an absolute gem, and which he had originally bought for himself from a small dealer, was resold to Mrs. Gardner in 1901 for £4,000—said to have been a handsome profit indeed.

There is a further example: two beautiful Pesellino panels, *The Seven Triumphs of Petrarch*. The original owner, a lady, had paid £100 each for them. Berenson went to see them in 1897 and admired them extravagantly. When the lady asked him how much he thought they were worth, Berenson did not hesitate. "Oh," he said airily, "I think they are quite as good as the . . . Panels which went for £8,000. Would you care to sell them for that?"

It was said, charitably in some circles, that Berenson was responsible for bringing the price of these rarities into an approximate correspondence with their real worth. There was no question that prices for such works were rising and that he himself was the victim of the vogue he had started. He complained to Mrs. Gardner in 1899 that a *St. George and the Dragon* ascribed to the Florentine painter Uccello, which he would not let her buy for £200, had just sold for £1,420. It was also being said, less charitably by those who presumably knew of Berenson's 5 percent commission that, "Berenson made a good thing out of Mrs. Gardner."

The Gardners first began to suspect precisely this in 1898, during the sale of a Raphael portrait of the sixteenth-century Italian nobleman Count Tommaso Inghirami, librarian to the Vatican and a familiar figure in the courts of three popes of the Renaissance. The count's portrait in the family castle at Volterra had, for many years, been the object of much speculation, since an identical portrait hung in the Pitti Palace. The Florentine museum officials naturally claimed to own the genuine Raphael, saying that the Inghirami family owned a copy. Since it was well-known that Italian families often had copies of their treasures painted as a keepsake at the time of a sale, the story seemed plausible. However, noble families had also been known to substitute the false for the genuine at the eleventh hour and the Inghirami family might well be guilty of such double-dealing.

Crowe and Cavalcaselle thought the Inghirami family was telling the truth and so did Morelli, although these experts also agreed that the painting was in indifferent condition and had been considerably overpainted. Berenson, convinced of its genuineness, offered the painting to Mrs. Gardner for £15,000 or $75,000.

Negotiations were proceeding well when a Florentine art dealer, Emilio Costantini, the apparent intermediary, contacted the Gardners directly and offered the same portrait for about $40,000. The Gardners sought Berenson's advice on whether they should not buy directly from Costantini. Berenson replied, a month later, that by good luck he had just managed to acquire the work for that price. He had happened to learn that the Inghirami family had tried to take out a loan in Siena for $40,000 and used this knowledge to beat them down. (There is a postscript to this tale. In the 1950s the Pitti Palace belatedly acknowledged that it owned a copy of a Raphael.)

The difference in price—$35,000—lodged itself in the mind of Mrs. Gardner's husband, a museum treasurer with, therefore, a close knowledge of market values. A second incident, in 1898, a few months later, added to his suspicions. Berenson offered Mrs. Gardner a Dürer portrait from the famous Czernin Collection for £12,000. Mrs. Gardner replied that she had already heard about the painting from friends in Paris and that a much lower price was being quoted. Berenson bowed out with the comment that the owners must be feeling a financial pinch and had lowered the price since his first contact with them. He politely hoped that her friend could buy the painting for less.

Perhaps Berenson's explanations sounded too much alike. The stage was set for a confrontation, and it came in the autumn of 1898. Mrs. Gardner wrote a sad little letter saying that people had been circulating ugly rumors about Berenson, which had reached her husband's ears. Gardner had again raised the issue of the Raphael and Dürer portraits and asserted that Berenson was inflating his prices. Mrs. Gardner hoped, more in sorrow than anger, that Berenson knew how many enemies he had. She did not add what she doubtless also hoped, that he would take the broad hint.

What reply Berenson made to all of this has not survived except in fragmentary form. Its tone of humble gratitude, along with some apparently convincing explanations, placated Isabella at least, and things returned to normal on the surface.

However, the matter was never satisfactorily resolved. She continued to haggle over differences of 1,000 lire and he to write testily of so-called agents who offered, for ridiculously small sums, paintings which they had no hope of actually buying.

The task of amassing a collection for Mrs. Gardner demonstrated that Berenson had all the shrewdness the game required, along with an uncanny ability to analyze and diagnose that was already highly developed. Matching his wits with those of dealers seemed to appeal to his love of intrigue and holding the trump card. He adopted the market's cloak-and-dagger aspects almost at once. No one must know for whom he was buying. He arranged in advance for the code word of acceptance that Mrs. Gardner was to send by cable whenever she wanted a particular painting.

Similarly, Berenson usually gave her little or no information on a painting, due to his suspiciousness of provenances in general and dislike of showing his hand in particular. One suspects that he also liked to demonstrate the triumph of the new method over archaic scholarship, of connoisseurship over conniving. When Mrs. Gardner insisted on knowing who the previous owner of a painting had been, Berenson reluctantly complied, with the curious comment that he was treating the seller as she herself would not wish to be treated.

Berenson learned not only the tortuous approach which would bring him on business terms with an Earl, but how to use the tactics of the Bond Street dealers against them. He began employing "scouts" to tell him the instant a good buy came on the London and Paris markets and began to talk about "double games," "syndicates," and "buying en bloc."

Except for the winter months, Berenson was constantly traveling to London, Paris, Rome, Frankfurt, Vienna, Amsterdam, and back again to Bond Street. In London he might start the day at 9:00 A.M. and end it at 1:00 the following morning. After a particularly exhausting set of negotiations was concluded successfully he complained that he was too worn out to celebrate.

He was cultivating anyone who might be remotely useful and was willing to put up with their boring company for years, even though he might never discover a single interesting tidbit of information. He even began to pronounce upon art with caution. In the summer of 1901, a Velásquez was being exhibited in London that he happened to know would soon be for sale. He was being besieged with demands for his opinion, he said, but was declaring that he did not know enough about Velásquez to have one. He had praised other paintings. In short, he had done everything in his power to discourage potential purchasers like the Rothschilds and the Berlin Museum so that Mrs. Gardner could buy the painting cheaply in a month's time.

The incident demonstrates that Berenson had mastered the most important ability which art dealing required, i.e., to make a convincing assertion while believing its reverse, to wear an impenetrable mask. In short, he was beginning to think of himself as a hell of a fellow and a power in the art world.

In 1898, Mrs. Gardner sent him a telegram asking him to go to the London dealer, Agnew's, to inspect a painting. He replied from Berlin that, even if he were in London, he would not be able to see the painting. The trouble was that he, Berenson, was considered too influential and dangerous. That firm would, as a result, prefer to lose Mrs. Gardner as a client rather than allow him on the premises.

What Berenson did not tell Mrs. Gardner was that Agnew's of Bond Street was in direct competition with Colnaghi's, and it was from Colnaghi's that Berenson bought paintings whenever they came on the London market. (He bought sixteen in all for her.) Berenson's contact there was Otto Gutekunst, a German-born connoisseur from a family of well-known auctioneers and himself a discriminating collector, who joined Colnaghi's in 1894. The two men became friendly, wrote to each other often (the correspondence was destroyed in the 1930s), and had a close business relationship. The Colnaghi records show that Berenson bought pictures from the company, sold pictures to them, and had a part interest in other pictures as well. He bought in his own name.

There is a persistent rumor that Berenson took a commission from Colnaghi's on paintings for which he found buyers, i.e., that he was being paid by the dealer as well as by Mrs. Gardner. John James Byam Shaw, a former director of P. & D. Colnaghi & Co., who had known Berenson since the 1930s, doubted that this was ever the case. "That is always considered a dishonorable thing," he said. In response to that same question, Sir Geoffrey Agnew, present head of the famous old firm, remarked, "We never paid Berenson a commission. I have always imagined that was why we never sold anything through him."

The rumor is perhaps based on the fact that Berenson did boycott Agnew's, at a time when it was selling Old Masters to wealthy collectors like H. G. Marquand of New York, Rodolphe

Kann of Paris, Cornelius Vanderbilt, and members of the Rothschild family, and for no apparent reason. Despite the possible
loss of valuable works for his client, Berenson continued to
belittle Agnew's to Mrs. Gardner. He also defended Colnaghi's
on several occasions when they displeased his benefactor and
continued to deal with them, despite her repeated commands.

It was from Otto Gutekunst that Berenson bought Mrs.
Gardner's famous *Rape of Europa*, and it was also from Gutekunst,
who had, in 1898, acquired a half-interest in the famous Hope
Collection of Dutch paintings, that Berenson was able to buy
three handsome additions for Fenway Court. Two of them were
Rembrandts: the famous portrait of *A Lady and Gentleman in
Black*, and *The Storm on the Sea of Galilee*; the third painting was an
interior scene by the seventeenth-century Dutch painter Gerard
Ter Borch. The total price was £30,000.

The sale was taking place just as Berenson was defending
himself against charges of overpricing, so he was particularly
anxious to strike a hard bargain. But he complained that, while
awaiting a reply from her, he had been bombarded with telegrams from the owners and, in the interim, the price shot up by
£3,000. He had wrestled it back down again, Berenson wrote, but
the effort had exhausted him.

A further aspect of dealing in Old Masters needed to be
learned, and that was the art of smuggling. As foreign millionaires
with a taste for Italian paintings moved into the market, the
Italian government began to impose belated export controls. The
millionaire buyers viewed the matter as a sporting proposition
and their ingenious solutions have been recorded: how one millionaire rolled canvases up and smuggled them out in the muffler
of his car, and how another concealed a small Old Master behind
a grandiose, recently painted portrait of himself.

Mrs. Gardner faced the same problem with the painting, *A
Head of Christ*, attributed to Giorgione, which she wanted to buy
from the Countess Loschi dal Veme of Vicenza in 1897. There
was some doubt whether the head was by Giorgione (Dr. Bode
gave the work to Giovanni Bellini) and Berenson tried to dis-
suade her, but the main problem seemed to be that the Italian
government was unlikely to let the painting be exported.

Mrs. Gardner was petulant, then furious. She blamed
Costantini, the dealer involved, who, she said, had promised to
deliver the work and then reneged. He had deliberately tricked
her into buying it. Meanwhile, Berenson was insisting that the

solution was to wait until her next trip to Italy and secrete the painting in the bottom of a trunk. He was willing to appear as the buyer and take the legal consequences, he wrote, even though these might be unpleasant. But he did not see how to smuggle the painting out in his one, modest, man's trunk. It would be much easier for her. Nevertheless, Berenson decided to solve the problem himself. He swaddled the *Head of Christ* up in a blanket and announced that friends had taken it safely to London. Perhaps the friend was Mary.

A Botticelli, *The Madonna and Child of the Eucharist*, required a similar sleight of hand; this time, Berenson did not have to arrange the matter himself. The painting was in demand since it was perhaps the last well-authenticated Botticelli for sale inside Italy, and a German emperor and a British group were bidding up the price. Mrs. Gardner proved the winner, at £13,500. Its owner, Prince Chigi, provided notice of the sale as required by law, but when the authorities arrived, the painting had been spirited away by Colnaghi's, the intermediary. The prince was taken to court. He escaped with a ludicrous fine.

In the meantime Berenson became adept at the art of making paintings disappear. When a series of new export laws was passed in Italy in 1902 Berenson complained that this would make it virtually impossible to buy any more paintings from that country. The law discriminated against the small collector like himself, who had invested his life savings in a few valuable works. The ritual of lamentation over, Berenson announced from London nine days later that his beautiful and rare Perugino *Madonna with Child and Bird in Hand* had left Italy and he was offering it to Mrs. Gardner for £4,500. (She declined.)

The brilliance of the collection at Fenway Court, that "wonderfully gathered and splendidly lodged" museum, as Henry James described it, has been established beyond question. Fenway Court is remarkable for its concentration of masterpieces, an eclectic mélange of rare jewels that is particularly strong in Italian Renaissance paintings. Since the fortune involved was relatively small and others, notably J. P. Morgan, were to spend much more to get far less, the credit for that culling of masterpieces belongs to Berenson, who chose over 60 of Fenway Court's 290 paintings. It is a monument to his skill, his enterprise, and his taste.

There were, nevetheless, a few errors of judgment, most due to inexperience. His inability to assess correctly the seriousness of the buyer was the reason why he believed that the Gainsborough portrait Mrs. Gardner wanted, the famous *Blue Boy,* was actually for sale. After offering £20,000 and then going as high as £30,000, Berenson had to concede that its owner did not intend to sell and had continued the flirtation out of curiosity.

A Titian portrait was the subject of another early miscalculation. The painting, reputed to be a portrait of Marie of Austria, daughter of Charles V and wife of Maximilian, with her daughter, was referred to him by Mrs. Gardner in 1896. She obviously wanted to buy it but Berenson suspected that the painting was not by Titian and therefore not worth the price.

Two months later, he allowed himself to be convinced that the portrait was by Titian, therefore worth its price tag of £10,000. He added, two weeks later, that the painting was in as good a condition as such works ever were and minimized its defects—discolored varnish and a few other unimportant matters.

In allowing his desire to please to get the upper hand, Berenson played false to his sense of scholarship and made an expensive mistake in the process. Almost at once, it was said that the painting had actually been bought from a private dealer in Rome who paid eighty francs for it, that Berenson himself pronounced it a Titian and sold it to Mrs. Gardner for a handsome sum, and that it was a fake. The rumor about Berenson's role is obviously unfounded but that the portrait was not by Titian, and in very poor condition as well, was soon believed. Eight years later Berenson refused to give it any attribution at all. The painting is now given to Alonzo Sánchez Coello, court painter to Philip II of Spain, and is not considered one of the jewels of Fenway Court.

There has been similar scholarly disagreement over a *Portrait of Michelangelo* by Sebastiano del Piombo.

The painting, Berenson wrote in 1899, was without doubt the only portrait of the Italian genius known to be authentic. Since it came from a well-known collection, that of George Vivian at Claverton, near Bath, and the price tag was a modest £700, Mrs. Gardner bought it.

Again, dissenting voices began to be heard. C. E. Norton declared that the drawing, which the sitter held in his hand, was by the less distinguished Florentine sculptor and painter Baccio Bandinelli, a contemporary of Michelangelo. Others with more faith in documentation than Berenson added that a similar portrait had been recorded, in an eighteenth-century Florentine publication, as being by Bandinelli himself. Philip Hendy, who made a detailed study of the Fenway Court attributions in 1931, traced the provenance of the painting and concluded that it had been considered a Bandinelli self-portrait until it reached the Vivian Collection. The price-enhancing notion that it was actually a portrait of Michelangelo took hold at that time. Long before the Hendy verdict was pronounced, Berenson told Mrs. Gardner that one could never be absolutely sure about portraits.

What he was ambitious to become, he told Mrs. Gardner, was the greatest living authority on Italian art. The statement is a significant indication that, in five years of art-market dealing, Berenson had abandoned hope of a phantasmal Goethian immortality in favor of the immediate rewards of position, fame, power, and money. Carl Snyder, the American sleuth, found indications everywhere that, by the winter of 1903–04, Berenson was indeed regarded as one of a handful of major authorities. Fenway Court had securely established his reputation.

Snyder also concluded that Berenson was someone one either liked or hated; there seemed to be no half measures. "No man has so many red-hot enemies—and good friends," he wrote. Part of the problem seemed to be self-made. Berenson appeared to disagree with every other expert in the field, and had an unpleasant way of belittling other men. His insistence that "he is the only one who really knows," was jarring.

It was also said that he was a hypocrite. Although posing as a disinterested scholar (his class report to Harvard in 1897 made no mention of any other activity), he was actually in the thick of the art market. He wore a false façade, in contrast to another expert on Italian painting, Langton Douglas, who had announced it honestly in the newspapers when he turned from pure scholarship to art dealing.

Berenson was undeniably conceited. When Snyder visited him in an attempt to persuade him to write for the book he and Jaccaci were preparing, "His feeling, as I understood it, was that he has developed a truly scientific method of judging pictures, and others who have not the advantages of this method stand in the same relation to him as, let us say, the astrologers of the days of Copernicus did to the discoverer of the true system of the heavens," Snyder explained to another art historian and friend of Berenson, Herbert Horne.

Berenson finally told Jaccaci that he would not write for their book because he and Mary were planning one of their own on the American collections. It seemed a reasonable explanation. However, Berenson threw up such a smoke screen of objections before revealing this that Jaccaci, who admired Berenson, knew his family, and had watched his spectacular rise from obscurity, had many reservations.

"I think," Jaccaci wrote, "that he is about the hardest person in the world to handle. . . . Now that you stumble against him, let me beg you pray . . . do not argue and do not talk pictures . . . because he is very sharp and would surely take advantage of the fact that you are not a connoisseur. . . ." While giving Berenson full credit for his accomplishments, Jaccaci's verdict on his personality was gloomy: "He is by nature arrogant, conceited and deceitful and his neurasthenia has made him more violently so."

Carl Snyder reported from London that he found the same negative verdict to be widespread. He quoted the remark of Claude Phillips, then art critic of the *Daily Telegraph* and considered "the cleanest man in London" because he gave his advice on paintings absolutely free. Phillips had said "that he never cared to meet Berenson, 'because he was a man . . . too much surrounded by an atmosphere of storm.' " But, Snyder added, "Phillips was the only man in England that Berenson had a good word for. . . ."

> It was whispered by Fry and consigned back to—Dell
> And Holmes on the subject will pleasantly dwell
> And B. B. at Boston
> Heard of the sell.

THE UNEASY
COMPROMISE

To suppose, as we all suppose, that we could be
rich and not behave as the rich behave, is like
supposing that we could drink all day and stay
sober.

—LOGAN PEARSALL SMITH, *Afterthoughts*

"**I** WAS STANDING on my head with the expectation of seeing Bernhard," Senda wrote to her family in the spring of
1900, four days after she had landed in Italy.

> I looked for him long before I could make out a dock—and
> when the dock heaved in sight every man I saw was that dear
> brother of ours. I got more and more nervous and at length . . . —
> we reached the dock—& Bernhard was not there!! . . . I was think-
> ing sadly of having to go to the hotel alone—when behold—he
> rushed into the station—and I in his arms.
> He is the same dear fellow—growing lovelier with the years. It
> makes the tears come to my eyes at the thought of his beautiful
> kindness to me—but I really can not speak of the thousand and one
> little things he has done for me to still make me feel I am in
> fairyland. I have already learned not to speak of things I like—for
> presto—I get them—or I am promised them—

Senda, at thirty-three, was unmarried and the most beautiful
of the sisters; with her brother's arresting cheekbones and the

same challenging, authoritative look in her eyes. At a garden party, where women wore straw boaters with elastic bands tied behind their buns and carried parasols, Senda was juggling lace and frills and poking uneasily at the large, floppy hat that was sliding off her luxuriant hair. But, in an everyday dress of some dark fabric with leg-o'-mutton sleeves and a single rose pinned to her bodice, or striding about in capes, she revealed her independence, her emphatic nature, and her innate if incoherent belief that a woman ought to amount to something.

Senda had been teaching gymnastics at Smith College for eight years. When she joined the faculty, an inarticulate instructor with a class of 400 girls, it was believed that physical exercise would damage the delicate female physique and the most that might be expected of young ladies, dressed in ruffled white muslin and skirts with trains, was a decorous stroll or a game of croquet. Senda strove energetically to change that view. The physical education curriculum at Smith was enlarged to include volleyball, archery, dancing, cricket, and hockey. Perhaps her greatest coup, and one which has earned her a modest niche in sports history, was her introduction of basketball as a girls' sport to America. Senda subsequently wrote the standard book of rules. By the turn of the century she was director of physical education at Smith, attended the faculty meetings, and walked in the processions, although she had no degree.

Bessie had followed in Senda's footsteps. She also graduated from the Boston Normal School of Gymnastics and went to Smith College under her sister, teaching dancing.

As the oldest girl, Senda had become surrogate mother to Abie, now twenty-seven and the very model of Edwardian manliness, Bessie, age twenty-one, tiny and deceptively fragile looking, and Rachel. At twenty, Rachel combined her mother's vivid charm with the father's irreverent intelligence. She had studied Greek and Latin and was a member of the Marlowe Club at the Girls' Latin School in Boston. Entering Smith College, her interest in Shakespeare led her to early triumph as an actress (she played the nurse in *Romeo and Juliet*). She had the reputation of a wit and her impersonations, said Eleanor Garrison, a fellow student, would make you roll on the floor.

Rachel and Abie had fought bitterly as children. Although seven years older, he was no match for her nimble tongue and, like her father and older brother, Rachel was equal to every occasion, with perhaps less malice and more humor. As she grew older Rachel gradually assumed the role of peacemaker. She was particularly upset by the constant battling between Abie and Father.

"Little Mother looked so much better," she wrote to Senda in the summer of 1903, "but I found Abie nagging at her about Father. I hate to worry you dearie—but I feel as if matters were reaching a crisis in regard to Abie and Father and the brunt of the blow naturally falls on Little Mother. I write you this because I *do* wish you'd write to Abie in whom the fault seems to me more glaring and tell him—for Mother's sake—to be decent to Father by ignoring him. Father can't open his lips without a scornful comment from Abie."

Senda must intervene, Rachel continued, because Rachel could not do it. "I haven't tact enough and force of character enough." What a shame it was, the whole business of Abie! He was so proud of them all really, but not enough "to make us reciprocally proud of him." Lingering faintly behind that remark was the hint of disappointments experienced, the unspoken regret they all felt because Abie couldn't be as cultured and successful as Bernhard was. "I hope you are as happy as you can't help being," Rachel wrote to Senda, teasingly, in that summer of 1900. "Abie would say to that, 'I give up—what's the answer?' "

Bernhard's importance in the family as firstborn male had been heightened by his successes. The immigrant Jewish culture had become one "utterly devoted to its sons." Parents, disappointed by their own meager inroads into their adopted society, transferred hopes to their male children. As the decades passed, dreams of collective fulfillment, the hope of centuries, narrowed to the more immediate goals of personal achievement. Bit by bit, they were all succumbing to the values of a materialistic society.

Hutchins Hapgood, an American journalist and writer who came to know the Berenson family before the turn of the century, may have been thinking of them when he observed, in *The Spirit of the Ghetto* (1902), that fathers were disappearing as figureheads, their traditional position of honor usurped by their sons. Acknowledged failures, fathers were expected to swallow their hurt feelings, applaud their son's successes, accept their lesser status, and try to forget the Jewish proverb that a father who accepted help from a son must mourn.

The position of the son was equally difficult. He dared not openly acknowledge these "nobodies," these "nothings," as the American society labeled the immigrants and as they came to assess themselves, particularly if he were socially ambitious. However, he could not ignore the oppressive burdens his father had carried. He owed his parents a heavy emotional debt.

"... in a real way the old people remain his conscience, the visible representatives of a moral and religious tradition by which the boy may regulate his inner life."

Berenson, the firstborn, temporized. While keeping his family origins a close secret, Berenson privately provided for them lavishly. Whatever inner feelings Alter and Abie may have harbored, it was the attitude of Eudice and the sisters that prevailed. The women praised, blessed, and adored, keeping Bernhard's memory verdant. The men were silent.

After Bernhard began to send his parents a regular monthly allowance, almost their first move was to leave 11 Minot Street (in 1896) for the sedate, middle-class environs of Roxbury, which were being favored by emerging Jewish families. A year or so later they moved again, to 39 Mellen Street, in the newly developed area of Dorchester, where middle-income houses were being built on rolling fields. Eudice could now afford some modest cleaning help about the house for the first time in her life.

The Little Mother had grown a bit stouter by 1900 but, her admiring son Abie declared, she was as nice as ever. "Hasn't she got a grand figure for a woman of her age," Abie wrote to Senda in June 1900. "If she had ... a few inches more in height, she would be a stunner."

Thanks to Bernhard's generosity, Rachel was attending Smith, the first girl in the family to go to college. Senda was spending summers in Europe, and when Abie, in some unnamed job in Providence, couldn't quite seem to find the right thing, Bernhard promised $10,000 to set him up in business.

The long, effusive travel diaries that Senda sent to her "dear children" at home document the first months of 1900. The turn of the century was a pivotal year. Its events illumine the changes that five years of undreamed-of prosperity had brought, not only in Berenson's style of living, but in the nebulous areas of his inner life.

On the surface the effect of success was to increase his cultivation of wealthy people, who had such freedom and must therefore live with more intensity. He liked their frivolous ways and the constant activity in their "coralline" world much more than he was prepared to admit. There was a further practical objective, since Berenson needed free access to their collections and buying whims. To mingle with society was tangible proof that he was accepted.

Skill in the marketplace had its price. It required him to turn a deaf ear to those idealistic inner protests with which he had observed the corrupting effects of wealth a few years before. At the same time, the transformation of the "Lithuanian ghetto prince" to an impeccable Edwardian aristocrat was receiving its finishing touches. His manners became even more polished, his charm ever more alluring, and his acts increasingly calculated. For Berenson, success had ushered in the era of the uneasy compromise.

Senda and Bernhard spent some weeks together in Florence and then drove to Rome, to a hotel perched on the Pincian Hills near the Medici Gardens.

Almost at once they plunged into a round of sightseeing. Berenson's favorite game with Senda, as with Mary, was The Surprise. He would lead her to some vista with her eyes closed to enjoy her reaction as she saw, for instance, the panorama of the Piazza del Populo in Siena spread out before her. "I have never seen anything to beat this!" she would write in rapture, or, "It is too beautiful, this place!" or, "But what can I say? Words fail me." Bernhard didn't seem to mind.

"B.B. is an angel—he really seems to like to show me things. He says I *feel* things so well!! *Now* what do you think!" she wrote. He kept such a pace that her neck stiffened from inspecting ceilings and her knees trembled from climbing stairs and her eyes grew glassy from staring at masterpieces. After a morning at the Accademia in Venice, she confided, "I get quite exhausted after two hours. There is nothing to take one's strength as enjoying pictures."

They also dived into the Roman social whirl. "We left cards at Mrs. McCreery with whom we were to dine in the evening. She lives in a new palace & *very* grand—I was a bit scared when we approached the gate and saw the porter in grand costume with a sort of major baton in his hand! We dined with her at half past eight (*such* an unearthly hour). . . ." The whole business of social calls was "too amusing." Senda confessed that she could not take it seriously.

> *Quite* an unforgettable day. The prince . . . has invited us to spend the day with him at his castle Duino—just outside of Trieste, Austria. . . . We took the train at seven o'clock and had a three-hour

journey to our destination. There horses were waiting for us—and before long the castle perched on the top of an immense rock overhanging the Adriatic came in sight. I never saw anything so wonderfully romantic as that place. We passed through three gates ... before we reached the court of the castle.

It is quite by itself, has a tower two *thousand* years old, of Roman times ... and it is so near the water— ... And the sea—such color! I thought I had already seen wonderful color in the sea—but *never* anything so marvellous—a liquid world of torquoise [*sic*] and violet and pearl. The princess and her sister came out to greet us— they were most cordial—and lead [*sic*] us to a terrace garden quite overhanging the sea—where we had a delicious breakfast. Then we spent the morning until two o'clock enjoying the castle. ... We exclaimed over everything until we were tired. But such a magnificent lunch was served us that our spirits soon revived. The princess is noted for her famous French chef—and she brings him from Vienna with her. ...

We had tea in the garden later on and I had the peculiar pleasure of meeting a white-haired most regal Austrian princess, who leaned back in her chair and smoked so large and thick and round a *cigar* that I was speechless for half an hour. ...

"I cannot tell you, dear kids," Senda wrote from Rome, "what a name your brother has— ... I fear people think him a 'snob'—for he happens to know so many great and titled people— but if one only knew how these people run after him—how renowned people come to see him even without letters of intro-duction—how 'society' people like him for himself—for he *is* brilliant—and all people court him—they would wonder how little it really counts with him. Society people amuse him—but his life is really that of a hard-working book maker." She concluded, "I never realized as now that he is really considered *the* living authority on painting!"

As one might expect, the Greatest Living Authority was looking at art. "We go to see the Layard collection of pictures in the afternoon," she wrote. "Sir Layard was a great lover of pictures and as Morelli advised him in his picture collecting—you may imagine how interesting they are—everyone is of mint— ... *À propos* of this collection it is told that a poor peasant brought a picture to Sir Layard who immediately saw it was a Carpaccio. ... The peasant of course was ignorant of its value and asked 50 francs. Sir Layard immediately said, 'I will give you 25'—and bought it! It can not be possible—for the picture could fetch

$50,000 easily—and he paid $5—to *think* of his beating the poor man down!"

Her brother was in great demand as an expertiser.

> . . . we all take the train for a small town. . . . A man had discovered that he had in his possession a wonderful Duccio—and wanted B.B. to see it. The news had evidently spread—for when we got off the train literally over a hundred people greeted us at the gate—and stood gaping while Mr. Perkins [Frederick Mason Perkins, an expert on Sienese painting] bargained with the cab man. . . . We walked to a small house—entered a room literally reeking with garlic—and there saw the wonderful picture.
>
> I really felt quite set up—for . . . I dared say that I thought the picture was of the school of Ambrogio Lorenzetti—and bless you, I was right! Well—the man asked a great price—B.B. shrugged his shoulders—Mr. Perkins looked wise but said nothing—and I was dying to get away from the garlic—so we all fled. . . . Our driver immediately asked us how much the man wanted for his picture and how much we offered. I was then told that the news within 10 minutes would reach even the gates of Siena that three millionaire Americans had come to purchase the wonderful picture—etc.—

As soon as they arrived in Venice Berenson went straight to the art dealers but had to report to Mrs. Gardner that there was nothing except the delightful little bagatelle of a painting whose photographs she had already been sent. While Bernhard was doing business, Senda was in ecstasy.

". . . what a world was opened to me as I ran to my window and saw the grand canal—broad and green and cool, with gondolas gliding silently yet gayly [*sic*] about—and such wonderful palaces. . . . We have an apartment in a palace [Palazzo Tiepolo, S. Toma] to ourselves . . . the first floor—on the grand canal. What a luxury it is to have these large, high rooms all to ourselves—our meals by ourselves, quite as if it were our home. B.B.—dear soul—has gone to the extravagance of hiring *two* gondoliers for the . . . month we shall be here."

They took a gondola trip to the Lido, along with the indispensable tea basket, so as to sip tea on the way while they read to each other aloud. Sometimes they were alone; at other times they might be joined by Flora Priestly, daughter of the chaplain at the English Church at Nice and a favorite subject of Sargent. She and her niece—"hang on every word B.B. says. Dear me—why isn't he absolutely spoiled?"

They had dinner with Prince Frédéric de Hohenlohe-Waldenburg in the Casetta Rossa, a tiny little jewel of a house on the Grand Canal so exquisitely accoutered in perfect eighteenth-century Venetian style that it was the only house that the Italian poet Gabriele d'Annunzio (who later rented it) did not further embellish. "Such a darling little bit of a house as he has," Senda wrote.

Senda taught Bernhard a new set of morning exercises, bought trinkets for all the family, and went for dress fittings in the afternoon. She had learned to forgo philosophical discussions with Bernhard, so likely to end in a fierce argument, just as she had accepted, with admirable resignation, those daily battles with the cabman that, for Bernhard, seemed *de rigueur*. But, when Bernhard fired the two gondoliers she protested, because one of them had eighteen children. The plight of children was always on her mind.

Earlier, they had encountered hordes of small beggars at Albano, running behind their carriage. "My heart melts, and I want to fling them money—but alas ... haven't a penny with me—and Bernhard doesn't look at a beggar with two feet. They have to have one foot or one arm ... before he will consider them at all."

Senda lunched with contessas and took tea with marchesas and dined with principessas and tried to look wise whenever the conversation shifted to French or Italian, which she did not speak. She also tried, dutifully, to like the society women she met. Her indignation at their idleness, however, sometimes got the better of her.

They celebrated Bernard's thirty-fifth birthday and she sympathized with his feelings of being played out and getting old, with so little time left for everything he wanted to do. "He really is a great personality," she wrote, "doomed to sadness because of wholesale misunderstanding by everybody but the very few good friends he has."

In mid-July they arrived at the Hotel Caspar Badrutt, Saint Moritz, the hotel to which Berenson had been making a yearly pilgrimage since the summer of 1897, when he had first arrived there with Senda. He was driven there by intolerable heat, he recalled, and found himself swept up in the Italian haut monde. In no time he was on friendly terms, he told Mrs. Gardner, with the

Colonnas, Pallavicini, Pasolinis, the Placcis, the Grazioli, and everyone who counted in Italy.

By the turn of the century Saint Moritz was an extremely fashionable Swiss resort for Americans as well as Italians, attracted by the cool temperatures, mineral water baths, known since the sixteenth century, and the glorious walks over the peaks of the High Engadine.

They had taken, Senda wrote, a three-room suite containing some rather dreadful plush furniture, but which could be made habitable with flowers, books, and photographs, and were not dining table d'hôte this time, but were sharing a table with Adelaide and Carlo Placci and the Marquesa Callabrini.

"The house is a bit upset today for Princess Pallavicini is expected and arrives in the evening—with her fat daughter Donna Bianca and her faithful tottering friend Conte Malatesta. *What* a team they are to be sure. The Princess has aged a good bit—and walks with difficulty—her daughter still has her two dogs—and her cigarettes—and is more laconic than ever."

The mornings were spent golfing and the afternoons taking "stiff climbs" with B.B. to mountains 7,500 feet above sea level where, with their remaining breath, they read scenes from *As You Like It* aloud. "We have tea there (all walks lead to a tea place) and with tired knees I reach home."

The leisurely pace was interrupted on July 30, six days after their arrival, by the news that Humbert I, King of Italy, had been assassinated at Monza the day before. The king, who had only reigned for two years, had inherited a strong antimonarchial opposition of republicans on the left and clericals on the right. His appointment of six military men to important government posts was violently resented by the republicans, who were responsible for his death.

"Our little hotel with so many distinguished Italians—is quite upset," she wrote.

Adelaide [Placci] greets me after breakfast with tears streaming down her face. . . . Carlo—who was a rabid socialist and is even now a great Popist—is greatly excited and groans with the crowd. . . .

At ten o'clock the faithful Marquesa Callabrini—fat and white-haired and gouty—a lady-in-waiting to the Queen and a great favorite of the King as well . . . began to pack immediately . . . and bravely starts for Monza. When we try to persuade her from going she says she sees no reason for accepting kindness from the King and Queen all her life and not being with them in trouble ... although we all think she is foolish we can not help admiring her. . . .

They chatted about the Vanderbilts, who had just arrived, and Mrs. Potter Palmer, and a certain Mrs. Shepherd, a rich American who had ruined all the servants by giving each of them fifty francs the moment she appeared. People came and went. The fascinating Duke Canasta was not staying at their hotel, "but is here so much that he considers [himself] one of us."

They gossiped about Alfred Dreyfus, the French officer who had been convicted of betraying his country but who Emile Zola claimed was innocent, and for whom Joseph Reinach, the brother of Bernhard's good friend Salomon, had campaigned so vigorously. Their efforts were successful; the French government had pardoned Dreyfus the year before and released him from prison.

Evidence that the Dreyfus Affair had not ended, in the minds of the French themselves, was provided during their stay at the Hotel Caspar Badrutt. The two French nephews of Placci, age seventeen and age nineteen, heard a rumor that someone named Dreyfus was in town. "A man by that name was registered at the Belvedere—and that was enough—they got all the French colony excited—they gathered in groups and gesticulated like mad—they thought of deep plots by which they could undo the 'damned traitor.' . . .

"And Adelaide spent the rest of the day—philanthropic—pious little goody-goody (I love her—too) by trying to convince me of the guilt of Dreyfus. I refused to speak of it to the boys—for if I did, I am sure I would never speak again," Senda wrote.

There they were, just like Isabella Stewart Gardner, in the midst of the crème de la crème, living the life of the idle rich. It was, for Bernhard, the summit of his social ambition. At last, he had arrived in that world of luxury and privilege whose advantages had impressed themselves on his mind ever since he had crossed the threshold of 152 Beacon Street.

But there were hidden threats to this eminence, won at the cost of so much energy and shrewdness, because the world they courted was so exclusive and so bigoted. Even so-called friends like the patrician Henry Adams might secretly condemn one on the basis of race alone and publish that one was "still reeking of the ghetto, snarling a weird Yiddish." They could never relax.

One spontaneous syllable, a single unguarded reference, a revelatory gesture, and the façade would collapse.

Take the two Placci nephews for instance, Senda wrote. They were such charming young men, so serious-minded, and with such elegant manners. Speaking of a young, very rich boy who had just arrived, the older said, " 'I don't want to meet him. Please don't introduce him.'

" 'Why?' said I.

"His face grew red with anger and hatred as he said, 'O, because he is a Jew!' And this boy . . . is one of the best. . . ."

ON THOSE EVENINGS IN VENICE when they all floated out toward the lagoons, observing the moon's iridescent wake and listening to the rhythmic plunge of the oars and the slap of the waves, the song that came quaveringly but clearly across the water was, "Vive l'Amour." The song was everywhere. A barge full of kindergarten children might heave into view and lilting childish voices proclaim the ascendance of love. At night, one could hear the rustle of laughter from floating palaces full of dancers and the faint strains of a violin playing the eternal and only theme that summer: "Vive l'Amour." How charming, how Italian, and how appropriate—since Bernhard and Mary had just decided to get married.

"I am ridiculously bashful about communicating it to anyone . . ." Berenson wrote to Mrs. Gardner in July 1900 from Promontogno. "I do not know why I am so. Perhaps it is that I had made up my mind to a continued bachelor existence. . . . She understands me and my needs and my interest as no other person, and I am sure she will try to make me happy. . . ."

Mary was a widow. Frank Costelloe had died in London in December 1899, at the age of forty-four. The event took everyone by surprise. The year before, Frank had run a race for Parliament and lost by only 187 votes. He was involved in dozens of liberal causes and had taken the girls to Belgium and France in the summer of 1899. But, in September, he complained of severe pains in one ear. A series of operations was performed and bone cancer discovered. In three months, Costelloe was dead.

There is no evidence that Mary had ever tried to resume her marriage with Frank. The decision for Berenson once taken, there was no turning back in her mind. However, relations continued to be cordial for a number of years. Frank was in constant touch with Hannah and Alys and quite willing to have his wife see her children. He seemed to have believed, against all evidence, that Mary would return. Then, in the final months of his life, Frank's position hardened. He refused to allow Mary to see the children in England in the summer of 1899. Writing to Alys, Hannah noted that Frank had only recently learned the true state of affairs in Florence.

In the ten years since Mary had left, Ray and Karin, living with their father at No. 41 Grosvenor Road, had spent the bulk of their time with their grandmother at No. 44, or "into Yours," as they said. They were so much her children that she might find herself signing a letter "Most lovingly thy mother," adding hastily, "I mean thy grandma."

Ray, now twelve, was nearly as tall as Hannah and would solicitously give Gram her arm to lean on now that Gram, age sixty-eight, was so troubled by rheumatism. To judge from Ray's account, the ten years had been exceptionally happy ones. The girls were delighted to see their mother and equally resigned to seeing her leave. From their Gram's point of view they were, as she never wearied of telling them, "angels of goodness," and as near perfection as girls could be.

It was comforting to have such unqualified approval in one's life, a "secure haven," particularly when one began to make forays into a cold outer world. Comforting, but not always comfortable. Ray and Karin, split between wanting to retain the familiar closeness of infancy and the independence of adolescence, used to joke about how they were always "just right." The phrase "came to mean, for us, being hopelessly in the wrong; but though we continually used it in this sense, we never discouraged her. . . ."

Hannah was so delightfully preoccupied with Ray and Karin that she hardly noticed it when Robert died in 1898. She took the news calmly, never knowing, because her three children generously provided her with an income, that Robert had effectively cut her out of his will.

Hannah did, however, discover the terms of Frank Costelloe's will and was indignant. Costelloe decreed that guardians should be appointed, the girls brought up as Catholics and sent to a convent. Hannah was ready for a battle, but the guardians capitulated without a fight. If she would agree to bring the girls up as Catholics, they could remain in her care. Early in 1900, the girls moved into "Yours."

"There is one thing which all this has accomplished," she wrote jubilantly, ". . . and that is that it has made me want to live! I feel as if I should be really needed for nine or ten more years, in order to make an English home for my grandchildren. . . ." Hannah continued to mother and adore and indulge her charges until 1911, when Karin, the younger, came of age. Then Hannah died.

The news of Mary's marriage unsettled Hannah, who worried that it might upset the hard-won custody agreement. Hannah was also convinced that Berenson would be transformed by the malevolent rites of marriage into that specter, The Husband. Logan and Alys argued successfully that this transformation only applied to the ordinary kind of lover and that, with "the tried companion, it would be different."

Logan continued, "Well anyhow, to-day mother seemed in the best of spirits—I have never seen her more full of jokes and I really cannot think that she is worrying about it. She . . . seems to intend being present at the ceremony. Convince her that B.B. really has money in solid investments!"

Mary wrote her first letter to Little Mother from Venice, that of a woman anxious to please. Bernhard was, she averred, the most fascinating man she had ever known. He had been an angel of kindness to her. He was, she declared, everything that was good, selfless, and noble. She would strive for his happiness and look after his health, since he was physically so fragile. Fortunately, she herself was strong.

To judge from his grudging little letter to Mrs. Gardner, the groom had decided misgivings. He was certainly relieved that, after years of dissembling, and being uncomfortably aware that they were being gossiped about, he could at last introduce Mary as his wife. Just the same, there is the mingled embarrassment and chagrin of a successful hunter who, after dreaming himself invincible, wakes up in the silken clutches of a triumphant partridge.

It was plain that Berenson was loath to give up the distance afforded by separate houses. People who were obliged to live apart and met only occasionally had an important compensation, that of intimacy. The "familiarity" of marriage acted as a narcotic, lulling to sleep that sense of mysteries unveiled and secrets confided that were the rewards of friendship at a distance. The essential charm of such moments was that they were fleeting.

"Did I marry for any reason more basic than that it was so much easier to drift along than to break and flounder about in search of another woman, or to hang around till another woman came and took me?" he wondered in 1950, at the age of eighty-five.

It is tempting to accept this explanation, but one suspects that more than simple inertia was involved. The best insights into his interpretation of the War Between the Sexes are contained in his review of Leo Tolstoy's books, written for *The Harvard Monthly*.

Discussing *Anna Karenina*, Berenson echoed the usual clichés. He asserted that love, for a womanly woman, satisfied every craving of her soul. However, for a "manly man," there was something deeply unsatisfactory about the bargain being struck.

"Most affairs of love have something in them of the compact between Faust and Mephistopheles. 'You serve me now assiduously,' the woman unconsciously is saying to the man, 'and I will return the favor hereafter.' " But, Berenson continued, "A man is not likely to be eaten up by a growing passion for a love that is assured him." He will return to his old carefree ways and the woman, sensing that his intellectual interests are her rivals, "will try to make [away] with them, and her attempts are bound to result at last in making her a bore and a burden."

Such arrogant chauvinism is a façade. Behind it is the outline of a son in the despairing thrall of smother-love. Passion is something that "eats one up"; similarly, the womanly woman will "drink up his soul." The unappeasable nature of her longing to merge completely with her lover, to cannibalize him, will end by his rejecting her. Although Berenson would like his readers to think that it is his superior sensibilities that have been offended, one recognizes here the fleeing silhouette of a man in fear of his life.

Given these deep inner doubts, why then did Berenson marry? There is the prosaic, if undeniable, fact that Mary was indispensable as secretary, librarian, filing clerk, and main picture scout. When Berenson was not in London, she went to the dealers and exhibitions, she sent the catalogues, and sometimes made the fateful decision to buy.

Would she please, Berenson wrote from Fiesole, go to Gutekunst and look at a Velásquez being considered for Mrs. Gardner? "I am very anxious that you should see it, as I do not like to deal in such big game without autopsy. . . . I should not ask you to do this, if I did not believe you as competent as any living person to have an opinion." That Berenson should think this highly of Mary is the sincerest compliment he could have given her.

There were other reasons having their origins in the subtle meshings and balances of their backgrounds and personalities. Mary was not Jewish. This was important, since she was therefore safely remote from any resemblance to mothers and sisters. Her impeccable social credentials were also important. So was the fact that she had an income of her own and was surrounded by some of the most intelligent men and women in England. She was grandly Junoesque, to compensate for his physical puniness, and had the bearing of a natural aristocrat.

Where Berenson tended to be emotionally inhibited, Mary was the reverse, blown with quixotic unpredictability by whatever impulse surfaced next. He could be capable of large generosities and small-scale stinginess; Mary tended toward the reverse. Berenson needed princely surroundings to bolster his self-image; Mary was perfectly happy in the dowdy comfort of an English country house. He imagined himself prey to a thousand ills; she optimistically believed herself incapable of sickness.

Even their inner contradictions bore uncanny resemblances; they mirrored each other. Berenson's male chauvinism might be expected, given his upbringing and the prejudices of his adopted class. He spoke contemptuously of women who tried to use their minds, and ridiculed their "half-masculine, half-hysterical aspirations." He praised the womanly women who "understand their business as females and know how to keep men." Even though he was prepared to forgive a very pretty, and silly, woman, he invariably picked, as friends and lovers, women of talent, intelligence, and accomplishment.

Mary, following Hannah's example, was an emphatic feminist. So was her sister Alys. Ray and Karin, combining marriage with careers, reflected to one extent or another the strong bias of their matriarchal upbringing. Yet the women in that family humored, babied, manipulated, and spoiled their men. Logan Pearsall Smith, as his friend Robert Gathorne-Hardy demonstrated, became monumentally selfish as a result.

In England, during World War II, "the three women in his household, Mrs. Russell, his sister, Mary, the cook, and Hammond, sacrificed themselves continually to him. If eggs came to the house, he had them all. Admirers from overseas sent him a steady succession of food parcels. Only leavings went to the others. He took these things as a right."

That, for Bernhard and Mary, the reality was at odds with the theoretical bias did not seem to occur to either.

Mary challenged and stimulated the intellectual in him, and flattered and indulged the spoiled child. She understood his unwillingness to share her with children, and never tried to have her daughters live with them (although, in later years, she was continually inviting her children and grandchildren. Berenson dreaded the visits). There were other ways in which they accommodated themselves to each other's crochets and quirks and, as he said, after ten years there were few surprises left. The slender evidence suggests that sex was never very satisfying and that, by 1900, it had ceased to be important. What was important was that they had successfully surmounted the dangerous quagmire of love and had arrived at the serene plateau of friendship. Given Berenson's fear of intimacy, one wonders whether he could have married under any other circumstances.

Meeting Mrs. Costelloe for the first time in 1900, Leo Stein was not impressed. In intelligence, she seemed a pale echo of Berenson, he told his sister Gertrude. Besides, she was well past her prime, a large and blowsy blonde of at least forty-five. (Mary was then thirty-six.)

Stein does Mary less than justice but, on one point, he was accurate. Mary was worried about her weight. She and her mother had been to Aix-les-Bains the summer before and, Hannah wrote, Mariechen had been "beguiled" into taking reducing exercises.

"The whole exercising is done by machinery, and . . . some of them are too funny for anything—such as little padded rollers revolving round and round the stomach, and little steel arms patting it all over. Then there are wriggling machines when she sits on a stool and her stomach and hips are wriggled about in the most absurd way." Bertie and Alys joined them, and then left with Mary to bicycle through Umbria.

Bicycling had become Berenson's passion. He had bought a machine early in 1898 and, as soon as he could look at his watch without wobbling, he was off on trips through forests and gorges to some mysterious ruined abbey, joking and talking of poetry and looking for pictures, with Mary and a crowd of friends. He would leave in the pale light of dawn, his pockets full of candles so that, when examining church frescoes inch by inch, he could light the dark corners.

He had moved that year to a suite of rooms on the second floor of 5 via Camerata, at San Domenico di Fiesole. It looked rather like a prison from the outside, according to Senda, but the rooms were exquisite. One room was green, furnished with old armchairs covered in mossy green. Its walls were covered with brown sacking and hung with all the green paintings that could be grouped together. Another room was red, the walls covered with a handsome damask of figured yellow on a red ground and furnished with his prize possession, a beautiful chest of tiny drawers. His bedroom was white and gold, his bed canopied with pale turquoise silk in the Louis XVI manner. Senda remarked, "It is for a fairy princess—not a man with a beard!"

Mary had taken rooms at Il Frullino, three doors away on the via Camerata, where she was frequently joined by Logan. He has left a charming description of that house in his diary. "I sit in the drawing room copying some beautiful lines of Milton. Someone was playing Mozart, there were sweet flowers, the sunshine and sweet air came in through the open window. It all impressed itself on me deliciously; the music and flowers and sweet air. . . ."

Almost effortlessly, Berenson had gathered a circle of friends around him. He was on intimate terms with the enigmatic and undemanding Countess Hortense Serristori and gossiped with his neighbor, the Countess Rasponi, and her twenty-year-old daughter, Rezia. He was visited by Frau Cosima Wagner, widow of the famous composer, who seemed to him as majestic as a work of art. Berenson talked art with Don Guido Cagnola, an aristocrat with an erudite interest in the Renaissance, and politics with the amiable Carlo Placci, through whom he met Gaetano Salvemini, who was to become famous for his opposition to Mussolini. Berenson argued with Vernon Lee and visited Janet Ross at her villa, Poggio Gherardo, where Boccaccio had begun to write the *Decameron*. Mrs. Ross adored Mary. She "used to say she was like a *rayon de soleil* when she entered the room."

Whenever Berenson traveled, the promising young critic Frederick Mason Perkins was among those invariably invited. Berenson liked to say that he had found Perkins on the streets of Siena, starving, and was apparently helping him financially. Senda wrote, "He is an interesting youth—just 26—an American who spent most of his life, until he was 16, with the Jesuits in Japan. . . . He is a musician—but gave music up to trail near the skirts of Art."

Another traveling companion was Lina Duff-Gordon, a young Scotswoman with the ethereal beauty of a Burne-Jones, who had come to live with her aunt, Mrs. Ross, some years before, after her mother died. Now, she was writing a book about

Assisi. Friendship with B.B. was her entrée from the staid backwaters of life at Poggio Gherardo into a stimulating world. She was captivated by "his charm, and the individual interest he seemed to take in everyone, while I felt he noticed everything in the room and assessed us all."

B.B. was their organizer and focus. For his part, Berenson's restless search for new faces seemed motivated by a desire to find the perfect friend. Speaking of Herman Obrist, a German sculptor whom he had recently met, Berenson wrote to Mary that he was "not quite the friend of my dreams, the one who will be different from me, yet at least as sensitive and intelligent."

Robert Trevelyan, a young English poet, was a more promising candidate for the role of perfect friend. Berenson had met this classical scholar, whose bohemian life-style and beguiling preoccupation were already the subject for endless anecdotes, through Logan. Trevy had an enthusiasm that delighted Berenson, along with a commendable ability to tolerate difference in his friends. Even this patience was occasionally strained. On one of their many walking tours of Scotland, Berenson had insulted the reputation of Gladstone and Trevy threatened to throw Berenson over a cliff.

Berenson told another story about the same walking tour. "They were dining at an inn," Julian Trevelyan wrote, "and my father was holding forth about Greek tragedy. The maid brought in a haggis and handed it round for all the guests to take a bit. When it came to my father's turn, he was so engrossed in what he was saying, that he took the whole lot, and everybody gasped."

Trevy is here, Logan wrote to Alys from Il Frullino, in the winter of 1898,

> and giving us one of the strange echoes or reports of his that always make the world seem so fantastic. . . [He] is a congenial addition— . . . and is becoming really wonderfully cultivated. . . . He has written some wonderfully charming things we all like very much.
>
> Just now, he is in a state of debate and cogitation, for we are going to take him over to the Gamberaia on Sunday and he has begun to show a faint dim sense that there are such things as conventions—It takes the form of a vague wonder whether, if you are going to call on a Princess, you ought to have your hair cut first.

Herbert Horne, an English art historian living in Florence, who sold paintings in a genteel way and was becoming a particular expert on Botticelli and the Florentine School, was perhaps a less likely candidate as perfect friend. "You will imagine to yourself one of the most ladylike gentlemen in the world, and really ever so nice a chap," Carl Snyder wrote to Jaccaci after meeting Horne.

Lina Duff-Gordon remembered Horne's rigidities—he changed his clothes according to the calendar, rather than the weather—and his unwillingness to venture an opinion. "The nearest he ever got to committing himself was when B.B. asked him in Siena if he liked the Sienese primitives and he answered, 'I should not like to have many of them.'" Similarly, B.B. grumbled (to Trevy) that Horne was far too fond of whipping out a notebook whenever he, B.B., began to expostulate, instead of seeing things with his own eyes. If not an ideal friend, Horne was "always endurable, which in dearth of better things is something in a travelling companion."

They went by train and ancient landaus to remote villages in the pursuit of art, ignoring the occasional fleas in hotel rooms and the eternal mosquitoes. As always on such trips, Berenson was indefatigable, good-humored, contagiously enthusiastic, and rarely angry. On one of their visits to Assisi, Lina Duff-Gordon discovered a beautiful fresco painted on a wall over a woodshed and hidden in a yard. In order to see it the party trooped into an adjoining nunnery and stood on chairs.

Logan Pearsall Smith wrote in his diary, "Soon we saw the towers of . . . our next town and, looking up, as we climbed the hill we could see the straight shadowy street leading to the church steps and sunny church. Here we lunched on simple, delicious things; figs, white cheese and salad, and then started out to explore, as we always explore, in all these towns, the churches, with the lovely, almost unknown pictures."

Logan continued,

> . . . Several people travelling together cannot avoid, of course, occasions of annoyance. . . . Bernhard especially was quick-tempered, and apt to be much put out if anyone was unpunctual. But this afternoon he was late in starting for the train. We had 18 miles to drive in order to catch the only train there was that afternoon; if we missed it, we should have no place, unless we returned the 18 miles, to spend the night. The carriage was ready; my sister and I sat in it, self-righteous, indignant, counting the culpable minutes with vindictive pleasure—at last Berenson and Herbert Horne appeared, sauntering along. "You are late"—"Not at all, not by my watch." "Well," I said with furious calm, "if we miss the train, it doesn't

matter" and although the discomfort would have been immense, I longed that we might miss it.

The Berenson–Logan Pearsall Smith relationship, precariously balanced between liking and loathing, was nevertheless a fruitful collaboration. Logan had been in leisurely preparation for a literary career for several years. He had published *The Youth of Parnassus*, a book of short stories, in 1895, and was to become well-known, with the publication of several anthologies, as a miniaturist of exquisite sensibility. Berenson was constantly in his company ("We potter and curse and bicycle and abuse our friends," Logan wrote) and was aware that they had common goals, idols, and ideals. Their conversations led to the creation of a new magazine, *The Golden Urn*, which they, along with Mary, wrote and had privately printed.

The magazine was dedicated to the cult of perfection. There were lists of "sacred" pictures, which had been elevated to the status of icons by virtue of their beauty, and which had become the nucleus for the first Lists. There were "perfect" cullings from the Bible and "perfect" quotations from Shakespeare, Milton, and Keats. Such exclusiveness doomed the magazine to a short life and it was discontinued after three issues. It is important only for an essay, in 1898, on "Altamura."

This essay, written by Logan but, Berenson insisted, on the basis of his ideas, developed the philosophic concepts expounded in *Marius the Epicurean*. Since Marius had lost the religion of his childhood, and with it any hope for survival after death, he must therefore make himself the measure of all things and place his faith upon what could be experienced subjectively in the present. Pater called that "healthfully sensuous wisdom." He was to be saved from hedonism by an innate sense of moderation in all things, including his tastes. His path toward insight would be that of culture.

"From that maxim of *Life as the end of Life*, followed, as a practical consequence, the desirableness of refining all the instruments of inward and outward intuition, of developing all their capacities, of testing and exercising one's self in them, till one's whole nature became one complex medium of reception, towards . . . the 'beatific vision' . . . of our actual experience in the world."

Berenson's manifesto for Altamura is based upon Pater's beatific vision. What was to be worshiped, in this remote monastery of "wealth and disillusion," was life itself, "life in its beauty and essence." It was a stylized society with a formal approach. Each month was devoted to an eternal theme, upon which Altamurans were to meditate. Since the year began in March for Altamurans, that month was dedicated to the God of the Deists, the moralists, and gnomic poets. In April, they contemplated youth in its springtime innocence.

May was sacred to lovers and June to the great achievers of the world, although the essay makes clear that, for Altamurans, virtue did not lie in emulating men of action but in contemplating the force they personified. In July, they celebrated the rich life. A few visiting monarchs were then allowed to enter the select cloisters of Altamura and "the tables are loaded with plate of gold. . . ."

August was given to the praise of pastoral beauty, September to elegiac regret, and October to a tempered hedonism—"not the young joy of fresh heart and senses, but the mature acceptance of what life has to give." In November they examined the inevitability of decay, in December, human brotherhood; in January, they evoked a golden world of art. The year ended in February with a study of religion and metaphysics.

Such a select group was much to be envied, Logan concluded. Since Altamurans had been liberated from love of the temporal and fear of death, they were free to see the enduring truths. They remained untainted by the clamor of worldly affairs and, in fact, had no contact with the world at all, except through the "hope that, by devout enjoyment, the burden of the world's joylessness can in some degree be lightened." The transparent emptiness of such a hope makes clear the obvious shortcomings and spiritual sterility of such a doctrine.

Nevertheless the religious parallels are so insistently drawn that one is forced to conclude that, for Berenson, Altamuran monasticism had become the new religion. His late-Victorian ideal of the scholar-poet, sober of mien and monkishly meditative of aspect, secure in his sanctuary, was a declaration meant for himself. It was an inner vow that he could somehow keep sordid reality at a safe distance, that he would remain true to the dreams of his youth, so beautifully stated in Pater's aesthetic, and the *Dahin*-ness of Goethe's poem. That such a dream become bricks and stone therefore had profound symbolic importance for him.

Scarcely had the concept of Altamura been defined and published, in the summer of 1898, than Berenson found the perfect site. It was a sixteenth-century villa, semiderelict, standing on a promontory, with a superlative view of the Arno almost as far as Aruzzo and Pisa, and surrounded by a thicket of cypresses and pines. Its aloof aspect, at once secluded and commanding, appealed to him at once. How he yearned, he told Mrs. Gardner, to bring it back to radiant life, plant flowers in its deserted garden and retreat to its exquisite solitude of stones and trees—with nothing but the wind to break the stillness—and contemplate the eternal poets.

Then, in the summer of 1900, Bernhard and Mary had to choose between renewing their leases on the separate villas or taking a house in common. The decision was made to marry and it was discovered that "i Tatti" was for rent. A lease was secured and repairs begun at once.

The villa overlooked the village of Ponte a Mensola, to the east of Florence. It was on the road to Settignano and in a distinguished literary ambiance: Boccaccio, John Addington Symonds, Mark Twain, and Gabriele d'Annunzio all were associated with the area. The house, a rectangular, three-storied, and classically simple building with gardens, was not pretentious by Florentine standards. Best of all, it was fragrant in spring with the smell of lemon trees. It was built in the sixteenth century as the modest home of the Alessandri family of Florence and its name, "i Tatti," is probably derived from the fact that the land on which it stands was given, three centuries before, to the Zatti family. The property was extensive. It contained vineyards and olive orchards, outbuildings, two or three small villas (villinos), and seven farms worked by peasant families.

One finds curious resemblances between the drawing rooms, hallways, dining room, and study of "i Tatti," and those interiors Mrs. Gardner was designing for Fenway Court at the same moment. Here are the same uses of brocade as wall hangings to provide the background for paintings in gilt Gothic frames; here is statuary flanking carved stone chimneypieces; here are leather-covered, seventeenth-century Venetian chairs, studded oak *cassónes* (marriage chests), and oblong carved tables, candelabra, and precisely placed vases of white lilies. The impression is the same: a stolid and austere grandeur, a formal and intimidating perfection.

The rooms are, in fact, almost interchangeable; but given the effect which the first sight of Mrs. Gardner's surroundings had on the young Berenson this is not surprising. He had accompanied Mrs. Gardner on shopping trips in Venice and Florence to be sure of buying in harmony with her taste. When the essay on Altamura was published Berenson urged Mrs. Gardner to read it because, he said, she was the only person in the world capable of actually living it.

That fall before their marriage, Berenson, Mary, and Logan were visiting the famous old villas around Florence. Almost every day they drove up the narrow, winding lane redolent of cypress and the hot, odoriferous smell of pine, and through the gate into the walled enclave of "i Tatti." All day long there would be smells of paint, hammering, crashing, and clouds of dust. From the terrace one could see the mist-shrouded, floating waters of the Arno and, sometimes in the later afternoon, when the mellow sunlight fell against the clear, delicate ceilings, they would have a sudden vision of the way it was going to look. ". . . and the blue view floats in the windows of those white rooms. . . ."

Janet Ross gave Berenson a lucky ring to see him through his two weddings: a civil marriage on December 27 in the Palazzo Vecchio and a religious ceremony in their tiny, seventeenth-century chapel on the grounds of "i Tatti" two days later. The morning of the twenty-seventh Bernhard and Mary were on time, but the court was late. Two clerks with their noses glued to paper wrote steadily for half an hour until the justice, with one cheek missing and a grotesque whistle for a voice, made his entrance in a dramatic sash of red, white, and green.

The religious ceremony was briefer and more agreeable. After Mass there was a wedding breakfast and a divine concert by Buonanicci. Logan was there. So was Hannah, serene and smiling, in a poke bonnet of black velvet, along with Ray and Karin. Everyone sat on the terrace after Mass and Mary's daughters crowned her with a garland of small oranges, instead of blossoms. Lina Duff-Gordon, another wedding guest, thought that in rather poor taste.

There was no honeymoon. They moved in at once and Mary began to explore some of the more obscure corners and to tackle three rooms full of caskets, trunks, and boxes. She had put all of B.B.'s possessions in apple-pie order, even to his ties, and he was at work preparing anthologies of his articles, a second volume of Lotto, and a major work, his book on the drawings of the Florentine painters. Mary began to have the occasional small lunch and dinner, with the help of a cook, but there were constant crises. First, the pipes in the house froze, then the well gave out, and, at the end of the winter, the heating system broke down. Herbert

Horne was designing a new façade for the lemon house and Mary was making plans to organize the chaotic garden into descending terraces, the first of grass and the remaining two of flowers, adding to the tulips, hyacinth, wild narcissus, sweet fresia, and pinks that were growing wild.

A Berenson family trip to England was being discussed for the summer but B.B. would not make definite plans. The problem, Mary told Senda, was that B.B. did not want his father to come, nor did he want to hurt his feelings; so he did nothing. Mary decided to intervene. If Senda would tell her exactly what to say, Mary would write the crucial letter herself. It would be ideal, Mary thought, if Mother and Bessie could spend a couple of months at Haslemere.

Mary had never felt healthier or more full of energy. Berenson, the poor boy from a Boston slum who had succeeded on his intelligence, energy, and wits, who, by the age of thirty-five, had made a fortune, acquired a handsome Italian estate, was being courted by European aristocracy, and had just made an eminently suitable marriage, should have been at the pinnacle of happiness. But his letters make almost no reference to his marriage or even his beautiful new house, and none to his state of mind. They focus on his health. He is tired, run-down, depressed. He does not know what. He must be overworked.

Berenson had been suffering from a strange malaise for several years. In the summer of 1896, after two years of concentrated buying, he had become ill, he told Barrett Wendell, and was recuperating with friends in the English countryside. He did not mention that his reason for being in London just then involved lengthy negotiations for Titian's *Marie of Austria* portrait.

A year later Berenson was still angling for the Titian portrait. *The Head of Christ* by Giorgione was another headache. The owner, Count Zileri, had taken advantage of a minor disagreement to withdraw from negotiations and Berenson was forced to swallow his wrath and pour on honeyed words, while feeling intensely humiliated. He was so desperately ill just then that the greatest specialist in Italy told him that his only hope was a Swiss rest cure.

By November of 1897 Lord Yarborough had decided not to sell his Holbein of the *Infant Edward* after all, and Berenson, in a desperate last-ditch attempt to regain his health, was undergoing three hours of massage a day.

The following year brought further crises. P. & D. Colnaghi had disobeyed Mrs. Gardner's express orders and she was making one of her periodic demands that Berenson stop dealing with them. He was involved with negotiations for another Holbein and felt in fragile health, perhaps because he had given up the daily massage.

A clue to his state of mind is contained in a letter to Mrs. Gardner in the spring of 1898. Berenson was ashamed of himself for being so apathetic. He felt strangely detached from life, as if he were a star, or a tree, or a cloud. He added, as if it were so obvious that it need hardly be mentioned, that he was tormented by the feeling that he had accomplished very little, yet, even so, that his best work was behind him.

In the summer of that year, Berenson was working sixteen hours a day as he plotted to acquire the Hope Collection paintings. In September the Gardners accused him of overcharging them. A month later, Berenson felt so low that he could hardly bring himself to do anything at all.

Neurasthenia, a disease first described in 1869, was a fashionable Edwardian complaint, and Berenson identified it as his own malady in 1901. Neurasthenia was characterized by feelings of persistent weakness, fatigue, and irritability. The sufferer felt depressed and had lost all interest in life. Often he could not sleep or eat. Rest was considered the only cure.

The term *neurasthenia* is no longer in use, since it is now believed that such symptoms have emotional origins. In Berenson's case, outer stresses caused the appearance of inner anxieties, which found their outlet in the self-torment of hypochondria, itself a mask for inadmissible emotions. Once in their grip, Berenson felt himself entitled to the utmost care since, in his eyes, he was in immediate danger of dying. Someone else must run his life while he recovered with a special diet and absolute freedom from care. Falling ill brought other benefits. It acted as a subtle and effective form of reproach.

In the winter of 1901, Mrs. Gardner fired off another salvo in her continuing battle with Colnaghi's. This time, the gallery had charged an entrance fee while exhibiting her Chigi Botticelli. Mrs. Gardner penned one of her most imperious letters and Berenson, in reply, reminded her that his health had been fragile for the last six or seven years and she must realize that the least angry word wounded a neurasthenic to the heart. So if Berenson seemed easily hurt, she must attribute it to his illness. For his part, he would be happy to die. He was too tactful to add that, in this event, she might blame herself.

The incident demonstrates that Berenson saw a relationship between his state of mind and recurring illness. He was, in fact, the victim of his own exorbitant demands upon himself. He had based his right to exist solely on his potential for accomplishment. That this was remarkable, he took for granted, but the moment he seemed likely not to achieve the impossible goals he had set for himself, he plunged into despair.

At such moments, Berenson's sense of dissatisfaction with himself was so all-pervasive that the anaesthetic of depression was the only solution. If he dared not vent his rage on Mrs. Gardner, his sole financial support, he could at least hate himself.

Berenson had his severest attack of neurasthenia shortly after his marriage and remained ill for the next two years. Uncharacteristically he would begin to lose things: his silver-topped bottle of mouthwash, two umbrellas, a nailbrush, his walking stick, or his luggage. Then he would become overwhelmed by fatigue and lose all interest in life. He would lounge about all day, unable to think or read, and lie awake all night. He would lose weight and accept injections of phosphorus, although these had no effect.

He was not in actual pain, he told Mrs. Gardner, but felt deadened and out of touch with himself. At the moment when he should have been reveling in his position of Greatest Living Authority, success had an ashen taste and even vindictive triumph eluded him. What a beautiful house "i Tatti" was, and how delicious the pine woods, and what a pity he was too ill to enjoy it.

"He needs something else," Mary told Senda. "I don't know what—a different childhood, I imagine."

Mary took a row house in London for the visit of Little Mother and Bessie to England; then they were all going to Haslemere. In London, B.B. and Mary took them to the Royal Academy where they dutifully found the contemporary painting "simply awful," and to the National Gallery, where they loved the Italian things. They went to the British Museum to hear a lecturer on art, George Zug, admiringly quote Berenson. They often went sightseeing with other friends because, "they are so rushed we see very little of them," Bessie wrote. B.B. looked "worn out," but was a perfect dear, and so was Mary. She came in one night just before going out to dinner, looking "simply stunning in a gorgeous black gown, low neck, and such lovely jewels."

When they arrived at High Buildings, Logan's handsome old house in Haslemere, there are hints that Bessie was becoming bored and Mary concluded that they were all too middle-aged for her. Little Mother was, however, blissfully content to be with her son who, for his part, was beginning to feel really ill. He slept constantly and his mother sat beside him, watching over him with utter happiness. Little Mother was even contemplating joining Mary and her daughters under the trees, where they slept every night. Learning of this nocturnal adventure, Don Guido Cagnola wrote to inquire why Mary used a bed and did not sleep in the branches like a bird. It would be deliciously cool, Cagnola observed, although "that old grumbler B.B." might not approve. Cagnola also wondered whether the balmy English climate had improved B.B.'s disposition.

Ray and Karin gave Berenson his first riding lessons on a white horse and ran alongside with encouraging shouts of, "See the proud Centaur!" At the suggestion of Little Mother, they decided to call him Uncle Bernhard. The four of them, Little Mother, Bessie, Mary, and Bernhard, posed for their portrait in a bucolic setting that summer of 1901. The resultant work is a tableau of family tension, as Strindberg might have dramatized it: Bessie, compositionally superfluous, simpering on the far right; Bernhard, nervously jingling small change in his pocket at far left; Mary leaning maternally over a wall, and in the stark center the impassive, black weight of Little Mother.

Being on such close terms with the hovering concern of Little Mother did nothing to improve Berenson's health. At the end of August he escaped to Saint Moritz, leaving Little Mother and Bessie behind in England. He was feeling so much worse, he wrote, that his mother and wife insisted he leave. Four days later he wrote to Senda that he had made a complete recovery.

In Oxford, where Mary had taken them to spend eight days alone, Little Mother was in tears. She felt utterly rejected. Mary appeared to suspect her of a martyr complex. What a pity it was that Little Mother made such problems for herself by her self-pity. There was another anguished scene the day Bessie and Little Mother sailed back to Boston. Mary saw them off and was so unnerved that she had to console herself with a large bowl of clam soup at Fuller's. Then she bought the girls an enormous walnut cake.

In Saint Moritz Berenson was seeing the old crowd and quarreling heatedly with his good friend Donna Laura Gropallo. Placci joked that they might as well be married. Meanwhile, Berenson asked insistently for the return of an umbrella, left on a visit to the Cagnolas. His host, to placate him, tried to replace it with one belonging to Placci. Learning of the plot, Placci was now sleeping with his umbrella clasped in his arms.

Like Cagnola and Placci, Mary was adopting a tone of jocular ridicule to tease Berenson out of his rages. Her determination to make light of things kept her in a sunny mood and often made all the difference to his young and impressionable visitors. When the young muralist, Allyn Cox, making his first visit to "i Tatti," told Mary that he was so afraid of Berenson that he wanted to crawl under the table, Mary gaily suggested that he do just that and, once there, that he give B.B.'s leg a good bite.

Mary's high spirits had no effect on Berenson's gloom, which was spreading to encompass everything: his life, his family, his house, his health, and his reason for being.

"I see now," he had written in the preface to *The Study and Criticism of Italian Art*, published that year, "how fruitless an interest is the history of art, and how worthless an undertaking is that of determining who painted, or carved, or built whatsoever it be. I see now how valueless all such matters are in the life of the spirit."

This realization, that he had completely lost interest in attributing works of art, the task to which he had so grandly dedicated his life in 1890, was not a new one. He had put it even more forcefully in a letter to the Michael Fields, five years before. "At bottom I no longer care a smart farthing who painted anything, and yea the archaeological, morphological, and even historical talk about pictures is like a wicked stench unto my almighty nostrils."

For the past five years, Berenson had been engaged in work that did not simply bore him, but that he found trivial and valueless and that smelled to high heaven, as far as he was concerned. So why had he continued despite everything? He must have known the answer.

ENHANCING LIFE

Perhaps the highest function of criticism is to tell
people why they like things.

—BERNARD BERENSON,
The Bernard Berenson Treasury

T HE ANCIENT TREE juts from the side of a slope some miles
north of Fiesole, near the valley leading to the Convent of
the Camaldoli. Its bark has the splintering rasp of flint, but its
scarred branches still thrust upward, bearing fruit. Its roots have
solidified into rock in their grip on the arid ground. They testify
to the blind strength of nature, its lavalike flow, its dark complexities.

Such a tree would not seem a particularly likely illustration of
nature's handiwork. The qualities it exemplifies, of weight, sub-
stance, and immobility, are the attributes of enduring things,
those of a force which, while it has asserted its blind power over
obstacles has also deformed itself into shapes that are more forbid-
ding than beautiful.

Yet this tree was, for Berenson, the focus of a pilgrimage. He
would drive up to the hills, catapulted around the erratic bends by
his chauffeur Parry, whose stubborn recklessness he had stoically
endured for half a century. Arriving at the tree, Berenson would
stand in rapt contemplation, his eye encompassing the lines of its
growth, its fixity, its relationship to the nice placement of farmhouses on the rising ground. Then he would bestow on its bark,
textured like the gnarled hand of age, his perfect and characteristic caress.

To say that Berenson found every manifestation of the natural world sublime, would imperfectly state the case. Rather, he went toward nature with an eye so rapturous and indiscriminating that everything, whether a root, a limb, a piece of bark, or a weed battered by the wind, had its own truth to impart. "How wonderful," he said musingly to Irene Worth, as they both stared into a fire, "how beautiful those flames are . . . and how much they have taught me about Botticelli."

Perhaps he was, as Rosamond Lehmann believed, not altogether human, an earth god, in his passionate appreciation of nature. Perhaps it was only that the beautiful first flowering of his responsive gift, tempered by years of training himself to really see, had led to an ability to perceive that thrust of nature with his whole being, to become one with the vision. The fact is that Berenson's theories of aesthetics originate in that childish impulse to make contact with that beauty and identify with it. "Contact is a desire for joining, love for the 'thing in itself,' of 'itness,' as I call it," he told Umberto Morra.

By the turn of the century Berenson, his reputation as an Authority made by Fenway Court, was also becoming known for his theories of aesthetics. In the books that followed his first, modest study of the Venetian painters in 1894: *The Florentine Painters of the Renaissance* (1896), *The Central Italian Painters of the Renaissance* (1897), and *The North Italian Painters of the Renaissance* (1907), these ideas were fully expounded. Although the core of Berenson's aesthetic is contained in the two books of 1896 and 1897, the four are usually considered as an ensemble, The Four Gospels, and were to bring him an international reputation. They are, in many ways, the most remarkable works he ever wrote.

Like the first book on the Venetians, Berenson's *Florentine Painters* takes the form of an essay followed by lists of paintings. His first theory concerns itself with the sense of touch. What is the particular magic of Giotto, unless it is that artist's ability to give his figures the illusion of dimension, and what is that quality that sympathetically comes into play in the viewer's mind, unless it is the illusion that we can touch his figures?

An artist's "first business, therefore, is to rouse the tactile sense, for I must have the illusion of being able to touch a figure . . . before I shall take it for granted as real. . . ." Berenson's irresistible impulse to touch became the basis for general conclusions about art. His term, "tactile values," became synonymous with his name and it was erroneously thought that he had named his house "i Tatti," after this first theoretical concept. He was also teased about it. Did she think, Salomon Reinach asked Mary, that her husband's theories about tactile values could be discussed with young girls?

Berenson continued that the effectiveness of a painting also depended upon its ability to arouse what he called "ideated sensations" in the viewer. It must evoke the illusion of movement, even bring the viewer to feel the same kinetic sensations. Speaking of Pollaiuolo's famous *Battle of the Nudes*, Berenson wrote, ". . . the pleasure we take in these savagely battling forms arises from their power to . . . heighten our sense of vitality. . . . The significance of all these muscular strains and pressures is so rendered that we cannot help realizing them. . . ."

The inner space of the painting must exert the same subtle power over the viewer, giving him the illusion that he can move, breathe, and have his being inside the work itself. Through such "ideated sensations," the viewer might make his own contact with a painting.

Such art must have, above all, a "life-enhancing" goal. The term came about after Edith Cooper, the younger member of the Michael Field writing team, used the term "enhance"; Berenson converted it to "life-enhancing." That expression, used to describe people as well as paintings, became a permanent part of Berenson's vocabulary, and has the ring of inevitability for one whose instinctive response to art was rapturous. His standards were Hellenistic. To him, the summit of human achievement was the Greek concept of the human form, and his criteria were those of the Golden Age: clarity, proportion, order, and harmony. That art might exert its power through its ability to evoke terror, primitive awe, fear, or disgust, was outside his philosophy. For Berenson, the beginning and end of art was Delight.

The emphasis in such theorizing is on the viewer. Technical mastery of color, form, and composition are taken for granted. What counts is how well the artist has communicated his message. This shift from object to viewer, or the subjective experience of art, is in marked contrast to the writings of Walter Pater, which, in *The Renaissance*, discuss the way in which a painting achieves greatness through the perfect fusion of subject and form.

Berenson's theories were derived in part from *The Problem of Form* (1893) by Adolf von Hildebrand, an analysis of the optical laws underlying a painting, which had a revolutionary effect on art criticism. They had most to do with the teachings of William James, the philosopher and psychologist whose lectures Berenson attended at Harvard. James rejected the notion that aesthetics could be "universal" or "objective" and taught that the aesthetic experience was private and subjective. To one who believed that the only way to make contact with a painting was to look at it directly: "A work of art is like women; *'il faut coucher avec'* " [One has to sleep with (it)], such an emphasis was long overdue.

James was, like other psychologists in the 1880s, including Dr. C. Lange of Copenhagen, advancing new theories about the bodily changes accompanying strong emotion, and even reached the conclusion that, without such changes, emotion was not possible. "We feel sorry because we cry, angry because we strike, afraid because we tremble."

"I owe everything to William James, for I was already applying his theories to the visible world. 'Tactile values' was really James's phrase, not mine, although he never knew he had invented it," Berenson said.

It was an idea whose moment had come. Other writers, notably Johannes Volkelt, in *Aesthetik des Tragischen* (1896), placed the same emphasis as Berenson did on the psychological and empirical. The Volkelt doctrine contains so many similarities that, "had I read Volkelt's 'Aesthetik,' . . . I should have had to acknowledge that he anticipated me," Berenson noted in *Rumor and Reflection* (1952).

Whatever their origins, Berenson's discussion of the psychology of aesthetic response was "the first, and remains the only demysticised aesthetic to command respect. . . . Compared to it, the 'plastic sequences' of Roger Fry and the 'significant form' of Mr. Clive Bell are pure mysticism—not to say incantation. And even the more respectable aesthetic theories of the past—for example those based on laws of proportion—end up in magic. . . ."

Berenson's writings make no reference to the subject matter of a work. A painting, whether of a Madonna, a Homeric legend, or a scene from the life of a saint, is treated in terms of its painterly values alone. In this respect, Berenson was in tune with his age and in revulsion against those mid-nineteenth-century tastes which had decreed that the only value of a painting was illustrative, and dependent upon its success in realizing a cliché or underlining a moral. In opposition to Ruskin, who taught that art must have an underlying moral purpose, Berenson was allying himself with the aestheticians who declared that form and color counted for everything. Whistler made his point clear by entitling his famous portrait of his mother as *Arrangement in Grey and Black No. 1.*

This emphasis on the nonillustrative elements of art was to lead, in the mid-twentieth century, to Abstract Expressionism. Illogically, Berenson detested the results of the doctrines he had espoused. He was in equal revolt against what became an inevitable swing of the pendulum in art history back toward a belated recognition of the importance of subject matter and the relation of the work to the times in which its creator lived. For Berenson, beginning from the vantage point of connoisseurship, these considerations were irrelevant. "The work of art," he wrote, "is the event."

It is inexplicable, but true, that this man, whose visual sensibilities were so finely honed, was born with no feeling for color. When he expounded his theories of aesthetics, color was a subordinate element. "In painting, color acts as form, in the chiaroscuro, in its passage from dark to light," he remarked to Umberto Morra in 1931. If one wanted pure color one should turn to the painted panels of the eighteenth century or lacquered carriages of the nineteenth, or the patterns of rugs.

Berenson changed that opinion one summer morning "tens of years later," in the nave of the upper church of St. Francis at Assisi, where he found himself "wrapped in an atmosphere of disembodied color." That moment of being bathed in color was so illuminating that he felt born to a new appreciation of this long-neglected element.

It is said that Berenson's writing, which shows traces of having been jerked and prodded into place by nimble fingers, had been emasculated by his wife, Mary, his brother-in-law Logan, and his friend Trevelyan. Because of their nit-picking, it is asserted, B.B.'s prose remained pedestrian and only rarely gave a hint of the passion behind it. Because Mary, Logan, and Trevy were so decidedly, perhaps arrogantly, sure of their mastery of style, they instilled such a complex in their writer that it took a heroic act of self-discipline for him to write at all. Or so he complained.

That Mary was a helpmeet in more than the routine chores of typing, filing, and taking notes, is clear from a letter Berenson wrote to Daniel Varney Thompson several decades later. In it he said that he was hard at work on a new book that seemed to say what he wanted; but now Mary was ripping it apart. She, poor invalid, apparently too ill for anything more mentally taxing than a card game or a detective novel, had seized on his words with as much energy as she unleashed upon them in her most vigorous years. Allowing for a certain ironic exaggeration, that is probably a fair description of the role Mary Berenson played in revising her husband's work.

One can only guess that Mary's contributions were an improvement, to judge from the tangled sentences one finds in Berenson's letters. It is equally likely that her revisions in no way obscured a native beauty of language. As has been noted, Berenson seemed deaf to the hidden music, the cadenced rise and fall, of an exquisite English sentence.

Yet, within their limits, Berenson's descriptions do give the reader a clear picture of the qualities he values. Berenson was a patient writer. He was willing to phrase and rephrase, and to present endless examples to demonstrate his points. His descriptions of artistic personalities are models of insight and his frames of reference far wider than those of his contemporaries. He once said that, until he discovered Italian art, he had been drawn to nineteenth-century French painting and considered that so promising that he predicted, in 1894, that we would soon dispense with the art of the past.

His writings frequently refer to such figures: "In spite of the exquisite modelling of Cézanne, who gives the sky its tactile values as Michelangelo has given them to the human figure, in spite of Monet's communication of the very pulse beat of the sun's warmth over the fields and trees, we are still waiting for a real art of landscape." The scope of his ideas, the fresh and vigorous theories of aesthetics—all were a revelation to his audience; and the fact that such ideas were simply expressed, in an area too often given, as Kenneth Clark notes, to mumbo-jumbo, added to their charm.

Art must, most of all, enhance life, Berenson wrote. From this original idea came a doctrine that eventually obsessed him, that art must have a civilizing influence. "No artifact is a work of art if it does not help to humanize us. Without art, visual, verbal and musical, our world would have remained a jungle." The visual arts must teach man how to behave, how to hold his body, look at the world, and the proper attitudes to take. All this would turn the ape into a civilized human being—eventually.

Such a grand and vaguely defined hope must owe something

to one of the early maxims Berenson adopted from Goethe: "To live resolutely in the good, the whole, the beautiful." "In my opinion," he told Morra, "if you begin investigating, you find the good at the root of the beautiful, just as you find the beautiful at the root of the good. ..." Leo Tolstoy made the same claim for the synonymity of the beautiful and good in *What is Art* (1896), in which he argued that good art fostered a feeling of unity and love, therefore furthering the kingdom of God on earth.

Another concept would have had an even more direct appeal on Berenson. This was the concept, expounded by Arthur Schopenhauer, that the essential aspect of the aesthetic experience was its ability to evoke a moment when the viewer became completely at one with the work.

Such a glimpse of Nirvana was the only one granted us in life, Schopenhauer argued. Through Delight, the viewer came to realize that the essential nature of Nature, and his own, were identical. As Byron wrote, "Are not the mountains, waves and skies a part/Of me and of my soul and I of them?"

This sense of identification with Art and Nature, terms which became interchangeable for Berenson, "eternity manifest in the light of day," was what he meant when he talked in lame terms of "IT-ness." At the moment when man's Will ceased to exist, he ceased to be at the mercy of his lower, animal self and those destructive passions responsible for the world's pain. This was the source of Berenson's belief that, through Art, man was somehow to be transformed from a beast into a human being.

One can also see why this doctrine took such a hold of Berenson's imagination, since it spoke directly to his deep inner longing to be free of the arrogant Will, the tyrannical "I," and to merge with the Ineffable. For a time, he had imagined that Catholicism would provide the escape. Disappointed, he took refuge in Art. He could not relinquish his longing, but he could appease it in those fleeting moments when he could merge ecstatically with the beautiful and good. At such moments he was "reconciled with life."

Berenson's theories were written as prefaces for the core of his work, lists of paintings by author and location that had begun with his volume on the Venetians. These Lists, the "whodunits" of Italian art, were revised and republished at intervals—the last appeared posthumously—and have provided the theoretical framework for much subsequent scholarship. "... on the whole our knowledge of who painted what in Renaissance art represents a solid, concrete advance, similar to an advance in chemistry or physics. Younger scholars take it for granted. . . ."

The Lists provided a structure that others could embellish, and altered the way in which certain artists have subsequently been viewed, sometimes radically. Like Pater, Berenson revered Giorgione but Botticelli, who is almost an afterthought in Pater's *The Renaissance*, is called "the greatest artist of linear design that Europe has ever had" by Berenson.

When Berenson turned to Italian art, the position of the Florentine fresco painter Domenico Ghirlandaio had been made secure by Crowe and Cavalcaselle, who considered him sublime. "Not a spark of genius," Berenson announced flatly. By contrast, the poetically beautiful work of Piero della Francesca seemed like a mere historical phenomenon to Crowe and Cavalcaselle and was not even mentioned by Ruskin. Berenson ranks him with Giotto and Masaccio as among the greatest artists of the fifteenth century.

It has already been noted that these early Lists made sharp inroads upon an inert mass of tradition. It has also been seen that their accuracy was uncanny. Berenson's book, *The Drawings of the Florentine Painters*, which was completed just as his Third Gospel (*The Central Italian Painters of the Renaissance*) went to print, and published six years later, is a model of precise scholarship whose judgments have survived unchallenged. Even before this book appeared, Berenson's position was assured. Discovering a supposed Antonello da Messina in Italy, Charles Ricketts noted in 1899 that it was "unmentioned by Baedeker Berenson."

Baedeker Berenson's most ambitious attempt was his decision to demonstrate the existence of certain anonymous artists on the basis of style alone. It was the kind of showmanship only a very confident performer would attempt, rather equivalent to a quadruple somersault from the high bar, and its audacious successes added further luster to his name. For example, Berenson might begin with a Nativity, now in the Fogg Museum of Art in Cambridge, whose author was unknown. The most that could be said for the painting was that it had been painted by a fourteenth-century Sienese. After a close study of the style, Berenson decided that the painter had begun as a pupil of Ugolino di Nerio and ended as a disciple of Pietro Lorenzetti, so he christened him "Ugolino Lorenzetti." A number of paintings in widely scattered collections have been tentatively ascribed to this Pirandellian figure.

Similarly, Berenson concluded that a number of designs for Florentine woodcut book illustrations of the late fifteenth century must all be by the same hand. The artist had studied with Domenico Ghirlandaio, Berenson decided, and called him "Alunno di Domenico." History has since demonstrated that Ghirlandaio had an assistant named Bartolommeo di Giovanni, the name by which "Alunno di Domenico" is now known.

However, Berenson's most ambitious artistic personality, "Amico di Sandro," was a failure. Berenson invented the name to identify a painter whose style reminded him of Botticelli, with aspects of Ghirlandaio and Filippino Lippi thrown in. A number of works in public and private collections were ascribed to this new artistic personality. "Amico di Sandro's" identity grew ever more secure, his market value soared, and private collectors bought on the gilt-edged guarantee of Berenson's connoisseurship.

Then Berenson began to have second thoughts. His mythical figure was not growing and maturing, as he had expected. On the contrary, "Amico di Sandro's" paintings displayed a consistent level of quality. When the 1931 Lists were published, "Amico di Sandro" had disappeared, his artistic personality dismantled and given back to Botticelli, Ghirlandaio, and Filippino Lippi. A similar fate was in store for "Polidoro Lanzani" and several others.

Berenson's mistakes look glaring only because he was so often right. When he was led astray it was often because of his refusal to consider any written evidence. He gave, for instance, a puzzling group of portraits, which had been ascribed to artists of such disparate styles as Holbein and Memling, to the Italian Alvise Vivarini. "Had he been less suspicious of names and documents," Kenneth Clark observed, "he would have found in Michiel's diary the name of Antonello's chief rival in the Veneto, Jacometto, and would no doubt have discovered the link which allows us to assign to him these otherwise unattributable portraits."

That the Lists began by naming only works that could be demonstrably shown to be authentic, and became radically more inclusive by 1932, is the subject for a later chapter. For the moment it is enough to note that they were full of booby traps.

Berenson often changed his mind, but this flexibility came into conflict with his need to appear omniscient at all costs, the ultimate arbiter. So Berenson temporized by publishing the new opinion without explanation.

"In some cases he silently concurred with tradition and the proposals of others; in other cases, he rejected these and placed the picture (without cross reference, of course) under the artist he believed correct. He might or might not have published this attribution before. In yet other cases he was the discoverer of the picture, had perhaps already launched it with his own attribution. (This in turn might win no acceptance from other scholars.) Hence the lists are dangerous ground for the unwary."

The terse pronouncements and apparently magical finality of the judgments inevitably added to the Berenson myth. Those who were simply trying to follow Berenson's labyrinthine trail found them exasperating. That a serious scholar should not provide footnotes was bad enough, but that he should show his judgments to be abrupt, arbitrary, and face-saving, made him some enemies.

The first casualty of Berenson's high-handedness was the writer Vernon Lee. Since Berenson misrepresented what happened, the actual sequence of events is worth considering.

Berenson, Vernon Lee, and Kit Anstruther-Thomson had been on close terms since late 1891. They met on his first trip to Florence in the spring of 1889. There was no further contact until Vernon Lee discovered Berenson studying the same painting in a Florentine gallery. From then on they took frequent trips to see art in Florence, Rome, and London. Vernon Lee visited the Velásquezes at Apsley House with "that little art critic who appears destined to be famous," as she wrote to her mother.

What seemed to develop between them was a lively sparring match of ideas. Berenson had harsh words for most women art historians. He seemed to believe, as Dr. Johnson did of women preachers, that they were "like a dog's walking on his hind legs. It is not done well; but you are surprised to find it done at all."

Vernon Lee, however, was respected for her intellect, since she was constantly asking questions about the nature of beauty and provoking Berenson to answer them. An established writer and a decade older than Berenson, she had been intrigued by the subject of aesthetics since adolescence, but had not yet written about it.

Vernon Lee and her friend had a theory that Andrea del Sarto had invented *plein air*. They would not look at Lotto and vastly preferred Rossetti to Manet. Berenson was thoroughly fed up with their "jabber"; none of it was worth remembering; it was just "sickening." It was, nevertheless, flattering that Vernon Lee was always ready to stop working to talk to him. Occasionally she even said something "worthy of me."

"I asked her had she not noticed how precocious had been all those painters who died young. 'Yes,' she said, 'otherwise we never should have heard of them.' "

He concluded, "She somehow makes you feel that she is intelligent."

Then, in the spring of 1896, Vernon Lee reviewed Berenson's *Florentine Painters of the Renaissance* for a magazine. The review was kindly and might even have been intended as a *volte-face* compliment, to repay Berenson for having reviewed her writings in *The Harvard Monthly*.

However, "Vernonia," as he called her, could not resist a short lecture. She thought the young writer had no particular literary gifts, but offered to give him some training. He needed to master a few rules of writing which she could teach in twenty minutes. Vernon Lee was equally condescending about his theories, which she thought lacked psychological insight, although she praised his scientific abilities. The tone, that of master assessing a pupil, was hardly calculated to appease one as ready to take offense as Berenson.

The gossip he heard rankled even more. Mary Costelloe, writing to Vernon Lee a year later, explained that Berenson began to hear reports from all sides that Lee and Thomson were dismissing his ideas and saying that they had the answers and would publish in due course.

In such an atmosphere, already poisoned by inner insecurities and gossip, the effect of Vernon Lee's first article on aesthetics was devastating. "Beauty and Ugliness," which she co-authored with Kit Anstruther-Thomson, was a discussion of theories that would, they believed, demonstrate how markedly they differed from Berenson. Unfortunately, the Lee-Thomson theories sounded exactly like the Berenson ones.

The Lee-Thomson aesthetic also took its point of departure from the James-Lange theory of emotions. Kit Anstruther-Thomson attempted to see whether this theory could be proved. She looked at a painting and was able to experience changes in breathing, sensations of muscular tension, and shifts in her body's equilibrium; all of which confirmed James's theories.

What, then, made a certain work of art pleasing or displeasing? Pleasing forms were those that awakened sensations of movement in the body and increased the vitality of the human organism. Ugly forms were those depriving us of an enhanced sense of life.

It seems extremely odd that Vernon Lee and Kit Anstruther-Thomson should have clung to the belief that their theories had nothing in common with those of their friend, traveling companion, and debating partner for the last five years. One can imagine Berenson's reactions when he read this article, which was to prove how superior their theories were to his own. He might have marveled at their myopia and dismissed them with the comforting thought that he had, after all, published first. Instead, he felt threatened. To take over such ideas and claim them was to rob him, he believed, of his most important achievement to date. So he wrote a letter. One can guess the extent of his anger by the insultingly polite way in which he suggested that they had plagiarized him.

Berenson wrote from Saint Moritz in the summer of 1897, "... Do you remember my sustaining [*sic*] that Miss Anstruther-Thomson was quite without a memory, while you opposed that she had a memory super-human, incapable of forgetting? I see from your paper that you were right. Her memory is indeed startling. I confess it inspires me with a certain awe; it is too much like conversing with a recording angel. ..." Berenson continued that he was delighted to meet so many familiar friends among the examples she had cited, made a veiled reference to an ethical conscience as the one hope for mankind, and concluded that their friends would be able to properly appreciate "the originality of your method. .."

Vernon Lee was not deceived by the ostensible politeness of Berenson's letter but addressed herself to its "sarcastic inuendo [*sic*]." He was accusing them, she wrote, of having stolen his ideas, and in plain terms such an accusation was slanderous. Although they might be looking at the same subject from the same direction they differed so markedly in their interpretation that she would not hold him responsible for the "wholesale robbery" of which he was accusing her.

Then Mary Costelloe insinuated herself into the argument. Mary wrote that Berenson did not want to think about the problem any more and had asked her to act for him. Vernon Lee must agree that it was much better for third parties to discuss the matter, since they could not be accused of having a stake. Her own involvement, she explained, was motivated by the realization that a friend had placed himself in an awkward position and, however much one might disagree with him, the least one could do was to help him get out of it.

Mary thought it reasonable to require proofs that the ideas had been stolen from Berenson's conversations. She proceeded to cite her journals to that effect. The evidence is inconclusive and not particularly revealing until Mary arrives at her main argument, which was that Vernon Lee was implying that Berenson's term, "life-enhancing," had been taken from her lectures at South Kensington in 1895. Since, however, Berenson had finished his manuscript by then, this could not be true.

If Vernon Lee privately believed Berenson to be an "ill-tempered and egoistic ass" (as she wrote to Carlo Placci some sixteen years later), she was beginning to think that she had risen somewhat too hastily to defend her friend who, at the time, had been too ill to defend herself. (Miss Anstruther-Thomson did not, as B.B claimed, flee to England in confusion.) Vernonia's letters become earnestly intent on demonstrating, from her own journals, that she had arrived at her views independently of Berenson. A letter in the Vernon Lee collection at Colby College, Maine, titled "Plagiarism" seems to be Lee's attempt to examine the arguments in her own defense. She asked herself whether the idea of psychology and the James-Lange theories were not in the air. It was outrageous for Berenson to act as if no one else might have opinions on the subject except himself.

Mary seemed to arrive at the same conclusion. She managed to wring an apology from Berenson and, in this particular case, Mary was able to effect a reconciliation between them, twenty-five years later.

Berenson, however, was never willing to concede that Vernon Lee's stimulating views on aesthetics ever helped him to formulate his own. He recalled to Morra (in 1931), "Vernon Lee thinks that I have a little secret key and that all I need to do is take it out of my pocket for her to see it and make use of it; a little key which, once possessed, would explain the mystery of all things."

This incident with Vernon Lee became the prototype for many subsequent disillusionments in the uncharted reefs of professional friendships that B.B. and Mary were to navigate together. The pattern was almost unvarying. First, enthusiasm, a delighted exploration of ideas, a burst of passionate meetings, confidences exchanged along with friends, and then second thoughts, qualifications, resentments, and corrosive suspicions. There would be a sudden flare-up and the former friends were in limbo; banished from the *unsereiners*.

The pattern was repeated with Herbert Horne. Horne is a paradoxical figure, an arid burrower among books, who supported a beautiful mistress. He was also a skilled art historian, an accomplished architect, and a book designer who produced a beautiful book on Botticelli.

The image of Horne as a scholarly introvert has tended to obscure the fact that he was modestly selling paintings as well as buying for his own collection (now in the Museo Horne in Florence) and had become a correspondingly shrewd observer of art-market dealings. He knew the history behind every painting Berenson sold to Mrs. Gardner and, since he had such a ringside seat at the amassing of this collection, he may have begun to suspect Berenson of making too much money at her expense.

Charles Loeser believed that Berenson had cultivated Horne only to absorb his impeccable scholarship and take advantage of it. Perhaps Horne began to share Loeser's opinion of Berenson's exploitive nature.

While regarding Horne with "distrust and absolute lack of confidence," B.B. and Mary were still in contact with him at the turn of the century. He was, they decided, a bona fide scholar and worth retaining as a professional acquaintance.

One does not know when even this gingerly contact ended but only that it did, and that there must have been no exchange between the two men for some years. Then, in 1916, Mary Berenson learned that Horne was ill, perhaps dying. She went to see him and found him anxious to be reconciled with his old enemy.

> . . . when B.B came, Horne held his hand & said he had been thinking of the old song—"The falling-out of faithful friends/ Renewal is of Love."
> Then B.B. said how much he regretted the coldness, for he had admired Horne's work & in the old days had loved him as a man, & that as they both had passions for the same things they ought to have been allies instead of enemies. Horne agreed to all this & said that B.B.'s visit had given him a few moments, in the midst of his

illness, of great pleasure & tranquility & peace. He was very tired
and lay awhile holding our hands, & then made B.B. promise to go
back & see him again.

In the night, he died. . . .

Loeser, the generous benefactor of Berenson's early years,
who made the first visit to the monastery of Monte Oliveto
Maggiore with him in 1890, who shared the same enthusiasms for
art, Morelli, and Harvard, had become, by the turn of the century, Berenson's foremost enemy.

Again, the reason for the enmity is unclear, but it was
mutual. Even by 1892, there seemed to be less warmth in
Berenson's affections. He complained to Mary that Loeser had
been hobnobbing with kings all over Europe and was telling
everyone about his friendships with Henry James and the painter
Bonnat. Such boasting was tedious and Berenson hoped to see
him as little as possible.

For his part, Loeser was keeping Berenson at arm's length.
"We come together often, but never to our mutual delight or
instruction," he wrote to a friend, Miriam S. Thayer, from Florence in 1895. "Our relations are a 'modus vivendi' which is at
least more useful than peace and less irksome than war."

Such careful comments gave way, by degrees, to active dislike. A year later they abandoned all effort to be friends, and, by
1900, Loeser was discussing Berenson with cheerful vigor as a
scoundrel of undeniable charm whose chief talent was his ability
to cajole information from others.

The men were doubtless in competition since Loeser, besides
collecting paintings for his Florentine villa, was also dealing in art.
Berenson felt the chill of rivalry for American dollars from his
personable compatriot. That he was also indebted to Loeser may
have placed him in a similar dilemma to that he faced with Mrs.
Gardner: duty bound to be grateful. Such a position breeds
rebellion.

Berenson, so alert to any challenge to his authority, so ready
to transform a friend into a foe, sometimes lost heart for the battle
once he had made himself emphatically clear. Mary was different.
Berenson noted, "Mary used to say she had to keep me from
meeting my worst enemies, because I was so completely the
victim of a present impression all my prejudices would vanish,
and all my defense. . . ." At such moments Berenson was charmingly ready to make amends.

In 1911, Mabel Dodge wrote to Gertrude Stein that she had driven to Saint Moritz for lunch with Loeser, when they happened to see Berenson on the sidewalk,

> who saw *us* but didn't catch sight of our companion! He hailed us & ran after the carriage, so Edwin & I tried to stop it & hop out in time to speak to him before he caught up to it & so avoid an unpleasant encounter! But the carriage was slow in stopping & B.B. swift in arriving & presently there he was at our carriage step directly in front of Loeser whom he *only then* noticed. I shivered for what would happen! To my amazement he pulled off his hat & put out his hand & said, "How are you Loeser," & they *shook hands*! Then we had some talk together—he all trembling & *quite pale*—& then drove off. "The first time in fifteen years," said Loeser meditatively! . . .

Mary was, in fact, mischievously delighted by B.B.'s battles, which appealed to her zest for intrigue. She seemed to share Logan's fondness for moral one-upmanship, and for telling "home truths." Lina Duff-Gordon observed that she could also be manipulative. With clandestine love affairs in particular, Mary was likely to fabricate situations for the pleasure of watching her puppets entangle themselves in her strings. " 'I want to be amuthed,' she would lisp. It was achieved sometimes at great cost to others."

The art-dealing world had split into camps for or against the Berensons. Among the members of the opposition was Sandford Arthur Strong, an Orientalist and art historian who was the target for more bitter words than almost anyone else. Again, one does not know why. Berenson's explanation, that the former curator of the Chatsworth Collection beguiled him into confiding all his ideas and then spread stories about him, seems incomplete. Mary always believed that Strong had never forgiven Berenson because his fiancée, Eugénie Sellars, broke her engagement to travel with the Berensons in Italy.

Miss Sellars, who eventually married Strong, found Berenson enchanting. Perhaps the affection was returned. They read Pliny together and she encouraged him to write about antique art, a notion he cherished for half a century afterward. To this *cherchez la femme* explanation of Mary's, one must add the possibility that the Englishman had criticized Berenson's possessiveness toward his own theories and discoveries. Years later, Berenson was still bitter about that. When Strong died of pernicious anemia in

Rome in 1903, Mary wrote, "That misshapen snake of a Strong is dead—Bernhard's worst enemy out of the way."

Another member of the opposition, Langton Douglas, was yet one more casualty in the subtle process by which friends were transformed into foes.

Again, Berenson at first welcomed this Anglican priest turned self-educated expert on Sienese art, invited him to make use of his photographic library, and gave him invaluable help in preparing his important study of Fra Angelico. Again, some unnamed incident turned the tables.

There is no doubt, however, that Douglas was also angling for wealthy American collectors and jockeying for position as Ultimate Authority. In 1903 Douglas, now making a study of Sassetta, was furious to learn that "his" discovery of a new painting by that artist was being bandied about by Berenson. Berenson, he told the British artist and critic Roger Fry indignantly, had stolen the discovery from him and was claiming it as his own. Nonsense, Mary Berenson wrote to Fry. B.B. had discovered it ages ago and it was sheer laziness that he had not published it. No doubt Perkins, who had been known to gossip, had leaked the news to Douglas. This must have been how Douglas found out, because he certainly never would have thought of it himself. Fry called such a controversy "the game of grab."

Douglas was also writing an article on Sassetta for the new *Burlington Magazine*, the brainchild of Fry, who, in 1903, was throwing his considerable energy and gifts toward shaping its course. In the same letter Mary transmitted the painful news that B.B. could not possibly appear in the same issue with Douglas and so would not be sending an article he planned.

Mary wrote, "The man should be driven out of Art, for which he has no talent, into historical work, editing etc. where he has real ability. He degrades the study of art, he makes the whole thing appear disgusting, and there is no use encouraging such a bounder. . . ." Mary blithely concluded, "he is, as you say, blind as a mole, and I may elegantly add, as furious as a poisoned rat."

Fry, in reply, argued that although Langton Douglas and Berenson were in opposite camps, the new magazine could not take sides. It should not be said that Berenson was capable of "political scheming to ring-fence Italian art." Much as he disliked Douglas, Fry considered him a serious scholar. What B.B. seemed to be saying was, "he is my enemy and I can't appear with him."

That, Fry thought, put things on a personal level and, "I think he descends to take it."

Berenson had known Fry for some years. They met through the Pearsall Smiths, since Fry's family were also prominent Quakers. Berenson had taken a benevolent interest in Fry's first book, an excellent study of Bellini, and was involved, financially and in matters of editorial policy, with the new magazine.

Fry was to discover that Langton Douglas was not the only man prepared to play "the game of grab." The matter began innocently enough when Fry took Berenson to see a collection of Italian art owned by Sir Hubert Parry of Highnam Court (now in the Courtauld Institute Galleries). Fry, with charming English diffidence, had ventured a few opinions. He was particularly anxious that Berenson pass judgment on a painting which Fry thought might be by Giotto. Berenson quickly amended it to "Pseudo-Giotto," i.e., one of Giotto's followers.

If at that point, Mary wrote severely, Roger had asked whether he might publish this as his own discovery, "B.B., who is really generous in such matters, would not only have agreed, but would have placed a wealth of information at your disposal." However, Fry had made the mistake of asking Berenson to co-author an article about the Parry Collection (making no exception for this particular painting) and Berenson agreed. Then Fry privately asked Horne's opinion about the Giotto. In the meantime, Fry sent photographs of all the Parry paintings except this one. The Berensons began to suspect a plot.

Mary wrote asking for the photograph. Fry was at last obliged to reveal that it had been sent to Horne and that Horne's opinion would be added to their article. Berenson took that as a personal affront and indignantly washed his hands of the matter.

Just as Hannah had defended her, Mary rushed to defend Berenson. It wasn't the matter of the attribution itself, she told Fry. Fry had handled him wrongly. Instead of being forthright and honest, as they trustingly believed, Fry had concealed information that Berenson had a right to know. They expected that from Horne—he was capable of anything—but coming from Fry, they were wounded to the quick.

Mary was looking for someone to punish and had pounced upon Fry. She went over the same ground for three more interminable letters, while Fry tried mightily to remain detached and friendly. He finally succeeded in calming her but, since Mary had tried so indefatigably to make Fry feel guilty, it would have been surprising if she had failed to arouse his resentment.

Berenson continued to write for the *Burlington Magazine* but his bid for editorial power failed. In order to vote in magazine affairs, Fry informed them, he would have to contribute £1,000. Temporarily discouraged, the Berensons made a second attempt when a new editor, C. J. Holmes, succeeded the first in 1907. This again failed and the matter ended.

Another friendship, which had begun so promisingly, dwindled to dislike. Fry had been disloyal and outrageous, Berenson wrote in his diaries. Fry had resented Berenson's authority on Bond Street "and had as good as declared war against me, if I did not leave London to him." In so saying Berenson conveniently forgot that Fry had left his early interest in the Italian Renaissance far behind, to become a painter himself and the leading champion of modern art in Britain. Of the book on Bellini that Fry published in 1899, Berenson once said, "Whatever is good in that book comes from me."

OUR DAILY IDEA

I was ... their offering to the strange new God;
I was to be the monument of their liberation from
the shame of being—what they were.

—ALFRED KAZIN, *A Walker in the City*

IN 1905 MAX BEERBOHM, already an accomplished caricaturist, dashed off a drawing on a visit to his friend Herbert Horne in Italy which the latter liked well enough to include in his archives. *Celestial Attributions* portrays a Virgin and Child in uncertain assessment of an anonymous painting. The object of their scrutiny bears a provisional label: "?Scuola di amico di Max," and, "?? Early venticento (sic)".

The Virgin comments, "That's a *very* doubtful Horne." The Child replies, "It seems to me rather as if it might be an early Berenson." The Virgin replies angrily, "Pooh! Nonsense! Bah! *Everything* points to its being a particularly late Loeser."

Besides aiming some artful barbs at the looking-glass world of art historians and their lunatic conclusions, the Beerbohm drawing attests to the position of eminence Berenson had achieved. No one in the art world dared ignore his opinion, however vulnerable a target he might be for some impish cartoonist. Berenson was complacently aware that his every move was the subject for speculation, even, or especially, when he wasn't there. Sibyl Colefax, who had traveled in Italy with Mary and B.B. some years before, and who was launched on her own career as a London hostess, followed his course with enthusiasm. "I doubt not that the American world like the rest is at the feet of B.B.!"

More than just teasing attention or uncritical admiration was involved in the response Berenson elicited. His exploits were becoming the raw material for fiction, as is shown by two short stories written about the same incident at almost the same moment, although the authors, one American and one French, were unaware of the coincidence.

The incident that inspired them centered around a baffling profile portrait of a girl, said to be by Leonardo da Vinci, which the famous critic Giovanni Morelli had owned but never allowed to be shown. In his will, Morelli did not leave the Leonardo with other paintings in his collection (which went to the Gallery of the Carrara Academy at Bergamo), but gave it to a friend, a certain Donna Laura Minghetti of Rome.

For years, the persistent rumor was that this was one of Leonardo's most beautiful paintings. Berenson managed to see it and, in the first flush of his enthusiasm for everything Morellian, declared himself enraptured. In his first Lists for the *Florentine Painters of the Renaissance* (1896), Berenson included the portrait under Leonardo's name, adding an "E" to indicate that it was an early work. He added, "(not quite finished)."

Berenson was not alone in his opinion. The critic J. P. Richter also called the work an early Leonardo and others praised it as one of the finest of his paintings.

Two years later, in 1898, the *Donna Laura Minghetti Leonardo* as it came to be known, was sold to the American collector Theodore Davis for 60,000 francs. In short order it was being said that the painting was a forgery and that an old Milanese restorer, Luigi Cavenaghi, knew the man who had painted it. In London, Richard Norton and Fairfax Murray said that Berenson had advised Davis to buy it, at a handsome profit to himself.

All of this was being indignantly denied by the Berensons and blame for the gossip given to the sinister Arthur Strong. Horne backed up Berenson's claim not to have been involved in the sale, asserting that Davis's advisor had been Richter.

Berenson, miserably aware how much trouble he had caused himself by his uncritical enthusiasm for Morelli, became convinced that the painting, if genuine, had been much overpainted by a modern forger, perhaps a certain Castagnolo who had recently died. Morelli must have known this, Berenson concluded, and this was why he had never exhibited the work and had not left it with his other paintings. It seemed obvious enough, but at the time, the painting's mysterious inaccessibility had only added to its allure and Berenson had succumbed to the myth, with everyone else.

When Davis died in 1915, the painting was not among those he left to the Metropolitan Museum of Art. It went to the Misses Janet and Mary Buttles and was seen, in 1963, in the New York apartment of Mrs. Paul de Schaeck. Its present whereabouts are unknown.

Those who knew the story relished the twist of fate by which a master of the scientific method had been bamboozled by a clever copyist. Or, had Morelli knowingly owned a fake? If he knew it, why did he allow everyone else, including his star pupil, to believe the reverse? The ironic possibilities of the plot were not lost on Frank Jewett Mather, who included the tale of "The Del Puente Giorgione" in his collection of short stories, *The Collectors*.

In Mather's version the narrator of the story was on his way to see a legendary early Giorgione which had been owned by the critic Mantovani and given to the Marquesa del Puente. She had sold it to a rich American and it was on exhibit in a New England museum. There were rumors that the painting was an inferior work, which the narrator brushed aside, since it had been praised by Mantovani's star pupil, a young Russian critic named Anitchkoff.

Once in front of the painting, the narrator was flabbergasted. "A slight inspection told all there was to tell. The paint was palpably modern; the surface would not have resisted a pin. . . . How could Mantovani have possessed such rubbish? How could Anitchkoff, enjoying the use of his eyes and mind, have credited it for a moment?"

The two men met for dinner and Anitchkoff explained that he did not see the painting until his mentor had died and he was invited to tea by the marquesa.

After the meal, as the light was fading, the marquesa conducted him up a winding staircase and into a room.

"The little octagon, a tower chamber I took it to be, was a prism of shadow enclosing a shaft of flying gold dust. Outside it must have been full sunset. Near the borderline of light and darkness," Anitchkoff saw the painting, which "swam in the twilight and became the most gracious that ever met my eyes." As a result of this enchanted and wholly misleading viewing, Anitchkoff wrote the praise he now bitterly regretted.

In his preface to *The Collectors*, Mather recorded that his account had been written in the winter of 1907. Paul Bourget wrote *La Dame Qui a Perdu son Peintre*, in August of 1906, but Mather did not know of it until 1911. Mather was thus careful to avoid a charge of plagiarism but his caution seems uncalled-for, since Bourget's ingenuity quickly transcended the limitations of the original plot to call into question the whole "science" of attribution.

In *The Lady Who Has Lost Her Painter*, Bourget told the story from the viewpoint of the man who painted the fake. His hero, Léon Monfrey, a distinguished French painter, went to visit an old count whose prize possession, a portrait by Leonardo, had just been downgraded by a young art critic, George Courmansel, who declared that the work was only by a talented pupil of Leonardo.

Another painting, which a relative of the old count had inherited, was for sale. It, too, was a portrait of a woman. Courmansel had attributed it to another of his inventions, "Amico d'Andrea Solario." Monfrey was taken to see it and was too amazed to utter a word. He found himself staring at one of his own paintings.

The portrait had been painted some twenty-five years before, while he was a poor student. An antique dealer offered him a handsome sum to fake a portrait in the style of Leonardo on an ancient piece of wood. Monfrey was in no position to refuse; but to assuage his conscience, he signed the panel with an abbreviation of "Pinxit Falsarius M . . . Parisiensis," meaning: "Monfrey, a Parisian and forger, painted this portrait." Monfrey sold the work and had not given it another thought until he found himself staring at it in a marchesa's drawing room.

Monfrey's immediate impulse to blurt out the truth was checked by the realization that to expose his fraud would be to ruin an engagement. An American collector was trying to buy the painting and so was a French collector whose daughter was engaged to marry Courmansel against her father's wishes. To expose the young critic would provide his fiancée's father with the excuse he needed to end the relationship. Monfrey, who had no great love for Courmansel, had been captivated by his fiancée. So the fateful moment passed.

However, when Monfrey learned that the owner was asking 50,000 francs for his fake, indignation triumphed over sentimentality. He went to the old count and told him what had happened, asking him to intercede so that the painting would be withdrawn, while protecting Courmansel from the humiliating truth. When approached, however, the owner was indignant. She preferred to think it a plot on the part of Courmansel and Monfrey to buy the painting themselves. So did the new owner, the American millionaire, when Monfrey went to present his case.

Monfrey reflected on the irony that the principals in the sale clung to a falsehood and rejected the less palatable truth. The comedy would be complete, he decided, if the critic also refused to believe him. Monfrey revealed everything to Courmansel except the fact that he himself had painted the portrait. Courmansel would not listen. Criticism had its own laws, he assured the painter, and one which was absolutely inviolable was that there was no such thing as an honest thief.

The one person who had instinctively divined the truth was Courmansel's young fiancée. She, however, feared its effect on her father. Monfrey capitulated. He assured her gallantly that the rumor that the painting was a fake was quite mistaken. His story, in the form of a long "letter" to Berenson's friend, the Countess Serristori, was signed, "Your useless servant."

Perhaps only the protagonists themselves could fully appreciate the elaborate twists of the plot. What is left for the reader is an adroit dramatization of the dangers of being emphatically sure of anything where paintings were concerned and the fact that the parties in a sale, buyer as well as seller and advisor, all have a vested interest in not having their assumptions questioned; the closed alliance against mankind about which the American critic Richard Offner was to write.

Artifice, in the story, has triumphed, and the genuine is dismissed. But behind the elegant irony, a young critic is getting his just deserts. The resemblance of Courmansel to Bourget's old friend Berenson was perhaps too obvious to bear mention and perhaps this is why Bourget chose not to refer to the original incident in his preface to the story.

The art world, Mary Berenson told Mrs. Gardner, was a clique of jealous, small-minded men and women. Berenson was detested for a number of reasons. In the first group were all the owners and buyers about whose optimistic attributions he had voiced doubts; in the second, all the collectors who had wanted the paintings he bought for Mrs. Gardner; in the third, all the dealers he was too scrupulous to deal with; and, finally, all the writers about Italian art who were envious of his success.

In similar letters to Roger Fry, Mary painted her husband and herself as innocents in a jungle, so badly treated that they were now quite resigned to it, and expected nothing better from Arthur Strong and Langton Douglas and Herbert Horne and Charles Loeser and the Austrian critic Franz Wickhoff and the German critic Hans Mackowsky, and even Frederick Mason Perkins. Fry, himself, and the German art historian George Gronau were the only honest men in "this accursed business."

Mary professed to consider the envy and enmity surrounding them a tribute to her husband's success. But B.B., she told Mrs. Gardner, was cut to the quick. He was often talking about dropping everything and settling in a remote corner of the American West.

In the summer of 1904, when B.B. and Mary had just returned from a winter spent traveling in America as far west as Chicago, and were in a nostalgic mood, full of America's promise, Berenson was telling everyone that America was the only place to be.

Berenson had also returned with a vague and splendid ambition. He intended to leave his precious collection of photographs and his rapidly growing library to his alma mater, Harvard University.

Weighing the respective merits of such contradictory aims was characteristic of him. Depending on the day, the weather, and his mood, he could announce his intention of emigrating at once, or his equal determination never to step foot outside "i Tatti" again, just as, a decade or so before, he had been seemingly torn by the dazzlingly different directions offered by his talents and interests. As before, words were at cross-purposes with his actions, which betrayed a fixed inner resolve. Having moved into "i Tatti," he clung to its rooms and gardens with tenacious single-mindedness for almost sixty years, and having once decided to make a great university his intellectual heir, that star set his course.

There was, therefore, never any real question of choosing. He had married and must earn a living, so as to support an impulsively generous wife, one accustomed to travel, servants, and entertaining; but that was the least of it. To perpetuate the Altamurean ideal would be to immortalize the pure, disinterested life of the scholar, selflessly dedicated to art, the great dream of life which Walter Pater had given poetic focus. A sanctuary of beauty, set against the world's sordid realities, would be the enduring proof that he had not "sold out." It symbolized his soul to himself.

Yet the irony was that to maintain this inner vision took a great deal of money. This monument of Altamura, born out of his intellect, sensibilities, energy, and wits, took, for a child who had been born poor, a continuing involvement in the very world he most feared and mistrusted. His determination to perpetuate that edifice guaranteed that he would never be free. He was caught in a dilemma of his own making, driven by circumstances he had unleashed.

It is perhaps no coincidence that one who had found a certain kind of solution in relegating his past to a small corner of his life, while adopting a new persona for the world, should again try to split his activities into corresponding divisions: the "real" world of the scholar, versus the hidden and covert world of the *marchand amateur*.

This attempt to maintain a truce between conflicting camps by keeping them distinctly separate accounts for that lifelong trait of his character of never discussing his business dealings (much less his origins), and of letting it appear that he was a gentleman of independent means. The same imperious need to keep warring factions at bay can be seen in a further trait of his character, which became marked: his insistence upon compartmentalizing his time.

At a certain moment, punctual to the second, he could be seen every day doing the same things in the same way. It gave him a marvelous mental discipline and an outlet for his agile brain, which required continual change, as long as it was predictably so. That the boxes became ever more locked, bolted, and fastened against the outside was his psyche's instinctive defense against an ever-present threat: the knowledge that such a solution, being artificial, was vulnerable to attack from within and without.

If people really knew how actively he was involved in art dealing, his whole façade of being a gentleman-aesthete would collapse. Berenson imagined that by maintaining a rigid silence he could hide that fact from the world, just as, earlier, he had thought that by cutting his links to the past, he could escape from it. Similarly, if he once allowed himself to examine the inner contradictions, the whole uneasy compromise might forever be destroyed, and with it whatever tenuous inner peace he still enjoyed. He dared not look at himself. Perhaps this explains a myopic refusal to see in himself those traits of character that he so freely denounced in others.

So there he was, imprisoned by the art market whether he willed it or not, inwardly vulnerable, constantly suspicious, and with his closest ally a tactless helper whose well-meant meddling and impulsive love of intrigue fed his doubts, kept old resentments evergreen, and added continuing evidence to an inner conviction that he was alone in a hostile world.

Isabella Stewart Gardner's collection was almost complete but that did not stop her advisor from showering her with new ideas several times a month. She was resisting them. Fenway Court had become an alarming drain on her purse and, in addition, her husband had died, leading her to conclude that only money was left to shield her from the world.

If Mrs. Gardner no longer needed him, Berenson must find a new source of income. He was speculating in the stock market and sometimes losing, as when he was obliged to borrow money from his mother-in-law in the summer of 1902.

Money was a constant worry, particularly since there was always some good cause in which it might be spent. He made no money at all in the winter of 1902, a situation exacerbated by the fact that he had sent $1,000 home and had promised a further $10,000 to Abie.

Mary was as warmly prepared to support her American family as was her husband, although her attitude toward money was much more relaxed; she had always had her own income. She didn't worry about being temporarily short, the way he did, telling him reassuringly that he was bound to make more. Their styles of life were based on differing needs.

"I don't quite know whether he means to be a great deal at Friday's Hill," she wrote to Senda of their plans for the summer of 1903. "It is quiet & comfortable for him there, but his presence makes life about twice as expensive—strange effect of one small man! We are content with a quiet, country way of life, an old trap to crawl about it, and simple meals. But he calls it 'mucking,' so I have to keep up there in that large house filled with people the standards we have here (and even here it isn't good enough for him!), and in England that is awfully expensive. My Mother pays half, but our half comes to far more than the running of this house...."

In 1902, Berenson discussed his financial cares with Mrs.

Gardner. If he were to exist he must make a living and the obvious road for him was to continue advising collectors. He could easily get control of the market and sell ten times as much, if he knew more people. Berenson begged Mrs. Gardner to recommend him to other collectors and perhaps she did, because, in the years that followed, Berenson began to advise other Americans.

Berenson knew that his main source of income lay on the other side of the Atlantic. Stories about a general eagerness to buy and lavish willingness to spend were common. One of the most popular, perhaps apocryphal, concerned the biggest spender of them all, Pierpont Morgan.

Morgan's chief advisor in the acquisition of objets d'art, a certain Mr. Fitzhenry, invited the collector for dinner. Morgan arrived with a group of adoring ladies. In honor of the occasion Fitzhenry ushered out his most beautiful Louis Quinze bibelots, worth £2,000. The ladies admired them. In that case, said Morgan, why didn't they just put the bibelots in their pockets. The ladies, nothing loath, did exactly as the millionaire suggested.

Their host, Fitzhenry, enjoyed the joke. But, as his guests prepared to leave, it became horribly clear that they had no intention of returning any of the items they had so gaily appropriated.

Fitzhenry spent a dreadful night and the next morning, with the courage born of desperation, bearded his employer at his office. Morgan was rather disdainful at the news that Fitzhenry could not afford such largesse, but grandly inquired how much the objects were worth. With daring, Fitzhenry quoted the sum of £7,000. Morgan summoned his secretary and, with an airy wave of his hand, commanded a check for that amount. He signed it with good humor.

Berenson's first objective, and one which he had largely· accomplished, was to gain introductions to visit the great European collections. These visits, as had been noted, had the advantage of adding to his scholarly knowledge and identifying potential buys, although, at first, they were not without comic-opera overtones. Mary Berenson recorded in her *Unfinished Life* of her husband that one Scottish lord threw them out of his castle and into a thunderstorm after Berenson made his doubts of that owner's claims to own a Leonardo and a Titian too apparent.

Berenson was just as tart-tongued about the collection of Mme. Édouard André in Paris who, he said, had designed her interiors in imitation of the shopkeeper Bardini, and who, apart from some excellent marbles and bronzes, had wretched paintings. He added ruminatively that he rather liked a Carpaccio and thought equally well of a Holy Family by Signorelli.

Berenson had continued his early contact with E. P. Warren, who consulted him whenever a Renaissance object was to be bought. He had become such an expert evaluator of Renaissance art that, in 1898, Warren sent him to Naples to report on the best possible buys from the ancient Sant' Angelo Collection of Naples.

Berenson's reply was that this generally undistinguished art collection had a single jewel: an exquisite Filippino Lippi, *Holy Family with S. S. Margaret and John*, which Berenson believed to be Lippi's third best-known work.

Berenson recommended offering £4,000 and thought it would be worth £6,000. Berenson included a group of the only other paintings in the collection he thought worth buying. The best solution, he told Warren, would be to buy the Filippino alone but if other paintings were a condition of the sale, he would suggest this group. He had given them low price tags (from £50 to £500 so that, if Warren had to bid £6,000 for the lot, he could be certain of recovering £2,000.)

If Warren did not want the Filippino Lippi, Berenson was sure Mrs. Gardner would take it for £6,000.

Berenson was continuing to advise Davis in the purchase of bronzes, plaquettes, and ivories, although he and Mary were contemptuous of that collector's acquisitions, which had not been bought with their advice. Davis had acquired at least five or six fakes, he wrote, at least one of them bought through Emilio Costantini and his handsome and rascally young son, who was adept at that ancient art. Mary Berenson made an exhaustive and gratuitous attempt to persuade Davis that the young Costantini had sold him a forgery of the central figure in Filippino's *Adoration of the Magi* at the Uffizi. Like the fictional hero of Bourget's tale, she was forced to give up. Davis continued to buy from the young scoundrel.

Mary's eagerness to prove Davis wrong and themselves right is an indication of the danger the fake posed to them all. Although everyone knew that Berenson had been misled by the *Donna Laura Minghetti Leonardo*, or perhaps because of it, Berenson was terrified of the threat to his reputation that the fake presented. He particularly did not want to sell one to Mrs. Gardner, or any other collector—it was bad enough if he bought one himself. The first painting Berenson bought was a fake, a stiff Madonna and Child of the Florentine School. He also bought what he took to be a genuine Sienese painting, from the Sterbini Collection in Rome, and blamed poor lighting for that misjudgment.

There may have been further errors. Taking his cue from Morelli, Berenson kept a group of what he called "Fool-o-meters" on display at "i Tatti" to see how well visiting professors knew their stuff. The joke occasionally backfired. Some historians, too polite to register shock in his presence, relieved their feelings by telling all their friends later that Berenson had fakes on his walls.

From past experience, Berenson knew how extremely difficult such fakes could be to detect. In the spring of 1902, a fake that he had actually seen on the easel of a "well-known Sienese forger" before it underwent the process of staining, cracking, and worm-holing, had sold at Christie's for a handsome price. Florence, he wrote to the London *Times*, was full of unscrupulous dealers who forged the works themselves and one's only defense was to learn to detect their particular style.

The "well-known Sienese forger" may well have been the famous G. F. Ioni who specialized in imitating the Italian quattrocento style. It is axiomatic, however, that a fake contains the indefinable stamp of the era in which it was painted. To Ioni's contemporaries his paintings perfectly expressed their own nineteenth-century vision of the Renaissance. Subsequent generations perceived the Renaissance differently; consequently, Ioni's traits and mannerisms became immediately visible. Berenson prided himself on being able to tell a fake Ioni while the latter, in his memoirs, protested that Berenson accepted his fakes as genuine and rejected the authentic paintings he offered. It is true that Berenson had bought a Ioni and also likely that he taught himself to recognize the Ioni style, as the following story suggests.

Ioni came to tell the Berensons that he had discovered a miraculous new painting hidden in a tiny church. They traveled miles together to reach the church and found it dusty and neglected. Ioni said, "There is the painting, over the altar." Mary and Berenson looked at the painting, then at each other, and said, "Oh Ioni, you old monster; now you have to pay for the cab."

Berenson was buying paintings as financial investments, but also because he liked them. He was obliged to sell a genuine, rare Pinturicchio in 1901 to offset some stock market losses, and a year later offered Mrs. Gardner his delicately beautiful Perugino

Madonna and Child with Bird in Hand for £4,500. By then he owned an even more beautiful Madonna and Child, one of the triumphs of his collection, and one he never dreamed of selling. Kenneth Clark called it one of the two most beautiful fifteenth-century pictures still in private hands.

Berenson had been asked to evaluate the possible sales prices for an old and famous collection of Italian art, the Panciatichi, and later wrote the catalogue. When asked to name his fee, Berenson selected the famous *Madonna and Child* which he, for decades to come, attributed to Alesso Baldovinetti. Mary wrote to Senda just after they had married and moved into "i Tatti" in 1901, about how exquisite the Baldovinetti Madonna looked in B.B.'s study, hung against a handsome piece of green silk.

Why Berenson should have insisted that the work was by the lesser Baldovinetti when the painting is given now to the more famous (and valuable) hand of Domenico Veneziano, is an interesting question with inconclusive answers. What is important about it, however, is that art has taken a quantum leap. Comparing it with another Madonna and Child in the Berenson Collection by Neroccio de' Landi, painted perhaps seventy-five years before, the difference becomes immediately apparent. The face of Neroccio's Madonna is more impassive than calm and her child is as emptily pretty as a Victorian wax doll. The painting's strength derives from its almost uncanny unity of design and its success in dealing with the clichés of a style, rather than in conveying any intensity of feeling.

The Domenico Veneziano Madonna is another species entirely. This mother is no symbol of a worn-out convention but a real human being, and the child she holds is an active baby. The poetic calm of her face, with its Botticelliesque curves, in contrast to the Child's impish look of inquiry, and the radiant luminosity of their flesh, set against gold halos and an arabesqued, gold and red background, enhance the spiritual, yet wholly corporeal, reality of these two people. Another, early fourteenth-century Madonna, Daddi's *Madonna of the Goldfinch*, which Berenson acquired, conveys the aching tenderness of mother and child; but none of his paintings fuse the human and divine into such a moment of exquisite harmony as his extraordinary Domenico Veneziano. Nothing could better illustrate the transforming influence of Renaissance thought on an outmoded medieval style, and Berenson gave this painting pride of place all his life.

Another remarkable addition to his collection was the most

dramatic to be discovered. More than one person took credit for finding it. Logan Pearsall Smith insisted that he was the one who discovered it on a cart, on its way to be broken up into a table. However, the Berenson account, which has the persuasive evidence of documentation, carries more weight.

According to Berenson he and Mary went to an antique dealer in the via della Spada in Florence, just after they moved into "i Tatti," to look for kitchen chairs, and Berenson found himself with his nose almost pressed against a wonderful painting. He had no idea what it was. He simply knew that it was marvelous, unique. So he bought it for 1,800 lire and put it on their landau and carted it home. The dealer said that he was going to saw it up the next day as artists liked old wood upon which to paint their fake Fra Angelicos.

The painting that so narrowly escaped destruction is a seven-foot panel from a polyptych of Saint Francis, painted by the then-forgotten Stefano di Giovanni Sassetta (fifteenth-century Sienese) and one of the most beautiful and best-documented Sassettas in existence. It was commissioned by the Cathedral at Borgo S. Sepolcro in 1437 and Sassetta completed it seven years later.

Berenson later wrote of this painting of Saint Francis, his arms outstretched and eyes lifted to heaven, that few paintings conveyed more dramatically the mystical sense of divine inspiration and universal harmony.

He continued, "The almost childlike simplicity of the arrangement, the crimson and gold and azure, the ecstatic figure of the saint . . . the flaming empyrean, the silvery green sea growing lighter as it approaches the silvery grey land, combine to present a real theophany, the apotheosis of a human soul that has attained to complete harmony with the soul of the universe by overcoming all that is belittling and confining, and opening itself out to all the benign influences of the spirit."

Another exquisite find, this one even more of a fragment, was *Head of a Virgin* by Gentile da Fabriano (fifteenth century), which Berenson discovered in worm-eaten form in Rome and placed into a perfectly chosen Venetian frame. Most of the Child's face can be seen at lower left and the slim-necked Madonna, bending in a supple arc toward her baby, registers a tender concern that is gracefully accentuated by the linked semicircles of their halos. The painting does not appear to have been restored and its fragmentary charm remains intact. Few, in fact, of Berenson's paintings were ever subjected to the mania for prettification that was to blight so many of the paintings that he later certified for Duveen.

Of the 100 paintings that Berenson collected, a considerable number bear the inevitable mark of a specialist's interest. This is in part due to natural inclination and in part *faute de mieux*, since the great Venetian painters he adored were already far beyond his pocketbook. So he specialized in making discoveries and, after this became known, some interesting "finds" arrived at his door, including a painting by Giotto, *Franciscan Monk Holding a Book*. Most of his acquisitions were made in the two years, 1909–11, when he was completing the furnishing of "i Tatti." Once this was done, he stopped buying. By 1915, his collection was worth half a million dollars.

Berenson also collected Oriental sculpture and scroll paintings. After the turn of the century, when Chinese painting, as distinct from its porcelains and lacquered objets d'art, began to reach the West, Berenson immediately saw its beauty and bought as much as he could from Vignier's in Paris. But he was already captivated by a beautiful collection of Chinese painting seen some six years before on a visit to America. These twelfth-century Chinese paintings had, he decided, what one never associated with Oriental art, i.e., the power to evoke character that sometimes surpassed Dürer and Gentile Bellini. They also had the tenderest qualities of love and humility and a mastery of line, color, and tone that left Europeans far behind.

"Fenollosa shivered as he looked, I thought I should die and even Denman Ross who looked dumpy Anglo-Saxon was jumping up and down. We had to poke and pinch each others' necks and wept. No, decidedly I never had had such an art experience," he wrote in 1894.

Long after his eternally verdant curiosity had taken him far afield of his original interest in Renaissance art, Berenson never lost that ability to feel art with his whole being. It marks him as a true aesthete, as does his ability to respond to a wide spectrum of art. "To be for ever learning—never to petrify—that is what I yearn for," he wrote at the age of twenty-four.

Berenson's very openness to artistic experience led him to espouse passions that were often fleeting. Speaking of such mutability of character, Iris Origo gave as an example his "wholly disproportionate appreciation," in the 1890s, for the minor painters of the Veronese School. He was later to remark of them, "They taste like vinegar." Iris Origo continued. "Sodoma was also accorded a measureless admiration, while all other Sienese painters after 1400 were dismissed as 'simply dull and meaningless.' "

" 'When you meet Berenson a second time,' his old friend Israel Zangwill used to say, 'you are beaten over the head for admiring what he taught you to admire the first,' and his wife's phrase, 'But Bernard, you *used* to think . . .' became so well-worn as to rouse all their friends to laughter and cause him to retort that his daily prayer had become: 'Give us this day our daily idea and forgive us all we thought yesterday!' "

One of the constant stars in Berenson's artistic firmament was his admiration for Cézanne. When Leo Stein first began looking at art and finding nothing worth buying, Berenson was the one who told him to look at the Cézanne paintings at Vollard's on the rue Lafitte. "This was the time when Piero della Francesca, Pollaiuolo, Castagno, Domenico Veneziano, and others of their kind and period were comparatively new and exciting. They formed a direct approach to the appreciation of Cézanne," Stein wrote.

Berenson rose even further in the admiring eyes of Leo, Gertrude, Michael, and Sally Stein when he sent a letter to the New York *Nation* defending Matisse against the charges that his sole aim was to shock the bourgeoisie and that his work contained nothing of value. This letter, Berenson later commented, convinced the Steins that he must leave all he had and dedicate himself to "expounding the merits of the new school. When I would not, they sadly put me down as having made the great refusal."

Matisse, Berenson had written, was a spectacular draftsman and a great designer. Berenson thought as highly of Picasso's early work and compared his draftsmanship to Raphael's. But Picasso's myriad twists and turns of style repelled him (in his postwar autobiography, Berenson called him "the most protean and acrobatic of painters. . .") and so did Picasso's personality. He was a demagogue, Berenson said, equating him with Huey Long in Robert Penn Warren's novel, *All the King's Men*.

Picasso had done more in those postwar years to corrupt art than anyone in history, Berenson said. He was vicious and unscrupulous. Berenson's low opinion of Picasso was paralleled by a comparable distaste and indecision when faced with modern art. Asked at what point he began to be unsure, Berenson replied, "After Matisse."

John Walker, Berenson's great friend, who found himself frequently defending contemporary artists against the latter's attacks, thought that the blind spot, if it were such, was easily explained.

"B.B. couldn't sympathize with contemporary art for a very simple reason. He couldn't understand how an abstraction could teach you anything about nature . . . he never realized that an artist, let's say like Rothko, could train . . . a viewer's eye to see . . . the blending of light at sunset; those . . . marvelous bands of color which occur in the sky occasionally . . . and though he could feel the tactile values in a sky by Cézanne because Cézanne belonged to his generation, he never could make the leap into an appreciation of contemporary art."

Furthermore, Berenson saw in the chaos of abstraction a mirror for the chaotic instability of the modern world and found parallels for that in other periods of historical crisis. One wonders, however, whether he could ever have come to like a movement so antithetical to the aesthetic he had inherited from Pater, or find anything commendable in a world in rebellion against the solid Edwardian virtues of tradition, stability, and permanence.

Neith Boyce Hapgood, her husband Hutchins, and their two-year-old son Boyce, arrived for a ten-day stay at "i Tatti" in the summer of 1903. They made the journey from Genoa to Florence, one hundred miles, in seven hours on a fast train and were met by Mrs. Berenson, who had a carriage waiting to take them to Settignano. The delicious drive took twenty minutes. Despite all the travel, Boyce behaved angelically, and went to bed, leaving his parents to dine with the Berensons at 8:30 p.m.

Hutchins Hapgood was an old friend of the Berenson family. He had become interested in the lives of Jewish immigrants in the course of newspaper reporting and had just published (1902) a series of studies, *The Spirit of the Ghetto*. He illustrated his book with some charming sketches by a then-unknown artist, Jacob Epstein.

Neith Boyce had written her first novel *The Forerunner*, which was published that year, and had just had her second accepted, *The Folly of Others*. She was to write a number of other novels and a play, *Enemies*, with her husband, which was performed by the Provincetown Players. That summer she kept a diary—never published—of her first trip to Italy.

Solidity, weight, permanence. It was a charming old villa, she wrote, with flowers in stone planters and potted lemon trees and exquisite small statues, the whole enclosed by a high wall. The house was perfectly finished to the last detail. The stucco walls were a wash of cool neutral colors, grays, greens, and buff, the stone floors hidden beneath Aubusson and Oriental carpets. The walls were covered with delicate hangings of old embroidery, and there were paintings of medieval saints and Madonnas with glittering gold backgrounds everywhere. Neith Boyce was particularly charmed by the Italian and French furniture as well as the atmosphere of serene living, the understated elegance.

People came to lunch, tea, and dinner, in small groups. Berenson told the Hapgoods that it was bestial to have more than six people at table and he also disliked "your American system of *tête-à-tête*." No matter how much he might be interested in his neighbor, Berenson always had the uncomfortable feeling that he was missing some other, more scintillating conversation. So he always insisted that the conversation be general. That was much more interesting; that was a work of art.

Neith Boyce sat on his right. After a day or so Berenson began to include her in the conversation, even if they were talking about such subjects as "progressive symbols" or English politics. Before that happened, however, she had been ignored. She explained that an Englishman named Horne had come to dinner. The whole evening, Horne and Berenson discussed their quarrels with some unknown art editor. Neith Boyce and Mrs. Berenson made feeble attempts to enter the conversation and were thrown out. So Neith Boyce ate her dinner in bored silence and was later told by the Berensons that she was as impersonal as an Englishwoman. It was meant as a great compliment, but Neith Boyce remained unmoved. She had no particular desire to seem impersonal. However, she reflected that a newcomer who was a compulsive talker would receive a very cool reception at "i Tatti" and a certain kind of American twang might well break the delicate crystal of the Venetian wine glasses.

She took a great liking to Berenson himself, enjoying his wit, his alertness, and authoritative air. He seemed unusually alive. Mary was more radiant and moved more slowly, but with a certain largesse, and followed her husband at a respectful intellectual distance. Even then, disparaging remarks were being made about their circle, and by 1912 Santayana said that "i Tatti" was full of "soulful tourists and weary dilettantes," but Neith Boyce liked it. It might be snobbish, but it encompassed a wonderful cross section of bizarre people.

There was a Miss Cracroft, an English girl who played Bach, Beethoven, and Gluck in the music room on Friday afternoons. There was the daughter of William Morris, in a fearfully strange "art gown," who had frizzy black hair, a long, sensitive face, and a black moustache, and who thought that people who were interested in the current notion that life should be lived for its own sake, were "terrible." There was Herbert Horne, whom Neith Boyce found a rather wooden kind of person, although she had heard that some found him interesting. Horne and Berenson talked about the fashionable artist John Singer Sargent and how his painting would not survive because the edges of his paintings were too brittle. At least, it sounded like that to Neith Boyce.

An elderly English scholar, a Mr. Benn, came for lunch. He turned out to be a great gossip and they all chatted about an elderly couple living on the hill who had just become parents. That aroused all kinds of derisive comment and Neith Boyce concluded that babies were quite out of favor at "i Tatti." There was a story about Vernon Lee. It seemed that a male guest of hers had arranged to go out for lunch every day. Then one day the weather was bad and he felt ill and wanted to stay in for lunch but Vernon Lee was adamant; an agreement was an agreement. This emboldened Neith Boyce to retell the story that Vernon Lee had said, "You don't know what love is, unless you have been loved by an Italian." Berenson said that was all nonsense, since Vernon Lee did not have affairs with men. Neith Boyce wondered how he knew.

There was more gossip about a wonderful Balkan princess who lived in a beautiful old villa with a woman companion, and how she had gone to visit Janet Ross in *déshabillé*, wearing hardly more than a few uncut rubies. Miss Maud Cruttwell, the art historian, asked why a lady should take such pains to dress up "for nobody." Berenson said, "You are innocent. There are no men in her life but that doesn't mean she dresses for nobody." Then Miss Cruttwell wondered how the princess could bear to live with such a commonplace person and Berenson replied, "She isn't commonplace. Miss X. is brutal and vulgar and wicked—but she isn't commonplace." Neith Boyce was amazed to find life so wonderfully dramatic.

On Saturday night, the Houghtons came to dinner and he told the frightful story that a mutual friend, Andrew G., had been arrested and imprisoned in Paris on the charge of being Jack the Ripper. He had even been convicted and sentenced to life imprisonment. Hutchins Hapgood wrote at once to his friend Leo Stein in Paris and found that it was all nonsense. Neith Boyce wondered how people could invent such gargantuan fictions and concluded that it must be the result of too many books and not enough exercise.

They all went up to Poggio Gherardo to visit Janet Ross, whom B.B. called "an epic person" and "an old dear." Neith Boyce found her, at almost seventy, a largish lady with white hair and impish black eyes, full of vigorous and scandalous stories, which she punctuated with a hearty slap to her thigh. Her gentle husband had just died, to Mrs. Ross's apparent relief. She had a son whom she never saw, and when she learned he was ill, she was gleeful. "I suppose you hope he'll die," Mary said to her. "Don't I!" Janet Ross replied. Mrs. Ross's niece, Lina Duff-Gordon, had fallen in love with Aubrey Waterfield, a penniless young painter, and Mrs. Ross had taken one of her irrational hatreds to the young man and abused him to everybody. They married anyway and now Mrs. Ross would not see them. They had a baby and Mrs. Ross told Mary, "Really, I'm very glad it wasn't born sooner. People thought the marriage was being hurried on a great deal."

The Berensons had been very tolerant of Boyce, even though having such a small child around must have been a great bother. But, Neith Boyce reflected, Mrs. Ross had not been very nice. They were talking on the terrace when Boyce ran up with something to show his mother. Mrs. Ross, enraged, roared at Boyce, "You are a very rude naughty little boy interrupting people like that!" Boyce looked at her in shocked silence and, when his mother took him away, he remarked, "Bad old 'ooman."

Berenson took Mrs. Hapgood to see his small white bedroom, which he said was the best room in the house, containing the same furnishings that he had had at the via Camerata, even to the small white bed, which, to Neith Boyce, looked more suitable for a girl. Here, Berenson said, he liked to sleep, "if possible, alone."

They left remembering the gracious entertaining, the exquisite beauty of the setting, the great cypresses on the terrace where they had tea, and the feeling of silence and serenity. Neith Boyce would always remember the old woman roasting coffee in a brazier outside her window, the cook, a formidable man in a tall white hat, and Roberto the butler, who was such a majestic snob, and whom she had encountered walking backward down the hall before that member of the old Italian aristocracy, the Countess Serristori, bowing from the waist at every step.

Neith Boyce Hapgood's diary, with its blend of wonder, admiration, amused interest, and detached observation, is valuable for the insight it provides into a visitor's reactions to Altamura. Her words attest to the warmth and generosity that was shown to people the Berensons liked, to the formal perfection of the house, and the blissful predictability of life within its walls. Her diary also bears witness to the numbers of people already drawn to this seductive and stimulating personality, and to the quality of the conversations, so erudite, so eclectic, and so ruthlessly personal. Behind her words one sees the restless figure of the host, declaring with an air of finality that Art was infinitely better than Life, or that Italian works of art were being allowed to go to rack and ruin, or that the only way to see Florence was at night, from the hillside, among the fireflies and quoting Browning.

Among other visitors in that same period were Mary's sister Alys and her husband Bertrand Russell. Alys's attitude had undergone a radical revision since the days when, despite her espousal of free love, she had been shocked to the marrow by her sister's behavior and had refused to meet Mary's lover.

Bertrand Russell, perceiving the contradiction, had reconciled her little by little to the idea of meeting Berenson. Once the ice was broken, an effortless friendship resulted. Berenson told Robert Trevelyan, "Bertie I . . . liked . . . better and better. His mind is exquisitely active. True it has yet perhaps not gone beyond picking up one moss-grown stone after the other to see what is under it, but that by itself is perfectly delightful. Were I really interested in metaphysics or he in art, we should be superhumanly well joined." As for Alys, she improved on acquaintance. "She has wit and good intentions and as her shyness wears off . . . she is charming."

The Russells spent Christmas of 1902 at "i Tatti" with the "Bee Bees," as H.W.S. called them. Alys was recovering from a terrible backache, put down to an excess of uric acid, rather than to the marital stresses which were the likely cause, and which would result in her divorce from Russell. Russell found the beauty of the countryside overwhelming and the house exquisite. He admitted that the cause of "existing beautifully" shocked his social conscience. He could not help thinking, he wrote to Gilbert Murray, about all those struggling young men and women in the East End. Just the same, he would not allow the thought to influence him, because someone should "keep up the ideal of beautiful houses." What did disturb him was the gulf separating the cult of exquisite living from the emotional tone at "i Tatti." ". . . I think one makes great demands on the mental furniture when the outside is so elaborate, and one is shocked at lapses one would otherwise tolerate. . . ."

Perhaps Altamura's air of aristocratic privilege was too tormenting for a well-born Englishman with an alert social conscience, or perhaps the contrast between the idyllic beauty of the scene and his own anguished state of mind was the cause. At any rate, while visiting the Berensons, Russell wrote perhaps his most famous essay, "The Free Man's Worship."

Beginning from the premise of Dr. Faustus's notorious pact with Mephistopheles, Russell went on to posit that we were living in a random and Godless universe. There was only one ray of hope for mankind: that by living up to an inner vision of "the good" man would wrestle a meaning from his life. Russell's moral imperative was thus juxtaposed against Berenson's more limited Paterian aesthetic; but if Berenson saw a challenge, he did not give evidence of it. He urged Russell to "write and write."

Berenson was also working hard. He had finished assembling two collections of essays and, in 1903, "a great big monster of a book" was going to press, the result of years of arduous study. He had been led to write about the drawings of the Florentine painters as a natural outcome of his study of painting, since clues to authorship, before the photograph, had routinely hinged upon the discovery of a preparatory sketch that could be attributed conclusively.

For Berenson, the principal charm of a drawing was its ability to demonstrate the evolution of an artistic personality, sometimes with breathtaking clarity. He studied 3,000 drawings, dealing with first one artist and then another, with "groans and moans." It took him ten years. Some of his attributions have been questioned since, but the bulk has withstood decades of challenge, and *Drawings of the Florentine Painters* is generally considered Berenson's "finest and most consistent critical work."

The completion of his Four Gospels and the publication of two volumes of the *Florentine Drawings* brought Berenson to a baffling halt. Two or three years from then, he would be reading widely on the influence of art on civilization and, in the final chapter of *The North Italian Painters*, he would make his first forays into a subject that was to fascinate him: the decline of art. These were vague and unformulated gropings, which did nothing to assuage his indecision. He explained to Hutchins Hapgood, "To continue doing the same thing is to do what others will do as well." Yet at the thought of expanding his aesthetic, he hesitated. "I'm less hopeful of that line, no longer sure I have anything to say which has not already been said. . . ."

Of one thing he was certain; he would not "walk a corpse all the rest of my life." As if in emphasis, he said it again in a letter two weeks later to the Michael Fields. "Give us this day . . ."

That summer of 1903 Berenson, who had finally recovered from his neurasthenia, was making plans to spend the winter in America. Mary was worrying less about her husband's health. She decided that a great deal of his exhaustion was self-induced by a tendency to push himself to the point of collapse. Emotional upsets always seemed to make him ill. They had talked about a trip to America since their marriage and he had constantly postponed it, pleading ill health. However, now that she was there to reassure him, he would have less irrational dread of the ocean crossing, she told his mother confidently.

They landed early in October and went straight to The Reef, the palatial home of Theodore Davis, in Newport, Rhode Island. Bernhard survived the journey extremely well and was disposed to view everything in a rosy light. He liked some of Davis's fine pieces, in particular an Egyptian object of 3,000 B.C. and was immensely taken with a piece of doggerel that he quoted forever afterward:

> There once was a monk of Liberia
> Whose existence grew drear and drearier
> So he broke from his cell
> With a hell of a yell
> And eloped with the Mother Superior.

However, when Davis began to eulogize interminably about his collection, Bernhard "turned perfectly grey . . . and I had to interpose and send him up to lie down," Mary wrote to Senda. "It is strange how much ingenuity the Creator has put into the making of bores! Mr. Davis is one of the most fancy varieties I ever met."

They traveled onward to 189 Grampian Way, Dorchester, to stay with Bernhard's parents. The "dear Little Mother" had her heart and hands full "trying to make her 'Prince' comfortable," Mary wrote. "Your father has been very nice and courteous so far. . . . If I didn't *know* all sorts of things, I should take a great fancy to him."

Later, Mary concluded that the visit home had been a success. They were concerned only for its effect on Little Mother, who had been obliged to do so much cooking, and it did put her "to great inconvenience as she had to try to sleep (but really lay awake) in the same bed with your father." They had almost decided to ask Little Mother to join them in Northampton, where they planned to visit Senda at Smith College. "B.B. would rather not have her, she tires him so dreadfully, but still a couple of days will not be too much for him."

Privately Mary told her journal that the Berensons were beginning to get on her nerves. B.B. realized this and was very understanding. He, too, confided that he dreaded the visit. Mary thought Little Mother "a rather depressing person, about whose life I cannot feel anything but hopeless." The girls, Senda and Bessie, felt trapped by the monotony of their school-teaching lives and looked at marriage as their only hope for escape. They worried continually about each other. "Senda is worried about Bessie and Bessie about her and both of them about Abie and all of them about the Mother and Father—I could not keep my spirits long with such life-diminishing people. The truth is Bernhard's career has given them all a vision of life they cannot themselves attain; and the contrast makes them discontented. . . ."

They went to visit Mrs. Gardner at Green Hill in Brookline and were taken to see the exterior of Fenway Court. They admired the picturesque Venetian garden which, although just planted, managed to look centuries old. There was no chance of seeing the interior until the museum opened in two months; on that Mrs. Gardner was adamant.

They were invited out constantly. They visited Mrs. Gardner's friends, dined with Santayana, were given a magnificent meal by Mrs. Norton, were having tea here and lunch there and dinner everywhere. "We are, I believe, being 'lionized'—we have quantities more invitations than we can possibly accept. There is, however, no direct 'business' in it so far."

While at Green Hill they went to a symphony concert and returned that evening, Mary wrote in her journal, "to a perfectly dark house, and had great trouble finding matches to light the gas in our rooms. Mrs. Gardner has a mania, evidently, for saving on lighting. The moment we leave our rooms a servant rushes in, not to turn down the gas, but . . . *out*, and in the music room, where we sit, there is only one lamp. . . . She lives very sparingly too, wearing old clothes and eating almost nothing." Thank goodness for the cakes Little Mother had given her, Mary added. "I should go ragingly hungry to bed, if it were not for that blessed tin box."

In November, Mrs. Gardner finally consented to show them around the rooms of Fenway Court and they were charmed by its beauty and taste. There was very little hanging on the walls that Bernhard had not chosen, but those few paintings "annoyed him intensely, and hurt him too," Mary recorded in her journal. The crowning blow was to discover, opposite the Chigi Botticelli, a poor school piece from the Duca di Brindisi's Palazzo Antinori in Florence that B.B. had refused to buy for her. Mrs. Gardner had bought it in spite of him and given it a place of honor.

"It turned poor Bernhard quite sick and cold. But he gave very little sign and the occasion went off so well that Mrs. Gardner presented me with a Chinese bracelet. . . ."

They arrived at the Plaza Hotel in New York just before Christmas and Berenson wrote to tell his Queen of Sheba that he, a Western Wise Man, stood ready to offer her myrrh and balsam.

The three met again in Chicago in January. Despite the gloom caused by the recent Chicago fire, Bernhard was delighted with the city and they had a splendid time. Adding to his euphoria was his discovery that the public libraries owned five copies of his *Florentine Drawings* (even though Harvard had not bought one).

Mary Berenson was invited to lecture before "all" the fashionable women and an unusual number of men. She used the occasion to condemn the work of Sargent, which neither of them liked. (They had been horrified by the new Sargents in the Boston Public Library.) The attack, she recorded in her journal, caused a great stir. She also lectured in Cleveland, where she was asked how much more she would charge for a "reception feature added." The phrase became a catchword at "i Tatti" to describe any onerous social occasion. Berenson was still using it half a century later.

In Chicago, the Berensons were invited to "squillionaire" dinners every night and were so flattered that,

> if we hadn't kept our minds steadily fixed on the reflection that Loeser & Douglas & all the rest would have just the same sort of reception, I think our heads would have been turned. Bernhard sat by a rollicking squillionairess, a great leader here, who flirted recklessly with him. She was very witty & he came out in quite a new phase, so that it made me feel it was really a pity to shut him up to the poverty-stricken denizens of the Florence hills. . . .
>
> Mrs. Gardner, thank heaven, is going today. She has been here all the time, lying on every subject, and plotting against Bernhard, but without success. She is disliked very much here. Her lying has become a pitiful spectacle. But noone [*sic*] is taken in. . . .
>
> She was, however, most gorgeous last night, with 2 enormous diamonds . . . fixed on her head like the antennae of a butterfly, and pearls innumerable around her neck, & a white & gold embroidered dress. She was so furious at *our* being the guests of honour instead of herself that she couldn't keep it in. Everyone went off together, & she shouted out in response to her hostess' polite remarks,—"O, *I* haven't counted here—it's all the Berensons," to which B.B. replied, "Oh Mrs. Jack—that's one of your most whopping fibs," and everybody grinned with appreciation.

Four days later, Berenson wrote to tell Mrs. Gardner that Chicago was very quiet now that she had left. Like Caesar, she had conquered all before her and there was nothing to do but sing her praise.

In reply, Mrs. Gardner spoke of her back taxes and her mood of depression. Thank heavens for the Berensons, she wrote. They made her feel as if they had a genuine affection for her and the thought was heartwarming. Just now she felt lonely and abandoned, without a friend in the world.

Berenson was as concerned about money as she was. "We are both worried at not having made any money this trip, and this leaves us so awfully short for all the things we want & need to do. It weighs on him a good deal, particularly about Rachel, to whom he hoped to be able to give, with ease, several years abroad. I myself think things will surely improve," Mary wrote to Senda.

Berenson was ostensibly visiting collections, including the Jarves Collection in Boston, where they caused a sensation when the word got around that "we" (Mary's description) had "changed every attribution!" It was also known that Berenson had paintings to sell.

"Of the lot of photos. of things for sale he had with him, Johnson told me no one in Phila. would pay 25 doll. for any picture. Now that Mrs. Gardner is not buying any more, he told, not to me alone, but to everybody (his wife also did) that she was a liar, a fiend and other choice things, with the result that everybody is shocked and disgusted by him," Jaccaci wrote.

Most of all, the Berensons were assessing future clients with a cool eye. "Mr. Loeb came to lunch, a handsome, fat, prosperous, philistine Jew, classmate of Bernhard's. He is founding a poetry prize, to be given to the best poet of each year. His idea is to have poems on 'modern' subjects—Panama, the Tammany victory, the strife of Labour and Capital, and so on. As he may be very useful to us financially, B.B. and I *listened politely* while he expounded on these views. It is astonishing," Mary noted in her journal, "how interesting and un-boring society becomes when you have something to get out of it."

Handsome, fat, prosperous, and philistine: these words came to describe the rich Jews whose company Mary Berenson and her husband disliked, even though they might take a cynical interest in them. The inference was that one might have to do business with such people but one did not have to like them. In condemning them the Berensons did not hesitate to employ terms in the vernacular of a bigoted age. "A Jew from the ghetto" became Berenson's catchall term to condemn any Jew he disapproved of. In so doing, he demonstrated that he, too, had assumed the anti-Semitism of the worlds of Henry Adams, Henry James, and Edith Wharton.

In these accounts of their American stay one searches in vain for a reference to the exchange that took place between Berenson and his father. Perhaps their contact was so perfunctory as not to be worth comment, or perhaps the emotions were too complex to bear close analysis. Speaking of his childhood, Berenson once remarked that Jerome and Jean Tharaud's novel, *L'Ombre de la Croix*, gave an exact portrait of the early years of his life. What the story describes is the gulf of generations separated by more than time.

The Shadow of the Cross concerns the plight of a pious Jewish couple who part with their sick son, a boy named Ruben, in deference to the Jewish belief that, if God brings illness to the family it is because he means to break the bonds between parent and child. Ruben goes to live with his grandfather, a rabbi, and dies in adolescence.

However, Ruben's ghost returns, to tell his grandfather that he wishes to learn about men of other ages and civilizations. The rabbi unsuccessfully tries to argue that such an idea will bring no happiness. The ghost vanishes and, when it reappears, his grandfather hardly recognizes the man, dressed as a Gentile, with a gold lorgnon on his nose, a gold chain around his stomach, and a stiff collar around his neck. Ruben, too, hardly recognizes the old man. He does admit, however, that from time to time, old memories surge up and a distant country appears through the mists, with tall black fir trees, where everything that once existed is preserved in amber.

"I see the square covered with snow, I see the house, I see the tombs in which an ancient happiness is buried, and to which one can never return." But, Ruben asks, why does he continue to dream such dreams? Why is the grandfather forcing him to remember things he would rather forget? For many years he has locked such memories in a casket with a double bolt. . . .

Heavy tears begin to roll down the old man's cheeks. Does he really believe, his ghostly grandchild continues, that Ruben intends to continue the old ways?

If you knew what a sigh of relief I gave when I saw the synagogue and the place of the scriptural commentaries disappear! What freedom! What gladness! I felt like fresh and sparkling water in which all of earth and heaven were reflected. . . . Since I have cut my locks and shortened my caftan, the world has opened its doors to me. How intelligent he is! they say. From whence does this subtle intelligence emanate? It must certainly come from you, old man. How well you prepared me for life! How well you taught me to seek the hidden meaning under the words. How well I benefitted from your saintly gymnastics! . . . One word from my mouth spells profit or ruin. . . . Next year in Jerusalem! The old cry of humiliated despair, which during centuries of trials you have hurled into the shadows, I also called out in the night. And now, the day has come. The gates of the City of Gold are opened before me! . . . I have found Jerusalem, I have rebuilt the ruined Temple, but in my own fashion, Reb Eljé! . . . All your life you have called for a miracle. But miracles, you know, don't come nowadays in the way that our ancient prophets used to predict, and in the way you hoped. Stop waiting for the Prophet Elijah to one day blow the shofar on the highest Carpathian mountain. The trumpet sounded a long time ago. . . . Look at me, Reb Eljé Lebowitz: I am the miracle! . . .

In misery, the old man begs Ruben to answer one last question. "Do you still say the Sh'ma Ysroel?" ("Hear, Oh Israel, the Lord is One.") A mocking laugh is his only reply. This time, the rabbi tells himself, his child is truly dead.

Early in 1907, Bernhard Berenson began to advise the great art dealer Joseph Duveen.

12

DORIS

A prostitute is anyone who does for money that
which, but for money, he would not do at all.

—BERNARD BERENSON,
The Bernard Berenson Treasury, circa 1939

"**D**ORIS," AS BERENSON CAME to be called under a code
name arbitrarily adopted for him, began to advise the
house of Duveen on the purchase of Italian Renaissance paintings
some time in 1906 and, in 1912, signed the first of a series of
contracts. In it, he was to receive 25 percent of the net profits
from the sales of paintings that he had attributed.

In the decade since he had bought heavily for Mrs. Gardner,
the tastes of scholars for hitherto unknown and neglected early
Italian Renaissance works had sifted down to the American
"squillionaires." In particular, four extremely wealthy men were
in the market: Benjamin Altman, P. A. B. Widener, J. P. Morgan,
and Henry Clay Frick, all of them being induced by shrewd
dealers like Joseph Duveen to bid against each other. The results
were spectacular.

Berenson, writing to the scholarly and comparatively penniless American collector John G. Johnson, observed, in 1911, that
the recent Abdy sale had made a great stir in London. Decorative
but inconsequential odds and ends that he would have advised
Johnson to buy for £300 were sold for ten times that price. In
particular, a much-repainted Botticelli had been bought by Langton Douglas for over £11,000.

The trend Berenson had complained about to Mrs. Gardner
in 1900 was accelerating, as a result of the enormous sums

Altman, Widener, Morgan, and Frick were willing to pay. The year he died, Altman paid Duveen £103,300 for a large Holy Family by Mantegna that came from Berlin, where it had been bought by Duveen for £29,500.

Widener paid Duveen £116,500 for a small Raphael Madonna. Benjamin Altman, who died before the sale could be completed, was preparing to pay £150,000 for an altarpiece that Morgan had bought for half that amount in 1900. The year 1913, according to Gerald Reitlinger in *The Economics of Taste*, has hardly ever been equaled for spectacular art sales. In all of this activity, the dealer most adept at exploiting the buying power of the American squillionaires was Joseph Duveen.

The story of Duveen's rise to glory has been told elsewhere, notably by S. N. Behrman in *Duveen*, and more recently by his associate, Edward Fowles, in *Memories of Duveen Brothers*. Duveen's extraordinary combination of brashness, showmanship, and guile, used to persuade, cajole, and bully rich Americans into buying incomparable masterpieces, and ones that grace our public collections today, is also known. It is a moot point whether Duveen is admired more for his achievements or his flair for flamboyant trickery, for being a lovable scoundrel.

What is less discussed is the reason why Duveen should wish to employ Berenson. Here one must recall that perfectly reputable scholars had miserable commercial reputations. As the late editor of the *Burlington Magazine*, Benedict Nicolson, pointed out, a great many scholars of Berenson's generation became involved with the trade and only a few, "to their eternal credit, refused to do so, because it was wrong."

Such an idea would have appeared preposterous to the art trade. Matters of principle hardly entered into it. Everybody gave certificates and the buyer was expected to take such affidavits with several tons of salt. If he didn't, he was a poor dupe whom everyone rather despised.

Until now, Berenson had not been closely identified with a single dealer, if one can discount his relationship with Otto Gutekunst of Colnaghi's, a relationship always tempered by the fact that Berenson represented the buyer. So dealers were desperate to hire him, because his word was untainted. They had resented him at first. They had resisted him and tried to trick him and drive him out. They failed. Berenson's position grew ever more secure and Duveen's offer was, in a sense, a capitulation, a recognition that the poacher must be made to turn gamekeeper.

There were practical considerations since, in the years 1907–09, Duveen had bought the great collections of Oscar Hainauer and Rudophe and Maurice Kann *en bloc* and was in urgent need of an authority under whose word the Italian items could be sold. Once Berenson joined the house of Duveen, it became in the prudent business interest of the owner to make that word appear infallible.

What is less apparent is why Berenson would wish to work for Duveen and take the momentous step of siding with the seller rather than the buyer, to represent what he had always considered the interests of the enemy. The evidence suggests that, although Berenson managed to replace Mrs. Gardner with other collectors, i.e., Davis, Johnson, Grenville L. Winthrop (chief benefactor of the Fogg Art Museum), and Henry Walters of Baltimore, none of them had the limitless resources that were becoming *de rigueur*. Berenson tried to woo Altman. When that collector made a buying trip to London and Paris in the autumn of 1909, Berenson was the one who guided him to the pinnacles, helped him to avoid the shallows, and desperately tried to impart some breadth and vision to the department store magnate's taste.

A month later he wrote from Paris to admit defeat. Altman, Berenson declared, had a perfect passion to acquire paintings that were not for sale, and adamantly refused to buy those that were. The only exceptions were late Rembrandts of half-length figures. Berenson tried in vain to interest Altman in Rembrandt's landscapes. Altman was, Berenson concluded, entirely a creature of habit and completely under the sway of Joseph Duveen's uncle Henry.

Berenson had also hoped to join the staff of the Metropolitan Museum as its chief buyer of Italian pictures, but when his principal advocate on the staff died suddenly in 1904, his hopes suffered a similar eclipse. Berenson was forced to conclude that, if he were to prosper, he would have to change sides.

In a remarkable letter to Johnson, probably written at the time when the first contract with Duveen's was being signed, Berenson managed to rationalize his decision. Duveen's, he wrote, were the only ones among the major dealers, with the notable exception of Arthur J. Sulley, of London, whom one could trust not to propose a shady deal. Since the squillionaires had resisted all his efforts to help them, they would be paying a great deal more for their masterpieces than they would otherwise have had to do. However, if he refused to aid the dealers, Altman and the rest would still be paying absurd prices but getting nothing in return.

Berenson would not pretend that he was not being paid handsomely. Nevertheless he had the consolation of helping bring to America some exceptional paintings that might never arrive if he were not involved. He ended with the consoling thought that it was not his business to prevent Mr. Altman from squandering his fortune.

The other factor in the equation was Altamura.

Early in the summer of 1905, the Berensons received notice that their landlord did not intend to renew the lease on "i Tatti." They had already invested a great deal of money in making the house habitable. There was a small fire the following summer, otherwise not described, but that presumably called for further repairs. After flirting with the idea of looking elsewhere, the Berensons began to negotiate for the purchase in 1907. They needed £6,000 down, "a very large sum for us," Mary Berenson wrote to the British artist and writer Sir William Rothenstein. Even though negotiations were not complete until December 1909, they began major repairs and additions in the autumn of 1908. At the same time, Berenson was trying to raise capital by selling some of his paintings. He offered a Borgognone to Winthrop, a Dosso Dossi to Johnson, and also the *Virgin and Child with Bird in Hand* by Perugino, which he had tried unsuccessfully to sell to Mrs. Gardner six years before for £4,500. Johnson bought it in 1908 for £2,000.

Whether Berenson actively sought a business relationship with Joseph Duveen, or whether they met by some random act of fate, is not known. One can only say that their association coincided with the acquisition of a handsome Italian property and that, in the years 1908–11, Berenson was furnishing, decorating, embellishing, renovating, and building an addition to the house that had come to personify his aesthetic ideal.

How much Johnson knew, or guessed, about Berenson's relationship with Duveen is impossible to tell. He probably did not know its true extent, since he wrote to Berenson in May of 1912 warning him to be extremely circumspect in dealing with a firm that he, for one, did not appear to trust in the slightest. But then, no one knew. The elaborate precautions of the house of Duveen followed a well-established tradition in the art market, which was that the sale of a painting must only be known after the fact. The dream of every dealer was to buy for nothing and sell for everything and to keep the extent of the disparity between the prices the secret of his bookkeeper. Such an idyllic business arrangement depended upon knowing where the paintings were and the art of appearing on the scene the instant they were for sale. Such cloak-and-dagger tactics appealed to the adventurer in Duveen. Like tornados, the principal protagonists were given female names: Sulley was "Bella," and other dealers were "Virginia" and "Sarah." Berenson would certainly not have chosen the name of "Doris."

Edward Fowles described the need for secrecy with characteristic circumspection. Berenson, he explained, always wanted Fowles to stay at "i Tatti" when he came to Florence, to avoid having their telephone conversations overheard. For the same reason, knowing the incurable gossipiness of the Florentines, Berenson hated to receive business telegrams. Fowles discovered the reason why.

"Joe telephoned me from New York ... [he] was feeling relaxed, and we talked for a full 45 minutes. I later left the hotel and as I was walking along the via Tornabuoni I heard a passerby say to his companion, 'That's the man who spoke to New York for 45 minutes this morning.'"

Berenson already had compelling personal reasons for wishing to maintain a façade. Duveen had compelling business ones. The contract worked so well that the fact that Berenson was the advisor for Sir Joseph Duveen was not generally known until he testified on the latter's behalf in open court in 1929.

However, the game of intrigue had certain pronounced disadvantages.

"Why do you play the game of suspicion with me?" Berenson once complained to the young British art dealer David Carritt, who replied, "Because I am perfectly aware that when I send you a photograph [of a painting for sale] it ends up being known by Wildenstein" (the dealer from whom Berenson worked until the end of his life).

In such a world one could never be sure that one's most innocent remark might not boomerang to one's spectacular disadvantage. The solution was to say nothing, or to cultivate a façade beneath which the truth could be hidden judiciously, to emerge piece by piece (as much as it was prudent for others to know), or in such a distorted form that one was safe from its ravages. Knowing Duveen, Berenson could never be sure that he was not being manipulated and, knowing Berenson, Duveen and Fowles

Above: *Berenson and Nicky Mariano sight-seeing at Athéras,
December 1928* (Courtesy of "i Tatti") Below: *Berenson on
the grounds of "i Tatti" with Nicky Mariano and Raymond
Mortimer in the spring of 1950* (Photo by Sam Hunter)

Kenneth Clark, the British art historian

John Walker with Bernard Berenson at Casa al Dono, Vallombrosa, August 1945 (Photo by Professor Frederick Hartt)

Left: *The British novelist Rosamond Lehmann in 1955* Right: *The Italian author Clotilde Marghieri, February 1950* (Photo by Derek Hill)

Left: *Former President Truman visiting "i Tatti," summer, 1956* (Courtesy of "i Tatti") Right: *Igor Markevitch* (Courtesy of "i Tatti")

Berenson and Nicky Mariano in old age (Photo by Derek Hill)

Berenson at Salzburg, 1936 (Photo by Elizabeth Percival)

Celestial Attributions, *a tongue-in-cheek tribute to the ruling connoisseurs at the turn of the century, which included Charles Loeser, Herbert Horne, and Bernard Berenson, drawn by Max Beerbohm (See page 204)*
(Courtesy of the Fondazione Horne, Florence)

The Portrait of a Man *by Titian, which Benjamin Altman bought as a Giorgione on Berenson's advice* (Courtesy of the Metropolitan Museum of Art, Bequest of Benjamin Altman, 1913)

Opposite top: *The* Madonna and Child *by Domenico Veneziano: the most famous painting in Berenson's collection at the Villa "i Tatti"* (Courtesy of the Soprintendenza Alle Gallerie Firenze)   Opposite bottom: *The famous* Adoration of the Shepherds, *known as the* Allendale Nativity, *which Berenson refused to call a Giorgione despite the urging of Lord Duveen, the art dealer he was advising. Now at the National Gallery of Art, Washington.* (Courtesy of the National Gallery of Art)

When Berenson first saw this painting at the turn of the century, he pronounced it a work of Andrea del Verrocchio's studio. Twenty years later, when Berenson was working for Duveen, the painting was sold to a New York collector by Duveen, as a genuine Verrocchio. The art critic Richard Offner saw it on exhibition and published a photograph of the painting side by side with its look-alike, establishing that the painting was an obvious copy. Now in the National Gallery of Art, Washington, the painting has since been demoted to "Style of Verrocchio." (Courtesy of the National Gallery of Art)

The Madonna and Child *by Andrea del Verrocchio, #104A in the Gemaldegalerie, Berlin, which Richard Offner published beside its likeness to establish that this was the original from which the Duveen painting was made* (Courtesy of the Staatliche Museen Preussischer Kulturbesitz)

were always ready to discover, behind the apparently innocent act, some veiled motive of revenge.

Berenson's jealousy of other art experts, Fowles and Duveen concluded, often influenced his professional decisions. Duveen Brothers acquired a fine Bellini from Douglas in 1913 and sent it to Italy at Berenson's request to be cleaned and restored. Some weeks later they received a letter from Berenson saying that Cavenaghi, the restorer involved, had discovered that the painting was a forgery. Berenson apologized for having authenticated it and offered to refund the money. Fowles was not deceived. He wrote, "Douglas responded to the spiteful mock-humility of BB's attack upon his reputation by furnishing a complete provenance for the picture, and the matter ended there."

In addition to suspecting each other, Berenson and Duveen were temperamentally at odds. "They said fine things in public . . . but behind the scenes there was constant bickering and at times outright antagonism." Because of this, Fowles became their intermediary, transmitting whatever Berenson wanted to Duveen and vice versa, for most of Berenson's association with the firm.

What Berenson thought of his new business partner may be ascertained from Mary Berenson's comment to Senda, written from Paris in 1909, that "he seems to have some very real friends here, who console him for the horror of the Dealer's World, which he says is a real inferno." Late in life, Berenson made the astonishing assertion to Behrman, upon which he was never to elaborate, that "Duveen was at the center of a vast, circular nexus of corruption that reached from the lowliest employee of the British Museum right up to the King."

Inevitably, the biggest source of tension was provided by the original agreement that Berenson would receive a percentage of the profits from every sale. Each painting thus sold with Berenson's authentication was to be entered into an "X book" which, to guard against tampering, was numbered in Berenson's own handwriting. So far, so good; but Berenson in Florence could never be certain what had just been sold by Duveen in London, Paris, and later New York, and was ready to believe that he was being shortchanged. This continual and festering source of suspicion and recrimination poisoned the atmosphere until 1927 when Berenson signed a new contract to guarantee him a yearly income of £15,000 ($75,000).

Another source of tension arose from the original agreement between Berenson and Duveen's that he would not expertise for other dealers unless, as it was reluctantly conceded, the request came from them. Again, it was impossible for Duveen to know the truth and he was always convinced that Berenson was breaking the spirit, if not the letter, of this agreement.

It is believed that Berenson never proposed paintings to Duveen's and simply passed judgment on those Duveen wanted to buy. However, Fowles's book makes clear that Duveen needed a resident expert in Italy to hunt up potential buys. One of Berenson's main functions, therefore, was to act as the link between the principal Italian dealers, such as Luigi Grassi, Paolo Paolini, and others, and Duveen Brothers or the French dealer Georges Wildenstein, with whom Duveen's sometimes worked in partnership.

"There was a kind of ritual they played when B.B. came to see a painting," said Marco Grassi, a New York restorer who is grandson of the Florentine art dealer. "If he said, 'This might interest my friends in New York,' he meant Duveen, and if he said, 'in Paris,' he meant Wildenstein. Sure enough, some time later a letter would arrive from Duveen or Wildenstein." Did Berenson take a commission from Grassi? "That would have been unconscionable," Grassi said. The relationship, he implied, was on a more personal footing. "Every Christmas my grandfather would select a beautiful antique binding and send it up to the [*sic*] Tatti as a Christmas card."

Other evidence that Berenson was in constant contact with the art market is provided by a letter to Johnson in which Berenson observed that, upon his return to Florence, he would no doubt find a backlog of new paintings that the dealers had been holding for his inspection. Until their relationship ended abruptly in 1922, Berenson was given an annual stipend by the Baltimore collector Henry Walters (in 1911–12 it was $75,000) to spend as he saw fit. It is clear from this correspondence that Berenson employed scouts, called "runners," to alert him to new buys. Finally, the Edward Fowles memoirs make constant reference to some new painting that Berenson discovered and wanted the firm to buy.

Berenson apparently reserved the impression that he was no longer directly soliciting clients or paintings for salesmen who were too persistent. Early in the 1920s the American author and artist Hendrik C. Andersen, an old friend of the Berensons, attempted to act as intermediary in the sale of a Velásquez belonging to Alessandro Contini of Rome, which, to judge from the correspondence, the Berensons concluded was a fake. In a letter politely detaching them from the affair, Mary Berenson wrote that her husband was curtailing his art-market activities because, it was "the most horrible of all businesses and one for which one gets only abuses and bother. And in his case it was too distasteful to be borne, unless it had been a matter of bread and butter. . . . The utmost he does is to pronounce on the authenticity of pictures submitted to him by one or two friends and a few dealers. . . ."

One must weigh this statement against one from Berenson himself to the French dealer René Gimpel in 1924, two years later. Berenson wrote from Rome that he did not understand why Gimpel was reluctant to ask his advice about prospective purchases. He had understood, Berenson continued, that they had a business agreement that if Gimpel sold a painting with Berenson's advice, the latter would receive 25 percent of the profits, and that this agreement held whether Gimpel proposed the painting, *or whether Berenson did himself.*

As before, a great many paintings made their way to Berenson's own door. Berenson might once have greeted the seller personally; now, a host of barriers was erected. Allyn Cox, then a young artist, who spent a whole summer in 1917 painting at "i Tatti" in the library, recalled that "if a dealer came to the house and had a Leonardo, he was turned away by the butler. If not, Mary would see him and weed out the obviously impossible paintings."

The emissary who managed to make his way to Berenson might find himself, as did the former director of the Walters Art Gallery, Edward S. King, one sunny afternoon in 1929, being "ushered into a dark inner sanctum to confront a gnomelike figure seated behind a lighted desk. It was quite Rembrandt-esque." Such a caller, whether he knew it or not, was at Berenson's mercy. "If he had someone in his study that he wanted to get rid of, he had a bell he could press with his knee, which rang in Mary's study. This is a fact," Cox said. "Then Mary would appear full of apologies, to tell him that he was needed elsewhere. . . ."

Working for the seller instead of the buyer placed Berenson in a radically different position. While advising the customer, Berenson needed to be on his guard to avoid the fake, the too-restored, or the marginal painting that (and he explained to Johnson that there were always some) refused to go into the witness box to be interrogated. In other words, working for the buyer, Berenson was in a position roughly analogous with that of the scholar. As a scholar, he cared only about identifying the hand of a painting's author. He did not care how minor that hand might be, and as an expert conscientiously advising a collector he dared not be sanguine, if he wished to have his client's trust.

However, once Berenson was subsidized by the man whose wares he was appraising, to borrow John Walker's phrase, his position was reversed. To any seller, "it mattered immensely that the work be by the biggest possible hand." For instance, the difference between a painting by Giovanni Bellini alone and one for which, it is concluded, Bellini sketched in the main outlines and perhaps painted the major figures, allowing the rest to be completed by apprentices, is minor to the enjoyment of a painting. It is, however, a major factor in the sale of that painting, involving, say, the difference between £50,000 and £500,000. A famous dealer was at pains not to sell a fake, which would have brought about a disastrous lack of confidence in his acumen, but whether Bellini painted all or most of a certain painting would have seemed like tedious hair-splitting. If the resident expert were to conclude that Bellini's hand was evident, the qualifying statement, "and apprentices," might be muffled in the interests of good business. The more that could be asserted on the painting's behalf, the higher the price asked, and vice versa, although, as the New York critic Richard Offner pointed out, "high prices are far from serving as a reliable criterion of quality. . . ."

However, the repetition of the favorable name, said often enough, would endow the particular painting with "an irresistible magic, and established it by irrefutable logic. Repeat the name often enough and you have rendered it a classic." That such a state of affairs was possible was a result of "our national voracity for culture, and, where men are possessed of wealth, by a fierce and blind efficiency in buying it up . . ."

The market, Offner continued (writing in 1941), had long since dried up. Nevertheless, "the accommodating Atlantic has until recently been washing up works of art on these hospitable shores with every incoming tide. To be sure great masterpieces have now and again turned up among the artistic flotsam, but on the whole the quality and, above all, the physical condition of available objects, have steadily declined. Nevertheless the aim of the trade had been to sustain the pretensions, and the prices, of these objects at an ever-rising level. . . ."

While Duveen pressed for the best possible attribution, the Berensons fought to maintain their position. It seemed a losing battle. It was hopeless for Mary Berenson to insist that her husband had his reputation to consider and that morality must dictate their actions. It was hopeless to try to explain the infinite shades of gray that colored any conclusion arrived at through connoisseurship. Joseph Duveen's mind was closed to such subtleties. What he wanted was a label. He did not want to have to deal with the news that to call a work a Raphael might only mean that it was just good enough to qualify. A major name from Berenson was the signal for a superlative salesman to begin beating his publicity drums; and Berenson was forced to watch in silence, with what inner feelings may be imagined.

Meanwhile, the ultimate responsibility for the attribution rested with the critic. "The seeming crudity of this undisguised preying of dealer upon buyer is tacitly regarded as humanly justifiable," Offner wrote in 1941. "For the buyer, himself a seasoned man of affairs, familiar with the technique of transaction, will recognize the intention, and treat it with the tenderest indulgence; while the 'expert,' the spiritual love-child of this union, is invested with the functions at once of priest and oracle, who may indeed err, but whose inspiration descends from unquestionable sources. Thus each of the three is drawn by a community of interest into a closed alliance against the rest of mankind."

When considering whether such a "vicious system" may or may not have troubled Berenson's conscience, one has to acknowledge the Old Testament tenor of his upbringing, that stern and uncompromising inner voice which declared that whatever one did for an advantage was "materialistic and almost bestial . . ." and that wealth choked up and killed what was finest in men. One can draw some conclusions about the way he felt about money so earned by the fact that he could not bear to touch it, and relied upon others—principally Nicky Mariano—to carry the purse.

Such uncompromising morality found its ally in an equal inner desire for flawless excellence in every area of his life. He must be the model of honorable and upright behavior, as befitted a natural artistocrat, a gentleman, and a scholar.

In conflict with these cultural and personal dictates was the equal inner imperative to win at all costs. To do so meant being the shrewdest player in a very unscrupulous game. "How much money would a business man make if he boggled at perjury, blushed to be caught in a lie and allowed himself to be affected by the inconvenient scruples of the wise concerning theft and usury?'' asked Erasmus, in a question of timeless relevance. To win under these conditions meant, for Berenson, being able to make a cynical appraisal of one's opponent and to prefer clever men who could be bought off rather than men whose very stupidity guaranteed their honesty.

To be at the mercy of such opposing inner dictates is intolerable unless one can keep the warring factions at bay by such distorted and Machiavellian reasoning as, "To tell lies because they are useful, or through sheer malice, is not a great sin; but to tell lies knowing that they are lies, and then, just because they've been said, to immediately take them for the truth and live accordingly, is a gross sin which falsifies all of life."

Berenson's inner unease might be further assuaged by the knowledge that serious scholars distinguished carefully between the private act of certification and the public act of a signed review in an arts magazine. For this alone was one held responsible. Berenson was aware of the distinction and observed it scrupulously, for the most part. So of course was Joseph Duveen. Again, Berenson was subjected to a relentless pressure that he resisted as best he could.

Did Berenson allow his business dealings sometimes to influence his attributions? The subject has been a matter of controversy almost since he died in 1959, and was whispered about before then. Sprigge, Berenson's first biographer, quoted his friend, the connoisseur F. Mason Perkins, that Berenson was "not capable of giving an attribution of which he was not convinced." The statement begs the question, since it gives rise to the assumption that Berenson might well convince himself, in the interests of good business.

However, Sir John Pope-Hennessy, the former director of the British Museum, who was a frequent visitor at "i Tatti," an admirer of Berenson's, and who has defended his reputation against attack, believes that when Berenson's judgment has been found at fault, this can be explained by his lack of knowledge about restoration and his tendency to work from photographs, particularly in later years. However, he was not "culpably wrong."

Prof. Ulrich Middeldorf, a distinguished Renaissance scholar, former professor of art at the University of Chicago and ex-director of the Kunsthistorisches Institut in Florence, was equally and emphatically sure that the charges were without foundation. Sir Ellis Waterhouse, a great British authority on the Old Masters, simply did not know. He added, "It may be impossible to tell." John Walker, former director of the National Gallery of Art in Washington, also did not know, but considered it most unlikely. However, a former disciple, David Carritt, now director of the International Art Investment Trust in London, believed it less damning to think that Berenson sometimes attributed against his conscience than to believe that he never did so. Almost the identical opinion was expressed by Kenneth Clark, the British art historian. Lord Clark remarked, "One has the choice of saying Berenson either made very bad choices or did it for money. I don't know which is more damaging."

Interestingly enough, the question of Berenson's attributions as a whole has not been subjected to a systematic study. No scholar has yet studied the complex evolution of Berenson's connoisseurship to see how well his Lists, which began in 1894 and appeared at intervals until 1968 (the last posthumously), have survived the light of subsequent knowledge. Creighton Gilbert, the Jacob Gould Schurman Professor of Art History at Cornell University, doubted whether such a study would have much statistical value.

"The trouble is that attributions are really only hunches and are not subject to any sort of testing, other than the long-term reactions of other art historians," he wrote in part.

Thus while on the one hand they are matters of feeling, they are also ego-trips (it's pretty wonderful to be able to say with assurance what an artist did and didn't do) and so there tends to be violent reaction to a denial of somebody's attribution; it's almost as if there was a proportion between the instability of the assertion and the indignation when it is denied.

One way, sometimes unfortunate, in which attributions do or do not gain adherence is through the relations of art historians as clusters; art historians who have studied under a professor tend to affirm the rightness of his work, though the best ones later on may gain some perspective. . . .

A possible way in which the correctness of attributions might be tested, in a few cases, which might or might not prove to be . . . representative, would be to locate those cases in which firm knowledge of authorship of works has been obtained after they had been attributed. One could then study the preceding attributions. . . .

Authorities are unanimous, however, about the extraordinary sensitivity of Berenson's eye and the enduring accuracy of his judgments. Rough guesses are proposed that Berenson was right 75 percent or 85 percent of the time, guesses based on familiarity with certain aspects of his oeuvre.

Any broad statistical survey, which is outside the scope of this book, would have to distinguish between those paintings with which Berenson was never commercially involved and those for which he received a compensation, sometimes substantial. Only with this clear distinction in mind can one fairly assess the reliability of Berenson's connoisseurship. Here again, no scholar has tried to determine which paintings entered private and public collections directly or indirectly through Berenson's business dealings and how well these judgments have withstood the test of time. Until recently such knowledge has been locked away in the files of art dealers and chief curators. The situation has changed markedly in the last decade, thanks to the scholarly and pioneering work of such art historians as Federico Zeri, who catalogued all the Italian paintings in the Walters Collection, Baltimore, and has completed two catalogues, on the Florentine and Venetian paintings at the Metropolitan Museum of Art (with two more in preparation), and the extraordinary three-volume study of the Kress Collection Italian paintings by Fern Rusk Shapley.

Mrs. Shapley is now working on a magnum opus, a catalogue of all the Italian paintings at the National Gallery in Washington, which will no doubt provide that institution with its first accurate tally of the number of paintings that have entered its collections through Berenson's business dealings. No such figure is available at present.

My study is limited by the published evidence provided by Zeri, Shapley, and others, i.e., paintings that are known to have entered collections through Berenson's aegis, either working directly for the collector, as in the cases of Johnson, Winthrop, Walters, and Mrs. Gardner, or as advisor to the seller, i.e., Duveen Brothers, Gimpel, and, after 1937, Wildenstein. In the final decades of his life Berenson also worked for the Italian dealer Contini-Bonacossi and thus probably had direct responsibility for a sizable number of other paintings in the Kress Collection. However, Berenson's attributions for him have been omitted because I have been unable to establish, from the scanty evidence available, exactly when Berenson acted as advisor to the sale.

As has been demonstrated, Berenson's purchases for Isabella Stewart Gardner are excellent. The same might be said for his dozen or so purchases, at the turn of the century, for Grenville Winthrop, who left his paintings to the Fogg Museum of Art at Harvard, and to a lesser extent for the extremely knowledgeable Philadelphia collector John G. Johnson who was, in any case, being advised by other experts and on a limited budget. The collection Berenson helped form for Walters raises some doubts and further questions begin to loom when one examines purchases made through Duveen, Wildenstein, and other dealers, with Berenson's expertise.

My study has identified sixty-nine paintings with problematic attributions from Berenson. They fall into four categories. In the first, I have found twenty-one paintings in public collections whose attributions changed from a lesser to a greater hand when Berenson became involved in their sale as expertiser for a dealer. In the second category are four definite or likely fakes. In the third category are forty-one paintings whose attributions would seem to have been too optimistic at the time of the sale, and which have been scaled down by other scholars. Finally I cite three instances in which Berenson made a verbal change of opinion.

This can only be a partial list because the evidence so far published is incomplete. For the same reason it is impossible to know the total number of paintings for which Berenson gave expertise in his role of dealer-critic. When this information is finally made public, it will be interesting to see how statistically significant these sixty-nine paintings may be. In the case of the Walters Art Gallery, for which the information is complete, it has been possible to identify thirty-six paintings bought through Berenson (including those marked "possible" or "very possible") and of that number, fourteen have since been scaled down, or somewhat better than one painting in three. This ratio may or may not be typical of Berenson's business attributions. A list of paintings and summary of their buying history is provided in the Appendix, pages 399–408.

I found numbers of other paintings with suspicious Berenson attributions. They were omitted because the evidence does not conclusively demonstrate that he had a financial interest in the paintings involved.

My intention in this chapter is not to argue for or against a Berensonian attribution. There are, I understand, numerous cases for which the optimistic Berenson attribution is plausible, as when he upgrades a painting from a Titian to a Giorgione, or from an Alvise Vivarini to a Giovanni Bellini. These arguments are for the specialists; I am not qualified to judge.

Nor do I claim that Berenson never held out for a lesser attribution, and lesser profit for himself, although I was only able to find a single purported example of this, the sale of the *Allendale Nativity*. I shall return to this issue later.

My intention is simply to present some circumstantial evidence for the thesis that Berenson gave attributions to the best possible hand when the work was for sale. And, in at least twenty-one cases, there is a published opinion that Berenson made earlier, before he had a financial stake in the matter, that is more conservative.

However I would like to propose that, if Berenson were trying to satisfy the demands of his dealer clients, as seems entirely likely, and if he were to attribute too optimistically, even his exalted position as an Authority would not save him. He had to make plausible attributions and in almost every case, each new attribution (as in the case of paintings in Category A) can be seen as an honest change of opinion when viewed by itself. Only in the aggregate can one begin to see a certain consistency.

IT HAS BEEN SUGGESTED that some of Berenson's early and negative conclusions, in particular those of 1895 for the Venetian paintings at the New Gallery, were a typical attempt to get even with uppercrust British families who had snubbed him when he tried to gain access to their collections. I have not found evidence of this. What is clear is the scrupulousness of Berenson's early work, the breathtaking accuracy of his judgments, and the exclusiveness of his approach. What he presented, in those first Lists of 1894, 1895, 1896, 1897, and 1907, was a relatively small group of works in public and private collections across Europe that he had seen himself. He was constantly revising such lists and enlarging upon them. His book on the *Florentine Drawings* (1903) adds to their number and so do his collections of essays, 1901 and 1902, and his new editions of The Four Gospels. (A list of Berenson's works of attribution is given in the Appendix.)

That such rigorous judgments were subsequently amended can be seen in the case of *Portrait of a Man*, also called *Ariosto*, which was shown at the New Gallery in 1895. When he saw the painting, then owned by A. H. Savage Landor of Florence,

Berenson was intrigued and impressed, but doubted that it was a Titian, as claimed. It must, he thought, be a very early work, or perhaps "only a copy after such a work . . . by Polidoro Lanzani." Berenson noted that the painting was in "deplorably bad preservation."

Seventeen years passed and, in 1912, the painting was for sale by Duveen Brothers. The prospective client was Altman. In a gushing letter of praise, Berenson wrote to Duveen's that the painting was actually by "the rarest, most wonderful, most fascinating and perhaps most discussed artist of the whole Renaissance—Giorgione!"

Why should a painting that Berenson had doubted as by the hand of Titian suddenly appear for sale as a genuine Giorgione? There is a choice of explanations. The first, that many years had passed and, in the interim, a noted critic had changed his mind, which he had a perfect right to do. The second, that the dealer wished to offer a painting to a wealthy buyer for the highest possible price, which meant attaching the best possible name to the work. Titians are plentiful and vary greatly in quality. There are only a few Giorgiones and they are priceless.

One can reasonably argue that Berenson happened by chance to revise his opinion in a direction that coincided with the needs of his new employer. What is more difficult to explain is how a painting could change, in the intervening seventeen years, from being in a deplorable state to being in "a miraculously fine state." What is even more odd is that Berenson, who proposed that Duveen buy the painting, and even made a reference to his 1895 opinion of it, neglected to point out the disparity. There is only one possible explanation for this curious omission and I shall expand upon it later.

In Berenson's Lists of 1932, about which I shall also have more to say, the Altman painting is listed as by Giorgione. It was shown as such in a large catalogue of paintings in American collections published by Duveen Brothers in 1941.

Since the *Portrait of a Man* entered the Metropolitan Museum of Art as an Altman Bequest, it has been cleaned. This cleaning has revealed an extensively damaged surface, whose color is so thinned that the underpainting shows through, especially on the face. It is now labeled as Titian and, the writer Prof. Francis Haskell of Oxford University declared, is a "sad, but still moving, ghost of a picture."

In October of 1897, Berenson published an article in the

Gazette des Beaux Arts of Paris in which he discussed several paintings that were, in his opinion, copies of lost Giorgione originals. One of them was a painting of a woman, *La Schiavona*, then owned by an M. Crespi of Milan and which the owner believed to be a Titian. Berenson did not, and went into some detail about his reasons for considering the painting a Giorgione copy.

In 1909–10, the same painting was for sale by a dealer in Venice named Balboni who offered it to the well-known Paris art dealer René Gimpel. Berenson acted as intermediary for the sale and was also consulted by Gimpel about a possible buyer for his "Titian."

Berenson confessed that his hands were tied, since he had published his doubts about the painting some years before. He castigated Balboni, the Venetian dealer, for spreading the word that Gimpel was buying the Titian on Berenson's advice, making it even more essential that he say nothing in print. Berenson added that he would be glad to write a letter of authentication to be shown to "Mr. A," or anyone else.

He had done more. His English secretary, Maurice Brockwell, wrote for an important London daily paper and was at that moment in London. Berenson had gone as far as he dared in urging Brockwell to write about the painting. He had also been in touch with the eminent art critic Claude Phillips and was sure that gentleman would spread the word.

Even more important than newspaper publicity was a well-placed word from the right people in society. Berenson was writing soon to his dear friends Edith Wharton and the Comtesse de Cossé-Brissac in Paris. He would urge them to see the painting in Gimpel's galleries and tell all their friends. In a matter of days, he assured Gimpel, all of Paris would be talking about his painting. One wonders whether Edith Wharton ever knew that her friendship was being used in so calculating a fashion.

The painting was bought by a wealthy English collector, Herbert Cook, as a Giorgione. He paid £36,000. At the famous Royal Academy exhibition in London in 1930 the painting was listed as "Giorgione or Titian." It was given to the National Gallery, London, in 1942. Its label: Titian.

The letters Gimpel has deposited at the Archives of American Art, 1909–24, provide another clue for the hypothesis that Berenson's assiduous cultivation of society and his regular appearances at their resorts was, at least in part, motivated by business interests. Replying to a letter from Gimpel evidently urging the direct approach, Berenson wrote that he could not deal with the Wideners (father P.A.B. and son Joseph) in that way. Collectors were naturally suspicious and to do so would put them on their guard. However, if Gimpel could manage to show the Wideners his painting, Berenson would be seeing the younger at Saint Moritz and would put in a word at the right moment.

René Gimpel, who married Joseph Duveen's youngest sister Florence in 1913, must have been told the nature of Berenson's relationship with Duveen Brothers. Despite their protracted business dealings, Gimpel appears not to have liked or trusted him.

Gimpel wrote in *Diary of an Art Dealer*, "If small, lithe tigers could speak, they would have the voice and intelligence of this feline Pole. Behind that calculated sweetness a high old roaring goes on. . . . He knows the whole gamut of society and its milieux, but everywhere he has only enemies. The hatred he expends he gets back in full measure; but if he were in a cage with one of his detractors, he would not be the one to be devoured."

The names of Titian and Giorgione are interchanged so frequently in the attributions Berenson gave during a sale that some other examples are worth considering. A *Portrait of a Venetian Gentleman*, now in the Kress Collection at the National Gallery of Art in Washington, provides a further case. This painting, which was sold as a Jacopo di Barbari in the ill-omened Henry Doetsch sale, was another in the group that Berenson believed to be copies of Giorgione originals. Berenson repeated that estimate in 1901. However, when the painting came into Duveen's hands sometime before 1920, Berenson attributed it to Titian and it was sold to Henry Goldman as such. Berenson's Lists of 1932 call the work a Titian.

The painting is shown at the National Gallery as a Titian and Mrs. Shapley's catalogue notes that subsequent cleaning supports this attribution. However, at least one expert on Titian, Harold Wethey, dislikes the strange and uncomfortable tilt of the *Venetian Gentleman*'s head and thinks the portrait should be attributed, as Berenson did in 1897, to a "Giorgionesque Painter."

Another example concerns a portrait, once called *Bust of a Young Woman* and now dubbed *Courtesan*. The picture was originally sold to the second Baron Melchett with Berenson's attribution to Titian and shown as such at the Royal Academy in 1930. It was subsequently "returned" to Duveen's and in 1957 was listed by Berenson as a Giorgione. The painting is now in the Norton Simon Museum of Art at Pasadena where it is labeled a Giorgione.

These examples provide three instances in which portraits by Titian have been called Giorgiones once Berenson had business dealings with them. There is a further case to be considered, the single example already cited in which Berenson steadfastly refused to improve upon a Titian to make it a Giorgione, with far-reaching consequences. The incident is widely believed to be the reason for his celebrated break with Duveen in 1937.

The painting, *The Adoration of the Shepherds* (also called *The Allendale Nativity*), had been owned by the Allendale family in Britain since the 1850s. It was seldom shown and in bad need of cleaning, but had always been considered a Giorgione, an attribution which (despite the sanguine expectations of most nineteenth-century owners) seems to have been accurate. Berenson listed it in 1894 tentatively by Catena (a pupil of the Bellinis much influenced by Giorgione).

When Kenneth Clark was helping to organize a large exhibition of Italian art at the Royal Academy in 1930, the painting was offered to the National Gallery for sale. The asking price seemed, at the time, exorbitant, and the gallery declined. However, the painting was shown at the exhibition and even though uncleaned there was no doubt in Lord Clark's mind that it was by Giorgione. Clark went with Berenson to inspect the painting at that time and Berenson "remained completely silent about it."

Some years later, in 1937, Duveen bought the Allendale Giorgione for 60,000 guineas ($315,000). John Walker was there when the cable arrived. "B.B. said, 'If Joe Duveen paid that much for the picture, he must think it is by Giorgione, and it isn't. It is by Titian.'" Berenson concluded that Duveen intended to sell the painting to Mellon, but the potential buyer was Samuel H. Kress. In 1938, Kress bought the painting as a Giorgione for £103,300, or $516,000.

Walker continued, "B.B. was furious. Thereafter he would have nothing whatever to do with Duveen Brothers, even though this meant the termination of his retainer." According to Walker, Berenson said that this was the only occasion upon which Duveen tried to influence his judgment.

However, there is another version for the reason behind the break with Duveen. It has been noted that Berenson's original contract with Duveen Brothers was amended in 1927. There were many such emendations. The contract was rewritten in the early 1930s, again in 1936, and was up for renewal on January 1, 1938. By the late 1930s, Berenson had become a close friend of Duveen's lawyer, Louis Levy. Shortly before the Berenson contract was to expire, Levy suggested that Berenson ask for a partnership in the firm and an equal share of the profits. The reply from Duveen was that he often sold paintings at a loss, and was Mr. Berenson willing to divide the losses equally? Mr. Berenson's reply to that was that profits were his only concern.

Berenson, Duveen, Nicky Mariano, Louis Levy, and Armand Lowengard (Duveen's nephew who was to become joint owner of the firm, with Edward Fowles) agreed to spend a holiday in Vienna together in the autumn of 1937. (Berenson stayed in Vienna for two months, October and November.) Instead of a vacation, however, Duveen was met with a contract drawn up by Levy on Berenson's behalf. The price of the attribution to Giorgione that Duveen wanted was the contract that Berenson wanted. Duveen refused and the two men parted acrimoniously, their relationship at an end. The painting remained a Titian in all of Berenson's public statements for the next seventeen years.

(Interestingly, the National Gallery of Art has always believed that it owned a Giorgione. In his 1957 Lists, Berenson finally conceded.)

When the Duveen-Berenson correspondence, sealed under the terms of Edward Fowles's will, and in the warehouses of the Metropolitan Museum of Art, is made public, it will be interesting to see how accurately the facts support this account. Partial support is provided by a letter from Berenson to Royal Cortissoz, the New York art critic, which reveals the reason for Berenson's unyielding position. Believing that "i Tatti" had already been accepted by Harvard University, Berenson wrote from Vienna to say that his request for more money was based on his need to establish a fund to give scholarship help to students who would work there after his death.

Lesser Titians were not the only Renaissance works whose attributions underwent a transformation in Berenson's years of expertising for dealers. Three paintings from the Benson Collection, all given Berenson labels as by the lesser-known Marco Basaiti were, once that collection was bought by Duveen in 1927, newly considered to be by the most famous and expensive of the three Bellinis, Giovanni.

St. Jerome Reading, sold by Duveen to Clarence H. Mackay of

Roslyn, New York, was shown as a Bellini in the 1930 Royal Academy Show and given to Bellini "in part" by Berenson in 1932, 1936, and 1957.

The Madonna and Child with Saints, which went to the Jules S. Bache Collection in 1927 with a letter from Berenson stating that it was "a late work" of Bellini, is now at the Metropolitan Museum of Art attributed to: G. Bellini and Workshop.

The Infant Bacchus, which Berenson in 1895 also thought to be by Marco Basaiti, and perhaps only a copy of another Bellini, was subsequently promoted to a Bellini.

Similarly, *Profile Portrait of a Boy* was considered to be by Boltraffio when it was owned by Gustave Dreyfus in Paris in 1907. After Duveen bought the painting Berenson reattributed the work to the better-known Jacopo Bellini, the father of the famous Giovanni. The National Gallery of Art's present label: "Attributed to Jacopo Bellini."

Perhaps the moment has come to discuss exactly what is meant by such labels. They reflect what the present director of the National Gallery of Art, J. Carter Brown, has called "shadings of uncertainty."

"Attributed to" is the accepted way of stating that the museum or gallery staff has inner reservations about the attribution. "Copy of" means that the painting is generally later, although it may be a contemporary of the original. "Follower of," or "circle of," usually indicates an artist trained or influenced by the great man, and "School, Shop, or Studio of" suggests that the work was executed in that artist's studio and is close to, but not on the same level with the master's hand. "Manner of" is used by Federico Zeri and Burton B. Fredericksen to describe a painting which resembles the artist's work but for which only a tenuous connection can be found. Last of all, "imitation" is often the polite label for a doctored-up painting or an outright fake.

This scale of increasing doubt can serve as a fairly reliable guide to labels at the National Gallery of Art, the Metropolitan Museum of Art, the Philadelphia Museum of Art, the Walters Art Gallery, and elsewhere.

Three other paintings, once thought to be by Alvise Vivarini, a Venetian painter under the influence of Giovanni Bellini, were given to the more valuable hand by Berenson once the paintings were for sale by Duveen. A painting once thought to be a work of Bellini's studio, *Madonna and Child in a Landscape*, was also promoted to a G. Bellini when Kress bought the painting in 1937.

"I can assure you," Duveen is reported as saying to his prospective clients, "that the stock of Giovanni Bellinis is absolutely inexhaustible."

The same apparent determination to place a painting in the best possible light can be seen in the case of a Verrocchio *Madonna and Child* that Berenson listed, in 1896 and 1912, as designed and superintended by that artist in his studio. After Duveen's sold the painting to the New York collector Clarence Mackay, the painting was exhibited, with fifty-two others, in a loan exhibition of works sold by Duveen's at the Duveen Brothers Galleries, New York, in 1924, as by Verrocchio himself.

The New York critic Richard Offner wrote at length about the exhibition in the May 1924 issue of *The Arts*. Offner did not mention the painting in the text but published a photograph of it beside an almost identical *Virgin and Child* (104A) in the Kaiser Friedrich Museum, Berlin.

It was abundantly clear from the comparison that the only painting that could be called genuine was the one in Berlin. Subsequently, in Berenson's Lists of 1932, and while Mackay still owned the painting, the work was listed under Verrocchio with the disclaimer, "Later replica of Berlin 104A."

Despite this admission from Berenson himself, the super salesman, who had in the interim bought the painting back again from Mackay, sold it again as a Verrocchio for the Kress Collection. In 1963, Berenson listed the work with a similar disclaimer. The painting is now "Style of Verrocchio" and is in storage.

There is very little evidence about paintings sold through Berenson that have subsequently been found to be fakes, for the understandable reason that museums are not anxious to draw attention to such flagrant examples of money wasted. One of the few examples in this category is *Madonna and Child with Angels*, attributed by Berenson as Central Italian, thirteenth century, and probably 1280. It was briefly shown at the National Gallery of Art in Washington and immediately criticized (by Offner) as being 600 years too early. The painting, now at the Fogg, is considered a modern pastiche in the style of Marcovaldo di Coppo.

The Walters Collection, about which Berenson had no very high opinion, and which he thought could provide a classic example of fake art, contains two possible fakes bought from Berenson. One is a small portrait of a female saint, a copy after a Luini, only a fragment and much overpainted. It was not catalogued and is not on view. The other is a Saint George and the Dragon, bought as a Carpaccio (late fifteenth or early sixteenth century), which has been found to have a sixteenth-century painting underneath. Zeri did not catalogue the work but the gallery has withheld judgment, pending further tests.

Published accounts refer to three occasions when Berenson is known to have had a change of heart (Category D). The first incident, which is well-known, centers around a Leonardo da Vinci, called *La Belle Ferronière*, which has been the subject of controversy for decades. Berenson was not alone in his opinion of No. 1600 when he noted, in 1907, "One would have to regret to accept this as Leonardo's own work."

Years later, an almost identical copy of the same painting came on the American market. Its owner, Mrs. Andrée Hahn, announced that it was the first genuine Leonardo to have come to the United States. Mrs. Hahn further claimed that she had been about to sell it (to the Kansas City Art Institute) when the (by then) Sir Joseph Duveen ruined the sale by publicly stating that the Hahn painting was an obvious copy and that the original was in the Louvre.

Mrs. Hahn sued. Duveen, knowing full well that the Louvre version's genuineness had been doubted for centuries, assembled a panel of experts to support his statement. The group, including Berenson, Roger Fry, and Sir Charles Holmes, then director of London's National Gallery, gathered in Paris in 1923 to compare both paintings and concluded that the Louvre copy was not a Leonardo. Fowles sent Duveen a telegram to that effect the same evening.

When the case came to court six years later, the same experts all testified that the Louvre Leonardo was indeed genuine. Mr. Justice Herman Black remarked, "It required a good deal of mental agility to follow some of the experts from their positive evidence on the stand, to the diametrically opposite views they had expressed in their books long before."

The trial incidentally established that Berenson worked for Duveen: "Later Sir Joseph Duveen was asked about his business relations with some experts he has called to his support for the trial," the *Times* of London reported in the winter of 1929. "One of these is Mr. Bernhard Berenson, who had said of the Hahn painting that it was not even a good copy. Sir Joseph Duveen said he had had business relations with Mr. Berenson. . . ."

The experts offered contradictory testimony. Berenson said

that he had come to the conclusion that the Louvre Leonardo was genuine in about 1914, but could not explain why he had never published his change of opinion. The jury could not reach a conclusion and, in his concluding remarks, Mr. Justice Black made pointed reference to experts who offered nothing better than their own sixth sense as evidence for a picture's genuineness. A retrial was set, but before it could take place, Duveen settled out of court.

Since then, the Louvre Museum officials have established that the museum owns a genuine Leonardo. In advance of its exhibition, "Homage to Leonardo," in 1952, the museum's conservation department took X rays of all the Leonardos and found preparatory sketches underneath the paint that were perfectly consistent in all cases, including that of its controversial *La Belle*.

In the interim, the Hahn *La Belle* has been the subject of a book, *The Rape of La Belle*, which argues heatedly in its favor. The painting was examined by the late conservator of the National Gallery of Art in London, Helmut Ruhemann, and pronounced genuine. The painting was in a vault at Coutts and Co., a London bank, for some time, and then shipped to the United States in care of Leon Loucks, a Wichita, Kansas, lawyer. All attempts to contact Mr. Loucks have failed.

The second published account of a Berenson change of heart took place just after World War II. John Walker, director of the National Gallery of Art in Washington, was attempting to persuade Rush Kress to acquire an extremely important fifteenth-century painting, *The Adoration of the Magi* by Fra Filippo Lippi. The collector replied that the price was far too high unless the painting could be authenticated as by Fra Angelico, Fra Filippo's master.

Walker recalled that, early in the 1930s, Berenson had published an article stating that the painting had been executed by Fra Angelico. Walker went to "i Tatti" to discuss the matter and found Berenson mournful. " 'I know I was wrong,' he declared solemnly. 'The painting is not by Fra Angelico. It is really by Fra Filippo Lippi!' "

Walker was in despair. He rushed to the library and unearthed all the relevant information. "We studied photographs—overall, detail, and microphotographs—and then ultraviolet, infrared and X rays. After a long time, stroking his beard, B.B. looked up and with a conciliatory smile said, 'Johnnie, I do think just before he died Fra Angelico may have painted one or two of the figures. . . ." The painting is now at the National Gallery, with a label: "By Fra Angelico and Fra Filippo Lippi."

The third incident involving a change of opinion involves two published accounts that are diametrically opposed.

According to Nicky Mariano, she and Berenson were on a trip to Berlin in 1922 where they were staying at the Hotel Bristol, and were joined by "the chief assistant to Sir Joseph Duveen" (Edward Fowles) who had some business to discuss. Nicky Mariano, in the bathroom, could not help overhearing.

"Duveen wanted B.B. to endorse the attributions of several pictures sold by him during the war and shipped to America without waiting for B.B.'s opinion and over which he was now having some trouble. B.B. refused categorically in spite of the financial advantage. . . . The chief assistant was a man whom B.B. admired for his seriousness and integrity, and I got the impression that he was not displeased over B.B.'s refusal of Sir Joseph's unreasonable demand. In the evening we went with him to a perfect performance of Offenbach's 'Orpheus in the Underworld.' . . ."

Edward Fowles, the pivotal figure in the drama, gave a conflicting account in his own memoirs. Fowles recalled that he was sent to Berlin to get Berenson to write a letter for the client in support of a Botticelli portrait that Duveen had just sold. Unfortunately the original attribution had come from a rival authority, Dr. O. Siren, whom Berenson disliked. Fowles was sure that Berenson would refuse but was persuaded to make the attempt.

As Fowles expected, when he broached the subject Berenson responded angrily and he did not press the matter further. However, after a performance of *Orpheus in the Underworld* they returned to the hotel for supper and, "as we approached the dinner table on that evening of September 7, 1922, Nicky said to me quietly, 'Edward, if you want a letter about that painting, you must ask BB for it now, before dinner.' I did as she suggested and BB meekly complied. Nicky produced a note-paper block and a fountain pen, BB dictated a letter suggesting that in his opinion the said painting was an unusually late work of Botticelli. I did the writing, he signed it, and we then sat down to an enjoyable meal."

THE 41 PAINTINGS in Category C belong to the heyday of Berenson's inclusivist spirit and many of their judgments are reflected in his famous Lists of 1932. These Lists, which combined The Four Gospels into one compendious book of tightly packed, tissue-thin pages for the first time, took years of preparation and revision. These pages naturally reflect judgments that Berenson had given for dealers and collectors.

Behind the laconic tables of artists by town, museum, and collection, one perceives that a philosophical change has taken place. Berenson has gone from a "contractionist" point of view, i.e., one allowing a work of art to be given the master's name only when it exhibits his genius to the smallest detail, to what might be termed an expansionist view.

Berenson now appeared to believe that ". . . since the style and conceptions of a master are transmitted to his students and assistants, any work that shows clear enough traces of his art may be judged to be his own, even if not executed entirely by his hand."

This expansionist stage, which many saw as a mellowing of a rigorous young critic's judgments from the arrogance of youth to the benignity of age (Berenson was then in his sixties), coincided with the period of Berenson's greatest art-market activity. It did not continue indefinitely. By the late 1950s when, it has also been noted, the majority of the paintings Berenson had authenticated were safely in public collections, one might discern, in his late Lists, a gradual tempering of this largesse.

Berenson appeared to be regretting his former inclusiveness at the end of his relationship with Duveen when, in connection with the Allendale Giorgione, he wrote to Walker that famous artists were subject to fads and that the only factor one could depend upon was quality. He expanded upon that theme later: "By loving too much the name of a great painter and bestowing it on mediocre and even vulgar works of art we dim his fame, diminish his value and reduce him to the rank of an unequal practitioner who had . . . moments of inspiration, but was often too disappointing. . . ."

That others apparently agree is evident from this list.

Paintings given without reservation to a master hand have, often since cleaning, been found unworthy of that hand alone and have been reattributed to, for instance, "G. Bellini and Assistant," or demoted to a minor figure around the great name. In some cases the painting has dropped to a general category, i.e., "Venetian Artist," meaning that this is the most that can confidently be said in its behalf. I have not included in this list many paintings still labeled as by the hand of the master, although no longer on view.

Such is the case, for instance, with a *Madonna and Child* sold before 1941 through Duveen to the Henry E. Huntington Library and Art Gallery (San Marino, California) as a Giovanni Bellini, with a provenance from the collection of Baron Michele Lazzaroni of Paris. According to the curator of art collections at the museum, Robert R. Wark, the Bellini has not been exhibited for years because of its poor condition. "The Bellini scholars who have seen it, regard it as the wreck of an authentic Bellini."

I have also not included many paintings whose attributions have been questioned by scholars but which are still accepted by the museum. One example is the *Madonna and Child with Angel* at the Norton Simon Museum, which a great authority on Botticelli, Yukio Yashiro, called a workshop copy of a Botticelli, an attribution which the museum does not accept. However, other cases in which the scholarly doubt seems general have been included, in order to give the reader an indication of the debate still in progress. This is particularly true for those paintings last to be sold by the house of Duveen.

Another factor that many of the paintings in all these categories share is their frequent poor condition. This was beginning to be a problem with paintings Berenson bought for Johnson. A *Virgin and Child with Saints Lucy and Nicholas* (No. 168), bought as a Montagna, is now considered too overpainted to be exhibited and so is *Portrait of Lorenzano* (No. 48), also from Berenson.

The problem became much more acute in the group of paintings Berenson bought for Walters. Of *The Madonna of Humility* (bought as an Antonio Vivarini but now downgraded to Giambono), Zeri's catalogue notes that the painting had been subjected to a great deal of tampering. Its size and shape had been altered, the original background scraped off and replaced with new gesso, and gold had been spread with a liberal and careless hand over the background, covering tops of trees and halos.

Of the *Madonna and Child* by Girolamo da Udine, bought through Berenson as a Cima, Zeri writes, "Cleaning (1965–67) revealed extensive losses, particularly in the faces of the Madonna and Child, the sky, the green curtain, and the Child's body. Examination of the Madonna's mantle under the microscope disclosed three layers: a modern blue on top, yellow with mauve shadows and, at the bottom, a dark blue. The dark blue was identified as azurite, the yellow as massicot. The modern blue overpaint was removed, but the yellow and mauve layer was allowed to remain, pending further study. . . ."

The case of *The Nativity*, bought through Berenson in 1915 as a Pinturicchio, presented an even more ominous example of the restorer's hand. Zeri wrote, "Taking advantage of the Pinturicchiesque elements in the composition of his painting, someone in modern times drastically changed and repainted much of the surface in order to suggest an attribution to Pinturicchio himself. . . ."—including the faces of the Madonna and Angels.

However, in terms of the problems they present to the restorer, perhaps the worst examples have to be paintings that passed through the house of Duveen. There are numerous examples; one can cite, for instance, *The Virgin and Child with Saint Catherine*, by Francesco Francia, and acquired by Norton Simon for his museum when he bought Duveen's in 1964. As originally painted, the Virgin held the Saint's hand steady as she accepted a ring from the Child. In the repainted version, the Virgin's hand has been relocated around the Child's waist, in an arbitrary alteration of the design apparently executed in order to make the painting look more "classical," and therefore more valuable.

In the case of a *Madonna and Child*, labeled as by Bellini (which also passed into the Norton Simon Museum of Art from Duveen's), making the picture salable involved an even more radical overpainting. The canvas has since been stripped of its modern additions and what remains, a shadowy outline staining the canvas, is considered to be by that master's hand.

Another of the paintings Berenson authenticated, now in the Kress Collection, was heavily restored in an apparently deliberate attempt to imitate the style of a famous artist, Alesso Baldovinetti. *Madonna and Child* passed through Duveen's and into Clarence Mackay's collection before being bought by Kress. Subsequent restoration has removed all trace of Baldovinetti's hand. The work has since been ascribed to Pier Francesco Fiorentino and is in storage.

Yet another painting in the Kress Collection, bought through Wildenstein's (1940–42), was subsequently shown to have been doctored to look like a Baldovinetti. *The Annunciation* is now ascribed to "Style of Alesso Baldovinetti" and is in the University of Notre Dame Study Collection, Notre Dame, Indiana.

Perhaps the most notorious illustration of this particular practice is Masaccio's *Madonna of Humility*. The painting had been on reserve at the Vienna Kunsthistorisches Museum and the museum's decision to sell may have been based upon some reservations about the painting's authenticity. In any event, Duveen took over and Berenson broke his rule never to write about a painting that was for sale when, in 1929 and 1930, he published articles stating that a new Masaccio had been discovered.

Berenson appeared to have no doubts whatsoever. Here, he wrote, was a painting without equal "since the builders of the Pyramids and the sculptors of the Chefrens, and Mycerinus, and Ranefers, and their contemporaries . . ."

Despite Berenson's enthusiasm, the painting did not sell. Behrman wrote, "Duveen had some of his major customers in for a look at it and exercised his panegyrics on it. They didn't work. A picture that wouldn't respond to Duveen's enthusiasm became in Duveen's eyes a picture that was too gross for civilized society. As it stayed on and on in his office, he gradually conceived for it an aversion that amounted to hatred. One day, feeling that he couldn't stand the unwanted guest a minute longer, he summoned his assistant, Boggis. 'Get me an axe!' he said. 'I want to chop up this picture.' 'Don't chop it up, Joe,' Boggis said. 'B.B. likes it.' "

Duveen did not chop up the Masaccio. Instead he had it restored in a last-ditch attempt to make a rather dour-looking Madonna fit the taste of the 1930s. That the repainting was extensive may be judged from "before" and "after" photographs of the work, published in *Masaccio* by Luciano Berti, and his comment that the Madonna's face seemed to be "a cross between the ovoid head painted by Francesco d'Antonio . . . wrongly attributed to Masaccio, and the face of the Virgin in the Pisa polyptych, and the look of an English lady of around 1930; the halo is out of proportion and badly foreshortened and seems made of malleable sheet iron rather than precious metal. . . ." The list is long and the result, everyone agreed, was a radically transformed work. Andrew Mellon approved and bought it in 1937.

"I spent a whole morning with the painting," Sir Ellis Waterhouse said, "and formed the impression that there was about two inches of undamaged paint." Other experts were of the same opinion. The painting has since been stripped down to its present ruined state, is no longer considered to be by Masaccio, and is in storage.

Duveen was already known for his fondness for repainting pictures before World War I. His youngest sister, René Gimpel's wife, liked to recall that her brother had come to visit them in Paris in their palatial mansion and, entering the pink marble hall, had wrinkled up his nose. "Your house, my dear Florrie, smells of the stables," he said with distaste. To which his sister retorted, "It's better than the smell of fresh paint on your pictures."

Edward Fowles defended Duveen's against the "unfair and inaccurate" charge that the firm had overrestored its paintings. Fowles, however, did not have a very high opinion of Baron Lazzaroni, a collector and restorer who was the original owner of the Bellini now at the Huntington Art Gallery, and, according to Sir Ellis Waterhouse, "one of Berenson's main sources" for paintings. The Baron was also the source for a *Portrait of a Youth* now at the Cleveland Museum of Art that is still thought to be by Bartolommeo Veneto, although "very much damaged and repainted."

Mrs. Jean Fowles, widow of the last owner of Duveen's, said that Baron Lazzaroni liked to give the impression that he was far above such matters as selling paintings, but provided Berenson with all kinds of works, including fakes. Such paintings were instantly recognizable, Mrs. Fowles added, because the "mouths were too pretty," in a style much favored in the 1920s. Others with an equally close knowledge of the art world have similar reservations.

In his review of the Italian paintings on view at the opening of the National Gallery of Art in Washington in 1941, Offner discussed the ruthless manner in which many of these paintings had been "patched and disguised by every resource available to man to approve them to the ingenuous taste of the buyer . . ."

Such repainting, he stated, is

> a cold crime of the heart. If the restorer's handiwork can be removed by cautious cleaning, no permanent harm has been done. But the more frequent result has been that the creeping course of the restorer's brush, which professes to replace what time or violence had removed, degrades a primitive beyond redemption. . . .
>
> Although restoration belongs to the unholy system of dealers, it originates in the still more profane desire of the collector—and, I am afraid, of many a museum director as well—to see the picture shine like a pair of new boots.

This, then, is the only possible explanation for the curious "before" and "after" condition of the so-called Giorgione portrait that Altman bought from Duveen: that it had been extensively repainted by Duveen's to improve its chances of being sold as (one might add) a Giorgione. One is also forced to conclude that Berenson knew full well what was happening and kept a calculated silence. Otherwise he would certainly have mentioned the obvious disparity.

Similarly, the "before" and "after" condition of the Masaccio *Madonna of Humility* is often cited as evidence of Berenson's lack of knowledge about restoration. Yet it is hardly a convincing example, since the possibility that Berenson did not know that the painting was being doctored is too remote to be worth considering. What these paintings do show, however, is the likely result when the objectives of dealer and collector are harmoniously meshed.

Offner pinpointed a problem whose full dimensions were only then beginning to be realized. It is now agreed that paintings in public collections should look as much as possible the way the centuries have left them. Styles of restoration vary and the amount of repainting that should be allowed is a subject of lively and continuing debate, but the broad principle, that to do too little is better than too much, appears well established.

This principle is, for the most part, of recent date. In the twenties and thirties, when the big collectors were buying, the reverse was true, as Offner makes clear. Rich men were never going to be persuaded to buy a noble ruin, no matter how authentic its tatters of remaining paint. They wanted it to "shine like a pair of new boots," and the dealers were prepared. How much restoration might be done depended entirely upon how much was needed to sell it.

That a trecento or quattrocento work has been extensively repaired in the course of its venerable existence seems obvious enough, although one's imagination may falter before the multitude of possibilities: fire, floods, wars (sword slashes), heat, mildew, and the normal ravages caused by centuries of encrusted dirt.

What is less appreciated is the extent to which such works were plundered in order to suit the whims of the epoch, particularly in nineteenth-century Italy. Much as Greek temples were dismantled to provide the building blocks for the hovels of savages, paintings were remade to suit the tastes of the times and the exigencies of the marketplace.

Large paintings were chopped down and small ones made large. Too-angular Christ figures were given pads of flesh and too-voluptuous nudes were clothed. It was decreed that Madonnas in the nineteenth century must all wear blue robes; those that did not were quickly made to conform. The same century took an arrogant dislike to Tintoretto's fondness for incorporating accompanying figures into his portraits and chopped them off. For this reason Tintoretto portraits, which have the added disadvantage of being plentiful, are worth even less than Titians.

Even restorations that were well-meant were tactlessly done, in what the Louvre restorer Lola Failland has called "a lack of respect" for the painting. It was common to cover a small loss by repainting a large area and, as an afterthought, to "prettify" the work. Before World War I, it was common for a restorer to repaint a Madonna's face. Paintings on wood often suffer most from centuries of expansion and contraction, and a technique was in use to take the painting off the wood and replace it on canvas, a process that frequently took with it the "soul" of the painting.

It is believed that, whenever Berenson erred in the attribution of a painting, that error can be traced to his unfamiliarity with the devilish cunning of the restorers. I have cited two examples that could tend to support the argument that this was not necessarily true, but, assuming that these are not typical, I would like to deal with the subject from two aspects. The first, How much did Berenson know about restoration?

From Berenson's letters to Mrs. Gardner one sees that he had been on his guard for years. In 1902 he wrote that he had already been studying the problem for fifteen years—which would mean that he began to be concerned about it during his first year in Europe, at the age of twenty-one. To that end he had cultivated the friendship of Luigi Cavenaghi, an old and highly respected restorer on the Corso Porta Nuova in Milan, who relied on a few primitive chemical tests and a finely honed intuition. Cavenaghi, Berenson wrote, had X rays for eyes. He crept over the surface of a painting millimeter by millimeter to determine how well, or badly, it had been treated, and repaired it with the delicacy and skill of a surgeon.

The evidence available to such an expert might be microscopic but revealing. Minute unevennesses of surface, conflicting stress marks as the paint had aged, or even subtle gradations in tone, indicating that a newer paint had supplanted the old, could serve as revealing signals. There are also those subtly jarring inconsistencies of style that are even harder to define. Detecting a too-restored painting is, according to Marco Grassi, "a knack, a bit like having a musical ear," something that can never be taught.

Cavenaghi was the one who had so skillfully removed the

grime and bad varnish from Mrs. Gardner's Chigi Botticelli, who had lovingly filled in the cracks and protected it with new varnish, to produce the miraculous transformation that graced Mrs. Gardner's collection. Cavenaghi was also the one who had effaced the effects of centuries of neglect from Berenson's Perugino Madonna, which had hung in a church for 400 years getting ever filthier, more blistered, and dried-up. In fact, Berenson routinely used Cavenaghi's talents to rescue his paintings.

There is no question, however, that the science of restoration was in its infancy. Twenty years later, restoration began to pass from the hands of the old craftsmen to those of the art historians and technicians, who combined scholarship with new methods and sophisticated techniques. Today's techniques vastly expand a restorer's craft. X rays will tell him whether other paintings are concealed beneath the surface, whether faces are new or features repainted. Ultraviolet rays will indentify venerable paint and its more recent replacements. Chemical analysis will, in some cases, pinpoint the actual paint used. Tests will date the age of the wood and the canvas in question although according to one restorer, this information is of limited value. Fifteenth-century wood and eighteenth-century canvas are still reasonably easy to find.

Since Duveen's main restorer, Madame Helfer, worked in Paris, Berenson could not have had the close knowledge of the actual process of restoration that he had watched at Cavenaghi's studio. Perhaps Berenson did not know what transformations Duveen was affecting on the paintings he had attributed, although he certainly had his suspicions. A letter is said to exist from Berenson to Duveen at the time of the 1930 Royal Academy show urging him not to let his clients lend their paintings in case some malicious person should say that they all seemed restored by the same hand. Or perhaps Berenson could not afford to inquire too closely. I shall return to this point shortly.

After World War II, Berenson again began to work closely with a restorer. His final mentor on all questions of condition, now retired and living outside Geneva in a handsome house with an atrium court filled with antiques and his own Degas-like paintings, is Prof. Jean (Giannino) Marchig. Professor Marchig is a former portraitist who became a restorer and worked with Berenson on paintings to be sold by Wildenstein following World War II. Marchig explained that they collaborated. A painting would be sent to his Florentine studio for cleaning and he and Berenson would jointly examine it.

Professor Marchig said, "Berenson knew and understood a great deal about technical problems. He had a great understanding of the painter, based on a sensibility that was absolutely exceptional, almost infallible. If he saw a false [forged] painting, he didn't need to look at it with a magnifying glass. He could sense it at once."

Professor Marchig continued that Berenson had a specialized knowledge of the painter's technique, as well as a keen awareness of those surface anomalies that betray a restorer's hand. However, Marchig emphasized that such refinishing might have been so expertly done that the surface revealed no clues. Here one needed a sense of style. Berenson had this to the highest degree.

That Berenson did not understand condition is "absolutely false," Professor Marchig insisted. "He could see it very well. If a painting is not in good condition, it lacks quality, and he could see it right away. He could see it."

If indeed Berenson's own knowledge of technique slowly improved over the decades, and one has no reason to doubt Professor Marchig, one arrives at the more difficult question: How much did Berenson care and, as a corollary, what were his standards? Again, one must return to the early correspondence with Mrs. Gardner. At an epoch when the most radical and brutal methods of restoring a work were perfectly accepted, we find him inveighing against such destruction of the painting and praising Cavenaghi because he added nothing of his own. Cavenaghi only removed the damage of the centuries, including subsequent repainting, and then left the picture alone. That Berenson should approve of this then-radical approach to restoration is sufficient indication of his own enlightened attitude, and one far in advance of his time.

Berenson was also at pains to protect Mrs. Gardner from a too-restored work. She should not buy one of the highest priced paintings in the Panciatichi Collection, a Crivelli, because, he said, the background had been completely repainted and that, for a Crivelli, meant half the painting. Berenson told Mrs. Gardner fervently that he would as soon sell her a doctored-up painting as hold up a bank.

However, once Berenson shifted from representing the interest of the buyer to representing the seller, his standards for a work underwent a gradual but perceptible slackening. Such a shift of viewpoint may be seen in an essay in which he argued that repainted heads were perfectly acceptable.

Discussing a Botticelli, *Madonna and Saints*, in the Accademia in Florence in 1926, Berenson wrote that he had dismissed the work when he saw it thirty years before because he had realized that the faces of the Madonna and Child had been repainted. Now, Berenson was ready to reevaluate the painting and reconsider his decision not to call it a Botticelli. Despite the repainting, "its unfortunate presence need not, as hitherto, prejudge the question whether the rest of the picture is by Botticelli." Instead, he called upon his long familiarity with the artistic personality of Botticelli and concluded that the painting could still be called an autograph work.

Berenson appears to have abandoned his purist perspective with the thought that every painting had been retouched somewhere. "The only painting in a pristine state which I know," he told Morra in 1931, "is Botticelli's 'Birth of Venus.' " One is led to wonder how much Berenson's liberalized standards were due to a genuine conversion, however misguided, and how much to the undeniable fact that the supply of well-preserved Italian paintings was almost exhausted, as Offner has noted, and that if he did not relax his standards there would be nothing left to sell.

The matter of repainted faces deserves a further examination since most museums nowadays would agree with the former restorer of London's National Gallery, Helmut Ruhemann, that the complete reconstruction of a major part of the painting, such as the head or an entire hand, is inadmissible. Ruhemann wrote, "However accomplished a draughtsman and painter the restorer may be, he can never match the original style, even if he were given a chance of practising his version a hundred times. . . ."

Asked about his philosophy of restoration, Professor Marchig said, "My theory is that one should recreate the harmony of the painting, to give the spectator a vision of unity; to show how the painting must have looked at the moment when it was created."

Exactly how would one do this? What would one replace and what leave untouched? Professor Marchig replied by giving the example of, say, an El Greco Christ whose features had been obliterated. El Greco's faces of Christ are numerous and very similar in style. Supposing, he continued, one found an almost identical painting in Madrid? One copied the missing features from this model and "the painting is saved." One is left wondering whether the painting was saved, or the dealer who sold it.

SEPARATE
BEDROOMS

Marriage is a sacrament tempered by adultery.

—BERNARD BERENSON,
The Bernard Berenson Treasury

ALTHOUGH OUTWARDLY EMANCIPATED, an impeccable example of the civilizing effect of Western culture, Berenson
remained influenced by customs and beliefs that had been incul-
cated during his earliest years. Of this, he seemed unaware. He
was conscious only of an inexplicable genuflection to an inner
inconsistency which he could neither identify nor explain, but
which had to be periodically appeased.

He felt compelled to look at the new moon, but never
through glass, to make three bows and turn over the loose cash in
his pockets, and did not seem to connect the observance of a
superstition with the *broche*, or blessing, that was a ritual of his
early training. For observant Jews, the *broche* must be recited on a
host of occasions, including the first sighting of the new moon. To
Berenson, the act remained an inexplicable quirk of his nature, "a
drag towards superstition in any and every one who was brought
up . . . in a magical world."

Similarly it was a sine qua non of his social code that men and
women should not spend the whole night in the same bed. This
doctrine had its probable origins in the same early indoctrination;
as has been noted, the Eastern European Jewish husband was
prohibited by law from remaining in his wife's bed overnight.

This view, which Berenson steadfastly maintained, was guaranteed to cause astonishment and shock among his friends after World War II. But, at the start of the marriage, it was consistent with the prevailing Edwardian code. Separate bedrooms were socially correct and, for the Berensons, symbolized the comfortable distance that ten years had brought about, as well as a freedom to act independently, which, it is believed, was the agreement when they married. Evidence that this was the case is provided in a letter that Mary wrote to Neith and Hutchins Hapgood in the early 1920s, in which she referred to the supposed agreement between Bertrand Russell and his new second wife that he might go on seeing his mistress. Such arrangements, Mary declared, never worked. "Our own haven't been truly satisfactory, though perhaps . . . inevitable."

It would be an error, however, to read too much into the amiable pact struck by the newlyweds. The strong indication is that it was designed to give ample scope to their joint need for an illusory freedom. Mary was too much the child of her feminist mother not to deeply suspect the havoc wrought by marriage, having heard all her life that husbands make the lives of women ". . . one long torture. What is invalidism compared to *that*?"

More to the point, Mary had grown up observing a relationship that turned an otherwise generous and loving woman into a shrew who pieced together the love letters sent by her husband's mistress and read them aloud to her children, obliging them to side with her in the unresolved battles of her marriage.

Such deeply planted suspicions found their counterpart in similar doubts of her husband's. In Berenson's culture, love was an undreamed-of luxury within marriage. His mother, the major target for the husband she had rejected, seduced her children into defending her against his rages. Berenson, too, had concluded that intimacy was only possible at a safe distance. Closeness was wounding. One must be protected from its devastations.

The limits of their pact were defined by loyalty. Family ties were unbreakable; it was part of his upbringing as well as hers. There were people who had become "one's own for ever," and one could grumble about them and inveigh against them but eventually one went on loving them, "as one does the people one has accepted without further chance of change." Flirtations were tolerable if they did not threaten the basic contract. To be married yet a free agent was, for someone who loved the thrill of the chase, and only dreaded entanglement, the perfect solution. By the same token, Berenson would have failed miserably as devoted husband, but was capable of an enduring loyalty toward those intimates who, sensing his needs, kept their demands to a minimum. Mary understood.

Their pact was also circumscribed by the fact that he needed her. She wrote many of his letters, spent four or five hours a day correcting his proofs and in the laborious and thankless task of indexing his books. She read, commented upon, and helped revise his manuscripts. She organized his photo collection, supervised his library, and even acted as preliminary reader, weeding out the new books not worth his trouble to read.

Mary paid all the bills. She managed the estate with its seven farms. She oversaw the restorations, additions, and repairs. She directed the household staff, composed the menus, and acted as tireless hostess. He would have been lost without her.

In part payment Berenson appears to have agreed to include Mary's name on his attributions, at least at first, since she spoke to his family of "our" conclusions. After Berenson began working for Duveen he also seems to have agreed to divide the profits. However, in 1917 Mary complained to Edward Fowles that their business agreement was not working. She wanted her share in order to provide for her daughters and, although agreeing in principle, "each time I ask for my share of our earnings, he makes a great fuss."

In those first years, they were making genuine efforts to tolerate each other. Berenson tried not to mind that Mary's gaze was always fixed at some distant spot on the horizon, toward England and "home" and heroically agreed to join her for summers at Friday's Hill (whose bucolic setting was genuinely attractive to him) despite the cacophony of her child-oriented life there. He even tried to accept philosophically the thought that she would always (probably) love her daughters more than she did him and to ignore, in himself, the imperious demands of a child once cheated of his mother's exclusive love by three younger sisters and a brother.

For her part, Mary tried to humor B.B. and accommodate herself to his needs. She would do the writing where detailed answers were required, "for I know from experience that he is no good at answering questions in a letter." She would manage his family and smooth the path for their visits. She understood the rigorous code required of Berenson's intimates, that they love whom he loved and condemn those he despised. She also understood how completely she was required to revolve around the sun of his whims.

"Maybe I spoil him, but I assure you I should regard it at present as a crime to let him suspect I was tired . . . or not quite happy, or to be half a minute late, or to leave even a handkerchief lying in a chair," she wrote to Senda in 1903, revealing how completely she was prepared to live up to his perfectionistic expectations.

Mary even took B.B.'s rages with indulgent fondness, saying of his invariable battles with station masters and porters, "I was delighted the dear thing had energy enough to fly into a rage." Mary was, in fact, "managing" her husband, just as Hannah advised. Men, Hannah wrote later, "are by nature unreasonable and have to be cajoled. They cannot be driven but must be coaxed. One feels undignified in descending to such methods, and yet I feel sure it is the best way. From the fact of their position of Lordship, encouraged at first by the wife's self-abnegation, they get to a place where they *have* to be managed; and the wives I have known who have made a success of marriage have always been women to pet and coax their husbands. . . ."

Mary appears to have made these concessions with great good humor and was irritated only by what looked like intractable meanness on her husband's part. She wrote to "dearest Senda" in 1903 that "he finds my housekeeping and way of spending money awful! The cook (really a good one, on whom everybody that stays here compliments me) is an idiot and beast, and everybody is cheating us. That I daresay is fairly true, and I suffer from it myself, but not half so much as if I spend my time haggling and beating people down."

Mary concluded thoughtfully, "I *think* this increasing irritation may be a sign of returning health. . . ."

In those first years of marriage, despite what Berenson liked to think of as his complete physical collapse, he demonstrated his usual zest for life by energetic expeditions to the art markets of London, Paris, and Rome, summers spent at Saint Moritz, and an indefatigable round of flirtations. Whether those flirtations were real or feigned or an inextricable mélange of personal inclination and good business practice, is impossible to determine. The ladies, however, seemed charmed and were "furious," Mary declared, to have her snatch this eligible bachelor from under their noses. Or they were not really furious, and Mary was embellishing the gossip that Donna Laura Cagnola and Adelaide Placci, the wives of his best friends, were secretly in love with him, and that Donna Carmelita, otherwise known as "The Zucchini," had vowed never to speak to him again or meet Mary, and that the Duchess Nicoletta—one more gay companion of his Saint Moritz summers—was heartbroken. The information in Mary's letters is given with such relish that it is difficult to extract the truth from so much victorious crowing.

Berenson's single-minded pursuit of married women of what the French delicately call "a certain age," who were wealthy and socially well-placed, was in no way affected by his own loss of eligibility. On his trip to Chicago in 1904, Berenson was flirting with a "rollicking squillionairess blazing with jewels," and by 1906, Berenson was becoming known in London as the *"séducteur de la cinquantaine"* (seducer of the fifty-year-old).

He had lunched or dined with Lady Aline Sassoon (who, Mary said, was even taller than she and much stouter) for fourteen days out of his sixteen days in London. The remainder of the time was spent with a Mrs. Leslie, said to be mistress of the Duke of Connaught, who was said to be insanely jealous of Berenson. Mary was delighted to see her "butterfly" husband enjoying himself because it would make him want to come to England more often.

Lady Sassoon, the daughter of the Baron and Baroness Gustave de Rothschild, known for her good works in Jewish charities and her emerald, sapphire, and gold jewelry, who made an equal practice of collecting scintillating young music and drama students, and who was important as a social connection, was one matter. It was, however, quite another affair to have B.B. enamored, in his heedless and incorrigible way, with the most beautiful girl in Europe.

She was Gladys Deacon, a ravishing twenty-year-old who descended upon "i Tatti" in February 1901, barely a month after their marriage. Even at that age, Gladys Deacon was notorious, the daughter of a Boston millionaire, Edward Parker Deacon, who shot his wife's lover in a hotel room in Cannes when Gladys was eleven years old. Gladys was promptly sent to a convent from which she was rescued by her mother, in defiance of a court order giving custody to her father.

Miss Deacon spent some years being "finished" in France, Germany, and the United States and was introduced into society to sensational effect. She was not only exquisite, with a Hellenic profile and large, lustrous blue eyes, but witty and high-spirited.

She was accompanied everywhere by her mother, now Mrs. Baldwin, who did her utmost to marry off her enchanting daughter to the highest bidder, and almost succeeded. (In 1902, Crown Prince Wilhelm of Germany, son of Kaiser Wilhelm II, gave Gladys a ring but the Kaiser made her give it back.) Despite, or perhaps because of, her mother's relentless maneuvering, Gladys held out until she was forty years old when, to everyone's surprise, she became the Dowager Duchess of Marlborough. (She died in 1977 at the age of ninety-six.)

Berenson, who enjoyed unlikely newcomers, was simply intrigued by this ravishing creature, around whom rumors seemed destined to hover like swarms of gnats. She was always about to be engaged or considered spoiled by her frivolous Paris life or corrupted by the ruinous success of her London season and said to be hated by every hostess in England. Mary was in a "dreadful scramble" to get the house in shape to receive Gladys and her mother, who arrived in midweek with their maid, their dog, their endless "toilettes," and the latest Paris gossip. Mary found herself cornered by Mrs. Baldwin, who wept sentimentally on her shoulder, while Berenson swept off with the other member of the party. All day long they were somewhere on walks or endless excursions to galleries. Mary thought Gladys was clever, "but very capricious and incapable, I should say, of intellectual discipline." However, realizing that B.B. was quite intrigued by this peerless example of the adolescent-minded woman he liked so much, Mary had the sense to keep her opinions to herself and managed to think that Gladys's visit was doing B.B. some good.

The Baldwin-Deacon visit to "i Tatti" a year later was less successful. Gladys came for a month, just as dazzling, with a beauty that made one breathless, and still capricious as a child. That, it transpired, was her undoing, as far as B.B. was concerned. "They couldn't take a drive together, but every few moments the carriage had to be stopped and he had to get out and pick up his hat which she had snatched off & thrown on the road, or over the hedge. . . ." Those constant ignominious descents, scrambling down to retrieve his hat, were too much for "Bibbins," as Gladys called him. Or perhaps it was the fact that she never read a book. Or that her only subject for conversation was herself. Whatever the cause, B.B. confessed that he was glad to see her leave.

Mary's gamble of letting events take their course had been a success. And it was a gamble, since the Reinachs, who had been with them at Siena, warned Mary plainly of the dangers of exposing B.B. to such a consummate charmer. But Mary was sure that Gladys was incapable of loving anyone.

In addition, "B.B. is of age, and must look after his own heart. Nothing could ever induce me to get into the position of keeping a person's affections that wished to stray elsewhere. I suffered too much from that myself, to inflict the same on anyone else!" Some years later, Mary was able to remark complacently of Gladys, now aged twenty-eight, "She is rather heart-breaking now, when you think what she was." When Berenson saw her again in 1919, "a sort of widow in weeds," he didn't recognize her.

Berenson was organizing "art pilgrimages" with his latest darlings, the ever-present, self-effacing Countess Serristori, Lady Sassoon (to Umbria), Mrs. Cooper Hewitt (Tuscany), and the right people everywhere. In the spring of 1907 they set off to explore Apulia, Berenson and Carlo Placci and Placci's nice French nephew Lucien Henraux, followed by a contingent of nobility in two other motors that included the Prince and Princess of Turn and Taxis and a wild and fascinating Pole named Rembrelinski. Berenson had discovered the motor car in 1905 and, from then on, intoxicated by the power it gave him to visit "just one more church," became more indefatigable than ever. In all of this he was abetted by the Welshman Parry, who had emigrated to Florence where he was discovered by Berenson to be the only mechanic in the city who understood cars. Berenson hired him as a chauffeur and Parry hurtled everywhere although, as people said, "he never really learned to drive."

At home there were people for every meal and the same idle, animated, and malicious conversations. Poor Mountenay Jephson, that hero who had been Stanley's chief on an expedition to rescue Emin Pasha in 1887–89, was involved in a homosexual scandal in Florence and Mary was single-handedly insisting that the gossips make a public retraction, while at the same time trying to marry him off. Mary was also organizing the private life of Israel Zangwill, to make sure that he did marry, even though he feared that his prospective wedding to a Gentile might hurt his new involvement in the Zionist cause. The hopeless Perkins had just married Miss Alcott on nothing a year, but fortunately she was "plucky," and they were still being invited everywhere by the Berensons. He had not yet metamorphosed into the "dreadful" Perkins who would try to cut B.B. out of the American market and hog it all for himself.

Janet Ross was as inimitable and eccentric as ever. Her husband having died, she was now directing her vigorous disapproval at Lina, still furious that she had married the penniless Waterfield, and finding energetic fault with the world in general. Logan told Hannah that he lunched with her in the spring of 1908 and that they had driven out to pay a call on Mrs. Mabel Dodge, a wealthy Buffalo woman who moved to Florence with her second husband and became known subsequently as a friend of the Steins and D. H. Lawrence.

Mrs. Ross was in one of her most genial cursing moods and Damiano was the most homicidal and monstrous driver she had ever known—the road to the Dodges' villa the most dangerous and difficult in Italy—the villa itself absolutely hopeless & uninhabitable, all their improvements terrible and they themselves the commonest people she had ever known.

As we drove away she almost popped out of the carriage in her anxiety to point out walls that were sure to fall down & she counted at least 60 trees that were certain to die. If any of them survive the effect of her evil eye it will be a wonder. She thoroughly enjoyed herself. . . .

There was plenty to gossip about. In that ceaseless round of new faces there were bound to be innocents abroad who were worth having for dinner if only to see them fall into the traps laid for them by that clever Zangwill. There was always some new story, such as the one about the husband of their friend "Rezia," said to have been a virgin when he married, or some new romance to be encouraged. When Gordon Craig, the talented young stage designer who was the illegitimate son of Ellen Terry, had the misfortune to fall for a married woman, Neith Hapgood, Mary was charmed.

"I took compassion on him and invited him to lunch tomorrow to go to La Gamberaia, & Neith will walk with him there through the woods," Mary wrote to William Rothenstein adding, "as she is going away on Wednesday, nothing can happen!" The plot was described in her neat, eminently sensible handwriting, and one imagines the letter being sealed with a wet flourish.

Berenson enjoyed the gossip as much as Mary did, but was less interested in manipulating the strings of the dramatis personae. For him the almost compulsive search for new faces had to do with his needs for conversation, the challenging kind that would "draw him out," for companionship, since, increasingly, he became incapable of being alone for any length of time, and toward the goal of some idealistic and unfulfillable union of complete oneness with another. Not only did he seek an "audience to whom one is always playing up," but he depended upon it in order to define himself. He indiscriminately needed people and took them on almost any terms, so long as they did not threaten his livelihood or his amour propre. Anything was better than the trapdoor of depression, or what he called accidie, into which he might hurtle with unnerving suddenness and whose presence manifested itself in continual stomach upsets, bouts of colitis alternating with just as painful bouts of constipation.

Berenson was reluctant to see "enemies" and, also, some of the great men of his day. The English essayist and caricaturist Max Beerbohm, for instance, who lived in Rapallo at the end of his life, might be praised by Berenson but never visited, because Berenson had a fixed notion that Beerbohm had hid under his bed when Berenson once visited him, to avoid seeing him. Nothing anyone said could change his mind.

An equal readiness to imagine himself ignored, if not actually slighted, can be seen in Berenson's ambivalent relationship with the philosopher Santayana. He and Santayana had just met in the Hotel Danieli in Venice, Berenson told Learned Hand in the winter of 1939. Santayana was occupying two rooms of the hotel and spent all day writing. He read the newspaper during dinner and went to the reading room afterward.

They spoke of old friends and Santayana asked Berenson what he was doing in Venice. When Berenson replied that he was there to see paintings, Santayana remarked, "Oh, I thought they had done all they could to advance you along the line of your ambitions," a remark hardly calculated to endear him to his listener. There was not another word about what he, Berenson, was thinking and doing, Berenson wrote indignantly.

Berenson concluded that Santayana was "a very self-satisfied, rather maliciously cynical, sniggering, sneering old man" who "kept his heart on ice." Yet Berenson felt bound to wonder how someone who lived utterly alone could be so content. When Santayana died in 1952, Berenson was still wondering about that.

Finally there was the Italian poet and dramatist, Gabriele d'Annunzio. Before they met, Berenson had seen D'Annunzio's mistress and chief source of inspiration, Eleanora Duse, acting in one of his plays. Berenson was intrigued but also repelled by its "aura of moral sultriness," as well as too garish a glitter in those precious jewels he strung together as words. Still, it was impossible to ignore such a towering personality, once D'Annunzio and La Duse took a villa a stone's throw from "i Tatti" at Settignano.

Carlo Placci, who knew D'Annunzio, arranged their meeting at Doney's, the famous Florentine pastry shop, and the men circled warily. Then they began to exchange visits.

Their opposed views of life were obvious from the start. ". . . the little D'Annunzio, his legs not reaching the floor, began to talk and as the lovely voice of crystal Italian reached the listeners they were subjugated. He expounded himself: his life as built on two masculine principles, Istinto and Orgoglio; and the two feminine principles, Volonta and Volutta. . . . Bernard, listening with a face of disgust, broke out, 'And where, Signor d'Annunzio, is the intellect?' There was a pause over all ears. 'I am the intellect,' replied the truculent insect in his bewitching tones."

It was La Duse Berenson liked, rather than her poet-lover, and this was why they were invited to "i Tatti" to listen to music. It was evident, to Mary, that La Duse adored D'Annunzio, but that he had only "affectionate contempt" for her. On the contrary, it was apparent to Berenson that D'Annunzio's famous women friends made him feel "small and unworthy," and this brought out the boastful and vulgar aspects of the poet's personality. What Mary and B.B. could agree upon was that D'Annunzio and Duse stayed far too long and were immune to hints.

Logan wrote to "Dearest Mother" from "i Tatti" in 1903, "We are all sleepy today as D'Annunzio and the Duse came last night for some music and stayed till 12 o'clock. Mariechen generally has a clock which she winds up when she wants people to go and as the winding makes a great noise, the hint—if hint isn't too mild a word for it—is always taken. But last night we were in the music room without the clock, so nothing could be done. . . ."

Berenson said subsequently that D'Annunzio had too many defects. He claimed that D'Annunzio took his false view of the gay life (women, wine, and song) seriously while being flippant about art. Not to take art with sufficient seriousness was the ultimate sin in Berenson's eyes, but the charge seems baseless. Worse still, Berenson sneered, D'Annunzio believed his own lies.

Behind the faultfinding one senses that Berenson found D'Annunzio too formidable. Or perhaps he saw too many unwelcome resemblances in this tiny man with such a mesmeric ability to charm, who monopolized the conversation, who chased women with relentless faithlessness, who was so bombastic, and such a poseur. Years later, when Berenson was traveling in northern Italy, D'Annunzio sent a telegram, *"Je vous embrasse et je vous attend"* ("I greet you and I await you"). Berenson would not go to see him. How horrible it was, he murmured, the day La Duse came to unburden her grief at losing D'Annunzio. She showed such a lack of restraint and such animal grief that it was quite repellent.

Berenson had published his *Drawings of the Florentine Painters*, his collections of essays, was preparing revised editions of The Four Gospels, and was contemplating a comprehensive index of all the Italian paintings that would result, twenty-five years later, in his Lists of 1932. Beyond that, he was at a crossroads, certain only that his intellectual curiosity was undimmed and his eagerness for experience as vigorous as ever. He had no right to complain, he told Hutchins Hapgood in 1905. "I dare say I shall be *wanderjahring* [wandering] it again for years. . . ."

In the Easter of 1906 Ray Costelloe, Mary's older daughter, was at Cambridge, where she had won a swimming championship and had written her first novel. Karin, at age seventeen, was having ear problems and had undergone the first of several operations in an unsuccessful attempt to retain her hearing. Both girls were expected at "i Tatti" for the Easter holidays and Mary, as indefatigable matchmaker, begged Alys for the names of two young men who would keep them company. Alys nominated John Maynard Keynes, then twenty-three, the future British economist, and an Oxford undergraduate, Geoffrey Scott, aged twenty-two.

Scott, who was destined to play a large role in the drama of "i Tatti," was born in 1884, the youngest of seven children. His father, Russell Scott, was a prosperous Unitarian flooring manufacturer, and his mother Jessie, "one of a large family of exceptionally strong and original characters." His uncle, C. P. Scott, was the famous editor of the *Manchester Guardian*.

Scott had been educated at private schools and, when he first visited "i Tatti," was at New College, Oxford, where he displayed an extraordinary literary talent, as well as a particular interest in architecture. He was tall, slim, and nearsighted (in later years, while attached to the British Embassy in Rome, he affected a monocle) and engagingly oblivious of the dashing impression he created.

His brown hair was usually casually rumpled or, on the rare occasion when it was combed, slicked down severely, and he conveyed the impression of a charming intellectual who was absentmindedly incapable of taking proper care of himself. ". . . for several days he shaved with his cigarette case as a mirror before he bothered to find one in my Mews flat," his close friend, W. H. Haslam, wrote. He was the most delightful of conversationalists, "the best raconteur I have known. So much so that he would hold people late into the night against their will."

No more talented and agreeable companions could conceivably have been chosen to amuse Mary's daughters and Keynes obliged by falling in love with Ray "a little bit . . ." Describing the house party to Lytton Strachey, Keynes wrote, "The comfort here is incredible; the cypresses and sun and moon and the amazing gardens and villas in which we picnic every day high above Florence have reduced me to a lump of Italian idleness. We go to bed later and later and gradually find methods of working five meals into the day. . . ."

Having invited Scott and Keynes for her daughters, Mary could not refrain from trying her own luck. Keynes responded with flattering promptness, his interest in Ray eclipsed by an even more eager interest in Ray's forty-two-year-old mother. He wrote to Strachey, ". . . she roars with laughter the whole time, allows you to laugh at her, and never worries one." When they all went motoring through Tuscany, Mary was "full of Italian and money and which hotel was best and what food they could cook best. We must have cost her pints of gold—for everything down to entrance fees to galleries was paid."

As for the long-legged Scott, with his perfect Botticellian good looks and his already pronounced susceptibilities (he was a "kindred spirit" of the opposite sex, his friend Haslam wrote), he came for a week and stayed for a month. A year later he was back at "i Tatti" in the somewhat tenuous role of secretary-librarian when William Rothenstein, a friend of his, came to paint Berenson's portrait in the autumn of 1907. Subsequently, Mary wrote to Rothenstein that "I heard of you from young Scott," revealing that she and Scott were in England together. In the spring of 1908, Scott was still at "i Tatti," "holding morning receptions in his bed and pouring out his length on garden chairs," Mary wrote to Rothenstein and, in the afternoons, reading Bergson in the library.

Bit by bit Scott was becoming a permanent addition to the court of Altamura. When the Berensons bought "i Tatti" and began to make extensive alterations, it seemed logical to transform Scott into the role of architect, a role in which he was joined by another talented young Englishman, Cecil Pinsent. They later went into an architectural partnership, one of complementary gifts, Pinsent wrote, ". . . Geoffrey Scott being intellectual, literary and brilliant, with the gift of words, but unpractical, and I practical, inventive, with an aptitude for things visible to the eye, but dumb."

When Scott began to think about writing on architecture (he published *The Architecture of Humanism* in 1914), it seemed natural that he should discuss his ideas with the Berensons. But B.B. liked to go to bed at a decent hour and so it was perhaps inevitable that Scott's confidante should become Mary, who was willing "to sit up till all hours of the night discussing it."

Perhaps it was no surprise that Mary was falling in love with Scott. At about this time she wrote a revealing letter to Berenson's youngest sister Rachel, who had just married Ralph Barton Perry, a young professor of philosophy at Harvard. Ray and Karin, Mary wrote, were becoming even more delightful, as children tended to do.

"Unfortunately this is seldom the case with one's husband. . . . I spend a good deal of time pondering this problem. If you have luck, you do get *fonder* of your life companion every year, and this is doubtless the most important & desirable thing. But it is *very* hard for the romance to last, & human nature does seem to want romance most desperately. The easiest way to get it is through a kind of transmuted sex feeling; and generally, after some years of married life, people know each other too well, bodily & spiritually, to weave romance of any kind about each other. . . ."

In the autumn of 1910 Scott was "traveling South" with Mrs. Berenson, having visited Paris, Nancy, and Munich. From La Haye, he wrote to Berenson's sister Bessie that the "Enchantress" kept changing her plans and their proposed trip to Spain together was off again.

That Mary was thoroughly disappointed in her marriage and looking elsewhere for romantic diversion, was soon plain to everyone. Everyone, apparently, but Berenson. He seemed to see "Young Scott" as a delightful addition, potential pupil and disciple. If Mary mothered him, well, she mothered a great many other people and it was entirely like her to draw the redoubtable Mrs. Scott into her circle with letters home chronicling, in detail, Geoffrey's latest ailments: "a line of little spots that looked like shingles, & he was in bed here for 2 days, but then seemed to get quite well ..." and to insist that he see Dr. Giglioli, who doctored everyone, whenever Scott came down with one of his nasty colds. "She certainly looks after me wonderfully," Scott wrote to his mother.

Mary finally found it necessary to spell out her feelings. She told Berenson that she no longer loved him and that she was in love with someone else, but she intended to stay with him. Berenson said later that she broke his heart.

From that moment on, Berenson apparently accepted the continued presence of Scott in their lives, but never forgave him. He vehemently denied, to Henry Hope Reed, who was to write a new foreword to Scott's book on architecture, that Scott deserved any credit for the design of their gardens. The truth of the matter was, John Walker told Reed, Berenson became very bitter about Scott, claiming that Scott had based his ideas on an early essay of Berenson's and had not given him adequate credit. There were, Walker also imagined, some emotional conflicts.

In *Sunset and Twilight* there is a reference to the "treacheries, disloyalties and calumnies" of people like "Geoffrey Scott, who owed me so much and whom I loved and trusted so much, not to speak of all I stood for 50 years from my own wife." Berenson, at the age of eighty-eight, was feeling in a self-pitying mood, but the fact that he linked Scott and Mary in the same sentence is perhaps significant.

In the spring of 1909, Geoffrey Scott and Cecil Pinsent, with "lists as long as their long legs," set to work on the first wave of wiring the villa, whitewashing the walls, and restoring all the floors, while Mary and B.B. took up temporary quarters in the Villa Linda. Mary had hoped that they might move back in a month and camp out while the work continued, but that hope was soon abandoned. The house was "noisy, dirty, disorderly, hopeless," she told Senda. In the interim they were moving to Poggio Gherardo to stay with Mrs. Ross. Entertaining stopped, except for an occasional invitation to lunch or tea under the trees, since not a single room was usable. A week later Mary wrote to say that they were having a H— of a time. The water system broke and had to be completely redone, ditto the electricity and floors and they were camping out in rooms full of dust and noise. "B.B. has rare days of resignation and some of desperation, when he vows never to return."

Berenson left. In June, he was in Paris, in September squiring Altman around London, and then back to Paris. He was making plans for Saint Moritz, Greece, and Constantinople. He contrived to spend his time in luxurious hotels but, whenever he returned, was confronted with some new disaster in the form of work incompetently done, which would have to be redone at vast expense. Arriving at the end of May, Berenson railed against the monumental stupidity and idleness of the workmen. When he returned to "i Tatti" six months later the house was still in a shambles, while fifty rascally incompetents sang opera arias, swigged wine, and did the least amount possible. Not a single window or door would shut and most of them were missing.

Berenson immediately came down with a bad cold and retired to bed where, at least, it was warm. The worst part, he wrote to Johnson, was that he couldn't make use of a single book or photograph and was stuck with the clothes he had been traveling in for a year and a half. And there was no end in sight.

There was a further disaster in store. In *Another Part of the Wood*, Kenneth Clark tells the story of murals that had been commissioned as a crowning touch for the former living room, now the new library. Or perhaps "commissioned" was too strong a word. René Piot, "a showy and conceited French painter," apparently took Mrs. Berenson's sigh of regret that the library walls were bare, as a command to execute a masterpiece. Piot locked himself into the room, had his food carried up to the ceiling, and for months, like Michelangelo, would not descend from his scaffold. But, ". . . when Pinsent was at last allowed to see them, his worst fears were confirmed. In front of a sky of the strongest lapis lazuli blue were groups of almost life-size naked figures in poses indicating strong sexual excitement. . . ." Berenson, returning home, entered the library and fainted. "He is said to have fallen flat on the floor, rigid with horror. He was carried to bed, where he remained for a week. When he had sufficiently recovered, the rows began. . . ."

Mary put it more sedately but with just as much horror, to B.B.'s mother. The fresco, she wrote, is "too awful for words! We cannot live with it. And the difficulty is how to tell the painter, & how to warn him that he must not go on to make designs for doing the other walls. . . . He thinks he is a Michelangelo at least, and he will be *Furious.* . . ."

Two years later, the work was finished. Architecturally, Scott wrote to Bessie, it was a great success. Even Berenson approved. "The house has been searched with a microscope from ground to roof & only revealed about six scratches, at a rage a piece. . . ."

Just as renovations were at their height Berenson fell ill. He wrote to his friend, the American novelist Edith Wharton, to say that he, too, suffered from neurasthenia, as did her husband, took all kinds of medicines and needed a daily massage. His struggles with Italian workmen had exhausted him, he wrote to Barrett Wendell at the same period, and he had been forced to spend a month in bed. Mary was less concerned about his health than his state of mind. "He is wearing himself out with his rages, which come on à propos of the smallest things. Indeed, I can no longer foresee or prevent them. Yesterday I was so afraid of what he might do to himself, that I locked him in his room. . . . He has taken the small things of the house *so* hard, that there is no peace for him. . . . He tells me many times a day that his life is nothing but agony. . . ." Three weeks later, Mary was trying to persuade him to take a rest cure, but he looked so "wickedly obstinate" against it that she had to laugh and give up. She concluded, "He is not easy to 'manage.' "

That Berenson was undergoing one more in a series of illnesses with emotional origins seems evident, but that the renovations were the cause is unlikely. The agony had another source.

In 1909 Belle da Costa Greene was the librarian for J. Pierpont Morgan and twenty-six years old. She had been suggested to him by Junius Morgan when she was an under-librarian at Princeton and invited to help build his collection of rare books. Morgan subsequently told another of his protégés, Langton Douglas, who was his advisor on Sienese paintings, that Belle Greene went on a buying trip and came back with wonderful finds, but presented a tremendous bill. Morgan sent for her and she defended herself so ably—those able to withstand the wrath of Morgan were already legendary figures—that, from then on, Belle Greene was his indispensable confidante. She may also have been his mistress.

Belle Greene was slim-waisted, had heavily lidded green eyes, and impeccable taste. She liked Renaissance gowns with matching jewels and always carried a large green silk handkerchief that she used to dramatic effect. Sir Harold Acton, an old friend of Berenson's, described her as having a yellowish complexion, with thick lips, and a sensual face and figure. It was frequently said, and her biographer, Mrs. Sherman Post Haight, thinks it entirely likely, that Belle Greene's family had crossed the color bar. Belle Greene herself tended to foster that impression.

A friend, taking her out to dinner one night, noticed in the taxi that the sleeve of her lace dress was torn to reveal the skin beneath. Belle Greene grinned and said, "The nigger blood shows through, doesn't it?"

She was, everyone agreed, an outrageous person. The Baltimore museum director Adelyn Breeskin recalled being taken up to her bedroom and seeing some beautiful drawings on the walls, most of them nudes, and being told by Belle Greene that she had posed herself. "In those days," Mr. Breeskin said, "that was something to admit." Mrs. Edward Fowles, widow of Douglas, remembered the day that Belle Greene began to ask her husband probing questions about his love life. Mrs. Fowles interrupted with, "I think you are the worst-mannered woman I have ever met."

Philip Hofer, former director of the Houghton Library at Harvard, who served as assistant director at the Morgan Library under Belle Greene, called her a formidable opponent. "B.B. was not half as ruthless as Belle Greene," he said. "I'd take on B.B. anytime in battle. She was a real tartar. You'd have to work under her to know it."

Belle Greene was avid for amusement. She loved "an exciting, semi-rowdy life, with endless cocktails and cigarettes and champagne suppers and practical jokes," Mary told Mrs. Gardner. She wanted, Mrs. Fowles recalled, to "sit on the floor and eat with her fingers à la Rousseau." Along with her exhibitionism, her spontaneity, and her daring, Belle Greene was known as a scholar of repute.

Opinions about her private life are in conflict. Some said that, following Morgan's death, she fell in love with his son. Others thought that her affairs with men were a façade for covert love affairs with her own sex, and that she used her undeniable charms to climb up the social ladder. She never married.

Belle Greene was capable of extraordinary advances. It was said that once, as she was shaking his hand, she slipped the key of her room to Count Umberto Gnoli, a well-known ladies' man and expert on Raphael. Whether her motive was business or pleasure is not known but, it is added, the count quietly slipped it back.

That she could also be ruthless may be judged from her comment that "if a person is a worm, you step on him." Yet she was capable of calling Roger Fry "that nice man," and, when Morgan died, she wrote, "I feel as if life had stopped."

Berenson met Belle Greene when he was on a business trip

to New York in 1908–09, and was evidently entranced by her intelligence, taste, and her imperious exhibitionism. Although the most sophisticated of *arrivistes*, they both had something to hide as they scaled the social summits. Yet, while he concealed his shameful secret, she seemed shamelessly defiant about her own; and while he calculated his every move, she was as defiantly impulsive as Isabella Stewart Gardner (whose handwriting her own curiously resembles). Belle Greene, however, did not think much of Berenson, at least at first.

She wrote to Sydney Cockerell, then director of the Fitzwilliam Museum, Cambridge, that ". . . like your friend, B.B., irritating and annoying . . . I have rarely heard him say a decent word for *anybody*, except some pretty lady. B.B.'s *pretences* are one of the things I hate most about him—someone truly said of him that he is a poisonous person."

Mrs. Haight, however, believes that Belle Greene eventually fell in love with B.B. It certainly was enough of an "affair" to alarm Mary, even though she thought the girl "a thoroughly good sort." If they married, B.B. would be swept up in her café-society life and made miserable. Mary did not intend to let that happen and so would not divorce him. But B.B. could not accept that Belle was wrong for him and was being made "thoroughly ill."

It seems clear that, if anyone was hopelessly in love, it was Berenson. When, in 1909 and 1910, Berenson raged against the incompetence of workmen, he was actually venting his frustration at being enmeshed in a hopeless love affair. In a fascinating letter to Neith Hapgood, written in the summer of 1911, Berenson explained what had happened to him. He had, he said, been hit by a wandering sun. He did not know what color it was, whether it was dark, or purple or, as it seemed to him, a radiant gold. It was a miracle that he was still alive.

Berenson continued that he didn't know what to do. Things might be easier if he were not so genuinely fond of Mary, or if Mary loved him. But, he told Neith, Mary had not loved him for a long time and hadn't even shared his interests for years. So there had been a void within him which he had tried not to feel. Unfortunately the heart, like everything else in nature, abhorred a vacuum.

Mary finally confided in Senda early in 1913. "He has been less well . . . since Carlsbad, but very much more tranquil in his nerves, so that everything has been calm & peaceful & harmonious, & even, when he is a *little* better, gay. Only, as he said to me this morning, 'It is an *awful* thing to be in love with a person three thousand miles away,' & as B.G. is by no means constant about writing or considerate in what she *does* write, she makes it no easier for him. Last winter her four months' silence drove him to despair. The same game has begun again, but he says he cannot get into such a state *twice*. . . ."

The Belle Greene affair, at its height, appears to have lasted for about four years and might be characterized as visits to New York (on his part) and to "i Tatti" (on hers), interspersed with letters coming promptly from him and erratically from her. It ended in a curious way. They had returned to New York for the winter of 1913–14, staying at the Ritz-Carlton Hotel on Madison Avenue, and B.B., as usual, was seeing Belle everyday, although with apparently less intensity than before, because Mary was beginning to think it would soon become "normal," just like his other friendships with women.

Then one morning Belle Greene came to visit Mary in her hotel room and they had a "real talk." "She said I must *make* B.B. understand that, while she is really devoted to him, she isn't one particle 'in love' with him, and never will be again. She is very straight & frank & I really like her. . . ."

Where B.B.'s love affairs were concerned Mary, often enmeshed with her own (in this case, Geoffrey Scott), liked to strike the pose of amused detachment. However, feelings of jealousy revealed themselves in her willingness to subtly disparage his mistresses. To do so with the blessing of one of them must have given her great satisfaction. Barely four days after Belle Greene's visit, Mary was declaring that Belle Greene was not the frank and candid person she seemed and was making B.B. very unhappy.

"B.B. is really having an awful time with Miss G. . . . He is so unhappy that I think the end must be near. He even longs to get home. . . . He tries to excuse her by thinking she is overworked & neurasthenic, & perhaps she is. . . . I feel deeply sorry for him."

That Belle Greene should engage the wife as an ally in her attempt to discourage the husband was, to say the least, original. She had taken proper measure of Mary who would have made some persuasive arguments. Berenson finally conceded that he had lost Belle, but was never quite able to let her go. He wrote her over 600 letters, almost to the day she died, in 1950.

Writing just after World War II, he asked whether she recognized the notepaper, adding that it was the remains of a huge stock she had given him, thirty years before. He was now an octogenarian, he said, but still capable of walking about the streets of Siena in ecstasy. It seemed such a short time since they had last met and yet it had been nine years. She must come and visit and stay for as long as she could stand him.

That letter is perhaps the only one from Berenson to Belle Greene that has survived. Just before Belle Greene died she burned all her diaries and letters, including Berenson's. "Well you know she had cancer," Mrs. Haight said. When Berenson heard the news he was distraught. "She has burned my autobiography."

He also said that Belle Greene had been an unusual woman, handicapped only by her part-Negro inheritance, and a wonderful lover. She was the only woman for whom he would have left Mary. When asked why he didn't, Berenson gave the tongue-in-cheek explanation, "I didn't want to stop my education." In fact, loving and losing Belle had the effect of causing Berenson to examine his own motives, for the first time in his life.

Introspection had never been one of his traits. While intensely interested in what people thought of him, he lacked the ability to confront his dragons that a successful self-analysis requires. His obstacle against self-knowledge was a remorseless inner censor, ready to pounce upon weakness and punish unacceptable feelings. Whenever he caught a glimpse of them, Berenson felt compelled to defend himself with excuses, however pathetically inadequate, and to ignore the implications of his own actions. Berenson also belittled and distrusted psychoanalysis. He argued that only inhibitions saved us from bestial animal behavior, a comment to be read for its revealing insight into his inner world.

In 1907, when he felt in danger of losing a close friend, Carlo Placci, he wrote a curiously placating and self-defensive letter saying that Placci would have to take him as he was, since he was forty-two and therefore too old. "I am what I am, and as a quality not likely to change much. . . ."

His failure to win Belle Greene, and her clear dislike of what seemed like his pretenses, which she may not have bothered to hide, plunged him into despair. The crisis had a fruitful outcome in leading him, in 1911, to examine his own heart. Because of it, he told Frances Francis some forty years later, he was saved from suicide.

He could not understand, he wrote to Neith Hapgood in

1911, how someone like himself, so aware and living such a well-ordered life, could be falling to pieces.

Perhaps, he continued, his passion for order was the result of a dim awareness that a great deal in his past must be covered up. He was like the giant in the fairy tale who had been obliged to hold the lid down tightly. For the first time since he wrote "The Death and Burial of Israel Koppel," Berenson began to confront some of the consequences of his momentous choice. For many years he did not dare to look further.

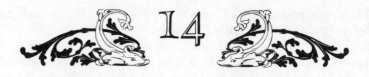

"PERCHED ON
THE PINNACLE"

A motto for the Library of this house, to be set
upon the chimney piece in bold letters for
remembrance and exhortation—
But little do men perceive what Solitude is, and
how far it extendeth. For a crowd is not company,
and faces are but a gallery of pictures, and talk but
a tinkling cymbal where there is no love.

—WILLIAM M. IVINS, JR.

ON THE AFTERNOON of June 28, 1914, Bernhard Berenson
was taking tea with the French portraitist Jacques Émile
Blanche when another guest arrived. She did not bother with the
usual formalities but blurted out, "There is terrible news; they
have assassinated the Archduke." The heir to the Austro-Hungarian throne, the Archduke Francis Ferdinand, had been killed at
Sarajevo. In a little more than a month, all of Europe would be at
war.

"For a minute everyone was struck dumb. Then, not even
the inflamed discussions of those first days were as alarming as the
silence which followed: a deathly silence, in which one felt the
presentiment of what was . . . to happen."

On the midnight of August 4, England declared war on
Germany and the rapid development caught Berenson resting in
the English countryside, and about to set off for North Germany
and the Baltic. Italy, which had an alliance with Germany and

Austria, had nevertheless declared its neutrality. The international art market and their main source of income was immediately disrupted. The Berensons could not go home because the banks were refusing to allow withdrawals, much less overdrafts, and Berenson owed $50,000, much of it to Italian creditors. On the other hand, "while B.B. has vast sums owing to him, he can't collect," Mary wrote to Senda. They did not even have enough money to return to Italy.

Berenson was "wild with worry" that their empty Italian villa might be commandeered to house refugees from the frontier. "It would . . . ruin . . . our peace & happiness . . . for he would worry about every inch of the floor & walls. . . ." Senda and her new husband, H. V. ("Bunny") Abbott, a Smith College professor, were similarly stranded in Florence and Mary was urging them to go and live at the villa. Fortunately, Cecil Pinsent was arranging to have the precious art collection moved to a bank vault and the safety of Carlo Placci's cellar. Despite Italy's neutrality, the Berensons expected it to enter the war on the German side.

The Berensons were preparing to live on one-tenth of their former income. They had dismissed their secretary and valet. The chauffeur was volunteering for the army. All further additions and repairs on the villa had stopped. In the meantime, since they could not return to Italy without paying some of their debts, Mary was trying to obtain access to money inherited from an aunt.

They stayed on through the autumn at Logan's house in Arundel. They were awakened every night at 3:00 A.M. by the "ominous iron rumble of trains of ambulance cars carrying the wounded soldiers" up from the coast and could never get back to sleep. Antwerp fell and London's lights were going out "in the fear of a Zeppelin raid. . . . Bernhard and I have nothing new to report," Mary wrote to his mother in the autumn of 1914. "We are still here & still waiting. . . ." The weather had never been more lovely. "The walled-in rose garden is all abloom, & Bernhard is sitting there in the sun—I can see him from my desk— reading the Sunday papers about Antwerp. . . ."

Bernhard was too obsessed by the war to sleep. He had, he told the Philadelphia collector Johnson, been fascinated by international politics since boyhood. His interest in the war now threatened to make him fit for nothing else even though he knew, he wrote, that his best course was to continue with his work.

He wrote to Barrett Wendell that he was reading nothing but history about the German nation, in order to understand how it could have become so fiendish, and his letters to his old friend T. S. Perry are passionate with indignation at America's refusal to enter the war against Germany that, to him, was a crusade against the devil.

Why, at least, didn't America treat Germany as an outlaw? Generations to come would be thoroughly ashamed if, in the most critical hour of world history, America refused to commit itself to what was right. The only declaration America had made so far was to tell Britain to go to hell. He was almost ashamed of being an American and wishing he were Italian. At least Italy had stopped supplying the Germans. As a lonely gesture of protest Berenson dropped the Germanicized "h" from his first name.

In November the Berensons traveled to Paris, where they stayed for two weeks. Berenson found that city inspiring, like a great cathedral at the moment of the elevation of the Host. They drove through France all the way to Florence and did not see a single horse or donkey, and seldom a car, nothing but soldiers. A million men were in readiness to go to the front.

Back at "i Tatti," Berenson worked in the library, took afternoon walks, and read all the papers while Mary tried to remain cheerful and find a "bright corner" for herself, even though "the bottom seems to have dropped out of everything" and, "we're no use in times like these—we belong to another kind of life." Commiserating with Senda over a foot ailment, Mary wrote, "Does it make it worse or better to think of the myriads of Italian soldiers whose feet ... are being so badly frozen that they have to be amputated?"

At home Mary tried to prevent Bernard from talking about the war on doctor's orders, although, "he might as well say I mustn't let him breathe!" The debate at Altamura was incessant. Italians had split into pro- and anti-German camps, and among the advocates Berenson was horrified to discover one of his oldest friends, the Countess Serristori. He refused to see her for the remainder of the war. He was almost as upset by Carlo Placci's enthusiasm to have Italy enter the war (Berenson would have preferred neutrality) but accepted it as the least of possible evils when Italy finally declared war on Germany. Discussions about the war were further strained by Mary's Quaker convictions.

She wrote to his mother, "Words cannot say how I hate war & all military ideals, including courage! Bernhard [*sic*] says my 'Quakerism' makes me a 'figure of fun'...." She concluded, "You can imagine what fights we have around the dinner table!"

Belle Greene had been urging Berenson to come to America. He decided against it, since the potential business was unlikely to justify the trip. Mary was rather glad of that. She suspected, she wrote to Senda, that a contributing factor might be a new romantic friendship "that has grown up between him & our neighbour in the Villa Medici, Lady Sybil Cutting. You can imagine I encourage that all I can! It begins to cast B.G. into the background, & Sybil is *such* an improvement on that horrible creature! She is really an awfully nice person who can have nothing but a good influence on anyone. . . ."

Lady Sybil Cutting was the daughter of an English nobleman, Lord Desart, and the widow of William Bayard Cutting, Jr., who was private secretary to the American ambassador in London when they married in 1901. A year later their only child, the writer Iris Origo, was born, and eight years later, Cutting died of tuberculosis. By 1915, Lady Sybil, still young, beautiful, and very rich, was living in the Villa Medici, on the southern slopes of the Fiesole hills, a short distance from "i Tatti." Its rooms, papered with Chinese flowers and floored with ornate Italian tile, were being further embellished with the help of two young architects, Pinsent and Scott, and the occasional Olympian word of advice from Berenson.

By May Italy was at war with Austria and the Berensons set off on a trip with Lady Sybil. Mary wrote from Perugia,

> Our goal is Rome, but we thought we might see some towns & their pictures on the way, especially in the Marches [East Coast] where Bernhard has some painters only half studied. We slept the first night at Urbino, where the hotel was full of people fleeing in fright from Ancona which the Austrians had been . . . bombarding. We had to present our papers at the Police Court, but had no other trouble.
>
> However, the next morning at our first stop . . . we were all arrested, & our motor-cars had to be rescued by the soldiers from a mob that wanted to wreck them under the impression that we were Germans! It took us hours to get free, & gave us such a fright that we came back here where we are known & everything comfortable. . . .

Three years of war passed with unusual tranquility at Altamura. There were days spent walking in the hills and driving to new places for picnics and then, as gasoline became unobtainable, they dispensed with a car.

Fortunately there was no shortage of food. They were growing their own potatoes and had their own eggs, chickens, rabbits, pigeons, strawberries, gooseberries, peas, beans, onions, and garden herbs. In Rome, things were much worse. Mary went there for a week with Mrs. Ross, "& we never even saw butter, & the bread was horrible." They were quite alone. Mary loved it, but Bernard sorely missed his conversational partners.

By the end of 1917 Berenson had had as much tranquility as he could endure and fled to Paris. He took an apartment at 40 avenue du Trocadéro and was swept up in a round of blissful reunions. He had not realized, he wrote to Edward Waldo Forbes of the Fogg Museum, how starved he had been for other human beings.

Berenson was casting about for some kind of role and found one as interpreter for the American Army. The camouflage allowed him to mingle with politicians (he was acquainted with Lord Balfour) and to subsequently imagine that he had played a role in the making of the Treaty of Versailles. Such an excuse to stay in Paris seemed heaven-sent. He told John J. Chapman that he couldn't bear to stay out of things a moment longer. There would be no more books for him for some time to come, he wrote. He seemed delighted.

One of the lures that drew Berenson back to Paris was the American novelist Edith Wharton who, by 1918, had become one of his closest friends. Berenson recalled that Mrs. Wharton, whose shyness was dinosaurian, had been so intent upon making a good impression that she inspired him with immediate revulsion. Six years passed. Then, invited to dine at Voisin's in Paris in 1909, Berenson sat down at a dimly lit table beside a lady "who immediately enchanted me by her conversation"; when the lights went up, he found himself beside Mrs. Wharton.

The truth, according to R. W. B. Lewis, Mrs. Wharton's biographer, is more prosaic. There was no problem of visibility and, in any case, Berenson had become reacquainted with her a few days before. Berenson could not resist adding a slight flourish to the facts of the reunion, but was being faithful to its emotional significance. It led to a friendship that lasted for almost thirty years.

Their remarkably close relationship seems to have contained nothing of the ambivalent flirtatiousness that muddied most of Berenson's friendships with women. Love, in the romantic sense, was out of the question. Edith Wharton was married to one man

and had fallen in love with Morton Fullerton, an American journalist; Berenson was launching upon the torturous ecstasies of his
affair with Belle Greene. The relationship seems to have been
precious for precisely that reason; they could be as unguarded and
cozily in contact as a sister and brother (Wharton was three years
his senior). Berenson's dependence upon adoring mothers and
sisters brought about such tender overtures to women like Edith
Wharton or, later, the American poet and hostess Natalie Barney,
who would not be misled when he commanded them to love him,
as he loved them.

One wonders how much Berenson's early friendliness was
motivated by the knowledge that Mrs. Wharton was a social lion.
Berenson's boasting letter to René Gimpel would suggest that
such was the case. One wonders, too, how much it would have
seemed like the ultimate social status symbol. To thus enter the
hallowed inner circles, even though a Simon Rosedale, was the
final triumph for a poor Lithuanian Jew who might so easily have
been "served up and rejected." And Mrs. Wharton did, indeed,
accept Berenson without reservation.

This was not the case for all of her friends. William R. Tyler,
son of her close friends Royall and Elisina Tyler, wrote, "Father
felt he had brains and ability to gain applause . . . in a world he
really lived *on*. No mean performance in light of his origins. I
think my father would have said, 'I still don't like the result. He's
not sound; not what he purports to be.' " Writing to his wife in
1916, Tyler said, "I know how agreeable B.B. is when he feels
like it, & as long as he thinks we're *solidaires* with people he wishes
to keep in with, he'll allow himself to like us & be polite. That's
what I think about it. But please, one thing; never accept an
invitation to . . . stay at 'i Tatti.' "

Berenson later said that he and Edith Wharton had been
sharing spiritual experiences long before they met, so that their
actual encounter had a curious déjà vu aspect for him. Their
interests in books, music, and people had followed the same paths
and because of this their common memory ranged back over sixty
years. She came to symbolize for him the America he grew up in
and loved, the America of Emerson, Hawthorne, Longfellow, and
Henry Adams. Since these were the only memories he could
openly be proud of, they were doubly precious to him.

They talked about the cunning little rock plants growing on
the walls and the stars in the heavens. He was in awe of her
knowledge of the human heart, and the delicacy with which she

phrased her insights, and was almost as delighted by her love of jokes, the broader and coarser the better.

She had been, he concluded, everything to a man a woman could be, who was neither wife nor mistress. Perhaps more, since he could confide in her, a luxury for one as well-defended as he was.

Paris in those days suited Berenson to perfection. Its wartime austerity, which banished trios and quartets playing tangos in restaurants, meant a dinner table conversation that was blissfully undisturbed. As he stayed on through that year of 1918, the uncertainty of the days when the Germans might make a dash for Paris intoxicated him with delicious terror. It aroused a renewed sense of life in him, and a longing for some calamitous event in which he could be the principal performer. In defiance of a "Big Bertha" that was firing directly overhead, he refused to leave his fifth-floor bedroom.

Mary was horrified. She was in London and her doctors insisted that he cross the Channel to spare her the anguish of believing him in danger. Mary had been completely broken down in mind and body since January, he wrote to T. S. Perry in the winter of 1918. It was a frightful business. Perhaps she would never be really well again.

If Geoffrey Scott had ever been deeply in love with Mary, that affection had been tempered, almost from the start, by an interest in other women. Bessie came to visit one summer while Scott was at work on restorations to "i Tatti" and they began to take so many long walks together that Mary's suspicions were aroused.

So she took Bessie off for a talk. If she and Scott were in love, then Bessie must marry him to "keep him in the family." Bessie replied that she found Scott fascinating, but was not in love with him. She added, in a letter to Frances Francis, that, of course, Mary was pretty smitten with Scott herself, underlining the words. Bessie wrote for B.B.'s opinion of the matter and received word that he would rather she marry a coal miner.

It has been noted that Mary, who had abandoned one husband, had decided not to repeat the pattern. Either she was unwilling to marry or, one suspects, Scott was. Mary knew that he was bound to depart one day unless, as she said, he could be kept in the family.

Scott's attraction to Berenson's sister must have seemed, to Mary, to present a desperate opportunity. Only a woman who was so in love that she would take a man on any terms would have accepted such a solution. To Mary, that Geoffrey loved someone younger and prettier whom he was prepared to marry meant little, if he could somehow be manipulated into staying. Bessie, however, refused to play the game. Despite this, Mary managed to keep Scott at her side for years to come. For a period during World War I he acted as Berenson's secretary.

One autumn day in 1913 a charming young woman of Italo-Baltic descent, Nicky Mariano, was invited to stay with her friend Byba Giuliani (later Coster) and her mother in their Florentine villa. Since the Florentine society of that time was closely interwoven it was inevitable that Byba should take Nicky to visit some friends staying in the Berenson villino. There, for the first time, Nicky met "a tall thin man," with "lank black hair . . . brushed back from his forehead. . ." whom she liked at once.

Geoffrey Scott would not make a boyfriend, Nicky decided; he did not appeal to her physically. But she liked his "voice, his laughter, his sense of fun, his whimsical expression. . . ."

In the weeks that followed, Nicky and Geoffrey saw each other frequently and Byba was sure that Geoffrey was in love. Nicky, accustomed to the more tempestuous approach of young Italians, found nothing remarkable about Geoffrey's guarded interest. "I assured [Byba] that even during our occasional *tête-á-têtes* not one word had been said . . . that could be interpreted as [a] . . . declaration of love."

Just before war broke out, in the spring of 1914, Nicky met Mary Berenson and was struck by the "world-embracing goodwill" that seemed to emanate from her. She also met Berenson, "looking elegant and aloof and somehow very intimidating." Mary sized up the situation between Scott and Miss Mariano and began to bombard the latter with invitations. She became "almost importunate in her eagerness" to have Nicky join her and Scott on a trip to the Dolomites. Nicky had already made plans to visit her sister Alda and her husband in the Baltic provinces of Russia and declined the invitation. She left Florence as war was declared and did not return for five years.

Nicky's subsequent account differs in one detail from that given by Alda von Anrep. According to the latter, Geoffrey had been waiting and hoping for Nicky's return. Then word was received that she had been killed. He, in bitter disappointment, married Lady Sybil Cutting. Nicky Mariano, however, makes no mention of this rumor in her book and states only that her first letter from Italy after the war, from Byba, brought the news that Gambe Lunghe (Long Legs, her nickname for Scott) had married.

Scott's marriage to Lady Sybil appears to have been viewed with general misgiving. Her daughter Iris Origo wrote only, "My instinct ... told me that her choice had not been wise. ..." Edith Wharton, who had adopted Scott as "a traveller after my own heart," was horrified that this extraordinary young man should ally himself with "that well-meaning waste of intelligence." In years to come, "probably none of Edith's acquaintances came in for more sheer venom than Lady Sybil."

Just what Mary had to say has not been ascertained, but that she had equally venomous remarks is plain. Scott subsequently told Nicky that she had written "very offensive letters ... to Geoffrey and Lady Sybil." She made no secret of her hatred. Cecil Pinsent talked about the "poison pen letters" she wrote and, when Berenson asked Mary some years later whether her interest in Lady Sybil's third and final husband, Percy Lubbock, was genuine, or only a substitute for her hatred for Sybil, Mary had to confess to the latter.

Geoffrey Scott's second book, published in the 1920s, was a biography of Madame de Charrière, who had a long liaison with the young Benjamin Constant and whose life was ruined when Constant married Madame de Staël. Scott, working on *The Portrait of Zélide* in the summer of 1922, wrote to Nicky that he was having problems because Madame de Charrière's reactions too much resembled Mary's when he had married. "I understand it almost too well to write about it in the detached and light manner which the tone of the book requires, and indeed I would much prefer not to write about it at all. ..."

Iris Origo saw some resemblances between Madame de Charrière and her mother (although, "the parallel must not be pressed too far. ..."). However, from Scott's comment about his emotional unease, one can perhaps conclude that this story of an older woman whose young lover leaves her bears a much closer resemblance to Mary Berenson's long affair with Scott.

In Zélide, Scott has painted an idealized portrait of Mary. There is a distinct physical resemblance; "... a face too florid for beauty, a portrait of wit and wilfulness where the mind and senses are disconcertingly alert; a temperament impulsive, vital, alarming; an arrowy spirit, quick, amusing, amused." There was, as Scott described Madame de Charrière, a contrast between an outward gaiety of manner and an inner skepticism; "she was disillusioned even before life had destroyed the illusions she artificially created."

For Constant, twenty-seven years her junior (Scott was twenty years younger than Mary), Madame de Charrière was the first person who understood him. She had intuitively comprehended his nature, "sensitive, complex, affectionate behind its mask of mockery." The attraction of their minds was immediate and obsessive. Madame de Charrière held him "as strongly as any woman could," using what Scott called a "tyrant benevolence," which found its "natural victim in his comic helplessness." No clearer description of the exact tenor of Mary's relationship with Scott is ever likely to be found.

Then Constant, goaded by Madame de Charrière's voracious and tyrannical jealousy, married Madame de Staël. It made her, his former mistress wrote, "jerk to think of it. . . . I did not accuse you of cruelty: a child will tear off the wings and legs of a fly without wishing to hurt. . . ." Madame de Charrière was determined to forget Constant, and succeeded. But she had lost the will to live. Not marrying Constant destroyed her. It was her way of punishing him.

Geoffrey Scott married Lady Sybil in April of 1918. Plans were announced at the end of 1917 and, in January of 1918, Mary Berenson became ill and remained so for the next year and a half.

There is no direct proof of a cause-and-effect relationship between Mary's illness, diagnosed as cystitis, a bladder complaint, and Scott's marriage. However, the temptation to see a link is irresistible, particularly when one considers the emotions of agonized rage and frustration that Mary must have been experiencing. A ten-year obsession had led, in Mary's eyes, to a kind of proprietary right to "manage" Geoffrey as she had tried to manipulate B.B. That he should resent her efforts and want to make his own decisions seems not to have occurred to her. She must have thought that he would never leave her.

The temptation to link the events becomes stronger when one considers Mary's emphasis on how much she was suffering. Cystitis, a common complaint, falls more in the category of a painful annoyance than a medieval torture, and yet Mary assured everyone that she was in agony.

She was taken at her word (it seems to have been a congenital weakness, since both Hannah and Logan suffered from it) and appears to have received the best medical care. Nothing helped. The pain was so unendurable, she insisted, that it broke her spirit. She had to be taken to England in the middle of a major war to be with her daughters.

Mary later wrote to Neith and Hutchins Hapgood, ". . . Of that 18 months I was horribly and torturingly ill for a whole year, always in bed, & when I got well I had four months of very distressing nervous break-down from the pain. . . ." Writing to Allyn Cox in the summer of 1918, Mary's sister Alys recorded laconically that her sister's disease was much improved, but that her "neurasthenia" was worse.

The effect of Mary's illness on Berenson was dramatic. Before it happened, he had referred to her with some detachment. She had, he told Edith Wharton in the winter of 1917, an attack of influenza and so he couldn't come to Paris just then. Since Geoffrey wasn't in the house, to leave her all alone didn't seem quite the thing.

Once he decided that she was really ill, Berenson thawed considerably. For years his chief asset had been her good health, he wrote—and apart from an attack of shingles ten years before and the usual winter colds, Mary seems to have been exceptionally healthy—and now the foundations of his life were threatened. When she left, he felt dazed and crushed and suddenly ill. Although Berenson avoided sickbeds and even to be near them made him uneasy, he showed his concern by his willingness to leave the enchantments of Paris for his wife's bedside.

Yet once in England, Berenson began to wonder why he had come, since his presence seemed to make her worse. She needed a rest cure alone. Yet he did not have the heart to leave her because she seemed in so much pain. He hoped it was not quite as bad as all that. Being Bernard Berenson, he began to think his wife was exaggerating to gain everyone's sympathy and there could only be one reason for that.

By the spring of 1919, Mary was much recovered. What followed then can best be seen as the impotent maneuvering of a very frustrated woman who was looking for someone to punish, even if the person who eventually suffered most should be herself.

Nicky Mariano was back in Florence. She was penniless. At the end of the war, the Bolshevik seizure of power had meant disaster for Nicky's land-owning brother-in-law, sister Alda, and their son Cecil. They had all fled and finally made their way to Germany. Nicky continued on to Florence.

As soon as Mary heard of Nicky's return, she offered her a job as librarian of "i Tatti." Although Nicky knew nothing about libraries she was desperate for any kind of work. So she wrote an effusive letter of thanks to "dear Mrs. Berenson," and set about learning her new job. Then she discovered from Geoffrey Scott that her new employment had little to do with her desirability as a librarian, or Mrs. Berenson's generosity of spirit, but with one goal in mind—to get even with Geoffrey.

Scott told Nicky, ". . . she wants to punish me by keeping to her end of our agreement" (which was that Scott marry Nicky and settle at the villino, she as librarian and he as general advisor), ". . . by employing you as librarian at 'i Tatti' in my nearest neighborhood, so that I should never stop regretting that I did not wait for your return."

Since Nicky Mariano was living and working a stone's throw from the Villa Medici, Scott did indeed repent at miserable leisure. At one time he threatened to kill himself. Nicky, however, was not about to run off with him to oblige Mary, and Scott eventually abandoned his hopes. His "ridiculous" marriage to Lady Sybil, as Mary called it, ended a few years later. He followed that with a brief inclination to marry Dorothy Warren, was subsequently enamored of the English poet Vita Sackville-West, and moved to London. While there, Scott was pronounced the ideal editor for the Boswell Papers, which had just been bought and were eventually published by a wealthy American, Lt. Col. Ralph H. Isham. Scott moved to New York, where he had a further bout of the pneumonia that periodically attacked him, and he died in the summer of 1929. At the time of his death Scott had embarked on yet another passionate affair, this time with the American lecturer, writer, and hostess Muriel Draper.

Nicky kept in touch with Scott until he died and even discussed him with one of his loves, a woman who may, to judge from the description, have been Vita Sackville-West. The latter revealed that she had broken off her relationship because of his "neurasthenic egoism." That Nicky should report the conversation rather indicates that she tacitly agreed with the verdict. Caught in an impossible position between Scott's needs, his wife's rights, and Mary's spitefulness, Nicky found it prudent to do nothing. However, Mary's tactic of punishing Scott with Nicky's presence had an ironic outcome that no one could have foreseen. Nicky Mariano, the enchanting lure for Mary's lover, became the next great love of her husband's life.

BY MIDDLE AGE Mary Berenson had lost all trace of the arrow-straight charm of womanhood and her body had collapsed into Brunhildean amplitude. She carried her weight in front, like the figurehead of a ship, arms akimbo, chest out, breasting the waves. She appeared to have abandoned all pretense at being what H.W.S. called "a milliner's block," and to have embraced the calculated drabness of her Quaker forebears, along with their almost perverse desire to make themselves as unattractive as possible.

Berenson was less changed. His head might be distinctly balder, his beard quite gray, and the lines around his eyes more marked, but his body was as slim and immaculate, his collars pulled as snappily taut, and his tie fastened with just as meticulous a knot as ever. There were, however, subtle differences. His eyes had narrowed perceptibly and his eyebrows were now lifted in an expression of permanent disbelief. The bridge of his nose had thickened markedly and his full lips, once curled in an expectant smile, were drawn into a thin line. The enchanting promise of youth had been replaced by something more than the usual disillusionments of maturity. Mary, as usual, tried to tease him out of it.

"B.B. is too funny when business is talked," she wrote to Senda from Köln in Germany, where they had gone to meet Duveen and his lawyer, Louis Levy. "His features fade into what Nicky and I call his 'Russian steppe' expression and he seems to be thousands of miles away. . . ."

The mask of pretense, maintained so consistently through the years, had become Berenson's single most valuable asset in the poker-playing game of the art market. Behind the impenetrable veneer of the connoisseur who had memorized every trick that cunning could devise, and beyond the façade of the gentleman-scholar who called more princesses by their first name than any man in Europe, was someone—but a human being whose actual feelings, memories, and instinctive responses were buried beneath a mask that he dared not let slip.

Berenson said of D'Annunzio that he believed his own lies. Perhaps it would be kinder to say of Berenson that this clear division, as Berenson remarked of Placci, between his private and public self, did not create the misguided beliefs he held about himself, but certainly contributed to them. Since he experienced himself as alone in a hostile universe, it followed that he was the injured party who gave love and generous help and was rewarded with snarls of ingratitude. In business, he was the one with his back to the wall and everyone else was trying to cheat him. He was friendliness itself, and therefore others must be lying when they complained of his asplike tongue. He never quarreled and therefore it must be others who started all the arguments. And so on.

Under these circumstances, Berenson was hardly aware that he was beginning to infuse his comments with special venom. Speaking of a wealthy man who had left his fortune to the "Necropolitan" Museum, Berenson commented to T. S. Perry that he had expected the man to be less subtly cynical than that, and found himself delightfully disappointed. His patience, never abundant, wore ever thinner. Taken to the house of a wealthy collector, Berenson was shown a doubtful painting for his approval. He turned to his host and with withering irrelevance remarked, "I wonder, could you let me have an elastic band?"

Most of all Berenson began to believe in his divine right to be right. His opinions, so amusing in a young man, outrageous certainly, but somehow charming in their presumption, hardened into the arrogance of dogma. Sweeping generalizations about art and aesthetics became pronouncements about life in general: i.e., no gentleman can be a painter. The English cannot draw. The poetry of the Middle Ages is a bore. Americans don't know how to think. The problems of the universe chiefly interest children between the ages of five and seven. Psychoanalysts are not interested in the mind, but only in a "cerebral intestine." The English have such bad manners; they insist on remaining silent in company, behind which everything could be hidden, "timidity, arrogance, virtue, vice. . . ." All of these verdicts were uttered with magical finality without discussion or elaboration.

At about this time, Berenson also began to make pessimistic statements about women in general and marriage in particular. Despite their ten-year "courtship," their solid friendship based on common interest and goals, and despite Mary's professed willingness to make him happy, the marriage had quickly disintegrated. There were, of course, aspects of her nature that had grated upon him from the start. He knew how ominously devoted she was to her family. He knew how frighteningly lavish she could be with money, as when she gave everyone around her £50 to celebrate her fiftieth birthday; and the time she had mailed a particularly fine tapestry, sent to "i Tatti" to be evaluated, to her daughter for Christmas, and then didn't want to give it back. He knew about what he called her *"oeil dénigrant,"* although this could scarcely have been a serious matter for concern, since her view that only intelligent people were interesting and that those who were merely simple and sweet were "sofa cushions," echoed his own. He knew about her mischievous ability to stir up trouble and her eternally wandering, flirtatious eye.

Nevertheless, marriage to Mary had satisfied a major part of his needs because there never was any doubt, at first, about the positions they held. He assumed the traditional role of an East European husband, benevolently meeting his financial responsibilities to his own family, his wife, and even to her daughters (who went on receiving an allowance from him for thirty years). He was the undisputed head of the household and leader of their intellectual interests.

Mary Berenson followed at a respectful distance, accepting her role as mother-wife, as well as their implicit agreement that she live up to his expectations. He would provide financial security and social respectability and she would contribute the mental, moral, and physical support that he so desperately needed.

It is difficult to escape the conclusion that Mary was the first to become dissatisfied, to resent the demands upon her, and wonder whether she were not getting the worst of the bargain. As the daughter of a feminist mother and with a sister now deeply involved in the cause of women's suffrage, Mary must have begun to wonder whether she were not, as Hannah maintained, trapped in the role of Wife, exploited by that ogre, the Husband.

A few years after their marriage she was complaining that nothing seemed left to her but the tedious daily ritual of housekeeping. That, she told Rachel, was "writ on water." The best she could hope for was that B.B. would not send away "dish after dish . . . saying it is pig's food, and there won't be dust in the corners and cobwebs on the ceiling."

As Mary became restive Berenson responded with a not-so-subtle teasing. He liked to wait until she was asleep and then blow a trumpet into her ear for the fun, no doubt, of seeing her startled and enraged reaction, even though, as Hannah Whitall Smith noted, there was a danger of "injuring thy ears. . . ." Berenson also liked to tweak Mary's nose. Alda von Anrep and Kenneth Clark were there on one occasion when B.B., in a good mood, strolled up to Mary and gave her nose such a twist that Mary burst into tears. It ended with them all clambering into the car in an embarrassed silence.

Mary was well prepared to cope with teasing and excelled in the art herself. Alice de Lamar, who traveled with them in Italy, recalled,

> In many of these villages in 1921, an automobile had never been seen before. Small boys were always swarming all over our cars; and, in fact, in the village square of one of the towns, when the Berenson chauffeur was endeavoring to change a flat tire, the crowd around him pushed until he could not work at all. At this point I saw Mary Berenson ... whisper something to one of the market women who had come close to our car window. Presently, the crowd melted away.... B.B. turned to Mary, "My dear, whatever did you say...?"
>
> "Don't you wish you knew!" Mary teased.
>
> "But really, what?"
>
> "Why, it was very easy. I simply said, 'Don't crowd too close.... My husband has the Evil Eye!' "

Alice de Lamar also recalled Mary Berenson telling her once that when she decided that B.B.'s interminable wrangles with a taxi driver had gone on long enough, she took her parasol, half-opened, and "dropped it over his head like a candle extinguisher!"

What Mary could not cope with was open hostility; and after she had launched on her affair with Geoffrey Scott, Berenson did not try to hide his antagonism.

Visiting "i Tatti" in the winter of 1911–12, Berenson's youngest sister Rachel wrote to Senda that she was enjoying everything except Berenson's explosive contradictions of anything Mary had to say. Count Umberto Morra, who was to become Berenson's close friend and an intimate of Altamura, recalled that there were remarks like, "Mary will drive me mad." Mary, for instance, had never learned to speak grammatically correct Italian. One day they had all been to Naples and were on their way back by car from an excursion to Pompeii, along with the director of excavation there.

"We were passing rocky country and the rocks were sprouting asphodels in bloom. Mary remarked, '*Come si chiamano questi pianti?*' " Mary meant to say, "What are those plants called?" However, she had used the wrong grammatical ending for the word "pianta," or plant, which should have been "piante." Instead, she had used the plural of "pianto," meaning tears. It seemed like a minor slip, but Berenson answered, "Mary, when you speak Italian this way you drive me to tears."

Berenson's frustrated anger then began to focus itself on Mary's management of the household. There, her inability (in his eyes) to give him the proper nourishment loomed large.

"I think we haven't had one single meal without complaints & even rages from Bernard," Mary wrote to Senda in 1916. "He all but rushes out at each meal to discharge the cooker of it on the spot." Mary knew it was important to have the right kind of food for his delicate stomach, but doubted whether a cook could ever be found to satisfy him.

"It cuts a deep gash into one's daily happiness. I think it makes people hate to take their meals with us. Certainly I would never go again to a house where my host lost his temper over the dishes. . . ."

To outsiders, the Berenson battles seemed incomprehensible. To Rachel and Senda the pattern seemed a terrible repetition of the unending faultfinding to which their father had subjected Little Mother, and to Berenson himself his angry outbursts must have seemed like the justifiable reaction of a man goaded beyond endurance. For her part, Mary had tried to survive by humoring Bernard, laughing at his pique and "managing" him, as Hannah advised. She had failed. By 1923 she had decided that there was a "serious cleavage" in their marriage and was simply trying to survive.

She wrote to Senda in the winter of 1923,

> He is always in love, & I put up with it all right, except when his mistress is an out & out vulgarian, like Belle Greene. Indeed, I sympathize in a way, for it is not the worst thing a human being can do, to find another human being supremely attractive. But what does me in are nasty little injustices & the betrayal of a suspicious, self-seeking, exacting egoism & scenes.
>
> B.B. rather likes scenes, they clear the air for him. Me they poison, & more & more since my break-down. [A reference to her illness in 1918.] However, it's no use repining. Such is my fate, & I am aware that if I went home to live among people whose lives are, at any rate outwardly, harmonious, I should miss his stimulating mind & his amusing talk.

It is quite silly of me to break out about it, for he will never change but only grow worse, but every six months or so I feel as if I couldn't bear it, as if I must live with "nice" people, who don't fly into unholy rages at little things & tell me that no man ever had a wife that did so little for him as I do, such a silly doddering incompetent imbecile, whose malice & stupidity have ruined his life, etc. The next day he may say affectionate things, then he wonders [why] I am not moved by them, but I cannot forget what has gone the day before. It is all so undignified & sordid. . . .

For many years to come the solution to their impasse would be separate lives. They both called "i Tatti" home, but they pursued different paths outside it and were parted much of the year by her visits to England or his business trips. For years, Berenson spent only four months of the year at "i Tatti." Even when traveling together, they often stayed at separate hotels. Mary was still fighting for equal partnership as an expertiser. She was partially successful in that it was generally thought that she had a better "eye" for a fake than her husband did, and some even said that her judgments were as shrewd as his. However, although Mary might call their marriage a "union of intellects," she never attained the same prominence.

If Mary had wanted to be accepted on equal terms, she had picked the wrong man. A woman who could hold her tongue, Berenson observed (in 1931), was precious. "Those who only know how to speak intelligently speak too much; the moment comes when they drive us mad with . . . an asinine interruption. Perhaps we love them even in these unpleasant moments, because they convince us of our superiority."

Berenson said that chance brought Nicky Mariano into his life and that his first impression was not a "very favorable one." She must have seemed to him as yet one more newcomer for whom Mary had taken an inexplicable, perhaps Machiavellian, liking, and, as he would say with a sigh, "Now Mary is again ready to cut us all up particularly fine in order to favour her new friends." Besides, Nicky Mariano had absolutely no experience as a librarian and one can imagine Berenson's irritation when she could not immediately find what he wanted with the help of his imperiously vague commands, "remembering the contents of a book but not the author nor the title."

Nicky, however, clung on desperately, goaded by necessity. She had never been trained to earn a living. She had been brought up in an uneasy half-world, socially correct but financially distressed, inheriting the aristocratic expectations of her mother, from a land-owning family in the Russian province of Livonia, and the straitened circumstances of her father, who barely made a living as a professor of church history at the University of Naples.

Nicky was one of three daughters. Alda, the oldest, was married by the time Nicky reached her teens, and another daughter, who is never mentioned, may have committed suicide. Their mother, whom Nicky adored, died when she was eight years old and her father, Raffaele Mariano, quickly married his wife's younger sister, "a Baltic old maid of limited intelligence," whom Nicky and Alda detested. Perhaps under her baleful influence Nicky's father became misanthropic, cut off from his friends and colleagues, self-pitying in his self-imposed isolation, and buried in scholarly studies on church history that no one wanted to read.

Nicky Mariano had, however, been trained to do something. Her father had used her quick, retentive mind and her patient willingness to fulfill any request in the aid of his studies and she had become an indispensable researcher. She cared for an increasingly lonely man, read to him in several languages, and led a life of genteel obscurity in Florence. Even though born in Italy, Nicky complained of "a slight inferiority complex due to my not 'belonging' anywhere. . . ."

From these slender clues one gathers the impression of a woman of great natural charm who received affection from a demanding parent, but at the price of her own self-effacement. Within her family, Nicky's habitual posture appears to have been that of determined cheerfulness. One can see this proud stance in an early photograph, in the stubborn lift of her delicate chin and the poignant smile, that of someone bravely hiding her pain. She was the peacemaker, according to the Princess Dina Lieven, who was Alda's niece. She hated disharmony and was "always ready to help wherever she could and prepared to do anything for those she loved. She would certainly always try to mediate and see to it that peace was established."

Not long after she arrived at "i Tatti," Nicky learned that the Berensons were looking for an honest estate agent to replace one who had embezzled considerable sums during World War I and whom it seemed urgently necessary to replace. Meanwhile, Alda and her husband, the Baron von Anrep, were eking out a living in Germany. "Alda sold motor bicycles and the Baron put a flower in his buttonhole and took the present Baron to school," said Luisa Vertova Nicolson, an Italian art historian and the divorced wife of Benedict Nicolson, who joined the circle at Altamura after World War II. "He did some shopping, went home, swept the floor and was the maid. . . ." It seemed natural that Nicky propose her brother-in-law as a replacement since he had such eminent qualifications as a former landowner. Then, as Nicky became official secretary, Alda moved into the job of librarian.

Stories about Alda von Anrep's reign in the library are legion. "She looked after B.B.'s books and never read one of them. She said that they could have been teacups," Mrs. Nicolson said. She treated her organizing role with the same cavalier cheerfulness. Philip Hofer, who became curator of the Harvard Library department of Printing and Graphic Arts in 1938, had been sent to "i Tatti" in an attempt to correlate Berenson's holdings with those of the university, and spent a considerable amount of time there.

"I always knew Alda was not a good housekeeper," he said, "but one day I heaved out two huge books and after them tumbled a plastic umbrella and two petrified sandwiches. They were almost certainly Alda's."

By contrast, the Baron seems to have been a pleasant, mild-mannered man who managed the Berenson estate paternal-istically, seeing to it that the peasant families working its farms had their first running water and electricity. Eventually, the Anreps rented an apartment on the Borgo S. Jacopo in Florence overlooking the Arno and the Ponte Vecchio where they gave delightful dinners and dances, all much enlivened by Alda's witty and irreverent comments.

Alda, Kenneth Clark observed, wasn't afraid of "old B.B. She gave him what she liked." Nicky Mariano's reaction was more subterranean. Soon after she began work at "i Tatti" Nicky Mariano realized that "B.B. was not easy to manage or to serve." Although Mary did not seem to understand his temperament, "through my father, I knew the workings of a Mediterranean temperament only too well and such was B.B.'s through and through, in spite of the coat of paint left on him by his Bostonian education." Nicky Mariano's extended visits to the Anrep estate in Livonia had made her familiar with life in an East European shtetl. She knew its traditions and could well see how Berenson, as firstborn male, had been "egregiously spoilt" by his family.

Because Berenson lacked a good kindergarten upbringing, Nicky decided, he had never learned to control his temper. References to Berenson as a child who needed the proper parental control are frequent in her reminiscences of life at "i Tatti." For instance, ". . . it was as easy to get him out of such moods as getting a child out of its tantrums with the help of a new toy." Elsewhere, Nicky speaks of herself as mother and of Berenson as her bearded (and undoubtedly spoiled) baby.

If Berenson was often angry, the problem, Nicky reasoned, was Mary. She seemed to "brush him the wrong way." She was always asking for more money for her daughters, broaching the subject at "the worst possible hour," early morning, when he invariably woke up in "an anxious and nervous state of mind."

Also, Mary lacked the remotest delicacy or tact. She would criticize Berenson's stumbling prose in "a disagreeable and contemptuous tone," and that would drive him "into stubborn defence of his own careless way of writing."

Realizing the gulf in temperament between their natures, Nicky did what was characteristic of her; she tried to restore harmony. "Sometimes they seemed to me like two musical instruments with a few of the highest and lowest notes out of tune. If one managed to play them without touching these unfortunate notes all was well." She did not call it "managing."

Almost from the start, her ministrations were very successful. Both needed an intermediary, or rather, a buffer. Berenson was delighted to discover in her a woman of similar cultural background: " 'Do you know Platen's "Busento Ballad"?' he asked me one day, and when I began reciting the first lines his delight was great and made me feel very close to him." Mary was transparently relieved to find their almost daily battles made light of, smoothed over, and otherwise robbed of their sting by Nicky's light-hearted charm. Nicky became adept at teasing Berenson, when he fell into a rage, by telling him that he was no good at making a scene because his voice did not carry. "When my father made a scene the whole house resounded from the power of his voice." And then Berenson would laugh.

"Nicky is the same old darling," Rachel wrote to Senda, "so merry and warm-hearted and *hard working*. I pray that B.B. may *never* have to live without her. It is really incredible how she understands B.B. and puts up with his crochets and adores him. And she makes Mary equally happy. . . ."

Mary called Nicky "our guardian angel." She was so thoughtful, so devoted, and so loyal, looking after her needs as meticulously as she did her employer's. Bit by bit Nicky was becoming indispensable to Mary's well-being. Nicky had temporarily "deserted her" for her own family, Mary wrote, and she felt like a "babe-in-the-wood with no kind Robin at hand." More to the point, Nicky was a congenial addition. On a trip to Turkey in 1928, Mary wrote that they were in love with all forms of Turkish art and were having such enchanting evenings, reading Gibbon aloud, "that we are furious if we're asked out. It is luck that we all three like the same things & the same way of life."

There were complicating factors. It was inevitable that each of the Berensons should attempt to enlist Nicky as an ally in their continuing battles with each other. Very early in her stay at "i Tatti," Nicky recalled that Berenson and Mary had quarreled over Belle Greene and that Mary had gone to hide in the sitting room while Berenson, very gloomy, begged Nicky to find her and "try to calm her."

On the other hand, Mary began to confide their financial worries to Nicky. From her point of view they were living foolishly, spending enormous sums to complete the library in the hope that it might one day be useful for some hypothetical student. Nicky agreed with Mary that it was not wise, and "often she actually does not order the books he marks in catalogues, and then he forgets about them."

Mary was also confiding in Nicky in the perpetually perplexing business of managing B.B., particularly when the atmosphere was so heavy that "Nicky and I go about trembling! Poor B.B. has had an internal 'upset,' but we think it is because he has begun to write again, & Nicky reminds me that last March, when he was writing his article on 'Antonello,' life wasn't worth living. . . ."

Most of all Mary began to manipulate Nicky into siding with her in the unending drama of Berenson's romances.

"Poor B.B.!" she wrote to her in 1921. "He had arranged his various honeymoons with his various ladies so very carefully . . ." and now, she continued, one of them had changed her dates and upset all his plans. "By the way a sweet young creature to whom he writes that the thought of her is like a gold thread woven through the unrolled tapestry of his life . . . is coming to us in October. I too thought her delightful. . . ."

The three of them were hammering out a certain *manière de vivre* in which Nicky was doing all of the accommodating. Like "a dog in a skittle alley," Nicky was the one who dodged the sharp edges of their natures, who soothed and ministered, who was the quintessence of tact and self-sacrifice and maternal nurturing. She was also enmeshed in the rules of Altamura which were that, when trouble arose, the person in difficulty went to a third party to air his or her grievances. The confidante, privileged to "know the truth," might hint at secrets divulged to others, but was honor bound not to confront the offender with them. A façade of propriety must be maintained. Beneath it, gossip might rage, and private grudges and recriminations flourish. So, too, might secret loves.

Someone caught in the cross fire, as Nicky was, would be intolerably torn, unless he or she could muster the strength to detach himself from the emotional demands being made, or otherwise resolve the dilemma by taking sides. Although she tried valiantly, and for the most part successfully, to appear neutral, Nicky seems to have made up her mind fairly quickly. She knew where her ultimate allegiance would lie.

She had been awed and even intimidated by Berenson's vast learning, she wrote. She trained herself to listen carefully, without comment, when the conversation turned to subjects that were over her head. However, it was not Berenson's "so-called brilliant conversation and witticisms or paradoxes" that attracted her to him but that other, quieter side that she saw when they were alone. "His comments on books, his analysis of the people he had seen during the day, his humane understanding of their shortcomings or difficulties, his freedom from any kind of fixed *Weltanschauung,* his boyish sense of fun, all that appealed to the whole of my being. . . ."

In the summer of 1921 Nicky was invited to go with Mary and B.B. on one of their many trips through Italy; she remembered one afternoon when Berenson took a detour to gaze at "two honey coloured Romanesque façades in the light of a late summer afternoon. . . .

"I was in the seventh heaven of joy, yet not aware of how much my responsiveness to everything we were looking at was due to B.B.'s presence."

Berenson showed no sign of being aware of her interest in him, she continued. That he was, however, very much aware of it is certain. From middle age onward he was more and more fascinated by women, or rather, by their reaction to him, particularly if they were younger. The most amazing thing had happened to him two nights before, he wrote to W. M. Ivins, Jr., in 1929. A delectable young woman of scarcely twenty sat next to him at dinner and by the merest accident, his fingertips had grazed her bare arm. He instantly had an erection. She spent the rest of the evening finding excuses to touch him and what he wanted to know was, why did she do it? Was she merely being a good granddaughter, or was there another reason? Did she do it unconsciously? Or deliberately? Was she only teasing him or (and he could have sworn she was) ready for ultimates?

One does not know when Berenson's self-absorbed and titillating musings about just what Nicky Mariano meant by that changed character. Neither can one know when his gallantry, by now almost involuntary (such as plucking a flower for his lady companion on a walk, or choosing the ripest fig to offer to his table partner), became more than a compulsive desire to charm and an expression of genuine emotion. One only knows that, at some point, he presented Nicky Mariano with the following poem by Werner (Werinher) vom Tegernsee, an eleventh-century monk:

> *Du bist min—ich bin din*
> *des solt du gewis sin*
> *du bist beslozzen*
> *in minem herzen*
> *verlorn ist daz sluzzelin*
> *du muost och immer darinne sin.*

> *You are mine; I am yours*
> *of that you may be sure.*
> *You are locked in my heart*
> *The key has been lost*
> *You must stay there for ever.*

Whenever he began a new flirtation, Mary said teasingly, Berenson always insisted upon reading poetry aloud with his new amour.

Mary knew. Nicky knew that she knew. Nicky was "caught in the net of his subtle charm," and so she stayed. She knew that the Berensons had been estranged for years, that theirs was only a "union of intellects," and that there was no reason to feel responsible. Being, however, the woman she was, Nicky felt an immense and obscure guilt, demonstrable in the lengths she went to appease it. She was the good aunt who had adopted Mary, and Mary's daughters and their children, and Berenson's parents and sisters and brother and nephews. By being selflessly devoted to them all, Nicky Mariano could somehow forgive herself for having stolen the affections, not only of Mary's lover, but her husband as well.

Berenson liked to say that Jehovah had seen that man could not live alone and so had created woman to be his helper, his audience, his stimulus, and, most important, his reflection.

Nicky Mariano perfectly fulfilled these requirements. She was the maternal embodiment of warmth, love, security, practical reality, and nourishment. She put one in mind of Cecily Grampion, the heroine of *The Third Category*, "goldenly mediocre, womanly, a little bit womanish even. He wished her to be beautiful, but not strikingly so. . . ." She must come from a respectable background, have a sweet smile, and be intelligent but not intellectual, a malleable disciple who would, like a magic mirror, transmit a most satisfying and idealized self-image.

However, Cecily Grampion had qualities of mind and heart that her young admirer sensed were on a far nobler and grander scale than his own. While in awe of her ecstatic readiness for self-sacrifice, he had no intention of letting himself be ensnared. The problem with womanly devotion, Berenson was to write, was that it was so oppressive. The man was bound to flee for his life and the woman to be heartbroken, "till she finds another 'rag baby' to build up into the most desirable object in the world. With the female in that case, the male is not . . . so much a *machine à plaisir* as an activity, a career." Some twenty years earlier, he had complained in a similar vein about women who soaked up the ideas of their men like blotters, allowing each new passion to change "their judgment, their scope, their aspirations and their values." Yet whenever such women dared to have an interest apart from him, Berenson reacted with petulant irritation. "*Me first* is the instinctive cry of little ones. . . ."

Meanwhile Mary was having a new grand passion of her own. Her eyes had been caught by Carl Hamilton, a young American of obscure origins—he chose to invent his name—whom Alice de Lamar, then a young heiress fascinated by Italian Renaissance art, found unprepossessing: "conservative, neat, slim, medium short, with a rather flat, round face and brown hair parted in the middle and neatly plastered down." Mary thought him a real prodigy, with a talent for appreciating art, "a mixture of Dionysus and Saint Francis, a mysterious awe-inspiring and love-compelling force and a kind of mystic genius," Geoffrey Scott sardonically informed Nicky Mariano.

This mysterious love-compelling force was an orphan who

grew up in a small Pennsylvania town. He had been cared for by a minister and subsequently came to the attention of Mrs. E. H. Harriman, the mother of Averell, who saw to it that he was educated at Andover and Yale. Early in the process, Hamilton demonstrated a flair for business, putting himself through university with the proceeds from a student clothes-pressing business, and so it was not too surprising that Hamilton should find a way to make money during World War I. When the war cut off the flow of oil to the United States and made soap scarce, Hamilton perfected a method of jelling copra from the Philippines so that it need not be shipped as a liquid and had made $5 million by the age of twenty-five. These financial returns were to dwindle to nothing after normal world trade was restored.

By 1920, Hamilton had acquired a handsome apartment at 270 Park Avenue, furnished with rare seventeenth- and eighteenth-century Persian rugs, cinquecento Florentine furniture from the Davenzatti Palace, sofas covered in Florentine brocade, and paintings.

"Here was a Cimabue, a fan-shaped altarpiece; a Piero della Francesca *Crucifixion* with bold background; a Fra Angelico *Annunciation* with two companion pictures of attending angels; a Fra Filippo Lippi *Madonna and Child*; a Botticelli portrait of a youth in a red cap; a fascinating Sassetta landscape with a figure in the snow; Mantegna's *Judith and Holofernes*; an Alvise Vivarini portrait . . . and, perhaps most impressive of all, the great Bellini *Feast of the Gods*," Alice de Lamar recalled.

Among the paintings also hanging on the wall at 270 Park Avenue was a small panel representing the young Saint John in the desert. It had been given to Hamilton in the first flush of her enthusiasm by Mary Berenson and, at that time, was thought to be by Pesellino. Mary was never able to understand why, when B.B. heard of the gift, he flew into "an unreasonable and undignified rage."

The painting was subsequently discovered on Hamilton's wall by the New York art critic Richard Offner, who asked for its attribution.

His widow recalled, "Richard told Carl Hamilton, 'Do me a favor, won't you? Send B.B. a cable telling him that I said the "St. John in the Desert" is by Domenico Veneziano.' The reply came back from B.B., 'Offner is right.' "

The painting now hangs in the National Gallery of Art in Washington.

The Hamilton style of life was so luxurious that Mary and B.B. had no reason to look below the surface. So, when they were planning to spend some months in New York in the winter of 1920, it seemed natural that Hamilton should invite them to stay in his "Aladdin's bower," as Mary called it, and that she should want to accept. Berenson, for some reason, was reluctant.

"But Carl had been persistent. He met them at the dock as they stepped from the steamer with his two Japanese servants. As they carried the Berensons' luggage, he explained that he had entirely moved out of his apartment and was, himself, installed in a hotel and that his staff of servants was prepared to take care of their every wish during their stay in New York. . . ."

Berenson's unwillingness to take advantage of the offer must have had some connection with the fact that Hamilton had acquired most of his masterpieces from Joseph Duveen.

> At that time, Duveen had in his vaults some of the finest paintings in the world. But the problem was, how could he lure such names as Mellon and Widener to come up to his gallery to see them? Collectors who will buy with almost reckless enthusiasm at auction, often developed great sales resistance to Duveen's own circus barker brand of merchandising. . . .
>
> Young Hamilton obviously admired and wanted . . . the best he had. If Duveen's credit search dug out the whole eccentric story, he must never have had the slightest idea Hamilton would ever be able to pay more than the small token payment with which he started his collection. But Duveen must have seen that he could conveniently use him as a prime showroom for his wares. It was a form of strategy, and it worked successfully. . . .

Any painting that Hamilton wanted was immediately delivered. Duveen paid to have every room appropriately decorated and, as soon as the apartment was finished, Hamilton dutifully invited Mrs. Harriman to give a series of dinners there and ask all of her friends. They came, returned for tea with their friends, and the fame of the Hamilton Collection began to spread. Mary even gave a lecture about it.

Hamilton, said Alice de Lamar, who followed his sad decline and knew him, years later, when he was living in a New York rooming house, had a *folie de grandeur* (delusions of grandeur). It never occurred to him to ask why Duveen was being so exceptionally accommodating (and, after all, Duveen was known for his generous tendency to insist that wealthy collectors hang the Rembrandt in their living room for a year or two to see if they could get to like it).

Belle Greene, who was privy to much of the art-market gossip of the twenties, was sure that Mary's and B.B.'s stay in the Hamilton apartment "had been nothing but a trap, skillfully arranged by Duveen who, realizing that Hamilton was not solvent any longer and would sooner or later return his treasures ... wanted the pictures to be well advertised through B.B.'s staying there and talking about them to his numerous guests," Nicky Mariano wrote.

Although Berenson denied that this was the case, his denial is not convincing. Allyn Cox, who was a confidant of Mary's during this period, went to 270 Park Avenue for dinner with her alone. "It was a dreadful situation. They didn't know what to do," he recalled. "They had discovered that Hamilton's pictures hadn't been paid for."

To be thus trapped into acting as a decoy for his employer's wares must have been an uncomfortable experience for Berenson who was at particular pains, during this period, to avoid having his business connections known. But that Duveen should be capable of such a maneuver would not have surprised him. Morever, the Berensons could hardly avoid fitting in with Duveen's plans, however unwillingly. They went to see collections, had daily luncheon parties, and were invited to large dinners followed by musicales almost every evening.

"We attended a millionaire dinner party the other night," Mary wrote to "dearest Nicky" early in 1921. "The table literally groaned under orchids, caviar, turtle soup and golden plate. Twenty-two gross old people sat around it guzzling champagne and all sorts of wine (in spite of Prohibition), the women all over 50 all fat and all except myself nearly naked and hung with ropes of pearls and diamonds. After dinner opera singers came in and yelled horrible music. B.B. nearly fainted away...."

There was no way to avoid the fact that B.B. had become "quite a lion," as his wife said. His books were popular and his eminent position as critic had made him indispensable to wealthy collectors, Americans in particular, who had been known to refuse paintings unaccompanied by certificates from Berenson. "We have seen a great many people this week," Mary wrote to Little Mother, "including a Mr. and Mrs. Straus. He is head of Macy's department store in New York and of course very rich. They collect, & word seems to have gone round among rich Jews that it is not safe to buy Italian pictures without Bernard's guarantee."

Berenson had been invited to Spain at the end of World War I to help rehang and catalogue the paintings at the Prado and had been given an audience with the Queen. In Paris, the officials of the Louvre had paid him the ultimate compliment of taking their masterpieces from the walls, unframing them, and standing them in sunlight, so that he might inspect them.

In Paris, as in New York, they lunched and dined out everyday or else invited the French cognoscenti to his hotel, the Beau Site at 4 rue du Presbourg. "At lunch, at tea, all evening, B.B. either talks with learned men or purrs to the admiration of Princesses and Countesses and Baronesses and Duchesses," Mary wrote.

While traveling, Berenson spared no expense to make himself comfortable and, in London, might well rent, as his temporary *pied-à-terre,* Lady Horner's Mayfair mansion in Lower Berkeley Street. Since the house had a staff of five servants and a genius of a cook, Bernard declared himself satisfied. "I often wonder if his Father wasn't secretly a Grand Duke! Do confess!! I never knew anyone with such luxurious and fastidious tastes as that blessed son of yours," Mary wrote to his mother.

Berenson could not help making an offhand reference to his prominence, particularly to other famous men. ". . . I have no objection to being known. On the contrary, I have a good human desire for 'fame'!" he wrote airily to Charles du Bos in 1926. His view of himself can best be seen in the following anecdote, related by the widow of Richard Offner.

"Many years before I met Richard he was quite young and in Paris, on his way to Italy. A friend said, 'Would you like to meet Anatole France?' Richard: 'I certainly would.' He called on France and had a short conversation. Richard very much admired him and when he got to Florence, he was still full of this. He said to B.B., 'Have you met him?' and B.B. replied, 'France? No, he's never been to see me.' "

Berenson's income, during the 1920s, averaged about £15,000 or $75,000 a year. Until the stock market crash of 1929 turned plutocrats into paupers overnight, the buoyant market for fine pictures was responsible for this handsome income. Mellon, Widener, Hearst, Bache, and Mackay were buying furiously. Berenson scouted and attributed and privately sneered. Art in America, he wrote to Royal Cortissoz, was unfortunately the plaything of the powerful financier, who did not like to be divested of his illusions. Although he, Berenson, had been trying for twenty years to talk some sense into such people, he found it a fruitless task. Such a man would rather listen to any kind of charlatan. "B.B. lived in perpetual fear of discredit," Edward Fowles observed; "his livelihood depended upon the maintenance of a delicate balance between his roles of critic and connoisseur of repute, and that of profitable intermediary."

The conviction that attributing paintings was valueless, in terms of the human spirit, had hardened into a profound disgust for his work, and even his writings were merely the evidence of his despair, he wrote. A suppressed yearning to "Burst from his cell with a hell of a yell/ And elope with the Mother Superior," began to surface at recurrent intervals in Berenson's letters. If he only had himself to consider, he told Frank Jewett Mather at the end of World War I, he would throw it all over.

To Ivins, Berenson was even more explicit. How he would like to give up this albatross of the imagination, he wrote from Altamura, which caused him so much trouble, difficulty, and cash, which was a cage, a prison, and a madhouse at times. How he wished he could sail the ocean and visit distant islands and take as his mistresses dark-skinned women with glinting teeth, languorous eyes, and beautiful shoulders. And, by golly, one day he would do it.

15

THE CON GAME

Do not make yourself so big. You are not so small.

—THEODOR REIK, *"Of Love and Lust"*

IN 1910, BERENSON WROTE to Edith Wharton from Rome
that he had long since lost interest in the sculpture of the
Renaissance and now, surrounded as he was by incomparable
examples, was losing interest in its architecture as well. He wondered whether he would eventually lose interest in the great love
of his life, Italian painting. In that event, Mary said, there was
only one course left. He would have to buy a box of paints and
take up art.

Since he had, however, never shown the slightest artistic talent, Berenson was casting around for a new interest, and found it.

"A problem that has interested me for the last 30 years," he
wrote in 1926, "is the problem of provincialism in art and its
close relation to, as well as its apparent identity with, most of the
phenomena of decline and decay. Surely it should seem as absurd
to construct a history of art without such enquiries, as it is to write
the history of language without the study of the dialects of the
backward communities and of the speech of uneducated people in
our midst. . . ."

His specific area of interest was the infinitely slow process by
which the glories of Greek and Roman art changed out of recognition into the art of the Middle Ages. To Berenson, that process
impoverished and barbarized classical art. It was a decadent art
and that, he found, "always repeats the same forms of evolution:
the enlargement, stiffening and geometricization of contours. . . ."

From the 1920s onward, Berenson's whole attention was turned to this problem. It led to an inner vow that he would write *the* book, the one upon which his reputation would finally rest, on "Decline and Recovery in the Figure Arts." (The book was never finished, although *The Arch of Constantine* [1954], and *Aesthetics and History* [1948] draw substantially from the ideas he developed for it.) But, Kenneth Clark said, Berenson had put himself in a false position.

"He wanted to call it the 'Deformation of Form'; i.e., to say that a change had occurred in the nature of form, from the human body to another kind of form based upon another system. However, when Byzantine and non-Classical art began to establish themselves, it was simply a new kind of form—not necessarily deformed. It's the great subject, how classical form died out and was replaced. But the subject was too big for him. It's too big for any of us. . . ."

The study on which Berenson had embarked involved a kind of artistic detective work, to identify artifacts throughout the Roman Empire that would support a patient reconstruction of what probably occurred over a thousand-year period. It was a reversal of the point of view which he, as a consummate appreciator of beauty, had followed to that moment. Instead of identifying and attributing works whose true worth needed to be uncovered, Berenson now proposed to discuss the process by which classical art had, in his opinion, been degraded past recognition. The passionate pilgrim in him was giving way to the historian, the archaeologist, and the would-be philosopher.

One might expect a historian of such art to begin his studies with Roman art, but he seems to have taken the more plausible (in his case) course of starting at the end and working backward. The *deus ex machina* in changing the Berenson course may well have been a Harvard University professor named Arthur Kingsley Porter. Porter, who was independently wealthy, was an assistant professor at Yale when they met (he shortly moved on to Harvard) and, during World War I, was the only foreigner on a French commission to study the preservation of monuments.

Porter subsequently became known for his heroic ten-volume study of Romanesque sculpture of the pilgrimage roads, but is perhaps best known for the mysterious manner of his disappearance some years later. He and his wife had bought a romantic Irish castle in County Donegal with the requisite number of haunted rooms and a suitably murky past, and were in residence in the summer of 1933. They decided to visit their tiny cottage on a nearby island just off the Irish coast. While Mrs. Porter was making lunch, her husband went for a walk. He never returned. He was declared to have been swept off the cliffs into the sea but his body was never found. There were persistent rumors that he had not died at all but merely, for some fathomless reason, dropped from sight. Henry P. McIlhenny, who bought the castle soon after that, said the servants told him that Kingsley Porter returned late at night to visit his wife. No one knows quite what to believe.

When Berenson met the Porters, undoubtedly in Paris at the end of World War I, they must have seemed simply like a well-to-do and well-educated couple of no particular idiosyncrasies apart from their obsession for some curious sculpture. "Porter and Berenson were fond of each other," said the late Walter Muir Whitehill, who was a friend of both, "but Berenson couldn't understand why he liked these old churches. To Berenson there was only Greece and the High Renaissance and everything in between was artistically debased. So he would join them on their trips to find out what it was all about. . . ."

They picked up Berenson at the Ritz in Paris on a fine, clear August morning and headed for Burgundy. Like Berenson, the two Porters were tireless in pursuit of choice specimens. There would be just enough time in the mornings to pack and buy food for the afternoon tea basket and they would be off, in their chauffeur-driven limousine, speeding through open country and green pastures and pine forests and vine-covered hills. They stopped at seven or eight small villages a day and, while B.B. and Lucy lunched at a small inn, Porter, to save time, would be huddled in a church taking notes and photos and would eat his lunch in the back seat on their way to the next.

While they worked, Berenson lounged in "comfortable chairs—feasting his eyes," Lucy Porter wrote in her diary, or went to storage centers for evacuated art objects and found a Sassetta, a school piece of Simone Martini, and a Lorenzetti Madonna, or expounded upon his favorite piece of philosophy, which was that achievement counted for nothing in life. The only goal was to become.

Years later, Berenson was to make a grateful reference to the new worlds Porter had opened for him. That the conversion was sudden seems likely. In the autumn of 1919, Mary wrote to his mother that, "Bernard doesn't quite know yet exactly what piece of work he will take up, but it may be something on Medieval Sculpture, which is the subject that interests him most at present."

Mary did not approve. Twelve years later, she wrote to the Lippmanns from Timgad, Algeria, that Berenson had finished his work on the Lists at long last and was preparing a more interesting study on "The Decline and Recovery of Art."

"N. Africa is a great place for the decline, & B.B. stands in ecstacy before every misunderstood Greek design, mishandled & degraded by provincial craftsmen here. Sometimes Nicky & I suspect that he actually loves ugliness. . . ."

Although Berenson was completely captivated by his self-imposed riddle, he was only able to give it sporadic study for almost two decades. He was, during the period between the wars, doing very little writing. His extraordinary first burst of publishing had been followed by what became a thirty-year gap, and, apart from *Venetian Painting in America* (1916) and *Three Essays in Method* (1926), Berenson's output was confined to new, foreign language or revised editions of his previous writings.

However, Berenson's influence was making itself felt in a new direction.

As he reached middle age, he became interested in the careers of younger men. All kinds of interesting youngsters who floated into his orbit might be invited to join the court of Altamura upon a sudden Berensonian impulse.

Bruno Molajoli, who was to become Italian director-general of Antiquities and Fine Arts, recalled that they met when he was a young student of art history studying in a little art gallery in Fabriano.

"He arrived there one day in an immense car—in my memory it was vast—with a chauffeur in furs and out stepped this very elegant little man with a large wife and pretty secretary, and came into the gallery. I realized that this must be an important man, but I didn't know who he was.

"He asked me, 'What are you doing here?'

"I answered, 'I'm studying.'

"He said, 'Come with us.' So I followed him while he walked around the gallery and caught a glimpse of his arresting personality and wicked wit.

" 'What is this painting?' he asked.

"I told him that the attribution was much disputed but some

said it was by the Maestro di Bambino Vispo. 'Who said that?' he wanted to know. I named a famous critic, and he smiled. 'Ah, these myth-makers!' he said."

Shortly afterwards, when Molajoli became a young officer posted in Florence, he was frequently invited to Sunday lunch at "i Tatti" and met all the great personalities of the day there. "Whenever I was invited, Berenson sent a car. I was in a tiny room in the old part of town and the third time it happened, the landlady raised the rent."

People were always meeting promising young men at Altamura and the Countess Elena Carandini, a friend from the 1930s onward, remarked upon his strong attraction to them. The attraction, if such, appeared to be admiration for their talents combined with a strong paternal impulse. To such young men, many of them eager disciples, Berenson was benevolent and generous and, most of all, directive, as if determined to prevent them from taking a wrong turn. He seemed to be reliving his youth in them.

In the case of John Walker, now retired as director of the National Gallery of Art in Washington, Berenson's response was spontaneous and uncomplex. Harvard University, he wrote to W. M. Ivins, Jr., in the winter of 1930, had just sent him a gilded youth who, but for the mercy of God, would be in training as a Grand Duke. Walker had contracted infantile paralysis at the age of eleven and now, at twenty-three, was sensitive, receptive, and stimulating, loving everything that pertained to the life of the spirit, in short, an *unsereiner*. Walker was invited to help Mary compile a short list of Italian "sacred pictures" from the Lists that were to be published in 1932, and was invited back again and again. By 1935, when Walker became assistant to Chester Aldrich at the American Academy in Rome, he had become "my" Johnnie and, Berenson told Learned Hand in 1940, he could not love him more if he were his own son. Perhaps Berenson's only disappointment was that Walker became director of the National Gallery, thus disqualifying himself for the role Berenson had hoped he would play as first director of "i Tatti."

Although Berenson never for a moment lost faith in Walker's judgment, that he should contemplate taking any kind of position worried him. In the spring of 1934 Berenson recalled that, as he looked back on life, worldly success had never brought him anything he valued. At best, it widened his opportunities; at worst, it had hampered him, since it denied him the only thing he ever really wanted, a sense that he was making the most of his abilities.

Quality, Berenson said, was the only thing that counted. He was saying this so that Walker might ask himself whether he, too, was not called by fate to renounce a career and live a life of inner development, one in which writing would take the place of administration or teaching.

Berenson made the same point even more forcibly with another pupil, and one for whom he had mixed feelings: Kenneth Clark. Like Walker and Molajoli, Clark has recalled their first meeting, how Berenson took a sudden, impulsive liking to him and invited him to help prepare a new edition of the *Florentine Drawings*. The invitation, the exact fulfillment of a boyhood dream, took Clark by such surprise that he fell ill.

What gave Clark reason for pause was the courtlike atmosphere of Altamura. As Berenson's sister Rachel had remarked a decade before that, "For diplomacy & intrigue the court of 'i Tatti' makes Henry of Navarre, Margot & Catherine de Medicis look like suckling babes." Meyer Schapiro, who was also to become a distinguished art historian, felt the same attraction-repulsion when he visited "i Tatti" in the 1920s and resolved it by deciding not to join the court, despite warm invitations. Clark decided in favor of Altamura and a new edition of the *Florentine Drawings* (although the collaboration was later abandoned). That his misgivings were well-founded is apparent from the following letter from Logan to his sister Alys:

> It is just like a little Court here, with favourites & changes of favour & jealousies—very amusing to look on & I think Mariechen & B.B. both enjoy it. Clark is the greatest favourite now & certainly seems to deserve his favour—his knowledge and reading and his power of expressing himself are certainly prodigious for his age. He likes it here immensely, loves the good talk, & appreciates the humour of the situation and his own to the full. . . . I have just left him sitting with the B.B.'s over a portfolio of photographs, emitting opinions about them which they seemed to listen to with respect.

Yet, despite this auspicious beginning, the proposed collaboration quickly floundered. As a young man, Umberto Morra recalled, Clark was already asserting himself. Even then he had a good deal of natural authority and a very clear mind. "I knew him at twenty-three and there was nothing adolescent about him."

Such qualities mark the born leader but are not conducive to the molding of an assistant, even at a cherished task, and Berenson quickly realized it. If Clark had some reservations about working with Berenson, Berenson had reservations of his own. He could not penetrate behind a façade of diffidence to find the man. To him Clark appeared, even at the end of Berenson's life, opaque and impenetrable.

What appeared to lurk at the heart of Berenson's unease was an emotion bound to color any relationship with a man born to every advantage—money, position, intelligence, and charm—and who was to be considered the best lecturer on art in English and the best art writer and critic. Berenson might have consoled himself with the thought that Clark could not be estimated a success while he, Berenson, was one, because he had been born poor and made a fortune. It did not help.

"He buys and sells works of art, and that counts only as a gentleman 'exchanging' a good thing for a better one. If I sold any picture I should at once be put down as a 'dealer,' because I started poor," Berenson wrote in 1952, still nursing his grievances. To be a gentleman: how much that name rankled, and how much he still wanted it.

The ostensible break between Berenson and Clark was caused by the latter's announcement that he was going to marry Jane Martin. Since Clark's future wife had just broken her engagement to Gordon Waterfield, son of Mary Berenson's lifelong friend Lina, the reaction at "i Tatti" might be predicted.

It did not help that Waterfield, then a penniless young journalist working in Egypt with no immediate hope of marrying, felt that Jane had behaved "very straight-forwardly and properly," and that the decision to break the engagement had been mutual. Mary rose to defend the Waterfields. She thought that Jane Martin had schemed to marry Clark. So did Berenson; he had, Rosamond Lehmann observed, "violent moral prejudices." After the marriage, he had some "very witty and sharp" things to say about Clark. When Clark left to get married, Mary took him to say good-bye to B.B. He was in the bathroom brushing his teeth.

" 'Bernard,' she said, 'Kenneth has come to say good-bye. He's going to get married.' Brush, brush, brush. 'Very well, Mary,' brush, brush, brush, 'I don't mind.' Being used to the undemonstrative behaviour of my mother, this did not seem strange to me."

The late Lady Clark reacted more spiritedly to the Berensonian chill. "I didn't like him because he was a terrible snob and I wasn't grand. He thought I had married K for his money and I hadn't. He was very rude."

Despite these reservations, Berenson went on writing to Clark and inviting him to Altamura. It almost looks as if he couldn't help himself. Behind the guardedly polite letters one finds the outline of a man who would, all of his life, long to know what happened next. In the case of this particularly independent pupil, Berenson did not have long to wait.

Books on art were followed by appointments as Keeper of Fine Arts at Ashmolean Museum, director of the National Gallery in London at the age of thirty and then surveyor of the King's Pictures. Such activism filled Berenson with alarm.

When Clark was offered the Ashmolean Museum post, and wrote for Berenson's opinion, he received a prompt reply from Rome. The offer seemed most tempting. However, the job would imprison Clark in the world of curators, collectors, and dons and he would be bogged down in it. And, Berenson said, Clark was so young. He begged him to reconsider.

If Clark really felt compelled to take the course of one who curated, collected, catalogued, made discoveries, praised novelties, and was, in other words, one more player in a sordid little game, then he must do so. Berenson clung to the thought that Clark could do better than that; that he could become a true student devoting his life to the humanization of mankind through art. This alone would give him lasting happiness, Berenson concluded poignantly. Clark took the job anyway and Berenson sent his polite congratulations.

Their chilly contact thawed noticeably once Berenson himself was no longer in the thick of the art market. A visit the Clarks made to "i Tatti" in the autumn of 1938 immediately established the friendship on a new footing. After the war, Berenson was most anxious to have Kenneth Clark write his biography and Clark agreed. ("What else could I say?") However, Clark later abandoned the idea. Although markedly more affectionate, Berenson, as has been noted, could never quite overcome rivalrous feelings and was known to say, "I love him but I don't like him."

Kenneth Clark has made a number of references to this thawing of the atmosphere in his autobiography and has recorded his appreciation for what was one of the formative influences on his life.

Berenson was to have other disciples, including Benedict

Nicolson, Sir John Pope-Hennessy, and William Mostyn-Owen, who expanded upon his ideas or departed from them; but the one whose life most closely mirrored his own, and who scrupulously upheld Berenson's strictures to avoid worldly contamination for the narrower paths of scholarship, was the one whose name inspired epithets of which "odious" and "toadlike" seem milder examples.

He was Richard Offner, born, like Berenson, of emigré Russian Jewish parents (in Vienna) and brought to the United States at a young age. Like Berenson, Offner went to Harvard and, also like him, "he was not a believing Jew; rather a citizen of the world, as B.B. was. He called himself an agnostic but actually he was an atheist," his widow remarked. "He never adopted the Christian faith."

Like Berenson, Offner was never at home in his adopted land, dividing his year between teaching positions at Chicago, Harvard, and later, New York University's Institute of Fine Arts, and his studies in Florence. Also like Berenson, Offner devoted his life to connoisseurship. The great work of his life is a critical and historical study of Florentine painting in several volumes.

Offner met Berenson when he was a young student at the University of Vienna and had just completed a doctoral thesis on Leonardo da Vinci. "He adored B.B. and spent a great deal of time at 'i Tatti.' One of the young men around the place," Mrs. Offner said. "B.B. was very generous with help and advice. He played the role of a spiritual father."

Offner had always attributed paintings although, his wife continued, Berenson advised him never to do so because one could no longer remain free from corruption. Offner's method of operation, however, differed significantly from that of his mentor.

"He charged a flat fee in advance, i.e., $150, the way a doctor would. He would always look at the painting before deciding and if it was a fake, he refused. He charged a fee to private collectors and dealers and, for museums, his advice was always free." The late Benedict Nicolson remarked that Offner was a man of complete integrity.

Then Offner committed the unforgivable act. In the early summer of 1924, Duveen decided to invite American collectors who had bought his Italian Renaissance paintings, all with attributions from Berenson, to exhibit in his New York galleries. Offner was invited by Forbes Watson, editor of *The Arts* magazine, to write a review. Offner hesitated. "If I were to write what I really think," he said, "you wouldn't publish it." Watson declared that he would. The article was published in May.

The review, as Philippa Offner observed, does not seem particularly "ferocious." The doubts expressed are gentlemanly. "The authorship of this 'Cimabue' seems to me still unsettled," Offner remarks of one painting and, of another, "the artistic savor of our panel is certainly not due to Bernardo Daddi," and, of a third, "the touching Deposition with some sensitive figures in it is inadmissible as an autograph work of Fra Angelico." However Offner did, wittingly or unwittingly, pinpoint paintings that, to judge from their subsequent history, were examples of too-optimistic attributing on the part of his mentor. Offner's article in *The Arts* was in effect the first serious challenge to Berenson's attributions.

Perhaps Offner was naïvely assuming that they were both dedicated to the disinterested pursuit of truth, as Berenson's generous response to his "St. John" attribution would suggest. However, to Berenson, Offner's article must have seemed like a direct attack upon his reputation, therefore a threat to his position, and therefore a profoundly disloyal act. Only the truth could have saved him but Berenson dared not speak. He was trapped.

"Richard went on writing to B.B. and there was no answer. He never heard from him," Mrs. Offner said. "He realized that it was the article. B.B. could not bear to have one of his disciples grow up and question the master. It was a betrayal."

At the close of World War II, Philippa Offner was sent to Florence as a writer for *Life* magazine and given a parcel of vitamins by mutual friends to take to Berenson. She sent it upon her arrival and, in due course, was invited for tea. Nicky Mariano was warm and welcoming; Berenson was enchanting. When the Offners returned to Florence to live the following year, Nicky Mariano telephoned and asked them both to visit. "It was over."

Offner, his wife continued, admired Berenson's early Lists in particular and always defended him as one of the most brilliant minds that ever touched the field.

"Richard was the last person B.B. spoke to. I was in New York and Richard in Florence when B.B. became really ill. He asked to see him and Nicky Mariano said, 'Yes, he's pretty far gone.' Richard went in. B.B. said, 'Good of you to come, Richard,' and I don't think he spoke after that. Richard of course went to his funeral. He really loved B.B."

Berenson had a highly developed ability to compartmentalize

his relationships, with men in particular. One of the longest lasting and in many ways least interesting of these is his correspondence with the American political commentator Walter Lippmann. The men met in Paris at the end of World War I and Berenson was delighted with this promising newcomer—he could, he remarked, recognize quality anywhere—and seized on the opportunity to vent a flow of political comment: fierce, denunciatory, emphatic, and invariably pessimistic. Lippmann's replies were distinctly dispassionate. They corresponded for decades yet talked of almost nothing else.

A similar impulse seems to have inspired Berenson to cultivate the friendship of Learned Hand. The distinguished American jurist loved to gossip about American politics and Berenson longed to feel privy to their inner workings. As with Lippmann, Berenson also made judicious use of his friendship with Hand when he needed help, for instance, on his status as an American citizen residing abroad.

However, the difference between their temperaments was marked. A clue to this may be glimpsed from the following reply of Hand to the standard Berenson railing against the imbecilities of politicians:

"I have no opinion," Learned Hand wrote; "indeed B.B. the congeries of relevant facts that become in the end a question of public policy is so vast and inaccessible that I always put it down as at best a 'Guess.' Quoting from one Bernard Berenson, I say: 'In the beginning was the Guess'. . . In short, while I agree that in retrospect we can say that A.B. was a silly ass when he declared, or didn't declare, war against Ruritania, I cannot see any reliable evidence in which he could have made his initial judgment in one way or the other."

What attracted Berenson was precisely this good-humored tolerance of human limitation. He liked Hand's disarming frankness, his willingness to appear as less than oracular, and his stimulating ideas. He was *haimish*, i.e., cozy, unspoiled, and unpretentious, qualities that Berenson valued highly. Berenson besieged Hand with invitations; Hand fended them off as best he could. His daughter, Mrs. Norris Darrell, said that her mother adored Nicky Mariano and was always eager to return to "i Tatti." But Hand hesitated, she thought, because he had been given reason to doubt the probity of Berenson's business dealings. Still, Berenson begged him to come, and, after another refusal, wrote that it really didn't matter because he held long, imaginary conversations with Hand every day in which he envisioned the comments Hand would make and the answers he would give. One is obliged to impress one's heroes and perhaps this is why Berenson's letters are so scrupulously unrevealing.

With Edward Waldo Forbes and Paul Sachs of the Fogg Museum, Berenson talked attributions and museum politics. With Daniel Varney Thompson, Frank Jewett Mather, and Royal Cortissoz, Berenson talked about art. These partial friendships had the advantage of keeping Berenson in contact with people whose sole interest for him appeared to be the link they all had in common. His letters are, perhaps inevitably, superficial and unrevealing. The exception was his correspondence with W. M. Ivins, Jr., the curator of prints and drawings at the Metropolitan Museum of Art.

The correspondence with Ivins is so unique among that of Berenson's male contacts that one seeks for explanations. Perhaps one reason is that Ivins, who was known as "Billee" after Thackeray's nonsense rhyme, "Little Billee," fitted into no conventional mold.

Ivins began with the intention of becoming an engineer, then switched to law and practiced it. By 1917, he had developed his amateur's interest in art so extensively that he was invited to become curator of a large print collection that the Metropolitan Museum of Art had just received.

Ivins approached the work with characteristic iconoclasm. "He was scornful of those who talked of beauty and always pronounced the word as a sneering 'beauteh.' He insisted that aesthetic could best be understood as the opposite of anaesthetic, and he bought for the collection many things he said he disliked intensely," his daughter, Barbara Ivins, wrote.

Little Billee's impudent, maverick spirit delighted Berenson. Here was someone with whom it was useless to sustain a façade since he would always, good-humoredly, make you laugh with him at yourself; he was someone with whom one could be real. Berenson's letters to Ivins are full of unguarded revelations about himself. They were met by Ivins's half-deriding, half-admiring replies, as the following draft of a letter now in the Archives of American Art would indicate:

"If ever I met an argument that was a phony—that a thing or quality is unimportant because it changes or because you haven't the scientifically exact vocabulary to deal with it! God knows that neither of these two objections ever stopped any man, let alone

my dear B.B., from talking ... about a lot of things—from the
Jewish profitts [*sic*] with sandburrs in their beards to the Greek
Thinkers. . . . You darned old mute inglorious faker. . . ." Ivins
closed by saying, "I dearly love a good rascal."

If Ivins charmed him with impudence, Berenson's brother-in-
law Ralph Barton Perry attracted that side of Berenson's nature
that would always be disarmed by a gentle and winning personality. Perry's authoritative comments on philosophy to one side—he
won a Pulitzer Prize for his biography of William James—the two
men had so many common interests that Berenson put up with his
rather-too-lively sister Rachel for the pleasure of her soothing
husband's company. At the end of Perry's life Berenson wrote
touchingly that he had always trusted him and loved him since
that day, a half-century before, when they became brothers-in-law.

While, with men, Berenson seemed to need a façade behind
which to hide his real thoughts and feelings, this was not true for
his friendships with women. If he was attracted at all, Berenson
trusted them, at least potentially, with everything: doubts, longings, whims, fantasies, and regrets. His friendships encompassed
every shade of feeling, from outrageous flirting to anxious protec-
tiveness. In most cases, it would have been difficult to separate a
parental concern from the more predictable attraction of the
sexes.

Young women like Pellegrina von Turco, an exquisite young
Florentine with the flowerlike face of a Piero della Francesca,
who was hired as a secretary in 1925, might be asked, "What do
you think of me?" Her response, that he was Dionysus with
whom every woman would have to be a bacchante, did not please
him; but Berenson responded to her other comments with such
wholehearted enthusiasm that, for Nicky Mariano, the world
turned black.

"Absurd as it may sound it never occurred to me that new
stars might rise up in his sky and the first time it happened I went
through agonies of despair and doubts and feelings of intense
inferiority," she wrote.

If others at the court of Altamura were, like Mary, merely
amused by the eternal round of shifting favorites, Nicky Mariano
was wounded to the heart. To have one's married lover turn to a
new and prettier face, while his wife watched, must have been
humiliating. It is difficult to understand why Nicky Mariano
continued to endure it. Only a woman who felt pathetically
inadequate as an independent being and inwardly convinced of

her unlovableness, would have accepted such meager fare.

Further evidence of her insecurity can be seen in the fact that Nicky even enlisted Berenson's aid to help her get over it. If she felt jealous (perhaps even outraged) it must be her fault since, by Nicky's confused reasoning, Berenson must be right. Nicky, riding roughshod over her feelings, discussed the problem with Berenson for hours. She seemed surprised that he was so angelically patient and sweet.

Like Berenson, Nicky Mariano was unable to envision a relationship of equals. One was condemned to the role of hopeless inferior, unless one could somehow float upward, out of reach of its pain, on the saintly wings of motherhood. From this point on she became, more than ever, the proud parent who watches the antics of its child with indulgence.

"It ended by my enjoying—as a mother enjoys a new toy for her baby—a new half-amorous friendship of his. . . ." At about this time (1926) Nicky Mariano had an operation for appendicitis and, in the years that followed, her slender silhouette disappeared, to be replaced by the ample bosom and wide spreading hips of middle age. By contrast Berenson seemed to grow tauter and ever more sinewy, his body tightening like a whip.

Berenson's infatuation with Pellegrina was destined to be brief. It was superseded by a longer-lasting interest in Pellegrina's Neapolitan friend, a young married woman and would-be writer who was already a habitué of the rival salons of Raffaello Piccoli and Benedetto Croce. Her name was Clotilde Marghieri. In her autobiography, *Il segno sul braccio* (1970), the Italian writer described at some length the process by which she was drawn into the circle of *unsereiners*. "The sovereign that met me the next evening, coming towards me with his busy little step, all minute and elegant, the carnation in the button-hole, and speaking to me with almost insolent familiarity, as if renewing a discussion interrupted the day before . . . wasn't anything like a bookworm. . . . I was . . . attracted to his eyes, which were so alive and magnetic that they could have revived a dead person; and I was quite alive, as far as I was concerned."

Mary, visiting her family in England in the summer of 1931, wrote to Senda to say that while she was away Bernard was flirting with a new romance, Clotilde Marghieri. "Mild flirtation is his distraction and if he chooses a nice person, *we none of us mind*. . . ." (Italics mine.)

Clotilde found excuses to leave her husband and visit "i

Tatti" alone. She wrote, "You represent for me all ... [that] is charm, and loveliness, and courtesy, apart from what I admire in your spirit, so when I am near you I do forget for a while what is difficult and hard and harsh. ...." She signed the letter, "For ever and ever yours."

Berenson, too, was entranced. He wrote to say that he adored people who, like herself, were willing to give themselves to others—in conversation. That, since childhood, had been the crowning joy of his life. He urged her to come and stay for as long as she liked. She must not despair. Even though she was young (there was a thirty-five-year difference in their ages) he was not yet decrepit, and might well live to join her often on her cherished island, Capri.

Once the first rapture of discovery had passed, her feelings for him took clearer outline. "B.B. was taken by my youth and I was much flattered, but to me he was a father figure. I couldn't be 'in love,' " she said. He challenged her ideas, made her think, and encouraged her to write. "I considered him like a tender, too tender father, a father I never had and for whom I was longing.

"You know," she continued, "B.B. was not a man of passions. He had his emotions under such control that he didn't much understand people who gave themselves to their feelings. I think he thought that was a sign of weakness. Love was important for him, but it always came second to his work, to a life dominated by reason."

She continued, "Was I one of his great loves? Love is an omnibus word. If love means a long, faithful, attentive, dedicated affection in which the need for sympathy and a dialogue together and helping one to be oneself and pushing one to work means anything, then it was love.

"It was not indispensable that it should be sexual. B.B. was not oversexed. He could master that. You know, if you refuse a Mediterranean man, he will vanish. But B.B. felt if that could not be, there were many other ways to love. He wished to possess a woman through his knowledge of her, not necessarily sexually. He has taught me a way of loving and being loved that is not common here."

As for Nicky, "Never in my head did I think that I could ever compete with her. Even when he loved others we all knew that there was Nicky. She was for him like the camel on which he traveled through the ways of life. She was the one he could not have lived without, the perpetual home. Others were the sightseeing." Therefore, there was no shadow on her friendship with Nicky. Clotilde Marghieri said she told Nicky that, if she wanted it, she would go away. Nicky replied, "No, don't go. Through you I have never suffered."

Bit by bit, what used to be a threesome in the work and travel plans at Altamura, was becoming two plus one. In Paris, B.B. and Nicky went out together and Mary did not mind being left behind because they enjoyed the social whirl so much, and "it is nice to see B.B. gay. He needs it from time to time." A year later, traveling together in Constantinople, Mary spent a great deal of time resting in her room, but fortunately Nicky was "about three-quarters" up to Berenson's traveling pace. During the Christmas holidays of 1929, Berenson faced a trip back from Mrs. Wharton's villa in Hyères all alone, and since that must not be allowed, Nicky was going to Hyères to "pick him up, buy his tickets and pilot him home."

Then, in the summer of 1931 Mary told Senda that, upon returning to Florence, she would avoid the heat by going up to their summer cottage at Vallombrosa, "even if they don't go."

Mary was chronically tired. A famous English specialist had told her that there was nothing wrong with her health and that her problems were caused by trying to keep up with a tireless husband. She should relax more, he said, spend a day a week in bed. She was also no longer interested in his work. Nicky, however, her "beloved Ersatz," adored Berenson's new subject and was as excited by it as he was.

"Nicky is the most splendid helper he has ever had," Mary wrote to Walter Lippmann in the summer of 1933. "What luck! I did the best I could for many years, but I never was as accurate & painstaking as Nicky. And now, since my illness, I am really laid aside. . . ."

The arrival of middle age brought with it a period of intense disillusion for Mary. That inner skepticism which, her perceptive lover had noticed, lay just beneath her outward gaiety, was rising to the surface, and with it the feeling that "there ain't going to be no core," as she wrote to Hapgood in 1920. Five years later she stated the feeling even more clearly. She was, she said, "stripped of the life-giving lies that made Youth so glorious. And work and fatigue are our dope." Travel was another anesthetic and, at such moments, she and B.B. were "almost happy."

Now, however, traveling with him wore her out. But B.B. had a better traveling companion, a younger woman who could almost keep up with him, and who shared his interest in the art Mary intensely disliked.

Mary must have realized that Nicky Mariano had gradually become a better companion, a better hostess, secretary, and housekeeper than she was. Nicky was peerless. However much Mary might have contributed to the process, she was now in the impossible position of being replaced in her own house. She felt old and "laid aside." She felt unloved.

Mary could have gone to England, but her daughters had their own lives. She could have turned on Nicky—but how could she hate a woman so selfless and so devoted, to her as well as B.B.? If Mary lacked the faith that had consoled and sustained her mother, there was another alternative for wives caught in an intolerable marriage and one that, her mother maintained, was almost bliss by comparison.

In the autumn of 1931 Mary went to the nursing home to have an operation for cystitis. She recovered slowly. She was impatient and bored and said the thought of food disgusted her, but she did not seem to be starving, her husband remarked sardonically to Edith Wharton. She had taken a dislike to Nicky, said that she couldn't stand her, and her mood of suppressed rage filled the house.

Then Mary contracted a bad case of influenza. This became worse and she was attacked by rheumatic pains. Then came a high fever and an abscess. She was recovering from all this when she had a sudden attack of erysipelas, a violent skin inflammation. Then, she later wrote in an account of her illness, she really was ill.

She was unconscious for two days and at the end of it she somewhere heard the doctors say, "She is going," and felt herself floating on a swift, smooth stream toward a precipice. She was not frightened, but enchanted by what seemed the most beautiful of all experiences in a life dedicated to Beauty. She wrote to the Lippmanns, "I have been feeling that . . . I had nearly reached the allotted span of years, three score and ten, and that I might as well go. In fact, I wished it. . . ."

Then she suddenly heard, as if from a vast distance, B.B. weeping and crying out, "Don't desert me! Oh Mary, don't desert me!" She wrote, "When I heard his voice and felt the love and despair in it I made a great effort of will and said to myself, 'I won't desert you after all our years together,' and began to swim against the current which was bearing me off. Orpheus, though no longer young, still had the magic to summon from Hades his aged Eurydice! The doctors felt as if a miracle had happened when I opened my eyes and said, 'I am going to get well.' "

Mary continued that her illness had the effect of making her reflect on spiritual matters for the first time. It also made her realize that B.B. loved her. She had always assumed, she wrote, that she was accepted only on B.B.'s terms, for what she could do for him. Now she realized that he loved her, and so did other people, and that was paradise.

The experience was equally wrenching for Berenson. She was so near death, he wrote to Ivins, that she had looked back over her life and had made the discovery, as she hardly ever had before, that the great thing in her life had been their love. In the past few days she had asked for him as often as she breathed, and looked happy, and held his hand. He had rubbed his beard against her cheek. No one could take that away from them.

Mary was still in pain although it was hard to know whether she suffered most physically or mentally. The nights, he said, were dreadful. The nurses were convinced then that she was losing her sanity. By day, she would sometimes ask for him, and then refuse to see him, or let him stay only briefly. Her eyes were full of tears and she would tell him how unhappy she was.

She didn't want to see Nicky and Nicky was dreadfully upset by Mary's coldness.

Three days after that, Mary's mood had lifted, and she looked lovelier than she had for years. Berenson was going to have her moved into his bedroom, since he thought the change might amuse her, and he was taking hers.

In March of 1932 Mary was slowly recovering and well enough to be wheeled into the library after lunch to talk to guests. Among them, one day, was the future British Prime Minister Winston Churchill.

"Churchill told us that he had gone crazy while writing his novels and that when he recovered he could not face the thought of writing any more, so he spends his time painting. This interested me very much and I hoped to have a good talk with him," Mary wrote to Neith Hapgood. Mary gave Churchill

one or two straight tips as to what I wanted him to tell me about; but he began a long discourse in which elementary metaphysics, mysticism, and various other unpalatable ingredients were beaten up together.

The consequence was that I went right off to sleep under his nose and everybody else saw that I was asleep and were afraid that he should find out. But he talked straight on for 20 minutes and at last, when he turned his face to me, and the others in the room were shivering with the dread of a catastrophe, I somehow managed to pull myself together and ask what the others said was a very intelligent question. . . .

Mary, who had always had a natural writing gift, was discovering its therapeutic benefits. She had written her first book, about their recent travels in Palestine and Syria, and to encourage her Berenson was trying to have the manuscript published, at his own expense if necessary. Now she was going to write her husband's biography. In the meantime, she was reading. B.B. "stretches out on a chaise-longue in my room & Nicky reads 'Middlemarch' to us, mixed pickles, it is! Edith," she wrote to Mrs. Wharton, "I can't complain of anything when I have two such companions."

· If Mary was too ill to think beyond her sick room, Berenson had other pressing worries. The late 1920s marked the pinnacle of his fame, power, and wealth in the art market. In 1929 the stock market crashed, and although some of the millionaires affected lived to recover their fortunes and spend as lavishly as before, tastes also changed and the market for Italian Renaissance paintings was never the same. The slump had its inevitable effect on Berenson's income, but there was no hint of financial disaster until January of 1932 when, in the midst of Mary's crisis, Berenson was cabling New York by the·hour to see what could be saved from the wreck of his finances.

Berenson never revealed exactly what disaster had hit, but it seems fairly well established that he, like thousands of others, made the monumental mistake of investing a substantial sum of money—perhaps the bulk of his fortune—in Kreuger-Toll Co. ·

Abie Berenson, who had become a one-man investment company for the Berenson family, wrote to Senda that he had been to see a stockbroker about investing her money. "Now—as to stocks—Kreuger-Toll Co. to my mind is a peach—it is 38¼ and in a reasonable time will sell 10 points higher, and for a good long pull will probably double itself—Bess has 20 shares, so has Ralph and I've bought a few—"

Everyone thought Kreuger-Toll was a "peach." Kreuger-Toll was the global invention of a Swedish financial genius, Ivar

Kreuger, called "the match king," who had managed to build an international financial empire by giving long-term dollar loans to countries short of foreign currency in exchange for a monopoly on the marketing of his matches. Since the demand for such was constant, even in poor countries, his business grew rapidly more successful and by 1928, Kreuger controlled more than half the world production of matches.

However, as the value of the dollar fell, Kreuger-Toll was subjected to increasing financial pressures from its creditors and it became disastrously clear that the bulk of its assets was on paper. The match empire began to totter and Kreuger committed suicide. Thousands of fortunes were lost. It was estimated that the financier's dubious international adventure cost his stockholders $720 million. Naomi Lofroth, the Berenson masseuse, who had invested her life savings, and Clotilde Marghieri, for whom Berenson had invested a million lire, were among the victims. So, it seems entirely likely, was Berenson.

By the afternoon of March 11, 1932, the day Kreuger shot himself in a Paris hotel bedroom, the Berensons had lost "nearly all our money," Mary wrote to the Lippmanns, and seriously doubted whether they could remain at "i Tatti." Just how much that fortune was is not known. However, in the mid-1920s, when Berenson was drawing up a will to leave "i Tatti" to Harvard to found an Institution for Humane Studies, Mary was worried that they were living far too extravagantly to provide an endowment for student scholarships. To do that, a lawyer had informed her, would take $1 million, which was more, she implied, than they had.

Now that he faced financial ruin, Berenson began to make alternative plans to persuade Harvard to take occupancy at once and allow them to live on the estate for the rest of their lives. It seemed as if they must survive on a quarter of their income and they had made drastic economies, including the withdrawal of the allowance Berenson made to Ray and Karin upon his marriage to Mary.

President James Bryant Conant of Harvard did not accept "i Tatti" on the terms Berenson hoped for. He made it clear that the estate would only be considered if it came with a substantial additional endowment for scholarships. By the time his letter of guarded acceptance arrived at the end of 1933, Berenson had spent six nightmarish days of wrangling with Duveen in Vienna and had managed to patch up his financial affairs for the next two years. Berenson's income slowly crept upward—by 1939 it was about $40,000 a year—but never equaled its pre-1929 magnificence.

He was considerably upset, Berenson wrote to Lippmann in the summer of 1933. It was not simply the disastrous financial loss he had suffered but the European political situation in general. His total Apollonian way of life—what Clotilde Marghieri called *"Luxe, calme et beauté* in a play on Baudelaire's famous verse— seemed to be threatened.

That threat to Altamura had been developing for several years. In 1925, two years after Mussolini came to power, "I cannot tell you how horrible things are here, worse and worse every day," Mary wrote to Walter Lippmann. "Not a newspaper is allowed to appear with even facts that might cause people to criticize the government. Two nights ago all the kiosks in Florence were burnt down, because they sell the expurgated editions of the Corriere della Sera, which is known to be an anti-F. journal. But that is nothing to the murders and beatings and general acts of violence."

A month later, the Berensons themselves became involved. Gaetano Salvemini, one of their closest Italian friends, a professor of history in the University of Florence, was in prison, denounced by a paid informer who claimed that he had heard his name coupled with that of a clandestine anti-Fascist newspaper. The arrest had caused "a commotion" in England and Mary's daughter was organizing a protest from people like Leonard Woolf, Gilbert Murray, John Maynard Keynes, and others.

Salvemini was not only involved with the anti-Fascist newspaper; he was the head of it. The Fascists, however, had no proof and Salvemini's wife hoped he would be freed. "She imagined he wouldn't be allowed to leave Italy," Count Umberto Morra said, "so she had this mad idea that, as he had a beard, B.B. could give him his own passport."

The young count, who had never been to "i Tatti" before, was dispatched there to make the suggestion.

"Nicky Mariano came to the door and I said, 'I am here with a message from Salvemini.' She replied, 'Don't say a word now because there will be others here for tea, but afterwards we'll take a walk in the garden.' "

When the moment for the walk came, Berenson took him by the arm. "He could be extremely kind and gentle when he wanted to be—or cutting. He asked me about the message.

"I answered that there was another part to the message, but that it was pure folly. I told him what it was, and he began to laugh heartily." Although the plot failed, that was not the end of Berenson's involvement with Salvemini since, a year later, Salvemini had managed to escape to England and was living with Logan Pearsall Smith and Alys Russell in London.

Perhaps this was the reason why Berenson was warned by the United States Consul that the Fascists were suspicious of him and that, the next time he left Italy, he might not be allowed to return. Mary hoped the agitation would die down. "B.B. remains a convinced, dyed-in-the-wool Liberal, which he says is the same thing as an Aristocrat in sympathy. . . ."

The Fascists, however, did not disrupt life at Altamura. As an art historian, Berenson was no direct political threat; Mussolini was anti-British rather than anti-American and the authorities in Florence were disinclined to prosecute. So Berenson, in the relative security of Altamura, went on railing against Mussolini's invasion of Abyssinia and the spectacle of forty-two million people apparently intoxicated by their lust for violence. If the highest aim of the state were the humanization of its citizens, there was no doubt that Mussolini and Hitler were the envoys of hell, who could truly declare, "Hell be thou my Heaven."

Berenson also railed against Mussolini's persecution of foreigners like himself who were having to pay fantastically high taxes, quite beyond his reduced means. Of course, if he were a dentist or a peddler, the United States government would spring to his defense, but since he was only a student living abroad, and with no commercial ties, he could hope for little.

Berenson inveighed against communism, since it heralded a world in which most of his values would be excluded, and all the other "isms" of the new world: the meaningless incantations of Gertrude Stein, the worthlessness of Picasso, and the daily evidence all around that the world was sinking into barbarity.

Berenson's Italian circle was limiting itself to ardent anti-Fascists like Morra and Placci and the amazing Benedetto Croce, whom he admired as a great liberal and historian despite his one-track mind and disorganized life-style or Luigi Albertini, the courageous editor of the *Corriere della sera*, and his daughter the Countess Elena Carandini.

Berenson had never associated much with the land-obsessed and culturally indifferent Italian aristocracy (their somewhat bigoted circles would, in any case, have excluded him) and was never accepted by Florentine society, which considered him "somewhat exotic and eccentric," Marco Grassi said. So he went on performing for galaxies of visitors from everywhere else and saying what he liked. "I remember going to a museum with him and the officials would give the Fascist salute," Professor Marchig said. "Berenson would say, 'Tell them to stop acting like Pagliacci.' "

While Berenson correctly saw the greater danger of Nazism long before his European and American friends—at the time of Hitler's beer cellar *putsch*, Berenson said, "This will turn into something that will make Mussolini look like a fairy tale"—his attitude toward fellow Jews who were fleeing Germany in the 1930s was so uncharitable that its sources deserve examination.

From the art-world gossip that his American friends assiduously provided, and from his wide reading, Berenson soon appreciated the threat to his aesthetic posed by the new art historians.

Art, he wrote, had nothing to do with the history and study of technique, or the history of artists, and especially not with iconographical research, which was nonsense. Similarly there was no such thing as an objective history of art, since every appraisal must be subjective.

The work of art was first and last the only phenomenon to be considered and, if there was anything to be taught at all, it must be the art of seeing, since, *"L'art le plus difficile à apprendre, c'est à voir."* ("The art of seeing is the most difficult one to learn"). Through the contemplation of masterpieces perhaps man might eventually become humanized, taught how to hold himself properly, how to look, what gestures to make, and what attitudes to take; and if it did not, there was nothing to be done.

Therefore Berenson could only view with alarm the teachings of Erwin Panofsky, leader of a new European movement that stressed the importance of a painting's inner meaning. One will look in vain in Berenson's writings for any reference to this issue, one he had dismissed, partly in rebellion against nineteenth-century Academism. Panofsky had fled from Hamburg in 1931 and was spreading his new gospel of iconographical research at New York University's Institute of Fine Arts at the invitation of Richard Offner. Panofskian followers from Germany were on their way, many of them Jews. Berenson saw such refugees only as carriers of an intellectual pestilence that would contaminate every American mind it touched.

Berenson's letters to Margaret Scolari Barr, wife of the director of the Museum of Modern Art, make clear that what also alarmed him was the extreme patriotism of the emigrés. They were not just Germans, they were 150 percent Germans, he wrote sarcastically. He almost seemed to be talking about a separate race of beings and indeed he was. German Jews who had established themselves in the New World made it clear that they were culturally superior to the tattered hordes of Russian Jews who arrived half a decade later; in Berenson's mind, he was merely returning the enmity. It would all end, he supposed, with German Jews taking over everywhere. He would not be surprised by an act of Congress requiring all lectures, lessons, articles, and books dealing with art to be given in Yiddish.

Clotilde Marghieri thought it paradoxical that he, who hated dictatorships so violently, should exhibit so many dictatorial traits himself. In the course of their friendship she timidly began to challenge his sweeping assertions and was swiftly accused of having a dialectical mind, or worse, forensic and destructive. Behind the pugnacious outlines of the Litvak, the *tsaylem kop*, one discovers another self, within whom raged a war of denial. What Berenson could not accept in himself, he experienced all around him. He saw his shortcomings, as if by some grotesque mirror, reflected everywhere in others. For him, the battle was to pounce upon that truth and annihilate it. In attempting to punish others he revealed the extent to which he despised and rejected such traits in himself, as well as his great distance from the truth, the labyrinthine course of his inner evasion and self-deceit.

The same battle to keep the truth at bay can be seen in Mary's case. Once she had retreated into the role of a querulous invalid, her cycles of recovery followed by inexorable cycles of decline, others around her began to discern a pattern that escaped his always fearful, sometimes exasperated gaze.

While Mary was undergoing her worst crisis her daughter, Karin Stephen, now a practicing psychiatrist, was writing a book, *The Wish to Fall Ill*. Its title immediately suggests that her daughter understood the weapon that illness had become in her mother's hands. Mary was repelled by the book's clinical detail but enthusiastic about the idea of writing one on the same theme for the general public. In the autumn of 1933 Mary began two-hour sittings with Leon Stein, Gertrude's brother, in an attempt at psychoanalysis.

That Mary might have deeply envied and resented Nicky never occurred to her husband. That she had been willing to court death to win an expression of his love, and was now using her illness in a final, desperate attempt to keep him riveted to her side, never crossed his mind. There is, however, ample evidence that in this respect at least, Mary was entirely successful.

Mary's illness, Berenson wrote, completely obsessed him, to the extent that he could only work in snatches. Again, he wrote that he could not be happy when someone he loved was in pain. By 1936, the thought that she might die made him feel depressed, alarmed, and dazed with fear. The problem, he said, was that Mary thought her illnesses were a visitation from the devil, whereas they were actually due to chills. Her weak spot was the bladder, while his was the intestine.

As each seeming improvement was followed by a relapse, Berenson began to conclude that part of her illness was certainly imaginary and therefore much harder to cure. Her fascination with Freud's "bowel psychology" was somehow at the root of all her troubles. And so the man who had a horror of the excretory functions of his own body, connecting them with dirt and guilt ("You cannot touch pitch. . ."), railed against the increasing trivialization of his wife's mind, as demonstrated by her fascination with such excretions, and complained about his hemorrhoids, his constipation, and his colitis.

Yet, almost in spite of himself, Berenson was beginning a belated self-examination. Even while he was working for Mrs. Gardner, Berenson had been periodically tormented by the idea that he had accomplished very little of value and that, nevertheless, his best work was behind him. This feeling recurred over the decades. In the middle of World War I, he was complaining to T. S. Perry about the wretched state of his health and his even more profound inner disappointment. Ten years after that, as he struggled to complete the Lists of 1932, he told Frank Jewett Mather that God had destined him for better things and that he would have a great deal to answer for.

By 1929 he reiterated the inner conviction that the man who had written those first four books on Italian Art should never have allowed himself to become sidetracked by connoisseurship. He "should have gone on to write the aesthetics of all humanistic art. That and that only would have meant success. As it is, I weep within me when I am ranked with the successful of my time. . . ."

These same themes: that he no longer believed in the value of his own work, that he was sick of attributing, and that art was made to be enjoyed, rather than analyzed (or exploited?), recur in his letters of the 1930s to D. V. Thompson. People who were still agonizing over questions of aesthetics after the age of thirty, he told W. M. Ivins, must be impotent.

Then, at the end of 1937, Berenson broke off his thirty-year relationship with Duveen Brothers, those business partners he called jackals. Returning to Vienna, he wrote his veiled conclusions to W. M. Ivins. When everything was said and done, art was a con game. He tried to do it decently, he wrote, but how he wished he had never done it at all.

In the summer of 1939 Berenson wrote again to exchange his decrepit musings for the still-youthful dreams of his friend Ivins. As he looked back on seventy-five years of life, he accepted everything that had happened, everything except his own meannesses. It was so much easier to forgive other people than to forgive oneself. At times, he would wake up in the morning, his eyes red with remorse at the thought of some dreadful act committed as a child. But what he had become was nothing to be proud of. He had just visited Benedetto Croce and found him surrounded by books, secretaries, and children—in the prime of life. What was he, compared to someone like Croce? Simply an arid, egotistical old man. He felt, if the truth were to be known, like a fraud.

In the politically ominous and emotionally wrenching atmosphere of the 1930s, Altamura had its compensations. One of the major interests of Berenson's life at that period became a baby boy.

Berenson, who had seen himself supplanted by four brothers and sisters, had consistently congratulated himself upon never having had children. When Kenneth and Jane Clark had twins, making three children in all, Berenson wrote reprovingly that they had now paid their debt to mankind. To continue having more children would be the grossest self-indulgence.

This theme, that to beget children amounted to parental selfishness, changed abruptly after Mary's great-grandchild Roger Hultin came to live with them. His mother Barbara, daughter of Ray, had married, just as quickly divorced, and left Roger in her grandparents' care while she established herself in a new career. Mary predictably found Roger "a fountain of silvery water springing up in a waste land." Berenson's reaction could not have been fantasized.

What fun a sixteen-month-old baby boy could be, Berenson wrote ecstatically to Ralph Perry. He had been playing with Roger for days at a time, but only that day had he discovered the way to the child's heart. He, Berenson, began to cluck like a broody hen. The child stood still, stared, suddenly understood, laughed, and threw himself into Berenson's arms.

Roger stayed for three years and Berenson's interest grew daily. Roger was so enchanting, he wrote to Margaret Barr, that it almost broke his heart. He was a work of art. Berenson almost wished he would die, so as not to develop into the beast he would probably become or, at any rate, have to live in a beastly world.

Logan wrote to Santayana in the winter of 1938, "Youth, that miracle youth, in that aged household—you can imagine what that means! That the child should not be allowed to remain there, but be recalled to London and live with his mother . . . is a view strongly held by the moral members of my family, among whom I am not numbered."

Nevertheless Roger was destined to leave. Mary threatened suicide. Berenson, who had been ready to adopt Roger himself, tried to make the best of it. Life, he told Mary, was still worth living. He meant it. There were its sacred compensations, and by that he meant his daily walk. The beauty of landscape was an enduring and continual source of happiness, and, as Mary observed, once in the country he seemed to "forget utterly his usually ailing body and he becomes all eyes and brain."

This was especially true of Vallombrosa. Every summer since 1924 Berenson had been going to the countryside above Florence where he rented Poggio allo Spino, a villa 4,000 feet up in the hills, some five miles from the small town of Vallombrosa. It stood alone at the edge of a beech forest and afforded endless opportunities for walks, excursions, and picnics.

That forest, with its luxuriant undergrowth, its mosses and wild flowers, encircled by a sky of Tuscan blue and with the most romantic distances, became one of the chief consolations of his life. Those woods looked and felt exactly like the forests of his Lithuanian childhood. Once there, he never wanted to leave.

He wrote to Ralph Perry in the early autumn of 1934 that he and Nicky were still at Vallombrosa, working as they used to in the good old days, walking and reading aloud. There was not a soul to disturb them. How he loved the uniform predictability of that life. How little one really needed at the age of seventy! All he asked for was someone willing to draw him out and listen whenever he excreted an obvious remark, and a companion for those idyllic, delicious walks.

At such moments he felt wafted back to the days of his youth, with all of its dreams and aspirations. "It is IT and why not abandon oneself, why wander, why act?" In the spring of 1941, he wrote to Royal Cortissoz to tell him that for days he had heard the birds tuning up and the night before there was a sound so fluid and so full-bodied that it could only be a nightingale.

16

"ESSENTIAL REALITIES"

The Hindu at forty was commanded by his
religion to retire from the world, to become a
"bhikshu," and to spend the rest of his days in
trying to find his soul.

—BERNARD BERENSON,
Sketch for a Self-Portrait

ISRAEL KOPPEL, the Lithuanian Jew whom Bernard Berenson
had laid to rest half a century before, was coming to life in the
grave of oblivion in which his author had buried him. As in the
story, the revival to awareness was involuntary; but the simile
cannot be carried any further, because Israel's sense of doomed
panic is far different from the indignation and outrage with which
Berenson, in those first years of World War II, read the laconic
accounts in the German papers of the systematic murder of millions of Jews.

"We heard from Rome a couple of days ago that Jews were
being penned into cattle vans to be transported to Germany," he
wrote in the winter of 1943 and, writing again of the Italian Jews
sent to Poland, "Why the expense and trouble of taking them all
the way to distant Lublin when they could so simply be put an end
to here! Or is it that the Gestapo has been trained to prolong
sadistically the agony of its victims?"

For the first time in his life, Berenson was looking for
reasons for what seemed a worldwide anti-Semitism and finding
few explanations, if endless examples. However, unlike Mary

Antin's mother, who stoically accepted the injustice, Berenson reacted with venom. He wrote, "... oh joy, the wave of anti-Semitism which reached America some time ago is rapidly rising and cries of 'Down with the Jews' are being painted on walls everywhere. ..."

The irony, he reflected, was that the Jews were absolutely harmless. No law-abiding citizen was ever more bourgeois or conservative than the average middle-class Jew. Why, then, were Jews the objects of such persecution? During his days of poverty in Vienna, Hitler had been insulted in the Jewish dormitory in which he took shelter and this, said Berenson, accepting the facile explanation, must be the reason for his hatred of Israel. "If that were so, it would be the most interesting case in history of a petty offense towards a ... helpless individual ending in horror to the like of which civilized humanity offers no parallel."

What was happening was indeed horrible and without parallel. As it became more and more obvious that war was inevitable, Berenson was fatalistically prepared to watch the end of his way of life. He was being urged to take Mary to the United States and Nicky was given a special permit to go with them, but he let the moment when they could have easily departed slip by. Mary was too ill to be moved, he said, despite the fact that she was in England when war started and survived the perilous journey back to Florence alone. Nicky Mariano, as an Italian subject, would be barred from leaving Italy and he was helpless without her. Behind his reluctance to leave was one conviction: "i Tatti" must be saved. If he left, the villa and its precious contents were doomed.

As the war drew nearer, Berenson was in Rome negotiating with the U.S. ambassador, William Phillips, and the Italian government, to again have "i Tatti" and all its contents given to Harvard at once. Harvard University declined to accept a property which might shortly be on alien territory, but again gave assurances that the gift would be accepted on his death, provided that it remained intact.

In the interim, Berenson was prudently using his excellent contacts to ensure their safety. Through the influence of Walter Lippmann, Berenson was given State Department protection and, in the spring of 1940, the U.S. ambassador told him that no American over the age of sixty who remained in Italy would be disturbed. Further assurances came in the autumn of 1941, when Phillips left Rome. The ambassador had recommended the Berensons to the powerful protection of Count Galeazzo Ciano, then Italian Minister of Foreign Affairs. The day after war was declared with the United States, a group of fanatical Fascists appeared before the Florentine chief of police demanding that Berenson be arrested. In reply, the chief showed them a telegram from Ciano ordering him to leave Berenson alone. The Fascists left in a rage.

The fact that he himself was in no immediate danger did not assuage the sense of outrage Berenson felt as he read the accounts of Jewish persecution. It seemed to have a reverse effect, as if he were asking himself why he alone should be saved, as if he were looking within himself for a sense of identification with them. To the Germans, that their Jewish population was loyally, even 150 percent German, as Berenson observed, meant nothing.

Assimilation, the doctrine Berenson fervently preached, had failed. Once a Jew, always a Jew, Hitler seemed to be saying; and Berenson was discovering the same truth, but from another vantage point. He began to ask himself what cultural, religious, and racial factors were pivotal to such a definition and would therefore qualify him as "one of them." He arrived at the conclusion that "at times I seem to myself to be a typical 'Talmud Jew.' . . ." At the height of the Holocaust, Berenson was coming to a belated recognition of what had been forfeited when he disowned his birthright.

Life went on as usual at "i Tatti," if more quietly. The usual crowd, Morra, Count Guglielmo degli Alberti, and Count Alessandro d'Entrèves came to stay at the house. People came for lunches and walks even if a great many Italians now declined because "their relatives think they had better keep away from us," Mary wrote to Senda and Bessie in the winter of 1940. Every evening Berenson put on a black tie, even if there was no one for dinner.

With the start of the war, Mary's health had dramatically improved confirming, Nicky wrote to Senda and Bessie, how much her suffering was caused by nerves. The shock of world events had ended her single-minded concentration upon her own woes. Mary had discovered a new doctor, whom she very much liked, and a new interest. The young composer-conductor Igor Markevitch had come to Florence to compose a new work, bringing his wife Topazia, the enchanting daughter of Nijinsky, and a dancer like her father. Both of them were temporarily immersed in their careers, and Mary, as always, stepped eagerly into the role of surrogate mother for their small son, nicknamed Funtyki.

Markevitch, who was invited to stay at the villino and spent seven years there during and after the war, remembers seeing Mary "lying in this very clean bed all day long and twiddling her toes under the sheets to keep her circulation going, while she told Funtyki stories from 'Winnie the Pooh.' One day I discovered Funtyki pretending to be a doctor and about to give Mary an injection with water he had just taken out of a vase of flowers. Mary was going to let him."

There was no gasoline for the car, so Nicky and B.B. drove about in a little horse and carriage, as in the good old days, and had plenty of simple, wholesome food, and took walks as usual every afternoon, either in the garden or adjoining woods. Mary, who would have stayed in bed all day long if they hadn't insisted, would get up two or three times a day after lunch or tea, and liked to read aloud. They had great fun rereading *Tom Jones* and *Amelia* and *Pendennis* and were trying to persuade her to read *Clarissa*, which she stoutly refused to do. In the morning Nicky read more mind-improving works to B.B. on the terrace. They had read a great deal of Pater and Burckhardt. B.B. had taken up his Greek and reread the whole of Plato with intense delight.

Berenson was also writing. He had begun to jot down "some glimpses into that chaos and . . . that stream of consciousness we are accustomed to call self." It became his *Sketch for a Self-Portrait*, and, episodic and fragmentary as it is, it provides an excellent insight into his state of mind as he approached his seventy-third year. The evidence is that a radical inner upheaval was taking place. As, on Yom Kippur, the devout Jew contemplates the ways in which he has sinned against God and man, so Berenson in those first years of the war seemed to be experiencing an inner day of atonement, in which he was attempting to purge himself, confess his sins to God, and beg the forgiveness of his fellow men. He wrote later, "A day scarcely passes without my feeling deeply penitential about my life. . . ."

One does not need to look far for the sources of his introspection. His break with Duveen, early in 1938, seemed to release all those uncomfortable feelings that he had not made the most of himself, and that he should have retired at the age of forty to a life of contemplation. His comment that he, one of the elect, had failed in his mission, makes that sense of guilt very plain.

The Talmud states, "God weeps over one who might have occupied himself with the Torah, but neglected to do so." He came, Berenson told Nicky, from a culture in which a profound respect for learning was uppermost, and which consequently made a sharp distinction between the learned and unlearned man. "I never noticed considerations of money or worldly values, but became aware of an almost ferocious idealism." A man equipped for a loftier role should have kept his intellectual gifts sacred for scholarship, if not for God.

The dissatisfaction with himself went deeper. For as long as he could remember, he had been trying to become someone else. "It has been a constant awareness of trying to live up to something, and a continuous self-reproach when I slipped, or lapsed into animality. So what I really am—is there such an animal? What should I have been, left to myself—but what self was mine?"

Elsewhere it becomes clear that Berenson is aware of wearing a mask: the mask of not being a Jew. "I even tried to pretend to what I was not. . . ." How wonderful it was, he later wrote, to "drop the mask of being *goyim* and return to Yiddish reminiscences, and Yiddish stories and witticisms! After all, it has been an effort . . . to act as if one were a mere Englishman or Frenchman or American. . . ."

One of the prices that such a false persona exacted was the feeling of being an exile, with no roots anywhere. Because of this, he had always felt an outsider, "not one of us"; elsewhere, he wrote that the Jew wants to side with "nice" people in the hope that ". . . he will attain complete assimilation, and cease to feel . . . not quite 'one of us.' "

A further price which the false persona had exacted was the feeling that he had had to amputate unacceptable parts of his personality, in order to arrive at what he now began to see was a spurious inner harmony: ". . . How much one has to put aside and ignore in order to integrate oneself into a magnet attracting what constitutes one's own universe." That a conscious attempt at integration was necessary points to a real feeling that he was in danger of falling apart.

That there was, indeed, a fundamental and underlying self-dissatisfaction is evident from the following: ". . . I have not yet learned to like myself as I am. I still wonder and question and look for flashes of hope that I am not so worthless as I often feel. . . ." It was because of this that he felt a fraud whenever people took him seriously; because of this that the whole world was rotten, stupid, and bad, himself included, and because of this that, he wrote, Jews need freedom from contempt. By that perhaps he meant self-contempt.

Disliking himself, it was easy to convince himself that others didn't like him either. He had a very uncomfortable feeling, he wrote to Arthur Kingsley Porter in 1930, that the latter preferred the idea of his company to his corporeality. He was, he continued, probably too much of an egotist and exhausted others around him. He was probably all kinds of things that made people uncomfortable, no matter how well they might think of him and even how fond they might be. "More recently, I mean in the last 20 years or so, I began to discover that I intimidated . . . people. Only the other day the husband of an old friend confessed that he had always been afraid of me. I looked at him with startled eyes. . . ."

Berenson summed up these feelings of inadequacy and lack of inner unity with a comment that reveals how much the assumption of a false person had cost him:

"At bottom I always longed to be loved rather than admired, to be appreciated for what I was and not for what others fancied I was."

Berenson's attempt at self-analysis, which is what the *Self-Portrait* is, was not altogether successful. Psychoanalysis tells us that any such attempt, if not impossible, is very difficult and, although Berenson was wholly sincere in his desire to be impartial, he could not help springing to his own defense. That he needed to do so implies the existence of what Karen Horney has called neurotic pride. Against an inner need to accuse, Berenson far too often appears in the role of chief defense attorney for the vulnerable self in the witness box.

Seen from another vantage point the presence of an inner judge and prosecuting attorney suggests the existence of an active self-hate, one which will try to sabotage any attempt on the part of the self to abandon whatever pathetic armor it still possesses.

Perhaps the crux of the problem is best expressed by Karen Horney: "A person attempting to analyze himself would simply fail to make any self-observations that would lead to insights as yet intolerable. Or he would interpret them in such a way as to miss the essential point. Or he would merely try to correct quickly and superficially an attitude conceived by him as faulty, and thereby close the door to further investigation."

So, for instance, one finds Berenson not only resistant to the idea that he might be competitive, but actually averring on several occasions that "I had scarcely any competitive impulse," and insisting that he had little or no "lust for power," despite his enormous satisfaction with the role of Ultimate Authority. One finds him vowing that he always tried to avoid argument and that it was others who dragged him into it, and that "I have deliberately and scrupulously avoided deriving benefit from friends," and finding himself, in the main, a completely faithful husband.

He is still far too often the victim of his perfectionistic inner dictates, using the *Self-Portrait* to goad himself to greater efforts. "I am lazy," he writes, finding that thought so alarming that he must immediately defend himself from the accusation with the reflection that he once had a nervous breakdown from overwork. He is judgmental: he is too "self-indulgent" and too "ease-loving" to enjoy "hard opposition."

Berenson is self-pitying: ". . . one with no claims to [genius] is apt to be more disliked and combated for his good qualities than for his bad ones. . . ." He tends to give himself compliments disguised as criticisms: "I have sinned and despite myself continue to sin because I cannot yet get rid of the notion that man is capable of being entirely rational, if only he wanted to be. . . ."

"I have not," Berenson also wrote, "borne the fruit that as a plant I should have brought to full ripeness." He had not become a second Goethe. He took the wrong turn when he swerved from intellectual pursuits to that of connoisseurship. "My only excuse is, if the comparison is not blasphemous, that like Saint Paul with his tent-making and Spinoza with his glass-polishing I too needed a means of livelihood. . . ."

The art historian Meyer Schapiro has phrased this same dilemma rather differently: ". . . worldly aims soon contaminated his intellectual goals. It was as if Spinoza and Saint Paul had tried to make a business and a way of social success out of philosophy and religion."

That he should not have become "that equivocal thing," an expert, is a refrain that haunts Berenson's *Self-Portrait*. That it was not a "spiritually profitable" field is also made clear, along with the belief that he should have developed and clarified his ideas about the enjoyment of art into the work of a lifetime.

Berenson also said that he discovered that he "ranked" with charlatans, speaks of his connoisseurship as a "trade," and continues that to begin work on the *Florentine Drawings* was "not only wrong, but sinful."

Berenson nowhere says what is clear from his letters and also from Mary's, that he thought the art world was a veritable inferno and that he felt spiritually contaminated by his association with it.

Neither will he have it said that he was an agent or dealer. Yet when one considers the evidence of the active manner in which he unearthed paintings for Duveen, Gimpel, and others, the distinction seems slight indeed.

Berenson never mentions Duveen's name in the *Self-Portrait* and predictably does not ask himself how he could hope to work, for thirty years, for a man in the center of a vast corrupt network, and not expect to be drawn into the web himself. He does not deal with the contradiction that he, who approached art with a mystical and reverential worship, had spent his life buying and selling it. He cannot deal with the question that he might have been seduced, as Offner wrote, "by a community of interest into a closed alliance against the rest of mankind." Neither is he able to address the question that his judgments might have been influenced by business considerations. Typically, he temporizes by deflecting his remorse onto what was publicly admissible—that he was destined for better things—and emotionally endurable. All that he can admit to one of his closest friends, "Billee" Ivins, is that he feels a fraud.

Finally, Berenson does not examine the possibility that his desire to perpetuate Altamura fatally bound him to the wheels of ambition and money making and that, when he wrote the *Self-Portrait* he was still bound, still advising dealers, and trying to endow "i Tatti" for Harvard. To question the goal of a lifetime was more than flesh could endure.

Reading the *Self-Portrait* one finds so much equivocation, if not outright self-deception, that one begins to regard anything Berenson has to say about himself with a very cool eye. One's suspicions are tempered, however, by the realization that, despite severe inner pressures, Berenson took a vital first step toward understanding himself better. The very detachment with which he viewed the world, that curious impersonality which others found so cold and unfeeling whenever they stumbled across an unguarded assessment of themselves, was an asset in viewing his own feelings. It is clear from the discoveries Berenson was making that the inner war of denial was no longer working, or perhaps the break with Duveen had sufficiently lightened his inner load that he could bring himself to illumine some dark corners. His self-analysis was, above all, an attempt to reconcile the deep inner divisions between the ascetic and the would-be Don Juan, the shtetl child and the Gentile aristocrat, the outer façade of scholar and the inner reality of businessman, the man ruled by logic and reason whose unruly emotions made him awaken every morning with tears in his eyes.

Berenson learned, for instance, that his bitterness had destructive internal aspects. That it was "corrosive," i.e., it destroyed that which it fed on. Similarly, he learned something about the "savage vindictiveness" that unfair treatment aroused in him, and that caused him to despair of ever becoming human. He learned that his self-confidence was a fragile flower, easily bruised, and that his own tendency to tear himself down added to such feelings of inner inferiority.

Despite Berenson's attempt to reassure himself that he approached people in a glow of warm feelings and it was others who rebuffed him, he came to realize that his overtures were not as unsullied as they seemed, but had their origins in an egotistical desire to show off. "... [I]t began to dawn upon me that perhaps I was exorbitant in supposing ... that others would accept the intrusion of my egoism, my claims upon their attention, my eagerness to be heard and ... appreciated and accepted." What seemed like sweet reasonableness to him might look like arrogance to others. "In short, and to use my own jargon, they may have felt my company to be more life-diminishing than life-enhancing."

It occurred to him to wonder whether he might not have a way of "rebutting what others have to say before they can enjoy the satisfaction of coming out with all that they want to say, thereby leaving them with a feeling of resentful frustration. . . ." He had not been willing to suffer fools gladly, and perhaps they were not really such fools, but "relatively innocent humbugs. . . ." Being admired by others for one's superior cleverness was flattering, "but if I have not ceased enjoying admiration, I have long since preferred affection."

How much better a world it would be, he mused, if, instead of hastening to blame others, we asked how much we ourselves had contributed. It would help to humanize us. Perhaps Berenson's most important self-insight was that he began to see how quickly he condemned in others those things which might "in great part if not wholly" be attributable to something in himself.

"It is not easy, for I flare up with indignation and can be only too vehement in resentment. I do try to understand why, and do not want like a child to blame it all on the piece of furniture against which, in his impetuous expenditure of energy, he barked his shins."

He also caught a glimpse of his inner demand to be perfect in the question of his inability to write. He had set the goal of writing something "enduring" and of permanent worth and, as a result, had prevented himself from doing anything. "Unless I could acquire the illusion that I had something to offer that would be lasting, it seemed only decent to do nothing."

How wonderful it would be, he wrote, if, instead of making such demands upon ourselves, we could teach the young to expect "a minimum from us poor bipeds.... What right have we to expect more from creatures who but a few thousand years ago were no better than ... beasts...."

One sees, running through the *Self-Portrait*, an immense nostalgia for the young man he had once been, so full of dreams and promise, so eager to live up to his potential, longing for "an earthly paradise, a state of adolescent bliss," who had come to earth with such a jolt in the sordid realities of the marketplace. One sees also an awakening to life's "essential realities" when, "all ambition spent and passion ... stilled," he could return to that sense of ecstatic identification with nature that he had lost.

"IT" came to have the broadest possible meaning for him: "IT is every experience that is ultimate, valued for its own sake...." Most of all, IT symbolized his adolescent vow to live life as a sacrament, and the realization that to live in any other way had been to do violence to himself.

Berenson did however discover that he still retained this ability for joyous experience. It made the introspective years of the war immensely rich and valuable ones. He could at least return to "my long interrupted ITness. Not merely to take it up where I had left it, but with an awareness, an understanding, a wonder, a gratitude, a joy that one could not have experienced young when one took as a matter of course what one found at hand...."

The *Self-Portrait* was finished at Casa al Dono, the house Nicky Mariano bought in Vallombrosa, in the summer of 1941.

B.B. was in very good form, Nicky told Senda and Bessie a year later. The quiet, almost idyllic nature of their life suited him to perfection, since he could spend all his time reading and working, and he was in a very optimistic and congenial frame of mind.

"B.B. is turning into a very genial and understanding sort of old man," Mary wrote to her family in the autumn of 1944, "instead of the fierce denouncer of his age we thought he might be. Besides being intensely interesting, as he always was, he has become more and more lovable. . . ."

The bucolic peace of life at "i Tatti" ended abruptly in the summer of 1943 following the Allied landing in Sicily and Mussolini's ignominious death. The Germans were about to take over and friends of Berenson realized that he would immediately be arrested as an American, an anti-Fascist, and a Jew. He must be made to disappear, and the opportunity to do so was offered by the Marchese Filippo Serlupi, whose tenuous diplomatic immunity as ambassador of San Marino to the Vatican would, as they rightly thought, be respected by the Germans.

A large proportion of the valuable books in the library were spirited away to basement hiding places in other houses. Many of them were tied in small bundles and sent off with peasants on bicycles. The most valuable paintings went with Berenson to the Serlupi mansion, "Villa delle Fontanelle" in Careggi, some two miles from "i Tatti," and thirty-two others to the basement of the Anrep building at Borgo San Jacopo in the heart of Florence. B.B. and Nicky did not tell Mary where they were going because "in her eyes it was all nonsense and she would have blurted out the name of our refuge to the first comer," Nicky Mariano wrote. However, Mary was left in the care of Nicky's sister and brother-in-law and her nurses, and told that a way would be found to get news to her. In the meantime it was spread abroad that Berenson had escaped to Portugal. They left in a car and arrived at the "Villa delle Fontanelle" just in time for tea.

Berenson was, the Marchesa Serlupi recalled, "a rather dangerous guest." She had told the servants that Berenson was an Austrian baron, but he was used to daily walks and would stop and talk to everyone, speaking Italian with such a dreadful American accent that she was sure no one believed her.

There was another problem. He used to write his diary everyday. He would sit in the living room with a small glass of brandy and water and write on big sheets of paper. The Marchese and Marchesa would innocently tell him all the local gossip. After about six months the Marchesa learned that these large bundles of paper had been sent to "i Tatti." After that, she said, they took care not to give him any names.

There was a further problem. "I found out that they used to

send their laundry to 'i Tatti.' I was much younger then and I took it for granted that it would be given to the maid. But Nicky was too embarrassed to ask, so she sent it off to 'i Tatti' on a bicycle—imagine these peasants going back and forth!—while I was trying desperately to keep their whereabouts a dark secret."

There were other anxious moments. The Marchesa added that she and her husband took care to discourage visitors. However, one afternoon as they were sitting in the drawing room alcove overlooking the terrace, she saw a neighbor approaching. "I rushed out to intercept him and took him in another door and upstairs where, as luck would have it, many of Berenson's paintings were hanging." "All these pictures! Who are they from?" the neighbor innocently inquired, and while the Marchesa struggled to invent an explanation her husband, on the floor below, "made B.B. and Nicky disappear."

Berenson remained imperturbable throughout their thirteen months in hiding at the "Villa delle Fontanelle," even during the final month of the war, when they found themselves in the front line of the German retreat and being shelled by the British. As soon as the Allies arrived, Berenson was taken to "i Tatti" by military jeep and found that, although it had been occupied by the Germans, it had not been sacked. Because of the Allied bombardment, every window in the house had been smashed, tiles had been taken off the roof, there were shell marks everywhere, and a peasant's house had been destroyed, but the damage could be repaired.

"He came back that day looking like a wreck," the Marchesa said. "He went to bed without any supper and the next day had violent diarrhoea. I didn't know how to stop it. We put him on grated apples and rice for three days."

The Marchesa thought the shock of seeing the damage to "i Tatti" had caused Berenson's alarming illness, but this seems not to have been the case.

Nicky Mariano wrote, "When we drove away, B.B. seemed sad and crushed and I thought it was over the condition of the house. 'Oh no,' he said, 'that can be remedied. What I am in despair over is Mary. The moment I entered her room she said that now everything was so changed and the house so heavily damaged she hoped I too would change my mind and give up my foolish plan of leaving it to Harvard. . . .'"

Mary had very little to sustain her during those last years of life. She had been cured of her troublesome cystitis and, since this had restored the use of her mind, had been reading her husband's manuscript, *Aesthetics and History*, which was finished in the autumn of 1941 but not published until 1948. However, her interest was focused elsewhere, on writing a life of her daughter Ray, who had died during an operation in 1940. She wrote to Ralph Perry early in 1941, "[I]n a way I bless the illness that still cuts me off from many of my activities, for it gives me the leisure to appreciate to the full all that I remember of Ray and all that her thousands of letters are telling me. . . . Sometimes when I cannot repress the tears of longing for her, I am nevertheless blissfully happy at the remembrance of what I have had. . . ."

A year before she died, Mary wrote Nicky a touching letter in which she expressed her love and admiration for her and hoped she would marry B.B. When Berenson found her in September of 1944 she seemed much reduced and her mind was wandering. She lived for a few months longer and died in the spring of 1945, at the age of eighty-one. Berenson was too ill to attend her funeral. Nicky went alone and the restorer Giannino Marchig kept him company.

"What was through life my own feeling about death? . . . I always have avoided seeing a corpse, and although I received my wife's last breath, I ran away the very instant. . . ."

The English architect Cecil Pinsent who had supervised much of the physical transformation of "i Tatti," now a captain in the British Army, arrived at "i Tatti" soon after the war. He found it amazing,

> in that welter of destruction and demoralization, to find the house intact, with all its pictures back in place and most of its books, and B.B. in the centre of a flood of visitors, looking older of course, but still with the old alertness of mind and keen interest in all that was going on. . . . The crowds that came to see him were astonishing, and if you went to tea you were lucky if you were able to push your way through just for a greeting. . . .
>
> B.B. was quite tolerant of it all, and glad to have this stream of life pour through his house once more. . . . but it was really odd to see B.B. "suffering fools gladly" when you think of what he used to feel about them in the old days. . . .

Pinsent's American counterpart in the monumental task of restoring damaged works of art in Italy was the art historian and author Frederick Hartt. Professor Hartt had visited Berenson just before World War II and had been dismayed and offended when

Berenson had attacked one of his teachers, a man he greatly admired, Meyer Schapiro. Professor Hartt said, "I learned later that this was standard operating procedure. This was what B.B. would subject a neophyte to when he came into the Presence. I also owed a great deal to Richard Offner and I remember Berenson turning to Nicky and saying, 'Oh Nicky, do you remember that insufferable little man?'

"After half an hour I could take no more and rose to leave. He took me by the right arm and sat me down and said, 'Don't go.' He changed the subject completely and turned on all his charm, but I made up my mind I wasn't going back."

When Professor Hartt was posted in Florence under Major Ernest de Wald, head of the American Military Government's Monuments and Arts Section, he was told by his superior that one of the monuments in his charge would be Berenson. So Professor Hartt dutifully made his way to the Serlupi villa, which, he noted, had been heavily damaged by shellfire. He was the second Allied soldier to reach Berenson.

"We found him on a chaise longue, looking pale and a bit shocked, covered with an ordinary Afghan even though it was a very hot day, but his feet were sticking out. They were bare, very clean, perfectly waxen, almost transparent feet. They looked like moth's wings. I looked at him and my heart melted."

17

THE SCHOLAR-GIPSY

If I am not for myself, who will be for me? And if
I am only for myself, what am I.... And if not
now—when?

—HILLEL

SOON AFTER WORLD WAR II Berenson was out on one of his
habitual walks in the hills of Settignano when a ten-ton truck
rumbled up the hill and drew to a halt beside him. A G.I. leaned
out of the window and began to ask questions in a pidgin Italian.
Berenson replied in impeccable English.

The G.I. stared at him blankly. "Are you an American?"

"Yes, I am."

"What's a guy like you doing in a dump like this?"

The answer to that question was already clear. Even before
World War II Berenson grumbled that he had become a local
monument, an obligatory stop on the road between the Bargello
Museum and the Pitti Palace, and now, with the Liberation, that
he had become a tourist attraction was more than ever ironically
evident. In a postwar letter to Sibyl Colefax, the famous London
hostess whom he had known since the turn of the century,
Berenson observed that English and American soldiers arrived
almost everyday. They were young and eager unknowns who had
read *The New York Times* and other news stories to the effect that
the "world-renowned art historian and expert" was safe after a
year in hiding. They had come to see the living legend.

Berenson told Lady Colefax that the young men often

brought gifts in the shape of sugar, coffee, candies, matches, and cigarettes. He received them all gratefully. When one could no longer get things for money, he wrote, one must essay the power of love.

Although the house had suffered no major damage there were no building materials available: no cement and, above all, no glass. The Nazis had destroyed their electrical generator and there was no light, no power for the electrical ovens, and no coal. They were obliged to sit in the dark and try to read by the light of improvised candles.

There was very little food. The household at "i Tatti," comprising as it did secretaries, librarians, two trained nurses for Mary, and servants, totaled twelve people, and there was almost nothing to eat. Captain Robert Berenson, aide-de-camp to General Clark and a relative on the Louis Berenson side, was among the first visitors (he arrived seven hours after the Germans left) and wrote to his family that they were all starving. He, Captain Berenson, had dined at the "Villa delle Fontanelle." The crystal was elegant, the china exquisite, the footmen were in full regalia, and the food was abysmal: bean soup, a main course of boiled and sliced potatoes, and a dried-up piece of cheese for dessert.

The Anrep apartment at Borgo San Jacopo had been completely destroyed and thirty-two paintings from "i Tatti" stored in the cellar had disappeared under the rubble. Berenson suffered intensely from the cold, even with sweaters and overcoats. Whenever he went out into "i Tatti's" drafty corridors he put on a muffler. He had rheumatism and barely slept for more than four or five hours. Yet, despite the fact that he tired easily, Berenson's mind was as alert as ever and his curiosity more verdant than it had been for years. He had sketched out two books, perhaps three, which he longed to revise, just as he was reading every periodical he could find to learn what the British, French, and Americans had been thinking during his enforced internment. He had emerged from his hibernation with a new appetite for life, and one sharpened by the ever-present thought that he was almost eighty.

Berenson engaged the skills of his restorer and friend Marchig to painstakingly repair the damage to the ruined paintings and as each was finished, it was returned to its customary position. The books in the library were back in place. The return to normality was so prompt that those who visited "i Tatti" could not believe their eyes.

Benedict Nicolson, who had received a commission in the British Intelligence Corps, was in Southern Italy and when Florence was liberated in September 1944 hitchhiked his way up the country by plane, jeep, and truck. "I saw all the damage: abandoned guns and vehicles beside the road. Then I got to Florence and the only bridge left standing across the Arno was the Ponte Vecchio. The city itself was relatively intact, although very untidy.

"I couldn't announce my arrival. I didn't know who was alive or dead. I walked up the via Vincigliata to 'i Tatti' wondering what I would find there. I rang the bell and the old butler Vittorio came to the door dressed in tails.

" 'Vittorio, I simply can't believe my eyes! There has been no war.' He was imperturbable; much more English than Italian. 'Is anyone here?' He replied, 'Yes. Upstairs you will find Miss Mariano and Mr. Berenson.'

"I walked up those stairs that I knew so well and into Nicky's room. There was a very emotional meeting. She rushed into B.B.'s room and said, 'Guess who's here!'

"I was astonished. There was no change! He was exactly the same. He was avid for any information I could give them. I was able to report the damage to the churches in Apulia right up to Viterbo and he wanted to know exactly what had survived and what was destroyed. Nicky, too, was quite unchanged. It all made a profound impression upon me.

"One of the first things Nicky said was, 'Would you like a bath?' Perhaps I stank. It was the first I'd had for four months. There was no hot water but they heated great bowls of water and carted them upstairs. I shall never forget that bath."

Like many others, Nicolson judged his first visit to "i Tatti" a failure. "I remember vividly that we talked about T. S. Eliot in whom I was passionately interested and B.B. couldn't bear the modern movement in painting or literature. He thought 'The Waste Land' was a betrayal of art." True to the pattern Nicolson had decided not to return but was lured back, partly because of his decision to become an art historian and partly because of Berenson's power to make each friend feel unique and cherished, a gift he shared with D'Annunzio.

Berenson's attitude was that of the generous, permissive host. He did not pontificate. He would not suggest, exhort, or direct. Instead he gave the newcomer full rein, trusting him to develop his own passion as he, Berenson, had found his. For Nicolson, that had become North Italian painters of the fifteenth century. Such an invitation to browse in the library, the superb collection of books that Berenson said was the only achievement of which he was proud, seemed heaven sent.

In all other respects the Nicolson experience was much more typical of the postwar atmosphere at Altamura than the prewar period. "To younger colleagues the words of the Chinese sage We-pu-fi are recommended: 'When you stand on another man's shoulders, try not to spit on his head,' " Berenson wrote for his preface to *Essays in the Study of Sienese Painting* in 1917. Such hostility had been the rule. It disappeared.

When Kenneth Clark wrote *Landscape into Art* and *The Nude*, Berenson wholeheartedly praised both books as magnificent accomplishments. Instead of the jealousy of a man who wishes the gods had given him such a gift of self-expression, there was the altruism of one who delights in the fruition of a promise he had seen so clearly. Young men who entered the Altamuran ambiance after the war: Sir John Pope-Hennessy, William Mostyn-Owen, Michael Rinehart, David Carritt, Frank Wright, and Carter Brown, have commented on the extraordinary kindness they received, as well as Berenson's gift for inspiring affection.

Berenson was capable of a subtle awareness of another's need. It was evident in his relationships with many aspiring young men, notably Sir Harold Acton. "My parents were extremely social," the poet and writer explained, "but they didn't like intellectuals. When I went to 'i Tatti,' Berenson was always extremely kind. The encouragement I didn't get at home I got from him." He concluded, "I have every reason to be grateful."

Promising young men were not the only ones taken into the fold. Luisa Vertova, a young Florentine and talented art historian, who arrived at "i Tatti" at the end of World War II, ill and starving, was nursed back to health, given full-time employment, and eventually became a second pair of eyes for Berenson's final Lists. Scholars like Ulrich Middeldorf were urged to come and go as they pleased and young Italian art-history students might, without too much difficulty, study in the library.

Writing about the future of "i Tatti," Berenson observed that he would like to have sixteen fellows engaged upon the humanistic study of the Muses. They must be postdoctoral students, avid for everything and committed to nothing except a common hatred for dry academism. As Berenson said, "[R]esearch for the lust of mere research is not to be encouraged. . . ." They were to have four years of leisure while they matured as "creative writers and teachers in the interpretation of art of every kind." That period of introspection while they had allowed their ideas to slowly mature and perfected their individual styles had been used to productive effect by Geoffrey Scott, Kenneth Clark, John Walker, and others. It was now to be institutionalized.

This was the pattern Berenson himself had followed, but it had certain implications that are only hinted at in his outline. To begin with, Berenson's concept was based on an elitist and Renaissance view of education which had pertained when he graduated from Harvard in the 1880s, but which had undergone a radical transformation in the succeeding decades. Then, art history barely existed as a discipline. As it had developed since, it was antithetical to Berenson's aesthetic ideal that the only function of such education was to achieve that exquisite moment "when we and the work of art are one. . . ." The age of specialization had also arrived, and to expect Fellows to have acquired Ph.D. degrees without having narrowed their fields in the scholarly manner Berenson detested, was similarly unrealistic.

Berenson was aware of the pitfalls. When a visitor suggested that Altamura's warm family atmosphere might be desiccated by Ph.D. holders chasing footnotes, Berenson answered that such a thought tortured him. America, he continued, must free itself from the dead hand of German scholarship and from people who knew more and more about less and less. Berenson continued to believe that Harvard would remain true to his dream of a center for humanists.

What Berenson really wanted as candidates were those gentlemen-scholars he had met at Harvard and Oxford in the 1880s, those "well-born attentives" who would, after some years of leisurely polishing, glide into one of the top jobs in their native lands. The pattern, if it ever existed, was vanishing fast in a post-elitist world.

Harvard's decision to accept Altamura was reluctant in the extreme. James Conant, then president, had accepted the gift, but his successors began to wish that he had not. To begin with, there were acute financial problems. Dumbarton Oaks, which the university had taken over, came with an endowment of $40 million. Even this, in an inflationary economy, was becoming too little on which to run the estate successfully. By contrast, Berenson was to leave "i Tatti" a little over $1 million. This was barely enough to maintain the house, grounds, and staff (with no provision for pensions for the low-paid servants) and at least $5 million was needed if the dream of student scholarships was to be realized.

Furthermore, the university saw the Berenson manifesto as a fin de siècle, Paterian concept out of tune with the times, an anachronistic Renaissance symposium. The university would, at best, be running a postdoctoral library, an ideal country club for scholars, but certainly not a place where college students could do research. What was left at "i Tatti" once Berenson had died, apart from Alda von Anrep in the library and Nicky Mariano pouring tea? He was the chief attraction.

The university was right in thinking that Berenson alone was the spool around which all the threads of Altamura were wound. He was the "one-man university," or, "university within one man." The strength of Berenson's personality alone could make real the concept of Altamura to which he clung with such desperate stubbornness.

The astonishing fact is that Altamura, in those postwar years, did become so largely what Berenson outlined for it in his turn-of-the-century manifesto. His edifice of *Luxe, calme et beauté* was his genuine creation. It flourished as it never had before or would again. In those last years of his life, it had become less cultist. There was a warmer mood, a more vivid concern for humankind. He had always welcomed new faces, but perhaps he had never been quite such a generous host or invited quite so many *oyrechs* (guests) to partake of his sumptuous holiday banquet. This liberal hospitality was one of Berenson's most ingratiating aspects.

"They extended an open invitation to visit," said Hugh Trevor-Roper, regius professor of modern history at Oxford, and a friend of the postwar years. "I took advantage of it. Staying with people can be an awful waste of time, but this wasn't. I was able to work and met all kinds of interesting people. The whole atmosphere of the house appealed to me. I felt it was a sophisticated, civilized world where the conversation was on an intellectual level. We didn't talk about paintings very much as it was too much his subject and he didn't want to be thought of as 'B.B. the picture man.' He wanted to be thought of as Goethe in old age. He wasn't, quite."

The writer Mario Praz said, "You must place him in the ritual of his house, as in a court. This is the impression that remains in my mind: an eighteenth-century atmosphere of kindness, ceremony, dressing up for dinner and the reflective, contemplative life." He added, "There was a very curious thing; sometimes Berenson put a shawl around his shoulders and you saw him exactly as a Jew in the synagogue."

As has been suggested, Berenson no longer had to solicit friends; they came in embarrassing abundance. His somewhat scholarly and abstruse postwar publications were not thought likely to make his name a household word, and yet this seemed to be happening. People were inventing any pretext, no matter how flimsy, to go to "i Tatti." Joan Hogg, who acted as a secretary there in the final years, recalled that, when a letter of condolence arrived from a stranger in connection with the death of Senda, Berenson's sister, Nicky Mariano wrote a routine letter that included the comment that, if the writer were ever in Florence, she should stop by. Shortly thereafter an article appeared in the writer's local paper to the effect that she had received an invitation to "i Tatti."

In the summer of 1948, Nicky Mariano commented to Berenson's sisters about the sudden burst of interest in him, as if he were a movie star. By the spring of 1949 people were arriving in such hordes that she was in despair. By the spring of 1950 Nicky Mariano was writing apprehensively of the expected avalanche and those dreaded telephone calls from hotels.

Two years after that, the problem was still acute. Berenson wrote to Frances Francis that, despite everything he and Nicky were doing to live quietly, he felt as if he had no privacy at all. He often opened his bedroom door to go to his morning bath and found people looking at paintings in the corridors. Or he would be politely interrupted by people wanting to inspect his study while he worked. And of course there was an avalanche of visitors for meals. He was beginning to feel like a spectator at a theatrical event in a foreign language.

Among the gallimaufry of friends and loves, adoring women tourists and returning veterans, whom Nicky shuffled and dealt out like complicated card tricks, were J. B. Priestley, Arthur Koestler, Robert Lowell, Sir Harold Acton, Raymond Mortimer, W. H. Auden, Stephen Spender, Katherine Dunham, Henry Moore, Hamish Hamilton, Yehudi Menuhin, Alberto Moravia, Renato Guttuso, Mary McCarthy, Sir Laurence Olivier, Vivien Leigh, Sinclair Lewis, Freya Stark, Derek Hill, Jacqueline Bouvier Kennedy, Harry S. Truman, and Billy Rose.

Few of them, however, created quite the flutter of the Crown Prince of Sweden, an archaeologist whom Berenson had known for decades. He arrived in the autumn of 1949 with a retinue of servants and chauffeurs and his traveling companion, a Chaucerian Swedish general, and the accompanying *frisson* of excitement made Nicky despair. She wrote to Jane Clark that she wished the old king would die and thus prevent his professorial son from visiting them, because even though he was a dear man, he was not a comfortable guest to have. He was hounded by so many reporters and photographers and police agents that "i Tatti" was turned into a circus. On the other hand, the collector Rush Kress, one of the chief benefactors of the National Gallery of Art in Washington, would have preferred no attentions at all. He was frequently invited to "i Tatti" but hated to accept because the servants insisted on unpacking his luggage and he didn't want it known that he brought his own toilet paper.

There were so many of the international intellectual elite that observers of Altamura looked for a pattern in the society Berenson chose and could find none. Any stray person might be invited and some thought, "the strayer the better." People of distinction were on a par with "feather-headed aristocrats" who used "i Tatti" as a "railway junction"; and lions of every persuasion might find themselves mingling with professional hunters of social game. The main requirement was that those invited be either clever, witty, famous, and titled, or adept at making Berenson himself feel clever, witty, famous, and titled.

If there was one quality that Berenson valued in a guest, it was the lack of what the English called "side." To find an American president, Harry S. Truman, so obviously unpretentious and approachable, delighted him. Similarly, when Alan Clark, Lord Clark's son, came to tea, was asked what he had been doing, and replied, "I've been driving a truck in Canada," Berenson was enchanted. Mrs. F. Carroll Taylor, a Quaker cousin of Mary Berenson and mother of a large family, recalled meeting Berenson and being asked, "And what do you do, my dear?" She didn't want him to think she was about to discuss culture, so she replied, "I scrub floors. I'm very good at it." "Thank God for that!" Berenson replied, and they walked off arm in arm.

Prince Clary of Venice recalled being invited for tea with his wife one afternoon. Their only reason for being there was a distant connection with Nicky Mariano's mother. They were in agonies of shyness and when it was the Prince's turn to sit beside Berenson, he couldn't think of a thing to say. Just then, a "very silly" Italian dashed up and began showering Berenson with the title of "Professore." Berenson, somewhat severely, replied that he was not a professor. The Italian switched to "Maestro." Berenson: "I'm not a musician either." The Prince could not repress his laughter. Berenson turned to him with a pleased smile. "What a fool!" he said. That, the Prince said, was the beginning of their friendship.

A friendship that had, perhaps, never ripened before the war might become a reality. Frances Francis recalled that she and her husband were invited to "i Tatti" several times before 1939 but that she had disliked Berenson intensely and refused to return, despite invitations. "I believed his enemies, that he was arrogant and money-centered."

When they returned after the war for tea, she was invited to sit next to Berenson. "He was sitting by the fire and all of a sudden I saw a sadness, a sense of deep loneliness about him that I would never have suspected. I fell hard, there is no question about it."

One of the most interesting and inconclusive of Berenson's friendships was with the writer Ernest Hemingway. The latter's fourth wife, Mary, had met Berenson in 1948 through their mutual friends Alan and Lucy Moorehead. She wrote to Berenson, he replied, and Hemingway preempted the correspondence. Hemingway had published *Across the River and into the Trees*, which had not been a critical success and was apprehensive about the reception of his new book, *The Old Man and the Sea.* He sent Berenson the galleys and asked for a few publishable comments. Berenson praised the work highly, finding a Homeric parallel, and predictably cementing their friendship.

If Hemingway's letters are ever published, they will demonstrate that the legend of Hemingway does an injustice to the reality of the man. His letters to Berenson are a delight, full of wit, anecdote, and imaginative invention. They are rambling and discursive, with much parenthetical exclamation and explanation, and are, in fact, so spontaneous that they will banish forever the image of Hemingway as an anguished writer painfully producing a sentence every third day. They are indomitable and life-enhancing letters, full of whimsical reminiscence and unguarded insights into himself, written in a labored hand, like a child learning to write. They show a wistful, tender, and loving man, transparently insecure, and one diametrically opposite to the almost ludicrous ultramasculine image offered to the world.

Berenson appeared not to see the man beneath the façade.

He seemed transfixed by the public view, as seen in the latest *Life* magazines, of a hard-drinking, hard-fighting, hard-whoring man. If living to the full meant nothing more than the exercise of one's animal functions, Berenson wrote, then he himself had not lived. He had loved much, but copulated little (although with the appreciation one would bring to a fine champagne). He, Berenson, had never been drunk in his life and didn't even like to drink. He had never fought in a war. In short, he had never been a he-man.

Hemingway's reply was gently conciliatory. He dismissed what people wrote about him as so much chaff and chided Berenson for calling him that kind of name. It wasn't polite. As for sex, once when Mary was ill Hemingway told her that if they only touched one another's feet, that contact was just as intimate as making love.

In contrast to the wit and irrepressible zest of Hemingway's letters, Berenson's sound drearily rational, recalcitrantly sane. They are full of self-doubts. To Berenson's lament that he had wasted his life, Hemingway countered with the advice that it was useless to waste time in regret, since it was in doing what one must that one had arrived at one's present insights. In contrast with Hemingway's life, Berenson wrote, his own seemed so pale, so lonely, spent only in reading, writing, walking, and romancing but seldom in making love. Berenson envied Hemingway that faculty.

Berenson, in fact, despaired of revealing his true self. He was so very different from the way he seemed, he wrote. He was even very different from the person he tried to describe in *Rumor and Reflection* and in his even more searching *Self-Portrait*. He seemed unable to get to the bottom of himself, or even come close. He was aware that his self-dredgings contained some elements of self-complacency and narcissism, but the overwhelming reason for even making the attempt was that he was the only person whom he could study continually and try to comprehend. Unfortunately, he made no progress.

Hemingway, for his part, saw Berenson as a sage. Berenson's way of evaluating art was one that Hemingway himself had tried and failed at. He perhaps admired Berenson's laconic, terse style, and the inner discipline that Hemingway felt he lacked. Berenson, he wrote in a burst of affection, was one of his heroes.

They exchanged impressions and prejudices about Santayana, Koestler, Gide, Claudel, the Steins, Malraux, and other writers and poets. Hemingway reminisced about his wars, about Africa and Venice and Italy in the spring. Would Berenson, he asked, please remember him to any large oxen, all of the cypress trees, twists in the road, and any hills Berenson might find?

They made plans to meet after an African safari, but Hemingway had not counted upon two plane crashes and a fire. He and his wife limped back to Venice and, once at the Gritti Palace Hotel, Hemingway assessed the damage: a major concussion, ruptured kidney, liver and spleen damage, collapsed intestines, and assorted burns and broken bones.

Nevertheless he was willing to make the pilgrimage to Florence to see Berenson and was *tutoyer*-ing him in the French fashion. He asked Berenson to remember, if he felt like it, that in some ways Hemingway was his offspring, since the former had helped educate him with his wonderful books. He, Hemingway, adored Bergamo before he ever heard Berenson's name and had not heard it only because he had disgracefully neglected being properly raised. Berenson never had to acknowledge him and could, if he liked, denounce him.

If Berenson ever wanted to be the father of a really worthless, truly bad boy, then here was this useless object who was willing to make the pilgrimage and promised faithfully not to embarrass him. Miss Mary would come with him, he wrote. She was under the impression that she maintained the necessary discipline in the ranks.

It was a pathetic, touching letter, the result of pain, fatigue, alcohol, and longing. Berenson recoiled just as he had the day Eleanora Duse poured out her agony over D'Annunzio. Hemingway's letters, he wrote, "seemed written when he was not quite sober, rambling and affectionate. I fear he may turn out too animal, too overwhelmingly masculine, too Bohemian. He may expect me to drink and guzzle with him, and write me down as a muff." They only knew each other through letters and books. What, Berenson continued, could Hemingway possibly know of the "real me? Has he seriously read anything I have written? Has he been taken by my myth?"

A day later, Berenson wrote a cool reply, saying that he would love to have them for meals but unfortunately could not house them at "i Tatti." Spring was the worst season and there were so many visitors that he would not be able to see them alone as much as he liked. He ignored the plea to his paternal feelings.

Hemingway, in reply, thought it best not to travel. He really was very ill. He would visit sometime when Berenson was not so busy and did not have so many admirers. That would probably be never. For his part, Hemingway did not know what value admirers might have. His were worthless. Berenson ignored the transparently hurt feelings and replied cordially, but something had ended between them. The two men never met.

Some might never become *unsereiners*. Others were patently so unworthy of the name that Berenson's friends had difficulty in reconciling their idea of him with his curious choices of companionship. Prof. Ulrich Middeldorf was invited for tea one afternoon, along with a well-educated American Episcopalian priest. He was settling down in the expectation of a fascinating conversation when a stately, still very good-looking lady came into the room. She sat beside Berenson, who took both her hands, and "the afternoon was completely wrecked by the childish small-talk of this horrible creature."

Berenson could, in fact, be amazingly tolerant. Frances Francis recalls that, one afternoon after lunch, the group was sitting in the living room when Berenson's lawyer Lawrence Berenson, another relative on the Louis Berenson side, fell asleep and began to snore. His wife went over to wake him. Berenson said, "Leave him alone, let him sleep." The wife protested, "But he is snoring." Berenson: "Oh, we all make some kind of noise."

There is general agreement that it took considerably more provocation to incite Berenson to rebellion than had once been the case.

Hannah Kiel, a close friend of Berenson's last years, recalled that one afternoon a party of Americans, two couples and a man, arrived unannounced just as tea was over, wanting to see Berenson. They were told that he was about to take a nap and could not be disturbed. Then they said that they had a message from one of Berenson's cousins. They were duly seated and more tea was ordered.

When tea arrived, Berenson inquired about the message. It was a very indirect one. It seemed that one of the men was in the same wholesale business as the cousin. Then someone pulled out a photograph of a so-called Raphael. Perhaps Berenson would be interested? Berenson said that he was not interested in Raphaels. The stranger was insistent. He wished Berenson would give an attribution. It would certainly improve the price. Still no response.

Finally one of the ladies asked for Berenson's autograph. "Certainly," Berenson said. "Which book of mine do you have?"

The woman pulled out an American Express guide to Florence. "You are mistaken, madam," said Berenson, returning the book, "I am not the author." The party left, not a moment too soon, and Berenson's parting comment was, "When you return to the States, don't be too prolific."

The famous Berenson squelch might appear less often than formerly but was still not robbed of its sting. There are several tales, perhaps apocryphal, of young girl students departing in tears, and Agnes Mongan, former director of the Fogg, recalled that Berenson attacked the late Aline Saarinen about a book on art that she had written. Saarinen begged Miss Mongan to defend her against him.

Daphne Hoffman Mebane, of the Frick Art Reference Library, went to visit "i Tatti" in the 1950s. When Berenson found that she knew Dr. Erica Tietze-Conrat, a well-known art historian, he "went into an arraignment of Dr. Erica, whom he considered a very spiteful and unfair person. The feuds of art critics are ... well-known, but his hope that she would die soon was not well received by me, since I admired her very much and was in fact a quite close friend of hers!"

Berenson was occasionally bested in turn. Frances Francis recalled that one of the few times when she saw Berenson at a loss for words was when she remarked that "Henry and I have discovered that we are descended from two Concord 'whores.'" Berenson: "That's nonsense! There were none in those days." "Yes there were," said the inimitable Frances, "I am descended from Elizabeth Hoare and Henry is from Mary."

"AND WITH CLEARER KNOWLEDGE of the shortness of life comes the great resolve to drain its cup before death comes. . . ." At an age when most men disappear from public life, Berenson burst upon the scene with renewed vigor, his thirty-year silence broken by a host of new books, the speculations, analyses, and philosophical musings of old age. *Rumor and Reflection* (dedicated to Nicky and prefaced with the quotation from Goethe, "Let man be noble, helpful and good") was his record of the war years. It revealed the extraordinary diversity of his play of thought: from Herodotus and the Persian Empire, and the Mesopotamian custom of burying young men alive, to the inability of England to comprehend Continental Europe, the uses of elastic-sided boots, and the reason why miracles happened. Among the kaleidoscope of subjects presented there were searching and often illuminating questions and observations, rather more often than conclusions.

Berenson had published another kind of diary, *One Year's Reading for Fun*, a chronicle of the equally diverse reading matter he had perused while in semi-isolation, and a short book on Piero della Francesca. He also published *Seeing and Knowing*, which, after discussing the compromise that the visual arts make between what is seen and what is known, launched an all-out attack on abstract art: those geometrical squares, lozenges, diagonals, trapezoids, and "disembodied lines and curves that can have none but a strictly encapsulated private meaning." This, too, would pass away, he predicted, to be followed by a Renaissance of sculpture and painting based on the human form.

Berenson's most ambitious work was *Aesthetics and History*, and since his main claim as a humanist rests on this work, it is worth examining. This, too, was more a compendium of reflections than a coherent philosophy, what he called "a pell-mell of stray thoughts." In it one meets the familiar themes: the discussion of tactile values, ideated sensations, movement, space composition, and the forcefully repeated message that art exists to be enjoyed. This, in fact, was a major dilemma for him, he wrote, since an art critic was bound to give the reader theoretical considerations, when his role must be to help the viewer to the direct experience of appreciation.

Such a work of art must have a narrowly defined effect. To be good, it must be beautiful or, "life-enhancing." It could not, therefore, be terrifying, as in the work of Goya, or anguished, as in the case of Käthe Kollwitz: ". . . representations that communicate feelings of dejection or nausea would be the less artistic, the more skillfully and successfully they were done."

One meets again Berenson's lifelong assertion that art must humanize mankind. A work of art may arguably be viewed as evidence of man's divinity and therefore serve to remind us of the transcendental nature of all great art. However, to ask art to take on the ennobling of the human race is surely to assume a more homiletical role than it can ever be expected to play. If one, however, views the word "art" as a substitute for that of "religion" in Berenson's philosophy, it becomes easier to comprehend. For him, art had preempted the function of religion. It had provided that path toward experiencing the ineffable that Catholicism had not given him. It had helped him become "reconciled with Life."

Berenson's ambitious claim for art was, however, very much in the postwar temper of the times. Against the brutalizing influence of totalitarianism, offering mankind freedom from nothing except independent thought, Berenson set his hatred of the irrational and despotic, his belief in the ancient roots of culture, in the power of reason, in order, continuity, and his faith in humanity. He defined humanism as the desire to build a world in which men, as instruments, might function to the "ever greater advantage of ourselves and of the universal House of Life.... Humanism consists in the belief that something worthwhile can be made of life on this planet ... that it is happiness to work toward that goal."

Berenson had become a symbol of resistance, an old man, alone and courageous, who had kept the flame of sanity alive in an insane world, "the last great humanist of Western Europe." When he spoke of humanism his contemporaries listened respectfully and perhaps did not realize that his view of it probably differed from theirs. Humanism in its general sense was a term embracing the betterment of mankind through the advancement of its welfare. In such socialist terms, Berenson was antihumanist, since he did not believe in equality for the masses.

Men, he believed, were hierarchical animals with pyramidal societies governed from the top and not from the ranks. The House of Life, as Berenson envisioned it, contained plenty of rooms at the bottom for those who were little better than domestic animals. One's duty was done to this level of mankind if one saw that they were properly housed, clothed, and kept clean.

Such people must, above all, be kept in their place. The local peasants, he wrote to Walter Lippmann in 1946, had grown indolent and resentful and were trying to get rid of the landowners and their money as well. Once industrial workers had destroyed the factories by their inordinate demands, they would have to be supported by the state. He had to confess that he felt not the slightest concern for the masses. Too many of them were still common clay and had not yet become human beings.

One day, he was sure, we would abandon the concept of a community of termites and return to an aristocratic society. When that day arrived man would produce to create and not merely to consume.

For Berenson, therefore, humanism was an "ideology of culture" inherited from the nineteenth century: "Beauty was separated from the ethical, the civic and the religious and lifted above these as a self-sufficient private goal. The aesthetic in itself could sublimate the imperfections of the world."

His astonishing network of friendships and the revival of interest in his books—in 1952, a new edition of his *Italian Painters* sold 60,000 copies—contributed to the renaissance of interest in Berenson. Honorary degrees were awarded to him in absentia (by the Sorbonne) but those that required his presence (one was offered by Oxford) were refused. Almost the only public ceremony Berenson forced himself to attend was in 1949, when Florence gave him honorary citizenship. He went to it as to major surgery and found it quite touching.

Berenson was, however, making numerous public appearances. He was still attending openings and still very much a power in the art world; still expertising for Wildenstein's at a retainer of $50,000 a year, although he no longer pursued paintings but waited for dealers' photographs to come to him. An indication of the commotion his presence could create is contained in the following description of Berenson's arrival at the Bellini exhibition in Venice in 1949:

> I had seen B.B. [Henry Sayles Francis wrote in his journal] flit across the background headed toward the sales desk, ostensibly intent on seeing the catalogue, but also staging his solo entrance, which pretty soon he effected—amazing, small, dapper and brisk with a pinched-in hat, smart suit and a bachelor's button. . . .
> . . . he caused the inevitable ripple, as planned [and] . . . after introductions all around, the royal progress commenced. It soon became evident that traveling in such an entourage was useless. . . . They all clustered about B.B. and he moved hither and yon like a humming bird, muttering wisdom to himself.

Sir Geoffrey Agnew met Berenson in Venice a year later at a major exhibition of Giorgione's paintings. Sir Geoffrey recalled, "I was looking at a very damaged landscape said to be by Giorgione when Berenson came up to me and said, 'What do you think of it?' I replied, 'Frankly, I don't think very much of it.' Berenson replied, 'You are wrong, absolutely wrong.' I stuck to my guns. He again repeated, 'You are absolutely wrong. It's a masterpiece—a masterpiece of the restorer's art.' "

Berenson said he disliked the attention he was receiving,

particularly since it seemed to be focused on him as a personality rather than on giving his books the scholarly appreciation they deserved. Yet there is evidence that he contributed to the myth, as the following curious story suggests.

News magazines of the postwar period had published the incidental information that, because Berenson was so physically fragile, his watch was warmed before it was placed on his wrist to minimize the shock of the cold upon his delicate constitution. Igor Markevitch, however, revealed that he made the story up.

"One day just after the liberation of Florence a journalist came to interview me about Berenson. He was so persistent that I got bored and, to amuse myself, started inventing stories. I said that Berenson was just like the princess and the pea, who felt the lump through seventeen mattresses, and that he even had to have his watch warmed for him. After the journalist left I told Berenson about it and we had a good laugh."

That the watch-warming story, the invention of a bored friend, had subsequently been perpetuated by journalists in search of telling detail and entered the realm of myth, seemed evident. However, there was more to come. A further twist to the tale was added by Bertram M. Goldsmith, who had served as military governor of Florence and had been among the first American soldiers to visit Berenson. He was regularly invited there for lunch and revisited "i Tatti" many times with his wife in the years that followed.

The watch-warming story was not a myth, he declared. "It's true! I saw it with my own eyes!" It seemed that, on one of their postwar visits, he and his wife were talking over aperitifs with Berenson and Nicky when, "all of a sudden, a butler arrived, carrying a red velvet cushion. On the cushion was a white towel and on that towel was a warmed watch. We asked about it and Nicky Mariano explained, 'We never let him put his watch on, because of the shock of the cold against his arm.' "

Whether Berenson really did decide that life might as well take its cue from fiction, and that a warmed watch felt better than a cold one, the fact that a minor matter of the toilette developed into an ostentatious ritual provided a further fillip to the myth that increasingly obscured the man. It was a process that Nicky Mariano, consciously or unconsciously, aided.

"Nicky Mariano was aware that Berenson was not the easiest person to deal with, but she made things worse because she was too subservient," Count Morra observed. He was referring to the atmosphere of reverential awe that Nicky Mariano insisted upon once she saw how much it flattered and soothed Berenson's ego. Thus guests were expected to stand deferentially as soon as Berenson appeared, even when he was entering his own living room.

Clotilde Marghieri remembered the particular way in which Nicky would preside over the tea ceremony. If her act of serving tea threatened to deflect attention from Berenson's next conversational serve, Nicky would pause with a cup held in midflight until the necessary silence had been reestablished; no jewel of thought, the Italian writer noted ironically, must ever be lost.

This exaggerated deference—in speaking Italian with Berenson, Nicky Mariano always used the impersonal "lei"—was offered to anyone with even remote family connections. Judith Friedberg, a writer whose grandmother was a first cousin of Berenson's mother, recalls that Nicky Mariano always insisted upon having her go through a door first because, "You're family."

To efface herself was intrinsic for Nicky Mariano. It was also natural for her to want to smooth out the rough edges of the Berenson image and establish him as "a disembodied sage, a sort of minor Confucius . . ." If Berenson and Roberto Longhi had quarreled, the fault must be with Mary. Nicky wrote that Mary's "heavy-handed" criticism of some translations into Italian of Berenson's early essays, made by Longhi, had probably offended him. Nicky was similarly determined that posterity view Berenson, as F. H. Taylor wrote, like a Buddha on a mountaintop. Nicky Mariano was given sole charge of Berenson's papers. After his death, some collections of love letters and others were returned and she wrote to Kenneth Clark asking for his advice on whether to retain or destroy Berenson's business correspondence. As a result there are no letters at all from Wildenstein and a number of files look incomplete, particularly those of other business contacts like Grassi, Contini-Bonacossi, Gutekunst, Marchig, and Duveen. When A. K. McComb came to edit a book of Berenson's letters, Nicky Mariano wrote an epilogue stating that their only disagreement had been over "the inclusion of the unfortunate exchange of letters between B.B. and Vernon Lee. It does no service to the memory of either of them."

Nicky Mariano's steely response to whatever might reflect unfavorably on Berenson had its fortunate aspects. If Mary had gleefully encouraged Berenson's feuds, Nicky Mariano was just as determined to reconcile old enemies. Thanks to her, Richard Offner was reinvited to "i Tatti" and Berenson discovered that he had improved vastly with age. Langton Douglas, another ancient foe, whose letters are also not at "i Tatti," was similarly reconciled shortly before he died and the long estrangement between Berenson and Longhi ended, three years before Berenson's death, when Longhi wrote a speech for the honorary degree awarded to Berenson by the University of Florence.

One of the subjects always sure of a lively discussion in Florence was the reason why Berenson and Nicky Mariano never married. It seemed, to the old guard, like an obvious reward for faithful services rendered, and the fact that they did not looked like base ingratitude on Berenson's part. There were a number of reasons given. Nicky Mariano usually told people that he had asked her and she had refused. Or, she ridiculed the idea: "It seems too silly at our age."

People said that Nicky also told them that Berenson never asked her. Berenson is quoted as having said, "I am ready to marry her if she wants me," and Nicky, "If he doesn't want to marry me, I am just as happy the way we are"; and, like characters in a Russian novel, each waited for the other to speak first for the rest of their lives. People also said that Berenson couldn't bring himself to ask because, "you can't marry your secretary."

Clotilde Marghieri said, "I asked Nicky this question and she replied, 'In a way, I would rather not be the second Mrs. Berenson because if I were and wanted to have my German relatives come into this house and he said no, if I am Mrs. Berenson I will resent it. But if I am Signorina Mariano, I will not resent it.'" Nicky Mariano must have known how determined Berenson was to leave "i Tatti" to Harvard, making it unlikely that he would wish to have any rights of inheritance entangling his estate. She continued to be his secretary until the day he died. She was provided with a small annuity in his will and she and her sister were given the right to live in the villino for life. Learning that Nicky Mariano was financially embarrassed, officials of Harvard University immediately put her on the payroll. When she died, in 1968, at the age of eighty-one, the inscription on Nicky Mariano's tomb was *"Visse per gl'altri"* ("She lived for others").

There was also the question of Berenson's lingering feelings about Mary. It is one that is impossible to settle. His comments at the time of her death are not revealing. Writing to Judge Learned Hand, he spoke only of the wonderful impression she always made, first as a college student, then (to the Germans) as a duchess, and (to the Egyptians) as the consort of a great feudatory. His late diaries, published posthumously in *Sunset and Twilight*, betray the fact that all love was not dead by his peevish references to her lovers and her ecstatic involvement with her offspring. She always, he said, put him last on the list. Yet Berenson would often speak of Mary in glowing terms. "How I wish you'd known my Mary!" he exclaimed to Frances Francis. In this connection there is a charming ghost story which, while it will shed no light on the problem whatsoever, is irresistible.

The British novelist Rosamond Lehmann said, "Some years ago I was in the College of Psychic Studies in London. As I came out of the library I saw a man, a psychic, standing in the library half looking at me. Finally he said, 'I must tell you this. There is a little man, very short and well-dressed, with a little beard, following you. He is saying that his name is "Bibi." Not "Baby" but "Bibi." He is obviously someone who is very fond of you, and he says he hopes you are happier now than you were when he last saw you. Now he is saying something very strange, I don't know if you will understand it: "I can't find Mary." ' " Rosamond Lehmann said that she had never met the psychic before and that he had known nothing at all about her.

Even though she never became the second Mrs. Berenson, the fact is that Nicky Mariano was the wife in everything but name. Nicky was captain of the ship, Berenson told Sibyl Colefax at the end of World War II, and he was one of the passengers with nothing to do but read, write, and see friends. Writing to Learned Hand he talked of what we, meaning himself and Nicky, would like, adding that she managed him as Mary had never dared to do. As the chief companion of a famous and aging man, Nicky Mariano was in an unavoidable position of power in deciding who could see him—Adlai Stevenson, Sir Harold Acton remarked, was given ten minutes. It was a role she played with great tact and grace.

It was true that she managed him. Flavia Colaccichi, who, with her husband Giovanni Colaccichi, was among the close circle of Florentine *unsereiners* said, "Berenson was terribly full of curiosity, like a little child. He adored walks. One time when we were out, he saw a little path through the wood and said, 'Nicky, we never went there. Can't we explore?' Nicky would never say, 'You are too old,' or, 'It's too rough for you.' She would reply in a reassuring voice, 'Of course we shall go—another day—' "

Nicky, another friend remarked, was for Berenson and for him only. "If Berenson said of someone, 'Oh, isn't he *sympathique*,' that guest would be showered with attention and invited to return. If Berenson gave the slightest hint of displeasure, that guest would never be asked back," Markevitch said. "During the receptions she watched him all the time and if she thought an exchange was not going well, she would immediately move the guest away."

Nicky, like Scheherazade, had read the *Thousand and One Nights* aloud to Berenson every night during the first months of their love, and was still reading to him aloud. One evening, Elizabeth Gates and her husband, staying at "i Tatti" with Rosamond Lehmann, recalled that they were all sitting around chatting after Berenson had gone to bed. His bedroom was directly overhead and suddenly they heard an imperious rapping on the ceiling. "Nicky said, 'Oh my goodness,' and went up like a shot to read to him."

He loved her. He would say, "No one loves me who doesn't love Nicky." One day Berenson invited Frances Francis for a walk with him. He suddenly realized that Nicky seemed a little sad and, quick as a flash, invited her to join them, "and made it all right." He was often gallant with her. As they settled themselves into a car, Nicky would say, "Wait until I get my big person in," and Berenson would reply, "Every ounce of which is precious, my dear." He was aware of his power over her. When he complained that he could no longer remember facts, Mrs. Francis reminded him that he had Nicky's excellent memory to prompt him. Berenson replied, "Yes, but I mesmerize her and she forgets."

Berenson's love for Nicky is one of the most charming themes of *Sunset and Twilight*. She was "the necessity, the solace, the happiness of my life," he wrote. "She works with me, she thinks with me, she feels as I do, she is the complete companion. . . ."

Nevertheless Nicky's selfless, single-minded devotion seemed sometimes more than Berenson could endure. "I ask her whether there is not somewhere in her make-up some secret closet, no matter how tiny & how remote, where she thinks, feels & lives for herself. No, all dedicated to my all-absorbingness," he wrote somewhat ironically to Margaret Scolari Barr at the end of World War II. Perhaps a need to establish a more comfortable psychic distance and avoid being smothered in the billowing maternal folds of Nicky's arms caused Berenson, at an age when most men have abandoned the idea, to imagine himself a Don Juan.

In theory, Nicky recognized that he needed the diversion of difference. "From me, who lived with him all the time, he could get complete devotion, tenderness, sympathy but no intellectual stimulus." It was natural that Berenson should seek intelligent companionship elsewhere; but when he seemed to be looking for more than that from his women friends, she reacted with the panic that betrayed a profound inner insecurity.

One of the women whom Nicky considered a threat to her position was Mrs. Otto Kahn, wife of a wealthy New York financier, who visited him every summer and, in fact, died of a heart attack while sitting at her desk writing a letter to Berenson. Addie Kahn and Berenson had known each other since World War I. Her visit to "i Tatti" was always accompanied by ten trunks and Nicky would say, "I can't see why she brings seventy-five dresses. They all look the same."

One summer in Venice, Mrs. Kahn hired a launch to take the Berenson party, which included Professor and Mrs. Frederick Hartt, to the island of Torcello. Professor Hartt said, "It was one of those afternoons in Venice when the sky is covered with a thin layer of gray and everything sweats and one's temper is foul. Then Nicky, in the launch, produced porcelain cups and little sandwiches and excellent tea from a basket. She was magical.

"Addie had a pair of marvelous binoculars, the first I had seen, a new ultraviolet type through which one could see in the dark. There was Addie, well in her seventies, snuggling up to B.B. in the middle of the Cathedral at Torcello saying, 'Shall I adjust these glasses for you?' and he was answering, 'My eyes are the same as yours. We have so much in common, don't we darling?' Nicky was in a rage.

"Next evening Nicky, my wife and I went to see a performance of the opera 'Don Pasquale.' It was exquisite and we were very happy, but Nicky was not happy. She was in tears. She was still upset about what happened the day before."

Nicky was equally jealous of Rosamond Lehmann. The novelist had published *The Ballad and the Source* at the end of the war and Berenson had been deeply impressed by it. He wrote a fan letter saying how much the principal character in the book reminded him of Mary and invited the author to "i Tatti."

"It was," she said, "a *coup de foudre* for both of us. I loved him and was fascinated by his life-enhancing conversation and since I was a great pet I never had the rough edge of his tongue." He seemed to see her as a potential replacement for Edith Wharton and confided that he had always wanted to be a writer himself. She thought he would have made a fine novelist because "he was very passionate and dramatic; he loved dramatic gossip about people."

She continued, "I wasn't sure, to tell you the truth, that Nicky liked me very much. Although she had no reason to be jealous. It was a fantasy of B.B.'s that I could ever have been interested in him romantically or sexually. One thing he said was that he would never forgive himself for not having married Nicky. He said, 'I should have given her children.' "

As with many other women friends, Rosamond Lehmann was involved in romantic entanglements of her own. That love affair ended unhappily and, some time after that, her daughter Sally died. Berenson wrote what was meant to be a helpful letter, "but it wasn't any good. For one thing, I have complete belief in survival after death and he had none. For another, he said, 'Absorb yourself in some mechanical work. Anything to keep yourself going,' which was the opposite of the way I was facing her death." Berenson's conventional response, which seemed to her without human insight or feeling, came at the end of his life. She never went back. "Well," she said, "I never did think he understood anything about human nature."

Berenson had a special fondness for women writers, like Freya Stark, or for writers manqué, like Frances Francis, who kept a meticulous record of their conversations and with whom he shared many of his most intimate thoughts. The first time they met, Patricia (Botond) Chapman, the former wife of Henry Luce III, in her twenty-three-year-old innocence, quoted Walter Pater's *Marius*. Berenson, predictably, fell hard. He seemed to see something of his own youth in her eyes, her full mouth, and small, agile body. He encouraged her to write poetry and plays, supervised her studies, and subjected her to a barrage of advice. They pleased and disappointed each other, she wrote in a charming memoir, as yet unpublished. She was fascinated by his ability to establish an immediate rapport, yet repelled by his determination to burrow into her secret thoughts. Yet he gave her something of value: the feeling that she was gifted.

He was, she noted, a joyful satyr, who seemed, even at the exalted age of eighty, to be appraising her sensually. He said that if only they'd met when he was younger he would have made love to her night and day. Others remarked upon Berenson's tendency to "pounce," as Rosamond Lehmann described it. Lady Lambe, the very respectable wife of a British naval officer, said that he tore her stockings, and Judith Friedberg recalled a similarly indiscreet lunge in her direction when Berenson was ninety. Such crude and wholly futile advances were so tempered by an otherwise courtly manner that his female admirers liked him nonetheless and flocked around him.

Professor Hartt recalled that, at one of what Berenson liked to call his Sunday afternoon "tea fights," he was surrounded by contessas, baronessas, and principessas in true Don Giovanni style. He was talking about Santayana and saying, "Santayana was always a year ahead of me. He came to the U.S. a year ahead, he graduated from Harvard a year ahead and published his first book a year ahead. . . ."

Professor Hartt interjected, "B.B., Santayana has entered a convent." Berenson said, "Santayana has entered a convent and I have entered . . . a harem."

He looked as fragile as Venetian crystal, but was surprisingly durable. He had been blessed with a heart as punctilious as a Swiss clock and the arteries of a young man, allowing him an agility of body to compare with his mind. He had minor complaints: hay fever, allergies to certain foods, and a tendency toward colitis, an inflammation of the colon that causes cramps and diarrhea and which is largely the result of nervous tension. Consequently he moved in a carefully controlled world, with a scarf for his shoulders, a blanket always tucked around his knees when he sat down, and a hot water bottle beneath the blanket.

Yet he still felt so coltish that, on one of his walks, he could leap across a small brook and mockingly offer his stick to Frank Giles, a British journalist, who followed behind. Berenson was then ninety years old and Giles twenty. At eighty-five or six, he felt full of vigor and as ready to venture forth as he had been in adolescence. Berenson seemed to be experiencing the enlightened old age of the sage in Lewis Carroll's poem who was performing antic feats that young men looked upon with alarm.

Then, in the summer of 1954, at the age of eighty-nine, Berenson had a freak accident. He and a party of friends had gone out on one of their afternoon "car walks." It was a windy day. Parry drove to the top of a hill and parked the car beside a steep bank. Berenson descended and was standing beside the car with Nicky, who suddenly decided to get back into the car in search of an extra scarf for B.B. As she climbed inside the wind caught the door, flung it open, and knocked Berenson off his feet. He rolled thirteen feet down the steep bank.

Berenson actually managed to laugh and get up, dusting off his hat. Prince Clary, who was among the party, said admiringly that he was wonderful and Berenson replied that he used to go mountain climbing as a young man and the mountaineers would say that he had the legs of a mountain goat.

It was worth an item on the Associated Press wire, which reported no bones broken. Berenson was put to bed with bruises and an aching back and stayed there for several months. By the winter of 1954 he was beginning to get up for meals. Although he complained that he tired easily and recovered slowly, he was still planning a fatiguing trip (his last) to Tripoli, then home by way of Sicily, Calabria, Naples, and Rome. Nevertheless, old age seemed to have caught up with him finally, he wrote to the Swedish archaeologist Axel Boethius. He was then ninety years old.

Bernard Berenson had once begun a will with the phrase, "If I die . . ." Now, even he began to realize that the Furies were behind him and rapidly gathering speed. He faced that eventuality with remarkable equanimity and the same impersonal curiosity with which he recorded the onslaught of old age in his diaries. Two years after his fall, he was attacked by an unknown virus. Periods of violent vomiting were followed by moments of extreme clarity. In one of them, Berenson heard his doctor whispering to Emma, his maid, and Nicky Mariano that he was about to die. The idea amused him so much that he burst out laughing. They were all certain that he had lost his mind. He had not; it simply struck him as absurd to be given up for dead when he felt so alive.

Although he complained of being too tired for sustained effort, his faithful friend Morra observed that he was still capable of brilliance and could take a half an hour's brisk walk, so long as it wasn't uphill. However, in the last two years, Berenson experienced a slow decline. There were problems with both eyes. Then he became hard of hearing. He told his close friend, the British publisher Hamish Hamilton, that a visitor had set Nicky Mariano and Willy Mostyn-Owen into gales of laughter but that he hadn't understood a word and had been obliged to fake amusement. Then there was a series of boils and a painful back ailment that prevented him from writing his own increasingly indecipherable letters. He dictated them instead. Paradoxically, these are among the best letters he ever wrote, since a stenographer could keep up with the spontaneous play of his thought the way he himself had never been able to do on paper.

Through it all, Nicky kept a smile "rouged" on her face. She refused to believe that he would not regain his old strength and when the days between his smiles grew longer and he became morose and difficult, she greeted old friends in tears. Late visitors were prepared to find a change, but not for its extent. Patricia Chapman, invited to "i Tatti," was taken to the small room called the French library, for lunch at a low table. Beside it stood an empty wheelchair. Berenson waited until they were all seated to arrive; she noted that he always loved to make an entrance. Then a nurse appeared in the doorway, carrying in her strong young arms a thin, elongated bundle with a head and hands as fragile as eggshell. She deposited him tenderly in the chair and proceeded to feed him pureed spinach with a spoon. Berenson tried to talk but he was already suffering from a staphylococcic infection that caused inner swellings in his mouth. After mumblings that Patricia Chapman barely understood, Berenson endured, with resigned patience, the face cleaning to which the nurse subjected him. Then he was scooped up and carried back to bed.

"His head turned to me as he . . . retreated through the door. His eyes were profoundly sad. . . .The white hand, like a wisp of a handkerchief, moved slowly on its frail wrist in a final farewell."

Berenson had remarked to Edith Wharton some fifty years before, after a freak accident, that he was in a euphoric, almost angelically blissful state. It reminded him of a prophecy that he would die in an aura of holiness. In the autumn of 1959, the swellings inside his mouth became markedly worse, and when he realized that no one, not even Nicky, could understand what he was saying, he lapsed into a tragic silence. Doctors, fearing that the infection would reach his throat, causing a death of slow suffocation, administered a powerful antibiotic. His heart failed and he died peacefully, in his sleep. He was laid out on a big table in the library, surrounded by flowers, with the cross painted by Vecchietta at his head and candles around him. He looked, Alda von Anrep wrote, like one of those saints one saw on the tombstones of ancient churches.

Richard Davis, former director of the Minneapolis Museum, said, "I happened to be sitting with Georges Wildenstein the art dealer one afternoon in the windows of his Bond Street gallery and we heard the newsboys shouting, 'Art Expert Dead.' Wildenstein said, 'It has to be B.B.'"

When Berenson died he was considered "at the pinnacle of his glory, a perfect example of a happy career and a successful life." To that, Berenson would doubtless have replied what he told the Countess Anna Maria Cicogna when she expressed a similar sentiment: "You only see the end of my life, but not what I could have been."

A more observant witness, S. N. Behrman, found no expression of serenity on Berenson's aging face. "When his face was in repose there was, at most, the suggestion of a fleeting truce between the warring of what he called his 'many selves.'" Berenson still felt, he wrote to friends, like one of the chosen who had failed to fulfill his highest function, which was to communicate his feelings to others. Although he might declare that there was no end to the unraveling of his personality, he fretted over his own attribution with a mental magnifying glass, as if reluctant to label himself "provenance unknown."

He had an old hat with holes in it, which he wore when in the company of his *unsereiners*, and liked to quote the haiku which he and Mary had discovered half a century before: "How heavenly falls the rain/ On the hat I stole from the scarecrow." At last he was beginning to feel something like a free tenant in his own House of Life.

"As I look back on 80 years of awareness I seem to myself to have tried strange garrets, icy, draughty, occupied by undesirables and almost becoming one, or to have attempted to insert myself into great ... houses where I was not invited to linger ...Only now ... have I a den all my own where I feel master, and can allow myself to recognize ... my own selfishness. ..."

So he found himself liking people better, and thinking that young people looked as lovely as flowers instead of the hideous freaks he had seen around him everywhere as an adolescent. He was becoming aware of the extent of his tendency to blame others, if not the extent to which he denounced and belittled himself. He even began to see the outlines of his self-deceptiveness.

In an uncanny echo of the charge he leveled against D'Annunzio, Berenson wrote, "[O]n the principle of 'What I say three times is true,' one may end by believing what one has said. ..." He continued, "I for instance never mean to lie, but often hear myself saying things that 'ain't quite so.' " The possibility that he had been deliberately deceptive weighed on his mind during those final years. When Berenson met Alessandro Brass, the son of an art dealer, Berenson asked him whether he had followed his father's footsteps. Brass replied that he was a lawyer. "Ah," said Berenson, "then we are colleagues." "Why is that?" said Brass. "Well, I am an art critic and you are a lawyer. Lying is common to both."

For some years before his death, Berenson was having nightmares. He would wake up hearing himself cry "Help, help," because assassins had come to kill him. For others, his nightmare was that money would corrupt them. When Luisa Vertova was considering a business career, Berenson told her that she would have to choose between peace of mind and money, and when Lord Clark became chairman of the British commercial television association in 1954, Berenson observed (to Hamish Hamilton) that Clark would have been better employed elsewhere, and that one could not touch pitch, etc.

This same apparent duality, *"vorrei e non vorrei"* ("I would like and I wouldn't like" [from Mozart's *Don Giovanni*]), can be seen in Berenson's attitude toward his own Jewishness. Thus we find him cheerfully exchanging Yiddish jokes with Sir Isaiah Berlin, Sir Lewis Namier, Bela Horowitz, and those others with whom one could drop the mask. Yet he still referred to himself as an Anglo-Saxon (in a postwar letter to Learned Hand). When he once spoke of "our Puritan forebears" to Professor Hartt, Professor Schapiro remarked, "His ancestors were Rabbis on the Mayflower." Even after World War II, he would not discuss his Lithuanian past with a Gentile.

The singer Mascia Predit, a refugee from Latvia who suffered terrible losses in the war—all her family died in Siberia, including her only son—remembered that Berenson would question her closely about her past, and "his eyes would fill with tears. Surely he, too, must have lost family in Lithuania?" she remarked. "I knew his background and gave him plenty of opportunity to tell me about himself. But he never said a word." Berenson never returned to Lithuania. He went as far as asking Judith Friedberg, then making a trip to Eastern Europe, to go to Butrimants on his behalf, but she never got there.

Similarly, he could complain to Frau Mally Dienemann, widow of the chief rabbi of Offenbach, Germany, with whom he had a long postwar correspondence, that German Jews seemed to have lost all pride in their Hebrew past and would prefer to be uneducated *goyim*; yet almost simultaneously argue that assimilation was the only solution for the Jewish race, and that Jews must learn to be as proud of Christ as the Greeks were of Socrates.

Berenson had reluctantly converted to the necessity of a Jewish state, but feared the influence of rabbinical orthodoxy. One finds frequent references to the dirt of the Middle Ages coupled with the rabbis of his childhood who "certainly never washed and used to wipe their noses on their sleeves." An almost irrational horror of dirt found its counterpart in a disgust of his body's animal functions; self-contempt fused with Jewishness, like sides of the same coin.

Yet, in spite of himself, the barriers between Berenson and his distant Lithuanian childhood were falling. When he became ill and could no longer wear his impeccably tailored Savile Row suits, Berenson had a dressing gown of burgundy velvet designed for him. With it he wore a matching cap which some people thought was a *cappèllo cardinalezio* (cardinal's cap).

"What do I remind you of?" Berenson asked Prince Clary and received an aristocratic shrug. Berenson continued, smiling, "An old Rabbi by Rembrandt."

Berenson acceded to Nicky Mariano's wish to have the last rites of the Catholic Church so as not to offend those who had nursed him with such devotion. However, in obedience to Jewish custom he was buried in a shroud.

"He was born a Jew and he died a Jew," Judith Friedberg declared. One day, John Walker and Nicky Mariano had returned from Mass and were talking ecstatically about its beauty. Berenson dug her in the ribs and said, "Don't these converts give you a pain?" Judith Friedberg replied, "That's a strange statement, coming from you." Berenson answered, "They got me to the door of the Church several times, but they never booted me in."

What did he really believe? Who was he? The question tormented him. He felt in purgatory, stumbling about, lost in a murky wood, where "there was no turning back, and the darkness was frightening...." There, a battle to the death was being waged between two kinds of trees, some with crooklike growths resembling question marks and some ending in mitres, those headdresses worn by bishops, which, some believe, have their origins in the liturgical headgear of the Jewish priesthood. The question-mark trees forced out the others. Then there was only an "infinity of question marks, nothing, nothing but question marks—questioning what and questioning whom?"

One can make sense of the pendulumlike swings and the apparently endless contradictions of Berenson's personality if one sees it in terms of a crumbling façade, behind which another persona was gradually emerging: the man Berenson might have been, left to himself. Late in life the split became marked. Or was it rather that the alter ego, so long submerged, began to be heard more and more insistently, giving us that tapestry of observation, aspiration, and longing that its counterpart, exhaustedly "climbing the ever-climbing way," could no longer ignore or silence. He was ashamed of the person he saw whenever he let down his guard. He seemed to be saying, "Is this *all* I am?" Yet, "when I can sink to rest, relax on my natural level, I like it . . . ."

> Still nursing the unconquerable hope
> Still clutching the inviolable shade,
> With a free, onward impulse brushing through,
> By night, the silver'd branches of the glade—
> Far on the forest-skirts, where none pursue.
> On some mild pastoral slope
> Emerge, and resting on the moonlit pales
> Freshen thy flowers as in former years
> With dew, or listen with enchanted ears,
> From the dark dingles, to the nightingales!

—Matthew Arnold, "The Scholar-Gipsy"

Berenson asked himself what the youth of twenty-five that he had once been would have thought of the old man he had become, and answered with: not much. He had become too conceited, spoiled, and self-indulgent for his once too-shy, too-proud self. Yet the miracle was that so much of the young man's vision, the "free, onward impulse," remained. A year before he died he could write testily to Frau Dienemann that he burned with eagerness to know what was happening in a world he despised, and yearned to pursue work he could no longer attempt.

That avidity for life never left him and he was delighted to find in himself, the older he became, a heightened appreciation of beauty. He and Nicky had been gadding about Northern Italy, he wrote to Learned Hand in the summer of 1949, and were bathed in domains of gold. He had never before had eyes to see what the country and towns now revealed to him: their luminousness, their grandeur, their picturesqueness, and the breathtaking beauty of their inhabitants, filled with vigorous life. He was finding again the disinterested student who was his "realest self," who crossed vast panoramas, both human and ideal, for the sake of the journey itself; content to live for living's sake.

"On some mild pastoral slope/ Emerge . . ." He went back to places like Ravenna where, when he visited it sixty-seven years before, the sound of a single footstep had set up echoes. He returned to Venice, that magical world he ought to have painted himself, and which brought him back to his first loves, the Giorgionesque Venetians. He wrote about these last journeys in his final book, *The Passionate Sightseer*, and was correcting the proofs when he died.

He had sought the enhancement of life, but even that began to fade and blur in his memory, like so much of his immediate past. What remained stood out in clear relief.

"What views of Ischia, of Procida, of more distant cameo-like Capri!" he wrote in Naples in the summer of 1955. *"Die alte Weise* [the old refrain], how it grips me still, but it is the grip now that counts, and not the message. Indeed, there is no more message. It is IT. IT is its own and only purpose; IT is intransitive."

APPENDIX

An Explanatory Note

The following list provides a brief buying history of a number of paintings now in public collections which, with one or two exceptions (Category D) passed through Berenson's hands as advisor to the sale, first for collectors and then for dealers. Berenson received a sometimes substantial percentage of the profits. Their history is cited as evidence in support of the thesis that Berenson attributed optimistically when a work was for sale, so that the painting involved might fetch the highest possible price.

Category A:

Paintings whose attributions changed to those of a more important painter after Berenson was involved in business dealings with the seller.

1) In 1897 and 1901, Berenson published *Portrait of a Venetian Gentleman*, (#369) National Gallery of Art, Washington (Kress Collection), as a copy after a lost Giorgione. Sold to Henry Goldman of New York by Duveen in the twenties as a Titian. Berenson, 1932 Lists: Titian. Now: Titian.

2) In 1895, Berenson thought *St. Jerome Reading*, (#328) National Gallery (Kress), to be by Basaiti. Sold in the Benson Collection to Duveen, 1927, then to Clarence Mackay of Roslyn, New York, as by Giovanni Bellini. In Berenson's Lists of 1932, 1936, and 1957: to Bellini in part. Now: Bellini.

3) In 1895, Berenson thought *The Infant Bacchus*, (#1362) National Gallery (Kress), to be by Basaiti and, even then, only a copy of another painting. In 1927, this painting from the Benson Collection sold to Duveen and finally to Kress. Berenson in 1957: Bellini. Now: Bellini.

4) In 1896 and 1912, Berenson thought *Madonna and Child*, (#502) National Gallery (Kress), a work designed and superintended by Verrocchio in his studio. Bought by Duveen's in 1924, who sold to Clarence Mackay in 1926 as a Verrocchio. Bought back by Duveen and sold to Kress in 1939 as a Verrocchio. Offner published in 1924 beside

the obvious original in the Kaiser Friedrich Museum, (#104A). In 1932 and 1963, painting listed with the caveat: "Later replica of Berlin 104A." Now: Style of Andrea del Verrocchio. Painting not on view.

5) When Berenson first listed *Portrait of a Senator*, also called, *Portrait of a Man*, (#448) National Gallery (Kress), he considered it a typical example of Alvise Vivarini's work. Berenson repeated the attribution in 1901 and 1907. Bought from the Comtesse de Béarn by Duveen in 1937 and exhibited in the Duveen exhibition of 1941 as by Giovanni Bellini. Berenson, manuscript opinion and 1957 Lists, gave to Bellini. Now: Vivarini.

6) When Berenson first saw *Madonna and Child*, (#367) National Gallery (Kress), he thought it was by Bernardo Daddi. Painting bought by Henry Goldman from Duveen sometime before 1924 and exhibited at the Duveen Galleries that year as by Giotto. Berenson in 1932 Lists: Giotto. Now: Giotto and Assistant.

7) When Berenson first saw *Portrait of a Condottiere*, (#335) National Gallery (Kress), he thought it by Alvise Vivarini. Bought by Duveen's and then Kress in 1936 and exhibited in New York in 1940 as by Gentile Bellini. Berenson, 1957, gave to Giovanni Bellini. Now: Giovanni Bellini.

8) In 1916, 1923, and 1927 Berenson published that *Madonna and Child in a Landscape*, (#373) National Gallery (Kress), was a studio copy of a Giovanni Bellini. The painting sold through Duveen's to Kress in 1937 as a Bellini. Berenson, 1957: Bellini. Now: Bellini and Assistant.

9) In 1894 and 1906 Berenson thought *Portrait of Vincenzo Capello*, (#1407) National Gallery (Kress), was by Tintoretto. Wildenstein's sold to Kress in 1954 as a Titian and in 1957 Berenson published as a Titian. Now: Titian.

10) In 1907, Berenson thought *Profile Portrait of a Boy*, (#374) National Gallery (Kress), by Boltraffio. The painting, then in the Dreyfus Collection, subsequently bought by Duveen's who sold to Kress in 1937 as a Jacopo Bellini. Berenson, 1957: Jacopo Bellini. Now: Attributed to Jacopo Bellini.

11) In 1895, Berenson thought Lord Pembroke's *Judith and Holofernes* an interesting work but not by Andrea Mantegna himself. In 1901, he repeated this verdict, citing the hard modeling of the head and "almost ludicrous" attitude of the attendant and gaudy colors. In 1902, he called it a school piece. In 1918, painting sold by Duveen's to Carl W. Hamilton of New York and Berenson published his change of opinion in *Art in America*, October 1920, saying that recent cleaning supported an attribution to Mantegna. Now in the Widener Collection, National Gallery of Art, (#638) as: Andrea Mantegna.

12) In 1895, Berenson thought *Portrait of a Man*, now at the Metropolitan Museum of Art, New York, a work by the young Titian, or only a copy of one by Polidoro Lanzani, and in poor condition. Painting sold to Altman through Duveen's in 1912 as by Giorgione, with praise from Berenson for its miraculous state. Subsequent cleaning has shown work to be so damaged that undercoating is visible. Present attribution: Titian.

13) In 1913 and 1916, Berenson thought *Portrait of a Young Man* by Alvise Vivarini. Sold through Duveen's to the collector Salomon in 1919, back to Duveen's (1922–28), and then to Jules Bache, as by Giovanni Bellini. Berenson, 1932 and 1957: Giovanni Bellini. Now at the Metropolitan (#49.7.3) as: Jacometto Veneziano.

14) When *The Madonna and Child with Saints*, (#49.7.1) at the Metropolitan, was shown at the New Gallery in 1895, Berenson thought it was by Marco Basaiti. He repeated the verdict in 1901. In 1916, he amended that verdict to: Studio of Bellini. Painting sold in 1927 with the Benson Collection to Duveen's and bought as a Giovanni Bellini by Jules Bache. Berenson, 1932: a "late work" of Bellini. Now attributed: Giovanni Bellini and Workshop.

15) In 1897, Berenson hesitantly listed *The Madonna and Child*, (#49.7.15) Metropolitan, as an early work by Domenico Caprioli. In 1907, he listed as an early Caprioli with a question mark. Painting sold to Duveen's in the Benson Collection in 1927 and a year later sold to Mellon. Berenson, in an article in *Art in America*, 1928, ascribed to Titian. Bought back from Mellon and sold to Bache, who gave it to the Metropolitan Museum in 1949. Berenson, 1932 Lists: An early work by Titian. 1957 Lists: Titian. Now: Titian.

16) In 1903, Berenson said that *The Madonna and Child*, (#14.40.647) at the Metropolitan, was entirely executed by assistants of Verrocchio. Duveen sold to Altman in 1912 as a Verrocchio and Berenson in a letter, 1912, gave to Verrocchio. 1932 and 1963 Lists: Verrocchio. Now: Workshop of Verrocchio.

17) When *Portrait of a Woman, 'La Schiavona' "* was in the collection of M. Crespi of Milan in 1897, Berenson called it a copy after a lost Giorgione. Painting bought by René Gimpel in 1911 and Berenson contracted to help sell the work as a Titian. Painting bought by H. L. Cook of Richmond, England, in 1914 as a Giorgione. Now at the National Gallery of Art, London, as: Titian.

18) When Berenson saw *A Member of the Este Family*, (#14.40.649) now at the Metropolitan, at the home of William Drury-Lowe, Locko Park, Derbyshire, he thought it should be listed as "Ferrarese, before 1500" adding, "Close to Fossa." Painting sold through Duveen's to Altman in 1911 as by Cosimo Tura and Berenson, 1932: Tura. Now: Tura.

19) When *Courtesan*, also called *Bust of a Young Woman*, was sold to Sir Henry Mond at Romsey by Duveen with Berenson's attribution to Titian, Berenson listed the work, 1932, as an early Titian. The painting later bought back by Duveen and in 1957, Berenson called it a Giorgione. Bought by the Norton Simon Museum of Art at Pasadena which lists it as: Giorgione. Not accepted by Wethey as a Titian or Pignatti as a Giorgione.

20) When Berenson saw *Saint Sebastian*, in 1907, in the collection of the Counts Larderel, Florence, and Leghorn, he thought the work a Botticini. Painting came on the market in 1945 and sold to the Metropolitan with assurance from Berenson that it was by Andrea del Castagno. Appears in his posthumous, 1963 Lists as: Tentatively, Castagno. Museum attribution: Follower of Castagno.

21) When the *Madonna and Child*, (#3370) (Kress), at the Philbrook Art Center, Tulsa, Oklahoma, was owned by Charles Butler in 1895, Berenson said the painting had been catalogued as a replica of a genuine Mantegna in Berlin and thought by an unknown artist somewhere between Mantegna and Vivarini. Painting sold by Wildenstein to Kress in 1949 as by Mantegna with an M. S. opinion from Berenson to that effect. Now: Follower of Mantegna.

Category B: Fakes

1) When the painting was sold to Kress sometime before 1940, Berenson dated *Madonna and Child with Angels* as Central Italian, thirteenth century. It was so displayed when the National Gallery of Art opened in Washington in 1941. The painting was attacked by Offner as a fake and subsequently sent to the study collection at the Fogg Art Museum as: A Modern Pastiche in the style of Marcovaldo di Coppo (Everett Fahy attribution).

2) Modern copy after Fra Filippo Lippi, K 516, indexed in the Kress Catalogue but not described. Sold through Duveen's.

3) Walters Art Gallery, Carpaccio, *St. George and the Dragon*, has been X-rayed and found to conceal a painting of the Last Supper underneath, sixteenth century. Not on view or catalogued pending further tests. Bought through Berenson.

4) Walters Art Gallery, painting of a female saint attributed to Luini, thought to be very much overpainted and probably a fake. Not on view. Bought through Berenson.

Category C:

Berenson's attributions at the time of a sale which have since been downgraded.

Appendix

1) Philadelphia Museum of Art, Johnson Collection, *Virgin and Child*, (#192), sold to Johnson by Berenson in 1910 as a Sebastiano del Piombo. Now: Follower of Cima da Conegliano.

2) Philadelphia, (Johnson) *Portrait of a Gentleman*, (#181), sold by Berenson in 1912 as by Basaiti. Now: Venetian artist.

3) Philadelphia, (Johnson) *Portrait of an Elderly Man*, (#228), sold 1911 as by Paolo Farinati. Now: Venetian artist.

4) Philadelphia, (Johnson) *Virgin and Child: St. Jerome*, (#153), sold in 1908 as by Bartolo di Maestro Fredi. Now: Sienese artist.

5) Philadelphia, (Johnson) *Scenes from the Legend of St. George*, (#174 & #175), sold in 1912 as by Bastiani. Now: Circle of Bastiani.

6) Walters Art Gallery, Baltimore, *Madonna and Child*, (#4), sold by Berenson in 1911 as by Bernardo Daddi. Lists, 1932: Daddi. Now: Workshop of B. Daddi.

7) Walters, *Madonna and Child with Angels and Two Donors*, (#33), bought through Berenson in 1911 as a Barnaba da Modena and Lists, 1932, ditto. Now: Attributed to Francesco Anguilla (School of Lucca—an imitation of B. da Modena and Taddeo di Bartolo).

8) Walters, *Madonna and Child with Saints*, (#79), bought in 1911 as a Giovanni di Paolo. Now: Giovanni di Paolo and Workshop.

9) Walters, *Madonna and Child with St. Nicholas of Bari and a Bishop Saint*, (#111), bought 1910 as by Raffaello dei Carli. Now: School of Umbria.

10) Walters, *The Holy Family with the Young St. John the Baptist*, (#118), bought between 1910 and 1915 as by Giovanni Battista Utili. Now: "School of Umbria (?)"

11) Walters, *The Nativity*, (#123), bought as by Pinturicchio in 1915 and found to have been restored in the manner of that artist. Now: Francesco da Monterale.

12) Walters, *Madonna and Child*, (#137), bought in 1913 as a Giorgio Schiavone. Lists, 1932 and 1936: School of. Now: School of Padua.

13) Walters, *Madonna and Child*, (#144), bought in 1911 as a Bramantino. Now: School of Ferrara.

14) Walters, *The Madonna of Humility*, (#158), bought in 1912 as by Antonio Vivarini, whom Berenson described in a letter, January 16, 1912 (gallery archives), as the founder of the Venetian School. Listed in *Art in America*, 1915, and *Venetian Painting in America*, 1916, as by Vivarini. Now: Michele Giambono.

15) Walters, *Madonna and Child*, (#173), bought in 1911 as by Cima da Conegliano. Berenson, 1916, called an early work of Cima. Now: Girolamo da Udine (direct follower of Cima).

16) Walters, *Portrait of a Young Man with Fur Collar*, (#177), sold in 1915 as by Marco Basaiti. Lists, 1916 and 1932: Basaiti. Now: Attributed to Basaiti.

17) Walters, *Profile Portrait of a Young Poet*, (#191), possibly bought from Berenson, as by Francesco Caroto. Now: School of Verona.

18) Walters, *The Holy Family with St. John the Baptist*, (#228), bought in 1911 as by Lo Spagno. Now: Umbro-Tuscan School.

19) Walters, *Madonna and Child with Saints Mark and Peter*, (#273), bought through Berenson in 1911 as by Polidoro da Lanzani. Now: Attributed to Polidoro da Lanzani.

20) In the early 1920s, Clarence Mackay was sold a *Madonna and Child* by Baldovinetti, (#325) National Gallery of Art (Kress), by Duveen's. Berenson listed as a Baldovinetti, 1932. Later bought by Kress. Now considered repainted in the style of Baldovinetti. Ascribed to: Pier Francesco Fiorentino and in storage.

21) In early 1920s, Henry Goldman bought *The Entombment*, (#371) National Gallery (Kress), as a Fra Angelico from Duveen and Berenson listed as such in 1932 and 1936. Now: Attributed to Fra Angelico.

22) *The Nativity*, (Kress) at Columbia Museum of Art, Columbia, South Carolina, originally in the Abdy Collection and bought by Duveen's in 1937; sold to Kress in 1946. In (undated) opinion Berenson gave to Botticelli. In 1963 posthumous Lists, to his Studio. Now: Attributed to Botticelli.

23) *Madonna and Child*, (Kress) at the El Paso Museum of Art, El Paso, Texas, came into Duveen's hands in the 1930s and exhibited in their 1941 show as by Botticelli. Berenson gave to Botticelli in (undated) opinion but later (1955) doubted the attribution. Now: Attributed to Botticelli.

24) *Madonna and Child with Saints*, (#538) National Gallery (Kress), bought from Duveen's as by Giovanni Bellini and exhibited as such in the Duveen Galleries, New York, 1924. Berenson, Lists of 1932 and 1936: A late work of Bellini. Subsequently bought for the Kress Collection and Berenson, 1957, gave to Bellini and Assistant. Now: Bellini and Assistants.

25) *St. John the Baptist*, (#402) National Gallery (Kress). Duveen bought early in the 1930s and sold to Kress in 1938 with an attribution from Berenson to Simone Martini. Exhibited at the Duveen exhibition of 1941 as by Martini. Now given to Martini's follower, Lippo Memmi.

26) *The Annunciation*, at the University of Notre Dame Study Collection, Notre Dame, Indiana, sold to Kress by Wildenstein in 1942 as by Alesso Baldovinetti. Painting discovered to have been repainted in the manner of Baldovinetti. Now: Style of Alesso Baldovinetti.

27) *Venetian Girl*, (#403) National Gallery (Kress), sold by Duveen's as by Titian and exhibited, under the name of *Giulia di Gonzaga-Colonna* in the Duveen show of 1941, as a Titian. Berenson, 1957 Lists: Titian. Now: Attributed to Titian. Not on view.

28) *Madonna and Child Enthroned with Saints*, now at the Rockhill Nelson Gallery of Art, Kansas City, Missouri (Kress), sold by Duveen's to Henry Goldman of New York, then to Kress, as by Bernardo Daddi. Berenson, 1963, gave to Daddi. Now: Bernardo Daddi and Assistants.

29) *Madonna of Humility*, (#7) National Gallery (Mellon). Berenson announced in articles, 1929 and 1930, that he had found a new Masaccio. Despite his enthusiasm, the work did not sell. Was heavily restored while at Duveen's and sold to Mellon in 1937 as by Masaccio. Repainting has been removed. When seen by author in March 1977, work was in a ruined state and, according to curator David Brown, is no longer considered to be by Masaccio.

30) *Christ Between St. Peter and St. James*, (#2) National Gallery (Mellon). Sold to Carl W. Hamilton by Duveen's as a Cimabue and published by Berenson in 1920, 1932, and 1936 as by Cimabue. Now: Attributed to Cimabue.

31) *Profile Portrait of a Lady*, (#23) National Gallery (Mellon). For sale in Paris in 1922 with the De Villeroy Collection and the young dealer, Germain Seligman, went to see it. Painting then labeled as by an unknown artist of the Italian fifteenth century. Seligman begged to buy it but his father adamantly refused. (G. Seligman, *Merchants of Art*, 1890–1960, Appleton-Century-Crofts, Inc., 1966.) Painting bought by Duveen's and sold to Clarence Mackay as a Pisanello. Berenson published as a Pisanello. Painting bought back by Duveen who sold to Mellon in 1937 as a Pisanello. Some years later the critic Max Friedlander suggested that the painting was not Italian at all. Berenson agreed and the National Gallery began inquiries leading to its present attribution: Franco-Flemish, early fifteenth century.

32) *Flight into Egypt*, (#28) National Gallery (Mellon). Sold through Sulley to Otto Kahn in 1927 with assurance from Berenson that the work an autograph Bellini, and subsequently bought by Mellon, 1937, as by Bellini. Berenson, 1932 and 1936, published as Bellini. Painting a reject from the Berlin Museums and largely repainted by Luigi Grassi (according to Sir Ellis Waterhouse). Now attributed: Carpaccio.

33) A profile portrait of *Cardinal Pietro Bimbo*, acquired by Wildenstein in 1952 and sold to the Putnam Foundation in 1955 as by Titian. Berenson published, 1957, as Titian. Painting left the Putnam Foundation in 1965 and present whereabouts unknown. Wethey says there are several copies of the same portrait and this one (X-11) definitely not a Titian.

34) *The Coronation of the Virgin*, (#49.7.4) Metropolitan Museum of Art. Bought by Duveen in 1927 and sold to Bache in 1928 as a Botticelli. Berenson, unpublished opinion, 1927, Botticelli; Lists, 1932 and 1936: Botticelli. Came to the Met after Bache's death in 1944 and now given to: Follower of Botticelli.

35) *Young Man* by Titian at the Norton Simon Museum of Art. Sold to Bache by Duveen in 1931 as a Giorgione and listed, Berenson, 1957 as a Giorgione. Bought back by Duveen's and subsequently came to Norton Simon Museum (1964). The expert on Giorgione, Pignatti, considers the painting to be in the style of Titian and the expert on Titian, Wethey, to be by a "Giorgionesque Painter." Both agree that it is not an autograph work by either painter.

36) *The Adoration of the Child*, bought by Duveen's, 1930, from the Gustave Dreyfus Collection (Paris) and sold to Edward D. Libbey, Toledo, Ohio, as a Filippino Lippi. Subsequently given to the Toledo Museum of Art and Berenson, letter, 1950, suggested the name of Raffaello Botticini. Now: Italian, Florentine School.

37) *The Resurrection*. When owned by Sir Joseph Duveen, painting exhibited as by Andrea del Castagno under the authority of Berenson in the 1930 Exhibition of Italian Art at the Royal Academy. Subsequently bought in 1939 and now at the Frick Collection, New York, as: Attributed to Andrea del Castagno.

38) *Portrait of N. Priuli*, now called *Portrait of a Venetian Procurator*, acquired by Duveen's sometime before 1923 and subsequently bought for the Frick Collection. Published in *Duveen Pictures in Public Collections*, 1941, as by Tintoretto and quoting Berenson to this effect. Now labeled: Circle of Tintoretto.

39) *Crucifixion* on loan to the Art Museum of Princeton University from the Frick Collection, discovered by Berenson who persuaded Duveen Brothers to buy the painting as a Piero della Francesca in 1915. Subsequently bought by Carl W. Hamilton who sold the painting in 1929 to John D. Rockefeller for $375,000 as a Piero della Francesca. Rockefeller bequeathed it to the Frick Collection, but it was never shown. Opinion of Sir Ellis Waterhouse that the work is by Francesca's studio. Present attribution: Workshop of Piero della Francesca.

40) In May 1928 Duveen bought, at a Berlin auction, a *Portrait of Giuliano de' Medici* from the Oscar Huldschinsky Collection. (Crowe and Cavalcaselle gave the conception of the painting to Raphael but not the execution.) Painting exported from Germany under a government permit ruling that the work was not by Raphael. Duveen sold to Bache as a Raphael, and Berenson, 1932 Lists, gave to Raphael. Subsequently entered the Metropolitan, and Keith Christiansen, assistant curator, Department of European Paintings, says, "The Giuliano de' Medici from the Bache Collection (#49.7.12) appears, from examination of X

rays, to be a contemporary copy after Raphael's lost original." (Letter to author, May 31, 1978.) Listed as: Contemporary copy after Raphael.

41) *Madonna and Child with Infant St. John* at the University of Miami, Coral Gables, Florida, bought by Duveen's in the Benson Collection, 1927, and shown by Duveen's, New York, in "Sixteenth Loan Exhibition of Italian Paintings" 1933 as by Andrea del Sarto; sold to Kress by Duveen in 1937. Now listed: Follower of Andrea del Sarto.

Category D:

Three instances in which Berenson made a verbal change of opinion:

1) When Berenson first saw the portrait of *La Belle Ferronière* in the Louvre, he wrote that he would regret to have to accept it as a work of Leonardo (1907). However, in 1929, Berenson was one of the main witnesses for Duveen in a trial to determine whether the Louvre Leonardo or an identical painting owned by Mrs. Andrée Hahn was the genuine Leonardo. Berenson: The Louvre.

2) With an almost unanimous group of critics, Berenson attributed *The Adoration of the Magi*, (#1085) National Gallery of Art (Kress), to Fra Filippo Lippi and listed it as such in 1909 and 1932 when in the Cook Collection at Richmond. In 1932, *Bollettino d'Arte*, Berenson advanced the idea that the work had been designed and partly painted by Fra Angelico, but had rejected this idea by the time the painting was offered for sale to the National Gallery after World War II. The then-director, John Walker, persuaded Berenson to amend his opinion and say that the work was partly painted by Fra Angelico so that Kress, the benefactor, would pay the high price asked. Now given to: Fra Angelico and Fra Filippo Lippi.

3) Nicky Mariano, Berenson's secretary, reported in her own memoir that, on a trip to Berlin just after World War I, Berenson indignantly refused to authenticate paintings for Duveen at the request of Edward Fowles, since he had not seen them. In his own memoir Fowles claims that Berenson did indeed give the necessary authentication and that Miss Mariano was present.

Reference Sources for Chapter 12 and Appendix:

Catalogue of Italian Paintings, John G. Johnson Collection, George H. Buchanan Co., Philadelphia, 1966.

Catalogue of European Paintings, in preparation, Toledo Museum of Art, Toledo, Ohio.

The Frick Collection, Volume II, Princeton University Press, Princeton, N.J., 1968.

Italian Paintings in the Walters Art Gallery, by Federico Zeri, two volumes, published by the Trustees, Baltimore, 1976.

Paintings from the Kress Collection, by Fern Rusk Shapley, three volumes, published in 1966, 1968, and 1973 by Phaidon Press, London.

Catalogue of Italian Paintings in the Metropolitan Museum, Florentine School, by Federico Zeri, New York, 1971.

Catalogue of Italian Paintings in the Metropolitan Museum, Venetian School, by Federico Zeri, New York, 1973.

Census of Pre-19th Century Italian Paintings in N. American Public Collections, by Federico Zeri and Burton B. Fredericksen, Harvard University Press, Cambridge, Mass., 1972.

Duveen Pictures in Public Collections of America, William Bradford Press, New York, 1941.

Giorgione, by Terisio Pignatti, Phaidon, London, 1971.

All the Paintings of Raphael, by Ettore Camesasca, Hawthorn Books, New York, 1963.

The Paintings of Titian, by Harold Wethey, two volumes, Phaidon Press, London, 1969.

Berenson Works:

1894 and 1906, *Venetian Painters of the Renaissance*, New York and London, G. P. Putnam's.

1895, *Lorenzo Lotto*, New York and London, G. P. Putnam's.

1896 and 1909, *Florentine Painters of the Renaissance*, New York and London, G. P. Putnam's.

1897 and 1909, *Central Italian Painters of the Renaissance*, New York and London, G. P. Putnam's.

1901 and 1902, first and second series of *Study and Criticism of Italian Art*, London, George Bell and Sons.

1903, *Drawings of the Florentine Painters*, London, John Murray.

1907, *North Italian Painters of the Renaissance*, New York and London, G. P. Putnam's.

1916, *Venetian Painting in America*, London, George Bell and Sons.

1932, *Italian Pictures of the Renaissance*, Oxford, The Clarendon Press.

1936, French edition of *Italian Pictures of the Renaissance*, Paris, Gallimard.

1957 and 1963, revised editions of *Italian Pictures of the Renaissance*.

1926, *Three Essays in Method*, Oxford, The Clarendon Press.

1895, *Venetian Painting, Chiefly before Titian, at the Exhibition of Venetian Art, the New Gallery*, reprinted in the *Study and Criticism of Italian Art*, 1901.

NOTES

ABBREVIATIONS USED IN THE NOTES:

APW   *Another Part of the Wood* by Kenneth Clark, John Murray, London, 1974.

AQG   *A Quaker Grandmother* by Ray Strachey, Fleming H. Revell Company, New York and London, 1914.

Archives   Letters deposited in the Archives of American Art, The Smithsonian Institution, Washington, D.C.

ARR   *A Religious Rebel, The Letters of "H.W.S.,"* edited by Logan Pearsall Smith, Nisbet & Co. Ltd., London, 1949.

BBT   *The Bernard Berenson Treasury*, selected and edited by Hanna Kiel, Simon & Schuster, New York, 1962.

BY   Letters deposited in the Beinecke Rare Book and Manuscript Library, Yale University, New Haven, Conn.

CB   *Conversations with Berenson* by Umberto Morra, Houghton Mifflin Co., Boston, 1965.

CC   Letters deposited in Colby College Library, Waterville, Maine.

Clark lecture   "Berenson," lecture by Kenneth Clark at Cambridge University, 1966.

FYB   *Forty Years with Berenson* by Nicky Mariano, Hamish Hamilton Ltd., London, 1966.

HA   Letters deposited in Harvard University Archives, Cambridge, Mass.

HHU   Letters deposited at Houghton Library, Harvard University, Cambridge, Mass.

KC   Letters deposited at King's College Library, Cambridge, England.

LPS Diary   Unpublished diaries of Logan Pearsall Smith on deposit at Kent State University, Kent, Ohio.

MDB   *Memories of Duveen Brothers* by Edward Fowles, Times Books, London, 1976.

PS   *The Passionate Sightseer* by Bernard Berenson, Thames and Hudson, London, 1960.

Collection BBP   Family letters in the possession of Bernard Berenson Perry.

NOTES

Collection RBP Family letters in the possession of Ralph Barton Perry, Jr.

R & R *Rumor and Reflection* by Bernard Berenson, Simon & Schuster, New York, 1952.

S & T *Sunset and Twilight* by Bernard Berenson, Harcourt, Brace & World, Inc., New York, 1963.

SL *The Selected Letters of Bernard Berenson*, edited by A. K. McComb, Houghton Mifflin Co., Boston, 1964.

SP *Sketch for a Self-Portrait* by Bernard Berenson, Constable Publishers, London, 1949.

Sprigge *Berenson* by Sylvia Sprigge, George Allen & Unwin Ltd., London, 1960.

VP *The Venetian Painters of the Renaissance*, G. P. Putnam's Sons, New York and London, 1895.

YUL Letters deposited in the Yale University Library, New Haven, Conn.

Page   *Chapter 1: High Walls*

2 "... feed on the shadows of perfection": "Altamura" by Logan Pearsall Smith, *Reperusals and Re-Collections* (London: Constable & Co., 1936), p. 84

3 living life "as a hard, gemlike flame": Sidney Alexander, *The Reporter Magazine*, September 1, 1960, p. 41

3 compared with Titian and Michelangelo: Francis Henry Taylor, "To Bernard Berenson on His 90th Birthday," *The Atlantic Magazine*, July 1955, p. 30.

4 "will kill me yet": Judith Friedberg, *The Reporter Magazine*, September 22, 1955, p. 43.

4 visit to "i Tatti" described: Alan Moorehead, *A Late Education* (New York: Harper and Row, 1970), pp. 150–51.

4 "the necessity ... the happiness of my life": S & T, p. 237

6 "the masculinity of the little jockey": Elizabeth Hardwick, *A View of My Own* (New York: Farrar, Straus & Cudahy, 1962), p. 204.

7 Berenson's manner of speaking described: Cyril Ray, *The Sunday Times* (London), August 22, 1954.

7 Berenson's game of conversation: Ibid.

7 "'... thought for the future'": *Encounter Magazine* (London), January 1960, pp. 62–63.

7–8 "someone to crank me up": Professor Ulrich Middledorf.

8 "... most brilliant strokes...": *Self-Portrait with Donors* (Boston: Little, Brown & Co., 1974), p. 87.

Page

8 "... seldom harmonious ...": APW, p. 152

8 "... long enough to be spoken": Clark lecture.

9 sharpening faculties: Introductions to S & T by Iris Origo, p. xii.

9 "... cemented our friendship ...": *Self-Portrait with Donors*, p. 83.

10 personal animosities: in *A View of My Own*, p. 212.

10 "... animal competitiveness": Introduction to S & T, p. xvi.

10 "stay afloat": *A Late Education*, p. 150.

11 "enough brains to feel fascinated": SP, p. 14.

11 "every day more dependent ...": S & T, p. 287.

12 "... I could bed with many ..." Ibid., pp. 432–33.

13 "... speechless with delight": APW, p. 154.

13 "... landscape in terms of art": BBC-TV program, "Bernard Berenson," 1971.

13 accusation is not valid: *The Letters of George Santayana*, ed. Daniel Cory (London: Constable, 1955), p. 342.

13 only guest at a banquet: Berenson to Frances Francis, November 15, 1955.

14 *Time* magazine, that the sale of his books made him wealthy: April 25, 1955, p. 80.

14 his books earned barely £100 a year: Mary Berenson, letter to Senda Berenson, August 3, 1902.

15 income estimated at $100,000 a year: William Mostyn-Owen.

15 "... 'I accept—for the sake of the library' ...": Cyril Connolly, "Love of Art and Love of Money," *The Sunday Times* (London), March 20, 1960, p. 17.

15 "... chose to be Mephistopheles": S. N. Behrman, *People in a Diary* (Boston: Little, Brown & Co., 1972), p. 274.

16 the art world was a jungle: letter, Berenson to Frances Francis, April 30, 1952.

16 we have touched pitch and been defiled: letter, Berenson to Frances Francis, September 18, 1951.

16 the question dream: S & T, p. 420.

16 "Yet who is the real *I* ..." Ibid., p. 160.

Chapter 2: Beyond the Pale

18 "ragged kingdom of the spirit": Irving Howe, *World of Our Fathers* (New York: Harcourt Brace Jovanovich, 1976), p. 8.

18 ". . . began life in the Middle Ages": Mary Antin, *The Promised Land* (Boston: Houghton Mifflin Co., 1969), p. xxi.

19 spelling of Bernard as Bernhard: Berenson changed the spelling during World War I.

19 information about his birthplace contained in a letter from Berenson to his brother-in-law Ralph Barton Perry. Berenson also sometimes said that he came from Vilna, the large town nearby, and from Dowig (Doig, Davgi), the town near Butrimants where his father was born. If not technically born in Butrimants, he went to live there at an early age. The village is so variously spelled that I have limited myself to those versions given in the *Encyclopedia Judaica* and have used Berenson's own version of the name.

19 his family name was actually Valvrojenski: Mary Berenson. His parents' names: Bernard Berenson.

20 by then, it is often too late: "I had no interest in the family history when I was young. Now I am curious, but I can't go back to the pale": Elizabeth Berenson Gates.

20 Eudice is related to Isaiah Hurwitz: from a family tree of the Hurwitz family compiled by David Lyon Hurwitz.

20 a boy might be told about his mother's family and not his father's: Ruth Landes and Mark Zborowski, "Hypotheses Concerning the East European Family," in *Psychodynamics of American Jewish Life*, ed. Norman Kiell (New York: Twayne Publishers, 1967).

20 ". . . anybody's social equal . . .": SP, p. 44.

20 unpublished memoir of Bella Wolfson: this manuscript was provided by his son, David Lyon Hurwitz.

23 close emotional ties: "Hypotheses Concerning the East European Family."

23 ". . . warmth, intimacy, food . . .": Ibid.

23 "looming figure . . .": *World of Our Fathers*, p. 174.

23 Eudice's height: about 5 feet 1 inch tall.

25 ". . . as old as Methusaleh . . .": letter to author, December 11, 1976.

25 ". . . the bold enquirer . . .": Henry Hurwitz.

25 ". . . a corner-cutting type . . .": Leo Rosten, *The Joys of Yiddish*, (New York: McGraw-Hill, 1968), p. 209.

Notes

25   an authority on the life of Jesus: Elizabeth Berenson Gates.

25   a follower of Swedenborg: Ruth Berenson Muhlen.

26   Shmarya Levin's memoirs: *Forward from Exile*, trans. and ed. Maurice Samuel (Philadelphia: The Jewish Publication Society of America, 1967).

26   "... a little schnapps too": memoir of Bella Wolfson.

26   poorer than the average Russian peasant: Salo W. Baron, *The Russian Jew Under the Tsars and Soviets* (New York: Macmillan & Co., 1960), p. 114.

26   "So poverty stood ...": *Forward from Exile*, p. 78.

26   "... too much the young girl ...": R & R, p. 28.

27   on his right shoulder: Ibid.

27   "... pity and tenderness": Ibid.

27   "the scheme of universal history ...": S & T, p. 468.

27   "the Russian mounted cavalry band": Ibid., p. 388.

27   "... drilling and parading": R & R, p. 118.

27   "... tiptoed around him": Bernard Perry.

27   center of the universe: CB, p. 67.

28   "... should be a saint": SP, p. 123.

28   "... odour of violets": S & T, p. 425.

28   autobiography by Serge Aksakoff: *Years of Childhood* (New York: Longmans, Green & Co., 1916).

28–29   "... the very air trembled": Ibid., p. 122.

29   "... It and I were one": SP, p. 21.

30   sound of the samovar: Mascia Predit.

30   "Ringing silence ...": CB, p. 275.

30–31   "... carried all the way": *Forward from Exile*, p. 45.

31   grew up at the age of seven: Sprigge, p. 26.

31   7,500 Jews left the Pale: *The Russian Jews under the Tsars and Soviets*.

32   "as one accepts the weather": *The Promised Land*, p. 5.

32   "a despairing sense of helplessness": SP, p. 49.

32   "drunken Cossacks ...": Judith Friedberg and Barton Perry.

33   "a long pilgrimage": SP, p. 122

33   "... feverish with excitement": PS, p. 94.

33   "... fun of going on and on": SP, p. 43, and Iris Origo,

Page

"The Long Pilgrimage," *Cornhill Magazine* (London), Spring 1960, p. 141.

Chapter 3: The Avenging Angel

34 Information about family departure from Berenson. Louis, the orphaned son of Albert's sister: letter, Lawrence Berenson to David Hurwood, June 17, 1968. Louis's name may have been Koussevitsky: Ruth Berenson Muhlen, James Berenson, Elizabeth Berenson Gates.

34 Boston an accidental choice: Sprigge, p. 21.

34 passports refused to emigrés: Salo W. Baron, *The Russian Jew Under the Tsars and Soviets* (New York: Macmillan & Co., 1960), p .58.

35 information on Boston Jews from the late Walter Muir Whitehill, Boston archivist and historian.

36–37 conditions in the Fort Hill area described by Oscar Handlin in *Boston's Immigrants*, (Cambridge: Harvard University Press, Belknap Press, 1959).

37 ". . . fleecing their Gentile neighbors . . .": Bernhard Berenson, "Contemporary Jewish Fiction," *Andover Review*, July–December, 1888, reprinted in *Yiddish* magazine, Vol. 2, No. 1, Fall 1975, p. 16.

37–38 ". . . shone glorious in our eyes": Mary Antin, *The Promised Land* (Boston: Houghton Mifflin Co., 1969), pp. 183–84.

38 first 32 Nashua Street and then 11 Minot Street: Sprigge.

38 precise information on the Minot Street area: Walter Muir Whitehill.

40 ". . . in front of this stove": Berenson, "The Death and Burial of Israel Koppel," *The Harvard Monthly*, July 1888, p. 178.

40 prices at Faneuil Hall: Boston *Evening Transcript*, January 3, 1875.

40 recipe for beef brisket: Harriet Perry.

41 ". . . studying Virgil": Irving Howe, *World of Our Fathers* (New York: Harcourt Brace Jovanovich, 1976), p. 171.

41 forage for manure: Berenson, letter to W. M. Ivins, June 11, 1948, Archives.

42 traveling fellowship application quoted: *Looking at Pictures with Bernard Berenson*, selected by Hanna Kiel (New York: Harry N. Abrams, 1974), pp. 21–27.

Page

42   anguish, and despair: "How Matthew Arnold Impressed Me," *The Harvard Monthly*, November 1887, p. 54.

42   named all the peddlers Berenson: Ruth Berenson Muhlen.

43   tea from a brass samovar: *Their Exits and Their Entrances*.

43   ". . . as cranky as 'ell . . .": letter, Abie Berenson to Senda Berenson Abbott, December 27, 1927, Collection RBP.

43–44   ". . . her children's love . . .": Rachel Perry, undated letter to Senda Berenson Abbott, circa 1927, Collection RBP.

44   ". . . *sotto voce*": Sprigge, p. 31.

44   "Sympathetic and consoling words . . .": Rachel Berenson to Senda Berenson, October 19, 1896, Collection RBP.

45   ". . . hubris of the Greeks": CB, p. 73.

45   ". . . all my fault . . .": Ibid., p. 42.

46   ". . . knowledge plus morality . . .": Leo Rosten *The Joys of Yiddish* (New York: McGraw-Hill, 1968), p. 86.

46   ". . . missed her day and night . . .": SP, p. 106.

47   ". . . temple of Ramses": Ibid.

47   ". . . hard to accept": Ibid.

47   ". . . terrible punishments": Ibid.

47   "It was unwise to think . . .": SP, p. 107.

47   ". . . brimstone of hell": Ibid., p. 117.

48   ". . . Hell disdains": BBT, p. 57.

48   "squalor and sordidness . . .": SP, p. 45.

48   "I had ears . . .": *The Apostate of Chego-Chegg*, 1899, as quoted in *The Promised City* by Moses Rischin (New York: Corinth Books, 1964), p. 144.

49   ignore Jewish customs: There is no evidence that Berenson attended services or was ever bar mitzvahed.

49   baptized at the age of fifteen: *Looking at Pictures with Bernard Berenson*, p. 43.

49   baptized by Phillips Brooks: Sprigge, p. 31.

49   ". . . European civilization": *The Joys of Yiddish*, p. 130.

49   ". . . scientific hypotheses": Berenson, "The Third Category," *The Harvard Monthly*, November 1886, p. 77.

49   ". . . than the Himalayas . . .": Ibid.

50–52   " 'Despising shalt thou be despised . . .' ": this and following quotations from "The Death and Burial of Israel Koppel," pp. 177–94.

NOTES

52 "... ritual-theological casuistry": Moses Mendelssohn, founder of the Haskalah movement.

52 " '... deserves to die' ": Jerome and Jean Tharaud, *L'Ombre de la Croix* (Paris: Librairie Plon, 1920), p. 142.

52 "... privately or in print": Sprigge, p. 31.

53 "... viewpoint of Goethe ...": *Listening with the Third Ear*, (New York: Farrar Straus & Co., 1949), p. 67.

53 "... not wanting to be oneself": Soren Kierkegaard.

Chapter 4: A True Gentleman

54 "... gone before": S & T, p. 308.

55 "... I'll marry a Christian ...": *Their Exits and Their Entrances*.

55 "I never would have ventured ...": Rachel to Senda, August 10, 1903, Collection RBP.

55 "I've read considerable ...": Abie to Senda, summer 1900, Collection RBP.

56 "was acutely painful ...": *Their Exits and Their Entrances*.

56 "... served up and rejected ...": *The House of Mirth* (New York: Charles Scribner's Sons, 1905), p. 16.

57 "... the puzzling character ...": Bernard Berenson "Contemporary Jewish Fiction," *Andover Review* July–December, 1888, reprinted in *Yiddish* magazine, Vol. 2, No. 1, Fall 1975, p. 15.

57 "... a ghetto Jew": Samuel Eliot Morison, *Three Centuries of Harvard* (Cambridge: Harvard University Press, 1946).

58 "... expected and imposed upon them": George Santayana, *Persons and Places* (New York: Charles Scribner's Sons, 1944), p. 154.

59 letter from Berenson to Lindsay, June 29, 1885, at "i Tatti."

59 letter from Berenson to Norton, December 23, 1886, HHU.

59 first Berenson letter to Perry, June 17, 1887, HHU.

59 second Berenson letter to Perry, December 3, 1925, CC.

61 "with radiant vividness": S & T, p. 315.

61 "... arm in arm": Senda to her family, June 1900, Collection BBP.

61 "... clever and original": *Isabella Stewart Gardner and Fenway Court* (Boston: I. S. Gardner Museum, 1925), p. 52.

Page

61   "Pandora's box . . .": SP, p. 45.

62   ". . . decorous system": CB, p. 74.

62   ". . . messy situations": Ibid., p. 167.

62–63   "ample time . . .": S & T, p. 458.

63   ". . . their own appearance": CB, p. 49.

63   "double dose" of Hebraism: SP, p. 28.

63   ". . . Lithuanian ghetto": S & T, p. 219.

63   ". . . more beautiful intrinsically . . .": R & R, p. 97.

63   ". . . a true gentleman": CB, p. 42.

64   ". . . history of culture": BBT, p. 39.

64   only worthwhile aim: Ibid., p. 43.

64   ". . . the whole, the beautiful": Ibid., p. 42.

64   He could speak German, Hebrew, and Yiddish: Berenson's application for a Parker Traveling Fellowship.

64   ". . . innermost heart": "How Matthew Arnold Impressed Me," *The Harvard Monthly*, November 1887, p. 54.

65   "I was not a creature apart . . .": Ibid.

65   ". . . epics of despair . . .": letter to Mary Costelloe, October 6, 1890; BBT, p. 37.

65   ". . . perhaps with Satan . . .": Ibid., p. 36.

66   ". . . the dramatic element . . .": Ibid., p. 60.

66   ". . . botannical experiments": Introduction by W. H. Auden and Elizabeth Mayer to Goethe, *Italian Journey* (New York: Schocken Books, 1968).

66   ". . . a new Goethe in short": SP, p. 51.

66   average freshman well prepared: *Three Centuries of Harvard*, p. 389.

66   "the best teacher of languages . . .": SP, p. 82.

67   Mount Auburn Street: Robert Nathan, *Peter Kindred* (New York, 1919), as reprinted in *The Harvard Book*, ed. William Bentinck-Smith (Cambridge: Harvard University Press, 1953).

67   ". . . the better of it": S & T, p. 465.

67   eschew originality": *Three Centuries of Harvard*, p. 422.

67   ". . . Harvard as I knew it": *Unforgotten Years* (Boston: Little, Brown & Co., 1939), pp. 115–16.

68   ". . . essence of literature": CB, p. 183.

NOTES

68 ". . . in a certain sense delusive": Ibid., p. 116.

69 " '. . . more ambition than ability' . . .": SP, pp. 44–45.

69 reading Dante aloud: told to Francis Henry Taylor, "The Summons of Art," *The Atlantic Monthly*, November 1957, p. 124.

69 "historical and illustrative": S & T, p. 526.

70 ". . . a single choice flower . . .": this and following quotations from *Marius the Epicurean*, Vol. I (London: Macmillan & Co., 1925), p. 33ff.

70 beautiful criticism: letter to Mrs. Gardner, July 4, 1888, Archives.

70 ". . . the funny feeling. . . .": Ronald W. Clark, *The Life of Bertrand Russell* (New York: Knopf 1976), p. 60.

70–71 ". . . wholesome and sweet . . .": SP, p. 129.

71 ". . . what was in me": Ibid, p. 46.

71 "against my will . . .": S & T, p. 526.

Chapter 5: A Painter's Eye

72 "Few men sleep less . . .": Sprigge, p. 59.

73 ". . . I feel myself weakest": Ibid., p. 60.

73 rescued by friends: *Self-Portrait with Donors* (Boston: Little, Brown & Co., 1974), p. 89.

73 "thirst for existence . . .": *Marcus the Epicurean*, Vol. I (London: Macmillan & Co., 1925) p. 157.

74 Senda on the benefits of exercise: Edith Naomi Hill, "Senda Berenson," *Research Quarterly*, October 1941; and Agnes C. R. Stillman, "Senda Berenson Abbott," Smith College, 1971.

74 Senda's first letter: at "i Tatti."

74 written the day after Berenson sailed: June 18, 1887. Dated from a letter to T. S. Perry, HHU.

74 Two days before that: June 17, 1887.

74 When Berenson wrote again: on August 24, 1887. From Berenson to Mrs. Gardner, Archives.

74 Montparnasse in those days: described in Logan Pearsall Smith, *Unforgotten Years* (Boston: Little, Brown & Co., 1939), p. 206.

Page

74   "... hide and seek within me": letter dated August 24, 1887. SL, p 1.

75   His second letter: dated September 30, 1887.

75   went to see *La Goseau*: December 11, 1887.

76   the National Gallery a revelation: letter of January 27, 1888.

76   brutes or fiendish rakes: letter of Professor Lindsay, March 14, 1886.

84–85   living aimlessly: January 27, 1888, and February 25, 1888.

85   visit to Ghent and Bruges described: letter of March 18, 1888.

85   The Venetians were incomparable: letter, April 19, 1888.

85   "... I could not resist mass emotion": R & R, pp. 356–57.

86   "... a nearness of relationship ...": May 23, 1888. Quoted, Sprigge, p. 88.

86   "... selling old clothes": quoted by Michael Fixler in "Bernard Berenson of Butremanz," *Yiddish* magazine, vol. 2, no. 1, Fall 1975, p. 34.

87   life lived more completely: letter, September 12, 1888.

87   "something apart, sacred almost": S & T, p. 84.

87   "... to caress with my eyes": S & T, p. 135.

87   "... act of aesthetic purity": CB, p. 210.

87   "... ripened spirit of the Renaissance": VP, p. 29.

87   "pictorial poetry": Walter Pater, *The Renaissance* (Glasgow: Fontana/Collins, 1961), p. 140.

88   "... a pure mysticism": CB, pp. 68–69.

89   intoxicated by a papyrus stalk: letter to Mrs. Gardner, November 28, 1888.

88   "like the satisfaction of a vow": BBT, p. 343.

88   "... to wander, absorb and dream": APW, p. 135.

89   hard-boiled, real world: SP, p. 45.

89   "... one compendious philosophy": Clark lecture.

89   "and Frank was ... an Italian": R & R, p. 157.

89   Everything Greek fascinated him: SP, pp. 83–84.

89   "a student of Greek letters ...": Ibid.

89   "... all the circumstances of death": *The Renaissance*, p. 108.

90   not one drawing authentic: Clark lecture.

NOTES

Page

90 influenced by Morelli's books most of all: letter, Berenson to Kenneth Clark, July 22, 1929.

90 definition of connoisseurship: *The Rudiments of Connoisseurship* (New York: Schocken Books, 1962), p. 113.

91 ". . . the work of art is the event": Ibid., p. 120.

92 visits to the surrounding countryside: described to Frances Francis, in the *Journals of Frances Francis*, April 14, 1949.

93 "I was in Florence for the first time . . .": CB, pp. 92–93.

93 " '. . . I will help you' ": George Santayana, *Persons and Places* (New York: Charles Scribner's Sons, 1944), p. 226.

93 "a friend has quite surprised me . . .": quoted in *Annual Report* (1972), Fenway Court.

94 "the opinion you must have had . . .": quoted in *Self-Portrait with Donors*, p. 90; and Louise Hall Tharp, *Mrs. Jack* (Boston: Little, Brown & Co., 1965), p. 176.

94 ". . . She is like an Indian . . .": *Reminiscences of Morris Carter*, printed at Industrial School for Crippled Children, Boston, 1964, p. 22.

Chapter 6: Enter Mary

95 "moment of perfect liberty": CB, p. 162.

95 the kind girls fell in love with: *Their Exits and Their Entrances*.

96 his yearning was idealistic: SP, p. 23.

96–97 "The Third Category": *The Harvard Monthly*, November 1886.

98 "suspiciousness, obsessive scrupulosity . . .": Erik Erikson, *Young Man Luther* (New York: W. W. Norton & Co., 1958), p. 61.

98 "the animal in me": S & T, p. 96.

98 ". . . disgust with everything that comes out of my body . . .": Ibid., p. 192.

98 the "not-lady" class: Ibid., p. 244.

99 ". . . occasion to fear for his sanity": Robert Gathorne-Hardy, *Recollections of Logan Pearsall Smith* (London: Constable, 1949), p. 27.

99 too gentlemanly to spit it out: Hannah Whitall Smith to her

Page

daughters, September 22, 1899, Collection of Jonathan Gathorne-Hardy.

99 "... a strain of insanity in all of them": *Ottoline at Garsington*, ed. Robert Gathorne-Hardy (New York: Knopf, 1975), p. 265.

99 "... tucked under their belts": memoir by Robert Gathorne-Hardy in ARR, p. xiii.

99 "race and romp and screech ...": Ibid.

99 "... young people *must* know better ...": AQG, p. 14.

99 hated a practical joke: Ibid., pp. 26–27.

100 "... salvation in the conviction of sin": Logan Pearsall Smith, *Unforgotten Years* (Boston: Little, Brown & Co., 1939), p. 34.

100 "... *could not* whip him any more ...": ARR, p. 8.

100 "... never ... the slightest twinge of conscience ...": *Unforgotten Years*, p. 40.

101 "A more sensitive ... man never lived": ARR, p. 30.

101 "it would burn your spirits up": quoted, Robert Gathorne-Hardy, draft of *Memoir*, p. 20.

101 "Don't be too unselfish": ARR, p. xxii.

101 "men are brutes and fools": *The Autobiography of Bertrand Russell, 1872–1914* (Boston: Atlantic Monthly Press, Little, Brown & Co., c. 1951), p. 224.

102 "... amid fits of laughter": Ibid.

102 "There was some trouble ...": Horace Traubel, *Walt Whitman in Camden*, vol. 4 (Philadelphia: University of Pennsylvania Press, 1953), pp. 53–54.

102 "tall ... and always smiling": quoted in John Russell, *A Portrait of Logan Pearsall Smith* (London: Dropmore Press, 1950), p. 7.

103 "One must not do ...": AQG, p. 26.

103 a waste of time to be "offended ...": Ibid., p. 28.

103 "'... thee coughed up that chair,'": ARR, p. 67.

104 "'... most notoriously immoral man who ever lived'": quoted, Robert Gathorne-Hardy, draft of *Memoir*, p. 62, note 1.

104 "... heroes shouted from afar": *Unforgotten Years*, pp. 110–11.

Page

104 "... the kingdom of Heaven down to earth ...": Ibid., p. 112.

105 "a high-flying courtship ...": Ibid., p. 113.

105 "furnished comfortably ...": letter, August 1891 from Dr. Richard Maurice Bucke to Walt Whitman, quoted in *The Letters of Dr. Richard Maurice Bucke to Walt Whitman*, ed. Artem Lozynsky (Detroit: Wayne State University Press, 1977), p. 244.

105 "strong reformers and liberals ...": letter, Mary Costelloe to Walt Whitman, January 25, 1889, from 40 Grosvenor Road, at the Library of Congress.

105 "into it heart and soul ...": Ibid.

106 "in low spirits": letter, Mary Costelloe to Walt Whitman, October 26, 1889, from Friday's Hill House, Haslemere, at the Library of Congress.

106 "My road has seemed so shut up ...": Ibid.

106 "Frank is an incurable Optimist ...": Mary Costelloe to Walt Whitman, January 25, 1889, from 40 Grosvenor Road, Library of Congress.

106 "very radical indeed": Horace Traubel, *Walt Whitman in Camden*, vol. 4 (Philadelphia: University of Pennsylvania Press, 1953), p. 188.

106 Mary's version told: Sprigge, pp. 102–104.

107 they all ordered photographs: Iris Origo, "The Long Pilgrimage," *Cornhill Magazine* (London), Spring 1960, p. 143.

107 "like a dry sponge ...": and "real values for me ...": and "... in which he hoped she would join him": Sprigge, pp. 102–104.

107 "It led to Mary Costelloe's falling in love with me": S & T, p. 168.

108 no very favorable first impression: Ibid., p. 169.

108 "... an unclaimed strip of the African coast": letter to Mary Costelloe, January 1892, quoted, SL, p. 12.

109 predicting great things for "Bertie": letter from Mary Costelloe to Robert and Hannah, November 11, 1894, Collection of Jonathan Gathorne-Hardy.

109 "She is at Verona ...": letter, September 14, 1891, *The Letters of Sidney and Beatrice Webb*, ed. Norman MacKenzie (Cambridge: Cambridge University Press, 1978), p. 297.

110 "... stronger than ever": September 13, 1891, Ibid., p. 295.

111 " 'One moment is enough . . .' ": Iris Origo, "The Long Pilgrimage," *Cornhill Magazine* (London), Spring 1960, p. 140.

111 "We must look and look . . .": Bernard Berenson, Preface to *The Italian Painters of the Renaissance* (London: The Phaidon Press, 1952), p. xiii.

112 "What a wonderful thing it is . . .": and ". . . I thought they would fall on me": quoted, "The Long Pilgrimage," p. 146.

112 ". . . pictures as . . . flowers": BBT, p. 35. "two unknown Giorgiones . . .": S & T, p. 65.

112 ". . . beautiful things are difficult": CB, p. 172.

113 ". . . so full of promise . . .": VP, p. 31.

113 ". . . kiss the stones in an Italian street": BBT, p. 35.

113 "I knew a Rome . . .": PS, p. 18.

113 two carabinieri on horseback: Ibid., p. 106.

113 ". . . spirit . . . so Mephistophelian . . .": BBT, p. 35.

114 ". . . fools of people generally": to Mary Costelloe from Berlin, October 5, 1890, BBT, p. 36.

114 wealth itself was corrupting: BBT, pp. 41–42.

114 ". . . every Cariani a Cariani": SP, p. 51.

114 ". . . dazzling hopes, shrunk": Ibid., p. 51.

114–15 ". . . the 'ultimate professorship' . . .": to Mary Costelloe from Venice, November 6, 1890, BBT, p. 45.

115 ". . . one exquisite and beautiful thing . . .": to Mary Costelloe from Venice, October 31, 1890, BBT, p. 43.

115 ". . . scarcely have any interest": Ibid., p. 38.

115 ". . . to earn my living": Ibid., p. 45.

115 "so wonderful, so delicate . . .": November 1890, quoted, APW, p. 136.

116 "I was far too Bostonian . . .": S & T, p. 261.

116 ". . . matured to manhood": SP, p. 66.

117 ". . . really 'mean business' . . .": to Mary Costelloe, February 3, 1891, from Perugia, SL, p. 31.

117 ". . . no feeling for the numinous . . .": R & R, p. 3.

117 ". . . deserted Italian city": LPS Diary 37, 1891–99, p. 09A.

118 ". . . a sort of Thélème": S & T, p. 74.

118 ". . . in a Bergamesque valley": PS, p. 44.

118 Lotto a poor choice: APW, p. 136.

NOTES

119 "The vaccination did not 'take' ": Sprigge, p. 110.

119 ". . . the fancied freedom": letter to Mary Costelloe, February 1, 1891, BBT, p. 57.

119 ". . . driving pigs and great oxen": LPS Diary 37, 1891–99, p. 92,

119 the game of "conosching": Lina Waterfield, *Castle in Italy* (London: John Murray, 1961), pp. 73–74,

120 ". . . naming those ancient paintings": "The Long Pilgrimage," p. 147.

120 ". . . ruined his stomach and temper . . .": Senda to her family from Ricti, Sunday, May 20, 1900, Collection BBP.

120 ". . . just going to kiss": "The Long Pilgrimage," pp. 146–47.

120 ". . . 'Oh, is that all!' . . .": SL, pp. 23–24.

121 ". . . may be by Jacopo de' Barbari": Ibid., p. 23.

121 ". . . skulked back to his kennel . . .": Ibid., p. 23.

121 "I can't get my feet warm . . .": Ibid., p. 17.

121 "thou precious darling": Ibid., p. 28.

121 ". . . a distant acquaintance": Ibid., p. 38.

121 "meet again to make it up . . .": "The Long Pilgrimage," p. 147.

122 ". . . less fond when they are away": SL, p. 21.

122 a ten-day idyll: from November 4–14, 1894.

122 ". . . making me talk about sexual morality . . .": Ronald W. Clark, *The Life of Bertrand Russell* (New York: Knopf, 1976), p. 55.

122 ". . . a meal in the woods": BBT, pp. 71–72.

122 ". . . flourish in the Millenium": Ibid., p. 42.

123 beauty more important than duty: Ibid.

123 philanthropy smacked of hypocrisy: letter to Mrs. Gardner, January 27, 1898.

123 gave other lectures in Paris: a letter from Charles Loeser to Miriam S. Thayer, 1895, HHU.

124 ". . . summons to intellectual instinct . . .": BBT, p. 59.

124 "a goat cropping . . .": SP, p. 92,

124 Edith Cooper "drew me out": S & T, p. 310.

124 "They knew few people . . .": Introduction by Sir William Rothenstein to *Works and Days, from the Journal of Michael*

Page

Field, ed. T. and D. C. Sturge Moore (London: John Murray, 1933).

125 "... Beaumont and Fletcher": SP, p. 72.

125 "... tell them I did": Ibid.

125 "All is not lost ...": Ibid.

125 a little house on Lord North Street: from M. A. de Wolfe Howe, *Barrett Wendell and His Letters* (Boston: Atlantic Monthly Press, 1924).

125–26 "We broke over Douglas ...": Journals of Frances Francis, April 5, 1951.

126 "... nothing but praise": S & T, p. 320.

126 "gave me a shock ...": Ibid. p. 497.

126 "I shouldn't have liked it": Journals of Frances Francis, April 5, 1951.

126 never approached him sexually: told to Frances Francis and Kenneth Clark.

126 "... picture was much restored": Clark lecture.

126 " '... we must have been in love' ...": Ibid.

127 "too professional ...": Sprigge, p. 113.

127 "Let us say Paolo Farinati": Clark lecture.

127 "... the few favourites": letter from Milan, January 19, 1890, in *The Nation*, New York.

128 "wielder of the photograph ...": letter to Ivins, November 19, 1951, Archives.

128 poor in Rome, PS, p. 26.

128 conducting tourists around the galleries: *Time* magazine, April 25, 1955, p. 80.

128 dabbling in the art market: SL, p. 19.

128–29 quotes from the diary of Emma B. Andrews: *A Journal on the Bedawin: 1899–1912: The Diary Kept on Board the Dahabiyeh of Theodore M. Davis During 17 Trips up the Nile*, on file in the Department of European Paintings, Metropolitan Museum of Art, New York.

129 "... if we shout loud enough": SL, p. 20.

130 the writer was misinformed: letter from Venice, October 4, 1892.

130 "... whose work he was reviewing": letter, January 31, 1893.

Page

130   dreaming of a book: letter to Mary Costelloe, quoted, BBT, p. 44.

130   ". . . in the Arno!": Mary Berenson to Kenneth Clark, October 29, 1928.

131   ". . . pleasure in each of the arts?": BBT, p. 89.

131   "they are more *painters* . . .": Ibid., p. 39.

131   "handsome, healthy . . .": VP, p. 14.

131   ". . . spirit of Japanese design . . .": Preface to VP, p. vii.

132   "and are often at variance . . .": Ibid., p. 79.

132   "No argument . . .": APW, p. 138.

133   "neither of a Lady . . .": "Venetian Painting Chiefly before Titian," reprinted in *The Sense of Quality* (New York: Schocken Books, 1962), p. 138.

133   ". . . justify the neglect . . .": Ibid., p. 105.

133   ". . . not worth notice": Ibid., note for p. 108.

133   "the hand that I recognize . . .": Ibid., p. 116.

133   "Another Alvisesque trick . . .": Ibid., p. 115.

133   "doubtless a second examination . . .": *Times* (London), January 5, 1895.

134   Bellini ran a factory: "Venetian Painting Chiefly before Titian," p. 123.

134   ". . . Palma to Amico di Nessuno!": Meyer Schapiro, *Commentary Magazine*, December 1949, pp. 614–16.

134   "a curious . . . innocence": Sprigge, p. 147.

134   "hunted down . . .": Francis Henry Taylor, "The Summons of Art," *The Atlantic Monthly*, November 1957, p. 126.

135   a well-aimed jab: letter to Mrs. Gardner, November 17, 1895, Archives.

Chapter 8: The Tsaylem Kop

136   posed for his photograph: now at "i Tatti."

137   considered a scholar's taste: this and other information from Gerald Reitlinger, *The Economics of Taste*, vol. I (London: Barrie and Rockliff, 1961).

137–38   the Henry Doetsch sale: information from Sir Ellis Waterhouse; *The Economics of Taste*; and the *Times* (London), issues of Monday, June 24, Thursday, June 27, and Saturday, June 29, 1895.

Page

139   their private dealings: P. & D. Colnaghi to Bernhard Sickert, quoted in a letter from Sickert to August Jaccaci, January 1, 1904, Archives.

139   ". . . not of any great value": Carl Snyder to Jaccaci, December 8, 1903, Archives.

140   "The Bond Street Ring": Snyder to Jaccaci, January 1904, Archives.

140   "Obach had an exhibition . . .": Snyder to Jaccaci, January 18, 1904, Archives.

141   ". . . portrait of Michelangelo by Titian": APW, p. 141.

141   " '. . . a Petrus Christus like this' ": MDB, p. 136.

141   ". . . venal critics": SP, p. 65.

141–42   hear the nightingales: letter to T. S. Perry, May 1, 1895, HHU.

142   ". . . effect on my career": S & T, p. 487.

143   "Predominantly mercantile . . .": Colin Eisler, *"Kunstgeschichte* American Style" in *The Intellectual Migration*, ed. Donald Fleming and Bernard Bailyn (Cambridge: Harvard University Press, 1969), pp. 554–55.

143   ". . . archaeological study of art": SP, p. 41.

144   ". . . pettily personal": letter to Carlo Placci, July 14, 1896, SL, p. 51.

144   For his first target: this and following information established from Berenson's letters to Mrs. Gardner, Archives.

145   pillows or ideas: letter from Mrs. Gardner to Berenson, February 18, 1898, Archives.

145–46   ". . . in good earnest": letter to Carlo Placci, November 27, 1907, SL, p. 72.

146   their ballads: letter, Berenson to Mrs. Gardner, July 29, 1896. Robert the Bruce unpleasant: letter, November 15, 1897.

148   bought it for £1 from a house in the country: Sir Ellis Waterhouse.

148   a handsome profit: Snyder to Jaccaci, January 27, 1904.

148   ". . . care to sell them for that?": Snyder to Jaccaci, January 11, 1904.

148   "Berenson made a good thing . . .": Snyder to Jaccaci, January 11, 1904.

NOTES

151   bought in his own name: letter from Lavinia Davies, P. & D. Colnaghi, to the author, August 18, 1977.

153   offering it for sale: June 8, 1902.

153   "wonderfully gathered . . .": Henry James in *The American Scene* (New York: Horizon Press, 1967), p. 254.

155   ambitious to become: letter, January 9, 1900.

155   ". . . red-hot enemies . . .": Snyder to Jaccaci, February 26, 1904.

155   ". . . the only one who really knows": Jaccaci to Snyder, March 16, 1904.

155   ". . . true system of the heavens": Snyder to Horne, March 25, 1904.

156   ". . . not a connoisseur": Jaccaci to Snyder, March 16, 1904.

156   ". . . conceited and deceitful . . .": Jaccaci to Snyder, April 1, 1904.

156   " '. . . atmosphere of storm' ": Snyder to Jaccaci, April 23, 1904.

156   ". . . Heard of the sell": cited are the first and last verses of "A Christmas Attribution," satirizing the wild guesswork and extravagant claims that accompanied the arrival of a work for sale on the London market. The poem was published as an anonymous work in *Robert Ross, Friend of Friends*, ed. M. Ross (London, 1952), p. 193–94. However, it has been recently established, in a competition held by the *Burlington Magazine*, that the author was Robert Ross himself and that the date was probably 1910. (The *Burlington Magazine*, March 1978, p. 166.)

Chapter 9: The Uneasy Compromise

157   "I was standing on my head . . .": this and other comments throughout this chapter from the travel diary of Senda Berenson to her family, 1900, Collection BBP.

159   ". . . scornful comment from Abie": Rachel to Senda, June 5, 1903, Collection BBP.

159   ". . . devoted to its sons": Irving Howe, *World of Our Fathers* (New York: Harcourt Brace Jovanovich, 1976) p. 251.

160   ". . . regulate his inner life": Hutchins Hapgood, *The Spirit of the Ghetto* as quoted in *World of Our Fathers*, p. 254.

160   ". . . a grand figure . . .": Abie to Senda, June 1900, Collection BBP.

160 promised $10,000: Mary Berenson to Senda, March 21, 1903, Collection RBP.

160 their coralline world: Berenson to Mrs. Gardner, March 5, 1900.

163 reported to Mrs. Gardner: on June 14, 1900.

164 driven there by the heat: S & T, p. 168.

164 on friendly terms: letter, August 15, 1897.

166 "still reeking of the ghetto . . .": privately printed edition of *The Education of Henry Adams*, 1906.

167 "I am ridiculously bashful . . .": Sprigge, p. 162.

168 ". . . thy mother": AQG, p. 140.

168 "just right": Ibid., p. 32.

169 ". . . for my grandchildren": Ibid., p. 71.

169 ". . . solid investments": Logan to Mary, June 13, 1900, quoted in John Russell, *A Portrait of Logan Pearsall Smith*.

169 Mary's first letter: July 1, 1900, Collection BBP.

169 intimacy of distance: CB, p. 128.

169–70 ". . . came and took me?" S & T, p. 50.

170 ". . . a bore and a burden": "The Writings of Count Leon Tolstoi," *The Harvard Monthly*, January 1887, p. 147.

170 ". . . to have an opinion": to Mary Costelloe, January 10, 1896, SL, p. 39.

171 ". . . half-hysterical aspirations": Sprigge, p. 86.

171 "understand their business . . .": S & T, p. 282.

171 "the three women . . .": Robert Gathorne-Hardy, *Recollections of Logan Pearsall Smith* (London: Constable, 1949), p. 216.

172 well past her prime: *Journey into the Self* (New York: Crown Publishers, 1950), p. 3.

172 "The whole exercising . . .": H.W.S. to "My darling Alys" from Aix-les-bains, August 25, 1899, Collection Jonathan Gathorne-Hardy.

172 without wobbling: Berenson to Mrs. Gardner, February 19, 1898, Archives.

172–73 5 via Camerata: described in a letter, Berenson to Mrs. Gardner, January 9, 1898, and Senda to her family, March 25, 1900, Collection BBP.

173 ". . . flowers and sweet air": LPS diary, February 1897.

Page

173 "... a *rayon de soleil* ...": Lina Waterfield, *Castle in Italy* (London: John Murray, 1961), p. 72.

173 "He is an interesting youth ...": Senda to her family, April 21, 1900, Collection BBP.

174 "... assessed us all": *Castle in Italy*, p. 72.

174 "... sensitive and intelligent": SL, p. 35.

174 "... and everybody gasped": Julian Trevelyan, letter to author, November 9, 1976.

174 "... your hair cut first": Logan Pearsall Smith letter in the Library of Congress.

175 so nice a chap": Carly Snyder to August Jaccaci, January 6, 1904, Archives.

175 "... Sienese primitives ...": *Castle in Italy*, p. 75.

175 "always endurable ...": letter, November 6, 1896, SL, p. 65.

175 stood on chairs: letter, Senda to family, May 20, 1900, Collection BBP.

175 "... unknown pictures": LPS Diary 39, vol. 1, p. 62.

175–76 "Several people ...": Ibid., p. 68.

176 "We potter and curse ...": letter, February 1898, Library of Congress.

176 on the basis of his ideas: to John Russell: "the hand was the hand of Logan, but the voice was the voice of B.B." Quoted in John Russell, *A Portrait of Logan Pearsall Smith* (London: Dropmore Press, 1950).

176 "... *Life as the end of Life* ...": *Marius the Epicurean*, pp. 142–43.

176 "wealth and disillusion": "Altamura," by Logan Pearsall Smith, *Reperusals and Re-Collections* (London: Constable & Co., 1936), p. 76.

177 "... plate of gold": Ibid., p. 79.

177 "not the young joy ...": Ibid., p. 81.

177 "... world's joylessness ...": "Altamura," p. 83.

177 concept of Altamura: dated from Berenson-Gardner correspondence, as the summer of 1898.

178 radiant life: letter, Berenson to Mrs. Gardner, November 19, 1898.

178 derivation of "i Tatti": theory advanced by the late Myron P. Gilmore in "The Berensons and Villa i Tatti," published

Page

in *The Proceedings of the American Philosophical Society*, vol. 120, no. 1, February 1976, p. 7.

179   actually living it: in a letter, July 31, 1898.

179   "and the blue view . . .": LPS Diary 39, vol. 3, 1900–1909.

179   a civil marriage on December 27 and a religious ceremony on December 29: dated from Berenson's letter to Mrs. Gardner, November 19, 1900, and Mary Costelloe's letter to Senda, received December 24, 1900, Collection BBP.

179   a grotesque whistle: Berenson to Mrs. Gardner, January 1, 1901.

179   rather poor taste: *Castle in Italy*, p. 76.

180   did not want his father to come: January 6, 1901, Collection RBP.

180   he had become ill: Berenson to Barrett Wendell, July 26, 1896, HHU.

180   a Swiss rest cure: Berenson to Mrs. Gardner, May 27, 1897.

180   three hours of massage: Berenson to Mrs. Gardner, November 14, 1897.

181   in fragile health: Berenson to Mrs. Gardner, January 20, 1898.

181   strangely detached: Berenson to Mrs. Gardner, March 21, 1898.

181   anything at all: Berenson to Mrs. Gardner, October 24, 1898.

181   another salvo: Mrs. Gardner to Berenson, November 22, 1901.

182   happy to die: Berenson to Mrs. Gardner, December 11, 1901.

182   would lose things: Mary Berenson to Senda, letters, 1901–03, Collections BBP and RBP.

182   felt deadened: Berenson to Mrs. Gardner, January 1, 1903.

182   too ill to enjoy it: Ibid., June 3, 1901.

182   ". . . a different childhood . . .": February 5, 1901, Collection RBP.

182   visit of Bessie and Little Mother to England: described in travel diaries of Bessie to family, July 1, 1901, Collection BBP.

183   too middle-aged for her; Mary to Senda, July 26, 1901, Collection RBP.

NOTES

183 utter happiness; Mary to Senda, Ibid.

183 "that old grumbler B.B.": letter of Don Guido Cagnola to Mary Berenson, July 25, 1901, Collection RBP.

183 Uncle Bernhard: Mary to Senda, August 2, 1901, Collection RBP.

183 feeling worse: Berenson to Mrs. Gardner, August 25, 1901.

183 Four days later: August 29, 1901, Collection RBP.

183 a martyr complex: Mary to Senda, September 3, 1901, Collection RBP.

184 clam soup and cake: Mary to Bessie, September 8, 1901, Collection BBP.

184 might as well be married: Mary to Senda, September 3, 1901, Collection RBP.

184 clasped in his arms: Mary to Senda, September 3, 1901, Collection RBP.

184 ". . . life of the spirit": preface, 1901, reprinted in *The Sense of Quality* (New York: Schocken Books, 1962), p. v.

184 ". . . a wicked stench . . .": October 24, 1895, BBT, pp. 88–89.

Chapter 10: Enhancing Life

186 "Contact is a desire . . .": CB, p. 240.

186 ". . . to rouse the tactile sense . . .": *The Italian Painters of the Renaissance* (London: The Phaidon Press, 1952), p. 40.

187 discussed with young girls?: CB, p. 259.

187 ". . . cannot help realizing them": Phaidon edition of *The Italian Painters of the Renaissance*, pp. 60–61.

187 his own contact: CB, p. 240.

187 converted it to "life-enhancing": letter, Mary Costelloe to Vernon Lee, November 7, 1897, CC.

188 ". . . il faut coucher avec": CB, p. 255.

188 "We feel sorry because we cry . . .": Ralph Barton Perry, *The Thought and Character of William James* (Cambridge: Harvard University Press, 1948), pp. 195–96.

188 ". . . he had invented it": Francis Henry Taylor, "The Summons of Art." *The Atlantic Monthly*, November 1957, p. 124.

188 ". . . he anticipated me": R & R, p. 73.

Notes

Page

188 "... end up in magic": Clark lecture.

189 "... color acts as form ...": CB, p. 40. "... disembodied color": SP, p. 127.

189–90 ripping it apart: Berenson to Daniel Varney Thompson, January 9, 1938, Archives.

190 dispense with the art of the past: BBT, p. 62.

190 "... real art of landscape": Phaidon edition *The Italian Painters of the Renaissance*, p. 122.

190 "... remained a jungle": Ibid., preface, p. xiii.

191 would transform the ape: letter, Berenson to D. V. Thompson, January 14, 1935.

191–92 "... root of the good": CB, p. 130.

192 "... take it for granted": Clark lecture.

192 "the greatest artist ...": Ibid.

192 "Not a spark ...": Ibid.

192 ranks him with Giotto: Ibid.

194 "... unattributable portraits": Ibid.

194 "... dangerous ground for the unwary": Michael Levey, "Wee Wotan," in the *New Statesman*, July 26, 1963.

194 misrepresented what happened: Sprigge.

194 "that little art critic ...": Peter Gunn, *Vernon Lee* (London: Oxford University Press, 1964), p. 149.

195 fed up with their "jabber": Berenson to Mary Costelloe, January 1892, SL, pp. 14–15.

195 "... never should have heard of them": Berenson to Mary Costelloe, 1892, SL, p. 17.

195 "... she is intelligent": Ibid., p. 24.

195 a year later: November 7 and 8, 1897, CC.

196 "... recording angel": August 24, 1897, quoted, SL, pp. 55–56.

196 "sarcastic inuendo": reply of September 2, 1897, quoted, SL, p. 57.

196 Mary wrote: to "Dear Miss Paget," on October 31, 1897.

197 help him get out of it: Mary to "Dear Miss Paget," November 7 and 8, 1897.

197 an "ill-tempered ... ass": Vernon Lee to Carlo Placci, SL, p. 16.

Page

197 ". . . mystery of all things": CB, pp. 92–93.

198 worth retaining: Mary Berenson to Roger Fry, June 19, 1903, KC.

198–99 ". . . In the night, he died": fragment of a letter, undated, from Mary Berenson to Roger Fry, KC.

199 his foremost enemy: Berenson to Mrs. Gardner, March 1898.

199 hobnobbing with kings: SL, p. 19.

199 ". . . a 'modus vivendi' . . .": Loeser Collection, HHU.

199 a charming scoundrel: Carl Snyder to August Jaccaci, February 10, 1904.

199 ". . . my worst enemies . . .": S & T, p. 87.

200 ". . . said Loeser meditatively!": letters written to Gertrude Stein, *The Flowers of Friendship*, ed. Donald Gallup (New York: Knopf, 1953), pp. 54–55.

200 a fondness for "home truths": Robert Gathorne-Hardy, *Recollections of Logan Pearsall Smith* (London: Constable, 1949), p. 155.

200 " 'I want to be amuthed' ": Lina Waterfield, *Castle in Italy* (London: John Murray, 1961), p. 73.

200 spread stories about him: Berenson to Frances Francis, July 6, 1954.

200 Eugénie Sellers, broke her engagement: Mary to Mrs. Gardner, January 21, 1904.

200 encouraged him to write: S & T, p. 193.

200 still bitter about that: letter to Maurice Brockwell, June 1909, Collection of Mrs. Michael Eland.

201 "That misshapen snake . . .": Mary to Senda, February 2, 1904, Collection BBP.

201 nonsense, Mary wrote: to Roger Fry, January 26, 1903, KC.

201 "the game of grab": *Letters of Roger Fry*, vol. I, ed. Denys Sutton (New York: Random House, 1972), p. 201.

201 ". . . a poisoned rat": Mary to Fry, January 26, 1903.

201 "political scheming . . .": *Letters of Roger Fry*, vol. I, p. 204.

202 ". . . descends to take it": Ibid.

202 ". . . information at your disposal": Mary to Fry, June 2, 1903.

203 "bid for editorial control": Jaccaci to Wilhelm von Bode, August 8, 1907, Archives.

203 contribute £1,000: Fry to Berenson, *Letters of Roger Fry*, vol. I, p. 214.

203 second attempt for editorial control: Jaccaci to Wilhelm von Bode, August 8, 1907, Archives.

203 Fry disloyal and outrageous: S & T, p. 233.

203 ". . . declared war . . .": Ibid., p. 455.

203 "comes from me": Meyer Schapiro

Chapter 11: Our Daily Idea

204 *Celestial Attributions:* published in the *Burlington Magazine* (London), June 1952.

204 especially, when he wasn't there: Berenson to Mrs. Gardner, March 5, 1900.

204 ". . . at the feet of B.B.!": Sibyl Colefax to Senda, December 8, 1903, Collection RBP.

205 painting a forgery: Snyder to Jaccaci, January 22, 1904.

205 Berenson advised Davis to buy it: Jaccaci to Snyder, January 2, 1904.

205 blamed on Strong: Mary to Mrs. Gardner, January 21, 1904.

205 Horne backed up Berenson: Snyder to Jaccaci, January 8, 1904.

206 succumbed to the myth: Berenson to Mrs. Gardner, May 4, 1898.

206 last seen in a New York apartment: letter to author from Sir John Pope-Hennessy, February 14, 1978.

206 "A slight inspection . . .": Frank Jewett Mather, "The Del Puente Giorgione," in *The Collectors* (New York: Henry Holt, 1912), pp. 29–30.

206 ". . . that ever met my eyes": Ibid., pp. 42–43.

208 envious of his success: letter, Mary to Mrs. Gardner, January 21, 1904.

209 "this accursed business": Mary to Roger Fry, June 19, 1903.

209 leaving "i Tatti" to Harvard: Mary to Mrs. Gardner, May 27, 1904.

211 stock market speculation: Mary to Senda, October 26, 1901, Collection RBP.

211 borrowed money from his mother-in-law: Mary to Senda, October 26, 1902, Collection BBP.

Page

211 Money was a constant worry: Mary to Senda, March 21, 1903, Collection BBP.

211 bound to make more: Mary to Senda, March 1901, Collection RBP.

211 ". . . running of this house": Mary to Senda, January 18, 1903, Collection RBP.

212 he must make a living: letter, August 9, 1902.

212 with good humor: Berenson to Mrs. Gardner, March 2, 1902.

213 wretched paintings: Berenson to Mrs. Gardner, June 18, 1898.

213 Berenson's reply: from 5 via Camerata, San Domenico, June 6, 1898.

213 would take it for £6,000: The painting was bought by Samuel D. Warren, president of the museum's board of trustees, and his wife, and has been in the Cleveland Museum of Art collection since 1928. It is worth "over $1 million," according to Henry Sayles Francis, former Cleveland Museum curator.

213 had acquired five fakes: Berenson to Mrs. Gardner, May 11, 1902.

213 an exhaustive and gratuitous attempt: Mary to Mrs. Gardner, November 10, 1902.

214 his first painting a fake: Derek Hill, "Berenson and 'i Tatti,'" *Apollo Magazine*, October 1967, p. 594.

214 blamed poor lighting: Berenson to Mrs. Gardner, July 12, 1902.

214 unscrupulous dealers: Berenson, letter to the *Times* (London), April 4, 1903.

215 one of the two most beautiful fifteenth-century pictures: Kenneth Clark, BBC-TV film, February 13, 1971.

215 When asked to name his fee: David Carritt.

215 hung against silk: Mary to Senda, January 6, 1901, Collection RBP.

216 Logan Pearsall Smith discovered it: Kenneth Clark, BBC film.

216 According to Berenson: four accounts, given by Frances Francis, Wiliam Mostyn-Owen, Derek Hill in *Apollo*, and Luisa Vertova in *Great Private Collections* (New York: Macmillan Company, 1963).

Page

216   completed it seven years later: other segments of the same polyptych are in collections at the National Gallery, London, the Louvre, the Musée Condé, and the Hermitage.

216   ". . . influences of the spirit": *A Sienese Painter of the Franciscan Legend* (London: Dent and Sons, 1909), as quoted in *Looking at Pictures with Bernard Berenson* (New York: Harry N. Abrams, Inc., 1963), p. 94.

217   worth half a million dollars: Mary to Senda, May 12, 1915, Collection RBP.

217   ". . . such an art experience": BBT, pp. 73–75.

217   "To be for ever learning . . .": quoted in Iris Origo, "The Long Pilgrimage," *Cornhill Magazine* (London), Spring 1960, p. 145.

218   "They taste like vinegar": Ibid.
"'Give us this day . . .'": Ibid.

218   ". . . appreciation of Cézanne": *Journey into the Self*, p. 204.

218   sent a letter: November 12, 1908.

218   ". . . the great refusal": SP, p. 40.

218   "the most protean . . .": SP, p. 41.

218   a demagogue: Journals, Henry and Frances Francis, March 17, 1949.

218   vicious and unscrupulous: Ibid.

219   "After Matisse": Ibid.

219   "appreciation of contemporary art": BBC-TV film.

219–23   unpublished diary: Hapgood papers, BY, by permission of Charles Hapgood.

221   "soulful tourists . . .": letter to Mrs. Frederick Winslow, December 6, 1912, *The Letters of George Santayana*, ed. Daniel Cory (London: Constable, 1955), p. 121.

222   the same furnishings: Luisa Vertova in *Great Private Collections*.

223   ". . . super-humanly well joined": SL, p. 65.

223–24   a terrible backache: letter, H.W.S., November 15, 1902, Collection of Jonathan Gathorne-Hardy.

224   ". . . shocked at lapses . . .": letter to Gilbert Murray, December 28, 1902, *The Autobiography of Bertrand Russell*, vol. I (Boston: Atlantic Monthly Press, Little, Brown & Co., c. 1951), p. 245.

NOTES

Page

224 "a ... monster ... book": Mary to Mother, February 5, 1901, Collection RBP.

224 "groans and moans": Mary to Senda, February 6, 1901, Collection RBP.

225 "... most consistent critical work": Sir John Pope-Hennessy, *Times Literary Supplement*, May 28, 1976.

225 reading widely: Mary to Senda, February 26, 1906, Collection BBP.

225 "walk a corpse . . .": BBT, pp. 116–17.

225 They landed early in October: this and other quotations from Mary's journal of their American trip, 1903–04, quoted in "The Berensons and Villa i Tatti" by Myron P. Gilmore.

226 "turned perfectly grey . . .": Mary to Senda, October 9, 1903, Collection RBP.

226 "... to make her 'Prince' comfortable": Mary to Senda, October 9, 1903, Collection RBP.

226 "... in the same bed . . .": Mary to Senda, October 1903, Collection BBP.

227 "... no direct 'business' . . .": Mary to Senda, November 22, 1903, Collection BBP.

227 "... that blessed tin box": Mary to Rachel, October 20, 1903, Collection BBP.

227 offer her myrrh and balsam: Berenson to Mrs. Gardner, December 23, 1903.

227–28 still using the phrase: Berenson to Frances Francis, March 3, 1950.

228 "... grinned with appreciation": Mary to Senda, January 9, 1904, Collection BBP.

228 sing her praise: Berenson to Mrs. Gardner, January 13, 1904.

228 a genuine affection: January 19, 1904.

228 "... so awfully short . . .": Mary to Senda, February 2, 1904, Collection RBP.

229 "changed every attribution!": Mary to Senda, November 3, 1903, Collection RBP.

229 "... disgusted by him": Jaccaci to Snyder, Archives, April 1, 1904.

Page

230–31   "I see the square . . .": this and following quotations from Jerome and Jean Tharaud, *L'Ombre de la Croix*, (Paris: Librairie Plon, 1920). Translated by the author.

Chapter 12: Doris

233   hardly been equalled: Gerald Reitlinger in *The Economics of Tate*, vol. I (London: Barnie and Rockliff, 1961).

234   trying to impart some vision: Berenson to John G. Johnson, September 7, 1909, Archives of the Johnson Collection, Philadelphia Museum.

234   a creature of habit: Berenson to Johnson, October 5, 1909, Ibid.

234   his hopes suffered an eclipse: Berenson to Johnson, October 22, 1904.

235   getting nothing in return: Berenson to Johnson, April 20, 1912.

235   a small fire: Mary to Mother, June 17, 1906, Collection BBP.

235   they needed £6,000: Mary to William Rothenstein, November 27, 1907, HHU.

235   major repairs in the fall of 1908: dated from letters to Johnson.

236   ". . . 'for 45 minutes this morning' ": MDB, p. 117.

245   ". . . spiteful mock-humility . . .": Ibid., p. 83.

245   ". . . outright antagonism": Ibid., p. 66.

245   ". . . a real inferno": Mary to Senda, June 29, 1909, Collection BBP.

245   ". . . a vast, circular nexus . . .": S. N. Behrman, *People in a Diary* (Boston: Little, Brown and Co., 1972).

246   Other evidence: letter to Johnson, September 25, 1911.

246   an annual stipend: Berenson to Henry Walters, May 13, 1912, Archives of the Walters Art Gallery, Baltimore.

246   employed scouts: Berenson to Henry Walters, October 21, 1912, Ibid.

247   politely detaching them: Mary to Hendrik C. Andersen, Andersen Collection, the Library of Congress, November 2, 1922.

NOTES

247 a business agreement: letter, Berenson to René Gimpel, November 9, 1924, Archives. (Also see René Gimpel, *Diary of an Art Dealer* (New York: Farrar, Straus and Giroux, 1966), p. 225.

247–48 refused to be interrogated: Berenson to Johnson, February 21, 1904.

248 "it mattered immensely . . .": David Carritt.

248 "high prices are far from serving . . .": "The Italians in Our National Gallery," unpublished article, 1941, permission of Philippa Offner.

248 "our national voracity . . .": Ibid.

248 ". . . an ever-rising level": Ibid.

249 ". . . a closed alliance . . .": Ibid.

249 "materialistic and almost bestial": "According to me, everything which one does for an advantage is materialistic and almost bestial. . . .": April 10, 1937, CB, p. 231.

250 clever men who can be bought off: "I prefer dishonesty to stupidity. One can make it worth while for the dishonest man to do the right thing, while the stupid man cannot be bought off." (circa 1939) Quoted, BBT, p. 192.

250 ". . . falsifies all of life": CB, p. 57.

250 "not capable of giving an attribution . . .": Sprigge, p. 210.

250 not "culpably wrong": interview, April 28, 1976.

251 did not know: *Self-Portrait with Donors* (Boston: Little, Brown & Co., 1974), p. 94.

251 ". . . very bad choices . . .": interview, April 23, 1976.

251–52 ". . . study the preceding attributions": letter to author, May 8, 1978.

255 "only a copy . . .": *The Sense of Quality* (New York: Schocken Books, 1962), p. 145.

255 "deplorably bad preservation": Ibid.

255 "the rarest, most wonderful . . .": letter, March 11, 1912, quoted in "The Benjamin Altman Bequest" by Francis Haskell, *Metropolitan Museum Journal*, vol. 3, 1970, pp. 259–80.

255 "a miraculously fine state": Ibid.

255 extensively damaged: Terisio Pignatti, *Giorgione* (London: The Phaidon Press, 1971).

255 ". . . ghost of a picture": Haskell article as cited.

Notes

256 all of Paris would be talking: letter, March 25, 1911, Gimpel Papers, Archives (Roll 417).

257 collectors suspicious: letter, Berenson to Gimpel, July 18, 1911, Ibid.

257 ". . . this feline Pole . . .": *Diary of an Art Dealer*, p. 4.

258 ". . . 'It is by Titian' ": *Self-Portrait with Donors*, p. 94.

258 bought for £103,300: Reitlinger, *The Economics of Taste*.

258 "B.B. was furious . . .": *Self-Portrait with Donors*, p. 94.

259 request for more money: letter from the Hotel Bristol, Vienna, November 17, 1937, YUL.

260 "shadings of uncertainty": Paul Richard in *The Washington Post*, August 5, 1975, p. B5.

260 used by Zeri and Fredericksen: in *Census of Pre-19th Century Italian Paintings in North American Public Collections* (Cambridge: Harvard University Press, 1972).

261 ". . . stock . . . is . . . inexhaustible": Sir Ellis Waterhouse.

261 a modern pastiche: attribution given by Everett Fahy in 1976, for a catalogue of the Fogg Collection.

261 a classic example of fake art: letter, Berenson to D. V. Thompson, September 16, 1933, Archives.

261 "One would have to regret . . .": *North Italian Painters of the Renaissance* (London: Putnam's & Sons, 1907), p. 260.

262 Fowles sent Duveen a telegram: *The Guardian*, January 9, 1977.

262 ". . . diametrically opposite views . . .": Harry J. Hahn, *The Rape of La Belle* (Kansas City, Mo.: Frank Glenn Publishing Co., 1946), p. 40.

262 ". . . had business relations . . .": *Times* (London), February 7, 1929.

263 " 'I know I was wrong' . . .": *Self-Portrait with Donors*, p. 149.

263–64 " '. . . may have painted one or two of the figures' ": Ibid.

264 ". . . refused categorically . . .": FYB, pp. 50–51.

264 ". . . BB meekly complied . . .": MDB, pp. 150–53.

265 ". . . clear enough traces . . .": Meyer Schapiro in *Commentary*, December 1949, pp. 614–16.

265 subject to fads: letter from Berenson to John Walker, October 28, 1937, collection of owner.

265 ". . . diminish his value . . .": from *Essays in Appreciation*, 1954, quoted, p. 355, BBT.

NOTES

Page

266 "... wreck of an authentic Bellini": letter to author, May 30, 1978.

266–67 "... pending further study": Federico Zeri, *Italian Paintings in the Walters Art Gallery*, published by The Trustees, Baltimore, 1976, p. 259.

267 "... to Pinturicchio himself": Ibid.

268 a new Masaccio: *Art in America*, February 1930.

268 "... sculptors of the Chefrens ...": Ibid.

268 "... 'B.B. likes it' ": S. N. Behrman, *Duveen* (New York: Random House, 1951), pp. 171–72.

268 "... malleable sheet iron ...": Luciano Berti, *Masaccio* (Pennsylvania State University Press, 1967), p. 94.

269 overrestored paintings: MDB, p. 123.

269 "very much damaged ...": from a museum catalogue being published in 1979.

269 "... shine like a pair of new boots": "The Italians in Our National Gallery."

271 X rays for eyes: Berenson to Mrs. Gardner, July 12, 1902.

273 Cavenaghi added nothing of his own: Berenson to Mrs. Gardner, July 2, 1902.

273 she should not buy a Crivelli: Berenson to Mrs. Gardner, June 10, 1900.

273 as hold up a bank: Berenson to Mrs. Gardner, July 2, 1902.

274 "... need not ... prejudge ...": *Three Essays in Method* (Oxford: The Clarendon Press, 1926), p. 80.

274 "The only painting a pristine state ...": CB, pp. 26–27.

274 "... the original style ...": *The Cleaning of Paintings* (London: Faber & Faber, 1968), pp. 256–57.

Chapter 13: Separate Bedrooms

275 "... a magical world": S & T, p. 117.

276 "... perhaps ... inevitable": Mary to Neith and Hutchins Hapgood, undated, BY.

276 "one long torture ...": ARR, p. 63.

276 one must be protected: CB, p. 128.

276 "one's own for ever": SL, p. 72.

276 "... without further chance ...": Ibid.

Page

277 a preliminary reader: Berenson to Barrett Wendell, July 16, 1919, HHU.

277 "...he makes a great fuss": MDB, p. 101.

277 "...answering questions...": Mary to Senda, February 5, 1901, Collection RBP.

278 "Maybe I spoil him...": Mary to Senda, March 21, 1903, Collection RBP.

278 "...fly into a rage": Mary to Senda, March 31, 1901, Collection RBP.

278 "...pet and coax...": ARR, p. 208.

278 "...beating people down": Mary to Senda, January 18, 1903, Collection RBP.

279 "...blazing with jewels": Mary to Senda, January 9, 1904, Collection BBP.

279 her "butterfly" husband: Mary to Senda, November 26, 1906, Collection BBP.

280 "...intellectual discipline": Mary to Senda, March 2, 1901, Collection BBP.

280 "...snatched off & thrown...": Mary to Senda, April 18, 1902, Collection RBP.

281 "B.B. is of age...": Mary to Senda, Ibid.

281 "...what she *was*": Mary to Senda, May 25, 1909, Collection BBP.

281 "a sort of widow in weeds": CB, p. 56.

281 a fascinating Pole: Mary to Mrs. Gardner, April 26, 1907.

282 "...thoroughly enjoyed herself": Logan Pearsall Smith, March 20, 1908, Library of Congress.

282 "...Neith will walk...": November 15, 1907, HHU.

283 could change his mind: S. N. Behrman, *A Portrait of Max* (New York: Random House, 1960), p. 198.

283 "...line of your ambitions": December 10, 1939, SL, p. 171.

283 "...sniggering, sneering old man": Ibid.

283 "...heart on ice": S & T, p. 276.

283 still wondering: Berenson to W. M. Ivins, October 4, 1952, Archives.

283 "...moral sultriness": S & T, p. 32.

Page

284 "... truculent insect...": *Works and Days*, from *The Journal of Michael Field*, T. and D. C. Stunge Moore, eds. (London: John Murray, 1933), pp. 255–56.

284 "affectionate contempt": Mary to Senda, March 22, 1903, Collection BBP.

284 "small and unworthy": S & T, p. 419.

284 "We are all sleepy today...": letter, Logan Pearsall Smith, March 22, 1903, Library of Congress.

284 believed his own lies: "One of D'Annunzio's great defects is that he believes his own lies." CB, p. 57.

285 lack of restraint: Ibid., p. 135.

285 "... *wanderjahring*...": BBT, p. 127.

285 "... exceptionally strong ... characters": Miss A. D. Scott, his eldest sister.

286 "the best raconteur...": W. H. Haslam, letter to E. D. Buchanan, October 9, 1975.

286 "... Italian idleness...": quoted, Robert Allerton Parker, *The Transatlantic Smiths* (New York: Random House, 1959), pp. 108–109.

286 "she roars with laughter...": Ibid., p. 109.

286 "... pints of gold...": Ibid.

286 "I heard of you...": September 6, 1910.

286 "... morning receptions...": Mary to Rothenstein, April 14, 1908, HHU.

287 "... literary and brilliant...": Cecil Pinsent to Henry Hope Reed, August 25, 1954, Collection Avery Architectural Library, Columbia University.

287 "... till all hours...": Ibid.

287 "... to weave romance...": Mary to Rachel, June 18, 1906, Ralph Barton Perry Collection, HA.

287 proposed trip was off: Scott to Bessie Berenson, undated letter, Collection RBP.

287–88 "... seemed to get quite well": Mary to "My dear Mrs. Scott," April 10, 1913, Collection of C. Russell Scott.

288 "... looks after me wonderfully": April 15, 1909, Ibid.

288 broke his heart: to Clotilde Marghieri.

288 emotional conflicts: John Walker to Henry Hope Reed, January 14, 1969, Collection Avery Architectural Library, Columbia University.

288 "... all I stood ...": S & T, p. 282.

288 "lists as long ...": Mary to Senda, April 23, 1910, Collection RBP.

288 "... disorderly, hopeless": Mary to Senda, May 16, 1909, Collection RBP.

288 tea under the trees: Mary to Senda, May 16, 1909, Collection RBP.

288 "... never to return": Mary to Senda, May 25, 1909, Collection BBP.

288 would have to be redone: to Johnson, April 25, 1909.

289 not a door would shut: to Johnson, November 8, 1909.

289 no end in sight: to Johnson, Ibid.

289 "a showy and conceited ...": APW, p. 154.

289 "... strong sexual excitement": Ibid., p. 155.

289 "... will be *Furious*": Mary to Mother, November 15, 1910, Collection BBP.

289 "... a rage a piece": Scott to Bessie Berenson, October 10, 1911, Collection RBP.

290 a daily massage: April 1910, BY.

290 "... nothing but agony": Mary to Senda, April 23, 1910, Collection RBP.

290 "wickedly obstinate": Mary to Senda, May 18, 1910, Collection RBP.

291 "... champagne suppers ...": Mary to Mrs. Gardner, Louise Hall Tharp, *Mrs. Jack* (Boston: Little, Brown & Co., 1965), p. 314.

291 "... as if life had stopped": Cass Canfield, *The Incredible Pierpont Morgan* (New York: Harper & Row, 1974), pp. 152–53.

292 "... a poisonous person": Ibid., pp. 147–48.

292 "a thoroughly good sort": Mary to Mrs. Gardner, quoted in *Mrs. Jack*, p. 314.

293 "... four months' silence ...": Mary to Senda, January 2, 1913, Collection RBP.

293 "... very straight & frank ...": Mary to Senda, January 19, 1914, Collection BBP.

293 "... an awful time ...": Mary to Senda, January 23, 1914, Collection BBP.

NOTES

294 come and visit: letter, Berenson to Belle Greene, in the D. V. Thompson correspondence at the Archives, dated July 11, 1945.

294 a wonderful lover: to Senda, August 28, 1950, Collection RBP.

294 ". . . stop my education": to Henry and Frances Francis.

294 "I am what I am . . .": SL, p. 72.

294 saved from suicide: April 29, 1950.

Chapter 14: "Perched on the Pinnacle"

296 "Perched on the Pinnacle": "He was perched on the pinnacle of a mountain of corruption. . . .": Kenneth Clark, *Another Part of the Wood* (London: John Murray, 1974), p. 114.

296 ". . . there is no love": William Ivins, Jr., writing at "i Tatti" in the 1920s, Archives of American Art.

296 ". . . a deathly silence . . .": CB, p. 44.

297 ". . . can't collect": Mary to Senda, August 20, 1914, Collection BBP.

297 ". . . he would worry . . .": Mary to Senda, Ibid.

297 "ominous iron rumble . . .": Mary to Senda, September 4, 1914, Collection BBP.

297 ". . . still waiting": October 11, 1914, Collection BBP.

297 his best course: letter to Johnson, December 8, 1914.

297 nothing but history: December 8, 1915.

298 thoroughly ashamed: January 16, 1915.

298 an inspiring city: Ibid.

298 a "bright corner": Mary to Senda, September 7, 1915, Collection RBP.

298 "we're no use . . .": Mary to Senda, October 6, 1914, Collection BBP.

298 ". . . Italian soldiers . . .": January 10, 1916, Collection RBP.

298 "he might as well say . . .": to Senda, March 6, 1915, Collection RBP.

298 ". . . 'figure of fun' . . .": February 14, 1915, Collection BBP.

299 ". . . a good influence . . .": November 8, 1914, Collection BBP.

299 "Our goal is Rome . . .": from Perugia, May 27, 1915, Collection RBP.

Page

300 "...bread was horrible": Mary to Senda, April 18, 1917, Collection RBP.

300 starved for companionship: January 2, 1918, Fogg Museum, Cambridge.

300 he told Chapman: on January 1, 1918, HHU.

300 "...enchanted me...": CB, pp. 54–55.

301 "'...what he purports to be'": interview with author.

301 "...never accept an invitation...": November 4, 1916, William R. Tyler Collection.

301 their actual encounter: to D. V. Thompson, August 15, 1937.

301 came to symbolize: to W. M. Ivins, October 25, 1930, Archives.

302 everything a woman could be: to Thompson, August 15, 1937.

302 a fascinating man: Bessie Berenson to Frances Francis, September 24, 1966.

303 "lank black hair...": FYB, p. 6.

303 "...sense of fun...": Ibid.

303 "...declaration of love": Ibid., p. 8.

303 "world-embracing goodwill": Ibid.

303 "...elegant and aloof...": Ibid.

303 "almost importunate...": Ibid., p. 9.

303 she had been killed: Alda von Anrep to Frances Francis, September 12, 1971.

304 "...had not been wise": *Images and Shadows* (New York: Harcourt Brace Jovanovich, Inc., 1970), p. 103.

304 "...after my own heart": R. W. B. Lewis, *Edith Wharton, a Biography* (New York: Harper & Row, 1975), p. 345.

304 "that well-meaning waste...": Edith Wharton to Mary Berenson, Ibid., p. 409.

304 "...sheer venom...": Ibid., p. 410.

304 "very offensive...": FYB, p. 15.

304 "poison pen letters": to Joan Haslip. Letter to author, January 5, 1978.

304 hatred for Sybil: Berenson to Edith Wharton, February 7, 1932, Tyler Collection.

304 "...I would...prefer not...": FYB, p. 23.

Page

304 "the parallel . . .": *Images and Shadows* (New York: Harcourt Brace Jovanovich, Inc., 1970), p. 105.

304 ". . . an arrowy spirit . . .": *The Portrait of Zelide* (New York: Charles Scribner's Sons, 1926), p. 1.

304–305 ". . . artificially created": Ibid., p. 9.

305 "sensitive, complex . . .": Ibid., p. 99.

305 "as strongly . . .": Ibid., p. 134.

305 "tyrant benevolence": Ibid.

305 ". . . wishing to hurt": Ibid., p. 183.

306 ". . . nervous break-down . . .": May 1, 1919.

306 "neurasthenia": August 28, 1918, Archives.

306 not quite the thing: February 19, 1917.

306 his chief asset: to Barrett Wendell, April 30, 1918.

306 foundations of his existence: to Barrett Wendell, December 6, 1918.

306 made her worse: to Barrett Wendell, July 10, 1918.

307 ". . . never stop regretting . . .": FYB, p. 40.

307 marry Dorothy Warren: Logan Pearsall Smith to Alys Russell, March 25, 1926.

307 "neurasthenic egoism": FYB, p. 158.

308 "a milliner's block": ARR, p. 189.

308 ". . . 'Russian steppe' expression . . .": August 21, 1927, Collection BBP.

309 as Berenson remarked of Placci: R & R, p. 17.

309 delightfully disappointed: Berenson to T. S. Perry, February 24, 1926, CC.

309 "timidity, arrogance . . .": CB, p. 19.

310 gave everyone $50: Mary to Mother, February 14, 1915, Collection BBP.

310 *"oeil dénigrant"*: R & R, p. 6.

310 "sofa cushions": Rachel Perry to Senda, March 14, 1930, Collection RBP.

310 ". . . pig's food . . .": Mary to Rachel Perry, December 30, 1909, Perry Collection, HA.

310 "injuring thy ears": to Mary Berenson, April 15, 1908, ARR, p. 198.

311 embarrassed silence: BBC-TV film.

Page

311 ". . . the Evil Eye!": Alice De Lamar, "Some Little-Known Facts about Bernard Berenson and the Art World," *Forum*, University of Houston, Winter 1975, p. 32.

311 ". . . candle extinguisher": Ibid.

312 ". . . lost his temper . . .": January 10, 1916, Collection RBP.

312 a "serious cleavage": letter to Nicky Mariano, FYB, p. 36.

312–13 ". . . undignified & sordid": January 7, 1923, Collection RBP.

313 separate hotels: MDB, p. 101. "a union of intellects": Ibid.

313 ". . . our superiority": CB, p. 38.

313 not a "very favorable one": S & T, p. 169.

313 ". . . particularly fine . . .": FYB, p. 9.

313 ". . . nor the title": Ibid., p. 22.

314 ". . . limited intelligence": Ibid., p. 2.

314 ". . . inferiority complex . . .": Ibid., p. 5.

314 ". . . always try to mediate . . .": letter to author, August 4, 1977.

315 ". . . not easy to manage . . .": FYB, p. 67.

315 ". . . Mediterranean temperament . . .": Ibid., p. 68.

316 never learned control: Ibid.

316 ". . . a new toy": Ibid.

316 mother and baby: Ibid., pp. 179, 260.

316 "an anxious and nervous . . .": Ibid., p. 69.

316 "a disagreeable and contemptuous . . .": Ibid.

316 "into stubborn defence . . .": Ibid.

316 ". . . unfortunate notes . . .": Ibid., p. 70.

316 ". . . feel very close to him": Ibid., p. 22.

316 ". . . the . . . house resounded . . .": Ibid., p. 69.

316 ". . . Mary equally happy": March 8, 1930, Collection BBP.

316 "our guardian angel": Giovanni and Flavia Colaccichi.

317 ". . . no kind Robin . . .": to the Hutchins Hapgoods, December 29, 1929.

317 ". . . same way of life": Mary to Senda, October 13, 1928, Collection BBP.

317 "try to calm her": FYB, p. 28.

317 ". . . forgets about them": Mary to Senda, June 9, 1924, Collection RBP.

Page

317 "... wasn't worth living": Mary to Senda, March 3, 1924, Collection RBP.

317 "... thought her delightful": FYB, p. 178.

317 "... in a skittle alley": Ibid., p. 15.

318 over her head: Ibid., p. 24.

318 "... brilliant conversation ...": Ibid.

318 "... *Weltanschauung* ...": Ibid.

318 "... Romanesque façades ...": Ibid., p. 39.

318 "... due to B.B.'s presence": Ibid.

318 to W. M. Ivins, Jr.: March 27, 1929, Archives.

319 his new amour: FYB, p. 96.

319 "... his subtle charm": Ibid., p. 177.

320 his reflection: letter to W. M. Ivins, Jr., November 12, 1949.

320 "... a career": S & T, p. 343.

320 "... their values": CB, p. 128.

320 "... plastered down": *Forum*, p. 25.

320 "... mystic genius": Geoffrey Scott to Nicky Mariano, FYB, p. 19.

321 "... the great Bellini ...": *Forum*, p. 25.

321 "... undignified rage": FYB, p. 20.

322 "... their every wish ...": *Forum*, p. 27.

322 "... worked successfully": Ibid., p. 26.

322 gave a lecture: at Bryn Mawr College, February 1921.

323 "... numerous guests": FYB, pp. 142–43.

323 "... fainted away": Ibid., p. 35.

323–24 "... without Bernard's guarantee": March 26, 1928, Collection BBP.

324 the ultimate compliment: Mary to Senda, November 10, 1927, Collection RBP.

324 "... Baronesses and Duchesses": Mary to Senda, November 10, 1927, Collection RBP.

324 "... fastidious tastes ...": Mary to Mother, October 3, 1927, Collection RBP.

324 "... a good human desire ...": BBT, p. 162.

325 "... fear of discredit": MDB, p. 130.

325 evidence of despair: Berenson to Frank Jewett Mather, February 26, 1925: at "i Tatti."

325 throw it all over: April 3, 1919.

325 a madhouse: January 20, 1928.

Chapter 15: The Con Game

326 buy a box of paints: Berenson to Edith Wharton, May 1910, BY.

326 "...provincialism in art...": from "Italian Illustrators of the Speculum Humanae Salvationis" in *Studies in Medieval Painting*, 1925, BBT, p. 161.

326 "...geometricization of contours": CB, p. 237.

327 "...artistically debased...": to the author, May 19, 1977.

328 "...feasting his eyes": on deposit, HA.

328 counted for nothing: Lucy Porter diary, August 16.

329 "...Medieval Sculpture...": Mary to Mother, October 25, 1919, Collection BBP.

329 "...loves ugliness": Mary to Walter Lippmann, Lippmann Papers, YUL.

330 an *unsereiner*: Berenson to W. M. Ivins, November 15, 1930.

330 told Learned Hand: October 3, 1940, Collection of Mrs. Norris Darrell.

331 quality counted: letter to John Walker, March 25, 1934.

331 "...suckling babes": Rachel Perry to Senda, February 2, 1912, Collection BBP.

331 "...with respect": January 9, 1926, Library of Congress.

332 opaque and impenetrable: Berenson to Frances Francis, March 25, 1954.

332 "...started poor": S & T, p. 283.

332 "...straight-forwardly and properly": letter to author, March 24, 1978.

332 "...witty and sharp": Count Umberto Morra.

332 "...Brush, brush, brush...": APW, p. 165.

332–33 "...very rude": interview with author.

333 lasting happiness: June 10, 1931.

335 "...autograph work of Fra Angelico": *The Arts* (New York), May 1924.

NOTES

343 rubbed his beard: Berenson to Mrs. Wharton, January 31, 1932, Tyler Collection.

343 full of tears: Berenson to Mrs. Wharton, February 5, 1932, Ibid.

343 change might amuse her: Berenson to Mrs. Wharton, February 8, 1932, Ibid.

343–44 ". . . very intelligent question": March 19, 1932.

344 her first book: *A Modern Pilgrimage*, published the following year, in 1933.

344 "I can't complain . . .": Mary to Mrs. Wharton, February 10, 1933, Tyler Collection.

344 ". . . is a peach . . .": Abie to Senda, January 11, 1929, Collection BBP.

345 "nearly all . . .": Mary to the Lippmanns, February 14, 1932.

345 more than they had: Mary to Senda, June 9, 1924, Collection RBP.

345 drastic economies: Mary to Lippmann, October 6, 1931.

346 considerably upset: July 19, 1933.

346 ". . . acts of violence": May 27, 1925.

347 ". . . Aristocrat in sympathy": Mary to Lippmann, April 19, 1926.

347 envoys of hell: Berenson to Lippmann, August 8, 1936.

347 no commercial ties: Berenson to Lippmann, February 26, 1936.

347 all the "isms": Berenson to the Hapgoods, May 15, 1937.

347 disorganized life-style: Berenson to Ralph Barton Perry, June 26, 1936.

348 ". . . a fairy tale": APW, p. 153.

348 nothing to be done: letters to John Walker and D. V. Thompson.

349 given in Yiddish: Berenson to Margaret Barr, December 29, 1939, "i Tatti."

349 forensic and destructive: *Il segno sul braccio*, p. 174.

349 two-hour sittings: Berenson to Mrs. Wharton, October 14, 1933, Tyler Collection.

350 work in snatches: Berenson to Ralph Perry, October 21, 1934.

350 could not be happy: to W. M. Ivins, October 23, 1934.

350 might die: to Edith Wharton, May 5, 1936.

350 Her weak spot: to Edith Wharton, August 13, 1933.

350 certainly imaginary: to Lippmann, February 26, 1936; seat of her troubles: to Ivins, September 5, 1934.

350 inner disappointment: October 1, 1916.

350 better things: March 5, 1926.

350 "... weep within me ...": to Mary Berenson, September 5, 1929, BBT, p. 163.

351 must be impotent: Berenson to Ivins, December 27, 1938.

351 a con game: December 13, 1937.

351 like a fraud: June 27, 1939.

351 grossest self-indulgence: October 10, 1932.

351 "... silvery water ...": Mary to Hapgoods, December 13, 1935.

351–52 What fun: March 11, 1936.

352 so enchanting: December 14, 1937.

352 "... not numbered": January 16, 1938, at the Library of Congress.

352 source of happiness: Berenson to Ivins, December 19, 1928.

352 "... all eyes and brain": Mary to Ralph Barton Perry, June 6, 1929.

352 his Lithuanian childhood: Berenson to Senda, August 3, 1937.

352 delicious walks: Berenson to Perry, July 31, 1935.

352 days of his youth: to Learned Hand, September 26, 1934.

353 "It is IT ...": BBT, p. 163.

353 a sound so fluid: April 5, 1941, YUL.

Chapter 16: "Essential Realities"

354 "Essential Realities": SP, p. 122.

354 "... cattle vans ...": R & R, p. 145.

354 "... prolong sadistically ...": Ibid., pp. 147–48.

355 "... painted on walls everywhere": Ibid., p. 211.

355 "... civilized humanity ...": Ibid., p. 159.

355 could have departed: Lawrence Berenson to Senda, December 17, 1940, Collection RBP.

Page

355 State Department protection: Berenson to Lippmann, May 12, 1938, YUL.

356 left in a rage: Nicky Mariano to Walter Lippmann, May 28, 1946, YUL.

356 ". . . 'Talmud Jew' ": S & T, p. 302.

356 ". . . keep away from us": Mary to Senda and Bessie, November 17, 1940, Collection RBP.

356 shock of world events: July 5, 1940, Collection RBP.

357 intense delight: Nicky Mariano to Senda and Bessie, August 25, 1942, Perry Collection, HA.

357 ". . . stream of consciousness . . .": SP, p. 9.

357 ". . . deeply penitential . . .": S & T, p. 400.

357 life of contemplation: CB, pp. 156–57.

357 failed in his mission: Berenson to Frances Francis, October 13, 1951.

358 ". . . ferocious idealism": FYB, p. 67.

358 ". . . left to myself . . .": S & T, p. 219.

358 "I even tried to pretend . . .": SP, p. 94.

358 ". . . mask of being *goyim* . . .": S & T, p. 323.

358 "not one of us": BBT, p. 335.

358 ". . . complete assimilation . . .": R & R, p. 145.

358 ". . . one's own universe": BBT, p. 263.

358 ". . . not so worthless . . .": Ibid., p. 292.

358 felt a fraud: Ibid., p. 344.

358 rotten and bad: letter to T. S. Perry, October 29, 1915.

358 freedom from contempt: S & T, p. 319.

359 too much of an egoist: to Arthur Kingsley Porter, January 5, 1930, HA.

359 ". . . with startled eyes": SP, p. 64.

359 ". . . loved rather than admired . . .": BBT, p. 392.

359 ". . . further investigation": Karen Horney, *Self-Analysis* (New York: W. W. Norton & Co., Inc., 1942), p. 33.

359–60 "I had scarcely any . . .": SP, p. 81. "lust for power': Ibid.

360 ". . . deliberately and scrupulously . . .": SP, p. 29.

360 completely faithful: Ibid., p. 30.

360 "I am lazy": Ibid., p. 31.

NOTES

360   "self-indulgent": Ibid., p. 25.

360   ". . . good qualities . . .": Ibid., p. 63.

360   ". . . entirely rational . . .": Ibid., p. 100.

360   ". . . full ripeness": Ibid., p. 35.

360   ". . . means of livelihood": Ibid., pp. 41–42.

360   ". . . social success . . .": Meyer Schapiro, "Mr. Berenson's Values," *Encounter Magazine*, January 1961, p. 58.

360   "that equivocal thing": SP, p. 35.

360   "spiritually profitable": Ibid.

360   "ranked" with charlatans: Ibid., p. 39.

360   a "trade": Ibid., p. 42.

360   "not only wrong . . .": Ibid., p. 51.

362   "corrosive": Ibid., p. 57.

362   "savage vindictiveness": Ibid., p. 112.

362   inner inferiority: Ibid., p. 25.

362   ". . . appreciated and accepted": Ibid., p. 62.

362   ". . . life-diminishing . . .": Ibid., p. 63.

362   ". . . resentful frustration": Ibid., p. 65.

362   "relatively innocent . . .": Ibid.

362   ". . . preferred affection": Ibid., p. 64.

362   help to humanize: Ibid., p. 78.

362   "in great part . . .": Ibid., p. 77.

362–63   ". . . barked his shins": Ibid.

363   ". . . acquire the illusion . . .": Ibid., p. 53.

363   ". . . poor bipeds . . .": Ibid., pp. 57–58.

363   "an earthly paradise . . .": Ibid., p. 45.

363   "IT is every experience . . .": Ibid., p. 120.

363   ". . . found at hand": Ibid., p. 122.

363   very optimistic: August 25, 1942.

364   ". . . more lovable": September 29, 1944, to "dearest family."

364   ". . . blurted out . . .": FYB, p. 255.

365   ". . . foolish plan . . .": Ibid., p. 263.

365   cured of cystitis: Mary to Simon Flexner, November 19, 1941.

Notes

Page

366   "... blissfully happy ...": Mary to Ralph Barton Perry, January 29, 1941.

366   hoped she would marry B.B.: FYD, p. 261.

366   "... I ran away ...": S & T, p. 376.

366   "... 'suffering fools gladly' ...": Cecil Pinsent to Bessie Berenson, March 28, 1946, Smith College Archives.

Chapter 17: The Scholar-Gipsy

368   postwar letter to Sibyl Colefax: December 8, 1944.

368   *The New York Times* article: September 8, 1944.

369   dried-up piece of cheese: September 6, 1944.

371   only achievement: Berenson to Axel Boethius, March 21, 1955.

371   "'... try not to spit ...'": Frederic Fairchild Sherman, *Essays in the Study of Sienese Painting* (New York, 1917), p. ix.

371   humanistic study: Berenson to Royal Cortissoz, February 5, 1927.

371–72   "... interpretation of art ...": "On the Future of i Tatti," *Art News*, November 1949.

372   "when we and the work of art are one": *North Italian Painters of the Renaissance* (New York & London: G. P. Putnam's Sons, 1907), p. 116.

373   the chief attraction: interview with a former Harvard University official.

373   the spool around which: S & T, p. 507.

374   scholarly and abstruse: Orville Prescott, *The New York Times*, September 29, 1952.

374   a foreign language: letter, January 26, 1952.

375   turned into a circus: letter, October 23, 1949.

375   "feather-headed ...": Hugh Trevor-Roper.

377   never been a he-man: March 12, 1953, Mary Hemingway Collection.

377   seldom making love: March 29, 1953.

377   made no progress: June 22, 1953.

378   twists in the road: March 6, 1953.

378   the necessary discipline: February 2, 1954.

Page

378 "... drink and guzzle ...": on March 25, 1954, S & T, p. 339.

378 a day later: March 26, 1954.

379 His were worthless: March 29, 1954.

380 "... a quite close friend ...": letter to the author, May 30, 1977.

380 "... the great resolve ...": "Altamura" by Logan Pearsall Smith, *Reperusals and Re-Collections* (London: Constable & Co., 1936), p. 81.

381 "... private meaning": *Seeing and Knowing* (London: Chapman & Hall, 1953), p. 28.

381 "a pell-mell ...": *Aesthetics and History* (Garden City, N.Y.: Doubleday and Co., 1954), p. 27.

381 direct experience: Ibid., p. 29.

381 "... feelings of dejection ...": Ibid., p. 77.

382 "... House of Life ...": Ibid., p. 139.

382 "... last great humanist ...": Iris Origo.

382 rooms at the bottom: Meyer Schapiro, "Mr. Berenson's Values," *Encounter Magazine*, January 1961, p. 64.

382 indolent and resentful: letter, January 3, 1946.

382 produce to create: letter to Learned Hand, June 6, 1958.

383 "... The aesthetic in itself ...": "Mr. Berenson's Values," p. 64.

383 "... muttering wisdom ...": Journal of Henry Sayles Frances, June 1949.

383 major surgery: Berenson to Senda, May 17, 1949.

384 scholarly appreciation: letter to Hugh Trevor-Roper, August 28, 1956.

385 expected to stand: Sprigge, p. 12.

385 no jewel of thought: *Il segno sul braccio*, p. 167.

385 "a disembodied sage ...": Stuart Preston, *The New York Times Book Review*, September 30, 1962.

385 probably offended him: FYB, p. 280.

385 to retain or destroy: June 23, 1960.

385 "... does no service ...": SL, p. 298.

387 as a duchess: SL, p. 216.

387 captain of the ship: December 8, 1944.

387 she managed him: February 4, 1947.

388 "Yes, but I mesmerize her . . .": this and preceding quotes from the Journals of Frances Francis of 1956.

388 "the necessity, the solace . . .": S & T, p. 237.

388 ". . . the complete companion": Ibid., p. 336.

388 ". . . all-absorbingness . . .": SL, p. 213.

389 ". . . intellectual stimulus": FYB, p. 274.

390 that she was gifted: "letter to B.B."

391 offer his stick: Hugh Trevor-Roper.

391 full of vigor: Berenson to Learned Hand, May 3, 1957.

392 rolled thirteen feet: S & T, p. 364.

392 caught up with him: August 14, 1955.

392 "If I die": Bruno Molajoli.

392 burst out laughing: Berenson, letter to Hugh Trevor-Roper, January 11, 1956.

392 still capable: Count Umberto Morra to Walter Lippmann, April 8, 1956.

392 a brisk walk: Morra to Learned Hand, October 8, 1956.

392 fake amusement: letter, Berenson to Hamish Hamilton, April 15, 1956.

393 "rouged" on her face: S & T, p. 415.

393 ". . . a final farewell": "Letter to B.B."

394 ". . . a successful life": Lili Rheims in *Réalites*, October 1957, p. 14.

394 ". . . a fleeting truce . . .": S. N. Behrman, *Duveen* (New York: Random House, 1951), p. 159.

394 his highest function: letter to D. V. Thompson, May 30, 1953.

394 ". . . my own selfishness": BBT, pp. 329–30.

394 lovely as flowers: SP, p. 114.

394 tendency to blame: BBT, p. 391.

394–95 ". . . 'ain't quite so' ": S & T, pp. 403–404.

395 ". . . Lying is common . . .": Journals of Frances Francis, June 14, 1949.

395 having nightmares: S & T, p. 519.

395 not touch pitch: September 25, 1954.

395 an Anglo-Saxon: letter, December 28, 1946.

396 "...noses on their sleeves": S & T, p. 520.

396 the last rites: Ibid., p. 533.

396–97 "...questioning what...": Ibid., p. 420.

397 "...ever-climbing way": Ibid., p. 251.

397 "...I like it": Ibid.

397 too-shy, too-proud: Ibid., p. 195.

397 no longer attempt: letter, Berenson to Frau Mally Dienemann, December 10, 1957.

397 domains of gold: letter, Berenson to Learned Hand, from
Modena, July 6, 1949.

398 "realest self": BBT, p. 271.

398 "...IT is intransitive": S & T, p. 390.

INDEX

INDEX

Art (*continued*)
  late 19th-cent. and 20th-cent. market, 136–141, 324–325
  methods of study, 89–91
  Pre-Raphaelites, 69, 76, 112
  smuggling, 152–153
  Venetian, 130–135
  see also Berenson, Bernard; Renaissance Art; *names of artists, dealers, historians*
The Arts, 334, 335
Ashburnham, Earl of, 144
Ashburton, Lady, 133, 134
Attributions to artists
  terminology defined, 260
  see also Berenson, Bernard: Biography: attributions
Auden, W. H., 9, 374

Balboni, 256
Baldovinetti, Alesso, 215
Bandinelli, Baccio, 154
Barney, Natalie, 301
Barr, Margaret Scolari, 348, 352, 388
Basaiti, Marco, 259, 260
Bassano, Jacopo, 138
Beaton, Cecil, 3
Beerbohm, Max, 283
  Celestial Attributions, 204
Behrman, S. N., 15, 245, 394
  Duveen, 233
Bell, Clive, 188
Bellini, Giovanni, 131, 132, 134, 152, 202, 203, 245, 259–261, 266, 383
Bellini, Jacopo, 260
Benn, Mr., 221
Berenson, Abram (Abie; brother), 34, 43, 55, 73, 158–159, 160, 344
Berenson, Albert (Alter Valvrojenski; father), 19–32, 55, 159–160, 180, 226, 312
  in Boston, 31–38, 41, 42–44, 49
  relationship with sons, 43–44
Berenson, Bernard (Bernhard)
—biography
  family background, 19–33
  birth, 19
  family move from Lithuania to U.S., 31–38

growing up in Boston, 38–73
education, 30–31, 41, 64; Boston Latin School, 57; Boston Univ., 59, 66; Harvard Univ., 59, 66–73, 96; poetry and art study, 68–71
Goethe as ideal of, 65–66, 68
appearance and general characteristics, 4–13, 42, 44–55, 116, 136–137, 155–156, 308, 315–316, 370
self-searching, 15–16, 294–295, 350–353, 356–363, 377, 394–398
relationship with parents, 42–53, 229–231
women, sex, morality and, 11–12, 60–61, 95–98, 122, 125–126, 275–281, 290–294, 299–302, 309–310, 318–319, 338–341
conversion to Christianity, 49–53
Isabella Stewart Gardner and, 59–62, 73–76, 91
Pater's influence on, 69–71, 87–88, 89, 111, 115, 176–177, 219
European "Grand Tour" (1887–90), 73–76, 85–94
first time in Italy, 86–93
on Florence, 92–93
Morelli's influence on, 90
break with Mrs. Gardner (1889), 93–94
meets Mary Costelloe, 106–110
connoisseurship as a career, 114–115, 350, 360
connoisseurship and photography, 127–128
early years as scout for collectors, 114–135
at Monte Oliveto Maggiore monastery, 117–119
conversion to Catholicism, 118, 119
"conosching," 119
visit to U.S. (1894), 122
lectures on Venetian paintings (National Gallery, London), 123–124
Michael Field and, 124–125
Oscar Wilde and, 125–126

Index

Index

Berenson, Senda, *see* Abbott, Senda Berenson

Berenson family name
  origin of, 21

Berlin, Sir Isaiah, 395

Berlin, Germany
  B.B. in (1880s), 85–86

Bernhardt, Sarah, 75

Black, Justice Herman, 262, 263

Blanche, Jacques Émile, 296

Boccaccio, 178
  Decameron, 173

Bode, Dr. Wilhelm von, 141, 147, 152

Boethius, Axel, 392

Boltraffio (Beltraffio), Giovanni, 260

Bonnat, L. J. F., 199

Borgognone, Ambrogio, 235

Bos, Charles du, 324

Boston Evening Transcript, 35

Boston Latin School
  Santayana on, 57–58

Botticelli, Sandro, 174, 181, 186, 192, 232, 266
  Birth of Venus, 274
  The Madonna and Child of the Eucharist, 153
  Primavera, 120
  The Tragedy of Lucretia (attrib.), 144

Bourget, Paul, 207–208, 213

Bradley, Katherine Harris, *see* Field, Michael

Brass, Alessandro, 395

Breeskin, Adelyn, 291

Brockwell, Maurice, 256

Bronzino, Il
  Madonna and Child, 115

Brooks, Phillips, 49

Brown, J. Carter, 260, 371

Browning, Robert, 76

Bucke, Dr. Richard Maurice, 105

Burlington Magazine, 201, 203, 233

Buttles, Janet and Mary, 206

Byron, Lord
  Don Juan, 1

Cagnola, Don Guido, 173, 183, 184

Cagnola, Donna Laura, 278

Carandini, Countess Elena, 330, 347

Carlton, Sir Dudley, 138

Carpaccio, Vittore, 262

Carritt, David, 236, 251, 371

Carter, Morris, 61, 94

Castagnolo, 205

Catena, 258

Cavalcaselle, Giovanni, 90, 91, 127, 132, 149, 192

Cavenaghi, Luigi, 205, 245, 271–272, 273

Cellini, Benvenuto
  bust of Altoviti, 147

The Century, 130

Cézanne, Paul, 218, 219

Chapman, John J., 300

Chapman, Patricia Botond, 390, 393

Charles I (England), 146

Charrière, Madame de, 304–305

Chigi, Prince, 153, 181

Chinese painting, 217

Churchill, Winston, 343

Ciano, Count Galeazzo, 355

Cicogna, Countess Anna Maria, 394

Cima da Conegliano, 147

Clark, Alan, 375

Clark, Jane Martin (Lady Clark), 332–333, 351, 375

Clark, Kenneth, 8, 9, 13, 64, 125, 126, 141, 190, 193, 215, 251, 311, 315, 327, 331–333, 351, 372, 385, 395
  Another Part of the Wood, 289
  Landscape into Art, 371
  The Nude, 371

Clark, Ronald W., 109

Clary, Prince, 375–376, 392, 396

Claudel, Paul, 377

Cockerell, Sydney, 292

Cocteau, Jean, 8

Colaccichi, Flavia, 387

Colaccichi, Giovanni, 387

Colefax, Sibyl, 204, 368, 387

Colnaghi & Co., 153, 181, 233
  B.B.'s contacts with, 151–152

Conant, James Bryant, 345, 372

Connoisseurship (art)
  B.B. on, 90–91
  defined, 90

Connolly, Cyril, 8, 15

INDEX

Index

INDEX

Hartt, Frederick, 366–367, 389, 391, 395

The Harvard Monthly, 49, 68, 92, 170, 195

Harvard University
"i Tatti" for, 13, 345–346, 355, 386

Harvard Univ. Center for Renaissance Studies, 13

Haskell, Francis, 255

Haslam, W. H., 286

Helen (Queen of Rumania), 6

Helfer, Madame, 272

Hemingway, Ernest, 3, 9, 376–379
Across the River and into the Trees, 376
The Old Man and the Sea, 376

Hemingway, Mary (Mrs. Ernest H.), 9, 376, 377, 378

Hendy, Philip, 154–155

Henraux, Lucien, 281

Hewitt, Mrs. Cooper, 281

Hildebrand, Alfred von
The Problem of Form, 187

Hill, Derek, 3, 374

Hillel, Rabbi, 368

Hitler, Adolf, 347, 348, 355, 356

Hitz, Gertrude, 107

Hofer, Philip, 291, 315

Hogg, Joan, 374

Holbein, Hans, 181
Infant Edward, 180

Holmes, Charles J., 203, 262

Honour, Hugh, 6

Horne, Herbert, 155, 174–175, 179–180, 198, 202, 204, 220, 221

Horney, Karen, 46, 359

Horowitz, Bela, 395

Howe, Irving
World of Our Fathers, 23, 34

Howes, Barbara, 9

Hultin, Roger, 351–352

Hurwitz, Reb Aryeh H., 20

Hurwitz, Bella, 40

Hurwitz, Henry, 20, 25, 26, 46

Hurwitz, Isaiah
Shene Luhot ha-Berit, 20

Hurwitz, Marks, 20

Ibsen, Henrik, 121

Ikhnaton, 128

Impressionism, 75

Inghirami family, 148–149

Ioni, G. F., 139, 214

Isham, Ralph H., 307

It-ness concept, 29, 353, 363, 398

Ivins, Barbara, 337

Ivins, William M., Jr. (Billee), 296, 318, 325, 330, 337–338, 343, 351, 361

Jaccaci, August, 139, 155–156, 175

Jacopo di Barbari, 257

James, Henry, 59, 63, 153, 199, 229

James, William, 123, 195
influence on B.B., 66, 187–188

Jephson, Mountenay, 281

Johns, Clayton, 60

Johnson, John G., 139, 232, 235, 246, 247, 266, 297

Journalists, B.B. on, 7

Jung, C. G.
Memories, Dreams and Reflections, 47

Kahn, Addie (Mrs. Otto K.), 389

Kann, Rodolphe, 151–152

Kazin, Alfred,
A Walker in the City, 204

Kennedy, Jacqueline, 3, 374

Keynes, John Maynard, 285, 286, 346

Kiel, Hannah, 379

King, Edward S., 247

Klaczko, Julian, 115–116

"Knock-out" art deals, 140

Koestler, Arthur, 374, 377

Kress, Ruth, 375

Kress, Samuel H., 258

Kreuger, Ivar, 344–345

Kreuger & Toll Co., 344–345

La Farge, John, 62, 64, 139

Lamar, Alice de, 311, 320, 321

Lambe, Lady, 391

Landi, Neroccio de', 215

Landor, A. H. Savage, 254

Lange, Dr. C., 188

Lanman, Charles R., 66

Lanzani, Polidoro, 255
Isabella d'Este, 147

Lawrence, D. H., 282

Lazzaroni, Baron, 269

Index

Index

Index